TM 1-1520-253-10

UH-60 BLACK HAWK PILOT'S FLIGHT OPERATING MANUAL

by Department of the Army

This manual is sold for historic research purposes only, as an entertainment. It is not intended to be used as part of an actual flight training program. No book can substitute for flight training by an authorized instructor. The licensing of pilots is overseen by organizations and authorities such as the FAA and CAA. Operating an aircraft without the proper license is a federal crime.

©2011 Periscope Film LLC
All Rights Reserved
ISBN #978-1-935700-61-6
www.PeriscopeFilm.com

TM 1-1520-253-10

TECHNICAL MANUAL

OPERATOR'S MANUAL
FOR

UH-60Q HELICOPTER

DISTRIBUTION STATEMENT A. Approved for public release; distribution unlimited.

HEADQUARTERS, DEPARTMENT OF THE ARMY

29 JANUARY 1999

TM 1-1520-253-10
C4

CHANGE

NO. 4

HEADQUARTERS
DEPARTMENT OF THE ARMY
WASHINGTON, D.C., 13 APRIL 2001

OPERATOR'S MANUAL
FOR

UH-60Q HELICOPTER

DISTRIBUTION STATEMENT A: Approved for public release; distribution is unlimited.

TM 1-1520-253-10, dated 29 January 1999, is changed as follows:

1. Remove and insert pages as indicated below. New or changed text material is indicated by a vertical bar in the margin. An illustration change is indicated by a vertical bar next to the figure title. Text that flows to the following page is indicated by a current change number.

Remove pages	Insert pages
a/(b Blank)	a/(b Blank)
A and B	A and B
i through iii/(iv Blank)	i through iii/(iv Blank)
2-9 and 2-10	2-9 and 2-10
2-13 and 2-14	2-13 and 2-14
————	2-14.1/(2-14.2 Blank)
2-17 and 2-18	2-17 and 2-18
2-21 and 2-22	2-21 and 2-22
2-25 and 2-26	2-25 and 2-26
2-27 through 2-30	2-27 through 2-30
2-43 through 2-48	2-43 through 2-48
2-55 and 2-56	2-55 and 2-56
2-73 through 2-76	2-73 through 2-76
3-17 and 3-18	3-17 and 3-18
3-33 and 3-34	3-33 and 3-34
3-93 through 3-96	3-93 through 3-96
4-3 through 4-6	4-3 through 4-6
4-17 and 4-18	4-17 and 4-18
————	4-18.1/(4-18.2 Blank)
4-21 and 4-22	4-21 and 4-22
4-22.1/(4-22.2 Blank)	4-22.1 and 4-22.2
4-23 through 4-28	4-23 through 4-28
4-39 and 4-40	4-39 and 4-40

TM 1-1520-253-10
C4

Remove pages	Insert pages
4-45 and 4-46	4-45 and 4-46
4-55 and 4-56	4-55 and 4-56
————	4-56.1/(4-56.2 Blank)
5-5 and 5-6	5-5 and 5-6
5-11 and 5-12	5-11 and 5-12
6-3 through 6-6	6-3 through 6-6
7-55 and 7-56	7-55 and 7-56
7-125 and 7-126	7-125 and 7-126
8-3 and 8-4	8-3 and 8-4
8-4.1/(8-4.2 Blank)	8-4.1/(8-4.2 Blank)
8-5 through 8-8	8-5 through 8-8
8-11 through 8-14	8-11 through 8-14
8-17 through 8-25/(8-26 Blank)	8-17 through 8-25/(8-26 Blank)
9-1 through 9-4	9-1 through 9-4
9-7 and 9-8	9-7 and 9-8
9-11 through 9-20	9-11 through 9-20
B-1 through B-3/(B-4 Blank)	B-1 through B-3/(B-4 Blank)

2. Retain this sheet in front of manual for reference purposes.

By Order of the Secretary of the Army:

ERIC K. SHINSEKI
General, United States Army
Chief of Staff

Official:

JOEL B. HUDSON
Administrative Assistant to the
Secretary of the Army
0103661

DISTRIBUTION:
To be distributed in accordance with Initial Distribution Number (IDN) 313811, requirements For TM 1-1520-253-10.

TM 1-1520-253-10
C3

CHANGE

NO. 3

HEADQUARTERS
DEPARTMENT OF THE ARMY
WASHINGTON, D.C., 27 NOVEMBER 2000

OPERATOR'S MANUAL
for

UH-60Q HELICOPTER

DISTRIBUTION STATEMENT A: Approved for public release; distribution is unlimited.

TM 1-1520-253-10, 29 January 1999, is changed as follows:

1. Remove and insert pages as indicated below. New or changed text material is indicated by a vertical bar in the margin. An illustration change is indicated by a vertical bar next to the figure title. Text that flows to the following page is indicated by a current change number.

Remove pages	Insert pages
A and B	A and B
2-13 and 2-14	2-13 and 2-14
2-55 and 2-56	2-55 and 2-56
2-75 and 2-76	2-75 and 2-76
2-83 and 2-84	2-83 and 2-84
3-11 through 3-14	3-11 through 3-14
3-33 and 3-34	3-33 and 3-34
-----------------	3-34.1/(3-34.2 Blank)
3-43 through 3-48	3-43 through 3-48
-----------------	3-48.1/(3-48.2 Blank)
3-51 through 3-54	3-51 through 3-54
3-57 and 3-58	3-57 and 3-58
4-5 and 4-6	4-5 and 4-6
-----------------	4-6.1/(4-6.2 Blank)
4-39 through 4-42	4-39 through 4-42
4-43 and 4-44	4-43 and 4-44
-----------------	4-44.1/(4-44.2 Blank)
4-47 and 4-48	4-47 and 4-48
9-1 through 9-4	9-1 through 9-4
9-7 and 9-8	9-7 and 9-8
9-19 and 9-20	9-19 and 9-20

2. Retain this sheet in front of manual for reference purposes.

TM 1-1520-253-10
C3

By Order of the Secretary of the Army:

Official:

ERIC K. SHINSEKI
General, United States Army
Chief of Staff

JOEL B. HUDSON
Administrative Assistant to the
Secretary of the Army
0019573

DISTRIBUTION:
To be distributed in accordance with Initial Distribution Number (IDN) 313811, requirements for TM 1-1520-253-10.

TM 1-1520-253-10
C2

CHANGE

NO.2

HEADQUARTERS
DEPARTMENT OF THE ARMY
WASHINGTON, D.C., 3 April 2000

OPERATOR'S MANUAL
for

UH-60Q HELICOPTER

DISTRIBUTION STATEMENT A: Approved for public release; distribution is unlimited.

TM 1-1520-253-10, dated 29 January 1999, is changed as follows:

1. Remove and insert pages as indicated below. New or changed text material is indicated by a vertical bar in the margin. An illustration change is indicated by a vertical bar next to the figure title. Text that flows to the following page is indicated by a current change number.

Remove pages	Insert pages
A(B blank)	A and B
1-1 and 1-2	1-1 and 1-2
2-9 and 2-1	2-9 and 2-10
2-25 and 2-26	2-25 and 2-26
---------------	2-26.1/(2-26.2 Blank)
2-37 and 2-38	2-37 and 2-38
2-41 through 2-44	2-41 through 2-44
2-67 and 2-68	2-67 and 2-68
2-79 and 2-80	2-79 and 2-80
4-3 through 4-6	4-3 through 4-6
4-31 through 4-34	4-31 through 4-34
4-39 through 4-42	4-39 through 4-42
---------------	4-42.1/(4-42.2 Blank)
5-5 and 5-6	5-5 and 5-6
5-17/(5-18 Blank)	5-17/(5-18 Blank)
7-1 and 7-2	7-1 and 7-2
8-3 and 8-4	8-3 and 8-4
---------------	8-4.1/(8-4.2 Blank)
8-9 and 8-10	8-9 and 8-10
---------------	8-10.1/(8-10.2 Blank)
8-13 and 8-14	8-13 and 8-14
---------------	8-14.1/(8-14.2 Blank)
9-19 and 9-20	9-19 and 9-20
---------------	9-20.1/(9-20.2 Blank)
A-1/(A-2 Blank)	A-1/(A-2 Blank)

TM 1-1520-253-10
C 2

2. Retain this sheet in front of manual for reference purposes.

By Order of the Secretary of the Army:

ERIC K. SHINSEKI
General, United States Army
Chief of Staff

OFFICIAL:

[signature]

JOEL B. HUDSON
Administrative Assistant to the
Secretary of the Army
9931323

DISTRIBUTION:
To be distributed in accordance with Initial Distribution Number (IDN) 313811, requirements for TM 1-1520-253-10.

TM 1-1520-253-10
C1

CHANGE

NO. 1

HEADQUARTERS
DEPARTMENT OF THE ARMY
WASHINGTON, D.C., 30 JULY 1999

OPERATOR'S MANUAL
for

UH-60Q HELICOPTER

DISTRIBUTION STATEMENT A: Approved for public release; distribution is unlimited.

TM 1-1520-253-10, dated 29 January 1999, is changed as follows:

1. Remove and insert pages as indicated below. New or changed text material is indicated by a vertical bar in the margin. An illustration change is indicated by a vertical bar next to the figure title. Text that flows to the following page is indicated by a current change number.

Remove pages	Insert pages
None	A/(B blank)
2-25 and 2-26	2-25 and 2-26
2-39 through 2-44	2-39 through 2-44
2-55 and 2-56	2-55 and 2-56
2-63 and 2-64	2-63 and 2-64
2-71 and 2-72	2-71 and 2-72
4-5 and 4-6	4-5 and 4-6
4-21 and 4-22	4-21 and 4-22
None	4-22.1/(4-22.2 blank)
4-39 and 4-40	4-39 and 4-40
5-11 and 5-12	5-11 and 5-12
7-3 and 7-4	7-3 and 7-4
7-139 and 7-140	7-139 and 7-140
7-145 through 7-147/(7-148 blank)	7-145 through 7-147/(7-148 blank)
8-11 through 8-22	8-11 through 8-22

2. Retain these sheets in front of the manual for reference purposes.

TM 1-1520-253-10
C 1

By Order of the Secretary of the Army:

>ERIC K. SHINSEKI
>*General, United States Army*
>*Chief of Staff*

OFFICIAL:

JOEL B. HUDSON
*Administrative Assistant to the
Secretary of the Army*
9917309

DISTRIBUTION:
 To be distributed in accordance with Initial Distribution Number (IDN) 313811, requirements for TM 1-1520-253-10.

TM 1-1520-253-10

Personnel performing operations, procedures, and practices which are included or implied in this technical manual shall observe the following warnings. Disregard of these warnings and precautionary information can cause serious injury or loss of life.

BATTERY ELECTROLYTE

Battery electrolyte is harmful to the skin and clothing. If potassium hydroxide is spilled on clothing or other material, wash immediately with clean water. If spilled on personnel, immediately flush the affected area with clean water. Continue washing until medical assistance arrives. Neutralize any spilled electrolyte by thoroughly flushing contacted area with water.

CARBON MONOXIDE

When smoke, suspected carbon monoxide fumes, or symptoms of anoxia exist, the crew should immediately ventilate the cockpit.

ELECTROMAGNETIC INTERFERENCE (EMI)

No electrical/electronic devices of any sort, other than those described in this manual or appropriate airworthiness release and approved by USAATCOM AMSAT-R-ECU, are to be operated by crewmembers or passengers during operation of this helicopter.

FIRE EXTINGUISHER

Exposure to high concentrations of extinguishing agent or decomposition products should be avoided. The liquid should not be allowed to come into contact with the skin, as it may cause frost bite or low temperature burns.

HANDLING FUEL AND OIL

Turbine fuels and lubricating oils contain additives which are poisonous and readily absorbed through the skin. Do not allow them to remain on skin longer than necessary.

HIGH VOLTAGE

All ground handling personnel shall be informed of high voltage hazards when making external cargo hookups.

NOISE

Sound pressure levels in this helicopter during some operating conditions exceed the Surgeon General's hearing conservation criteria, as defined in DA PAM 40-501. Hearing protection devices, such as the aviator helmet or ear plugs are required to be worn by all personnel in and around the helicopter during its operation. When flights exceed 100 minutes during any 24 hour period or when speeds are above 120 knots, helmet and ear plugs shall be worn by all crewmembers.

ELECTROMAGNETIC RADIATION

Potential radiation hazard exists at the TACAN antenna when the TACAN is turned on. Make sure that no person is within three feet of the antenna when power is applied to the helicopter. The HF radio transmits high power electromagnetic radiation. Serious injury or death can occur if you touch the HF antenna while it is transmitting. Do not grasp, or lean against the antenna when power is applied to the helicopter.

ALQ-144

Do not continuously look at the ALQ-144 infrared countermeasure transmitter during operation, or for a period of over 1 minute from a distance of less than 3 feet. Skin exposure to countermeasure radiation for longer than 10 seconds at a distance less than 4 inches shall be avoided.

Change 4   a/(b Blank)

TM 1-1520-253-10

LIST OF EFFECTIVE PAGES

Insert latest change pages; dispose of superseded pages in accordance with applicable policies.

NOTE: On a changed page, the portion of the text affected by the latest change is indicated by a vertical line in the outer margin of the page. Changes to illustrations are indicated by a vertical line in the outer margin of the page next to the illustration title.

Dates of issue for original and change pages are:

Original 0 .... 29 January 1999
Change 1 .... 30 July 1999
Change 2 .... 28 January 2000
Change 3 .... 27 November 2000
Change 4 .... 15 June 2001

The total number of pages in this manual is 566 consisting of the following:

Page No.	*Change No.	Page No.	*Change No.	Page No.	*Change No.
Title	0	2-27	4	2-76	3
Blank	0	2-28	0	2-77 - 2-78	0
a	4	2-29	4	2-79	2
b Blank	4	2-30 - 2-34	0	2-80 - 2-82	0
A - B	4	2-35	1	2-83	3
i - iv	4	2-36 - 2-37	0	2-84 - 2-86	0
1-1	2	2-38	2	3-1 - 3-10	0
1-2	0	2-39	0	3-11	3
2-1 - 2-8	0	2-40 - 2-41	1	3-12 - 3-13	0
2-9 - 2-10	4	2-42 - 2-43	2	3-14	3
2-11 - 2-12	0	2-44 - 2-45	4	3-15 - 3-16	0
2-13	4	2-46 - 2-47	0	3-17	4
2-14	0	2-48	4	3-18 - 3-32	0
2-14.1	4	2-49 - 2-54	0	3-33	3
2-14.2 Blank	4	2-55	3	3-34	4
2-15 - 2-16	0	2-56 - 2-63	0	3-34.1	3
2-17 - 2-18	4	2-64	1	3-34.2 Blank	3
2-19 - 2-20	0	2-65 - 2-66	0	3-35 - 3-43	0
2-21 - 2-22	4	2-67 - 2-68	2	3-44 - 3-45	3
2-23 - 2-24	0	2-69 - 2-71	0	3-46	0
2-25	4	2-72	1	3-47 - 3-48.1	3
2-26 - 2-26.1	2	2-73	0	3-48.2 Blank	3
2-26.2 Blank	2	2-74 - 2-75	4	3-49 - 3-50	0

* Zero in this column indicates an original page.

Change 4   A

TM 1-1520-253-10

LIST OF EFFECTIVE PAGES (Cont)

Page No.	*Change No.	Page No.	*Change No.	Page No.	*Change No.
3-51	3	4-56.2 Blank	4	8-9 - 8-10.1	2
3-52 - 3-53	0	4-57 - 4-61	0	8-10.2 Blank	2
3-54	3	4-62 Blank	0	8-11 - 8-13	4
3-55 - 3-56	0	5-1 - 5-4	0	8-14 - 8-14.1	2
3-57 - 3-58	3	5-5	4	8-14.2 Blank	2
3-59 - 3-92	0	5-6	2	8-15	0
3-93 - 3-94	4	5-7 - 5-11	0	8-16	1
3-95	0	5-12	4	8-17	4
3-96	4	5-13 - 5-16	0	8-18 - 8-19	0
4-1 - 4-2	0	5-17	2	8-20 - 8-21	4
4-3	2	5-18 Blank	2	8-22	0
4-4 - 4-5	4	6-1 - 6-2	0	8-23 - 8-25	4
4-6 - 4-6.1	3	6-3	4	8-26 Blank	4
4-6.2 Blank	3	6-4	0	9-1 - 9-3	4
4-7 - 4-16	0	6-5	4	9-4 - 9-6	0
4-17 - 4-18.1	4	6-6 - 6-19	0	9-7	4
4-18.2 Blank	4	6-20 Blank	0	9-8 - 9-10	0
4-19 - 4-20	0	7-1 - 7-2	2	9-11 - 9-12	4
4-21 - 4-25	4	7-3	1	9-13	0
4-26 Blank	4	7-4 - 7-54	0	9-14 - 9-15	4
4-29 - 4-30	0	7-55	4	9-16	0
4-31	2	7-56 - 7-124	0	9-17 - 9-18	4
4-32	0	7-125	4	9-19	3
4-33	2	7-126 - 7-139	0	9-20	4
4-34 - 4-38	0	7-140	1	9-20.1	2
4-39 - 4-40	4	7-141 - 7-145	0	9-20.2 Blank	2
4-41	2	7-146 - 7-147	1	9-21 - 9-26	0
4-42 - 4-44.1	3	7-148 Blank	1	A-1	2
4-44.2 Blank	3	8-1 - 8-3	0	A-2 Blank	2
4-45	0	8-4 - 8-4.1	4	B-1 - B-3	4
4-46	4	8-4.2 Blank	4	B-4 Blank	4
4-47	3	8-5	0	Index-1 - Index-46	0
4-48 - 4-54	0	8-6 - 8-7	4		
4-55 - 4-56.1	4	8-8	0		

* Zero in this column indicates an original page.

B   Change 4

TECHNICAL MANUAL

NO. 1-1520-253-10

TM 1-1520-253-10

**HEADQUARTERS
DEPARTMENT OF THE ARMY
WASHINGTON, D.C. 29 JANUARY 1999**

Operator's Manual
for
UH-60Q HELICOPTERS

REPORTING ERRORS AND RECOMMENDING IMPROVEMENTS

You can help improve this manual. If you find any mistakes or if you know of any way to improve the procedures, please let us know. Mail your letter, DA Form 2028 (Recommended Changes to Publications and Blank Forms), or DA Form 2028-2 located in the back of this manual, direct to: Commander, US Army Aviation and Missile Command, ATTN: AMSAM-MMC-MA-NP, Redstone Arsenal, AL 35898-5230. A reply will be furnished to you. You may also send in your comments electronically to our E-mail address: ls-lp@redstone.army.mil or by fax 256-842-6546/DSN 788-6546. Instructions for sending an electronic 2028 may be found at the back of this manual immediately preceding the hard copy 2028.

DISTRIBUTION STATEMENT A. Approved for public release; distribution unlimited.

TABLE OF CONTENTS

Chapter & Section		Page
CHAPTER 1	INTRODUCTION	1-1
CHAPTER 2	AIRCRAFT AND SYSTEMS DESCRIPTION AND OPERATION	2-1
Section I	Aircraft	2-1
Section II	Emergency Equipment	2-17
Section III	Engines and Related Systems	2-19
Section IV	Fuel System	2-28
Section V	Flight Controls	2-30
Section VI	Hydraulic and Pneumatic System	2-38
Section VII	Powertrain System	2-43
Section VIII	Main and Tail Rotor Groups	2-45
Section IX	Utility Systems	2-47
Section X	Heating, Ventilating, Cooling, and Environmental Control Unit	2-52

Change 4   i

TABLE OF CONTENTS (Cont)

Chapter & Section		Page
Section XI	Electrical Power Supply and Distribution Systems	2-55
Section XII	Auxiliary Power Unit	2-61
Section XIII	Lighting	2-64
Section XIV	Flight Instruments	2-67
Section XV	Servicing, Parking, and Mooring	2-75
CHAPTER 3	AVIONICS	3-1
Section I	General	3-1
Section II	Communications	3-15
Section III	Navigation	3-45
Section IV	Transponder and Radar	3-90
CHAPTER 4	MISSION EQUIPMENT	4-1
Section I	Mission Avionics	4-1
Section II	Armament	4-30
Section III	Cargo Handling Systems	4-31
Section IV	Mission Flexible Systems	4-36
CHAPTER 5	OPERATING LIMITS AND RESTRICTIONS	5-1
Section I	General	5-1
Section II	System Limits	5-2
Section III	Power Limits	5-6
Section IV	Loading Limits	5-8
Section V	Airspeed Limits	5-9

TABLE OF CONTENTS (Cont)

Chapter & Section		Page
Section VI	Maneuvering Limits	5-12
Section VII	Environmental Restrictions	5-16
Section VIII	Other Limitations	5-17
CHAPTER 6	**WEIGHT/BALANCE AND LOADING**	**6-1**
Section I	General	6-1
Section II	Weight and Balance	6-3
Section III	Fuel/Oil	6-5
Section IV	Personnel	6-7
Section V	Mission Equipment	6-10
Section VI	Cargo Loading	6-13
Section VII	Center of Gravity	6-15
CHAPTER 7	**PERFORMANCE DATA**	**7-1**
Section I	Introduction	7-1
Section II	Maximum Torque Available	7-5
Section III	Hover	7-8
Section IV	Cruise	7-12
Section V	Optimum Cruise	7-131
Section VI	Drag	7-134
Section VII	Climb - Descent	7-137
Section VIII	Fuel Flow	7-140
Section IX	Airspeed System Characteristics	7-142

Change 4   iii

TABLE OF CONTENTS (Cont)

Chapter & Section		Page
Section X	Special Mission Performance	7-145
CHAPTER 8	NORMAL PROCEDURES	8-1
Section I	Mission Planning	8-1
Section II	Operating Procedures and Maneuvers	8-3
Section III	Instrument Flight	8-19
Section IV	Flight Characteristics	8-20
Section V	Adverse Environmental Conditions	8-22
CHAPTER 9	EMERGENCY PROCEDURES	9-1
Section I	Aircraft Systems	9-1
Section II	Mission Equipment	9-23
APPENDIX A	REFERENCES	A-1
APPENDIX B	ABBREVIATIONS AND TERMS	B-1
INDEX	INDEX	INDEX-1

CHAPTER 1
INTRODUCTION

1.1 GENERAL.

These instructions are for use by the operator. They apply to the UH-60Q helicopter.

1.2 WARNINGS, CAUTIONS, AND NOTES.

Warnings, cautions, and notes are used to emphasize important and critical instructions and are used for the following conditions:

WARNING

An operating procedure, practice, etc., which, if not correctly followed, could result in personal injury or loss of life.

An operating procedure, practice, etc., which, if not strictly observed, could result in damage to or destruction of equipment.

NOTE

An operating procedure, condition, etc., which it is essential to highlight.

1.3 DESCRIPTION.

This manual contains the complete operating instructions and procedures for the UH-60Q helicopter. The primary mission of this helicopter is that of medical evacuation (MEDEVAC), transport medical teams, deliver medical supplies, and provide support for combat search and rescue missions within the capabilities of the helicopter. The observance of limitations, performance, and weight and balance data provided is mandatory. The observance of procedures is mandatory except when modification is required because of multiple emergencies, adverse weather, terrain, etc. Your flying experience is recognized and therefore, basic flight principles are not included. IT IS REQUIRED THAT THIS MANUAL BE CARRIED IN THE HELICOPTER AT ALL TIMES.

1.4 APPENDIX A, REFERENCES.

Appendix A is a listing of official publications cited within the manual applicable to and available for flight crews, and fault isolation/trouble references.

1.5 APPENDIX B, ABBREVIATIONS, AND TERMS.

Abbreviations listed are to be used to clarify the text in this manual only. Do not use them as standard abbreviations.

1.6 INDEX.

The index lists, in alphabetical order, every titled paragraph, figure, and table contained in this manual. Chapter 7 performance data has an additional index within the chapter.

1.7 ARMY AVIATION SAFETY PROGRAM.

Reports necessary to comply with the safety program are prescribed in AR 385-40.

1.8 DESTRUCTION OF ARMY MATERIEL TO PREVENT ENEMY USE.

For information concerning destruction of Army materiel to prevent enemy use, refer to TM 750-244-1-5.

1.9 FORMS AND RECORDS.

Army aviators flight record and aircraft inspection and maintenance records which are to be used by crewmembers are prescribed in DA PAM 738-751 and TM 55-1500-342-23.

1.10 EXPLANATION OF CHANGE SYMBOLS.

Changes, except as noted below, to the text and tables, including new material on added pages, are indicated by a vertical line in the outer margin extending close to the entire area of the material affected: exception; pages with emergency markings, which consist of black diagonal lines around three edges, may have the vertical line or change symbol placed along the inner margin. Symbols show current changes only. A vertical line alongside the title is used to denote a change to an illustration. However, a vertical line in the outer margin, is utilized when there have been extensive changes made to an illustration. Change symbols are not used to indicate changes in the following:

a. Introductory material.

b. Indexes and tabular data where the change cannot be identified.

c. Blank space resulting from the deletion of text, an illustration, or a table.

d. Correction of minor inaccuracies, such as spelling, punctuation, relocation of material, etc., unless such correction changes the meaning of instructive information and procedures.

1.11 SERIES AND EFFECTIVITY CODES.

Designator symbols listed below, are used to show limited effectivity of airframe information material in conjunction with text content, paragraph titles, and illustrations. Designators may be used to indicate proper effectivity, unless the material applies to all models and configuration within the manual. Designator symbols precede procedural steps in Chapters 8 and 9. If the material applies to all series and configurations, no designator symbol will be used.

DESIGNATOR SYMBOL	APPLICATION
ES	Aircraft with External Stores Support Systems.
ERFS	Aircraft with Extended Range Fuel System.

1.12 HIGH DRAG SYMBOL.

This symbol will be used throughout this manual to designate information applicable to the high drag configuration described in Chapter 7.

1.13 USE OF WORDS SHALL, SHOULD, AND MAY.

Within this technical manual the word shall is used to indicate a mandatory requirement. The word should is used to indicate a nonmandatory but preferred method of accomplishment. The word may is used to indicate an acceptable method of accomplishment.

CHAPTER 2

AIRCRAFT AND SYSTEMS DESCRIPTION AND OPERATION

Section I AIRCRAFT

2.1 GENERAL.

This chapter describes the UH-60Q helicopter's systems and flight controls. The functioning of electrical and mechanical components is simplified where more detailed knowledge is not necessary.

2.2 UH-60Q.

The UH-60Q (BLACK HAWK) (Figure 2-1) is a twin turbine engine, single rotor, semimonocoque fuselage, rotary wing helicopter. Primary mission capability of the helicopter is MEDEVAC. Secondary missions include transport of medical teams, deliver medical supplies, and provide support for combat search and rescue missions. The main rotor system has four blades made of titanium/fiberglass. The drive train consists of a main transmission, intermediate gear box and tail rotor gear box with interconnecting shafts. The propulsion system has two T700-GE-700 engines operating in parallel. The nonretractable landing gear consists of the main landing gear and a tailwheel. Detailed descriptions of these systems are given in these chapters. For additional weight information, refer to Chapters 5, 6, and 7. Kit installations for the helicopter consist of range extension tanks, rescue hoist, medical evacuation, infrared suppression, blade anti-icing/deicing, and blackout devices. Refer to this chapter and Chapter 4 for kit descriptions.

2.3 DIMENSIONS.

Principal dimensions of the helicopter are based on the cyclic stick and tail rotor pedals being centered and the collective stick being in its lowest position. All dimensions are approximate and they are as shown on Figure 2-2.

2.4 TURNING RADIUS AND GROUND CLEARANCE.

Main rotor clearance in Figure 2-3 is shown with cyclic centered and level ground. Cyclic displacement or sloping terrain may cause rotor blade clearance to be significantly less.

For information on turning radius and ground clearance, see Figure 2-3.

2.5 COMPARTMENT DIAGRAM.

The fuselage is divided into two main compartments, the cockpit and cabin. The cockpit (Figure 2-4) is at the front of the helicopter with the pilots sitting in parallel, each with a set of flight controls and instruments. Operation of electrical controls is shared by both. The medical interior contains space for the seating of three medical attendants, two independent medical stations are designed to transport six littered patients or six ambulatory (seated) patients or crew members. The litter platforms can also be moved up, out of the way to transport cargo. Restraint of cargo is by tiedown rings installed in the floor. A medical cabinet provides storage for carry on equipment. Provisions for securing carry on medical equipment and supporting intravenous fluid bags are mounted throughout the cabin. A gust lock control, APU accumulator handpump and pressure gage, and APU ESU are also installed (Figure 2-5).

TM 1-1520-253-10

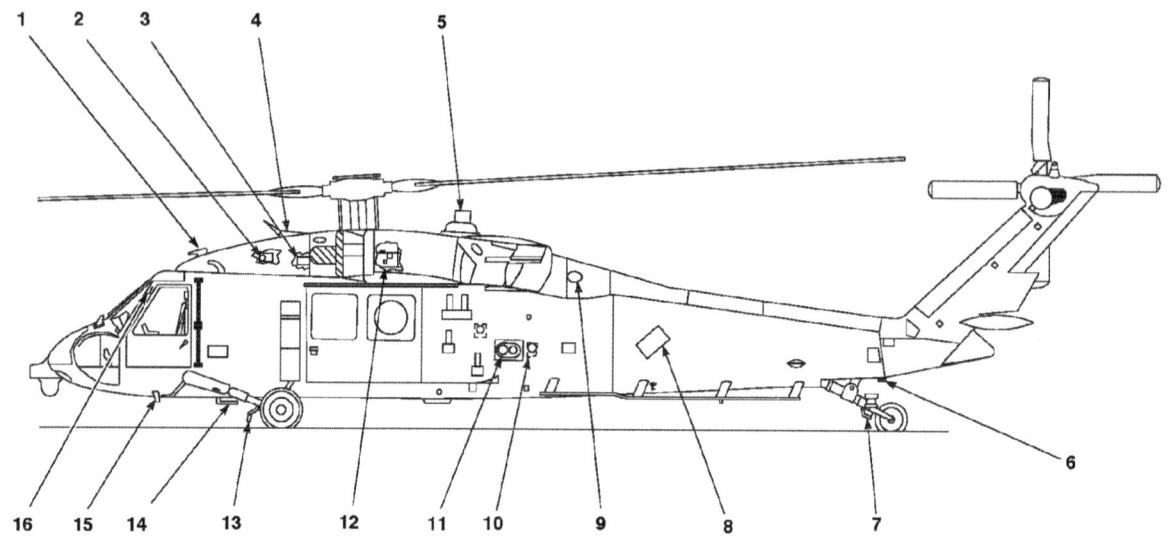

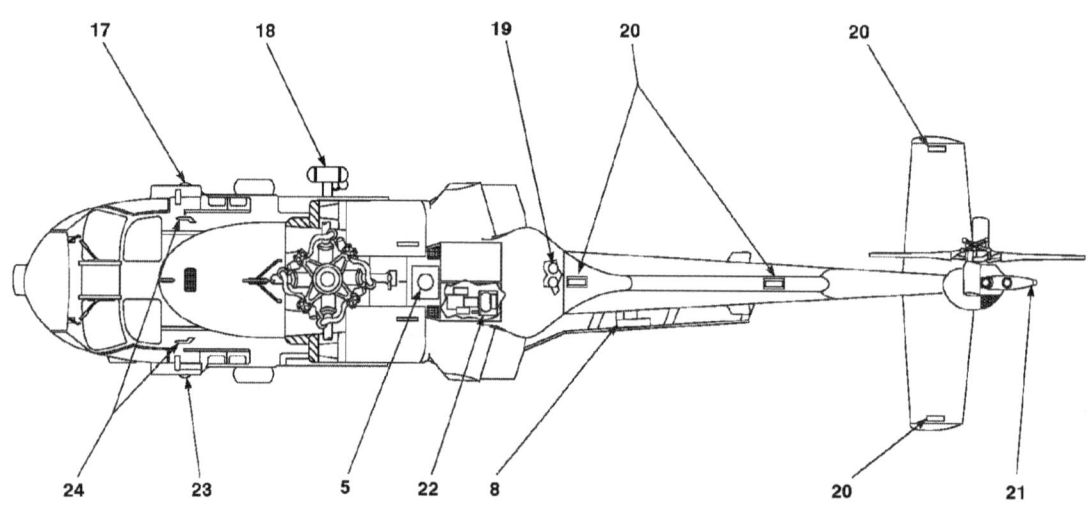

1. PITOT CUTTER
2. BACKUP HYDRAULIC PUMP
3. NO. 1 HYDRAULIC PUMP AND NO. 1 GENERATOR
4. UPPER (ROTOR PYLON) CUTTER
5. INFRARED COUNTERMEASURE TRANSMITTER
6. AFT MAINTENANCE LIGHT RECEPTACLE
7. TAIL LANDING GEAR DEFLECTOR
8. CHAFF DISPENSER
9. APU EXHAUST PORT
10. PNEUMATIC PORT
11. PRESSURE AND CLOSED CIRCUIT REFUELING PORTS
12. NO. 1 ENGINE
13. MAIN LANDING GEAR DEFLECTOR / CUTTER
14. LANDING GEAR JOINT DEFLECTOR
15. STEP AND EXTENSION DEFLECTOR
16. DOOR HINGE DEFLECTOR
17. RIGHT POSITION LIGHT (GREEN)
18. RESCUE HOIST
19. FIRE EXTINGUISHER BOTTLES
20. FORMATION LIGHTS
21. TAIL POSITION LIGHT (WHITE)
22. APU
23. LEFT POSITION LIGHT (RED)
24. PITOT TUBES

AB0691_1

Figure 2-1. General Arrangement (Sheet 1 of 2)

TM 1-1520-253-10

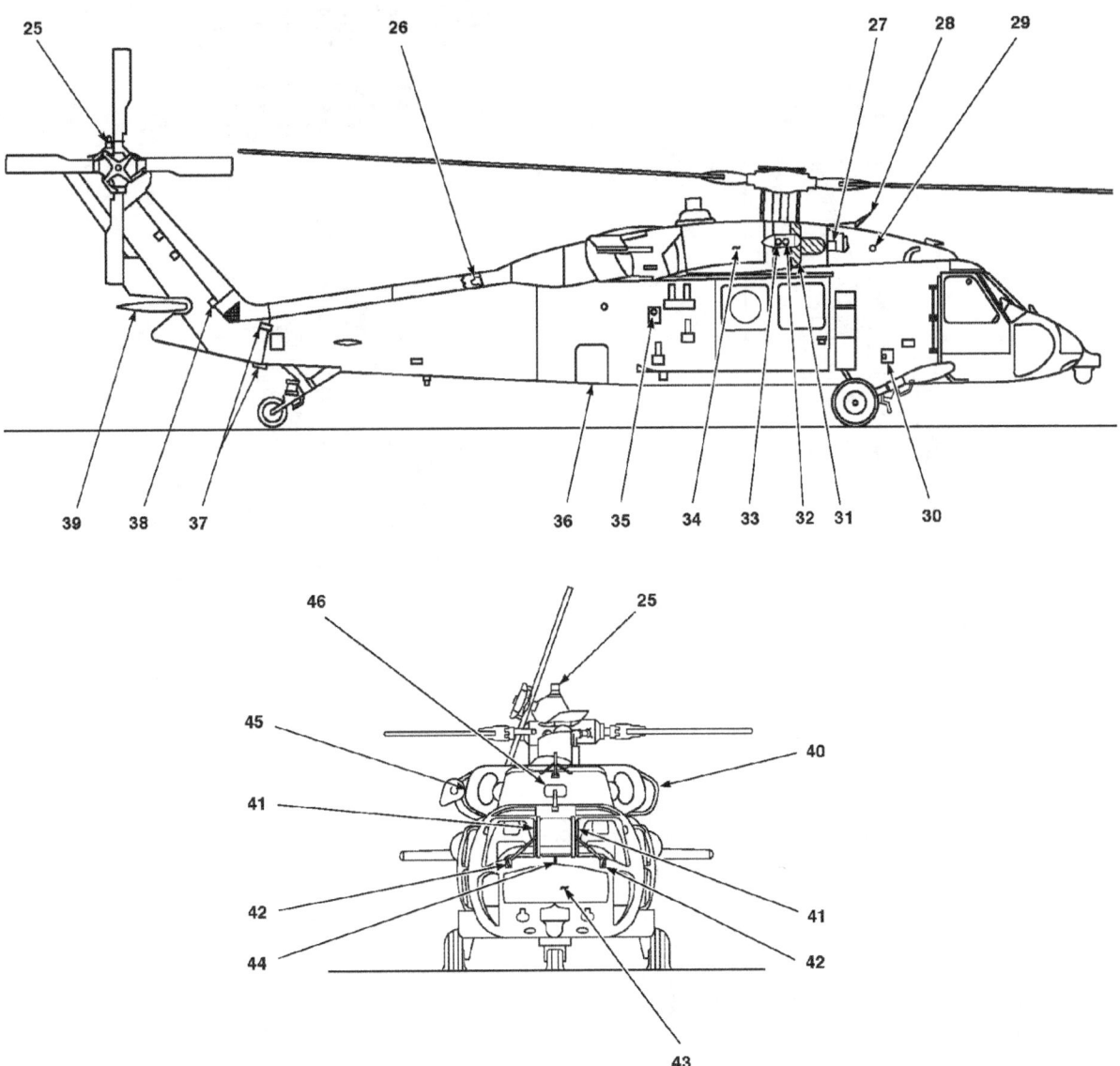

25. UPPER ANTICOLLISION LIGHT
26. TAIL DRIVE SHAFT
27. NO. 2 HYDRAULIC PUMP AND NO. 2 GENERATOR
28. PYLON CUTTER
29. HEATER AIR INTAKE PORT
30. EXTERNAL ELECTRICAL POWER RECEPTACLE
31. NO. 2 ENGINE INLET
32. ICE DETECTOR
33. AMBIENT SENSE PORT
34. ENGINE FAIRING / WORK PLATFORM (SAME BOTH SIDES)
35. GRAVITY REFUELING PORT (SAME BOTH SIDES)

36. AFT AVIONICS COMPARTMENT DOOR
37. TAIL PYLON FOLD HINGES
38. TAIL PYLON SERVICE LADDER (SAME BOTH SIDES)
39. STABILATOR
40. ENGINE BAY AREA COOLING AIR INTAKE (SAME BOTH SIDES)
41. WINDSHIELD POST DEFLECTOR
42. WINDSHIELD WIPER DEFLECTOR
43. AVIONICS COMPARTMENT
44. OAT SENSOR
45. ICE DETECTOR
46. PYLON COOLING AIR INTAKE

AB0691_2

Figure 2-1. General Arrangement (Sheet 2 of 2)

2-3

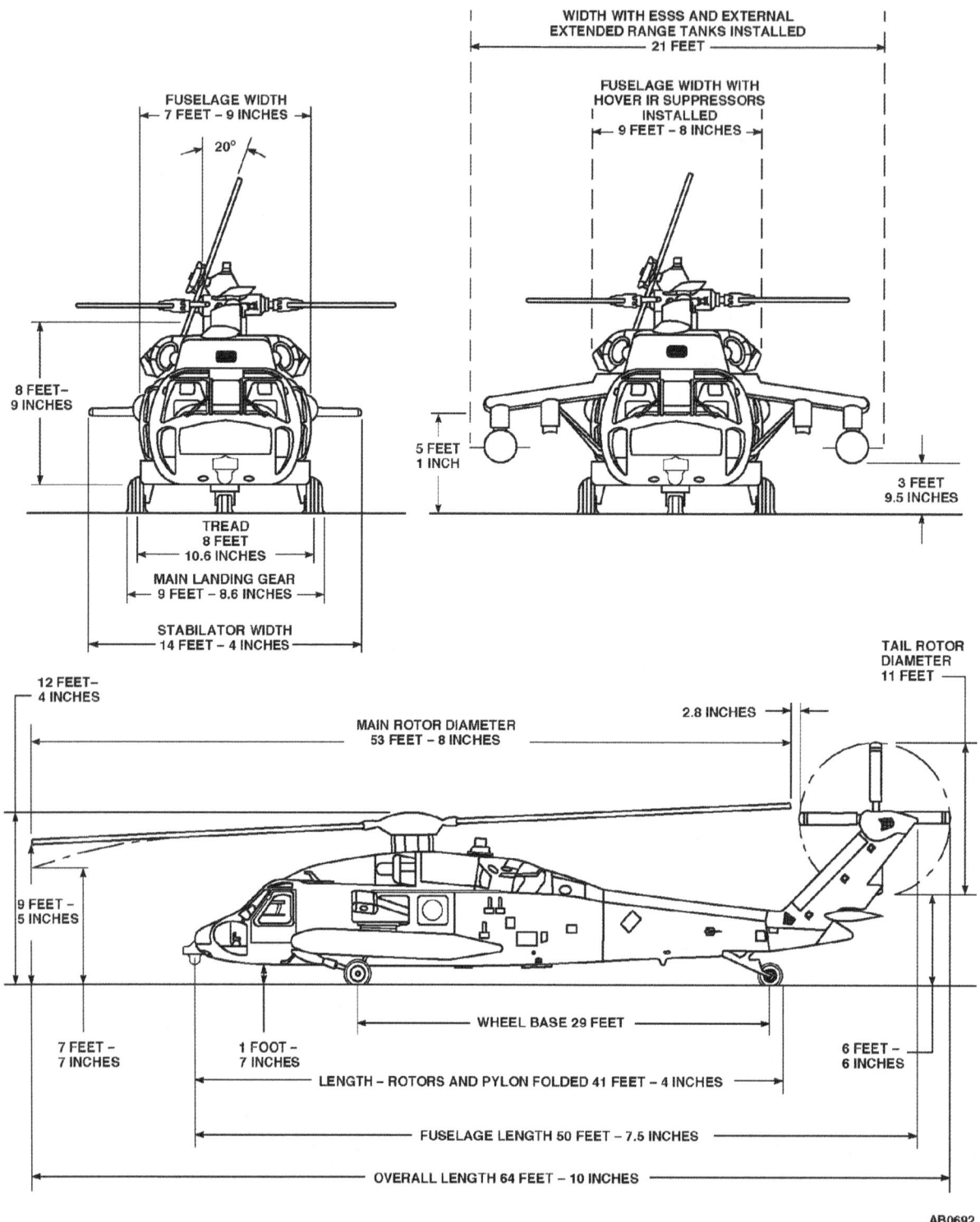

Figure 2-2. Principal Dimensions

TM 1-1520-253-10

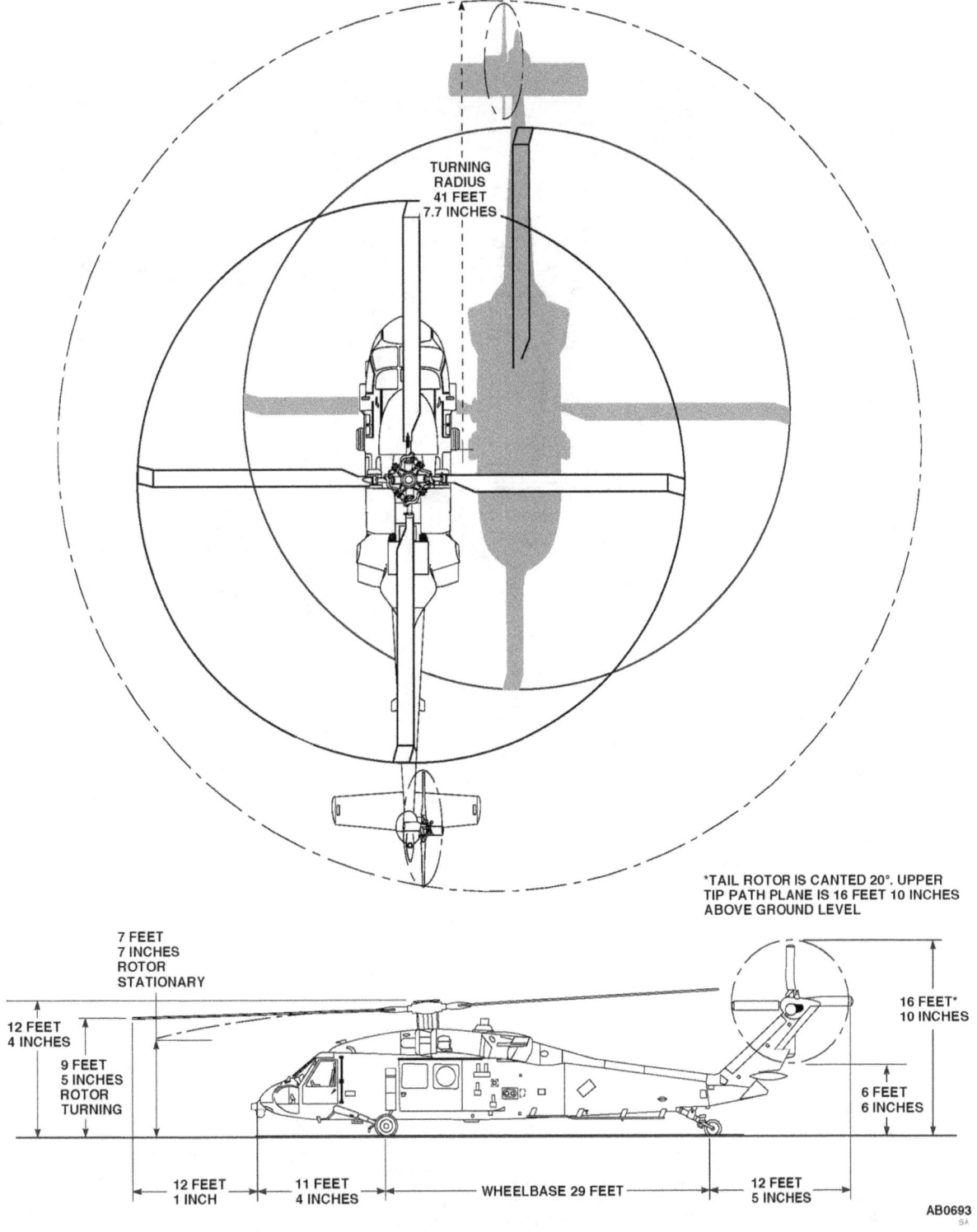

Figure 2-3. Turning Radius and Clearance

2-5

TM 1-1520-253-10

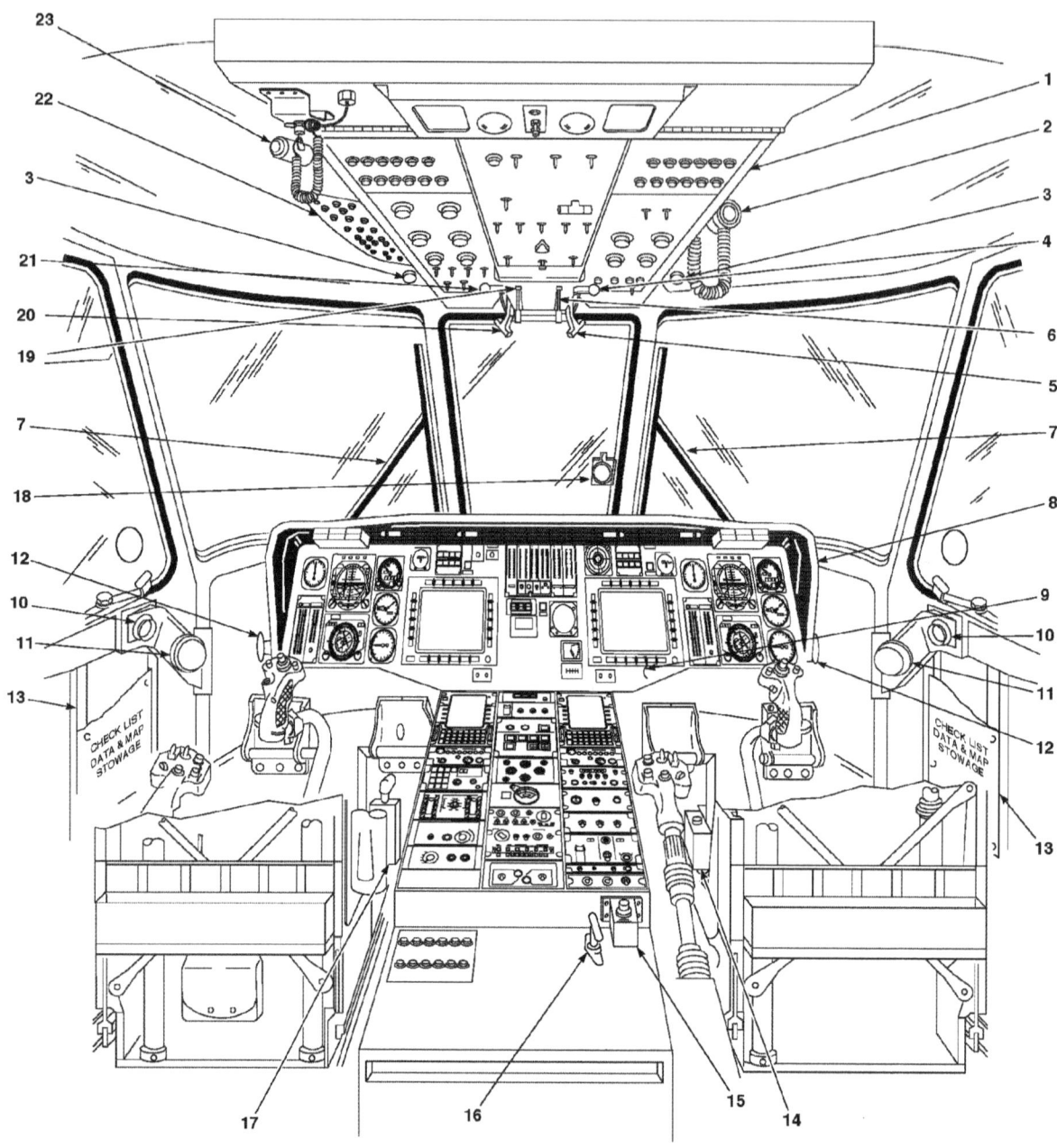

1. UPPER CONSOLE
2. PILOT'S COCKPIT UTILITY LIGHT
3. FREE-AIR TEMPERATURE GAGE
4. NO. 2 ENGINE FUEL SELECTOR LEVER
5. NO. 2 ENGINE OFF / FIRE T-HANDLE
6. NO. 2 ENGINE POWER CONTROL LEVER
7. WINDSHIELD WIPER
8. INSTRUMENT PANEL GLARE SHIELD
9. INSTRUMENT PANEL
10. VENT / DEFOGGER
11. ASHTRAY
12. PEDAL ADJUST LEVER
13. MAP / DATA CASE
14. CABIN DOME LIGHTS DIMMER
15. CHAFF RELEASE SWITCH
16. PARKING BRAKE LEVER
17. LOWER CONSOLE UTILITY LIGHT
18. STANDBY (MAGNETIC COMPASS)
19. NO. 1 ENGINE POWER CONTROL LEVER
20. NO. 1 ENGINE OFF / FIRE T-HANDLE
21. NO. 1 ENGINE FUEL SELECTOR LEVER
22. AUXILIARY CIRCUIT BREAKER PANEL
23. COPILOT'S COCKPIT UTILITY LIGHT

AB0694_1

Figure 2-4. Cockpit Diagram (Sheet 1 of 2)

2-6

TM 1-1520-253-10

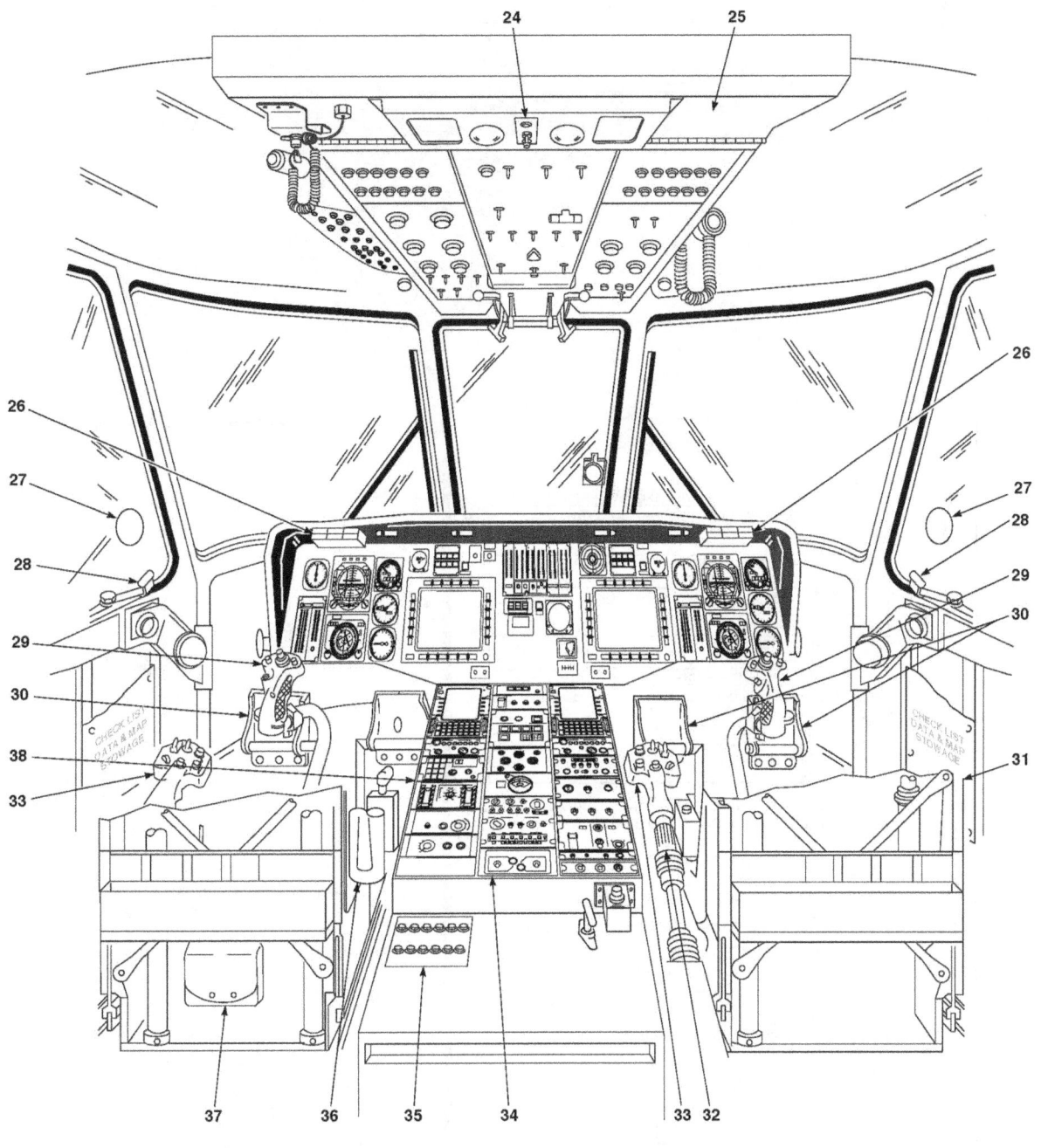

24. COCKPIT FLOODLIGHT CONTROL
25. UPPER CONSOLE
26. MASTER WARNING PANEL
27. WINDOW
28. COCKPIT DOOR EMERGENCY RELEASE
29. CYCLIC STICK
30. DIRECTIONAL CONTROL PEDALS
31. PILOT'S SEAT
32. COLLECTIVE STICK FRICTION CONTROL
33. COLLECTIVE STICK GRIP
34. LOWER CONSOLE
35. BATTERY / BATTERY UTILITY BUS CIRCUIT BREAKER PANEL
36. FIRE EXTINGUISHER
37. FIRST AID KIT
46. ENGINE IGNITION KEYLOCK LOCATED ON SIDE

Figure 2-4. Cockpit Diagram (Sheet 2 of 2)

2-7

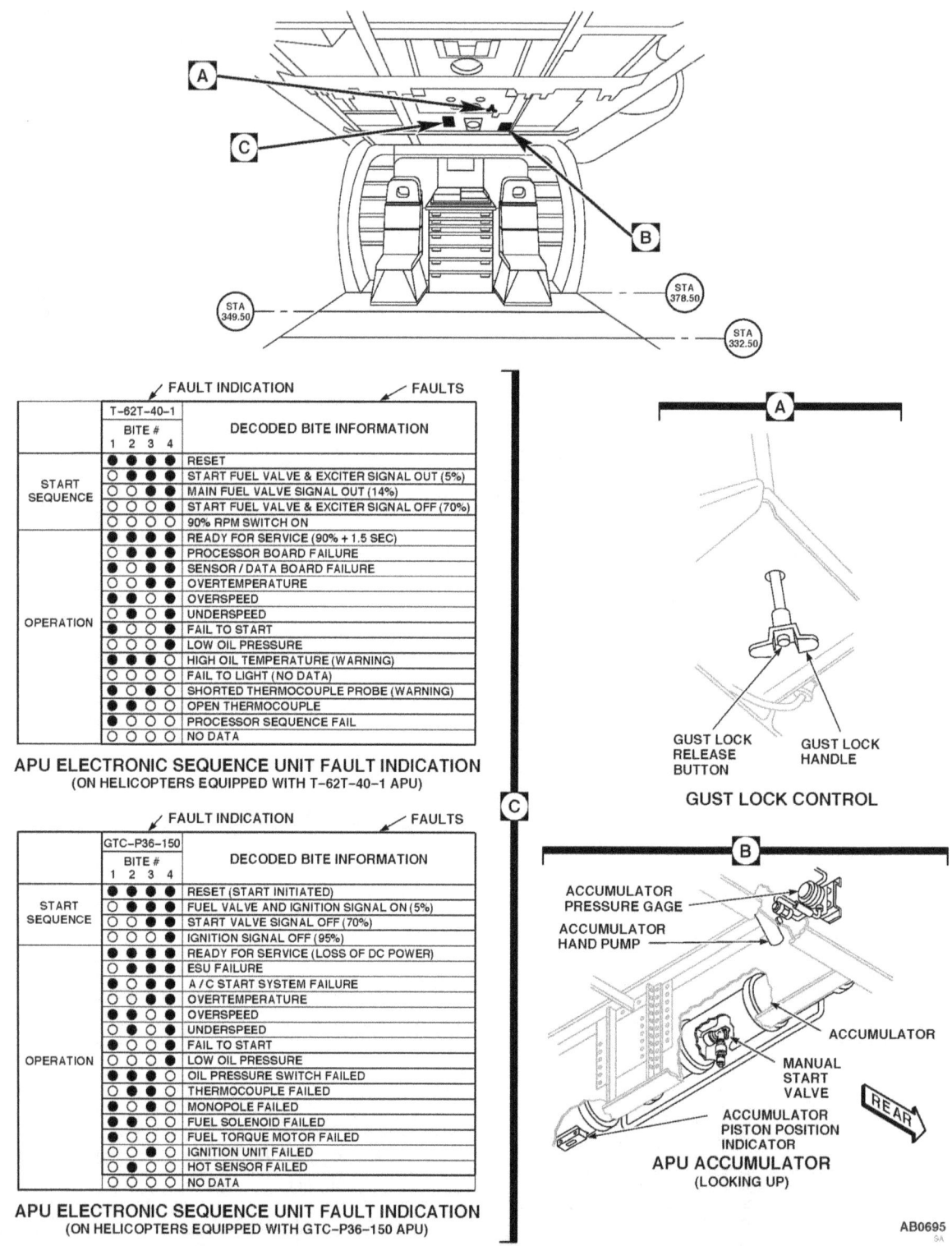

Figure 2-5. Cabin Interior

2.6 UPPER AND LOWER CONSOLES.

All cockpit electrical controls are on the upper and lower consoles and instrument panel. The upper console (Figure 2-6), overhead between pilot and copilot, contains engine controls, fire emergency controls, heater and windshield wiper controls, internal and external light controls, electrical systems and miscellaneous helicopter system controls. The rear portion of the upper panel contains the dc essential bus circuit breaker panels. The copilot's side of the upper console contains the auxiliary circuit breaker panel. The lower console (Figure 2-7) next to the base of the instrument panel and extending through the cockpit between the pilot and copilot, is easily reached by either pilot. The console is arranged with communication panels, navigational panels and flight attitude/stability controls. The rear part of the console houses the battery bus and battery utility bus circuit breaker panels, and parking brake handle.

2.7 LANDING GEAR SYSTEM.

The helicopter has a nonretractable landing gear consisting of two main gear assemblies and a tailwheel assembly. The landing gear permits helicopter takeoffs and landings on slopes in any direction. The system incorporates a jack and kneel feature that permits manual raising or lowering of the fuselage for air transportability. A landing gear weight-on-wheels (WOW) switch is installed on the left landing gear to control operation of selected systems (Table 2-1). The switch is deactivated when the weight of the helicopter is on the landing gear. WOW switch is also installed on the right landing gear drag beam to provide ac underfrequency cutout and external stores jettison. The left WOW switch provides all other WOW functions as without ESSS provisions and the **EMER JETT ALL** capabilities. See Table 2-1 for reference.

2.7.1 Main Landing Gear. The main landing gear is mounted on each side of the helicopter forward of center of gravity (Figure 2-1). Each individual landing gear has a single wheel, a drag beam, and a two-stage oleo shock strut. The lower stage will absorb energy from landings up to 10 feet-per-second (fps). Above 10 fps the upper stage and lower stage combine to absorb loads up to 39 fps (about 11.25 Gs).

2.7.2 Wheel Brake System. Main landing gear wheels have disc hydraulic brakes. The self-contained self-adjusting system is operated by the pilot's and copilot's tail rotor pedals. The brakes have a visual brake puck wear indicator. Each wheel brake consists of two steel rotating discs, brake pucks and a housing that contains the hydraulic pistons. The parking brake handle, marked **PARKING BRAKE**, is on the right side of the lower console (Figure 2-7). A hand-operated parking brake handle allows brakes to be locked by either pilot or copilot after brake pressure is applied. The parking brakes are applied by pressing the toe brake pedals, pulling the parking brake handle to its fully extended position, and then releasing the toe brakes while holding the handle out. An advisory legend will go on, indicating **PARKING BRAKE ON**. Pressing either pilot or copilot left brake pedal will release the parking brakes, the handle will return to the off position and the advisory

Table 2-1. Weight-On-Wheels Functions

WOW SWITCH FUNCTION	ON GROUND	IN FLIGHT
Backup Pump Automatic Operation	Disabled (Except when APU accumulator is low)	Enabled
Hydraulic Leak Test System	Enabled	Disabled
Backup Pump Thermal Switch	Enabled	Disabled
Low % RPM R Audio Warning	Disabled	Enabled
SAS/FPS Computer	Degraded	Enabled
Generator Underfrequency Protection	Enabled	Disabled
IFF Mode 4 Operation	Disabled Automatic Zeroize	Enabled Automatic Zeroize
External Stores Jettison ES	Disabled	Enabled
M130 Control	Disabled	Enabled

legend will go off. Power for the advisory legend comes from the No. 1 dc primary bus through a circuit breaker marked **LIGHTS ADVSY**.

2.7.3 Tail Landing Gear. The tail landing gear (Figure 2-1) is below the rear section of the tail cone. It has a two-stage oleo shock strut, tailwheel lock system fork assembly, yoke assembly, and a wheel and tire. The fork assembly is the attachment point for the tailwheel and allows the wheel to swivel 360°. The tailwheel can be locked in a trail position by a **TAILWHEEL** switch in the cockpit indicating **LOCK** or **UNLK** (Figure 2-7). The fork is locked by an electrical actuator through a bellcrank and locking pin. When the pin is extended, the switch will indicate **LOCK**. When the pin is retracted, the switch will indicate **UNLK**. Power to operate the locking system is by the dc essential bus through a circuit breaker marked **TAILWHEEL LOCK**.

2.8 INSTRUMENT PANEL.

Engine and dual flight instruments are on the one-piece instrument panel (Figure 2-8). The panel is tilted back 30°. The master warning panels are mounted on the upper instrument panel below the glare shield, to inform the pilot of conditions that require immediate action.

2.8.1 Vertical Instrument Display System (VIDS). The VIDS (Figure 2-8) consists of a vertical strip central display unit (CDU), two vertical strip pilot display units (PDU), and two signal data converters (SDC). Those readings are shown by ascending and descending columns of multicolored lights (red, yellow, and green) measured against vertical scales which operate in this manner: the segments will light in normal progression and remain on as the received signal level increases. Those scales will go off in normal progression as the received signal level decreases. Scales with red-coded and/or amber-coded segments below green-coded segments operate in this manner: When the received signal level is zero or bottom scale, the segments will light in normal progression and will remain on. When the first segment above the red or amber range goes on, all red-coded or amber-coded segments will go off. These segments will remain off until the received signal level indicates a reading at or within the red or amber range. At that time all red-coded or amber-coded segments will go on and the scale display will either go on or go off in normal progression, depending upon the received signal level. The CDU and PDUs contain photocells that automatically adjust lighting of the indicators with respect to ambient light. If any one of the three photocells should fail, the lights on the vertical scales of the PDU's or CDU may not be at the optimum brightness for the ambient conditions. The **DIM** knob on the CDU contains an override capability which allows the pilot to manually set the display light level. The SDCs receive parameter data from the No. 1 and No. 2 engines, transmission, and fuel system; provides processing and transmits the resulting signal data to the instrument display. The No. 1 engine instruments on the CDU and copilot's PDU, receive signal data from the No. 1 SDC (CHAN 1). The No. 2 engine and main transmission instruments on the CDU and pilot's PDU, receives signal data from the No. 2 SDC (CHAN 2). If either SDC fails, the corresponding **CHAN 1** or **2** light will go on, and it is likely the pilot's or copilot's PDU and the corresponding instruments will fail. Failure of a lamp power supply within an SDC will cause every second display light on the CDU to go off. Both SDCs receive % **RPM 1** and **2**, % **RPM R** and % **TRQ** information from both engines. Therefore if one SDC fails only one PDU will provide % **RPM 1** and **2** and % **TRQ** for both engines.

2.8.2 Central Display Unit (CDU). The CDU (Figure 2-8) contains instruments that display fuel quantity, transmission oil temperature and pressure, engine oil temperature and pressure, turbine gas temperature (TGT), and gas generator speed (Ng) readings. Those readings are shown by ascending and descending columns of multicolored lights (red, yellow, and green) measured against vertical scales. If the instrument contains low range turnoff (red or yellow lights below green lights) they will go off when the system is operating within the normal range (green). If the instrument contains yellow or red lights above the green range, the green as well as the yellow or red will stay on when operating above the green range. The operating ranges for the different instruments are shown in Figure 5-1. Digital readouts are also installed on the **TOTAL FUEL** quantity, **TGT**, and **Ng** gages.

2.8.2.1 Lamp Test System. The lamp test provides a means of electrically checking all CDU scale lamps, digital readouts, and % **RPM RTR OVERSPEED** lights on the PDUs. When the **PUSH TO TEST** switch on the CDU is pressed, all CDU scale lamps should light, digital readouts

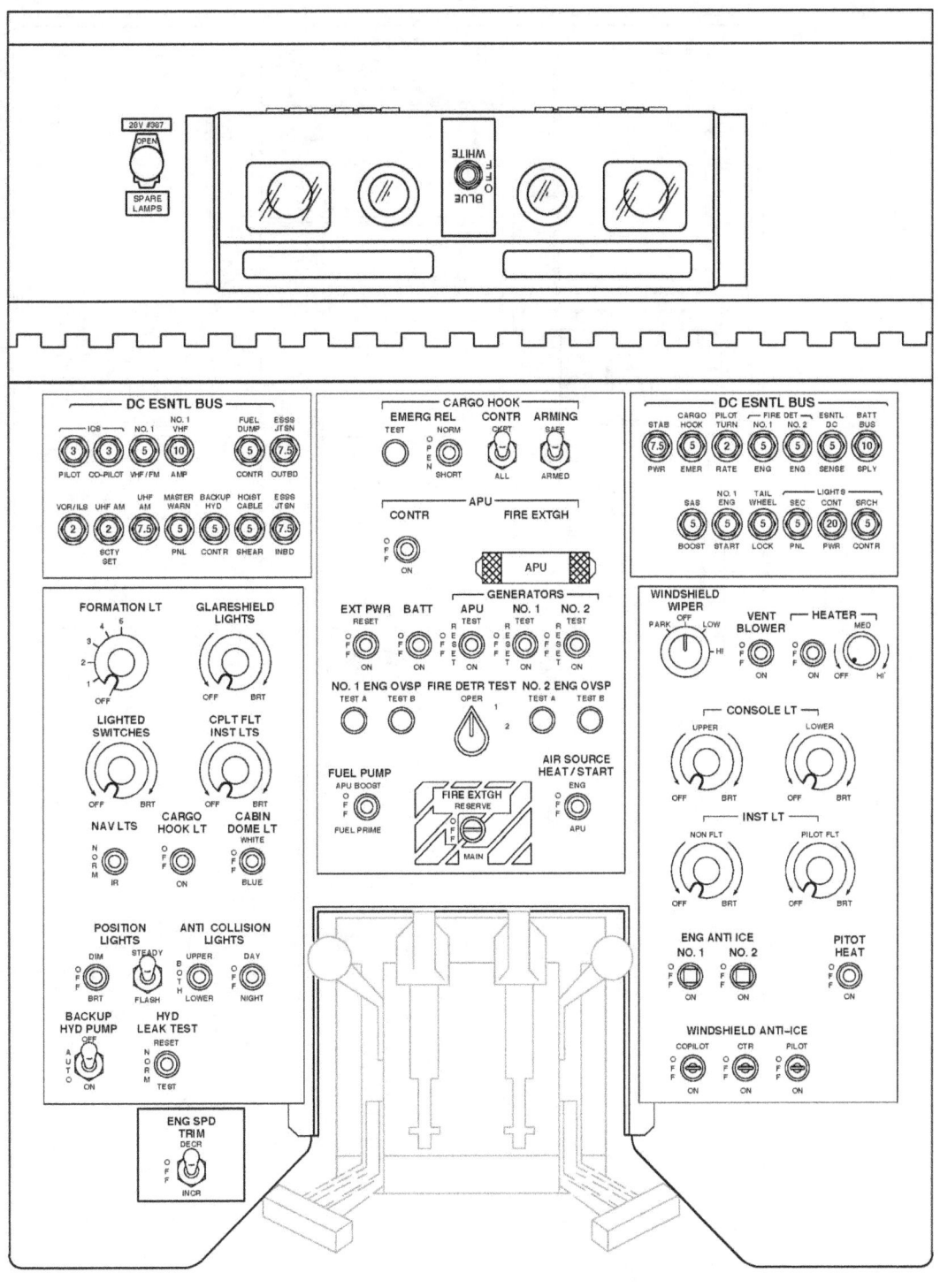

Figure 2-6. Upper Console

2-11

TM 1-1520-253-10

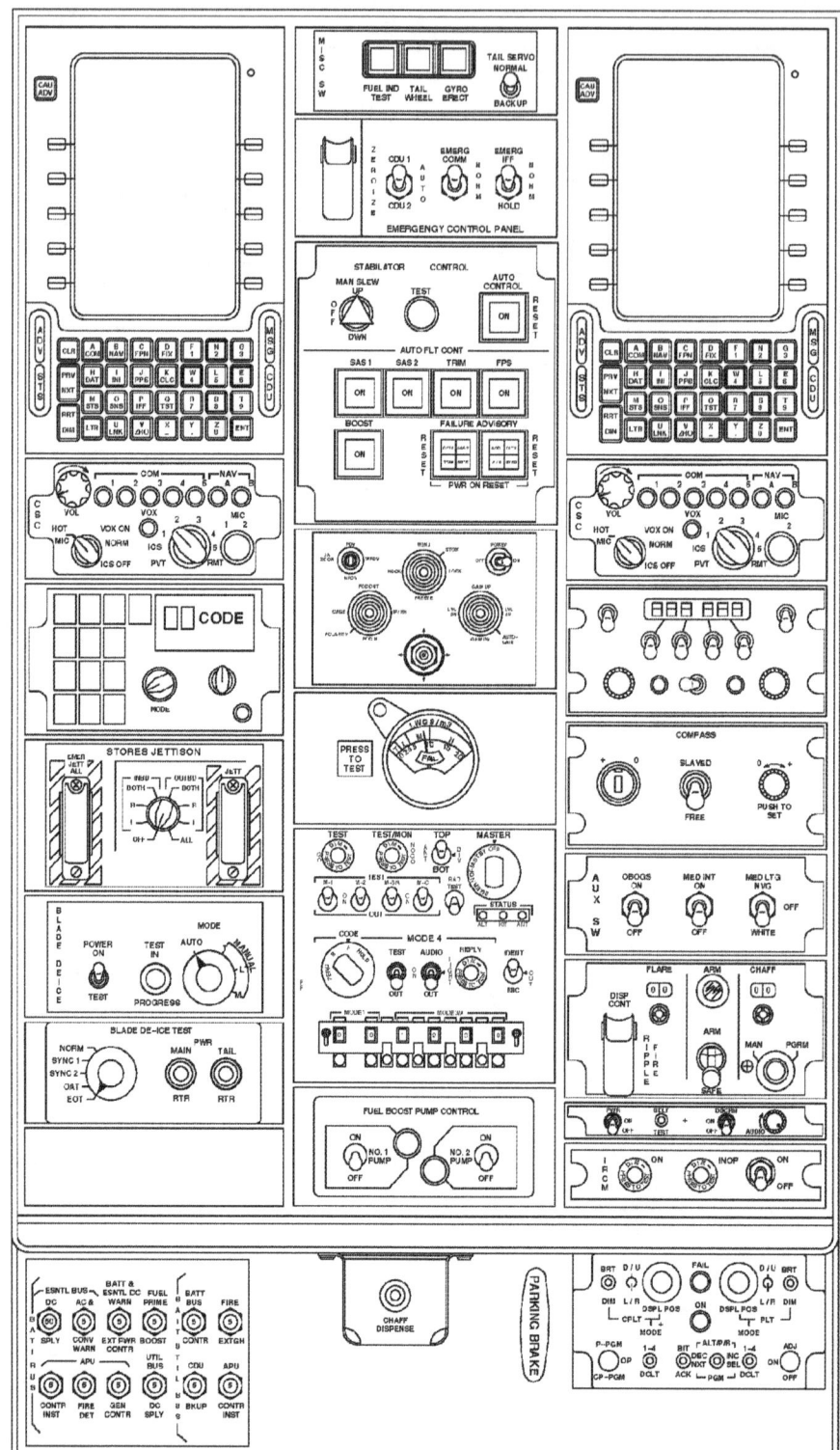

NOTE

IGNITION SWITCH IS LOCATED ON LEFT SIDE OF CENTER CONSOLE.

Figure 2-7. Lower Console

should display **888**, and three **RTR OVERSPEED** lights on the PDUs should be on.

2.8.2.2 Dim Control. The **DIM** control allows the pilot to set a desired display light level of the CDU and PDUs in accordance with the ambient light, or override the auto-dim sensors. If the auto-dim circuitry should fail or malfunction, turn the **DIM** control fully clockwise to regain illumination of the CDU and PDUs.

2.8.2.3 CDU and PDU Digital Control. An **ON, OFF DIGITS** control switch is on the CDU (Figure 2-8) to turn on or off the digital readout displays on the CDU and PDUs. If a digital processor fails, all digital displays will go off.

2.8.3 Pilot's Display Unit (PDU). The PDU (Figure 2-8) displays to the pilot engine power turbines speed (% **RPM 1 and 2**), rotor speed (% **RPM R**), and torque (% **TRQ**). Readings are shown by ascending and descending columns of multicolored lights (red, yellow, and green) measured against vertical scales. A **TEST** switch provides a means of electrically checking all PDU scale lamps and digital readouts. When the **TEST** switch is pressed, all PDU scale lamps should light and digital readouts should display **188**. The % **RPM** indicators contain low range turnoff below the normal operating range. Three overspeed lights at the top will go on from left to right when a corresponding rotor speed of 127%, 137%, and 142% is reached. Once a light is turned on, a latch prevents it from going off until reset by maintenance. Power for the PDUs is from No. 1 and No. 2 ac and dc primary buses through circuit breakers marked **NO. 1 AC INST/NO. 1 DC INST** and **NO. 2 AC INST/NO. 2 DC INST** respectively. See Figure 5-1 for instrument markings.

2.9 DOORS AND WINDOWS.

2.9.1 Cockpit Doors. The crew compartment is reached through two doors, one on each side of the cockpit. The doors swing outward and are hinged on the forward side (Figure 2-1). Each door has a window for ventilation. Installed on the back of each door is a latch handle to allow unlatching the door from either inside or outside the cockpit. Emergency release handles are on the inside frame of each door (Figure 9-1). They allow the cockpit doors to be jettisoned in case of an emergency. There is an emergency release pull tab on the inside forward portion of each cockpit door window for pilot egress.

2.9.2 Cabin/Cargo Doors.

CAUTION

Do not put pressure on bubble during observation. Excessive pressure or loading could cause bubble seal to loosen, causing loss of window.

During operation of the air conditioner system, the right cabin door should remain closed. If opening is required, the right cabin door should not remain open for more than one minute, due to heat from ECS.

Aft sliding doors are on each side of the cabin/cargo compartment (Figure 2-1). Single-action door latches allow the doors to be latched in the fully open or fully closed positions. Each of the two doors incorporate two jettisonable windows, for emergency exit (Figure 9-1). One window on each side is a bubble window to allow the hoist operator/crew to observe the hoist pick up point as well as the area behind the aircraft, without opening the cabin/cargo door.

2.9.3 Door Locks. Key door locks are installed on each of the cabin, cockpit and avionics compartment doors. A common key is used to lock and unlock the doors from the outside to secure the helicopter.

2.10 CREW SEATS.

2.10.1 Pilots' Seats.

WARNING

Do not store any items below seats. Seats stroke downward during a crash and any obstruction will increase the probability and severity of injury.

The pilots' seats provide ballistic protection and can be adjusted for the pilots' leg length and height. The pilot's seat is on the right side, and the copilot's is on the left.

TM 1-1520-253-10

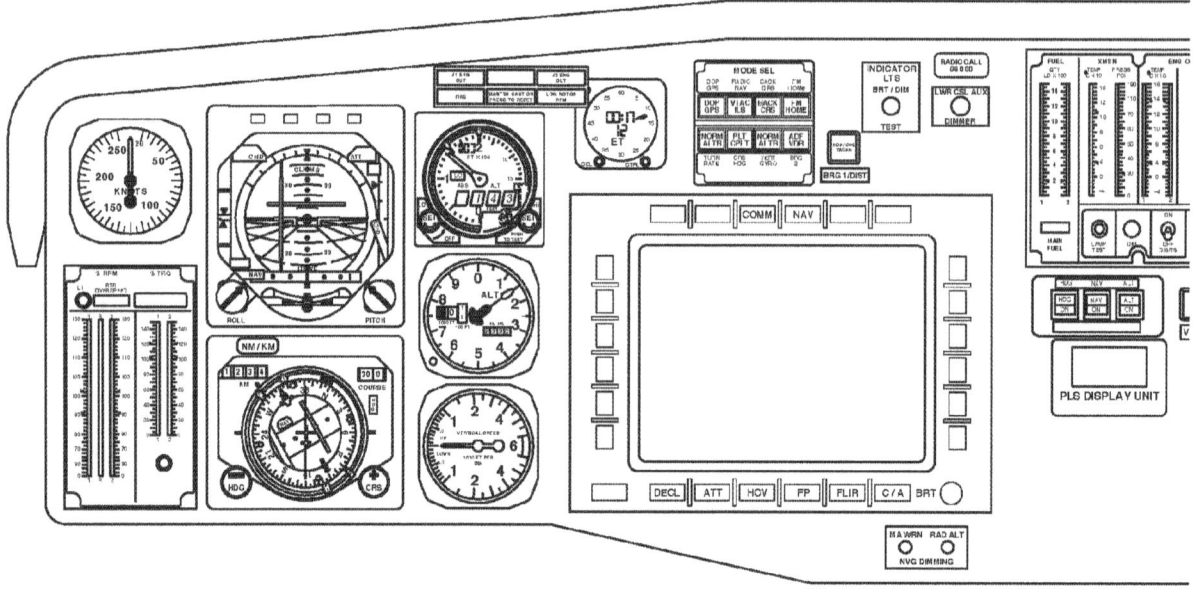

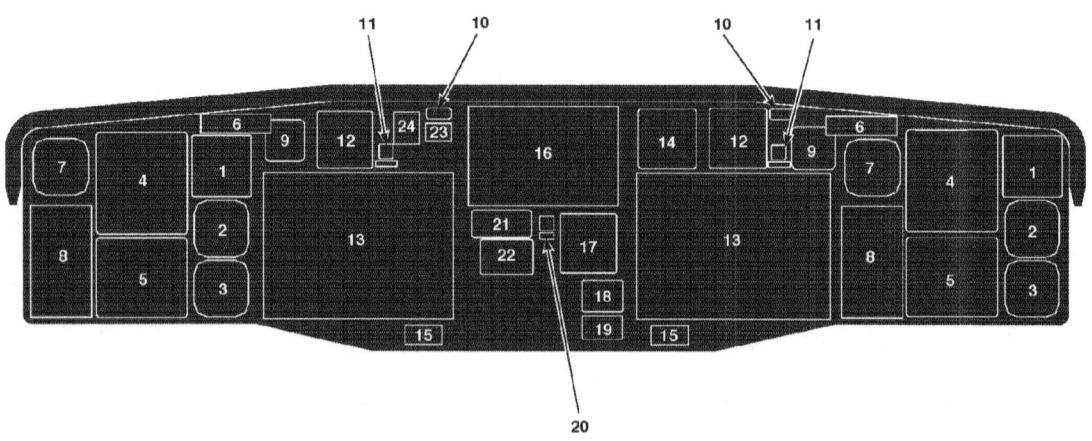

Figure 2-8. Instrument Panel (Sheet 1 of 2)

Each seat has a one-piece ceramic composite bucket attached to energy absorption tubes. Each seat is positioned on a track with the bucket directly above a recess in the cockpit floor. Crash loads are reduced by allowing the seat and occupant to move vertically as single unit. Occupant restraint is provided by a shoulder harness, lap belts, and a crotch belt.

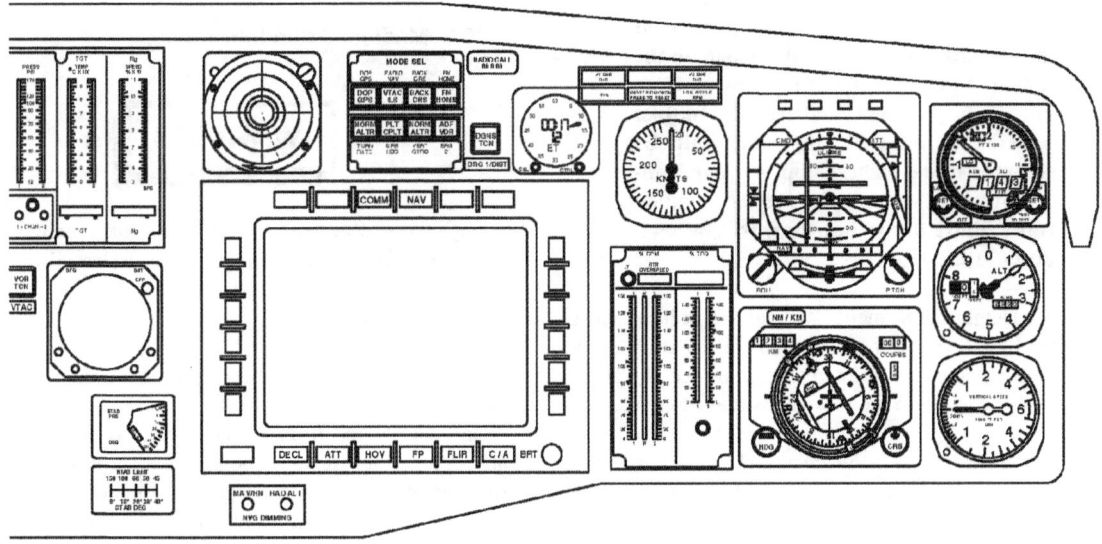

1. RADAR ALTIMETER
2. BAROMETRIC ALTIMETER
3. VERTICAL SPEED INDICATOR
4. VERTICAL SITUATION INDICATOR
5. HORIZONTAL SITUATION INDICATOR
6. MASTER WARNING PANEL
7. AIRSPEED INDICATOR
8. PILOT'S DISPLAY UNIT
9. CLOCK
10. RADIO CALL PLACARD
11. GPS / TACAN SELECT BUTTON
12. VSI / HSI MODE SELECTOR
13. MULTIFUNCTION DISPLAY
14. RADAR WARNING INDICATOR
15. NVG DIMMING CONTROL PANEL
16. CENTRAL DISPLAY UNIT
17. STORMSCOPE
18. STABILATOR INDICATOR
19. STABILATOR POSITION PLACARD
20. VOR / TACAN SELECT BUTTON
21. CIS MODE SELECTOR
22. PERSONNEL LOCATOR DISPLAY
23. LOWER CONSOLE DIMMING CONTROL PANEL
24. INDICATOR LIGHTS CONTROL / TEST PANEL

Figure 2-8. Instrument Panel (Sheet 2 of 2)

WARNING

To prevent injury to personnel, do not release either the normal or emergency vertical adjust levers unless someone is sitting in the seat. The extension springs are under load at all times. With seat at lowest position, the vertical preload on the seat could be as high as 150 pounds. If no one is in the seat and vertical adjust lever(s) is released, the seat will be snapped to the highest stop. Anyone leaning over the seat or with hands on guide tubes above linear bearings, will be seriously injured.

a. Seat Height Adjustment. Vertical seat adjustment is controlled by a lever on the right front of the seat bucket. Springs are installed to counterbalance the weight of the seat. The lever returns to the locked position when released.

b. Forward and Rear Adjustment. The seat is adjusted for leg length by a locking lever on the left front of the seat bucket. The lever is spring-loaded and returns to the locked position when released.

c. Emergency Tilt Levers. The emergency tilt release levers are on each side of the seat support frame. The seat may be tilted back into the cabin for removal or treatment of a wounded pilot. Seat tilting can be done from the cabin, only with the seat in the full down and aft position by pushing in on the tilt handles, and pulling the seat top rearward.

d. Emergency Vertical Release Lever. The emergency vertical release permits the seat to drop to the lowest adjustment point for tilting. The release lever is on the upper center back of the seat, and is actuated by pulling right on the lever.

e. Seat Belts. The pilot's and copilot's seats each contain a shoulder harness, seat belt, and a crotch strap connected to a common buckle assembly. All belts and straps have adjustment fittings. The attachment buckle has a single-point release that will be common in configuration on the pilots and copilots seats; they may be of the lift lever or rotary release configuration, when the lanyard is pulled or the release is turned all belts and straps will release simultaneously.

2.10.2 Protective Armor. Armor protection is provided for the body of the pilot and copilot against 7.62 mm rounds from the side and from the back and below. Armored wings, attached to the cockpit interior, consist of a sliding panel at the outboard side of each seat. A release lever at the front of each panel permits sliding the panel aft to allow rapid entrance and exit, as well as freedom of movement for the seat occupant.

2.10.3 Medical Attendant Seats.

WARNING

To enable emergency exit, keep center medical seat facing to rear, unless litter pans and/or ambulatory seats are in full up position.

Two forward facing seats (Figure 2-5), one on each side of the helicopter at the rear of the cabin and one rearward facing seat at the front of the cabin, are for the medical attendants. Each seat can be adjusted forward or rearward from it's center position. Each seat has a complete lap belt and dual torso-restraint shoulder harness attached to a dual action rotary release buckle. The shoulder harness is connected to inertia reels on the seat back and bottom. This gives the wearer freedom to move about his station. The restraint system is equipped with a single action rotary release buckle with a guard. A release plate must be pressed to allow rotation of release, preventing inadvertent handle rotation from contact with equipment etc. The inertia reel lock control is replaced by a shorter push/pull manual locking control. Push in and the inertia reel is manually locked in place. When the control is pulled out, the reel will lock on sudden pull.

2.10.4 Medical Attendant Seat Belt Operation.

1. Extend shoulder strap and attach shoulder strap fittings to buckle.

2. Extend lap belt and place across body.

3. Place lap belt fitting into buckle and make certain of positive lock.

4. Adjust lap belt tension adjustments and shoulder strap adjustments for a comfortable fit.

Section II EMERGENCY EQUIPMENT

2.11 FIRE PROTECTION SYSTEMS.

Fire detection and fire extinguishing systems are installed so that a fire may be detected and put out at either engine or the APU installation, without affecting the remaining two. The engines and APU are monitored by infrared radiation type sensing units, and protected by a main and reserve high-rate discharge type fire extinguisher installation.

2.11.1 Fire Detection System. A detection system provides fire warning to the cockpit in case of fire in either main engine compartment or in the APU compartment. The system consists of five radiation-sensing flame detectors, control amplifiers, and a test panel. Two detectors are installed in each main engine compartment and one detector is in the APU compartment (Figure 2-1). The flame detectors are solid-state photoconductive cells providing continuous volume optical surveillance of the monitored areas. In case of fire, the detectors react to the infrared radiation and send a signal to one of the three control amplifiers which in turn signals the fire warning assembly lighting the proper T-handle (Figures 2-6 and 2-10). Also, the master **FIRE** warning lights will go on if a fire is detected (Figure 2-8). The detector system automatically resets itself, with warning lights off, when the infrared radiation source ceases to emit.

2.11.2 Fire Detector Test Panel. A test switch on the **FIRE DETR TEST** panel on the upper console (Figure 2-6), when moved to positions **1** or **2**, sends a test signal through the system to put on the fire warning lights and verify proper system operation to, but not including, the photo cells. The No. **1 TEST** position lights #**1** and #**2 ENG EMER OFF** T-handles and APU T-handle and checks all firewall mounted detectors. The No. **2 TEST** position lights #**1** and #**2 ENG EMER OFF** T-handle only, and checks all deck mounted detectors. The engines and APU are completely enclosed within their own firewall compartment, thus reducing the possibility of a false fire warning from outside sources. Electrical power to operate the No. 1 and No. 2 detector system is by the dc essential bus through circuit breakers marked **FIRE DET, NO. 1 ENG** and **NO. 2 ENG**, respectively. Power to operate the APU detector system is by the battery bus through a circuit breaker marked **APU FIRE DET**.

2.11.3 Fire Extinguishing Systems. A high-rate discharge extinguishing system provides a two-shot, main and reserve capability to either main engine compartment or APU compartment. Two containers are each filled with liquid and charged with gaseous nitrogen. The containers are mounted above the upper deck, behind the right engine compartment (Figure 2-1). Both containers have dual outlets, each with its own firing mechanism. Each extinguishing agent container has a pressure gage, easily viewed for preflight inspection. The system also has a thermal discharge safety port that will cause a visual indicator on the right side of the fuselage to rupture, indicating that one or both containers are empty. Electrical power to operate the No. 1 main and No. 2 reserve outlet valves is by the No. 2 dc primary bus through a circuit breaker, marked **FIRE EXTGH**. Power to operate the No. 2 main and No. 1 reserve fire bottles outlet port valves and the directional control valve is by the battery utility bus through a circuit breaker on the lower console marked **FIRE EXTGH**.

2.11.4 Fire Extinguisher Arming Levers (T-Handles). One APU T-handle is on the upper console (Figure 2-6) marked **APU**, and two engine fire extinguisher T-handles are on the engine control quadrant, marked **#1 ENG EMER OFF** and **#2 ENG EMER OFF** (Figures 2-6 and 2-10). The handle marked **#1 ENG EMER OFF** is for the No. 1 engine compartment, the handle marked **#2 ENG EMER OFF** is for the No. 2 engine compartment, and APU is for the auxiliary power unit compartment. When a handle is pulled, dc power actuates the fire extinguisher logic module to select the compartment to which the fire extinguisher agent is to be directed, and also energizes the circuit to the fire extinguisher switch. The ends of the handles house fire detector warning lights.

2.11.5 Fire Extinguisher Control Panel.

CAUTION

In case of fire when ac electrical power is not applied to the helicopter, the reserve fire extinguisher must be discharged. Fire extinguisher agent cannot be discharged into No. 2 engine compartment if ac electrical power is not applied to helicopter.

The switch, marked **FIRE EXTGH**, on the upper console (Figure 2-6), has marked positions **RESERVE-OFF-MAIN**. The switch is operative only after one of the **ENG EMER OFF** or **APU** lever (T-handle) has been pulled. When the switch is placed to **MAIN**, after an **ENG EMER OFF** lever has been pulled, the contents of the main fire extinguisher bottle are discharged into the corresponding compartment. When the **FIRE EXTGH** switch is placed to **RESERVE** after an **ENG EMER OFF** lever has been pulled, the contents of the opposite fire extinguisher bottle are discharged into the selected compartment. The contents of the fire extinguisher bottle discharge into the compartment of the last lever pulled.

2.11.6 Crash-Actuated System. A crash-actuated system is part of the fire extinguisher system. An omnidirectional inertia switch is hard-mounted to the airframe to sense crash forces. Upon impact of a crash of 10 Gs or more, the switch will automatically fire both fire extinguishing containers into both engine compartments. Electrical power is supplied from the battery utility bus through a circuit breaker on the lower console, marked **FIRE EXTGH**.

2.11.7 Hand-Operated Fire Extinguishers.

WARNING

Exposure to high concentrations of extinguishing agent or decomposition products should be avoided. The liquid should not be allowed to contact the skin; it could cause frostbite or low temperature burns.

One hand-operated fire extinguisher (Figure 9-1) is mounted on the medical cabinet. A second fire extinguisher is on the copilot's seat.

2.12 CRASH AXE.

One axe (Figure 9-1) is installed on medical cabinet.

2.13 FIRST AID KITS.

Three first aid kits (Figure 9-1) are installed, one on the back of the left pilot seat, one on the back of the right pilot seat, and one on the medical cabinet.

Section III ENGINES AND RELATED SYSTEMS

2.14 ENGINE.

The T700 engine (Figure 2-9), is a front drive, turboshaft engine of modular construction. One is mounted on the airframe at either side of the main transmission. The engine is divided into four modules: cold section, hot section, power turbine section, and accessory section.

2.14.1 Cold Section Module. The cold section module (Figure 2-9), includes the inlet particle separator, the compressor, the output shaft assembly, and line replaceable units (LRU's). The inlet particle separator removes sand, dust, and other foreign material from the engine inlet air. Engine inlet air passes through the swirl vanes, spinning the air and throwing dirt out by inertial action into the collector scroll, after which it is sucked through by the engine-driven blower and discharged overboard around the engine exhaust duct. The compressor has five axial stages and one centrifugal stage. There are variable inlet guide vanes and variable stage 1 and stage 2 vanes. LRU's mounted on the cold section module are the electrical control unit (ECU), anti-icing and start bleed valve, history recorder, ignition system, and electrical cables.

2.14.2 Hot Section Module. The hot section module (Figure 2-9) consists of three subassemblies; the gas generator turbine, stage 1 nozzle assembly, and combustion liner. LRU's on the hot section module are primer nozzles and ignitors. The gas generator turbine consists of a gas generator stator assembly and a two-stage air cooled turbine rotor assembly which drives the compressor and the accessory gear box. Stage 1 nozzle assembly contains air cooled nozzle segments. The nozzle assemblies direct gas flow to the gas generator turbine. The combustion liner is a ring type combustor cooled by air flow from the diffuser case.

2.14.3 Power Turbine Section Module. The power turbine module (Figure 2-9), includes a two stage power turbine, exhaust frame, and the shaft and C-sump assembly. The LRU's mounted on the power turbine section module are the thermocouple harness, torque and overspeed sensor, and Np (% **RPM 1** or **2**) sensor.

2.14.4 Accessory Section Module. The accessory section module (Figure 2-9) includes the top mounted accessory gear box and a number of LRU's. The LRUs mounted on the module are the hydromechanical unit (HMU), engine driven boost pump, oil filter, oil cooler, alternator, oil and scavenge pump, particle separator blower, fuel filter assembly, chip detector, oil filter bypass sensor, radial drive shaft, fuel pressure sensor, and oil pressure sensor.

2.15 ENGINE FUEL SUPPLY SYSTEM.

The engine fuel supply system consists primarily of the low pressure engine driven boost pump, fuel filter, fuel filter bypass valve, fuel pressure sensor, hydromechanical unit (HMU), pressurizing and overspeed unit (POU).

2.15.1 Engine Driven Boost Pump. A low pressure suction engine driven boost pump is installed on the front face of the engine accessory gear box (Figure 2-9). It assures that the airframe fuel supply system is under negative pressure, lessening the potential of fire in case of fuel system damage. Lighting of the **#1** or **#2 FUEL PRESS** caution legend at idle speed and above could indicate a leak, or failed engine driven boost pump.

2.15.2 Fuel Filter. The fuel filter is a barrier type full flow filter with integral bypass. An electrical switch lights the **#1 FUEL FLTR BYPAS** or **#2 FUEL FLTR BYPAS** caution legend to indicate filter bypass. In addition, a red button on the filter housing pops out when filter element differential pressure indicates impending bypass. Power for the fuel filter bypass legends is from the No. 1 and No. 2 dc primary busses through circuit breakers marked **NO. 1** and **NO. 2 ENG WARN LTS** respectively.

2.15.3 Fuel Pressure Warning System. The engine fuel pressure warning system for each engine consists of a pressure switch that turns on the **FUEL PRESS** caution legend. Fuel pressure caution legends, marked **#1 FUEL PRESS** and **#2 FUEL PRESS** will light when fuel pressure drops below 9 psi. This legend can go on when fuel pressure drops, due to failure of the low pressure boost pump or an air leak in the suction fuel system. The effect will vary depending upon the size of the leak. The effect will be more serious at low engine power. A large enough leak may cause a flameout. Power for the No. 1 engine fuel pressure warning system is supplied by the No. 1 dc primary bus through the **NO. 1 ENG WARN LTS** circuit breaker. Power for the No. 2 engine fuel pressure warning system is supplied by the No. 2 dc primary bus through the **NO. 2 ENG WARN LTS** circuit breaker.

2.15.4 Engine Fuel System Components. Control of fuel to the combustion system is done by the HMU. The HMU, mounted on the rear center of the accessory gear box (Figure 2-9), contains a high pressure pump that delivers fuel to the POU. Various parameters are sensed by the

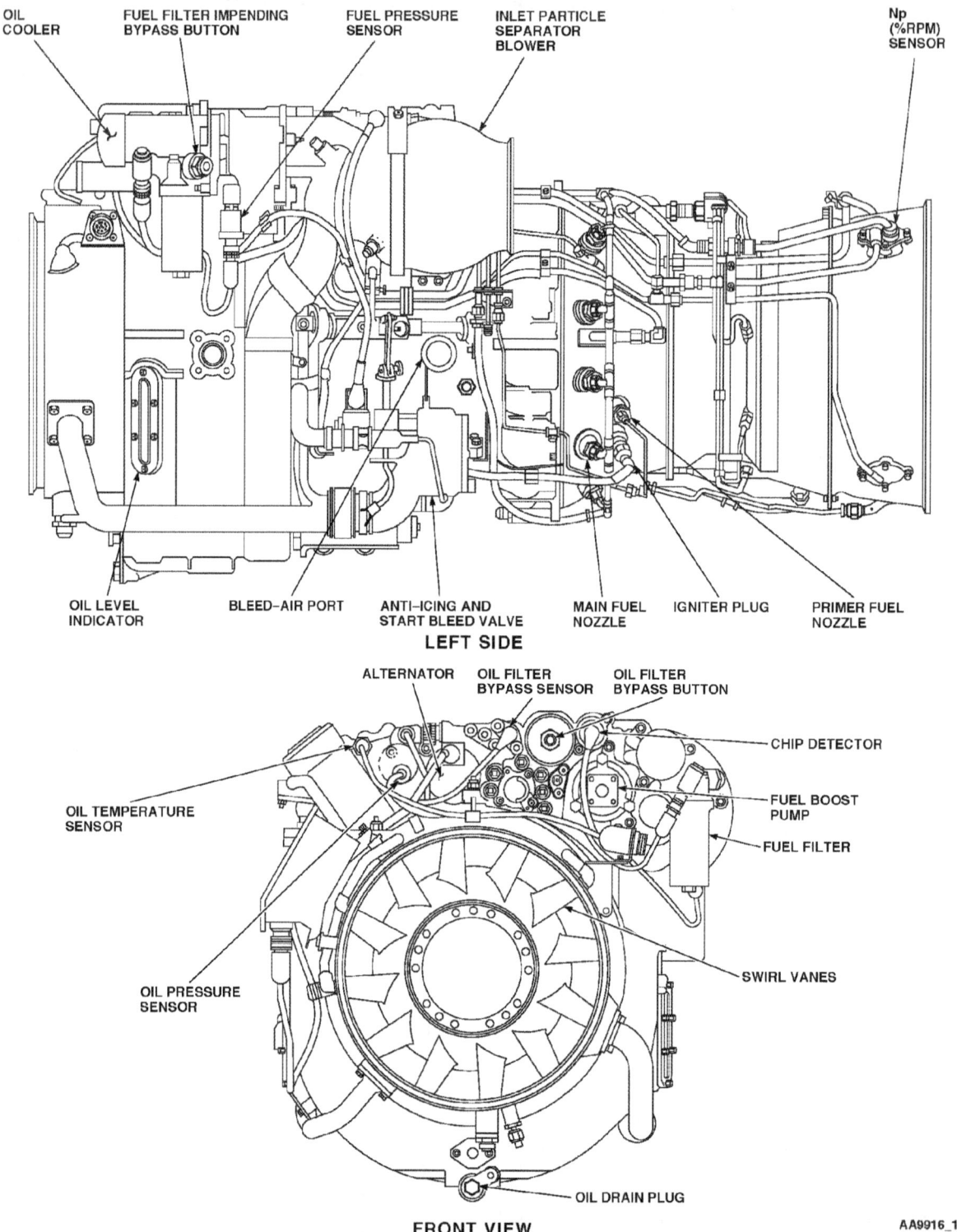

Figure 2-9. Engine T700 (Sheet 1 of 2)

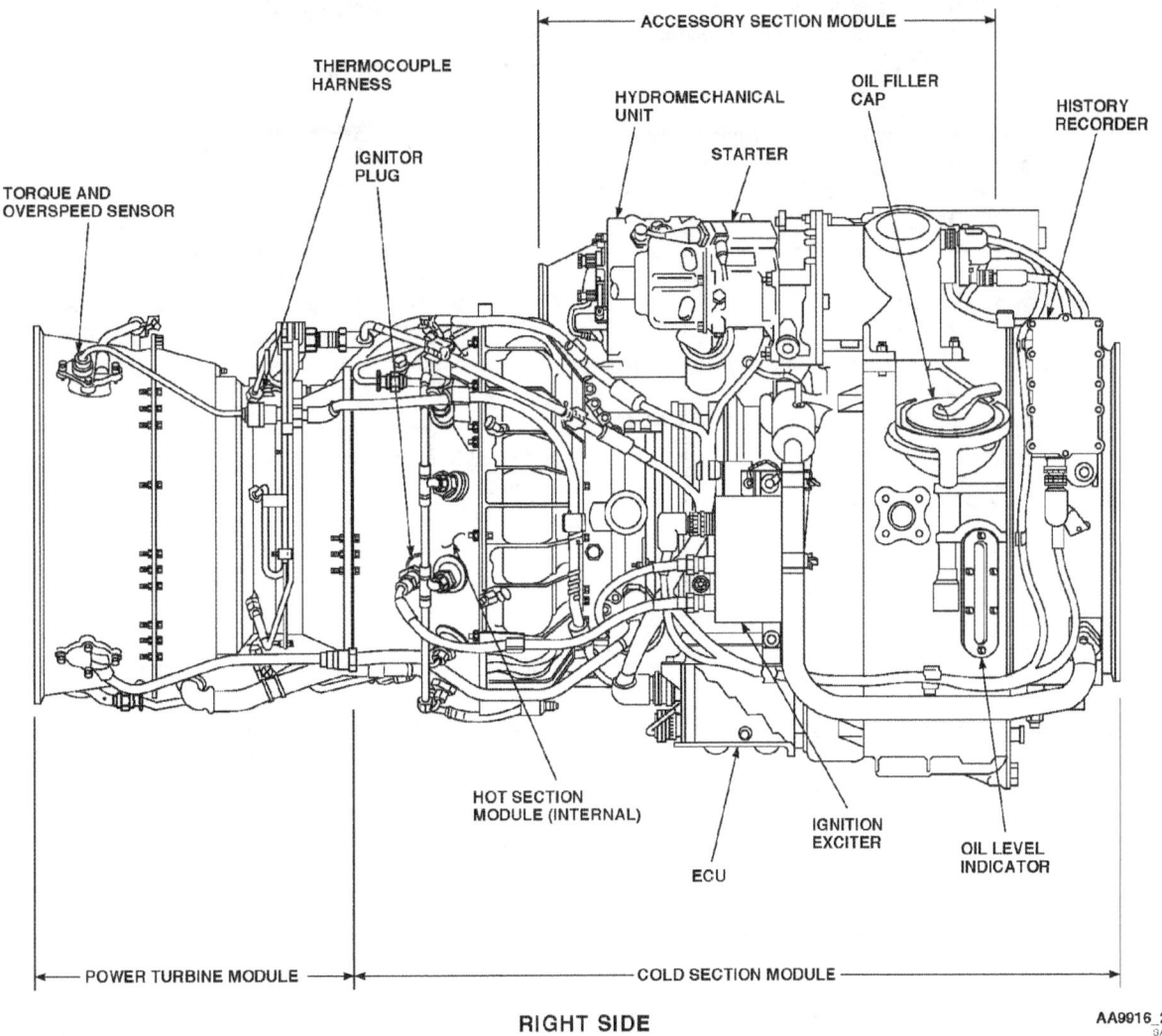

Figure 2-9. Engine T700 (Sheet 2 of 2)

HMU and influence fuel flow, variable geometry position, and engine anti-ice start bleed valve operation. Fuel from the HMU flows to a POU.

2.15.4.1 Pressurizing and Overspeed Unit. The POU sends some of the fuel through the fuel start manifold tube to the primer nozzles and allows back flow of high pressure air for purging. The rest of the fuel is sent through the main fuel manifold to the injectors for starting acceleration and engine operation. It purges fuel from the primer nozzles after light off. It purges fuel from the primer nozzle and main fuel manifold on shutdown. It also reduces fuel flow to prevent an engine overspeed when the overspeed system is tripped as sensed by the ECU.

2.16 ENGINE ALTERNATOR.

2.16.1 Engine Alternator. The engine alternator (Figure 2-9) supplies ac power to the ignition exciter and electrical control unit (ECU). It also supplies a signal to the **Ng SPEED** cockpit indicator. All essential engine electrical functions are powered by the alternator.

a. When the alternator power supply to the ECU is interrupted, a loss of % **RPM 1** or **2** and % **TRQ** indications will occur, with corresponding engine(s) increasing to maximum power (high side).

b. When the alternator Ng signal is interrupted, a loss of Ng cockpit indication will occur with a corresponding **ENG OUT** warning light and audio.

c. A complete loss of engine alternator power results in affected engine(s) increasing to maximum power (high side) with a loss of cockpit indications of % **RPM 1** or **2**, % **TRQ**, **Ng SPEED**; and **ENG OUT** warning light and audio will occur. Overspeed protection is still available.

2.17 IGNITION SYSTEM.

The engine ignition system is a noncontinuous ac powered, capacitor discharge, low voltage system. It includes a dual exciter, two igniter plugs, ignition leads, and **ENGINE IGNITION** keylock switch.

2.18 HISTORY RECORDER.

The engine history recorder is mounted on the right side of the swirl frame (Figure 2-9). It displays four digital counters which records information for maintenance purposes only. The history recorder will only operate with an ECU.

2.19 THERMOCOUPLE HARNESS.

A seven probe harness measures the temperature of the gases at the power turbine inlet. It provides a signal to the ECU, that relays it to the history recorder through the signal data converter (SDC) to the cockpit temperature gage.

2.20 TORQUE AND OVERSPEED AND % RPM SENSORS.

Two sensors are installed on the exhaust frame of the engine. One sensor provides the power turbine governor and tachometer signal to the ECU. The other sensor feeds the torque computation circuit and overspeed protection system.

2.21 ENGINE BLEED-AIR SYSTEM.

Two bleed-air ports are incorporated on the engine. The outboard port supplies bleed-air to the engine air inlet anti-icing system as described in Section III. The inboard port ties into the pressurized air system. Air from this port is supplied to the cabin heating system and can be supplied to the other engine for crossbleed starts.

2.22 ENGINE ANTI-ICING SYSTEMS.

2.22.1 Engine Anti-Icing.

CAUTION

The engine can incur FOD by improper use of these systems and the other anti-ice/deice systems. For example, ice shedding off the windshield can cause FOD damage to the engines.

a. The engine is anti-iced by two systems; the first described in subparagraph b is called an engine anti-ice system and a second described in paragraph 2.22.2 is called the engine inlet anti-icing. Both of these systems are turned on by the **ENG ANTI-ICE NO. 1** and **NO. 2** switch (Figure 2-6).

b. Engine anti-icing is a combination of bleed-air and heated engine oil. Anti-icing is controlled by a solenoid-operated air valve. The engine anti-ice/start bleed valve opens during starting and will remain open at low power settings until engine reaches 88 to 92% Ng, depending on the outside air temperature, with anti-ice **OFF**. The engine anti-ice/deice system is designed so that in the event of an electrical failure the valve reverts to the anti-icing mode and turns on an advisory legend indicating **#1 ENG ANTI-ICE ON** or **#2 ENG ANTI-ICE ON**. Axial compressor discharge air is bled from stage five of the compressor casing, routed through the anti-icing/bleed valve, and delivered to the front frame through ducting. Within the swirl frame, hot air is ducted around the outer casing to each swirl vane splitter lip and inlet guide vanes. The hot air is directed within each vane by a series of baffles. Hot engine oil passing within the scroll vanes in the main frame prevents ice buildup. Water, snow, and solids are carried out through the inlet particle separator discharge system. Switches marked **ENG ANTI-ICE NO. 1** or **NO. 2 OFF**, and **ON**, control engine and inlet anti-ice. At the **ON** position, compressor bleed-air is supplied continuously. Power to operate the anti-icing system is by the No. 1 and No. 2 dc primary buses respectively, through circuit breakers, marked **NO. 1 ENG ANTI-ICE** and **ANTI-ICE WARN**, **NO. 2 ENG ANTI-ICE** and **ANTI-ICE WARN** respectively.

2.22.2 Engine Inlet Anti-Icing.

a. The engine air inlets are anti-iced by bleed-air from the engines. Four advisory legends, marked **#1 ENG ANTI-ICE ON**, **#2 ENG ANTI-ICE ON**, **#1 INL ANTI-ICE ON** and **#2 INL ANTI-ICE ON** are provided for the engines. The **#1** and **#2 ENG ANTI-ICE ON** advisory legends will go on when the **ENG ANTI-ICE NO. 1** and **ENG ANTI-ICE NO. 2** switches are placed **ON**. When the anti-ice system is operating and an engine is started, the inlet anti-ice valve for that engine will close. The **#1** and **#2 INL ANTI-ICE ON** advisory legends operate from temperature sensed at the engine inlet fairing. When the temperature reaches about 93°C (199°F), the temperature switch will turn on the appropriate **INL ANTI-ICE ON** advisory legend. If this legend goes on with the switches at **ENG ANTI-ICE NO. 1** and **NO. 2 OFF**, it indicates that heat is being applied to that engine inlet and a malfunction exists. Inlet anti-icing will turn on if dc primary power failure occurs; dc electrical power is applied to keep the valve closed. Functioning of ENG INLET ANTI-ICE is controlled as follows:

(1) Above 13°C (55°F) - Illumination of the **INL ANTI-ICE ON** advisory legend indicates a system malfunction.

(2) Above 4°C (39°F) to 13°C (55°F) - The **INL ANTI-ICE ON** advisory legend may illuminate or may not illuminate.

(3) At 4°C (39°F) and below - Failure of **INL ANTI-ICE ON** advisory legend to illuminate indicates a system malfunction. Do not fly the aircraft in known icing conditions.

b. At engine power levels of 10% **TRQ** per engine and below, full inlet anti-ice capability cannot be provided due to engine bleed limitations. Power to operate the valves is normally provided from the No. 1 and No. 2 dc primary buses, respectively, through circuit breakers marked **NO. 1** and **NO. 2 ENG ANTI-ICE**, respectively. During engine start, power to operate the No. 1 engine inlet anti-ice valve is provided from the dc essential bus through a circuit breaker marked **NO. 1 ENG START**. The **#1** and **#2 INL ANTI-ICE ON** advisory legends receive power from No. 1 and No. 2 dc primary buses, through circuit breakers, marked **NO. 1** and **NO. 2 ENG ANTI-ICE WARN**, respectively.

2.23 ENGINE OIL SYSTEM.

Lubrication of each engine is by a self-contained, pressurized, recirculating, dry sump system. Included are oil and scavenge pump, emergency oil system, monitored oil filter, tank, oil cooler, and seal pressurization and venting. The oil tank is a part of the main frame. Each scavenge line has a screen at the scavenge pump to aid fault isolation. A chip detector with a cockpit warning legend is in the line downstream of the scavenge pump.

2.23.1 Engine Emergency Oil System.
The engine has an emergency oil system in case oil pressure is lost. Oil reservoirs built into the A and B sumps are kept full during normal operation by the oil pump. Oil bleeds slowly out of those reservoirs and is atomized by air jets, providing continuous oil mist lubrication for the bearings. A **#1 ENG OIL PRESS** or **#2 ENG OIL PRESS** caution legend will go on when indicated oil pressure drops below 25 psi on helicopters without modified faceplates on the instrument panel or below 20 psi on helicopters with modified faceplates. Power for the caution legend comes from the No. 1 and No. 2 dc primary buses through circuit breakers marked **NO. 1** and **NO. 2 ENG WARN LTS** respectively.

2.23.2 Oil Tank.
The oil tank is an integral part of the engine. Tank capacity is 7 US quarts. The filler port is on the right. Oil level is indicated by a sight gage on each side of the tank. Servicing of the tank is required if the oil level reaches the **ADD** line. Overservicing is not possible because extra oil will flow out the filler port. The scavenge pump returns oil from the sumps to the oil tank through six scavenge screens, each one labeled for fault isolation.

2.23.3 Oil Cooler and Filter.
The oil cooler (Figure 2-9) cools scavenge oil before it returns to the tank. Oil from the chip detector passes through the oil cooler and is cooled by transferring heat from the oil to fuel. After passing through the oil cooler, oil enters the top of the main frame where it flows through the scroll vanes. This further cools the oil and heats the vanes for full-time anti-icing. The vanes discharge oil into the oil tank. If the oil cooler pressure becomes too high, a relief valve will open to dump scavenge oil directly into the oil tank. Oil discharged from the oil pump is routed to a disposable-element filter. As the pressure differential across the filter increases, the first indicator will be a popped impending bypass button. As the pressure increases further, this indication will be followed by an indication in the cockpit **#1** or **#2 OIL FLTR BYPASS**, after which a filter bypass will occur. Power for the caution legends is from the No. 1 and No. 2 dc primary buses respectively, through circuit breakers marked **NO. 1** and **NO. 2 ENG WARN LTS**. During cold weather starting, or on starting with a partially clogged filter, the high-pressure drop across the filter will cause the bypass valve to open and the caution legends to go on. The impending bypass indicator has a thermal lockout below 38°C to prevent the button from popping. A cold-start relief valve

downstream of the filter protects the system by opening and dumping the extra oil to the gear box case.

2.23.4 Engine Chip Detector. The chip detector is on the forward side of the accessory gear box. It consists of a housing with integral magnet and electrical connector, with a removable screen surrounding the magnet. The detector attracts magnetic particles at a primary chip detecting gap. A common oil discharge from the scavenge pump is routed to a chip detector wired to a cockpit caution legend marked **CHIP #1 ENGINE** or **CHIP #2 ENGINE**. If chips are detected, a signal is sent to the cockpit to light a caution legend, marked **CHIP #1 ENGINE** or **CHIP #2 ENGINE**. Power to operate the engine chip detector system is from the No. 1 and No. 2 dc primary buses respectively, through circuit breakers marked **WARN LTS**, under the general headings **NO. 1 ENG** and **NO. 2 ENG**.

2.24 ENGINE START SYSTEM.

The pneumatic start system uses an air turbine engine start motor for engine starting. System components consist of an engine start motor, start control valve, external start connector, check valves, controls and ducting. Three pneumatic sources may provide air for engine starts: the APU, engine crossbleed, or a ground source. When the start button is pressed, air from the selected source is directed through the start control valve to the engine start motor. The **#1 ENGINE STARTER** or **#2 ENGINE STARTER** caution legend will go on at this time and remain on until the starter drops out. As the engine start motor begins to turn, an overrun clutch engages causing the engine to motor. As the engine alternator begins to turn, electrical current is supplied to the ignition exciter. Ignition will continue until either the **ENGINE IGNITION** switch is moved to **OFF** or starter dropout occurs. The **ENG POWER CONT** lever is advanced to **IDLE** detent for light-off and acceleration. A starter speed switch terminates the start cycle when cutoff speed is reached (52% to 65% **Ng SPEED**) and turns off the starter caution legend and engine ignition. Malfunction of the starter speed switch may be overcome by manually holding the start button pressed until reaching 52% to 65% **Ng SPEED**. To drop out the starter, manually pull down on the **ENG POWER CONT** lever. To abort a start, pull down on the **ENG POWER CONT** lever and move to **OFF** in one swift movement. Power to operate the No. 1 engine start control valve is from the dc essential bus through a circuit breaker marked **NO. 1 ENG START**. Power to operate the No. 2 engine start control valve is from the No. 2 dc primary bus through a circuit breaker marked **NO. 2 ENG START CONTR**.

2.24.1 Engine Ignition Keylock. An **ENGINE IGNITION** keylock is installed on the side of the lower console (Figure 2-7), to short out and prevent ignition exciter current flow when the switch is **OFF** and the starter is engaged. The switch is marked **ENGINE IGNITION OFF** and **ON**. When the switch is **ON**, the shorts are removed from both engine alternators, allowing exciter current to flow when the engine alternator begins to turn. The **ENGINE IGNITION** is normally **ON** during flight and turned **OFF** at shutdown. One switch serves both engines. If the switch is **OFF**, neither engine can be started, although motoring capability remains. When an engine is to be motored without a start, make certain the **ENGINE IGNITION** switch is **OFF**. To prevent a possible hot or torching start never turn the **ENGINE IGNITION** switch **ON** after motoring has started. Abort start procedures must be done to remove excess fuel from the engine if a start was attempted with the switch **OFF**.

2.24.2 APU Source Engine Start. The APU provides an on-board source of air and auxiliary electrical power. The APU bleed-air output is enough to start each engine individually at all required combinations of ambient temperatures and enough to start both engines simultaneously within a reduced range of ambient temperatures (Figure 5-2). The **AIR SOURCE HEAT/START** switch must be at **APU**. Refer to Section XII for complete APU description.

2.24.3 Crossbleed Engine Start System. Crossbleed engine starts are used when one engine is operating and it is desired to start the other engine from the bleed-air source of the operating engine. To make a crossbleed start, the operating engine must be at least 90% **Ng SPEED**. When the **AIR SOURCE HEAT/START** switch is placed to **ENG**, both engine crossbleed valves will open. Pressing the start button for the engine not operating will cause the start valve for that engine to open at the same time the crossbleed valve for the starting engine will close, and remain closed until starter dropout occurs. At 52% to 65% **Ng SPEED**, the starting engine start valve will close, stopping bleed-air flow to the starter. Power to operate the bleed shutoff valve is from No. 1 dc primary bus through a circuit breaker marked **AIR SOURCE HEAT/START**.

2.24.4 External Source Engine Start. The external start pneumatic port (Figure 2-1) is on the left side of the fuselage. It is the attachment point for a bleed-air line from an external source for engine starting or helicopter heating on the ground. The assembly contains a check valve to prevent engine or APU bleed-air from being vented. The external air source pressurizes the start system up to the engine start control valves, requiring only that electrical power be applied. If an emergency start is made without ac electrical power, No. 1 engine must be started first because the No. 2 engine start control valve will not operate without dc primary bus power.

2.25 ENGINE CONTROL SYSTEM.

The engine control system consists of the ECU, engine quadrant, load demand system and speed control system.

2.25.1 Electrical Control Unit (ECU). The electrical control unit controls the electrical functions of the engine and transmits operational information to the cockpit. It is a solid-state device, mounted below the engine compressor casing. The ECU accepts inputs from the alternator, thermocouple harness, Np (% **RPM 1** and **2**) sensor, torque and overspeed sensors, torque signal from opposite engine for load sharing, feedback signals from the HMU for system stabilization, and a demand speed from the engine speed trim button. The ECU provides signals to the % **RPM 1** and **2** indicators, % **TRQ** meter, **TGT TEMP** indicator, and history recorder.

NOTE

Phantom torque may be observed on the Pilot Display Unit (PDU) torque display of a non-operating engine while the aircraft's other engine is operating during a ground run. Phantom torque readings of up to 14% have been observed on the PDU of the non-operating engine. During startup of the non-operating engine, its ECU will produce a normal, positive torque signal which displays the correct torque signal on the respective PDU.

a. In case of an ECU malfunction, the pilot may override the ECU by momentarily advancing the **ENG POWER CONT** lever to the **LOCKOUT** stop, then retarding it to manually control engine power. To remove the ECU from lockout, the **ENG POWER CONT** lever must be moved to **IDLE**.

b. The torque matching/load sharing system increases power on the lower-torque engine to keep engine torques approximately equal. The system does not allow an engine to reduce power to match a lower power engine. If an engine fails to the high side, the good engine will only attempt to increase torque upward until its Np is 3% above the reference Np.

c. The temperature limiting system limits fuel flow when the requirement is so great that the turbine temperature reaches the limiting value of 837°C to 849°C. Fuel flow is reduced to hold a constant TGT. It is normal to see a transient increase above the 850°C **TGT TEMP** when the pilot demands maximum power (Figure 5-1 transient limits). TGT limiting does not prevent overtemperature during engine starts, compressor stall, or when the engine is operated in **LOCKOUT** (Paragraph 9.3e).

d. Overspeed protection protects the power turbine from destructive overspeeds. The system is set to trigger at 106%±1% **RPM 1** or **2** and will result in an initial reduced fuel flow and will cycle until the cause of the overspeed is removed or % RPM is reduced manually. Two momentary switches marked **NO. 1** and **NO. 2 ENG OVSP TEST A** and **TEST B** on the upper console (Figure 2-6), are used to check the circuits. Testing individual circuits A and B indicates that those systems are complete and performing correctly. Dual closing of A and B serves to check out the actual overspeed system itself, the overspeed solenoid and the POU. This check must be done only on the ground by designated maintenance personnel. The overspeed protection is not deactivated when in **LOCKOUT**. Power to operate the overspeed system is from two independent sources: the engine alternators as the primary source, and the No. 1 and No. 2 ac primary buses as alternate backup source in case of alternator failure. Circuit protection is through circuit breakers marked **NO. 1 ENG OVSP** and **NO. 2 ENG OVSP**.

2.25.2 Engine Control Quadrant. The engine control quadrant (Figure 2-10) consists of two **ENG POWER CONT** levers, two **ENG FUEL SYS** selector levers, and two **ENG EMER OFF** T-handles. A starter button is on each **ENG POWER CONT** lever. Each **ENG POWER CONT** lever has four positions: **OFF-IDLE-FLY-LOCKOUT**. Movement of the **ENG POWER CONT** levers moves a cable to mechanically shut off fuel or set available Ng SPEED. The lever is advanced to **FLY** for flight. This **ENG POWER CONT** lever setting represents the highest power that could be supplied if demanded. Power turbine speed (% **RPM 1** or **2**) is not governed until the power lever is advanced from **IDLE**. The engine quadrant secondary stop, two stop blocks, the quadrant assembly, and a latch on each **ENG POWER CONT** lever prevent moving the levers below **IDLE** detent. When shutdown is required, the **ENG POWER CONT** lever must be pulled out slightly, at the same time the latch release must be pressed, then the **ENG POWER CONT** lever can be moved below **IDLE** detent. After being moved momentarily to **LOCKOUT**, the **ENG POWER CONT** lever is used to manually control **Ng SPEED** and % **RPM 1** or **2**. With the **ENG POWER CONT** lever at **LOCKOUT**, the automatic TGT limiting system is deactivated and TGT must be manually controlled. The overspeed protection system is not deactivated when at **LOCKOUT**.

TM 1-1520-253-10

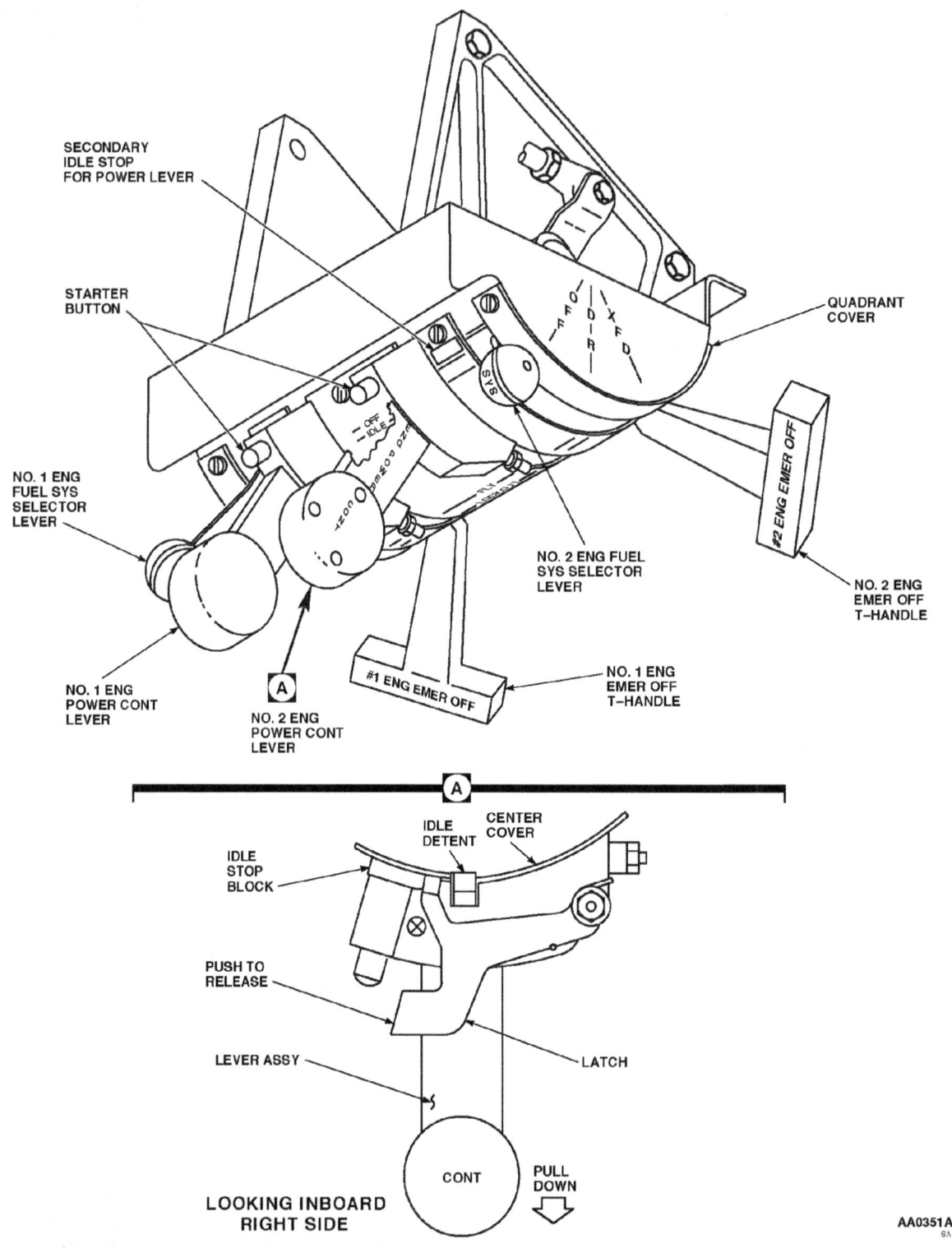

Figure 2-10. Engine Control Quadrant

2-26 Change 2

2.25.3 Load Demand System. With **ENG POWER CONT** lever at **FLY**, the ECU and HMU respond to collective signals to automatically control engine speed and provide required power. During emergency operations, when the **ENG POWER CONT** lever is moved to **LOCKOUT** and then to some intermediate position, the engine will still respond to collective signals.

2.25.4 Engine Speed Control System. An engine RPM control switch on the upper console (Figure 2-6) controls the speed of both engines simultaneously. There is no individual trim capability. It is used to supply a signal to the ECU for controlling % **RPM 1** and **2** as required. The **ENG RPM** control switch allows adjustment between 96%

and 100%. Power for **ENG RPM** control system is from the No. 2 dc primary bus through a circuit breaker marked **SPEED TRIM**.

2.26 HOVER INFRARED SUPPRESSOR SUBSYSTEM (HIRSS).

The hover IR suppressor (Figure 2-2) provides improved helicopter survivability from heat-seeking missiles throughout the flight envelope. The HIRSS kit has no moving parts. It contains a three-stage removable core which reduces metal surface and exhaust gas temperature radiation and prevents line-of-sight viewing of hot engine surfaces. The HIRSS channels hot exhaust gasses through the three-stage core and inner baffle to induce the flow of cooling air from the engine bay and the inlet scoops. The three-stage core and inner baffle cold surfaces are coated with low-reflectance material. For further cooling, hot exhaust gas is ducted outboard and downward by the engine, away from the helicopter by the exhaust deflector, where additional cooling air is provided by the main rotor downwash. Installation of each HIRSS module requires removal of the standard engine exhaust module and aft cabin door track fairings. HIRSS modules are installed on the basic airframe equipped with HIRSS fixed provisions by two airframe mounts. The aft fairings are installed using existing mounting points and hardware. While operating in a non-hostile environment, the inner baffle can be removed to enhance helicopter performance.

2.27 ENGINE INSTRUMENTS.

The instrument displays (Figure 2-8) consist of **ENG OIL TEMP** and **PRESS**, **TGT TEMP**, gas generator **Ng SPEED**, power turbine speed (**% RPM 1** or **2**), rotor speed **% RPM R**, engine torque **% TRQ**, and **FUEL QTY** to provide the pilots with engine and subsystem monitoring. Continuous indications of those parameters are indicated on vertical scales, digital readouts and caution lights. Instruments without low range turn-off feature: **% TRQ**, **TGT TEMP**, **Ng SPEED**, **ENG OIL TEMP** and **XMSN TEMP** will remain on as parameter increases and go out as it decreases (Figure 5-1). Power for lighting the displays is from the No. 1 and No. 2 ac primary and No. 1 and No. 2 dc primary buses through the signal data converters.

2.27.1 Engine Oil Temperature Indicator. Each engine has an oil temperature sensor wired through the signal data converter to a vertical scale instrument, marked **ENG OIL TEMP**, on the central display unit; and to an engine oil temperature caution light, marked **ENGINE OIL TEMP**.

2.27.2 Engine Oil Pressure Indicator. Each engine has an engine oil pressure transmitter, downstream of the oil filter, that sends readings to a vertical scale indicator, marked **ENG OIL PRESS**, on the instrument display panel; and to an engine oil pressure caution legend, marked **ENG OIL PRESS**. The lower precautionary and prohibited ranges will go out when reaching the bottom of the normal range. It may be possible that during **IDLE** operations, the **ENG OIL PRESS** caution legend will go on. If **ENG OIL PRESS** caution legend comes on at **IDLE**, verify oil pressure is acceptable by setting **Ng SPEED** at 90%, check that engine oil pressure is at least 35 psi. As pressure increases above 100 psi the respective prohibited scale changes to red.

2.27.3 TGT Temperature Indicator. The TGT indicating system consists of thermocouples transmitting to a **TGT TEMP** indicator. The indicator assembly has two digital readouts that indicate precise temperatures.

2.27.4 Gas Generator Speed (Ng) Indicator. The Ng speed indicating system shows Ng speed for each engine. The system consists of one alternator winding and **Ng SPEED** vertical scale instrument, on the instrument panel, giving percent rpm. Digital readouts for **Ng SPEED** are at the lower section of the instrument face plate. The three-digit readouts provide a closer indication of **Ng SPEED**.

2.27.5 Engine Power Turbine/Rotor Speed Indicator. Power turbine and rotor speed are indicated for each engine on a single instrument marked **% RPM 1 R 2** on the display panel with three vertical scales (Figure 5-1). Power turbine speed is indicated in **% RPM 1** or **2** and rotor speed **% RPM R**. Rotor speed is sensed by a speed sensor on the right accessory module. Power turbine speed is sensed by a speed sensor on the engine exhaust frame. At the top of the panel are three warning lights that indicate varying degrees of rotor overspeed. These lights remain on, once tripped, and must be manually reset.

2.27.6 Torque Indicator. The torque system shows the amount of power the engine is delivering to the main transmission. A torque sensor mounted on the exhaust case measures the twist of the power turbine shaft, and transmits this signal to the ECU and signal data converter into the torque indicator marked **% TRQ** on the display panel, displaying readings for both engines. Digital readouts giving torques for each engine are at the top of the indicator. A photocell on the lower center of the display will automatically adjust the lighting of the **% RPM** and **% TRQ** indicators with respect to ambient light.

Section IV FUEL SYSTEM

2.28 FUEL SUPPLY SYSTEM.

A separate suction fuel system is provided for each engine. Fuel is stored in two interchangeable, crashworthy, ballistic-resistant tanks. The fuel system consists of lines from the main fuel tanks, firewall-mounted selector valves, prime/boost pump and fuel tanks, and engine-driven suction pumps. The prime/boost pump primes all fuel lines if prime is lost, and also acts as an APU boost for APU starts and operation. A selector valve, driven by cable from the **ENG FUEL SYS** selector lever on the engine control quadrant (Figure 2-10) permits operation of either engine from either fuel tank. The engines and APU are suction fed, the APU is fed from the left main fuel tank by a separate fuel line. All fuel lines are routed in the most direct manner. The fuel line network includes self-sealing breakaway valves that contain fuel in case of helicopter crash or malfunction. All engine fuel lines are self-sealing with the exception of the APU fuel line.

2.28.1 Fuel Tanks. Both main fuel tanks are crashworthy, self-sealing and interchangeable. Each tank contains a pressure refuel/defuel valve, fuel quantity and low-level sensors, high-level shutoff valve, low-level shutoff valve, check valve sump drain, and a self-sealing breakaway vent valve. (Refer to Table 2-4 for tank capacity.) Fuel tank drains are in the sumps to permit removal of sediment and water and provide fuel sampling.

2.28.2 Engine Fuel System Selector Control. Each fuel system has a selector valve which is manually operated through the **ENG FUEL SYS** selector lever on the overhead engine control quadrant (Figure 2-10). There is an **ENG EMER OFF** T-handle on each side of the quadrant which is arranged so that pulling the handle engages the **ENG FUEL SYS** selector lever, bringing it to **OFF**. The **ENG FUEL SYS** selectors are connected to the fuel selector valves with low-friction flexible push-pull cables. Each lever can be actuated to three positions: **OFF**, **DIR**, and **XFD**. With the selectors at **OFF**, the control valves are closed, allowing no fuel flow to the engines. When the selectors are moved forward to **DIR**, the selector valves are opened, providing fuel flow for each engine from its individual fuel tank. If a tank is empty, or you wish to equalize fuel in the tanks, the **ENG FUEL SYS** selector of the engine that normally feeds from the empty or low-level tank is moved to **XFD**. This connects that engine to the other tank through the crossfeed system. A check valve in each crossfeed line prevents air from an inoperative engine's fuel line crossing to the operating one.

2.28.3 Fuel Filter. The engine fuel filter has a bypass valve and bypass warning device. The filter is mounted on the forward left side of the engine accessory gear box. An impending bypass warning is incorporated on the filter housing in the form of a popout button. The bypass valve opens to assure continuous fuel flow with a blocked filter. At the same time the valve opens, an electrical switch closes to light the **#1** or **#2 FUEL FLTR BYPAS** caution legend. Power to operate the bypass warning system is from the No. 1 and No. 2 dc primary buses through circuit breakers marked **NO. 1** and **NO. 2 ENG WARN LTS**, respectively.

2.29 ENGINE FUEL PRIME SYSTEM.

NOTE

Priming engines using sump mounted fuel boost pumps is described in paragraph 8.41.3.

A toggle switch on the upper console, marked **FUEL PUMP, FUEL PRIME, OFF** and **APU BOOST** (Figure 2-6), when moved to **FUEL PRIME**, energizes the prime/boost pump and solenoid valves to each main engine fuel supply line and to the solenoid valve for the APU fuel feed system. An advisory indication is displayed during this mode by a legend marked **PRIME BOOST PUMP ON**. Prime pump capacity is not enough to prime an engine when the opposite engine is running. Engines should therefore be primed individually with both engines off. The prime/boost pump is actuated and the engine prime valve is opened whenever the engine starter is operating. This provides fuel pressure to aid in a successful engine start. When the engine speed reaches starter dropout speed, engine fuel prime valve will close and the prime/boost pump will also stop operating if the **FUEL PUMP** switch is **OFF**. Power to operate the prime boost system is from the battery bus through a circuit breaker marked **FUEL PRIME BOOST**.

2.30 FUEL QUANTITY INDICATING SYSTEM.

All internal fuel is continuously gaged with the **FUEL QTY** gage system (Figure 2-8). The system consists of two tank unit sensors (probes), one in each tank, a dual channel fuel quantity gage conditioner, and a dual channel low-level warning system. The tank units are connected to the fuel quantity gages marked **FUEL QTY 1-2** on the central display panel. A separate total fuel quantity readout numerically displays the total quantity of fuel on board. The system may be checked out by pressing the **FUEL IND TEST** pushbutton on the miscellaneous switch panel. The vertical scales of the **FUEL QTY** indicator and the digital readout should show a change, and the #1 and #2 **FUEL LOW** caution legends should flash. When the button is released, the scales and digital readout will return to the original readings. The fuel quantity indicating system is powered by the No. 1 ac primary bus through a circuit breaker, marked **NO. 1 AC INST**.

2.30.1 Fuel Low Caution Legend. Two low-level sensors, one on each probe, provide signals which activate two low-level caution legends indicating #1 **FUEL** or #2 **FUEL**. Those legends flash when the fuel level decreases to approximately 172 pounds in each tank. The illumination of these legends does not mean a fixed time period remains before fuel exhaustion, but is an indication that a low fuel condition exists The fuel-low caution legends are powered by the No. 1 dc primary bus through a circuit breaker marked **FUEL LOW WARN**.

2.30.2 Fuel Boost Pump. The helicopter fuel system contains an electrically-operated submerged fuel boost pump in each fuel tank. When the pumps operate, they provide pressurized fuel to the engine fuel inlet port. Each boost pump is controlled by a switch on the **FUEL BOOST PUMP CONTROL** panel (Figure 2-7). The two-position switch for each pump, marked **ON-OFF**, activates the pump for continuous operation to maintain a head of fuel pressure at the engine fuel inlet port, regardless of engine boost pump discharge pressure. An advisory light near each control switch indicates pump pressure and operation. A check valve in each pump discharge line prevents fuel recirculation during fuel boost operation, and prevents loss of engine fuel line prime. #1 or #2 **FUEL PRESS** caution legend going on is also an indicator to turn on boost pumps. Power to operate the boost pumps is provided from the No. 1 and No. 2 ac primary buses through circuit breakers marked **NO. 1** and **NO. 2 FUEL BOOST PUMP**, respectively.

2.30.3 Refueling/Defueling. A pressure refueling and defueling system provides complete refueling and defueling of both tanks from one point on the left side of the helicopter (Figure 2-23). Closed circuit refueling uses the pressure refueling system and its components. No electrical power is required for the system during refueling or defueling. The tank full shutoff valve is float-operated. A dual high-level shutoff system acts as back up for each other. The two high-level float valves close, causing a back pressure to the fueling/defueling valve at the bottom of the tank, closing the refuel valve. The tank empty automatic shutoff system is a function of the low-level float valve opening to allow air to be drawn into the line, closing the defuel valve. A filler neck between the fuselage contour and the fuel cell is a frangible (breakaway) connection. Gravity fueling is done through filler neck on each side of the fuselage for the respective tanks. Gravity defueling capability is provided through the drains.

Section V FLIGHT CONTROLS

2.31 FLIGHT CONTROL SYSTEMS.

NOTE

Flight near high power RF emitters such as microwave antennas or shipboard radar may cause uncommanded AFCS and/or stabilator control inputs. Electromagnetic interference (EMI) testing has shown that the master caution light may illuminate before or simultaneously with any uncommanded stabilator trailing edge movement, with 4° or 5° of movement being the maximum.

The primary flight control system consists of the lateral control subsystem, the longitudinal control subsystem, the collective pitch control subsystem, and the directional control subsystem. Control inputs are transferred from the cockpit to the rotor blades by mechanical linkages, and hydraulic servos. Pilot control is assisted by stability augmentation system (SAS), flight path stabilization (FPS), boost servos, and pitch, roll and yaw trim. Dual cockpit controls consist of the cyclic stick, collective stick and pedals. The pilot and copilot controls are routed separately to a combining linkage for each control axis. Outputs from the cockpit controls are carried by mechanical linkage through the pilot-assist servos to the mixing unit. The mixing unit combines, sums, and couples the cyclic, collective, and yaw inputs. It provides proportional output signals, through mechanical linkages, to the main and tail rotor controls.

2.31.1 Cyclic Stick.
Lateral and longitudinal control of the helicopter is by movement of the cyclic sticks through push rods, bellcranks, and servos to the main rotor. Movement in any direction tilts the plane of the main rotor blades in the same direction, thereby causing the helicopter to go in that direction. Each cyclic stick grip (Figure 2-11) contains a stick trim switch, marked **STICK TRIM FWD, L, R** and **AFT**, a go around switch, marked **GA**, trim release switch, marked **TRIM REL**, a panel light kill switch, marked **PNL LTS**, a cargo release switch, marked **CARGO REL**, and a transmitter ICS switch, marked **RADIO** and **ICS**. Refer to major systems for a complete description of switches on the cyclic grip.

2.31.2 Collective Pitch Control Stick.
The collective sticks change the pitch of the main rotor blades, causing an increase or decrease in lift on the entire main rotor disc. A friction control on the pilot's lever can be turned to adjust the amount of friction and prevent the collective stick from creeping. The copilot's stick telescopes by twisting the grip and pushing the stick aft to improve access to his seat. Each collective stick has a grip (Figure 2-11) with switches and controls for various helicopter systems. These systems are: landing light control, marked **LDG LT PUSH ON/OFF EXT** and **RETR**; searchlight controls, marked **SRCH LT ON/OFF BRT, DIM, EXT, L, R,** and **RETR**; servo shutoff control switch, marked **SVO OFF 1ST STG** and **2ND STG**; a cargo hook emergency release switch, marked **HOOK EMER REL**, a radio select switch marked **RAD SEL UP-DN** and **HUD** control switch, marked **BRT-DIM-MODE-DCLT**. All switches are within easy reach of the left thumb. For a complete description of switches and controls, refer to major system description.

2.31.3 Mixing Unit.
A mechanical mixing unit provides control mixing functions which minimizes inherent control coupling. The four types of mechanical mixing and their functions are:

   a. Collective to Pitch - Compensates for the effects of changes in rotor downwash on the stabilator caused by collective pitch changes. The mixing unit provides forward input to the main rotor as collective is increased and aft input as collective is decreased.

   b. Collective to Yaw - Compensates for changes in torque effect caused by changes in collective position. The mixing unit increases tail rotor pitch as collective is increased and decreases tail rotor pitch as collective is decreased.

   c. Collective to Roll - Compensates for the rolling moments and translating tendency caused by changes in tail rotor thrust. The mixing unit provides left lateral input to the main rotor system as collective is increased and right lateral input as collective is decreased.

   d. Yaw to Pitch - Compensates for changes in the vertical thrust component of the canted tail rotor as tail rotor pitch is changed. The mixing unit provides aft input to the main rotor system as tail rotor pitch is increased and forward input as tail rotor pitch is decreased.

2.31.4 Collective/Airspeed to Yaw (Electronic Coupling).
This mixing is in addition to collective to yaw mechanical mixing. It helps compensate for the torque effect caused by changes in collective position. It has the ability to decrease tail rotor pitch as airspeed increases and the tail rotor and cambered fin become more efficient. As airspeed decreases, the opposite occurs. The SAS/FPS computer commands the yaw trim actuator to change tail rotor pitch as collective position changes. The amount of tail rotor pitch change is proportional to airspeed. Maximum mixing occurs from 0 to 40 knots. As airspeed

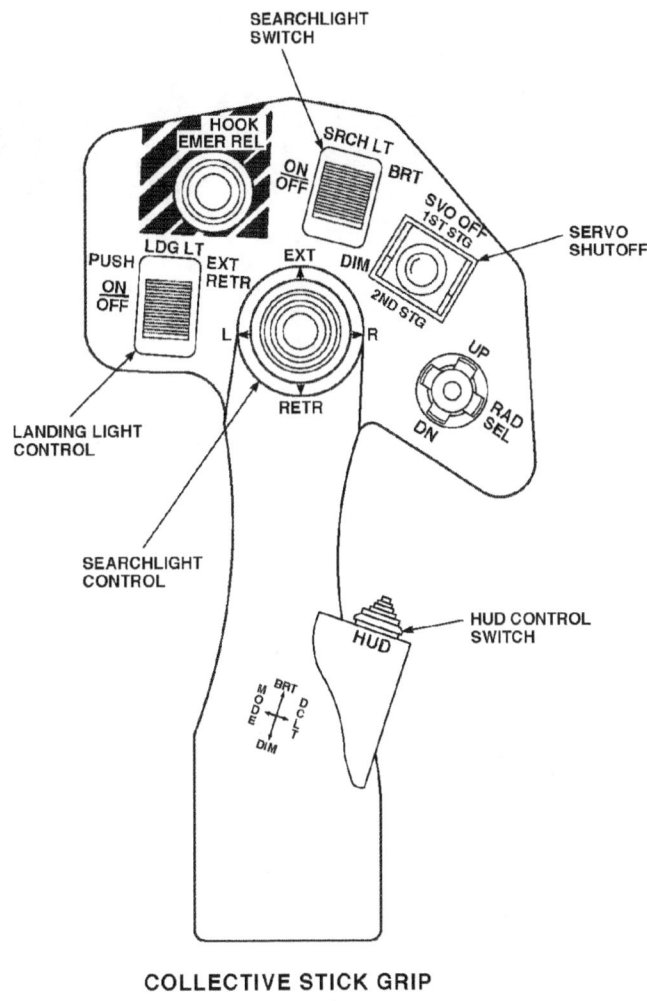

Figure 2-11. Collective and Cyclic Grips (Sheet 1 of 2)

increases above 40 knots, the amount of mixing decreases until 100 knots, after which no mixing occurs.

2.31.5 Tail Rotor Control. The tail rotor control system determines helicopter heading by controlling pitch of the tail rotor blades. Inputs by the pilot or copilot to the control pedals are transmitted through a series of control rods, bellcranks, a mixing unit, control cables and servos to the pitch change beam that changes blade pitch angle. Hydraulic power to the tail rotor servo is supplied from No. 1 or the backup hydraulic systems.

2.31.6 Tail Rotor Pedals. The pedals contain switches that, when pressed, disengage the heading hold feature of FPS below 60 KIAS. Adjustment for pilot leg length is done by pulling a T-handle, on each side of the instrument panel, marked **PED ADJ**. The pedals are spring-loaded and will move toward the operator when unlocked. Applying pressure to both pedals simultaneously will move the pedals for desired leg position. The handle is then released to lock the pedal adjusted position.

2.32 FLIGHT CONTROL SERVO SYSTEMS.

The servos are mounted on the upper deck above the cabin area forward of the main gear box in the control access. Three main rotor servos with two independent redundant stages have only the input linkage in common.

2-31

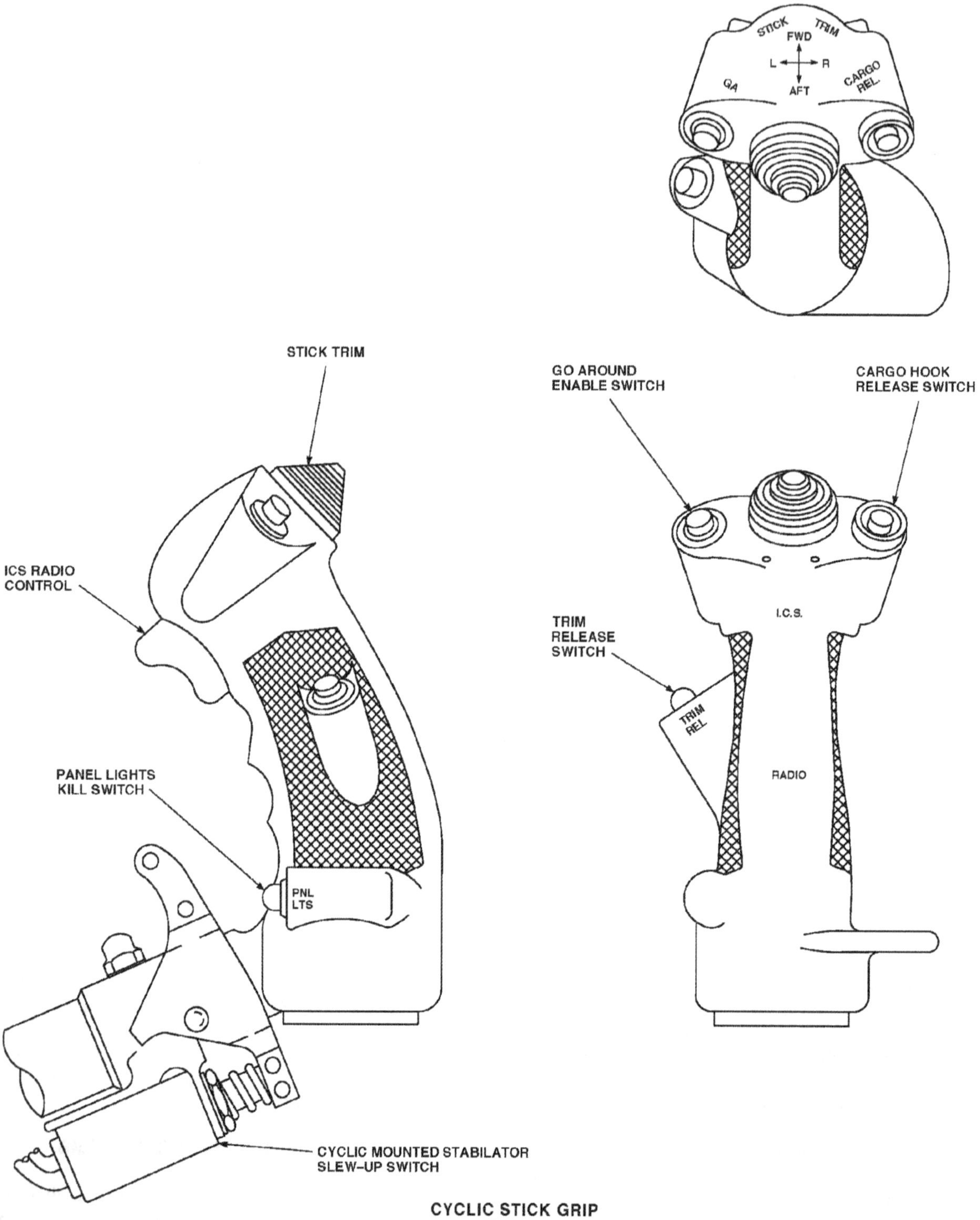

TM 1-1520-253-10

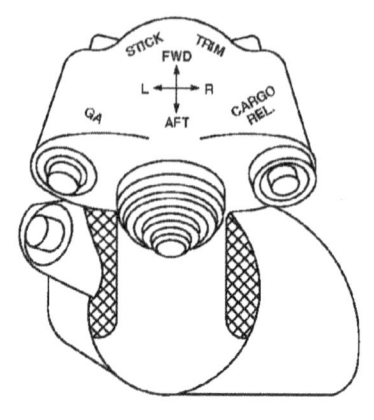

CYCLIC STICK GRIP
(TYPICAL)

Figure 2-11. Collective and Cyclic Grips (Sheet 2 of 2)

2-32

Should one stage become inoperative due to pressure loss, a bypass valve within the depressurized stage will open, preventing a hydraulic lock. Tail rotor control loads are reacted by a two-stage tail rotor servo mounted on the tail gear box. With the **TAIL SERVO** switch at **NORMAL**, the first stage of this servo is powered by the No. 1 hydraulic system; the second stage is powered by the backup system when the switch is at **BACKUP**. Should the first stage become inoperative, the backup pump will come on and power the second stage. All aerodynamic loads are then reacted by the second stage. Electrical interlocks prevent both flight control servos from being turned off simultaneously. The servo switches marked **SVO OFF**, **1ST STG** and **2ND STG** are on the pilot and copilot collective stick grips (Figure 2-11). If the input pilot valve to the servo becomes jammed, bypass automatically occurs. Automatic bypass is indicated to the pilot by lighting of the associated **PRI SERVO PRESS** caution legend.

2.32.1 Flight Control Servo Switch. First and second stage primary servo systems are controlled by the servo switch, marked **SVO OFF**, on the pilot's and copilot's collective stick grips (Figure 2-11). The marked switch positions are **1ST STG** and **2ND STG**. The servo systems normally operate with the switch in the unmarked center (on) position. To turn off the first stage primary servos, the **SVO OFF** switch is placed to **1ST STG**. To turn off the second stage servo, the switch is placed to **2ND STG**. The systems are interconnected electrically so that regardless of switch position, a system will not shut off unless there is at least 2350 psi in the remaining system. The servo shutoff valve operates on current from the No. 1 and No. 2 dc primary buses through circuit breakers marked **NO. 1** and **NO. 2 SERVO CONTR** respectively.

2.32.2 Flight Control Servo Low-Pressure Caution Legends. The first, second, and tail rotor stage servo hydraulic low-pressure caution legends are marked **#1 PRI SERVO PRESS**, **#2 PRI SERVO PRESS**, and **#1 TAIL RTR SERVO**, and will go on if the pressure is below its respective switch setting, or if the servo pilot valve becomes jammed. The servo switches and warning legends operate on direct current from the No. 1 and No. 2 dc primary buses through circuit breakers, marked **NO. 1 SERVO WARN** and **NO. 2 SERVO WARN**, respectively.

2.32.3 Pilot-Assist Servos. Pilot assist servos are normally powered by the No. 2 hydraulic system. If the No. 2 hydraulic pump fails, the pilot assist servos and pitch trim actuator are powered by the backup hydraulic pump. The following units are pilot-assist servos: collective, yaw, and pitch boost servos, which reduce control forces; and three (pitch, roll, yaw) SAS actuators which transfer the output of the SAS controllers into control actuations.

2.32.4 Boost Servo. There are three boost servos, collective, yaw, and pitch, installed between the cockpit controls and mixing unit, which reduce cockpit control forces. The collective and yaw boost servos are turned on and off by pressing the button marked **BOOST** on the **AUTO FLT CONT** panel (Figure 2-12). The pitch boost servo is turned on when **SAS 1** or **SAS 2** is **ON**. The boost shutoff valves receive power from the dc essential bus through a circuit breaker, marked **SAS BOOST**.

2.32.5 Pilot-Assist Controls. An **AUTO FLT CONT** panel (Figure 2-12), in the lower console, contains the controls for operating the pilot-assist servos and actuators. The panel contains **SAS 1**, **SAS 2**, **TRIM**, **FPS**, **BOOST** and the **FAILURE ADVISORY/POWER ON RESET** lights/switches. **STICK TRIM** and **TRIM REL** switches on the cyclic sticks, are manually operated by either pilot or copilot.

2.33 AUTOMATIC FLIGHT CONTROL SYSTEM (AFCS).

The AFCS enhances the stability and handling qualities of the helicopter. It is comprised of four basic subsystems: Stabilator, Stability Augmentation System (SAS), Trim Systems, and Flight Path Stabilization (FPS). The stabilator system improves flying qualities by positioning the stabilator by means of electromechanical actuators in response to collective, airspeed, pitch rate and lateral acceleration inputs. The stability augmentation system provides short term rate damping in the pitch, roll, and yaw axes. Trim/FPS system provides control positioning and force gradient functions as well as basic autopilot functions with FPS engaged.

2.33.1 Stability Augmentation System (SAS).

NOTE

As the vertical gyro comes up to speed or when the system is shutdown, the derived pitch/roll rate signal which feeds **SAS 1** will cause small oscillations in pitch and roll SAS actuators. This is a temporary situation and can be eliminated by turning **SAS 1** off.

The SAS enhances dynamic stability in the pitch, roll, and yaw axes. In addition, both **SAS 1** and **SAS 2** enhance turn coordination by deriving commands from lateral accelerometers which together with roll rate signals are sent to their respective yaw channels automatically at airspeeds greater than 60 knots. The **SAS 1** amplifier circuitry operates on 28 vdc power from the dc essential bus through a circuit breaker marked **SAS BOOST** providing excitation for the electronic components within the amplifier. AC power from the ac essential bus through a circuit breaker marked **SAS AMPL** is also required for normal operation of the SAS. The SAS amplifier uses the vertical gyro roll output to derive roll attitude and rate for the roll SAS commands and an ac-powered yaw rate gyro for the yaw SAS commands. Loss of ac power to the vertical gyro or SAS amplifier causes erratic operation of **SAS 1** due to loss of the reference for the ac demodulators. When this condition is encountered, the pilot must manually disengage **SAS 1**. In case of a malfunction of the **SAS 2** function, the input will normally be removed from the actuator and the **SAS 2** fail advisory light on the **AUTO FLT CONT** panel will go on. If the malfunction is of an intermittent nature the indication can be cleared by simultaneously pressing **POWER ON RESET** switches. If the malfunction is continuous, the **SAS 2** should be turned off. With **SAS 1** or **SAS 2** off, the control authority of the stability augmentation system is reduced by one-half (5% control authority). Malfunction of the **SAS 1** system may be detected by the pilot as an erratic motion in the helicopter without a corresponding failure advisory indication. If a malfunction is experienced, **SAS 1** should be turned off. SAS actuator hydraulic pressure is monitored. In case of loss of actuator pressure, or if both **SAS 1** and **SAS 2** are off, the **SAS OFF** caution light will go on.

2.33.2 Trim System. When the **TRIM** is engaged on the **AUTO FLT CONT** panel, the pitch, roll and yaw trim systems are activated to maintain position of the cyclic and tail rotor controls. Proper operation of the yaw trim requires that the **BOOST** on the **AUTO FLT CONT** panel be on. The tail rotor and lateral cyclic forces are developed in the electromechanical yaw and roll trim actuators. Both yaw and roll trim actuators incorporate slip clutches to allow pilot and copilot control inputs if either actuator should jam. The forces required to break through the clutch are 80-pounds maximum in yaw and 13 pounds maximum in roll. The longitudinal force is developed by an electrohydromechanical actuator operated in conjunction with the SAS/FPS computer. When the pilot applies a longitudinal or lateral force to the cyclic stick with trim engaged, a combination detent and gradient force is felt. The pilot may remove the force by pressing the thumb-operated **TRIM REL** switch on the pilot/copilot cyclic grip. The pedal gradient maintains pedal position whenever the trim is engaged. By placing feet on the pedals, the pedal switches are depressed and the gradient force is removed. The pedals may then be moved to the desired position and released. The pedals will be held at this position by the trim gradient. The pedal trim gradient actuator also includes a pedal damper. The pedal damper is engaged continuously, independent of electric power and the **TRIM** switch on the **AUTO FLT CONT** panel. Operation of the trim system is continuously monitored by the SAS/FPS computer. If a

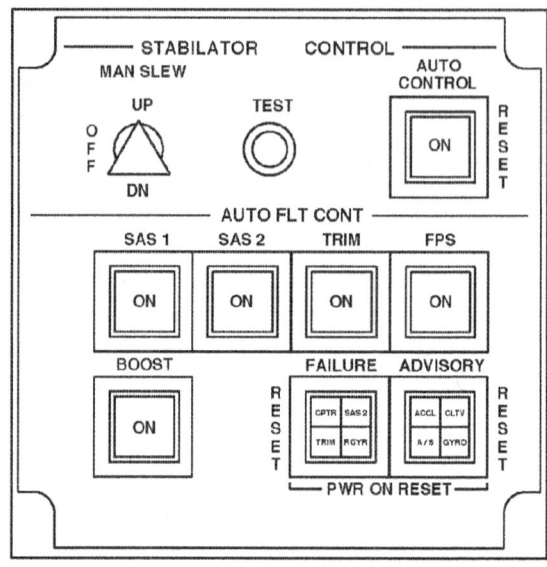

Figure 2-12. Automatic Flight Control System (AFCS) Switch Panel

malfunction occurs, the SAS/FPS computer will shut off the trim actuator(s) driving the affected axis, and the **TRIM FAIL** and **FLT PATH STAB** caution legend will illuminate. If the malfunction is of an intermittent nature, the indication may be cleared by simultaneously pressing both **POWER ON RESET** switches. In addition to the trim release switch, a four-way trim switch on each cyclic stick establishes a trim position without releasing trim. With trim engaged, the trim position is moved in the direction of switch movement. The cyclic is moved by the trim switch in one direction at a time. When **FPS** is engaged, the **TRIM** switch changes the pitch and roll attitude reference instead of the cyclic stick position reference. The trim system release feature permits the pilot or copilot to fly the helicopter with light stick forces. The push-on/push-off **TRIM** switch on the **AUTO FLT CONT** panel or the **TRIM REL** switches on the pilot/copilot cyclic grips may be used to release trim. When the switch is **ON**, the trim system provides gradient and detent holding force for pitch, roll, and yaw. When turned off, the trim system is released and light cyclic control forces are present.

2.33.3 Flight Path Stabilization (FPS).

a. Proper FPS operation requires that the **BOOST**, **TRIM** and **SAS 1** and/or **SAS 2** functions have been selected on the **AUTO FLT CONT** panel. Although not required for proper operation, the FPS performance will be improved by the proper operation of the stabilator in the automatic mode. To use the FPS features, the pilot first assures that **BOOST**, **SAS** and **TRIM** are on and operating, and then turns the **FPS** switch **ON**. The desired pitch and roll attitude of the helicopter may be established in one of these ways:

    (1) Pressing the **STICK TRIM** switch to slew the reference attitude to the desired attitude.

    (2) Pressing the **TRIM REL** switch on the pilot/copilot cyclic grip, manually flying the helicopter to the desired trim condition, and releasing the **TRIM REL** switch.

    (3) Overriding the stick trim forces to establish the desired trim condition, and then neutralizing stick forces by means of the trim switch.

b. The trim attitude, once established, will be automatically held until changed by the pilot. At airspeeds greater than 60 knots, the pitch axis seeks to maintain the airspeed at which the trim is established, by variation of pitch attitude. When pitch attitude is changed by means of the **STICK TRIM** switch, there is a delay from the time that the **STICK TRIM** switch input is removed until the new reference airspeed is acquired. This is to allow time for the helicopter to accelerate or decelerate to the new trim speed. The yaw axis of the FPS provides heading hold at airspeeds less than 60 knots and heading hold or turn coordination at airspeeds greater than 60 knots. For heading hold operation at airspeeds less than 60 knots, the helicopter is maneuvered to the desired heading with feet on pedals. When trimmed at the desired heading, the pilot may remove feet from pedals, at which time the existing heading becomes the reference, which is automatically held. To change heading, the pilot may activate one or both pedal switches, trim up on the desired heading and remove feet from pedals. At airspeeds greater than 60 knots, heading hold will be automatically disengaged, and coordinated turn engaged under these conditions:

    (1) **STICK TRIM** switch is actuated in the lateral direction.

    (2) **TRIM REL** switch is pressed and roll attitude is greater than prescribed limits.

    (3) About 1/2 inch cyclic displacement and a roll attitude of about 1.5°. Heading hold is automatically reengaged and turn coordination disengaged upon recovery from the turn when the lateral stick force, roll attitude, and yaw rate are within prescribed limits.

c. To make a coordinated turn, the pilot enters a turn in one of these ways:

    (1) Changing reference roll attitude by pressing the **STICK TRIM** switch in the desired lateral direction.

    (2) Pressing **TRIM REL** switch on the cyclic grip and establishing the desired bank angle with feet off pedal switches.

    (3) Exerting a lateral force on the cyclic stick to achieve the desired bank angle, and then neutralizing the force with the **STICK TRIM** switch.

    (4) Keeping a lateral force on the cyclic stick for the duration of the turn.

d. In each of these ways the ball should remain automatically centered during the entry and recovery from the turn. If feet are on the pedals, care must be taken not to apply too much force to the pedals to oppose their motion. If the pilot intentionally miscoordinates the helicopter, the result will be a pedal force roughly proportional to sideslip. The pilot may release the pedal force by pressing the cyclic **TRIM REL** switch with feet on pedals. During transition through 60 knots airspeed, the pilot may feel a slight pedal motion due to a switching transient which may occur when the commanded coordinated turn pedal position differs slightly from the pilot-commanded position. The FPS monitoring is automatic. If a malfunction is detected, the **FLT PATH STAB** caution legend will go on and the FPS will either continue to operate in a degraded mode, such as without heading hold, or without airspeed hold; or may cease to function altogether. The pilot must take over manual flight of the helicopter, and may either turn the FPS off or evaluate performance to determine the degree and type of degradation, and continue flight with the remaining features. To help evaluate the nature of the degradation, eight failure advisory indicators are displayed on two **FAILURE ADVISORY** switches on the flight control panel. These tell the pilot the type of sensor or actuator which has experienced the failure. If a light goes on, it may be turned off by pressing the lighted switch. All failure advisory lights will be on at initial application of power. The pilot may attempt to clear the indication of temporary malfunction by simultaneously pressing both **FAILURE ADVISORY** switches. If the **FLT PATH STAB** caution legend goes off, it may be assumed that normal operation is restored. All FPS functions are provided by automatically moving the cockpit controls.

2.34 STABILATOR SYSTEM.

a. The helicopter has a variable angle of incidence stabilator to enhance handling qualities. The automatic mode of operation positions the stabilator to the best angle of attack for the existing flight conditions. After the pilot engages the automatic mode, no further pilot action is required for stabilator operation. Two stabilator amplifiers receive airspeed, collective stick position, pitch rate, and lateral acceleration information to program the stabilator through the dual electric actuators. The stabilator is programmed to:

(1) Align stabilator and main rotor downwash in low speed flight to minimize nose-up attitude resulting from downwash.

(2) Decrease angle of incidence with increased airspeed to improve static stability.

(3) Provide collective coupling to minimize pitch attitude excursions due to collective inputs from the pilot. Collective position sensors detect pilot collective displacement and programs the stabilator a corresponding amount to counteract the pitch changes. The coupling of stabilator position to collective displacement is automatically phased in beginning at 30 KIAS.

(4) Provide pitch rate feedback to improve dynamic stability. The rate of pitch attitude change of the helicopter is sensed by a pitch rate gyro in each of the two stabilator amplifiers and used to position the stabilator to help dampen pitch excursions during gusty wind conditions. A sudden pitch up due to gusts would cause the stabilator to be programmed trailing edge down a small amount to induce a nose-down pitch to dampen the initial reaction.

(5) Provide sideslip to pitch coupling to reduce susceptibility to gusts. When the helicopter is out of trim in a slip or skid, pitch excursions are also induced as a result of the main rotor downwash on the stabilator. Lateral accelerometers sense this out of trim condition and signal the stabilator amplifiers to compensate for the pitch attitude change (called sideslip to pitch coupling). Nose left (right slip) results in the trailing edge programming down. Nose right produces the opposite stabilator reaction.

b. The above features are provided via inputs to dual actuators which position the stabilator. Failure of one actuator will restrict total maximum movement of the stabilator to about 35° if failure occurs full down, or about 30° if failure occurs full up. The stabilator actuators receive power from the dc essential bus and No. 2 dc primary bus through circuit breakers marked **STAB PWR**. Since the dc essential bus is powered by the battery, it is possible to manually slew one actuator using battery power only. If the stabilator is slewed up, regain automatic control by manually slewing stabilator full down, then push **AUTO CONTROL RESET** twice. Otherwise, when only one actuator is slewed, it causes a very large mismatch between the two actuator positions. This is detected by the fault monitor and shuts down the automatic mode upon attempted engagement. Automatic control function sensors, airspeed sensors, pitch rate gyros, collective position sensor, and lateral accelerometer receive power from the ac essential bus and No. 2 ac primary bus through circuit breakers marked **STAB CONTR**.

2.34.1 Stabilator Control Panel. The stabilator control panel (Figure 2-8), on the lower console, provides electrical control of the stabilator system. The panel contains a **MAN SLEW** switch, a **TEST** button, and **AUTO CONTROL RESET** switch with a push-to-reset feature. The automatic mode will allow the stabilator to be automatically operated from about 39° trailing edge down to 9° trailing edge up. Manual operation is also restricted to these limits. If a malfunction occurs in the automatic mode, the system will switch to manual, **ON** will go off in the **AUTO CONTROL** window, and the **STABILATOR** caution legend and **MASTER CAUTION** light will go on and a beeping tone will be heard in the pilot's and copilot's headphones. It may be possible to regain the auto mode by pressing the **AUTO CONTROL RESET**. If the automatic mode is regained, **ON** will appear in the **AUTO CONTROL** switch window and the caution lights will go off. The stabilator automatic mode is held in the energized state within the stabilator control amplifier. On certain occasions during interruption of dc power, such as switching of generators, it is possible to have conditions where the stabilator automatic mode may shut down. If the automatic mode shuts down during flight because of an ac power failure, the helicopter shall be slowed to 80 KIAS before power is restored. In this case the **AUTO CONTROL RESET** switch may be pressed to reengage the auto mode. If the automatic mode is not regained, the **MASTER CAUTION** must be reset, which turns off the beeping tone, and the stabilator controlled throughout its range with the **MAN SLEW** switch. When initial power is applied to the stabilator system, it will be in automatic mode. The **TEST** switch is used to check the AUTO mode fault detector feature and is inoperative above 60 KIAS. When pressed, control of the stabilator should go to the manual mode.

2.34.2 Stabilator Position Indicator. A **STAB POS** indicator (Figure 2-8) is on the instrument panel. It gives pilots a remote indication of stabilator position. The indicator range is marked from 45° **DN** to 10° up. The stabilator position indicator system is powered from the ac essential bus 26V through a circuit breaker marked **STAB IND**.

2.34.3 Cyclic-Mounted Stabilator Slew Up Switch.
Installed on each cyclic stick below the grip (Figure 2-11) is a pull-type stabilator manual slew up switch. The switch provides the pilot and copilot with rapid accessibility to stabilator slew up. The cyclic slew switch is wired in parallel with the stabilator panel **MAN SLEW-UP** switch position. When the switch is actuated, the stabilator trailing edge will begin to move up and continue until the up limit stop is reached or the switch is released.

Section VI HYDRAULIC AND PNEUMATIC SYSTEM

2.35 HYDRAULIC SYSTEM.

The three hydraulic systems are designed to provide full flight control pressure. The components of the hydraulic systems are three hydraulic pump modules, two transfer modules, a utility module, three dual primary servos, one dual tail rotor servo, four pilot-assist servos, an APU accumulator, an APU handpump, and a servicing handpump. There are three hydraulic pressure supply systems, number 1, number 2, and backup. All are completely independent and each is fully capable of providing essential flight control pressure for maximum system redundancy. Complete redundancy is accomplished by the backup pump providing hydraulic power to both number 1 and/or number 2 systems if one or both pumps fail. If two systems lose pressure, there will be a slight restriction in the maximum rate of flight control movement due to only one pump supplying both stages with hydraulic power. An automatic turnoff feature is provided. When the **SVO OFF** switch (Figure 2-11) is moved to **1ST STG** or **2ND STG** position, that stage of the primary servos is turned off. When the **SVO OFF** switch is moved to **1ST STG**, the first stage of the primary servos is turned off. A malfunction in the second stage will cause first stage (which was turned off) to automatically turn back on in case the backup system does not take over the function of the failed second stage. If the second stage is initially turned off, the sequence is reversed. An additional hydraulic handpump is provided for APU start system.

NOTE

The following listed caution legends may momentarily flicker when the applicable listed switch is activated; this is considered normal.

SUBSYSTEM	CAUTION LEGEND
SAS 1 or SAS 2 switch ON	#2 PRI SERVO PRESS #2 HYD PUMP BOOST SERVO OFF
BOOST switch ON	#2 PRI SERVO PRESS #2 HYD PUMP SAS OFF
TAIL SERVO switch BACKUP	#1 PRI SERVO PRESS #1 HYD PUMP
HYD LEAK TEST switch NORM after RESET	#1 and #2 PRI SERVO PRESS #1 and #2 HYD PUMP

2.36 HYDRAULIC PUMP MODULES.

The hydraulic pump modules are combination hydraulic pumps and reservoirs. The No. 1, No. 2, and backup pump modules are identical and interchangeable with each other. The No. 1 pump module is mounted on and driven by the left accessory module of the main transmission. The No. 2 pump module is mounted on and driven by the right accessory transmission module. The backup pump module is mounted on and driven by an ac electric motor. The reservoir part of each pump module has a level indicator window marked, **REFILL**, **FULL**, and **EXPANSION**. A pressure relief and bleed valve protects the pump from high pressure in the return system. The pump has two filters: a pressure filter and a return filter. A red indicator button on each filter will pop out when pressure goes up 70 ±10 psi above normal. The pressure filter has no bypass. The return filter has a bypass valve that opens when return pressure reaches 100 ±10 psi above normal. Each pump has three check valves: one at the external ground coupling, one at the pressure side, and one at the return side. A fluid quantity switch, mounted on top of each pump module, senses fluid loss for that system. When the piston in the pump module moves down to the **REFILL** mark, the piston closes the switch, turning on a caution legend marked **RSVR LOW**. Each hydraulic pump has two temperature sensitive labels mounted on the side. When a temperature level is reached a circle turns black. There are two types of labels used on the pumps. When the temperature label indicates that a temperature of 132°C (270°F) has been exceeded, an entry shall be made on DA Form 2408-13-1. The aircraft should not be flown until appropriate maintenance action has been taken.

2.36.1 Number 1 Hydraulic System. Number 1 hydraulic system operates with the rotor turning, and supplies the first stage of all primary servos and the first stage of the tail rotor servo. The system components are an integrated pump module, a transfer module, first stage primary servos, and first stage tail rotor servo. The primary servos are controlled by the **SVO OFF** switch (Figure 2-11). The switch can turn off either first or second stage of the primary servos but not both at the same time. First stage tail rotor servo can be manually turned off by a two-position switch marked **TAIL SERVO**, on the miscellaneous switch panel (Figure 2-7). If the fluid quantity of the number one pump reservoir becomes low, a microswitch will complete an electrical circuit to close the first stage tail rotor servo valve. If fluid continues to be lost and the **#1 HYD PUMP** caution legend goes on, the first stage tail rotor shutoff valve will open, allowing backup pressure to supply first stage tail rotor. The logic modules automatically control the hydraulic system. The tail rotor servo is a two-stage servo but, unlike the primary servos, only one stage is pressurized at a time.

2.36.2 Number 2 Hydraulic System. The number 2 hydraulic system, which also operates with the rotor turning, supplies the second stage primary servo and the pilot-assist servos. System components are the integrated pump module, transfer module, second stage primary servos, and pilot-assist modules. Second stage primary servos can be manually turned off by the **SVO OFF** switch. The pilot-assist servos cannot be turned off collectively, but **SAS**, **TRIM** and **BOOST** servos can be manually turned off by switches on the **AUTO FLT CONT** panel. If fluid quantity of the number two pump reservoir becomes low, the pilot-assist servo becomes inoperative. If fluid continues to be lost, the **#2 HYD PUMP** caution legend will go on.

2.36.3 Backup Hydraulic System.

Whenever the No. 1 ac generator is inoperative (failed, or not on line) and the BACKUP PUMP PWR circuit breaker is out for any reason, ac electrical power must be shut off before resetting BACKUP PUMP PWR circuit breaker. Otherwise, it is possible to damage the current limiters.

The backup hydraulic pump system supplies emergency pressure to the number 1 and/or number 2 hydraulic systems whenever a pressure loss occurs. It also supplies pressure to the number 2 stage of the tail rotor servo in case of a loss of pressure in the first stage of the tail rotor servo or **#1 RSVR LOW** indication. This system supplies hydraulic pressure to all flight control components during ground checkout. The backup system also provides a hydraulic pressure for automatic recharging of the APU start system accumulator. The backup hydraulic system pump module is driven by an electric motor which can be powered by any adequate three-phase ac power source. An internal depressurizing valve in the backup pump module reduces the output pressure of the pump upon startup of the electric motor. This valve unloads the electric motor by reducing torque requirement at low rpm. After about 0.5 second when main generator is operating, or 4 seconds when operating from APU generator or external power, the valve is closed and 3000 psi pressure is supplied to the hydraulic system. This sequence reduces the current demand during backup system startup. Pressure sensing switches in the number 1 and number 2 transfer modules constantly monitor the pressure output of the number 1 and number 2 pumps. Loss of pressure initiates the backup operation. The system then provides emergency pressure to maintain full flight control capability. A WOW switch on the left main landing gear provides automatic operation of the backup pump when the helicopter is in the air, regardless of **BACKUP HYD PUMP** switch position, and disables the backup pump ac thermal switch. A pressure sensing switch at the tail rotor monitors supply pressure to the first stage tail rotor servo. The backup pump can supply pressure to the first stage tail rotor servo if the number 1 pump loses pressure. This gives the pilot a backup tail rotor servo even with the loss of the primary hydraulic supply, or **#1 RSVR LOW**. If a leak in a primary servo system depletes the backup system fluid, the backup reservoir level sensing switch will turn on the **BACK-UP RSVR LOW** caution legend, and the pilot must manually turn off the leaking primary system.

2.37 HYDRAULIC LEAK DETECTION/ISOLATION SYSTEM.

The leak detection/isolation (LDI) system protects the flight control hydraulic system by preventing the further loss of hydraulic fluid in case of a leak. The LDI system uses pressure switches and fluid level sensors for monitoring pump hydraulic fluid level, and pump pressure for primary and tail rotor servos, and pilot-assist servos. When a pump module reservoir fluid level switch detects a fluid loss, the logic module follows the sequence detailed in Figure 2-13 to isolate the leak. To accomplish this, the logic module operates the required shutoff valve(s) to isolate the leak and turns on the backup pump when required. In the cockpit the **RSVR LOW** caution legend for that system lights. Backup pump and shutoff valve(s) operation is automatic through the logic module. If, after the isolation sequence, the leak continues, the leakage is in the stage 1 or 2 primary servos and the appropriate **SVO OFF** switch must be moved to the off position by the pilot. By placing the **HYD LEAK TEST** switch to **TEST**, all leak detection/isolation system components are checked electrically. After a leak test has been made, the **HYD LEAK TEST** switch must be moved to **RESET** momentarily, to turn off caution and advisory legends that were on during the test. The

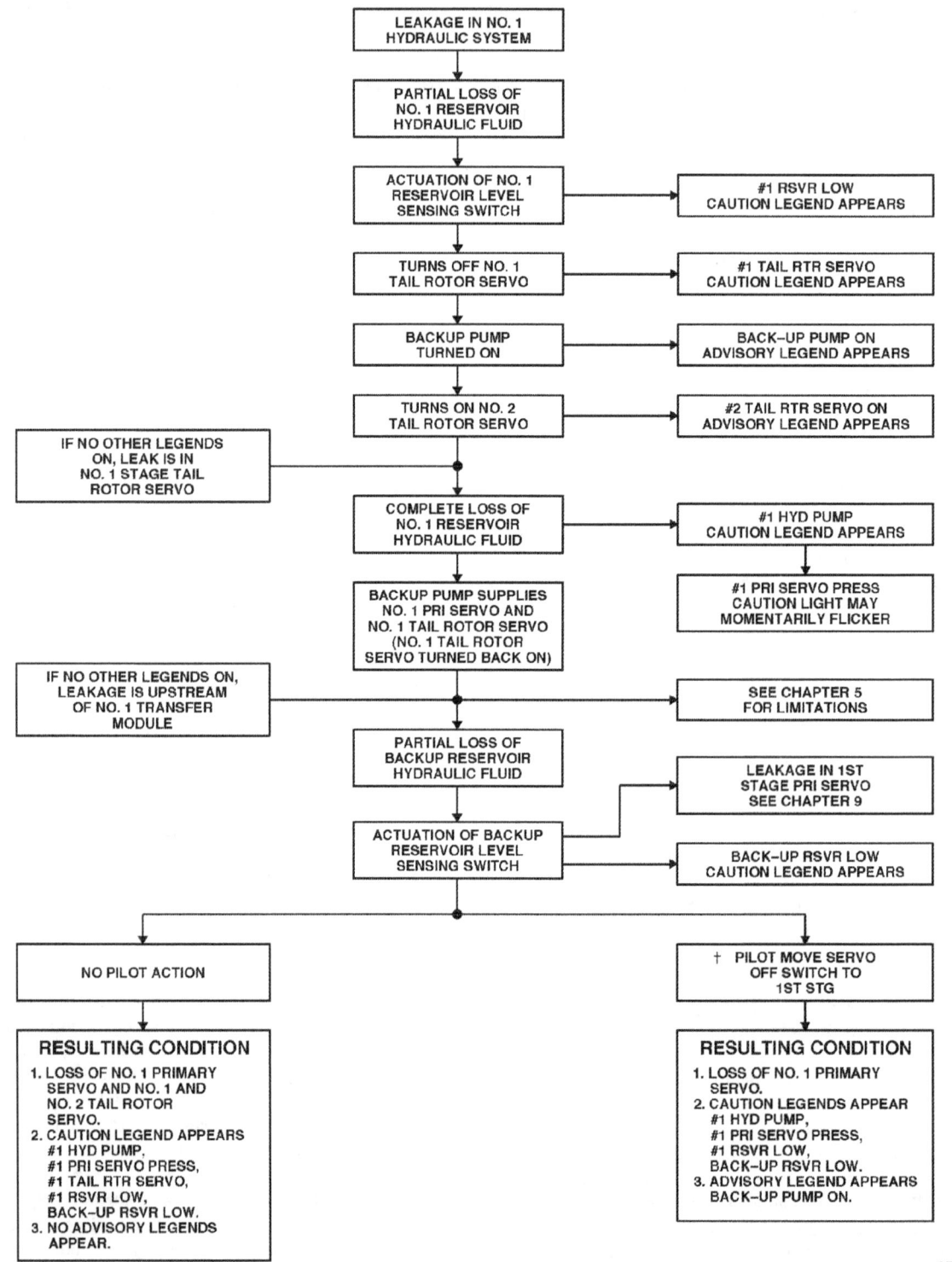

Figure 2-13. Hydraulic Logic Module Operation Principle (Sheet 1 of 2)

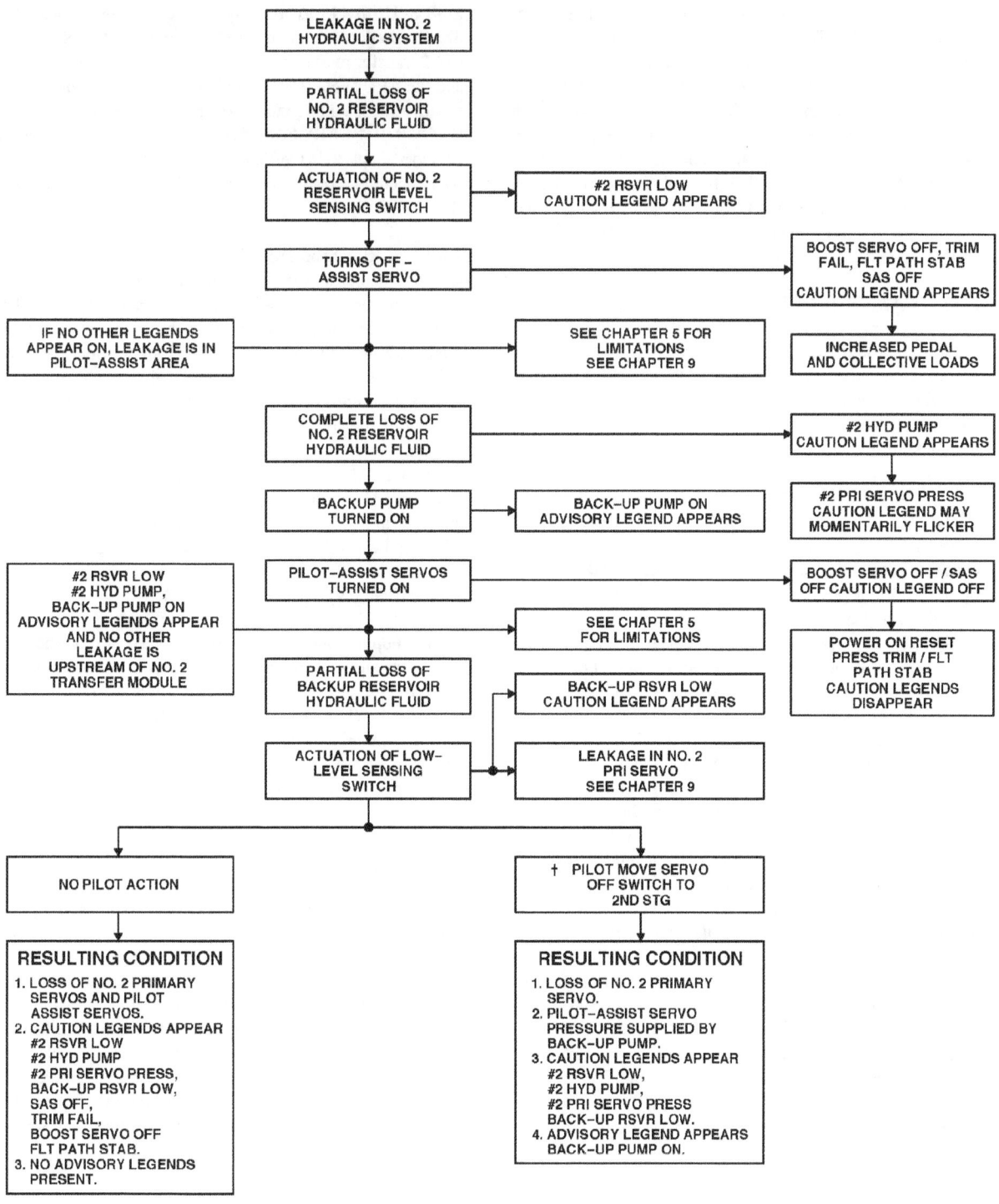

Figure 2-13. Hydraulic Logic Module Operation Principle (Sheet 2 of 2)

BACK-UP PUMP ON advisory legend will remain on for about 90 seconds. Refer to Chapter 8 Section II for test procedure. Except for the **HYD LEAK TEST** switch, the hydraulic leak system consists of components of 1st stage, 2nd stage and backup hydraulic systems. A WOW switch contact prevents hydraulic leak tests from being made in flight. Power to operate the hydraulic leak test system is from the No. 2 dc primary bus through a circuit breaker, marked **NO. 2 SERVO CONTR** and dc essential bus through a circuit breaker, marked **BACKUP HYD CONTR**.

2.38 TRANSFER MODULES.

The No. 1 and No. 2 transfer modules connect hydraulic pressure from the pump modules to the flight control servos. Each module is an integrated assembly of shutoff valves, pressure switches, check valves, and restrictors. The modules are interchangeable.

2.38.1 No. 1 Transfer Module. This module has a transfer valve, a pressure switch, a 1st stage primary shutoff valve, a 1st stage tail rotor shutoff valve, a restrictor, and check valves. The transfer valve is spring-loaded to the open or normal position. If 1st stage hydraulic pressure is lost, the valve automatically transfers backup pump pressure to the 1st stage system. The 1st stage primary shutoff valve lets the pilot or copilot shut off 1st stage pressure to the primary servos and prevents both stages from being shut off at the same time. The pressure switch lights the #1 **HYD PUMP** legend on the caution advisory display when pressure drops below 2000 psi and also sends a signal to a logic module that pressure is lost in the 1st stage hydraulic system. The restrictor allows fluid to circulate for cooling under no-flow conditions. If a fluid leak develops past the transfer module, the check valves prevent fluid loss on the return side of the transfer module.

2.38.2 No. 2 Transfer Module. The No. 2 transfer module is like the No. 1 module except that it supplies 2nd stage pressure. The pilot assist shutoff valve turns off pressure to the pilot assist module. The 2nd stage primary servo shutoff valve turns off pressure to the 2nd stage of the primary servos. The pressure switch turns on the **#2 HYD PUMP** caution legend on the caution/advisory display when 2nd stage system pressure is below 2000 psi, and also sends a signal to a logic module that pressure is lost in the 2nd stage system.

2.38.3 Utility Module. The utility module connects hydraulic pressure from the backup pump to the No. 1 and No. 2 transfer modules, the 2nd stage of the tail rotor servo, and the APU accumulator. A pressure switch on the module senses the backup pump operating and turns on the **BACK-UP PUMP ON** advisory legend on the caution/advisory display. If the flow rate through the module to the APU accumulator goes over 1-1/2 gpm, a velocity fuse shuts off flow.

2.38.4 Logic Modules. Two logic modules, one in the left relay panel and the other in the right relay panel, are used to control the operation of the hydraulic systems. The logic modules continually monitor the operation of the hydraulic systems by inputs received from pressure switches, fluid level switches on the pump modules, and inputs received from control switches in the hydraulic system. The outputs of the logic modules will either turn on lights on the caution/advisory panel notifying the pilot of a failure, and/or turn off one or more valves due to a system malfunction. All switching functions of the hydraulic logic modules are automatic, except as shown by a dagger (†) which indicates crewmember action (Figure 2-13).

2.39 RESERVOIR FILL SYSTEM.

A handpump and manual selector valve are on the right side upper deck of the helicopter for system servicing. Refer to Figure 2-23 for servicing. The three hydraulic system reservoir levels can be seen from the fill pump location. The handpump reservoir contains a sight gage above the handpump crank. A 1-quart level mark indicates a requirement for refill. Refer to Section XV this chapter for servicing.

2.40 PNEUMATIC SUBSYSTEM.

A pneumatic subsystem operating from bleed-air furnished by the main engines, the APU, or an external pneumatic power source, is used to drive the main engine starter, for heating system operation and external extended range tank fuel transfer. Bleed-air from the main engines is used for engine inlet anti-icing subsystem operation. The heating subsystem and the extended range fuel tanks use bleed-air supplied by the main engines during flight, and on the ground by the main engines, APU, or external source. The subsystem contains check valves at each bleed-air source, and a shutoff valve at each main engine.

Section VII POWERTRAIN SYSTEM

2.41 POWERTRAIN.

The powertrain consists of inputs from two engines, a main transmission, intermediate gear box, tail gear box and connecting drive shafting. Power from the engines is transmitted to the main transmission module through input modules. The main transmission is mounted on top of the cabin between the two engines (Figure 2-1). It mounts and powers the main rotor head, changes the angle of drive from the engines, reduces rpm from the engines, powers the tail rotor drive shaft and drives the accessory module. The main transmission consists of five modules: two input modules; the main module; and two accessory modules. The main transmission has a built-in 3° forward tilt.

2.41.1 Input Module. The input modules are mounted on the left and right front of the main module and support the front of the engines. They contain an input bevel pinion and gear, and a freewheel unit. The freewheel unit allows engine disengagement during autorotation, or in case of a nonoperating engine, the accessory module will continue to be driven by the main rotor. The input module provides the first gear reduction between engine and main module.

2.41.2 Accessory Module. One accessory module is mounted on the forward section of each input module. Each accessory module provides mounting and drive for an electrical generator and a hydraulic pump package. A rotor speed sensor is mounted on the right accessory module and provides signals for the VIDS.

2.41.3 Main Module. The main module contains the necessary gearing to drive the main rotor and tail rotor systems. It provides a reduction in speed from the input module to the main module and the tail drive shaft.

2.42 MAIN TRANSMISSION LUBRICATION SYSTEM.

Prolonged nose-down attitudes of 5 degrees or more may cause high main transmission oil temperature.

The transmission incorporates an integral wet sump lubrication system that provides cooled, filtered oil to all bearing and gears. The ac generators on the accessory modules also receive oil for cooling. Oil under pressure is supplied through internally cored oil lines, except for the pressure and return lines of the oil cooler. Refer to servicing diagram for oil specification and servicing (Table 2-4). The lubrication system includes two lubrication pumps that are combination pressure and scavenge types operating in parallel. The main transmission may run at cruise flight for 30 minutes with loss of all oil. Main transmission oil pressure may fluctuate when the aircraft is known to be in a nose-up attitude (i.e., slope landings or hover with an extreme aft CG). Pressure regulating and bypass valves protect the lube system by returning excess high pressure oil back to the inlet side of the pump. A two-stage oil filter and various strainers in the sump prevent contamination. The oil filter has a visual impending bypass indicator (red button) that protrudes when the first stage filter becomes contaminated. When the button pops the filter element must be replaced to reset. A thermal lockout prevents button popping when oil is cold and thick. The oil cooler uses a blower driven by the tail rotor drive shaft to cool oil before it enters the various modules. The oil cooler has a thermostatic bypass valve that directs oil flow around the cooler when the oil temperature is below 71°±1°C. Other warning and monitoring systems on the main transmission are: **MAIN XMSN OIL TEMP** and **PRESS** caution legends, and **XMSN TEMP** and **PRESS** oil temperature gages. An oil pressure switch on the left accessory module, the farthest point from the pumps, causes the **MAIN XMSN OIL PRES** caution legend to go on when the pressure drops to 14±2 psi. The transmission oil temperature warning system is triggered by an oil temperature switch at the oil cooler input to the main module, near the tail takeoff drive shaft flange. A caution legend, **MAIN XMSN OIL TEMP** goes on when transmission oil temperature reaches 120°C. Temperature for the gage is sensed between the sump and the pump. Pressure readings are taken at the main module manifold. Electrical power for the warning systems, except chip detection, is from the No. 2 dc primary bus, through the **MAIN XMSN** circuit breaker on the overhead circuit breaker panel.

2.42.1 Transmission Oil Temperature Indicator. The transmission oil temperature indicator marked **XMSN TEMP** is a part of the central display unit (Figure 2-8). Refer to Chapter 5 for limitations. Power to operate the temperature indicator and **MAIN XMSN OIL TEMP** caution legend is provided from the No. 1 and No. 2 ac primary buses through the signal data converters and the No. 2 dc primary bus through a circuit breaker, marked **MAIN XMSN**.

2.42.2 Transmission Oil Pressure Indicator. The transmission oil pressure indicator, marked **XMSN PRESS**, is a part of the central display unit (Figure 2-8). Refer to

Chapter 5 for limitations. Power to operate the pressure indicator and **MAIN XMSN OIL PRES** caution legend is provided from the No. 1 and No. 2 ac primary buses through the signal data converter and No. 2 dc primary bus through a circuit breaker marked **MAIN XMSN**.

2.42.3 Transmission Chip Detector System. The transmission chip detector system consists of chip detectors on the left and right input modules, left and right accessory modules, the main gear box module, and caution legends marked **CHIP INPUT MDL-LH, CHIP INPUT MDL-RH, CHIP ACCESS MDL-LH, CHIP ACCESS MDL-RH** and **CHIP MAIN MDL SUMP**. These detectors provide warning of chips in any of five areas of the main transmission system. Each chip detector incorporates a self-sealing provision so that it can be removed for visual inspection without loss of oil. The magnetic plugs on each chip detector attract ferrous particles at any of the detector locations. The fuzz burn-off feature prevents false warnings by burning off small chips and fuzz. The fuzz burn-off feature is deactivated when oil temperature reaches 140°C. Deactivation of the fuzz burn-off feature does not disable detection and illumination of caution lights. The main transmission chip detector is also connected to a 30 second time delay relay to allow small chips and fuzz to burn off and/or wash away. Chips that are too large to burn off or wash away trigger the detection system which illuminates a caution light on the caution/advisory panel. The pilot or maintenance personnel must check the caution/advisory panel before removing power to determine the location of the chip. The system is powered by the dc essential bus through a circuit breaker on the upper console circuit breaker panel marked **CHIP DET**.

2.42.4 Deleted.

2.43 TAIL DRIVE SYSTEM.

Six sections of drive shaft connect the main module to the tail rotor gear box. The shafts drive the oil cooler blower and transmit torque to the tail rotor. Each shaft is dynamically balanced tubular aluminum. Multiple disc (flexible) couplings between sections eliminate universal joints. The shafts are ballistically tolerant if hit by a projectile and are suspended at four points in viscous-damped bearings mounted in adjustable plates and bolted to fuselage support brackets.

2.43.1 Intermediate Gear Box. Mounted at the base of the pylon is the oil-lubricated intermediate gear box (Figure 2-1). It transmits torque and reduces shaft speed from the main gear box to the tail gear box. The intermediate gear box may run at cruise flight for 30 minutes, with loss of all oil. An internal metal fuzz suppression chip/temperature sensor detects metal particles and gear box overtemperature conditions, to light caution legends marked **CHIP INT XMSN** and **INT XMSN OIL TEMP**.

2.43.2 Tail Gear Box. The oil-lubricated tail gear box (Figure 2-1) at the top of the tail pylon transmits torque to the tail rotor head. The gear box mounts the tail rotor, changes angle of drive and gives a gear reduction. It also enables pitch changes of the tail rotor blades through the flight control system. The gear box housing is magnesium. The tail gear box may run at cruise flight for 30 minutes with loss of all oil. An internal fuzz suppression metal chip/temperature sensor detects metal particles, and gear box overtemperature conditions, to light caution legends, marked **CHIP TAIL XMSN** and **TAIL XMSN OIL TEMP**.

2.43.3 Intermediate and Tail Gear Box Chip/Temperature Systems. The intermediate and tail gear boxes contain identical chip/temperature sensors that indicate in the cockpit when the gear box temperature is too high, or a chip is present. The chip detectors incorporate a fuzz burn-off feature which eliminates false warning due to fuzz and small particles. When a chip is detected and will not burn off, a caution legend on the caution/advisory display will go on, indicating **CHIP INT XMSN** or **CHIP TAIL XMSN**. The oil temperature sensor is a bimetal strip that reacts to temperatures. When the oil temperature reaches 140°C a switch closes to turn on a caution legend in the cockpit, marked **INT XMSN OIL TEMP** or **TAIL XMSN OIL TEMP**. Power to operate the oil temperature system is from the No. 2 dc primary bus through a circuit breaker marked **MAIN XMSN**.

Section VIII MAIN AND TAIL ROTOR GROUPS

2.44 ROTOR SYSTEMS.

The rotor system consists of a main rotor and tail rotor. Both systems are driven by the engines through the transmission system, with pitch controlled by the flight control system.

2.45 MAIN ROTOR SYSTEM.

The main rotor system consists of four subsystems: main rotor blades, hub, flight controls and the bifilar vibration absorber. Four titanium-spar main rotor blades attach to spindles which are retained by elastomeric bearings contained in one-piece titanium hub. The elastomeric bearing permits the blade to flap, lead and lag. Lag motion is controlled by hydraulic dampers and blade pitch is controlled through adjustable control rods which are moved by the swashplate. When the rotor is not turning, the blades and spindles rest on hub mounted droop stops. Upper restraints called antiflapping stops retain flapping motion caused by the wind. Both stops engage as the rotor slows down during engine shutdown. Blade retaining pins can be pulled from the blade spindle joint and the blades folded along the rear of the fuselage. The bifilar vibration absorber reduces rotor vibration at the rotor. The absorber is mounted on top of the hub and consists of a four arm plate with attached weights. Main rotor dampers are installed between each of the main rotor spindles modules and the hub to restrain hunting (lead and lag motions) of the main rotor blades during rotation and to absorb rotor head starting loads. Each damper is supplied with pressurized hydraulic fluid from a reservoir mounted on the side of each damper. The reservoir has an indicator that monitors the reserve fluid. When the damper is fully serviced, the indicator will show full gold.

2.45.1 Main Rotor Blades. Four main rotor blades use a titanium spar for their main structural member. The structure aft of the spar consists of fiberglass skin, Nomex honeycomb filler and a graphite/fiberglass trailing edge. The leading edge of each blade has a titanium abrasion strip, the outboard portion of which is protected by a replaceable nickel strip. Electro-thermal blankets are bonded into the blades leading edge for deicing. A Blade Inspection Method (BIM®) indicator (Figure 2-14), is installed on each blade at the root end trailing edge to visually indicate when blade spar structural integrity is degraded. If a spar crack occurs, or a seal leaks, nitrogen will escape from the spar. When the pressure drops below minimum the indicator will show red bands. A manual test lever is installed on each BIM indicator to provide a maintenance check. The blades are attached to the rotor head by two quick-release expandable pins, that require no tools to either remove or install. To conserve space, all blades can be folded to the rear and downward along the tail cone. When mooring, the blades can be tied down with a fitting on the bottom of each blade.

2.45.2 Main Rotor Gust Lock. The gust lock prevents the blades from rotating when the helicopter is parked. The gust lock is designed to withstand torque from one engine at **IDLE**, and thus allow engine maintenance checks independent of drive train rotation. The locking system consists of a locking handle at the rear of the cabin (Figure 2-5), a **GUST LOCK** caution legend on the caution/advisory display (Figure 2-8), and a locking device and teeth on the tail rotor takeoff flange of the main transmission. The lock shall only be applied when the rotor system is stationary; it can only be released when both engines are shut down. Power to operate the caution light is provided from the No. 1 dc primary bus through a circuit breaker marked **LIGHTS ADVSY**.

2.46 TAIL ROTOR SYSTEM.

A cross-beam tail rotor blade system provides anti-torque action and directional control. The blades are of graphite and fiberglass construction. Blade flap and pitch change motion is provided by deflection of the flexible graphite fiber spar. This feature eliminates all bearings and lubrication. The spar is a continuous member running from the tip of one blade to the tip of the opposite blade. Electro-thermal blankets are bonded into the blade leading edge for deicing. The tail rotor head and blades are installed on the right side of the tail pylon, canted 20° upward. In addition to providing directional control and anti-torque reaction, the tail rotor provides 2.5% of the total lifting force in a hover. A spring-loaded feature of the tail rotor control system will provide a setting of the tail rotor blades for balance flight at cruise power setting in case of complete loss of tail rotor control.

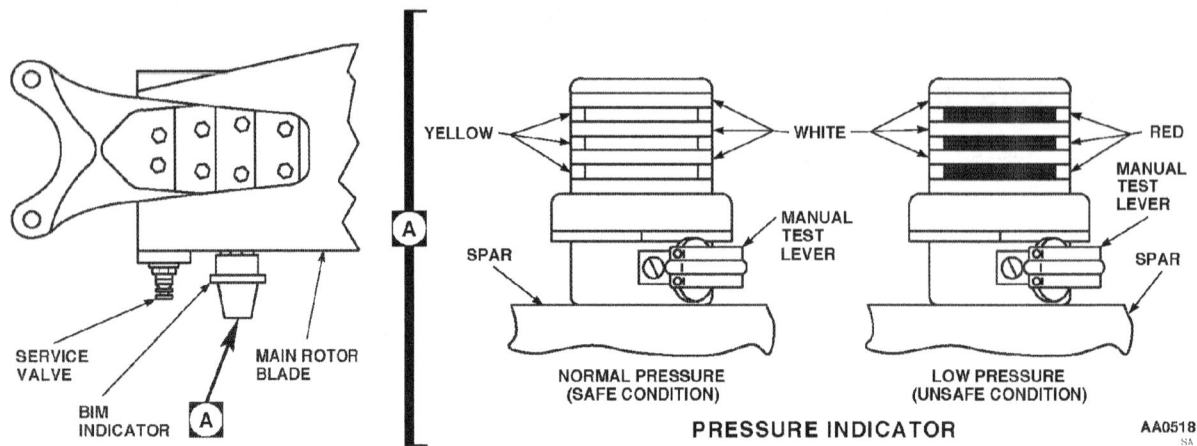

Figure 2-14. Main Rotor Blade and BIM® System

2.47 TAIL ROTOR QUADRANT/WARNING.

The tail rotor quadrant contains microswitches to turn on a caution legend marked **TAIL RTR QUADRANT** if a tail rotor cable becomes severed. Spring tension allows the quadrant to operate in a normal manner. Electrical power to operate the warning system is provided from No. 1 dc primary bus through a circuit breaker marked **T RTR SERVO WARN**. If the helicopter is shut down and/or hydraulic power is removed with one tail rotor cable failure, disconnection of the other tail rotor cable will occur when force from the boost servo cannot react against control cable quadrant spring tension. The quadrant spring will displace the cable and boost servo piston enough to unlatch the quadrant cable.

Section IX UTILITY SYSTEMS

2.48 WINDSHIELD WIPERS.

Two electrically-operated windshield wipers are installed, one on the pilot's windshield and one on the copilot's windshield (Figure 2-1). Both wiper arms are driven by a common motor through flexible drives and converters. Power to operate the windshield wiper system is from No. 1 ac primary bus through a circuit breaker, marked **WSHLD WIPER**.

NOTE

The use of rain repellent on the windshields will improve visibility above speeds of 50 KIAS.

2.48.1 Windshield Wiper Control.

To prevent possible damage to windshield surface, do not operate windshield wipers on a dry windshield.

Control of the windshield wipers is through a spring-loaded rotary switch on the upper console (Figure 2-6). The switch is labeled **WINDSHIELD WIPER**, with marked positions **PARK-OFF-LOW-HI**. When the switch is turned from **OFF** to **LOW** or **HI**, the wipers will operate at the corresponding speed. The wipers will stop at any position when the switch is turned **OFF**. When the switch is turned to **PARK**, the wipers will return to the inboard windshield frame and stop. When the switch is released, it will return to **OFF**.

2.48.2 Windshield Anti-Ice/Defogging System.

Continued use of a faulty windshield anti-ice system may result in structural damage (delamination and/or cracking) to the windshield.

Do not allow ice to accumulate on the windshield, as ice shedding can cause engine FOD.

Pilot's, copilot's and center windshield are electrically anti-iced and defogged. Transparent conductors imbedded between the laminations provide heat when electrical power is applied. The temperature of each panel is controlled to a heat level of about 43°C (109°F). The windshield anti-ice system fault monitoring circuit prevents windshield burnout when the windshield surface heat is above 43°C (109°F). If heat increases, the monitor circuit will turn off the system. Three switches, one for the pilot, one for the copilot and one for the center windshield are on the upper console (Figure 2-6) with markings of **WINDSHIELD ANTI-ICE-PILOT-OFF-ON**, and **COPILOT-OFF-ON** and **CTR-OFF-ON**. Power to operate the anti-icing system is provided by the No. 1 and No. 2 ac primary buses through circuit breakers marked **PILOT WSHLD ANTI-ICE**, **CPLT WSHLD ANTI-ICE** and **CTR WSHLD ANTI-ICE**. Power to control the anti-ice system is provided by the No. 1 and No. 2 dc primary buses through circuit breakers marked **CPLT WSHLD ANTI-ICE** and **WINDSHIELD ANTI-ICE PILOT** and **CTR**. If the APU generator is the sole source of ac-generated power, the backup pump and the windshield anti-ice cannot be used simultaneously.

2.49 PITOT HEATER.

Pitot tube heat is provided by heating elements within each pitot tube head. Power to operate both heating elements is controlled by a single switch on the upper console, marked **PITOT HEAT OFF** and **ON**. When the switch is placed **ON**, current flows to the heating elements. Current sensors in the circuits sense the current flow and keep the caution legends, marked **LFT PITOT HEAT** and **RT PITOT HEAT**, turned off. If a heating element fails, the current sensor will detect no current flow, and turn on the caution legend for that pitot tube. Power to operate the pitot tube heaters is provided from the No. 2 ac primary bus for the right pitot tube, through a circuit breaker marked **RT PITOT HEAT**, and from the No. 1 ac primary bus for the left pitot tube, through a circuit breaker marked **LEFT PITOT HEAT**. Power to operate the caution lights is provided from the No. 1 dc primary bus through a circuit breaker, marked **NO. 1 ENG ANTI-ICE**.

2.50 ROTOR BLADE DEICE KIT.

Blade deice operation with erosion strips installed may cause blade damage.

The rotor blade deice kit (Figure 2-15) consists of the following: deice control panel, deice test panel, system controller, power distributor, main and tail sliprings, main and tail blade heating elements, droop stop heaters, caution legends, outside air temperature (OAT) sensor, a modified ambient temperature sense line and an icing rate meter subsystem. The blade deice system provides improved mission performance in icing conditions by applying controlled electrical power to integral heating elements in the main and tail rotor blades, causing the ice bond layer to melt, allowing symmetrical ice shedding. Droop stop heaters apply heat to the droop stop hinge pins, to prevent icing and permit proper operation. The heaters are electrically powered continuously whenever the blade deice system is operating, either with the power switch **ON**, or the system in the **TEST** mode. The blade deice system, excluding element-on-time (EOT) failure, may be ground checked using the APU generator. To prevent generator overload when only the APU generator is operating, an interlock system is installed to inhibit blade deice test if the backup pump is operating. If the backup pump should go on during the test cycle, the **MR DE-ICE FAIL** caution legend will go on immediately, alerting the crew to an invalid test attempt. The test cycle must then be initiated again. The OAT sensor, installed below the windshield, provides a signal to the controller for heating EOT of the rotor blades. The lower the OAT, the longer EOT will be. To reduce power requirements, the blades are deiced in cycles. Power to operate the blade deice is provided from the No. 1 and No. 2 ac primary buses and No. 2 dc primary bus through circuit breakers, marked **ICE-DET**, **DE-ICE CNTRLR**, and **DE-ICE PWR TAIL ROTOR**, on the mission readiness circuit breaker panel in the cabin. Main blade deice power is routed through current limiters in the deice junction box. When one main generator is inoperative, deice power can be supplied by the APU generator.

2.50.1 Blade Deice System Operation. The ice detector is operational anytime power is applied to the helicopter. The ice detector senses ice accumulation on a vibrating probe by a change in probe frequency. The frequency change is processed by the ice rate meter. The ice rate meter provides a visual display of icing intensity, T (trace), L (light) blue, M (moderate) yellow, and H (heavy) red. Also, the ice rate meter sends a signal to the **ICE DETECTED** caution legend when the **BLADE DE-ICE POWER** switch is off, informing the pilot of the requirement to turn on the system. When the system has been turned on by placing the **POWER** switch **ON**, the ice detector aspirator heater is turned on, and the **ICE DETECTED** caution legend is turned off. If the **MODE** switch is at **AUTO**, the rate meter sends an ice rate signal to the controller. The controller processes the ice rate signal to produce heater element-off-time, and the OAT signal to produce the heater EOT. The controller sends command signals through the main rotor sliprings to the system distributor which responds to controller signals by switching power in sequence to the main rotor blade heater zones. Tail rotor blade power is switched directly by the controller and sent through the tail rotor sliprings to the tail rotor blades. A tail blade distributor is not required since the power is applied to the four tail blades simultaneously. The deice control panel contains a rotary switch which allows automatic or manual control of blade heater element-off-time. In **AUTO** (automatic), the ice rate signal is passed on to the controller, which results in off-time variations proportional to the ice rate. In **MANUAL**, T, L, or M, fixed signals are transmitted to the controller, resulting in fixed element-off-time. Ice rate subsystem malfunctions are indicated by the appearance of a **FAIL** flag on the rate meter face, requiring operation of the blade deice system in one of the three manual modes. **MANUAL** mode should also be used when the rate meter has no indicated malfunction, but any of these three conditions has occurred: 1. Pilot has determined by his judgment of ice intensity that the ice rate system is inaccurate. 2. Torque required has increased to an unacceptable level. 3. Helicopter vibration has increased to an unacceptable level. During a single main generator failure, blade deice will be dropped until the APU is started and the **APU generator** switch is placed **ON**. Even though the **APU generator** switch is **ON** and providing power to the blade deice system, the **APU GEN ON** advisory legend will not be on because of one main generator operating.

2.50.2 Blade Deice System Control Panel. All controls for operating the rotor blade deice system are on the **BLADE DEICE** system control panel (Figure 2-15). Controls are described as follows:

CONTROL/ INDICATOR	FUNCTION
POWER switch **TEST**	Electrically test main and tail rotor deice system for one test cycle.
ON	Turns on power to blade deice controller and turns off **ICE DETECTED** caution legend.
OFF	Turns off deice system.

TM 1-1520-253-10

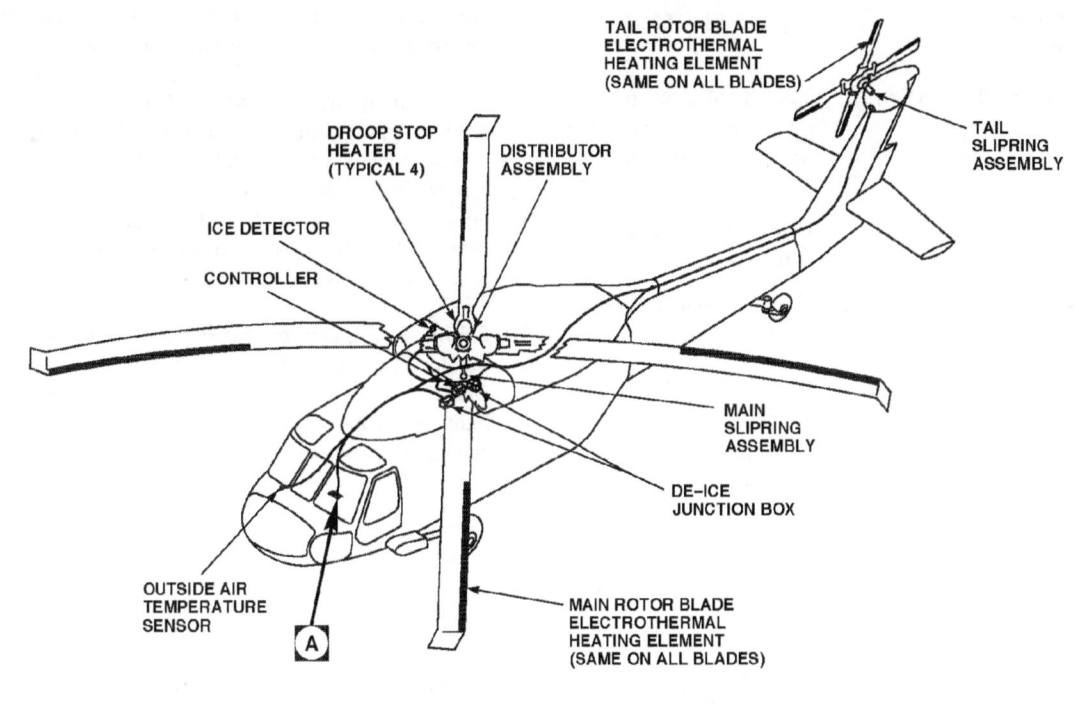

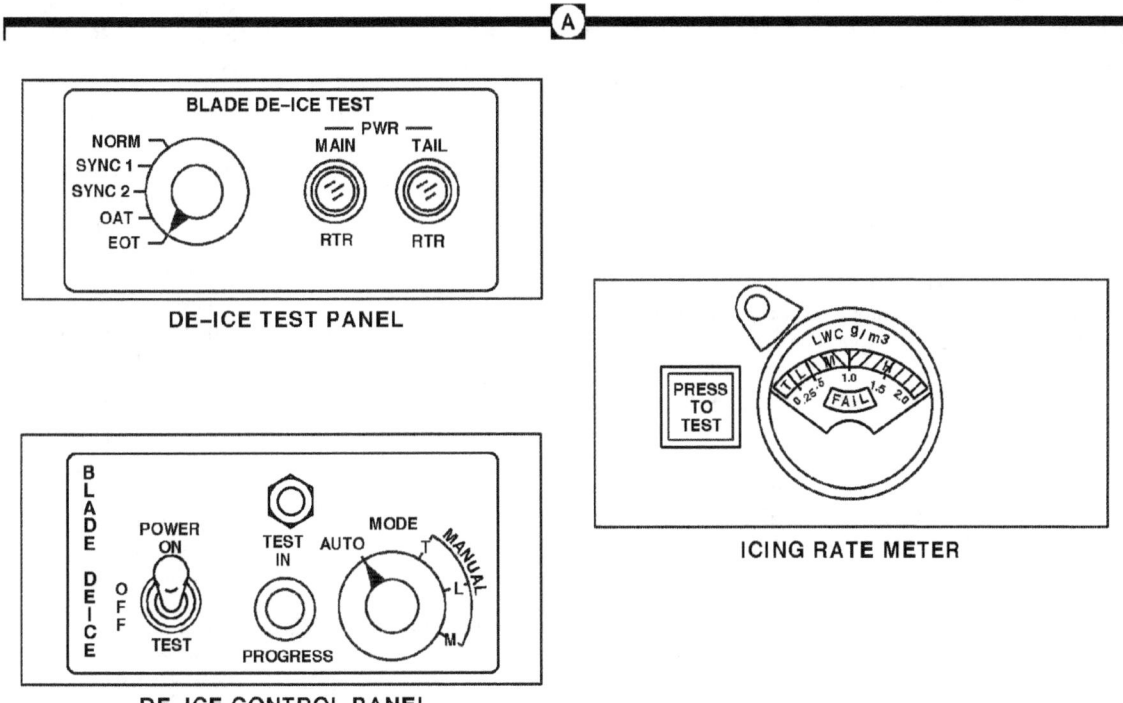

Figure 2-15. Rotor Blade Deice Kit

2-49

CONTROL/ INDICATOR	FUNCTION
TEST IN PROGRESS	Green light goes on during test cycle. At end of test cycle, light should go off.
MODE selector	
AUTO	System off-time is controlled by ice rate signal.
MANUAL	Gives pilot manual control of system off-time.
T	Sets a fixed element-off-time for trace icing.
L	Sets a fixed element-off-time for light icing.
M	Sets a fixed element-off-time for moderate icing.

2.50.3 Blade Deice Test. The **BLADE DE-ICE TEST** panel (Figure 2-15) allows the pilot to check the blade deice system for failures that are otherwise dormant during the normal **TEST** mode, but that can allow abnormal operation during use. The panel accomplishes this by introducing selected failure signals into the system and requiring the deice controller built-in-test circuitry to function in a specific manner. The blade deice test should be done during the ground checkout before each flight when blade deice use is anticipated. In the **NORM** position, the test panel allows system test to be done without the introduction of false failure signals. Thus, the system should complete its self checkout cycle without failure indications on the caution display. In the **SYNC 1** and **SYNC 2** positions, the test panel interrupts the distributor sync line and provides the controller with a false sync input. The controller must interpret these false signals as indications of distributor failure, and produce **MR DE-ICE FAIL** caution legend for both cases. In the **OAT** position, the test panel short circuits the OAT sensor input to the controller. BITE circuitry within the controller must sense the simulated failure and turn on both the **MR DE-ICE FAIL** and **TR DE-ICE FAIL** caution legends. In the **EOT** position, the test panel biases BITE circuitry in the controller and the OAT sensor to simulate malfunctioning primary EOT timing circuits. The biased BITE circuit is thus deceived into believing that the primary circuits are in error. The controller must turn on both the **MR DE-ICE FAIL** and **TR DE-ICE FAIL** legends when this occurs. The test panel also functions automatically during blade deice system use to sense contradictory signals from the deice power circuits. If electrical power remains applied to either the main or tail rotor heating elements after the controller signals a **FAIL** condition or when the system is **OFF**, then the corresponding **PWR** monitor light on the **BLADE DE-ICE TEST** panel turns on. The light informs the crew that further action is required to isolate the deice loads indicated. The test panel provides a reliability check of critical deice system functions. The pilot, after doing the indicated tests properly, can be confident that the deice system primary and BITE electronics are functioning within specified tolerances.

2.50.4 Blade Deice Test Panel. The control for selecting test functions of the blade deice system is on the **BLADE DE-ICE TEST** panel (Figure 2-15). Two **PWR** lights on the panel warn of power malfunctions of the main and tail rotor deice. Control and indicators are as follows:

CONTROL/ INDICATOR	FUNCTION
NORM	Provides a signal path for normal operation.
SYNC 1	Provides a signal to the controller to verify operation of synchronization check circuitry when **POWER** switch is at **TEST**.
SYNC 2	Provides an open circuit to the controller to verify operation of synchronization check circuitry when **POWER** switch is at **TEST**.
OAT	Short circuits the OAT sensor to check BITE circuit sensing a fault when **POWER** switch is at **TEST**.
EOT	Disables BITE circuits in controller and OAT sensor to simulate a malfunctioning primary EOT timing circuit when **POWER** switch is **ON** and **MODE** select switch is at **M** (moderate).
PWR MAIN RTR light	Indicates a malfunction has occurred in the main rotor primary power.

CONTROL/INDICATOR	FUNCTION
PWR TAIL RTR light	Indicates a malfunction has occurred in the tail rotor primary power.

2.51 BLACKOUT CURTAINS.

Curtains are provided to cover the cabin windows and the opening between the pilot's compartment and the cabin. Velcro tape is bonded to the cabin structure and the curtains with an adhesive. Loops are attached to the curtains to aid removal.

2.512.52 WIRE STRIKE PROTECTION SYSTEM.

On helicopters equipped with wire strike protection provisions, the system (Figure 2-1) is a simple, lightweight, positive system with no motorized or pyrotechnic components used to cut, break, or deflect wires that may strike the helicopter in the frontal area between the tires and fuselage, and between the fuselage and main rotor in level flight. The system consists of nine cutters/deflectors located on the fuselage and landing gear/support. They are: upper cutter on the rear of the sliding fairing, the pitot cutter/deflector on the front of the sliding fairing, windshield post and wiper deflectors, door hinge deflector, step extension and step deflector, landing gear joint deflector, main landing gear cutter/deflector, and tail landing gear deflector.

2.53 DATA COMPARTMENTS.

Data Compartments are on each cockpit door (Figure 2-4).

Section X HEATING, VENTILATING, COOLING, AND ENVIRONMENTAL CONTROL UNIT

2.54 HEATING SYSTEM.

The subsystem consists of a heated air source, cold air source, mixing unit, temperature sensing unit, overtemperature sensor, controls, ducting and registers. The heating system is a bleed-air system and bleed-air supplied in flight by the main engines, and on the ground by the main engines or the APU. An external connector allows connection of an external ground source in to the pneumatic system, that can provide heat when connected. Power to operate electrical components of the heating system is by the No. 1 dc primary bus through a circuit breaker, marked **AIR SOURCE HEAT/START**.

2.54.1 Heat and Ventilation Controls. A variable control air mixing valve assembly is used to control the temperature of air for cabin heating in the helicopter. Bleed-air from the engine, APU, or external source is mixed with ambient air to obtain the desired temperature determined by the setting of the sensor in the downstream air flow. Regulation of the diaphragm position is by a solenoid. Should the **HEATER** control switch (Figure 2-6) be turned **OFF**, or dc power fail, bleed-air will shut off. The valve also has a thermal protective switch that deenergizes the solenoid if mixed air temperature is over 90° to 96°C (194° to 205°F). The mixture temperature sensor downstream of the mixing valve regulates flow output temperature. The sensor is regulated from the cockpit through a control linkage at the overhead console. The temperature control is marked **HEATER OFF**, **MED**, and **HI**. Ventilation is controlled through a panel on the upper console marked **VENT BLOWER**. When the switch is placed **ON**, dc power to the solenoid allows bleed-air to mix with outside air.

2.54.2 Normal Operation.

1. APU or engine - Start .

2. **AIR SOURCE HEAT/START** switch - As required. **ENG** if engine is operating; **OFF** for heat from external air source.

3. **HEATER ON-OFF** switch - **ON**.

4. **VENT BLOWER** switch - **OFF** for maximum heat.

5. **HEATER** control - As desired.

2.55 VENTILATION SYSTEM.

2.55.1 Ventilation System. The helicopter is ventilated by an electrically-operated blower system controlled through the **VENT BLOWER** control panel on the upper console (Figure 2-6). The **VENT BLOWER** switch is marked **OFF** and **ON**. When **ON**, the blower forces ambient air into the cabin ducts. The No. 2 ac primary bus powers the blower through a circuit breaker, marked **HEAT & VENT**. It is also controlled by dc power from the No. 2 dc primary bus through the **VENT BLOWER** switch protected by a circuit breaker, marked **HEAT VENT**. Ram air vents for cooling the cockpit area are on each side of the upper console and at the front of the lower console (Figure 2-4) and are controlled by turning the nozzle to control the opening.

2.55.2 Normal Operation.

1. APU, rotor or external power - Operating.

2. **VENT BLOWER** switch - **ON**.

2.56 Air Conditioner System.

CAUTION

ECS operations involving the use of the heat mode: do not remove main power from the ECS without first turning the ECS switch to OFF and waiting **60** seconds. Failure to do so may result in an extreme over temperature condition of the heater element surface.

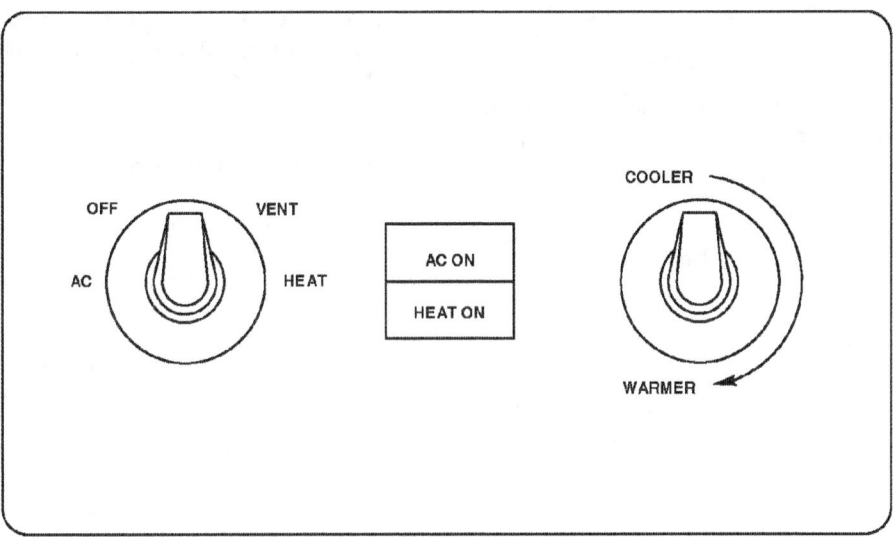

Figure 2-16. ECS Control Panel

NOTE

ECS air conditioning requires that the rotor head be turning to facilitate use due to being bussed on the main generators. Either main generator or ground power unit must be connected to the aircraft for operation.

All ECS EMC data is currently not available. Operation of the ECS causes an approximate one percent loss in aircraft maximum power available. Additionally, there are ECS design concerns. Use of the ECS may cause an inadvertent power-on reset command to the SAS/FPS computer, illuminating the FPS and TRIM cautions on the MFD and the CPTR failure advisory on the AFCS control panel.

The environmental control system (ECS) heats, ventilates, and cools the cabin and cockpit areas. Its main components are an evaporator pallet and condenser pallet located over the main fuel tanks, and an electrical pallet mounted on the bulkhead behind the right main fuel tank. Ducting directs air to the cabin and cockpit. The cooling subsystem is a vapor cycle system, whose compressor is electrically powered. Electrical resistance heating elements in the evaporator pallet heat the air, when required. A single speed fans draws air from the cabin through a filter, heats or cools the air in the evaporator pallet, and returns the air to the cabin or cockpit through the ducts. Power to operate the air conditioner system is provided from the No. 1 ac primary bus through a circuit breaker marked **ECS/HEAT POWER** and controlled from the No. 1 dc primary bus through a circuit breaker marked **ECS CONTR** on the auxiliary circuit breaker panel. Power is removed from the environmental control system when the rescue hoist power switch is in the **ON** position.

2.56.1 Controls Control of the ECS system is through the ECS control panel in the cabin (Figure 2-16). Functions of controls are as follows:

CONTROL	FUNCTION
Mode switch	Changes temperature of heated or cooled air.
AC	Selects air conditioning mode.
OFF	Removes power from ECS system.

2-53

CONTROL	FUNCTION
VENT	Selects ventilation mode.
HEAT	Selects heating mode.
COOLER - WARMER knob	Changes temperature of conditioned air.
AC ON	Air conditioning mode has been selected.
HEAT ON	Heat mode has been selected.

2.56.2 Modes of Operation.

a. In the heating mode, air is circulated through the evaporator pallet where it is heated by the resistance heater, and directed to the cabin through ducts.

b. In the air conditioning mode, air is circulated through the evaporator pallet where it is cooled and dried, and directed to the cabin through ducts. The major components of the air conditioning system are started in spaced intervals to prevent power surges, which results in a delay of up to 30 seconds between turning the system on and feeling cooler air at the vents. Load shedding (Table 2-2) protects the electrical system from overload when the air conditioning is operated and the main generators are not supplying power.

b. In the ventilation mode, air is circulated through the evaporator pallet, and directed to the cabin through ducts. No heating, cooling, or drying occurs in the evaporator in this mode.

2.56.3 Normal Operation.

1. Heating Mode.

    a. Mode switch - **HEAT**. **HEAT ON** light will illuminate.

    b. **COOLER ♦ WARMER** knob - Adjust to a comfortable temperature.

2. Air Conditioning Mode.

    a. Mode switch - **AC**. **AC ON** light will illuminate.

    b. **COOLER ♦ WARMER** knob - Adjust to a comfortable temperature.

2. Ventilation Mode.

    a. Mode switch - **VENT**.

Table 2-2. Air Conditioning System Power Source Priority

POWER SOURCE	AIR CONDITIONING SYSTEM OPERATION
APU GENERATOR (AIRCRAFT ON GROUND)	•AIR CONDITIONING INTERRUPTED IF: (1) BACKUP PUMP IS ON. OR (2) WINDSHIELD ANTI-ICE IS ON. •WINDSHIELD ANTI-ICE INTERRUPTED WHEN BACKUP PUMP IS ON.
APU GENERATOR (AIRCRAFT IN FLIGHT)	•AIR CONDITIONING INTERRUPTED WHILE AIRCRAFT IN AIR. •WINDSHIELD ANTI-ICE INTERRUPTED WHEN BACKUP PUMP IS ON.
DUAL MAIN GENERATOR (NO. 1 AND NO. 2) (AIRCRAFT IN FLIGHT OR ON GROUND)	•AIR CONDITIONING, BACKUP PUMP, AND WINDSHIELD ANTI-ICE CAN OPERATE SIMULTANEOUSLY.
SINGLE GENERATOR OR EXTERNAL AC POWER (WEIGHT ON OR OFF WHEELS)	•AIR CONDITIONING INTERRUPTED IF: (1) BACKUP PUMP IS ON.
ANY POWER SOURCE OR COMBINATION	•ECS POWER (AIR CONDITIONING AND HEATER) INTERRUPTED WHEN HOIST POWER IS ON.

Section XI ELECTRICAL POWER SUPPLY AND DISTRIBUTION SYSTEMS

2.57 ELECTRICAL POWER SYSTEMS.

Alternating current (ac) is the primary source of power. The primary electrical system consists of two independent systems, each capable of supplying the total helicopter power requirements. The prime source of each system is a 115/200 vac generator. A subsystem feeds two independent ac primary buses and an ac essential bus. A portion of each ac primary bus load is converted to 28 volts direct current (vdc) by two 200 ampere ac/dc converters. The 28 vdc is distributed by two independent dc primary buses and a dc essential bus. Emergency power is provided by a generator driven by the auxiliary power unit (APU). The APU generator is capable of supplying all flight-essential ac and dc bus loads. In addition, the APU generator can supply power to the blade deice system (when installed) if one main generator should fail. Should a second generator fail, the blade deice load will be dropped and the APU generator will power the remaining ac bus loads. An electric power priority feature allows either the No. 1 or No. 2 main generator to automatically supersede the APU generator, which, in turn, automatically supersedes external power. A 24-volt battery provides backup dc power when the #1 generator fails or is turned off.

2.58 DC POWER SUPPLY SYSTEM.

Primary dc power is obtained from two converters (transformer-rectifiers) with a battery as the secondary power source. There is no external dc power connector (Figure 2-17).

2.58.1 Converters. Two 200-ampere converters, each normally powered by the No. 1 and No. 2 ac primary buses respectively, turn ac power into dc power and reduce it to 28 volts. The converter output is applied to the No. 1 and No. 2 dc primary buses whenever ac power is applied to the ac primary buses. If one converter's output is lost, the converter load will be transferred to the operating system, and a caution legend, marked **#1 CONV** or **#2 CONV** will go on. Power to light the caution legend is provided by the battery bus through a circuit breaker marked, **AC CONV WARN**.

2.58.2 Battery. A 24-volt dc 9.5 ampere hour battery provides secondary or emergency dc power. The sealed lead acid battery (SLAB) is in the cabin section below the floor panel accessable from the exterior of the aircraft. It supplies dc power to the battery bus, the battery utility bus and the dc essential bus (Figure 2-172-19) for operating dc essential equipment during primary dc malfunction. Power to the battery bus is controlled by the **BATT** switch on the upper console. It has marked positions **OFF** and **ON**. The battery utility bus is connected directly to the battery. The battery powers the dc essential bus when both converters have failed. When only battery power is available, the battery life is about 38 minutes day and 24 minutes night for a battery 80% charged. The **BATT** switch should be **ON** when either external power, APU generator or main generator power is applied to the helicopter. This will recharge the battery. When the battery is the sole source of dc power, the **BATT** switch should be turned **OFF** immediately upon obtaining a **BATT LOW CHARGE** caution legend to conserve battery power for APU starts. A malfunction of both dc primary sources will light caution legends marked #1 and **#2 CONV**. If the **BATT** switch is left **ON**, the battery will be completely discharged in less than 6.0 hours. Power to light the caution legend is from the battery bus through a circuit breaker marked **BATT & ESNTL DC WARN EXT PWR CONTR**.

2.58.3 Battery Low Sensing Relay. The system charges the battery through the battery charging relay with one or both converters on. A caution legend indicating **BATT LOW CHARGE** lights when the battery charge lowers to 22.7 volts ± 2%. At this capacity the battery can provide two APU starts.

2.58.4 DC and AC Circuit Breaker Panels. The circuit breaker panels (Figure 2-18) protect the power systems. One is above and to the rear of each pilot and copilot, one is on the lower console, and two are on the upper console, an auxiliary circuit breaker panel is located on the copilot's side of the upper console, a mission readiness panel is located in the cabin area above the left window and there is a left and right side circuit breaker panel for the medical interior. The ac essential bus contains one additional panel. The circuit breakers provide both ac and dc protection. Popping of a circuit breaker indicates too much current is being drawn by a component in the circuit that is powered through the circuit breaker. Unnecessary recycling of circuit breakers, or using circuit breakers as a switch should not be done.

2.59 AC POWER SUPPLY SYSTEM.

A primary ac power system (Figure 2-17) delivers regulated three phase, 115/200 vac, 400 Hz. Each system contains a 30/45 kilovolt-ampere generator mounted on and driven by the transmission accessory gear box module, a current transformer, a generator control unit, and current

TM 1-1520-253-10

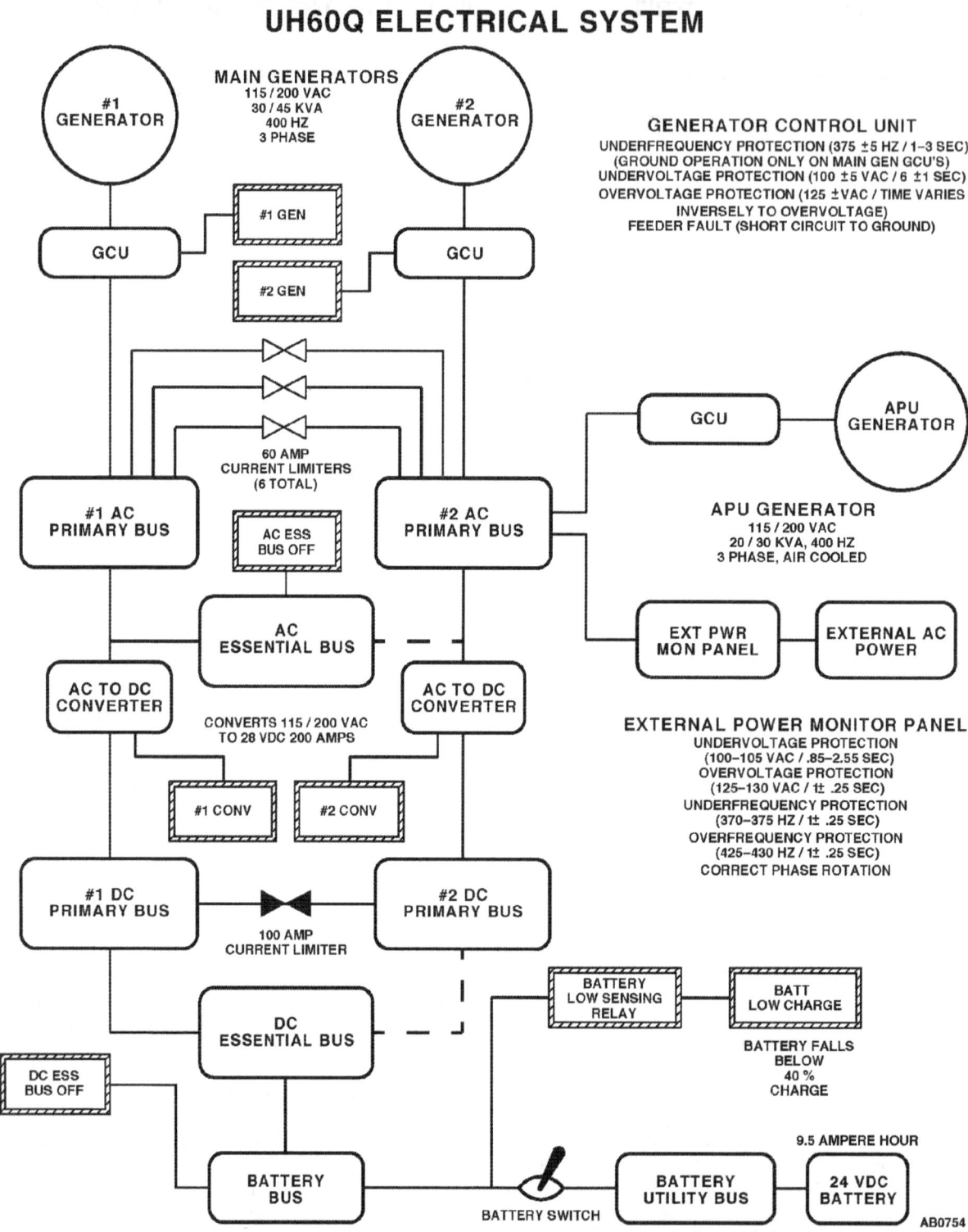

Figure 2-17. Electrical System

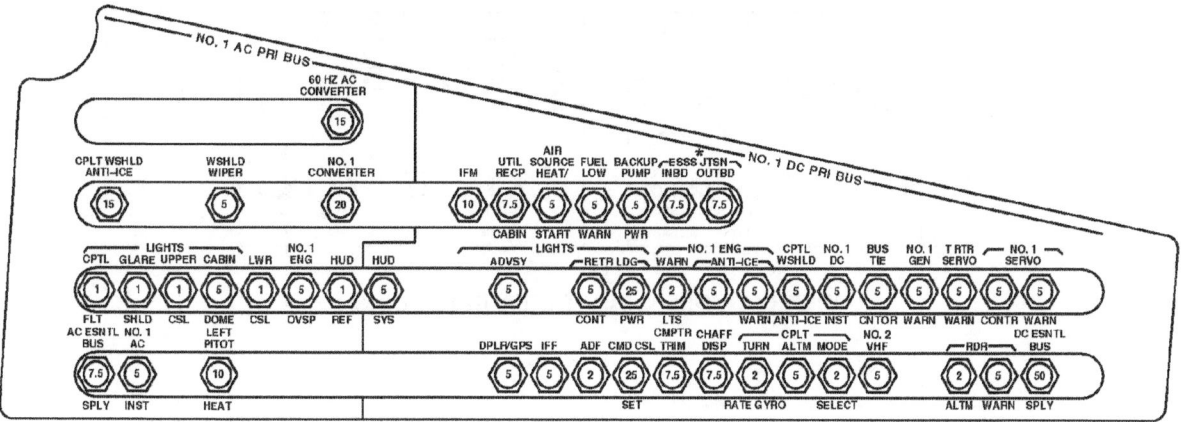

COPILOT'S CIRCUIT BREAKER PANEL

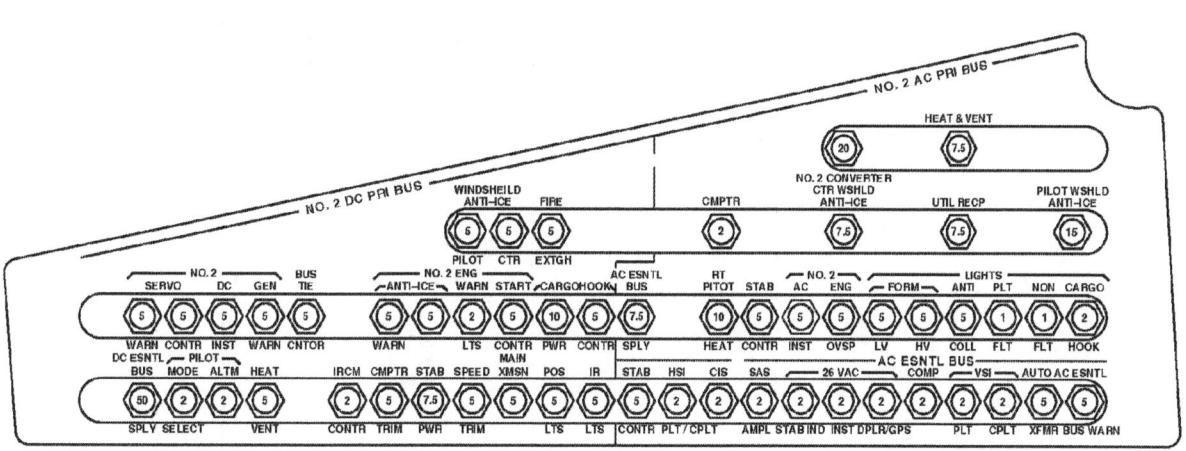

PILOT'S CIRCUIT BREAKER PANEL

Figure 2-18. DC and AC Circuit Breaker Panels (Sheet 1 of 3)

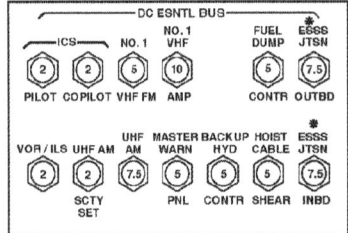
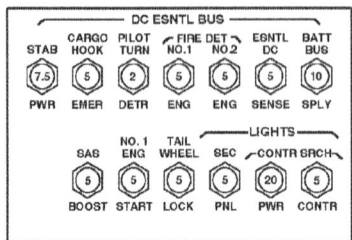

UPPER CONSOLE CIRCUIT BREAKER PANEL

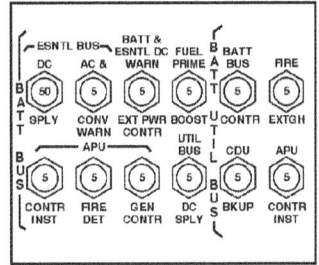

BATTERY AND BATTERY UTILITY
BUS CIRCUIT BREAKER PANEL

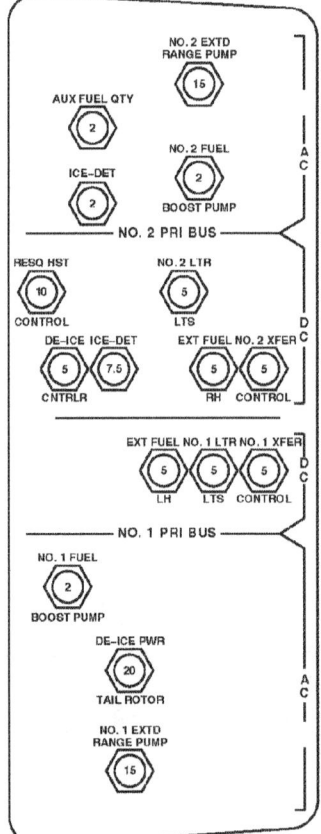

MISSION READINESS CIRCUIT
BREAKER PANEL

Figure 2-18. DC and AC Circuit Breaker Panels (Sheet 2 of 3)

TM 1-1520-253-10

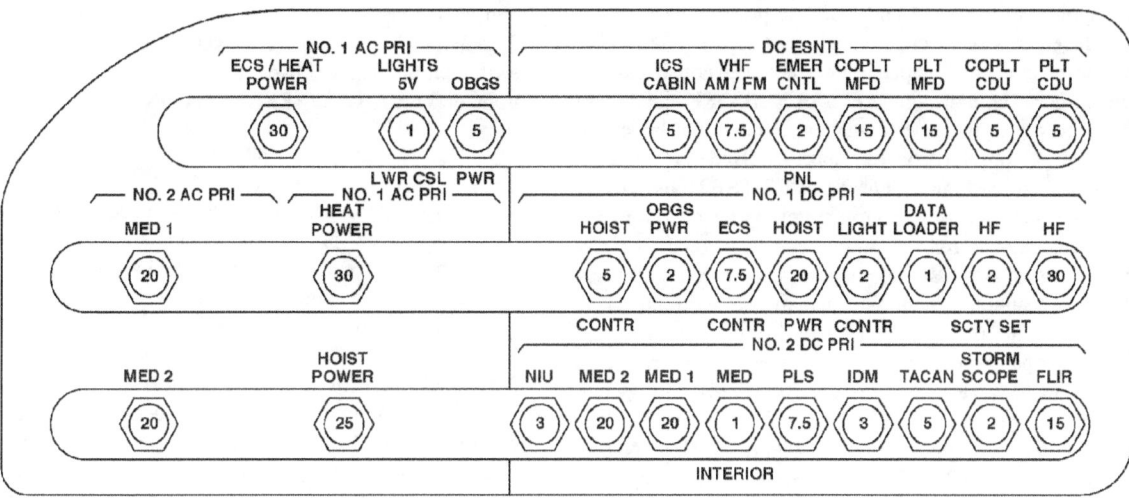

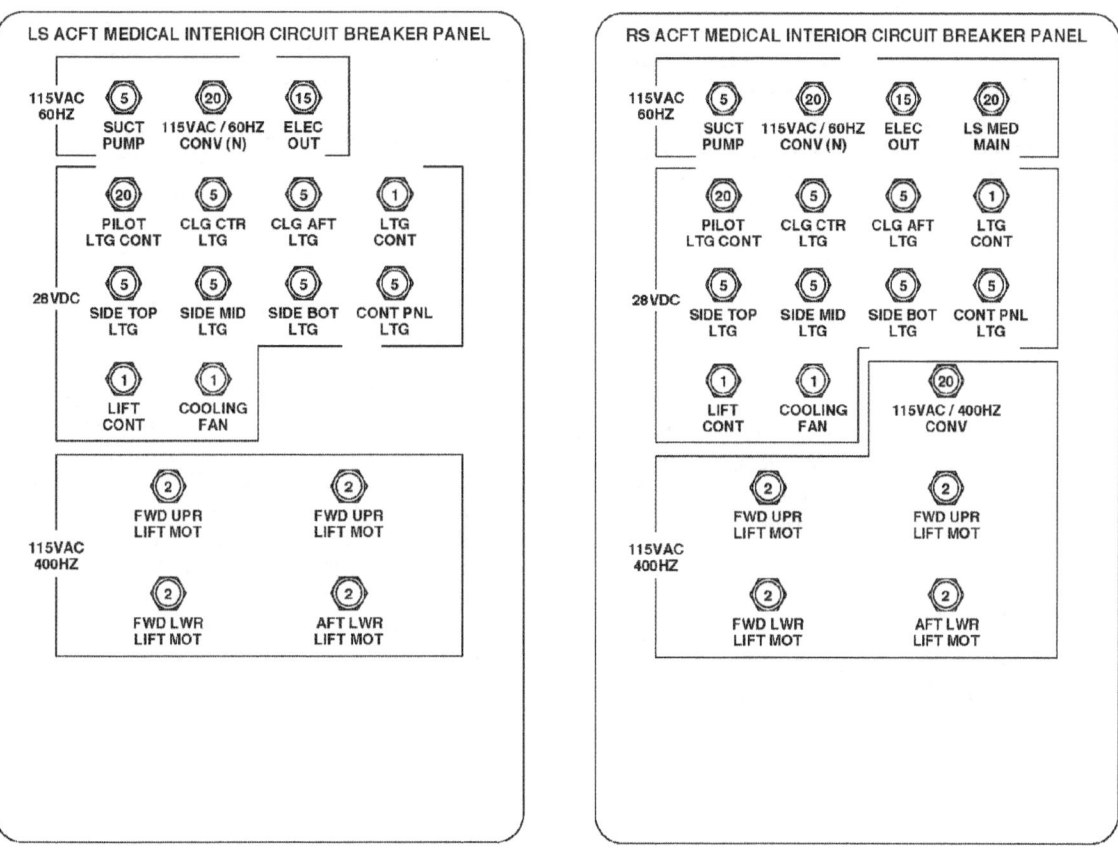

Figure 2-18. DC and AC Circuit Breaker Panels (Sheet 3 of 3)

2-59

limiter, all of which are interchangeable. System outputs are applied to the No. 1 and No. 2 ac primary buses. Caution legends will go on, indicating **#1 GEN** or **#2 GEN** whenever generator output is interrupted. Another caution legend goes on, indicating **AC ESS BUS OFF** when there is no power to the ac essential bus. Individual generator controls are provided on the upper console (Figure 2-6), with marked positions of **TEST, OFF/RESET,** and **ON**. A generator main bearing caution system is installed on each main generator to light a caution legend, marked **#1 GEN BRG** or **#2 GEN BRG**, to indicate a worn or failed bearing. The caution legend will remain on until power is removed. The auxiliary bearing will allow 10 additional hours of operation after the legend goes on. Therefore, it should not be a cause for mission abort. Power to operate the caution system is provided from the No. 1 and No. 2 dc primary buses, through circuit breakers, marked **NO. 1 GEN WARN** and **NO. 2 GEN WARN**, respectively.

NOTE

When the **GEN BRG** caution legend remains on for more than 1 minute, make an entry on the DA Form 2408-13-1.

2.59.1 Generator Control Units (GCU). The GCUs monitor voltage from the No. 1, No. 2 and APU generators and take the generator(s) off-line where malfunctions occur. Underfrequency protection is disabled in flight by the WOW switch.

2.60 AUXILIARY AC POWER SYSTEM.

An auxiliary ac power system (Figure 2-17), is a backup ac power source, providing electrical power for ground checkouts. The system consists of a 115 vac three-phase, 400 Hz 20/30 kVA, air-cooled generator mounted on and driven by the APU, a current transformer and a generator control unit. If the primary ac generators are not operating, the auxiliary ac power output will be applied through contactors to the No. 2 ac primary bus and through contactors and current limiters to the No. 1 ac primary bus. An advisory legend on the caution/advisory display will go on, indicating **APU GEN ON** when the APU generator is operating, and the APU generator switch is **ON**. **APU GEN ON** legend will be on only when supplying power to the system, it will be off at any time either No. 1 generator or No. 2 generator is supplying power. The generator control switch on the upper console (Figure 2-6), has marked positions of **TEST, OFF/RESET,** and **ON**.

NOTE

If the APU generator is the sole source of ac generated power, all equipment may be operated, except that when the backup pump is on, the windshield anti-ice is prevented from being used.

2.60.1 Generator Control Switches. Generators are controlled by a three-position generator switch on the upper console (Figure 2-6). The switch **ON** position energizes the generator and permits connection of generator ac output to the ac loads. **TEST** permits you to test the generator ac output without connecting to the generator loads. **OFF/RESET** deenergizes the generator and permits generator recycling if the generator is disabled and disconnected from its loads. The control switch is manually placed to **RESET** and then back to **ON**.

2.60.2 External AC Power System.

Do not connect a source of dc power to the external ac connector.

An external ac power connector, on the right side of the helicopter (Figure 2-1), accepts ground source of 115 vac, three-phase, 400 Hz power. The system is controlled by a switch on the upper console (Figure 2-6), marked **EXT PWR-RESET-OFF** and **ON**. External power will be introduced into the system if acceptable external power is connected, the **EXT PWR** switch is **ON**, and no other generating source is operating. An advisory legend on the caution/advisory display will go on, indicating **EXT PWR CONNECTED**, whenever external power is connected to the helicopter.

Section XII AUXILIARY POWER UNIT

2.61 AUXILIARY POWER UNIT (APU) SYSTEM.

The auxiliary power unit system (Figure 2-19) consists of an auxiliary power unit (APU), accessories, controls, a monitoring system, and a starting system. The APU system provides pneumatic power for main engine starting and cabin heating, and electrical power for ground and emergency in-flight electrical operations.

NOTE

The APU is not qualified for normal inflight use.

APU system accessories include a prime/boost pump, hydraulic accumulator, hydraulic handpump, hydraulic start motor, and ac generator. The hydraulic accumulators and handpump, in the aft midsection cabin ceiling (Figure 2-5), provide the hydraulic pressure for driving the APU starter. If the APU does not start, the hydraulic accumulator can be recharged by pumping the hydraulic handpump. The hydraulic utility module and backup pump, on the left forward deck within the main rotor pylon, will automatically recharge the depleted hydraulic accumulator for the next APU start. The APU controls are in the cockpit on the upper console. Indicator legends on the caution/advisory display provide cockpit monitoring of the APU. An indicator panel in the cabin will indicate reason for APU shutdown on BITE indicators. The BITE indicators are incorporated in the APU electronic sequence unit (ESU), and will indicate reasons for APU shutdown. Those indicators can be monitored during APU operation without interrupting normal operating systems. During a start, the ESU compares input signals from speed, time, and temperature sensors on the APU to specified values stowed in the ESU memory, and performs functional steps as a result of the comparison. The system also provides for APU protective shutdown in case of turbine overspeed, underspeed, high exhaust temperature, low oil pressure, or loss of electrical power or sequence failure. Each major sequence step will have a visual indication of go/no-go. The ESU samples predetermined parameters of exhaust temperature, turbine speed and oil pressure. If any one of the predetermined values are exceeded, the APU will shut down, and appropriate BITE indication is made. If a momentary malfunction occurs (i.e., a power interruption other than switching of the **APU CONTR** switch) the APU will shut down and the **APU CONTR** switch must be placed at **OFF** and then back **ON**, to restart the APU. There is also an output signal to the caution/advisory display to turn on the **APU ON** advisory legend, indicating the APU is operating. Power to operate the APU and ESU is provided from the battery bus through a circuit breaker marked **APU CONTR INST**.

2.62 APU.

The auxiliary power unit (Figure 2-19) consists of a gas turbine shaft power section, a reduction gear drive, and appropriate controls and accessories. The accessory gear box provides an axial pad with a 12,000 rpm output drive for the APU ac generator, rpm pad for mounting the APU start motor, rpm drive pad for the APU fuel assembly. A magnetic pickup mounted on the accessory gear box senses engine speed. The APU is lubricated by a self-contained oil system. Refer to Figure 2-23 for servicing.

2.62.1 APU Controls. The APU control, on the upper console (Figure 2-6), consists of a **CONTR** switch and an APU fire extinguisher T-handle. The **APU CONTR** switch, with marked positions **OFF** and **ON**, controls the operation of the APU. Placing the switch **ON** starts the APU and allows it to operate. The APU is off when the switch is **OFF**. The **APU FAIL** caution legend will be on any time the APU automatically shuts down. The **APU OIL TEMP HI** caution legend is on when APU oil temperature is above normal range. During ground operation at high ambient temperatures the **APU OIL TEMP HI** caution legend may go on. If this occurs, the APU should be shut down immediately to prevent damage. After a 30-minute cooling period, the oil level should be checked. If OK, the APU may be restarted. The control system receives electrical power from the battery bus through a circuit breaker marked **APU CONTR INST** on the lower console. When illuminated, the **APU** T-handle warns the pilot/copilot of a fire in the APU compartment. When the T-handle is pulled, it turns off fuel to the APU, sends a stop signal to the ESU, arms the fire extinguisher system, and sets the extinguisher direction control valve to the APU. During APU starts using battery power, if the fire extinguisher is required, **FIRE EXTGH RESERVE** must be used. The T-handle microswitch receives electrical power from the battery utility bus through a circuit breaker marked **FIRE EXTGH** on the lower console circuit breaker panel.

2.62.2 APU Fuel Control System (Helicopters equipped with (T-62T-40-1 APU). This system consists of a fuel pump and a control assembly. The fuel pump is protected by a filter. Fuel pump output flow passes through another filter before entering the control assembly. A governor and flow metering valve controls fuel flow to the engine during ignition, permitting automatic starting under

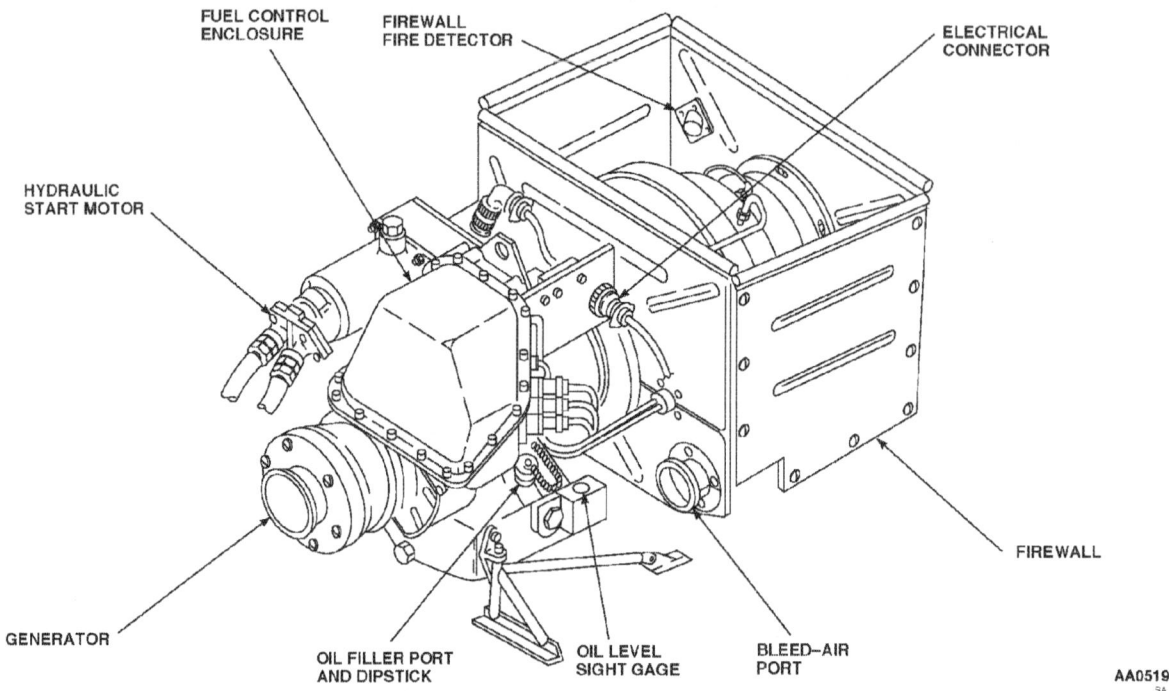

Figure 2-19. Auxiliary Power Unit (APU)

all ambient conditions, and controls the turbine at a constant speed once it has accelerated to operating speed. An electronic speed sensing device provides automatic fuel flow, ignition, and operation of the APU.

2.62.3 APU Fuel Control System (Helicopters equipped with GTC-P36-150 APU). The fuel control system includes a fuel pump and metering section. The fuel pump is protected by an integral inlet filter. Fuel pump output flow passes through a filter screen before entering the metering assembly. Fuel pump discharge pressure is limited by an ultimate relief valve which, when activated, bypasses fuel flow back to the pump inlet. Fuel metering is accomplished by the torque motor metering valve as a function of an electrical signal from the electronic sequence unit (ESU). For accurate fuel metering, a constant, pressure drop across the metering valve is maintained by the differential pressure regulating valve. The fuel solenoid valve is energized by the ESU following the initiation of APU start. This allows fuel to flow to the engine. The fuel control assembly subsequently provides fuel according to a preprogrammed schedule to effect efficient acceleration. The fuel solenoid valve will close completely without visible leakage from the minimum operating fuel pressure to 110% of the maximum operating fuel pressure.

2.62.4 APU Fuel Supply System. APU fuel is supplied to the APU from the left main fuel tank. The **FUEL PUMP** switch must be at **APU BOOST** for all APU operation, except engine priming. The APU prime/boost shutoff valve is a two-position, open-closed unit mounted on the APU compartment firewall where it also functions as a firewall shutoff valve. The valve is pilot-operated from the upper console **FUEL PUMP** switch as well as by the **FIRE EXTGH APU** T-handle. If the APU does not start and the **APU ACCUM LOW** advisory legend is not on, the manual override lever on the accumulator manifold should be pulled to attempt another start, and held until the APU has reached self-sustaining speed.

2.63 ACCUMULATOR RECHARGE.

The accumulator recharge cycle starts when the APU has reached operational speed and the APU-driven generator comes on the line. The pressure switch for the accumulator causes the **APU ACCUM LOW** legend to go on and the backup system pump to develop pressure. The APU accumulator pressure should be at least 2800 psi before attempting an APU start. The accumulator is recharged from the backup pump which runs for 90 seconds after the accumulator low-pressure switch is actuated. When the winterization kit is installed, an additional identical accumulator is installed in parallel with the original accumulator. Discharge and recharge of the added accumulator is the same, except a 180-second recharge cycle for the two accumulators will take place when the accumulator pressure switch senses low accumulator pressure. Both accumulators are charged or discharged simultaneously. If the accumulators do not fully charge during the first 180 seconds of the backup pump operating cycle, the pump will continue to operate in 180-second segments, or until the **BACKUP PUMP PWR** circuit breaker is pulled, or 115 vac power is removed. The backup system pump shuts down after recharge, unless required for other purposes. Should the accumulator pressure drop, the backup system pump restarts to replenish the accumulator charge. The rate of accumulator charge is limited to protect the backup system from possible depletion due to ballistic damage to the APU start system. Should the APU not start, the accumulator may be recharged by these methods, after the **APU CONTR** switch is **OFF**. An electric ground cart powering the backup hydraulic pump or a hydraulic ground cart connected to the backup hydraulic system through the ground test quick-disconnects or by using the handpump in the aft upper cabin. The **APU CONTR** switch should not be turned **ON** again or the **BATT** switch turned **OFF** until after the ESU BITE indicators have been checked. The handpump may also be used to top off the accumulator charge if the charge has dropped due to a low temperature condition. A pressure gage mounted in the aft cabin (Figure 2-5) indicates the charge. Check valves prevent draining of the accumulator charge through the system.

Section XIII LIGHTING

2.64 INTERIOR LIGHTING.

The interior lighting system consists of cockpit dome lights, utility lights and a cabin dome light (Figure 2-4). NVG blue-green lighting can be selected for the cockpit dome, instrument panel glare shield, utility lights and cabin dome light. For medical interior lighting description refer to Chapter 4.

2.64.1 NVG Lighting System. The NVG lighting system consists of interior NVG blue-green lighting. Exterior lighting consists of cargo hook well area electroluminescent lighting, infrared formation and position lights, and attachable/detachable controllable searchlight filter. A dimming feature is incorporated in the searchlight system to provide dimming through the collective **SRCH LT PUSH ON - OFF**, **BRT**, **DIM** switch. The position and formation lights have IR emitters installed within close proximity to the regular installed lights to enhance outside viewing with night vision goggles.

2.64.2 Cockpit Floodlights. Two blue-green and two white cockpit floodlights are on the overhead cockpit floodlight panel, marked **BLUE**, **OFF** and **WHITE** (Figure 2-6). Power is supplied from the dc essential bus through a circuit breaker marked **LIGHTS SEC PNL**. Six lights installed in the instrument panel glare shield provide secondary lighting for the instrument panel. The lights are mechanically dimmed by a control on the upper console labeled **GLARESHIELD LIGHTS** with marked positions **OFF** and **BRT**. Power to operate the glare shield lights is provided from the No. 1 ac primary bus through a circuit breaker, marked **LIGHTS GLARE SHLD**.

2.64.3 Flight Instrument Lights. Instrument lights are grouped into flight instrument and nonflight instruments. The flight instrument lights are divided into pilot's and copilot's. Lights are controlled by individual rotary intensity controls (Figure 2-6), marked **INST LT PILOT FLT**, **OFF** and **BRT**, and **CPLT FLT INST LTS**, **OFF** and **BRT**. The nonflight instrument lights operate in the same manner as the flight instrument lights. The nonflight lights intensity is controlled by a rotary control, marked **INST LT NON FLT**, **OFF** and **BRT**. Instrument lighting is provided by instrument bezels with NVG lights. The radar altimeters lighting incorporates dimming controls on the instrument panel, marked **RAD ALT DIMMING** for pilots radar altimeters (Figure 2-8). The vertical instrument display system has NVG information panel lighting to make those instruments compatible with the NVG system. Power to operate the instrument lights is provided by the No. 2 ac primary bus through circuit breakers marked **LIGHTS PLT FLT** and **LIGHTS NON FLT**, and No. 1 ac primary bus, through a circuit breaker marked **LIGHTS CPLT FLT**.

2.64.4 Lighted Switches Dimmer. A dimmer control labeled **LIGHTED SWITCHES** (Figure 2-6) is provided on the upper console to reduce illumination level of the following panel lighted switches: Pilot and copilot **MODE SEL**, **TAILWHEEL LOCK**, **CIS MODE SEL**, **AUTO FLT CONT** and **NO. 1** and **NO. 2 FUEL BOOST PUMP** on lights.

2.64.5 Upper and Lower Console Lights. NVG lights for the upper console, cockpit flood secondary lights, engine control quadrant, flight control panel, miscellaneous switch panel, boost pump control panel, ESSS related panels, range extension fuel management panel, rescue hoist panel, and compass are illuminated from the No. 1 ac primary bus through dimmer controls marked **CONSOLE LT UPPER** and **LOWER**. Circuits are protected by circuit breakers marked **LIGHTS UPPER CSL** and **LIGHTS LWR CSL**. All other lower console panels are illuminated by the lower console auxiliary utility light next to the copilot's seat.

2.64.6 Utility Lights. All utility lights are dual (blue/green-white) (Figure 2-4). One portable cockpit utility light with coiled cord is attached to the upper console by removable brackets, on the pilot's side of the console. The light may be adjusted on it's mounting to direct the light beam or it may be removed and used portably. The utility light is controlled by a rheostat or a pushbutton on the end of the casting. The lens casting of the light may be turned to change from white to blue/green and/or spot to flood. The copilot's utility light, located at the right rear of the copilot's seat, is used to illuminate some panels on the lower console for night flight. A transition equipment bay utility light is installed on the bay shelf to provide bay lighting. All utility lights operate in the same manner as above. The utility lights operate from the battery bus through a circuit breaker marked **UTIL BUS DC SPLY**.

2.64.7 Cabin Dome Lights. One dome light is provided for cabin lighting (Figure 2-5). Control of cabin lights is from the upper console by a control marked **CABIN DOME LT** (Figure 2-6). The light color selector switch has marked positions **WHITE**, **OFF**, and **BLUE**. To place the switch from **OFF** to **WHITE**, the switch must first be pulled out to clear a detent. This prevents accidentally placing the switch to **WHITE**. The cabin lighting is enabled through the **CABIN DOME LT** switch. The side medical lights only operate when the **CABIN DOME LT** switch is in the **WHITE** position. The ceiling medical lights operate when the **CABIN DOME LT** switch is in the **WHITE** or **BLUE** position. For a complete description of the cabin lighting refer to Chapter 4. Dimming control for the cabin dome light is from a control on the left side of the pilots seat (Figure 2-4), marked **CABIN DOME LT**, with marked positions **OFF** and **BRT**. Power to operate the cabin dome light system is provided from the No. 1 ac primary bus through a circuit breaker marked **LIGHTS CABIN DOME**.

2.64.8 Maintenance Light. A portable 20 watt floodlight, in the cabin is used by the crew for maintenance work. The light has a 20-foot cord, allowing its use within the cabin and around the main transmission. A switch on the rear end of the light with marked positions, **DIM**, **OFF**, and **BRIGHT**, controls the light intensity. Another maintenance light receptacle, in the aft tailcone, allows the light to be used around the tail section. Power to operate the light is from the battery bus through a circuit breaker marked **UTIL BUS DC SPLY**. The maintenance light is stowed in a bag at the back of the pilot's seat. Power to operate the maintenance lights is provided from the battery bus through a circuit breaker, marked **UTIL BUS DC SPLY**. Make sure the maintenance and cockpit utility lights are **OFF** when not in use.

2.65 EXTERIOR LIGHTS.

2.65.1 Searchlight.

Landing and searchlight have less than one foot ground clearance when extended. Use caution when ground taxiing over rough terrain when landing light and/or searchlight are extended.

The searchlight is mounted on the right bottom of the nose section, and is controlled from either collective pitch stick. The 150 watt light can be moved forward through a 120° arc from the stow position. It can also be turned 360° in either a right or left direction on its axis. The light is operated by a switch labeled **SRCH LT ON, OFF, BRT, DIM** (Figure 2-11). Directional control of the light is provided through the four-position searchlight control switch, labeled **EXT** (extend), **RETR** (retract), **L** (left), and **R** (right). When the **SRCH LT** switch is placed **ON**, the lamp will go on, arming the control switch. Placing the control switch to **EXT** causes the light beam to move forward at a rate of about 12° per second. If the switch is placed to **OFF** the light will extinguish. To retract the searchlight, place the switch to **RETR**. Refer to Chapter 5 for extend/retract limitations. An infrared filter can be installed on the controllable searchlight to enhance viewing objects outside the helicopter when wearing the night vision goggles. The dimming feature provides a variable light level through a switch on each collective grip marked **SRCH LT ON - OFF**. Push **BRT - DIM** to control power to the light and the **DIM/BRT** mode selector. When the light is on, the **BRT DIM** switch may be moved to select the desired light level. When the desired level is reached, the switch is released to the center position. Power to light and control the searchlight is provided from the dc essential bus through circuit breakers, marked **LIGHTS, CONTR PWR** and **SRCH CONTR**. The IR filter may be removed for unaided night flight.

2.65.2 Landing Light. One 600-watt landing light is mounted on the left side beneath the nose section and is controlled from both collective pitch stick grips (Figure 2-11). The light can be extended 107° from the stowed position. A dual function switch is used to operate the light. The **LDG LT PUSH ON-OFF** switch controls lighting and **EXT, RETR** controls light position. When the light is **ON** (**LDG LT ON** advisory legend should be on) and the switch is at **EXT** detent, the light can be positioned at any point between stowed and fully extended, or it will continue to extend until reaching its limit and power is removed. When the switch is held at **RETR** the light retracts to the stowed position. When the light reaches its stowed position, power is automatically removed from the motor. The **LDG LT PUSH ON-OFF** switch must be pushed **OFF** (**LDG LT ON** advisory legend should go off). Refer to Chapter 5 for extend/retract limitations. During extension, the travel speed is about 12° per second, and during retract, about 30° per second. Power to light and control the landing light is supplied from the No. 1 dc primary bus through circuit breakers, marked **LIGHTS, RETR LDG, CONT** and **PWR**.

2.65.3 Anticollision Lights. This light system contains four strobes in two separate units, one beneath the aft fuselage and one on top of the aft pylon section. The lights are controlled by two switches on the upper console (Figure 2-6) labeled **ANTI COLLISION LIGHTS UPPER, BOTH, LOWER** and **DAY, OFF, NIGHT**. The system consists of a dual power supply and two interchangeable day/night anticollision lights. The dual supply system provides separate outputs for the aft fuselage light and the pylon mounted light. Each anticollision light assembly contains two lamps, the upper lamp within a red lens for night operation and the lower within a clear lens for day operation. Proper operation is selected by placing the switch to

DAY or **NIGHT**. The desired strobe(s) is selected by placing the switch to **UPPER**, **LOWER** or **BOTH**. If at **BOTH**, the lower fuselage and the aft pylon lights will alternately flash. If the selector switch is placed to **UPPER** or **LOWER**, only that light will flash. To discontinue operation of the anticollision light(s), the **DAY-NIGHT** switch is placed to **OFF**. Power to operate the anticollision light system is provided from the No. 2 ac primary bus through a circuit breaker, marked **LIGHTS, ANTI COLL**.

2.65.4 Position Lights. Position lights (Figure 2-1) are outboard of the left and right landing gear support and top tail pylon. The lights are red on the left, green on the right, and white on the tail. Control of the position lights is through the upper console panel containing two switches, marked **POSITION LIGHTS, DIM, OFF, BRT,** and **STEADY, FLASH**. When the intensity switch is placed to **DIM** or **BRT**, all three lights go on at once. If the **STEADY-FLASH** switch is placed to **FLASH**, the three lights will flash. The **STEADY** position causes the lights to remain on continuously. Power to operate the position lights is provided by No. 2 dc primary bus through a circuit breaker, marked **POS LTS**. Infrared position lights are installed within close proximity of the standard position lights. NVG operation is selected through a toggle switch on the upper console (Figure 2-6) marked **NAV LTS**, with switch positions **NORM** and **IR**. Position lights are to be selected through a switch marked **POSITION LIGHTS, DIM, OFF,** or **BRT,** and mode of operation through a switch marked **STEADY** or **FLASH**. Power for control of the IR lights is from the No. 2 dc primary bus through a circuit breaker marked **IR LTS**.

2.65.5 Formation Lights. These lights (Figure 2-1) are on top of the main pylon cowling, tail drive shaft cover, and horizontal stabilizer. The system consists of four green electroluminescent lights. The lights are controlled by a single rotary selector switch, marked **FORMATION LT**, with marked positions **OFF** and **1** through **5**. Position **5** is the brightest. When NVG operations are required, IR lights may be used to enhance viewing outside the helicopter. IR lights are selected through a toggle switch on the upper console (Figure 2-6) marked, **NAV LTS, NORM,** and **IR**. This switch shares operation with the IR position lights when operating in a NVG environment. Dimming of the IR lights is done with the **FORMATION LT** control, as used with the electroluminescent formation lights. Selection of position **1** through **4** causes the IR formation lights to illuminate at the same intensity. Position **5** causes the lights to illuminate brighter. Power to operate the formation lights is provided from the No. 2 ac primary bus through two circuit breakers, marked **LIGHTS, FORM LV** and **HV**.

Section XIV FLIGHT INSTRUMENTS

2.66 PITOT-STATIC SYSTEM.

Two electrically-heated pitot tubes with static ports are aft and above the pilot's and copilot's cockpit doors. The right pitot tube is connected to the pilot's instruments and the left pitot tube is connected to the copilot's instruments. Tubing connects the pitot tube static pressure ports to the airspeed indicators and the altimeters. In addition to standard instrumentation, airspeed data is sensed for operation of stabilator, flight path stabilization, and command instrument system. Refer to Section IX for pitot tube heater system.

2.67 ATTITUDE INDICATING SYSTEM.

Helicopter pitch and roll attitudes are sensed by the pilot's and copilot's vertical displacement gyroscopes, that apply attitude signals to the vertical situation indicators (VSI) for visual display (Figure 2-8). Signals are applied through the **VERT GYRO** select switches to the remote indicator on the vertical situation indicators. Helicopter pitch and roll attitudes are shown on the pilot's and copilot's vertical situation indicators. The indicator face contains a fixed bar, representing the helicopter, a movable sphere with a white horizon line dividing the two colors, white above and black below, a fixed bank angle scale and a bank index on the moving sphere. Relative position of the fixed bar (helicopter) and the horizon line indicates the helicopter's attitude referenced to the earth horizon. A **ROLL** trim knob on the lower left of the VSI permits adjustment of the roll index about 14°±6° right and left from zero. A **PITCH** trim knob on the lower right of the VSI permits adjustment of the indicator sphere 14°±6° for dive and 7°±3° for climb from zero index. If a power failure or unbalance occurs in the pilot's or copilot's vertical displacement gyroscope, a gyroscope power failure flag will appear, indicating **ATT**, warning the pilot or copilot that pitch and roll attitude signals are not being sent to his indicator. To restore attitude information to the indicator, the pilot or copilot should press his **VERT GYRO** select switch on the **MODE SEL** panel so that **ALTR** appears in the switch window. This causes the **ATT** flag on the indicator to disappear, and pitch and roll signals are supplied from the operating gyro, restoring attitude information display. Refer to Chapter 3 for description of **VERT GYRO** select switch.

2.68 TURN RATE INDICATING SYSTEM.

A 4-minute turn rate (turn and slip) indicator is at the bottom center of each VSI (Figure 2-8). The pilot's and copilot's indicators operate independent of each other through **TURN RATE** switches on the **MODE SEL** panels. Each system consists of a rate gyro, a turn slip indicator and a select switch. The VSI contains a moving turn rate needle and a fixed turn rate scale for indicating rate and direction of turn. During straight flight the needle is positioned at the center of the scale. When the helicopter turns, the rate-of-turn signal from the rate gyroscope deflects the needle in the proper direction to indicate the turn. Amount of deflection is proportional to the rate-of-turn. A one-needle width deflection represents a turn of 1.5° per second. The VSI also contains a slip indicator that shows uncoordinated turns. If a power failure or unbalance occurs in the pilot's or copilot's rate gyroscope, the associated VSI signal will be lost. To restore rate-of-turn information to the indicator, the pilot or copilot will press the **TURN RATE** switch on his **MODE SEL** panel so that **ALTR** appears in the switch window. This applies alternate rate gyroscope signals from the operating gyroscope to the indicator. Power to operate the pilot's turn rate system is provided from the dc essential bus through a circuit breaker, marked **PILOT TURN DETR**. The copilot's system is powered from the No. 1 dc primary bus through a circuit breaker, marked **CPLT TURN RATE GYRO**. Refer to Chapter 3 for a description of the **TURN RATE** select switch.

2.69 AIRSPEED INDICATOR.

Two airspeed indicators (Figure 2-8), are installed on the instrument panel, one each for the pilot and copilot. The indicators are differential pressure instruments, measuring the difference between impact pressure and static pressure. Instrument range markings and limitations are contained in Chapter 5, Section II, System Limits.

2.70 ALTIMETER/ENCODER AAU-32A.

Two altimeters are installed on the instrument panel (Figures 2-8 and 2-20). The altimeter encoder functions as a barometric altimeter for the pilot and a barometric altitude sensor for the AN/APX-100 transponder in mode C. The copilot's functions only as a barometric altimeter. The system is equipped with a continuously operating vibrator to improve altitude measuring accuracy. The altimeter's operating range is from -1000 feet to 50,000 feet. The face of the instrument has a marked scale from zero to nine in 50-foot units. The operating indicators and controls are a 100-foot pointer, 100-foot drum, 1,000-foot drum, 10,000-foot drum, barometric pressure set knob, barometric pressure scale window and warning flag. The warning flag is only used in conjunction with the encoder. A counter window next to the sweep hand contains the three digital drums

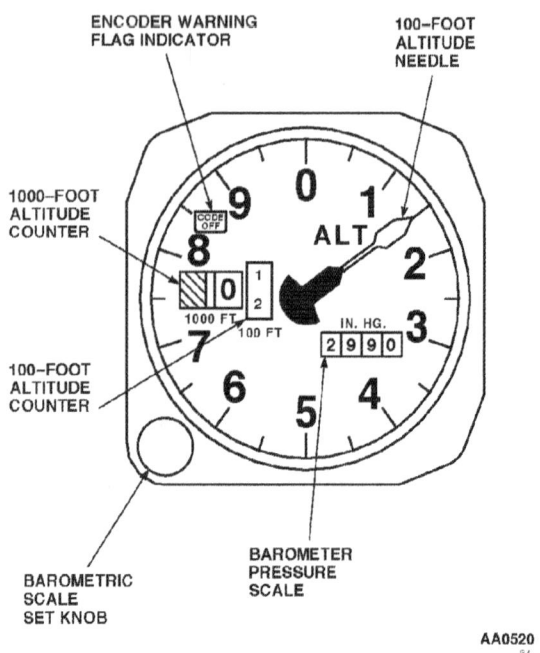

Figure 2-20. Altimeter Encoder AAU-32A

that rotate to indicate the altitude of the helicopter. Another window in the upper left section of the instrument face indicates the normal code operation. When the system fails to transmit signals to the transponder, a flag marked **CODE OFF** will appear in the window. A window on the lower right section of the instrument face indicates barometric pressure setting. The barometric pressure set knob is on the lower left corner of the indicator bezel. Power to operate the encoder system is provided by the No. 2 dc primary bus through a circuit breaker, marked **PILOT ALTM**.

2.71 VERTICAL SPEED INDICATOR.

Two indicators are installed, one each in front of the pilot and copilot (Figure 2-8), to indicate rate of climb or descent.

2.72 STANDBY MAGNETIC COMPASS.

A magnetic compass is installed above the instrument panel on the right center windshield frame (Figure 2-4). The compass is used as a standby instrument for heading references. A compass correction card with deviation errors is installed on the right side of the upper console.

2.73 FREE-AIR TEMPERATURE (FAT) INDICATOR.

The free-air temperature indicator is a direct reading instrument marked **FREE AIR**, and reads in degrees Celsius. Two FAT indicators are installed through the overhead windows (Figure 2-4).

2.74 CLOCK.

Two digital clocks (Figure 2-8) may be installed on the instrument panel. The clock incorporates a six digit liquid crystal display, 24 hour numerals and sweep second indication. A battery allows continuous operation for a minimum of one year when aircraft 28 vdc power is not applied. The clock has two modes of operation, clock mode (C) and the elapsed time mode (ET). Power to operate the clock is provided by the No. 1 dc and No. 2 dc primary buses through circuit breakers marked **CPLT ALTM** and **PILOT ALTM** respectively.

2.75 MASTER WARNING SYSTEM.

Master caution lights will not illuminate if both MFDs have failed.

Two master caution lights (Figures 2-8 and 2-21) one each side for the pilot and copilot, marked **MASTER CAUTION PRESS TO RESET**, are on the master warning panel. They light whenever a caution legend goes on. These lights alert the pilots and direct attention to the caution/advisory grid. The master caution lights should be reset at once to provide a similar indication if a second condition or malfunction occurs while the first is still present. The master caution light can be reset from either pilot position. Four amber warning lights, also on the master warning panel, require immediate action if they go on. The markings are **#1 ENG OUT**, **#2 ENG OUT**, **FIRE**, and **LOW ROTOR RPM**. The **LOW ROTOR RPM** warning light will flash at a rate of three to five flashes per second if rotor rpm drops below 96% **RPM R**. In addition, if % **RPM R** drops below 96% or Ng drops below 55%, a low steady tone is provided. The low rotor rpm tone is inhibited on the ground through the left landing gear weight-on-wheels switch. The engine Ng steady tone is not inhibited. The **ENG OUT** warning lights and tone will go on at 55% **Ng SPEED** and below. Refer to paragraph 2.11.1

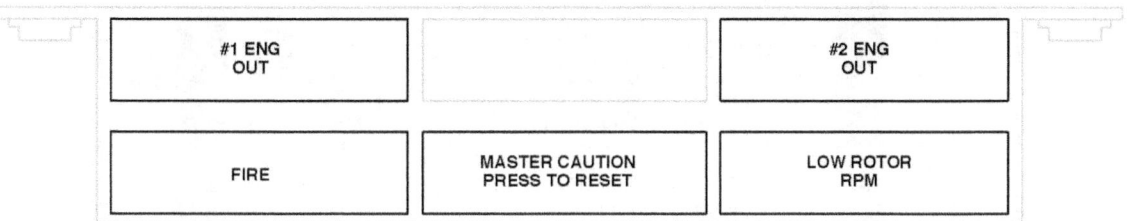

Figure 2-21. Master Warning Panel

for description of the FIRE warning lights. Power for the master caution lights is provided from the No. 1 dc primary bus through a circuit breaker, marked **LIGHTS ADVSY**.

2.75.1 Caution/Advisory Legend System. Caution and advisory legends appear in the MFDs and CDU. Pressing **ILLUM ALL** soft key on the MFD displays the caution/advisory grid. Caution legends indicate malfunctions or unsafe conditions, and are displayed in yellow. Noncritical advisory legends are displayed in green. Some cautions will also generate a **LAND ASAP** message in the MFD. Caution legends appear in reverse video until acknowledged, which is done by pressing **ACK** soft key. When the MFD has other displays active, cautions and advisory messages are displayed in a pop up window. Cautions appear in "last in, first displayed" order, with the most current caution at the top of the list. The most recent advisory is at the top of the advisory list, which is below the last caution. Cautions are separated from advisory legends by a row of asterisks. Refer to major systems for a complete description of caution-advisory legends. Refer to Table 2-3 for a brief description of each fault.

2.75.2 CDU Caution/Advisory Grid. A caution/advisory grid is also displayed on the CDU as a backup to the MFD grid. Press **CAU/ADV** fixed function key to view active caution and advisory legends. When the caution advisory display is present, the CDU keyboard is disabled. Press **CAU/ADV**, or acknowledge the caution legend from the MFD to return to the previous display. Caution and advisory legends have the same meanings as those on the MFD (Table 2-3).

2.75.3 Caution/Advisory BRT/DIM - TEST Switch. Testing of the caution/advisory display is done through a momentary spring-loaded to center switch marked **INDICATOR LTS BRT/DIM** and **TEST**, on the instrument panel (Figure 2-8). Placing the switch to **TEST** simultaneously checks legends on the caution/advisory display and the master warning panels. The **LOW ROTOR RPM** warning lights will flash. During caution/advisory test, when the **TEST** switch is released from the **TEST** position, the master caution lights will flash approximately 16 times to indicate that the transmission drive train chip caution panel circuits are going through self-test. An existing malfunction within those circuits will prevent flashing of the master caution lights and the respective chip caution legend will flash. The master caution warning lights should be reset at once to provide a similar indication if a second condition or malfunction occurs while the first condition is present. When the pilot's **PILOT FLT** rotary intensity control is moved from the **OFF** position, placing the **INDICATOR LTS BRT/DIM-TEST** switch to **BRT/DIM** causes the caution/advisory legends and master warning lights to change intensity. When the lights are dim and power is removed, the light intensity will return to bright when power is reapplied. The **TEST** switch position receives power from the No. 1 dc primary bus through a circuit breaker, marked **LIGHTS ADVSY**. Dimming of the cockpit indicator lights operates with the caution dimming system.

Figure 2-22. MFD Caution/Advisory Grid

Table 2-3. Caution/Advisory and Warning Light Lighting Parameters

LEGEND	ILLUMINATING PARAMETER OR FAULT
	CAUTION LEGENDS
#1 FUEL LOW	Flashes when left fuel tank level is about 172 pounds.
#1 FUEL PRESS	Left engine fuel pressure between engine-driven low-pressure fuel pump and high-pressure fuel pump is low.
#1 ENG OIL PRESS	Left engine oil pressure is too low for continued operation.
#1 ENGINE OIL TEMP	Left engine oil temperature is above 150°C.
CHIP #1 ENGINE	Left engine chip detector in scavenge oil system has metal chip or particle buildup.
#1 FUEL FLTR BYPAS	Left engine fuel filter has excessive pressure differential across filter.
#1 ENGINE STARTER	Left engine start circuit is actuated.
#1 PRI SERVO PRESS	First stage pressure is shut off, or has dropped below minimum, or servo pilot valve is jammed.
TAIL RTR QUADRANT	Goes on when a tail rotor cable is broken or disconnected.
MAIN XMSN OIL TEMP	Main transmission oil temperature is above 120°C.

2-70

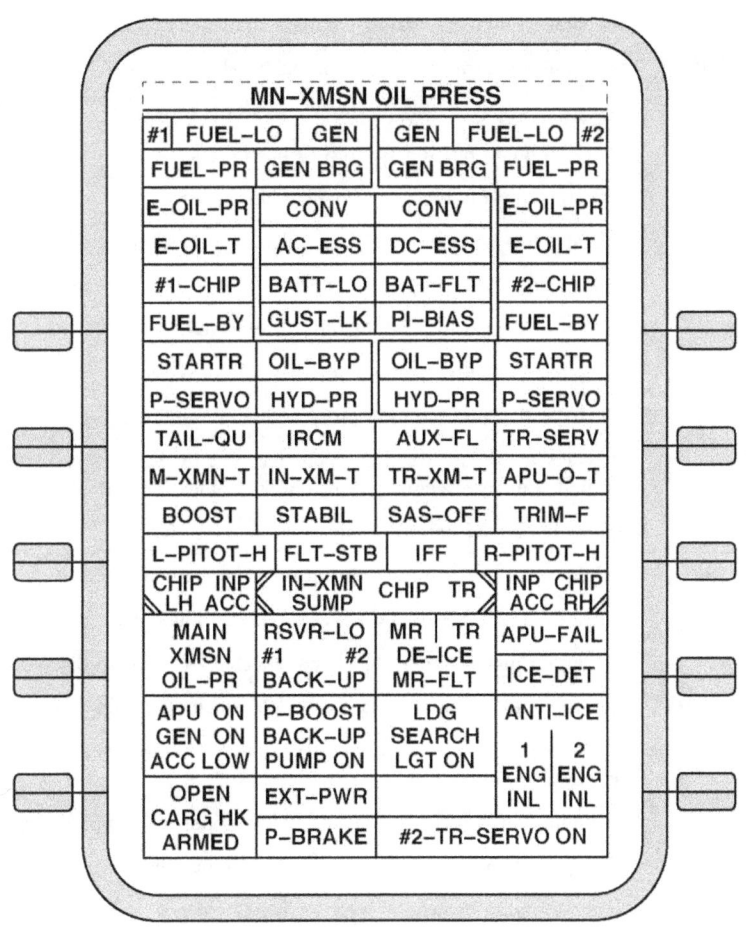

Figure 2-23. CDU Caution/Advisory Grid

Table 2-3. Caution/Advisory and Warning Light Lighting Parameters (Cont)

LEGEND	ILLUMINATING PARAMETER OR FAULT
BOOST SERVO OFF	Indicates loss of second stage hydraulic pressure to the boost servo, or a boost servo jam.
LFT PITOT HEAT	Indicates left pitot heater element is not receiving power with **PITOT HEAT** switch **ON**.
CHIP INPUT MDL-LH	Indicates a metal particle has been detected by the chip detector.
CHIP ACCESS MDL-LH	Indicates a metal particle has been detected by the chip detector.
MR DE-ICE FAIL	Indicates a short or open in the main rotor deice system, which will disable the system.
MAIN XMSN OIL PRES	Main transmission oil pressure is below about 14 psi.
#1 GEN	Left generator is not supplying power to the buses.
#1 GEN BRG	Generator main bearing is worn or has failed.
#1 CONV	Left converter (ac to dc current) has no output.
AC ESS BUS OFF	Indicates that no power (115 vac, phase B) is being supplied to the ac essential bus.
BATT LOW CHARGE	Indicates that the battery charge state is at or below about 40% of full charge state.
GUST LOCK	Indicates the gust lock is not fully disengaged.
#1 OIL FLTR BYPASS	Left engine oil filter pressure differential is excessive.
#1 HYD PUMP	Left hydraulic pump output pressure below minimum.
IRCM INOP	Indicates a malfunction has been detected by the infrared countermeasure system or infrared countermeasure system is in a cooldown cycle.
INT XMSN OIL TEMP	Intermediate gear box oil temperature is excessive.
STABILATOR	Stabilator system is turned on but is in the manual mode.
FLT-PATH STAB	Indicates that FPS is inoperative in one or more axis.
CHIP INT XMSN	Indicates a metal particle has been detected by the chip detector.
CHIP MAIN MDL SUMP	Indicates a metal particle has been detected by the chip detector.
MR DE-ICE FAULT	Indicates partial failure of the blade deice system. Uneven shedding of ice can be expected.
#1 RSVR LOW	Hydraulic fluid level has dropped below about 60% of full capacity.
#2 GEN	Right generator is not supplying power to the buses.
#2 GEN BRG	Generator main bearing is worn or has failed.
#2 CONV	Right converter (ac to dc current) has no output.
DC ESS BUS OFF	Indicates that no power is being supplied to the dc essential bus.
BATTERY FAULT	(No longer used)
PITCH BIAS FAIL	(No longer used)
#2 OIL FLTR BYPASS	Right engine oil filter pressure differential is excessive.
#2 HYD PUMP	Right hydraulic pump output pressure below minimum.
ERFS AUX FUEL	Indicates one or more auxiliary fuel tanks are empty and/or a degraded mode of system operation.

Table 2-3. Caution/Advisory and Warning Light Lighting Parameters (Cont)

LEGEND	ILLUMINATING PARAMETER OR FAULT
TAIL XMSN OIL TEMP	Tail gear box oil temperature is excessive.
SAS OFF	Hydraulic pressure supplied to the SAS actuator is below minimum.
IFF	Mode 4 is not capable of responding to interrogation.
CHIP TAIL XMSN	Indicates a metal particle has been detected by the chip detector.
APU FAIL	APU was automatically shut down by the electrical sequence unit.
TR DE-ICE FAIL	Indicates a short or open in a tail rotor blade deice element.
#2 RSVR LOW	Hydraulic fluid level has dropped below about 60% of full capacity.
#2 FUEL LOW	Flashes when right fuel level is about 172 pounds.
#2 FUEL PRESS	Right engine fuel pressure between engine-driven low-pressure fuel pump and high-pressure fuel pump is low.
#2 ENG OIL PRESS	Right engine oil pressure is too low for continued operation.
#2 ENGINE OIL TEMP	Right engine oil temperature is above 150°C.
CHIP #2 ENGINE	Right engine chip detector in scavenge oil system has metal chip or particle buildup.
#2 FUEL FLTR BYPAS	Right engine fuel filter has excessive pressure differential across filter.
#2 ENGINE STARTER	Right engine start circuit is actuated.
#2 PRI SERVO PRESS	Second stage pressure is shut off, or has dropped below minimum, or servo pilot valve is jammed.
#1 TAIL RTR SERVO	Pressure to the first stage tail rotor servo is below minimum, or servo pilot valve is jammed.
APU OIL TEMP HI	APU oil temperature is above the maximum.
TRIM FAIL	Indicates that yaw, roll, or pitch trim actuators are not responding accurately to computer signals.
RT PITOT HEAT	Indicates right pitot heat element is not receiving power with **PITOT HEAT** switch **ON**.
CHIP INPUT MDL-RH	Indicates a metal particle has been detected by the chip detector.
CHIP ACCESS MDL-RH	Indicates a metal particle has been detected by the chip detector.
ICE DETECTED	Indicates that ice has been detected.
BACK-UP RSVR LOW	Hydraulic fluid level has dropped below about 60% of full capacity.
	ADVISORY LEGENDS
#1 ENG ANTI-ICE ON	Indicates that No. 1 engine anti-ice/start bleed valve is open.
APU ON	APU is operative.
APU ACCUM LOW	APU accumulator pressure is low.
#1 MFD MALF	IO code failure of MFD.
#1 INL ANTI-ICE ON	Indicates that No. 1 engine inlet anti-icing air temperature is 93°C or above.
APU GEN ON	APU generator output is accepted and being supplied to the helicopter.

Table 2-3. Caution/Advisory and Warning Light Lighting Parameters (Cont)

LEGEND	ILLUMINATING PARAMETER OR FAULT
SEARCH LT ON	Either pilot or copilot has selected **SRCH LT** switch is on.
CARGO HOOK OPEN	Indicates that cargo hook load beam is not latched.
PARKING BRAKE ON	Indicates that **PARKING BRAKE** handle is pulled.
#2 INL ANTI-ICE ON	Indicates that No. 2 engine inlet anti-icing air temperature is 93°C or above.
PRIME BOOST PMP ON	Prime boost pump switch is at **PRIME** or **BOOST**.
LDG LT ON	Either pilot or copilot has selected **LDG LT ON**.
HOOK ARMED	The cargo hook release system is armed.
EXT PWR CONNECTED	Indicates that external power plug is connected to helicopter's EXT POWER connector.
#2 ENG ANTI-ICE ON	Indicates that No. 2 engine inlet anti-ice/start bleed valve is open.
BACK-UP PUMP ON	Backup pump pressure is being supplied.
#2 TL RTR SERVO ON	Pressure to 2nd stage tail rotor servo is above minimum.
#2 MFD MALF	IO code failure of MFD.
MASTER WARNING PANEL	
#1 ENG OUT	No. 1 engine **Ng SPEED** is below 55%.
FIRE	Indicates a fire detector has actuated a fire warning circuit.
MASTER CAUTION PRESS TO RESET	Indicates a caution light on the caution panel has been actuated by failed system.
#2 ENG OUT	No. 2 engine **Ng SPEED** is below 55%.
LOW ROTOR RPM	Rotor speed is below about 96% **RPM R**.

Section XV SERVICING, PARKING, AND MOORING

2.76 SERVICING.

Servicing information is given by systems or components. Points used in frequent servicing and replenishment of fuel, oil and hydraulic fluid are shown in Figure 2-24. Fuel and lubricant specifications and capacities are in Table 2-4. Table 2-5 contains a listing of acceptable commercial fuel.

2.77 SERVICE PLATFORMS AND FAIRINGS.

Service platforms are a part of the engine cowlings, providing access to the engines. Each service platform is about 46 inches long and 18 inches wide. It is capable of supporting a static weight of 400 pounds on any area without yielding. The platform is made of composite metal and fiberglass with a honeycomb core. The engine cowling is opened by releasing a latch on the side and pulling outward on a locking handle. The cowling is opened outward and down, providing a standing area at the lower section. When closed, the cowling lock prevents opening in flight.

2.78 FUEL SYSTEM SERVICING.

a. Both tanks (Figure 2-24) may be serviced simultaneously through pressure refueling or closed circuit refueling. They may be serviced individually by gravity refueling through refueling ports on the left and right sides of the helicopter.

b. **ERFS** The external extended range tanks can only be serviced by gravity refueling through refueling ports on the forward top of each tank.

2.78.1 Fuel Types. Fuels are classified in Table 2-5.

2.78.2 Use of Fuels. Mixing of fuels in fuel tanks. When changing from one type of authorized fuel to another, for example JP-4 to JP-5, it is not necessary to drain the helicopter fuel system before adding the new fuel. Fuels having the same NATO code number are interchangeable. Jet fuels conforming to ASTM D-1655 specification may be used when MIL-T-5624 fuels are not available. This usually occurs during cross-country flights where helicopters using NATO F-44 (JP-5) are refueled with NATO F-40 (JP-4) or Commercial ASTM Type B fuels. Whenever this condition occurs, the operating characteristics may change in that lower operating temperature: slower acceleration, easier starting, and shorter range may be experienced. The reverse is true when changing from F-40 (JP-4) fuel to F-44 (JP-5) or Commercial ASTM Type A-1 fuels.

2.78.3 Gravity Refueling.

1. Ground helicopter to fuel truck or other suitable ground.

2. Plug hose nozzle ground into the helicopter grounding jack, marked **GROUND HERE**, above refueling ports.

3. Remove fuel filler caps and refuel. Refer to Table 2-4 for fuel quantities.

2.78.4 Pressure Refueling.

1. Ground helicopter to fuel truck or other suitable ground.

2. Ground fuel dispenser nozzle to the helicopter grounding point marked **GROUND HERE**, above refueling ports.

Damage to the fuel system could result if refueling hose pressure exceeds 55 psi during pressure refueling or 15 psi during closed circuit refueling.

3. Connect fuel dispenser nozzle to pressure refueling adapter.

NOTE

The system is designed to restrict fuel flow to 300 gpm during pressure refueling at a nozzle pressure of 55 psi and 110 gpm at a nozzle pressure of 15 psi during closed circuit refueling.

4. Start fuel flow from fuel dispenser and refuel helicopter.

If fuel is observed flowing from vent, discontinue refueling and make an entry on DA Form 2408-13-1.

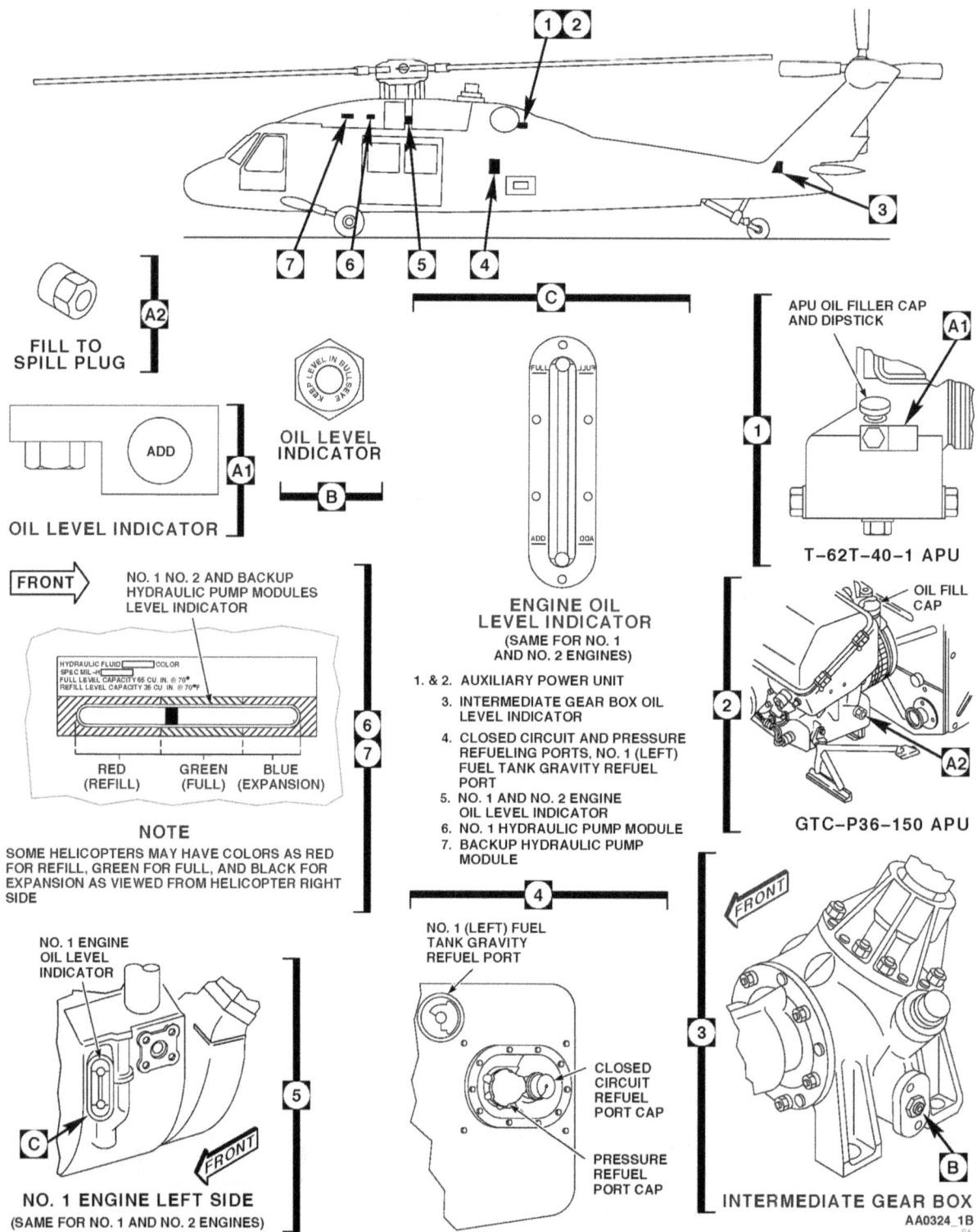

Figure 2-24. Servicing Diagram (Sheet 1 of 3)

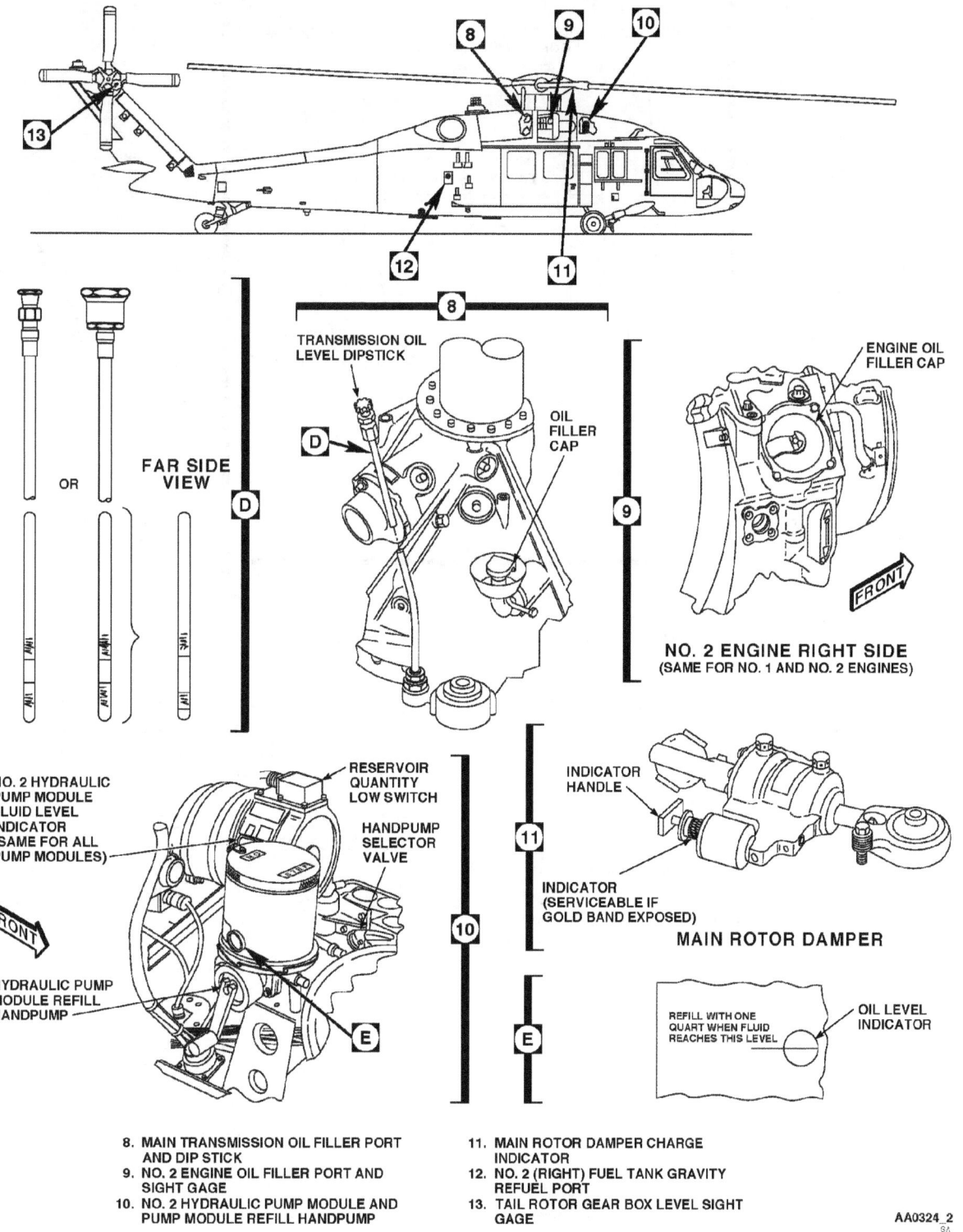

Figure 2-24. Servicing Diagram (Sheet 2 of 3)

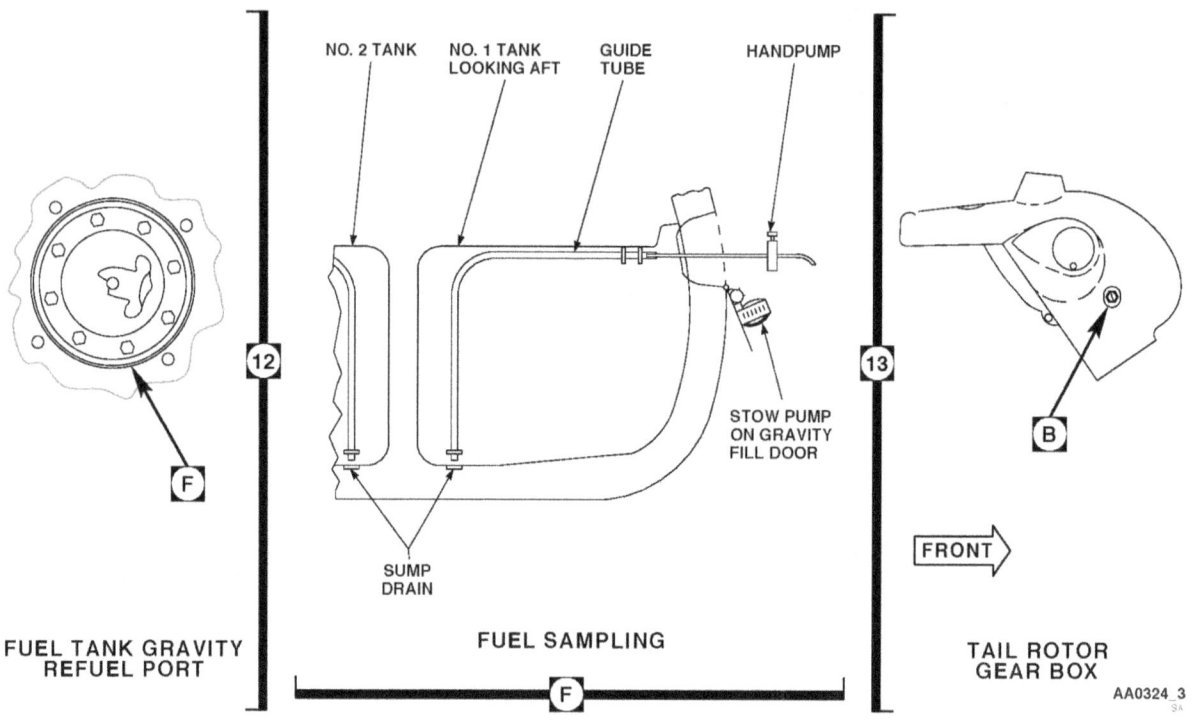

Figure 2-24. Servicing Diagram (Sheet 3 of 3)

5. Once fuel has reached the desired level, remove the fuel dispenser nozzle from the refueling adapter and cap pressure fueling adapter.

2.78.5 Fuel Sampling System. Fuel sampling is done with a thumb-operated handpump (Figure 2-24) containing 5 feet of plastic tubing. The tubing is placed in a guide tube inside the fuel tank and is directed to the bottom of the tank. The handpump is stroked and fuel is drawn from the tank, with contaminants at the bottom. When sampling is completed, the tubing is emptied, rolled, and stowed with the pump on the gravity refueling door. **ERFS** Fuel sampling of the external extended range fuel system is done by taking the sample with a fuel sampler tube from the sump drain located at the bottom aft of each tank.

2.79 EXTERNAL AIR SOURCE/ELECTRICAL REQUIREMENTS.

Refer to Chapter 5 for limitations.

2.80 ENGINE OIL SYSTEM SERVICING.

The helicopter must be level to get accurate oil tank readings. When the helicopter is parked on a slope, the downslope engine will read higher oil level than actual, and the upslope engine will read lower.

NOTE

Do not service the engines with DOD-L-85734 oil. If DOD-L-85734 oil is inadvertently added to the engines, drain the oil and add MIL-L-7808 or MIL-L-23699 oil. Flushing the system before refilling is not required.

The engine oil tank (Figure 2-24) is within the main frame. When the oil level reaches the **ADD** mark, oil should be added to bring the level to the full mark on the sight gage. Wait at least 20 minutes after engine shutdown before checking engine oil level. Before adding oil, determine whether system contains MIL-L-7808 oil or MIL-L-23699 oil. If flights of over 6 hours are made, engine oil level must be at the full line of sight glass before flight.

Table 2-4. Fuel and Lubricants, Specifications, and Capacities

SYSTEM	SPECIFICATION	CAPACITY
Fuel	Primary: Grade JP-4 (NATO Code F-40) (Note 5) Alternate: Grade JP-5 (NATO Code F-44) (Notes 1 and 6) Grade JP-8 (NATO Code F-34) (Note 1)	Main Tanks usable U. S. Gallons of fuel are: 360 gravity, 359 pressure, and 356 closed circuit. External Tank Gravity Refueling: 230 U. S. Gallons each tank.

WARNING

Lubricating oils MIL-L-23699, DOD-L-85734 and MIL-L-7808 contain materials hazardous to health. They produce paralysis if swallowed. Prolonged contact may irritate the skin. Wash hands thoroughly after handling. Oils may burn if exposed to heat or flames. Use only with proper ventilation.

Engine oil	MIL-L-23699 (NATO Code O-156) MIL-L-7808 (NATO Code O-148) (Notes 2, 3 and 7)	7 U. S. Quarts
Auxiliary power unit	MIL-L-23699 (NATO Code O-156) MIL-L-7808 (NATO Code O-148) (Notes 2, 3 and 7)	3 U. S. Quarts (T-62T-40-1) 2 U. S. Quarts (GTC-P36-150)
Transmission oil	MIL-L-23699 (NATO Code O-156) MIL-L-7808 (NATO Code O-148) DOD-L-85734 (Notes 2, 3, 6, and 8)	7 U. S. Gallons

Table 2-4. Fuel and Lubricants, Specifications, and Capacities (Cont)

SYSTEM	SPECIFICATION	CAPACITY
Intermediate gear box oil	MIL-L-23699 (NATO Code 0-156) MIL-L-7808 (NATO Code 0-148) DOD-L-85734 (Notes 2, 3, 6, and 8)	2.75 U. S. Pints
Tail gear box oil	MIL-L-23699 (NATO Code 0-156) MIL-L-7808 (NATO Code 0-148) DOD-L-85734 (Notes 2, 3, 6, and 8)	2.75 U. S. Pints
First stage hydraulic reservoir	MIL-H-83282 MIL-H-5606 (NATO Code H-515) (Note 4)	1 U. S. Quart
Second stage hydraulic reservoir	MIL-H-83282 MIL-H-5606 (NATO Code H-515) (Note 4)	1 U. S. Quart
Backup hydraulic reservoir	MIL-H-83282 MIL-H-5606 (NATO Code H-515) (Note 4)	1 U. S. Quart

SOURCE	PRIMARY OIL	ALTERNATE OIL	
APPROVED COMMERCIAL OILS			

NOTE

Commercial oils listed below are approved alternates for engines and gear boxes except as indicated.

U. S. Military Oil NATO Code No.	DOD-L-85734 (Note 7)	MIL-L-23699 or 0-156	MIL-L-7808 0-148
COMMERCIAL OIL		TYPE II	TYPE I
Castrol Inc.		Castrol 5050 Castrol 5000 Aerojet 5	Castrol 399
Exxon Co.	Turbo Oil 25	Turbo Oil 2380	Turbo Oil 2389 Turbo Oil 2391
Hatco Corp.		HATCO 3211 HATCO 3611 HATCO 1639 HATCO 1680	HATCO 1278 HATCO 1280
Mobil Corp.		Mobil Jet Oil II Mobil Jet Oil 254	
Royal Lubricants	Royco 555	Royco 500 Royco 560 Royco 899 Royco 899HC	Royco 808

Table 2-4. Fuel and Lubricants, Specifications, and Capacities (Cont)

SOURCE	PRIMARY OIL	ALTERNATE OIL	
Shell Oil Company	Aeroshell 555	Aeroshell 500 Aeroshell 560	Aeroshell 308

NOTE

1. When starting in ambient temperatures below -34°C (-29°F), do not use JP-5 or JP-8.

2. When starting in ambient temperatures of -34°C (-29°F) or below, lubricating oil MIL-L-7808 must be used. It is not advisable to mix MIL-L-23699 or DOD-L-85734 oil with MIL-L-7808 oil.

3. If the type oil being used is not available, another authorized type oil may be added. When one type oil is mixed with another, it is not necessary to drain the system and refill with one type oil. No mixing is allowed for cold temperature operation. For transmissions and gear boxes, when one type of oil is mixed with another, it is not necessary to drain the system and refill with one type oil.

4. For operation below -34°C (-29°F), MIL-H-5606 (NATO Code H-515) shall be used. Mixing MIL-H-5606 with MIL-H-83282 degrades fire-resistant qualities of MIL-H-83282.

5. Fuel settling time for jet (JP) fuel is 1 hour per foot depth of fuel. Allow the fuel to settle for the prescribed period before any samples are taken (about 4 hours for proper settling).

6. DOD-L-85734 oil is the preferred oil for use in the main transmission, intermediate gearbox, and tail gearbox, except for cold temperature operation.

7. DOD-L-85734 oil should not be used in the engines or the auxiliary power unit (APU). If DOD-L-85734 oil is inadvertently added to the engines or APU, the system should be drained and the correct oil added. There is no need to flush the system.

8. When changing from MIL-L-7808 or MIL-L-23699 oil to DOD-L-85734 (and vice versa), drain the oil from the system and refill with desired oil. There is no need to flush the system before refilling.

Table 2-5. Approved Fuels

SOURCE	PRIMARY/STANDARD FUEL	ALTERNATE FUELS	
U. S. Military Fuel	JP-4	JP-5	JP-8
NATO Code No.	F-40	F-44	F-34
COMMERCIAL FUEL (ASTM-D-1655)	**JET B**	**JET A**	**JET A-1**

Table 2-5. Approved Fuels (Cont)

SOURCE	PRIMARY/STANDARD FUEL	ALTERNATE FUELS	
American Oil Co.	American JP-4	American Type A	
Atlantic Richfield Richfield Div.	Arcojet B	Arcojet A Richfield A	Arcojet A-1 Richfield A-1
B. P. Trading	B. P. A. T. G		B. P. A. T. K.
Caltex Petroleum Corp.	Caltex Jet B		Caltex Jet A-1
City Service Co.		CITCO A	
Continental Oil Co.	Conoco JP-4	Conoco Jet-50	Conoco Jet-60
Exxon Co. U. S. A.	Exxon Turbo Fuel B	Exxon A	Exxon A-1
Gulf Oil	Gulf Jet B	Gulf Jet A	Gulf Jet A-1
Mobil Oil	Mobil Jet B	Mobil Jet A	Mobil Jet A-1
Phillips Petroleum	Philjet JP-4	Philjet A-50	
Shell Oil	Aeroshell JP-4	Aeroshell 640	Aeroshell 650
Sinclair		Superjet A	Superjet A-1
Standard Oil Co.		Jet A Kerosene	Jet A-1 Kerosene
Chevron	Chevron B	Chevron A-50	Chevron A-1
Texaco	Texaco Avjet B	Avjet A	Avjet A-1
Union Oil	Union JP-4	76 Turbine Fuel	
INTERNATIONAL FUEL	**NATO F-40**	**NATO F-44**	**NATO F-34**
Belgium	BA-PF-2B		
Canada	3GP-22F	3-6P-24C	
Denmark	JP-4 MIL-T-5624		
France	Air 3407A		
Germany	VTL-9130-006	UTL-9130-007 UTL-9130-010	
Greece	JP-4 MIL-T-5624		
Italy	AA-M-C-1421	AMC-143	
Netherland	JP-4 MIL-T-5624	D. Eng RD 2493	
Norway	JP-4 MIL-T-5624		
Portugal	JP-4 MIL-T-5624		
Turkey	JP-4 MIL-T-5624		
United Kingdom (Britain)	D. Eng RD 2454	D. Eng RD 2498	

Table 2-5. Approved Fuels (Cont)

SOURCE	PRIMARY/STANDARD FUEL	ALTERNATE FUELS

NOTE

Commercial fuels are commonly made to conform to American Society for Testing and Materials (ASTM) Specification D 1655. The ASTM fuel specification does not contain anti-icing additives unless specified. Icing inhibitor conforming to MIL-I-85470 or MIL-I-27686 (Commercial name PRIST) shall be added to commercial and NATO fuels, not containing an icing inhibitor, during refueling operations, regardless of ambient temperatures. Icing inhibitor conforming to MIL-I-85470 is replacing the MIL-I-27686 version. The use of MIL-I-27686 icing inhibitor is acceptable until all supplies are depleted. Adding PRIST during refueling operation shall be done using accepted commercial mixing procedures. The additive provides anti-icing protection and also functions as a biocide to kill microbial growths in helicopter fuel systems.

2.81 APU OIL SYSTEM SERVICING.

NOTE

Do not service the APU with DOD-L-85734 oil. If DOD-L-85734 oil is inadvertently added to the APU, drain the oil and add MIL-L-7808 or MIL-L-23699 oil. Flushing the system before refilling is not required.

a. The APU oil supply is in the APU gear box assembly. The sump filler/oil dipstick port (T-62T-40-1) or cap and fill to spill plug (GTC-P36-150) (Figure 2-24) are on the left side of the gear box housing.

b. When the APU is cool to the touch the **COLD** side of the dipstick may be used, if the APU is hot to the touch the **HOT** side of the dipstick may be used.

2.82 HANDPUMP RESERVOIR SERVICING.

CAUTION

Do not allow reservoir level to fall below refill line.

Servicing of the refill handpump is done when fluid level decreases to the refill line on the fluid level sight gage, on the side of the pump tank. When fluid level decreases to the refill line, 1 quart of hydraulic fluid can be poured into the reservoir after removing the refill cap. Handpump reservoir level should be replenished only in 1 quart units.

2.83 HYDRAULIC SYSTEMS SERVICING.

Reservoirs (Figure 2-24) for the hydraulic systems are on the hydraulic pump modules. Fluid level sight gages are visible on the side of each pump. All hydraulic pump reservoir capacities are 1 U. S. quart to the blue (black on some pumps) mark. When the indicator reaches the red area (refill) point, 2/3 of a pint is required to return the indicator to the green mark. The fluid level indication is the 1/8 inch wide gold band at the outboard edge of the level piston. To refill the reservoirs, the fluid is supplied from the manual handpump. After flight, fluid in hydraulic systems will be hot. Piston movement of up to 3/8 inch into the blue (black on some pumps) (overfill) zone is acceptable. When piston is beyond this limit, bleed off enough fluid to bring piston back to 3/8 inch above fill limit. To replenish the pump reservoir fluid, do the following:

1. Unscrew handpump lid and pour in clean hydraulic fluid, MIL-H-83282, until pump is full. Make sure you can always see oil in pump reservoir window while servicing, so not to pump air into pump module's reservoir. Keep filling.

2. Make sure pump cover is clean, then screw lid on tight.

3. Turn selector valve to desired reservoir to be filled. **OUT 1** is left pump module, **OUT 2** is right pump module, and **OUT 3** is backup pump module.

4. While holding selector valve handle down, crank pump handle on handpump clockwise and fill desired hydraulic pump module until forward end of piston in reservoir window is at forward end of green decal on reservoir housing.

5. Check that reservoirs stay full (forward end of piston at forward end of green decal), with fluid at ambient temperature 1 hour after flight.

6. Make sure area remains clean during procedure.

7. Stow selector valve handle in **OUT 4** (capped off) position.

8. Turn on electrical power.

9. Check caution panel for #1 **RSVR LOW**, #2 **RSVR LOW**, and **BACK-UP RSVR LOW** lights are off.

2.84 MAIN TRANSMISSION OIL SYSTEM SERVICING.

The transmission oil supply is in the sump case with the filler port and dipstick gage (Figure 2-24), on the right rear of the main module. When filling is required, oil is poured through the filler tube on the main module case, and oil level is checked by a dipstick, marked **FULL** and **ADD**, or **FULL COLD** and **ADD** on one side of the dipstick and **FULL HOT** and **ADD** on the other side. Check oil level as follows:

NOTE

Remove the dipstick, clean and reinsert to obtain correct reading.

a. Single scale dipstick is for checking cold oil levels. Wait at least 2 hours after shutdown to check oil. If oil level must be checked when hot (immediately to 1/2 hour after shutdown), oil level will read about 1/2 inch low (halfway between full and add mark or 1/2 inch below add mark).

b. Dual scale dipstick is for checking cold or hot oil levels. Use appropriate scale when checking oil level. Read hot side of dipstick when checking hot oil (immediately to 1/2 hour after shutdown), or cold side of dipstick when checking cold oil (at least 2 hours after shutdown).

2.85 TAIL AND INTERMEDIATE GEAR BOX SERVICING.

The intermediate gear box oil level sight gage (Figure 2-24) is on the left side of the gear box. The tail gear box oil level sight gauge is on the right side.

2.86 PARKING.

The methods used to secure the helicopter for temporary periods of time will vary with the local commands. The minimum requirements for parking are: gust lock engaged and wheel brakes set, tailwheel locked, and wheels properly chocked. For extended periods of time, engine inlet covers, exhaust covers, and pitot covers should be installed, and stabilator slewed to 0°. When required, the ignition system and the doors and window should be locked.

2.87 PROTECTIVE COVERS AND PLUGS.

The covers and plugs (Figure 2-24) protect vital areas from grit, snow, and water. The protected areas are avionics compartment air inlet, engine air inlet/accessory bay, engine and APU exhausts, pitot tubes, IRCM transmitter and APU air inlet and main transmission oil cooler exhaust. Covers and plugs should be installed whenever the helicopter is to be on the ground for an extended period of time. Each cover may be installed independently of the others.

2.88 MOORING.

Mooring fittings are installed at four points on the helicopter (Figure 2-25). Two fittings are at the front of the fuselage, one above each main landing gear strut, and two at the rear, one attached to each side of the aft transition section. These fittings are used to tie down the helicopter when parked, and wind conditions require it.

2.88.1 Mooring Instructions. Refer to TM 1-1500-250-23 for mooring instructions.

2.88.2 Main Rotor Tiedown. Tiedown of the main rotor should be done when the helicopter will be parked for a period of time or when actual or projected wind conditions are 45 knots and above. To tiedown main rotor blades, do this:

1. Turn rotor head and position a blade over centerline of helicopter. Install tiedown fitting into receiver while pulling down on lock release cable. Release cable when fitting is installed in blade receiver.

2. Uncoil tiedown rope.

3. Repeat steps 1. and 2. for each remaining blade.

4. Turn blade to about 45° angle to centerline of helicopter and engage gust lock.

Do not deflect main rotor blade tips more than 6 inches below normal droop position when attaching tiedowns. Do not tie down below normal droop position.

5. Attach tiedown ropes to helicopter as shown in Figure 2-25. To release tiedown fitting, pull down on lock release cable and remove fitting from blade.

TM 1-1520-253-10

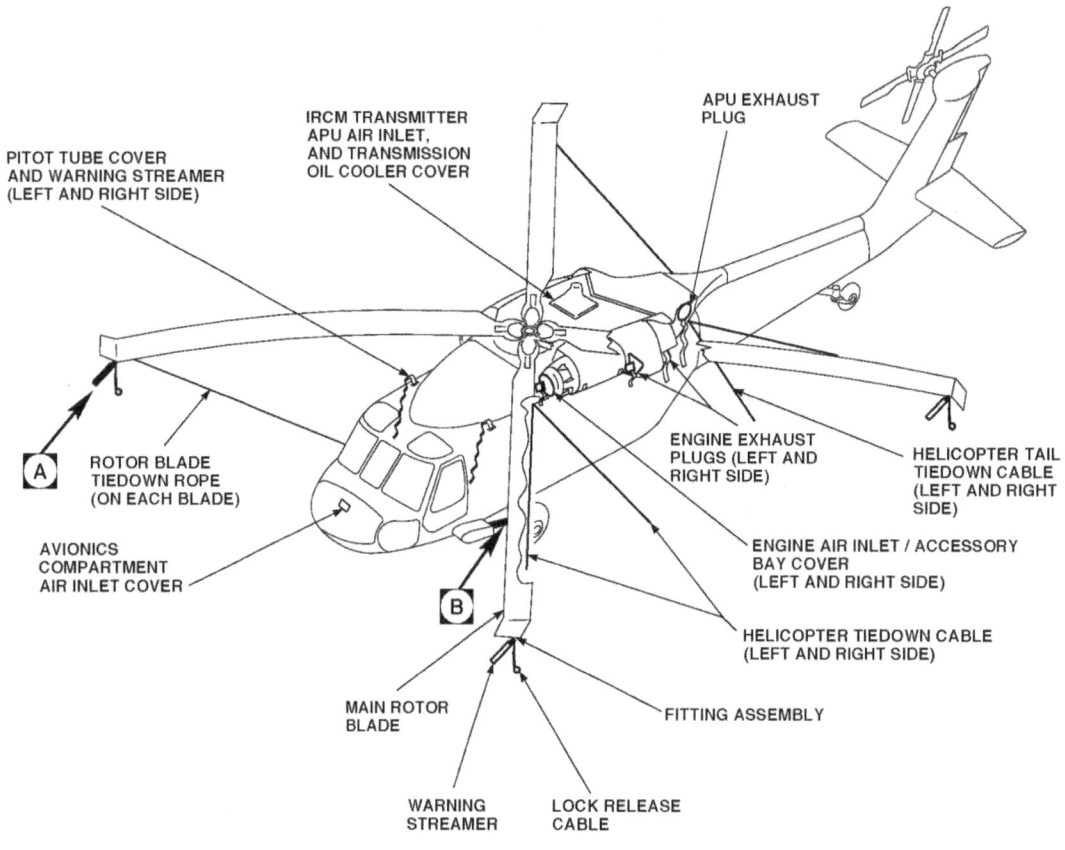

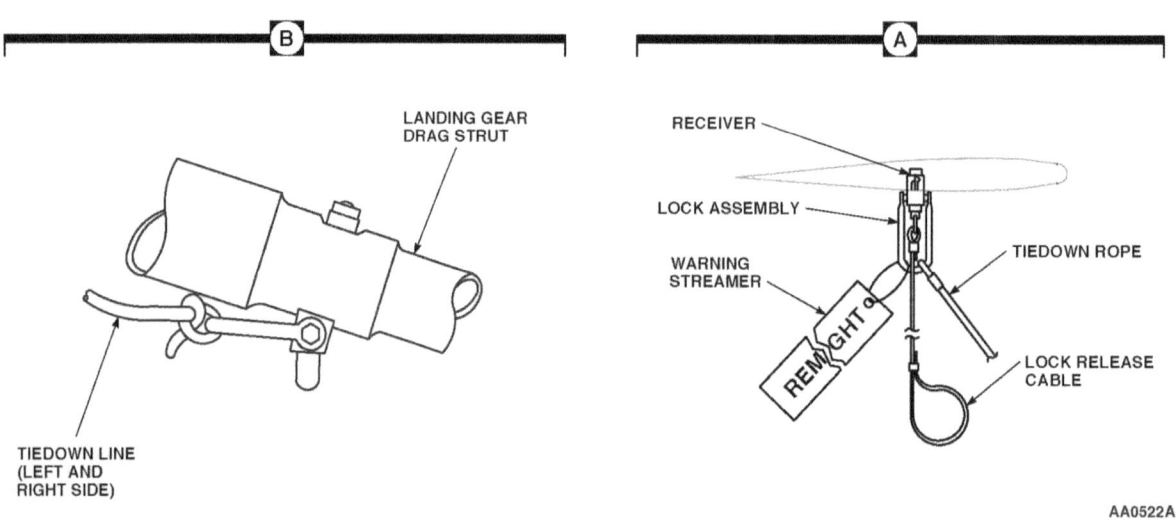

Figure 2-25. Mooring

2-86

CHAPTER 3
AVIONICS

Section I GENERAL

3.1 DESCRIPTION.

The avionics subsystem consist of the communications equipment providing VHF-AM, VHF-FM, and UHF-AM communications. The navigation equipment includes LF-ADF, VOR, ILS, marker beacon, TACAN, and Doppler/GPS. VHF-FM homing is provided through the No. 1 VHF-FM communication radio. Control of the majority of the navigation and communication radios is provided by the Avionics Management System (AMS). Transponder equipment consists of a receiver-transmitter with inputs from barometric altimeter for altitude fixing. Absolute height is provided by a radar altimeter. Each antenna will be described with its major end item, and locations as shown in Figure 3-1.

3.2 AVIONICS EQUIPMENT CONFIGURATION.

Equipment configuration is as shown in Table 3-1.

3.3 AVIONICS POWER SUPPLY.

Primary power to operate the avionics systems is provided from the No. 1 and No. 2 dc primary buses and the dc essential bus, and No. 1 and No. 2 ac primary buses (Figure 2-17). When operating any of the avionics equipment, helicopter generator output must be available or external ac power connected. Function selector switches should be at **OFF** before applying helicopter power.

Table 3-1. Communication/Navigation Equipment

FACILITY	NOMEN-CLATURE	USE	RANGE	CONTROL LOCATION	REMARKS
Intercommunication system	Interphone control C-11746	Intercommunication between crewmembers and control of navigation and communication radio.	Stations within helicopter	Cockpit lower console, crewchief and medic's stations	
FM communications	Radio Set AN/ARC-201 VHF-FM	Two-way voice communications, homing, frequency hopping in 30.0 - 87.975 MHz range.	*Line of sight	Lower console via AMS CDU	COM 1 and COM 4
VHF/AM communications	Radio Set AN/ARC-222	Two-way voice communications FM in frequency range of 30-87.975 MHz, AM in frequency range of 108-139.975MHz, police and marine band in frequency range of 136-174 MHz.	*Line of sight	Lower console via AMS CDU	COM 3

Table 3-1. Communication/Navigation Equipment (Cont)

FACILITY	NOMEN-CLATURE	USE	RANGE	CONTROL LOCATION	REMARKS
UHF communications	Radio-Transmitter Radio, RT-1614/ARC-164(V) UHF-AM	Two-way voice communications in the frequency range of 225.000 to 399.975 MHz with HAVEQUICK.	*Line of sight	Lower console via AMS CDU	COM 2
High frequency communications	Radio Set AN/ARC-220	Two way voice communications in the frequency range of 2 to 29.9999 MHz.	*Over the horizon	Lower console via AMS CDU	
Voice security system	TSEC/KY-58	Secure communications.	Not applicable	Lower console via AMS CDU	Used with UHF-AM.
Voice security system	TSEC/KY-100	Secure communications.	Not applicable	Lower console via AMS CDU	Used with HF.
Automatic direction finding	Direction Finder Set AN/ARN-149	Radio range and broadcast reception; automatic direction finding and homing in the frequency range of 100 to 2199.5 kHz.	*50 to 100 miles range signals.	Lower console via AMS CDU	
VOR/LOC/GS/MB receiving set	Radio Receiving Set AN/ARN-147(V)	VHF navigational aid, VHF audio reception in the frequency range of 108 to 126.95 MHz and marker beacon receiver operating at 75 MHz.	*Line of sight	Lower console via AMS CDU	
Doppler/GPS navigation set	Doppler/GPS Navigation Set AN/ASN-128B	Provides present position or destination navigation information to AMS.		Lower console via AMS CDU	
Tactical Navigation, distance measuring	AN/ASN-153(V)	Navigational Aid.		Lower console via AMS CDU	
Pilot locating	Personnel Locator System AN/ARS-6(V)	Navigational Aid.	Line of sight (60 miles)	Lower Console	

Table 3-1. Communication/Navigation Equipment (Cont)

FACILITY	NOMEN-CLATURE	USE	RANGE	CONTROL LOCATION	REMARKS
Magnetic heading indications	Gyro Magnetic Compass AN/ASN-43	Navigational Aid.		Lower console	
Identification friend or foe	Transponder Set AN/APX-100(V)	Transmits a specially coded reply to a ground-based IFF radar Interrogator system.	*Line of sight	Lower console	
Absolute altimeter	Radar Altimeter AN/APN-209	Measures absolute altitude.	0 to 1500 feet	Instrument panel	

NOTE

*Range of transmission or reception depends upon many variables including weather conditions, time of day, operating frequency, power of transmitter and altitude of the helicopter.

3.4 AVIONICS MANAGEMENT SYSTEM.

a. The avionics management system provides the pilot with a means of controlling the avionics communications and navigation systems, and displays information on the Multi Function Displays (MFD), the Horizontal Situation Indicators (HSI), and Night vision goggle heads up display (NVG HUD). The CDU is the primary controller for communication and navigation radios and sensors, and displays mission and system data as well as permitting operator entry and modification of mission data. The CDU front panel provides a data display, a keyboard composed of alphanumeric keys, two rocker keys, software-programmed keys (soft keys) whose functions depend on the adjacent display, and annunciators that indicate failures, status changes, or message alerts. The CDU keyboard is used to access top level menus or screens of the system functional areas and to enter or edit displayed data. Power for the AMS is provided from the dc essential bus, through circuit breakers marked **CPLT CDU** and **PLT CDU**, and from the battery utility bus through a circuit breaker marked **CDU BKUP**. The dc power from the battery utility bus acts only as a backup power source, maintaining power on AMS to for up to 10 seconds in the event of a dc essential bus power interruption.

3.4.1 CDU Controls and Functions. Controls for the AMS are on the front panel (Figure 3-2), and on the collective stick (Figure 2-11). The function of each control is as follows:

CONTROL	FUNCTION
Fixed Function buttons:	
CAU/ADV button	Toggles between caution advisory and normal screen of CDU.
CLR	Clears all data present in the scratch pad, and ends the edit.
COM	Access main communication screen.
NAV	Access main navigation screen, to select modes of navigation and tune radio navaids.
FPN	Access flight planning screen.
FIX	Access screen to update position, and create waypoints.

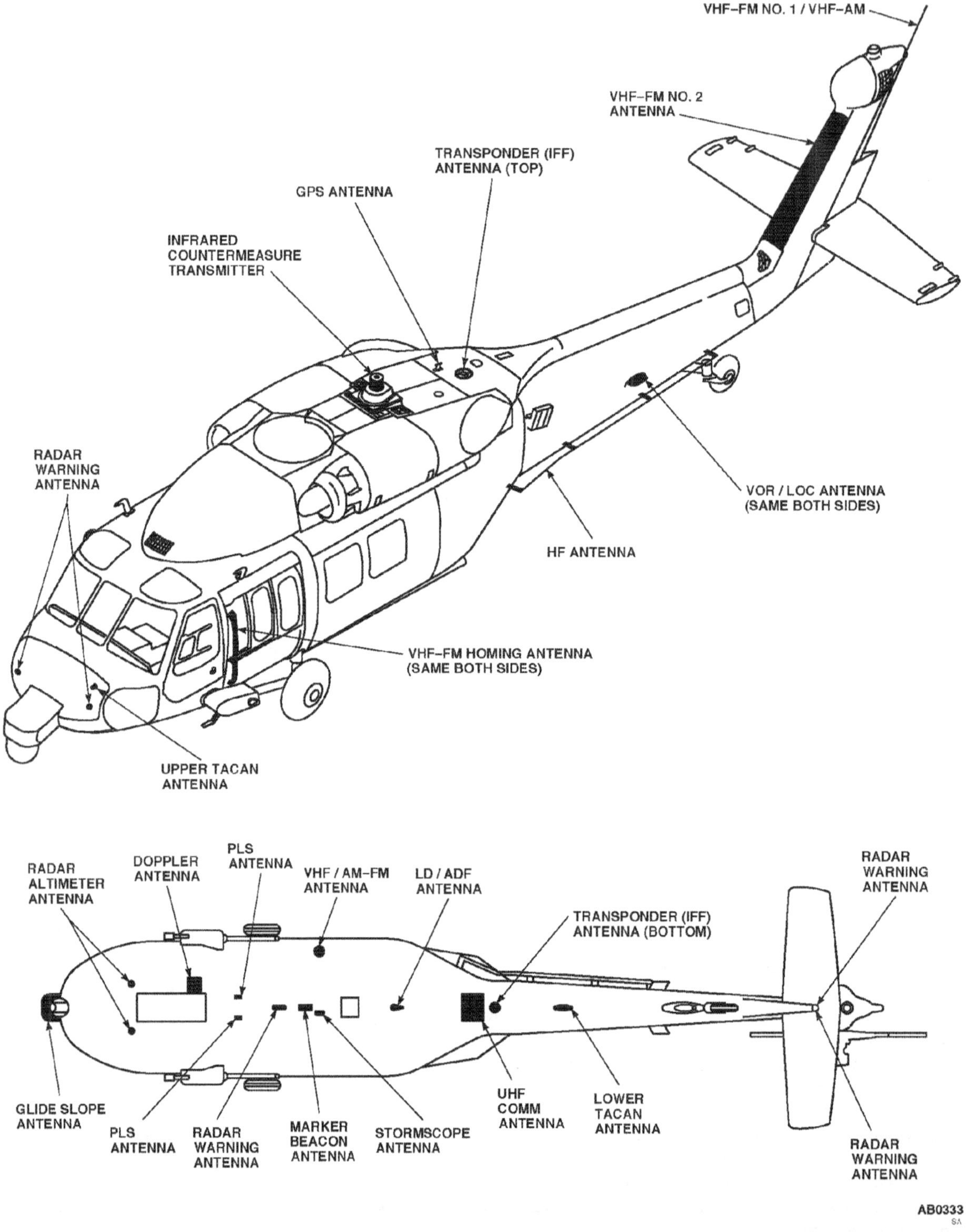

TM 1-1520-253-10

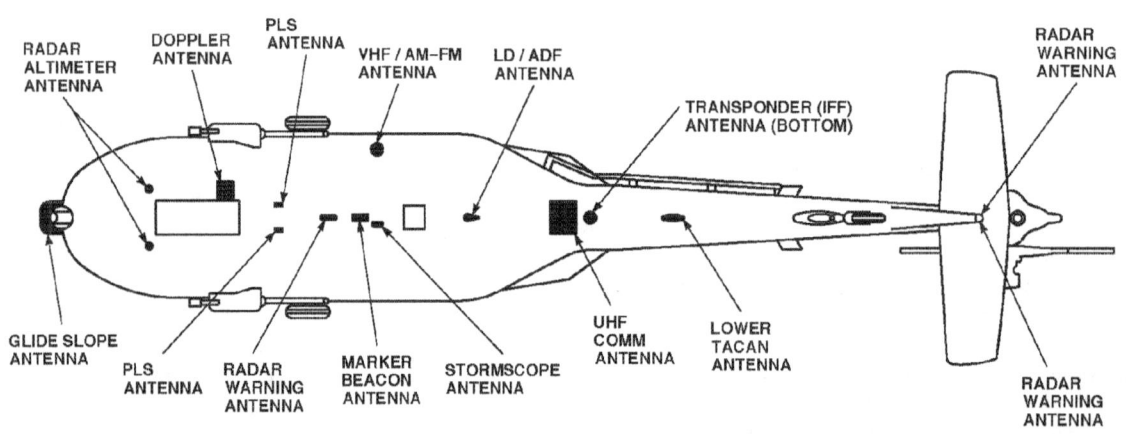

Figure 3-1. Antenna Arrangement

3-4

TM 1-1520-253-10

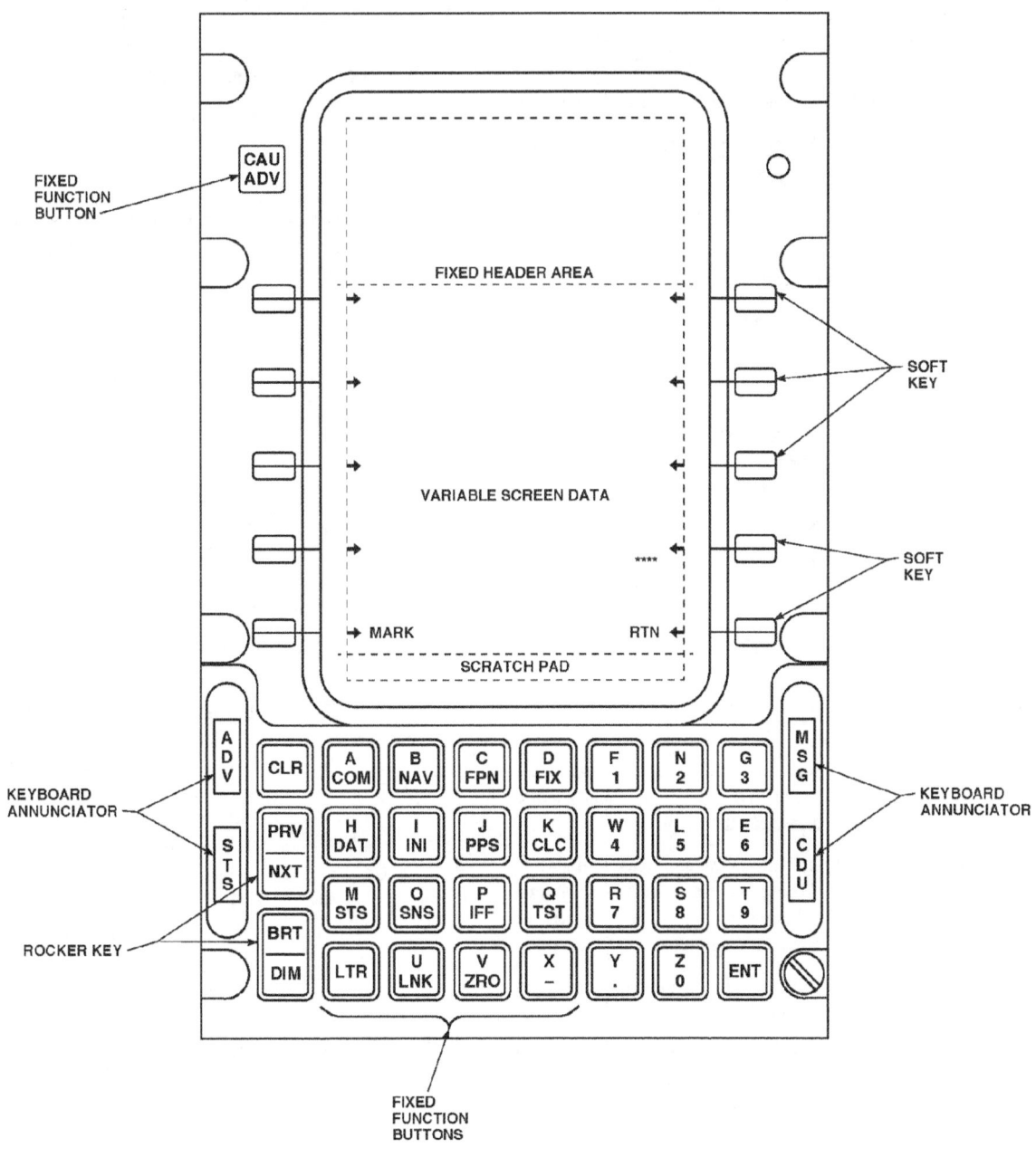

Figure 3-2. AMS Control Display Unit

3-5

CONTROL	FUNCTION
DAT	Access screen to enter, edit and review mission data.
INI	Access screen to initialize system, and download mission data.
PPS	Access present position screen.
CLC	Access navigation calculation screens.
STS	Access system status screens.
SNS	Access navigation sensor status and control screen.
IFF	Not used.
TST	Access test and maintenance screens.
LTR	Toggles between upper and lower functions of dual alphanumeric - mode keys.
LNK	Not used.
ZRO	Access screen displaying choices of equipment to be zeroized.
ENT	Enters data from scratchpad to the selected data field.
Keyboard annunciators	
ADV	Indicates an advisory condition. Press **ADV** key to acknowledge and clear the annunciator.
STS	Indicates a change in system status. Access system status screen, or acknowledge from the screen to clear the annunciator.
MSG	Indicates that a message has been received, but not viewed.
CDU	Indicates a built in test (BIT) failure within the CDU. Access system status screen to clear the annunciator.
Rocker keys	
PRV NXT	depending on CDU software, accesses previous or next screens, or choices in a list.

CONTROL	FUNCTION
BRT DIM	Adjusts brightness of CDU display screen.
Collective Stick	
UP DN	Scrolls edit box through selections.
RAD SEL	Accesses **COM** screen from **INIT**, then selects radio.

3.4.2 CDU Display Screen Conventions. Some display items have special meaning, no matter where they appear on the screen:

INDICATION	FUNCTION
RTN	A soft key, always located in the lower right key position, returns the display to the lowest priority menu screen from which the current screen was selected.
MARK	Allows the operator to mark an event or specify when data should be transferred.
∗∗∗∗	Indicate a calculated value exceeds the limits of the display fields, or no data is available for display fields, or no data is available for display. A range value beyond 999.9 miles is displayed as ∗∗∗∗∗ and a cross-track error with no valid TO waypoint will be displayed as ∗∗∗∗∗.
	Indicates that **PRV NXT** key (or collective switch) is operational for paging functions. These include changing records (as in stepping through preset or waypoint records) or stepping through flight plan or quick review screens.

3.4.2.1 CDU Display Screen. The display screen is divided in three parts (Figure 3-2). The top is the fixed header area, followed by variable screen data area. At the bottom of the screen is the scratchpad, where entries are made with the keyboard.

3.4.2.2 Box Around Text.

a. Indicates selection of a parameter for editing, the selection to be activated/initiated, or the active mode/item. At the same time the scratch pad displays the format that the entry is expected to follow: i.e., time [--:--:--].

b. A parameter which is not editable but instead is related to edit conditions may be boxed. For example, a boxed **ACTIVE** on the flight plan screens indicated that any attempt to edit this entry will be ignored as that leg of the flight plan is active.

c. Move the box from editable item to item by pressing **ENT**. No entries will be made if the scratchpad is empty. An item may also be selected for editing by pressing the adjacent soft key.

3.4.2.3 Inverse Video.
Inverse video is used to highlight soft key switch settings, alert conditions on the status line, new alert conditions, or to stale or invalid data. (i.e. if the nav system fails, the last known present position will be displayed in inverse video).

3.4.2.4 Soft Keys.
Soft keys border the left and right sides of the display. Soft key functions depend on the current screen being displayed. In text, a soft key is identified by its position and adjacent item. Soft keys only perform a function when there is an arrow displayed beside the key. Arrows which point inwards are for soft key functions performed on the screen (i.e. switch selections, or editing). Arrows which point outwards bring the operator to a new screen.

3.4.2.5 Alphanumeric Keys.
The numeric key are available in lower case which is default mode. The system will automatically shift to alpha keys (indicated by a boxed **L** on the scratch pad line) when it expects a letter entry. If the system cannot determine what is expected (i.e. call signs) the operator may use the **LTR** key to shift cases.

3.4.2.6 Editing.
A box drawn around a parameter indicates that it is selected for editing. While on a screen the operator can step through the editable fields by pressing the **ENT** key if there is nothing in the scratchpad, or by pressing the soft key adjacent to the parameter. When the box is around the field to be edited, enter the new values in the scratchpad, and press **ENT** to change the field.

3.4.2.6.1 Error Messages.
During edit, the expected format of the entry is shown on the scratch pad. If an error in entry is detected, **ERROR** will be displayed in inverse video in the scratch pad line for two seconds followed by a description of the expected entry.

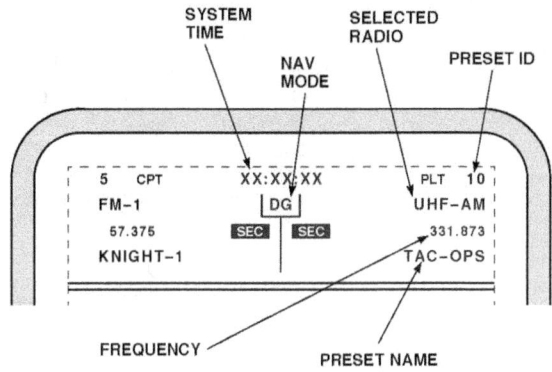

Figure 3-3. COM Header

3.4.2.6.2 Editing Using Fixed Function Keys.
During entries **CLR** clears the scratch pad and terminates the edit. **ENT** accepts the entry. **PRV** deletes the last key stroke and **NXT** pulls characters down from the current parameter value. For special format entries (i.e. lat/long, zone/coord, date/time) the editor will fill unentered positions with blanks or zeros as appropriate. Entries are alined based on their decimal point position. If no decimal has been entered, one is assumed after the last character keyed.

3.4.2.7 Fixed Header.
The fixed header functions independently from the rest of the screen. Its purpose is to provide continuous display of essential navigation and communication information. Direct entry into the header is not permitted. Headers are either in **COM** or **NAV** format.

3.4.2.7.1 COM Header.
Display communication radio status for copilot and pilot radios as selected on the ICS control panel. The Com header is divided into two halves, showing communication radio selections for the pilot (**PLT**) and copilot (**CPT**) (Figure 3-3).

INDICATION	FUNCTION
System Time	Indicates system time.

INDICATION	FUNCTION
PLT	Indicates pilot's side of display. In inverse video when the ICS selected radio is keyed.
Preset ID	Shows selected preset. Blank if manual tune, or ICS mode, ***EMERG*** when emergency selected.
Selected Radio	Type of radio selected with ICS mode selector switch.
Frequency	Frequency or channel display. Area displays **SCAN** when in scan mode and is blank when in ICS selection mode.
Preset Name	Name of preset chosen.
Nav Mode	Indicates navigation mode of the AMS.
SEC	Appears in inverse video when the selected radio is in CIPHER mode. When operating in PLAIN mode, the display is **MHZ** or blank.
CPT	Indicates copilot's side of display. In inverse video when the ICS selected radio is keyed.

3.4.2.7.2 NAV Header. Displays navigation status of AMS, giving summary of position of TO waypoint (Figure 3-4).

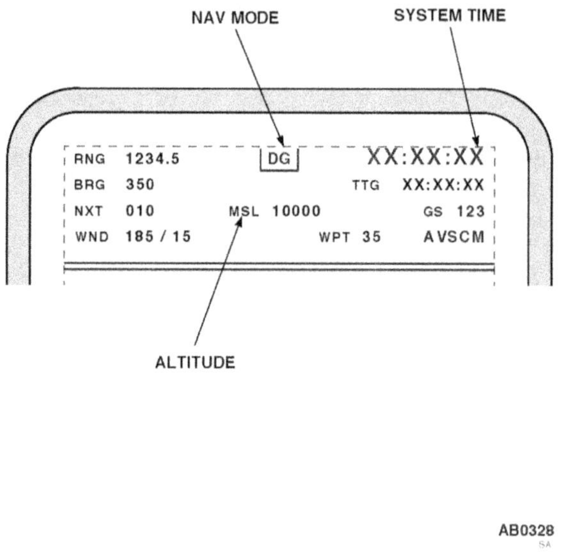

INDICATION	FUNCTION
RNG	Distance in nautical miles to the parent waypoint. Displays are 0 to 9999.9 or ****.* if beyond range. 0.0 is displayed when there is no active steering.
BRG	The magnetic bearing to the parent waypoint.
NXT	The initial desired magnetic course of the next leg of the flight plan with the parent waypoint as the FROM point. Blank when there is no next leg.

Figure 3-4. NAV Header

INDICATION	FUNCTION
WND	Computed wind direction and velocity in knots
Time	System time.
TTG	Time to go to the parent waypoint at current ground speed.
Altitude	Either Planned Enroute Altitude (**PEA**, expressed in MSL) or Planned Ground Clearance Altitude (**PGC**, expressed in AGL). Blank if no altitude is in flight leg data.
GS	Ground Speed in knots

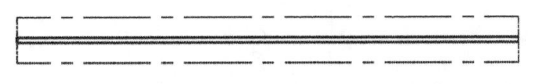

NORMAL STATUS LINE ON REMOTE TERMINAL CDU

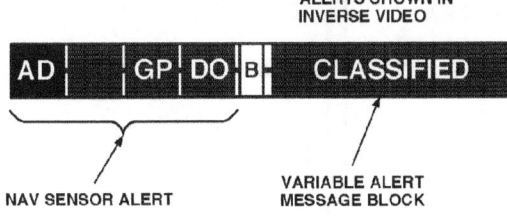

ALERTS SHOWN IN INVERSE VIDEO

NAV SENSOR ALERT

VARIABLE ALERT MESSAGE BLOCK

AB0329
SA

Figure 3-5. Status Line

INDICATION	FUNCTION
WPT	The identifier of the present TO waypoint. Displays **WPT** for regular waypoint or **MOB** for a mobile waypoint. The indicators blink several times prior to waypoint capture. Labels will flash between normal and inverse video when a waypoint is captured (minimum 3 seconds).

3.4.2.8 Status Line. The status line is between the fixed header and variable screen data of the CDU (Figure 3-5).

INDICATION	FUNCTION
Bus Control indicator	Boxed **B** indicates that the CDU is the bus controller.
Nav Sensor Alerts	
AD	Air data source failed.
GP	GPS failed.
DO	Doppler failed.
Variable Alert Message block	See below for meanings.
CLASSIFIED	COMSEC data (i.e. WODS) in CDU.
CUE	SINCGARS Cue frequency reception alert.
DEGR RDY	Degraded nav ready provision.
EMERG COM	Emergency control panel (ECP) activated.
INCM-CALL	ALE/ECCM incoming call.
UPDT RQD	Update required to Doppler.
WPT	Waypoint capture alert (minimum 3 seconds).

3.4.3 Operation.

3.4.3.1 Normal Start-up. When power is first applied to the system, the following sequence of events occurs:

1. Each AMS unit perform a internal built in test (BIT).

    a. AMS annunciators will flash, indicating a lamp test.

    b. The display screen will display the software version loaded. This will remain for approximately 10 seconds.

    c. The display screen will then change to the initialize screen, which shows the status of system time and navigation sensors.

2. The first CDU to finish up BIT (normally the copilot's) becomes the bus controller (BC), while the other becomes the remote terminal (RT). The BC CDU responds to inputs marginally faster than the RT CDU. The BC CDU performs all the required communications and control sequences to tune the radios, and computes navigation information for display. The RT CDU passes its commands to the BC CDU for coordination of full systems operation.

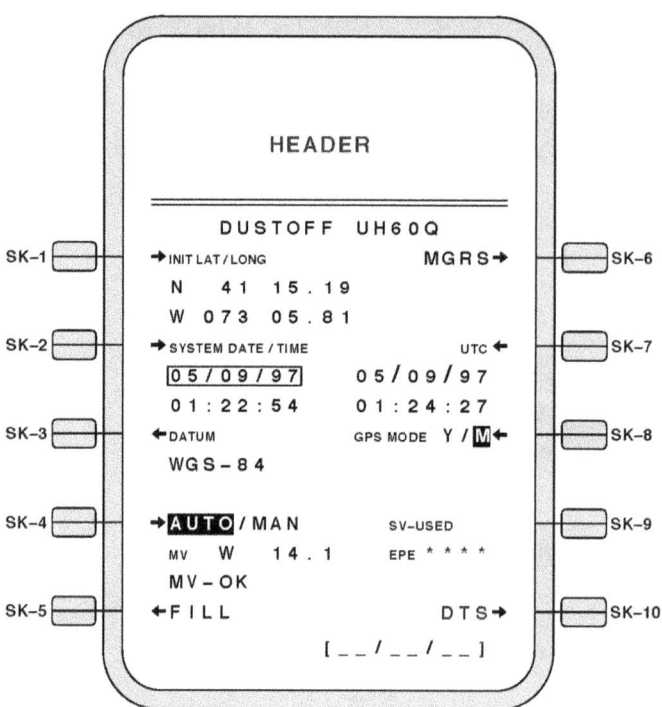

Figure 3-6. Initialization Screen

3.4.3.2 Initialization. The initialization screen is the first default screen upon power up (Figure 3-6). After the CDU first powers up, if the DGNS is reporting its GPS time and date, the CDU system time and date will default to the GPS reported values. This date is in UTC. System time may be changed after this first update to local time, if desired. If the GPS time and date are not available, then the system date will default to 01/01/9X and the time field will default to 00:00:00.

3.4.3.2.1 Initialize Position. The initial position default will be the position as stored by the CDU in non volatile memory on shutdown. This position is stored so long as the system position was valid for at least 1.0 minute with weight-on-wheels at shutdown.

NOTE

If the aircraft has been moved since shutdown, it may be necessary for the operator to reenter the new initial position for normal start-up.

1. **SYSTEM DATE/TIME** soft key - Press to correct date time, if not correct in screen. Enter correct date and time in scratch pad.

2. **ENT** - Press to enter date and time in system.

3. **INIT LAT/LONG** soft key - Press to correct location, if not correct in screen. Enter correct coordinates in scratch pad.

4. **ENT** - Press to enter position in system.

3.4.3.2.2 Initializing the Doppler Sensor. As the system powers up and the screen is first displayed, the initial position (as determined from non volatile memory) is used to initialize the Doppler portion of the DGNS. When the GPS completes an initial fix in the DO/GPS blended mode (the default mode) the Doppler sensor will be updated to the GPS position.

3.4.3.2.3 Initialization of the GPS Sensor. At power up the GPS sensor will automatically attempt to perform a first fix using its internal stored position, time, and almanac data. If the helicopter is moved from its shutdown position, this will cause delay in initializing. The GPS position will be updated each time the initial position fields are edited on screen. The CDU will not modify the GPS time or date but will echo back the GPS reported time and date on the initialization screen. A full initialization of the GPS sensor (i.e. position, time, date, and almanac if necessary) requires that the operator command a GPS initialization via the sensors **SNSGPS** screen.

3.4.3.3 Horizontal Datums. The CDUs store and processes position information based on WGS-84 datum and spheroid. Each pilot must individually select the local datum for CDU position entry and presentation that corresponds to the horizontal datum listed on the tactical map being used for the mission. Navigation information is processed based on the BC CDU active datum, ignoring the datum of the RT CDU.

1. To change a horizontal datum in CDU go to the local datum screen from the **DUSTOFF UH60Q** screen (Figure 3-6), enter the desired datum number in the scratchpad, and **ENT** key - Press.

3.4.3.4 Magnetic Variation.

> **CAUTION**
>
> An improper MAG VAR setting will affect the navigation accuracy of the Doppler present position (PPS).

Use the AUTO setting whenever the ASN-43 Compass System is set to **SLAVED** (i.e. Magnetic Heading) (Figure 3-7). If the ASN-43 is set to **DG** and manually slewed to true north, then the CDU **MAG VAR** should be set to **MAN** with an entered variation of 0.0 degrees.

3.4.3.5 Load Data.

NOTE

Waypoints, presets, flight plans, etc. will be changed on the cartridge only if the **DTS STATUS** screen **SAVE** soft key is pressed.

If a cartridge is placed in the DTS after power up the pilot must initiate a mission data load. A full mission data load takes about a minute (about 30 seconds for the mission data and the balance for maintenance data). The pilot does not have to wait for the full load to finish before using the data, and may leave the download screen and do other operations. COM presets, for example, are available almost immediately. The DTM mission is loaded in the following order:

a. COM presets.

b. Nav-points data.

c. Radio Nav Presets.

d. Flight plans.

e. Recorded fault histories.

NOTE

The following steps are required only if the DTC cartridge was not loaded prior to power up.

1. DTC cartridge - Load in DTS.

2. On CDU, **INI** - Press.

3. **DTS** soft key - Press.

4. **LOAD** soft key - Press, to initiate mission data load.

3.4.3.6 Load ECCM and COMSEC Data.

NOTE

The following steps are required to load classified key codes in AMS.

1. Fill device - Attach to fill port for appropriate radio.

2. On CDU, **INI** - Press.

3. **FILL** soft key - Press.

4. Soft key adjacent to radio designator, or **KY-58**, or **KY-100** soft key - Press, to initiate fill.

3.4.3.7 Status. Status screens give the pilot quick review of the status of all equipment controlled by AMS (Figure 3-8).

3.4.3.7.1 DTS Status. This screen is accessed by pressing **DTS** soft key on the **DUSTOFF UH-60Q** screen (Figure 3-6). Refer to table below for annunciators and their meanings.

INDICATION	FUNCTION
DTS	Displays status of system. (**OK** or **FAIL**).

Change 3   3-11

TM 1-1520-253-10

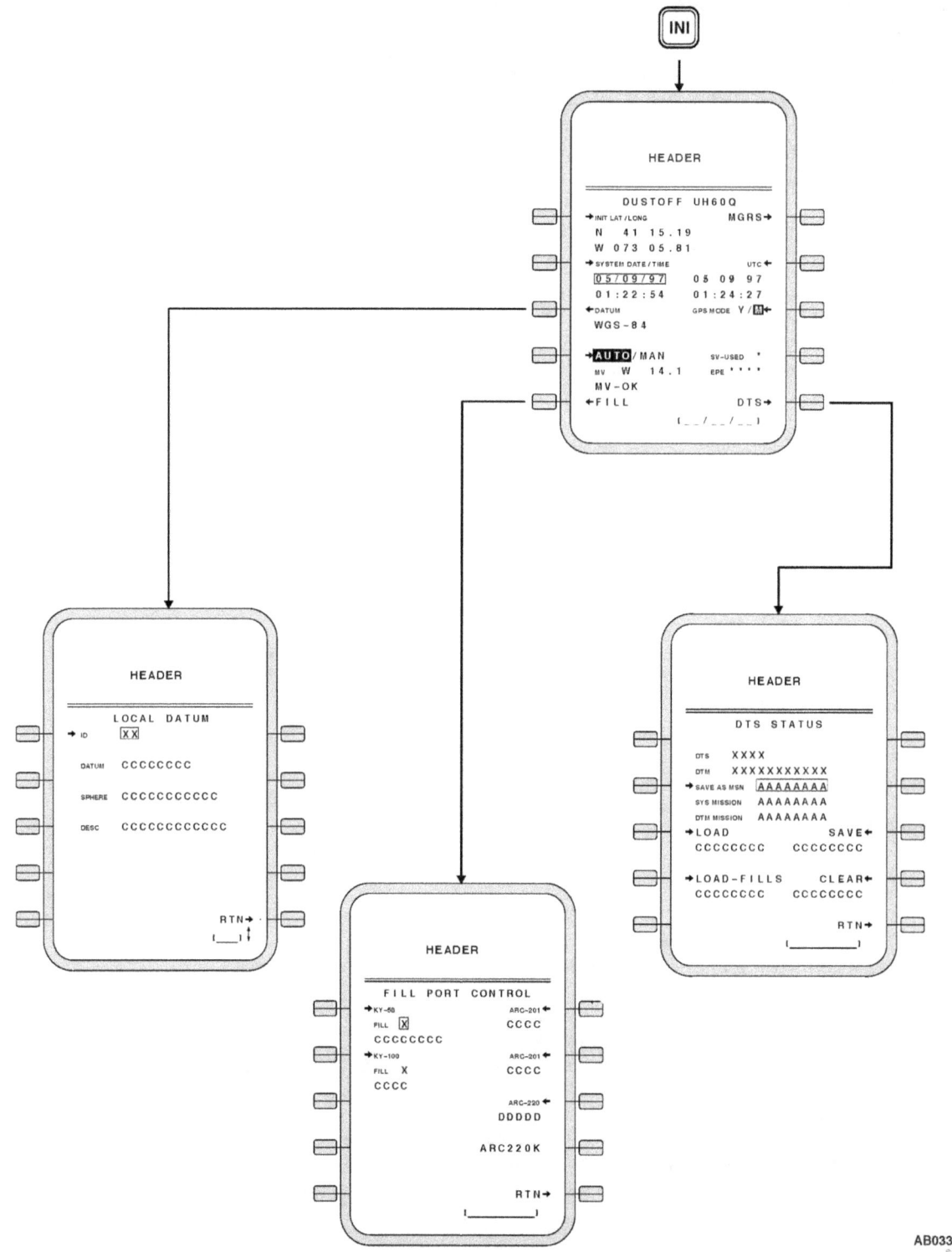

Figure 3-7. INI Screen Flow

3-12

TM 1-1520-253-10

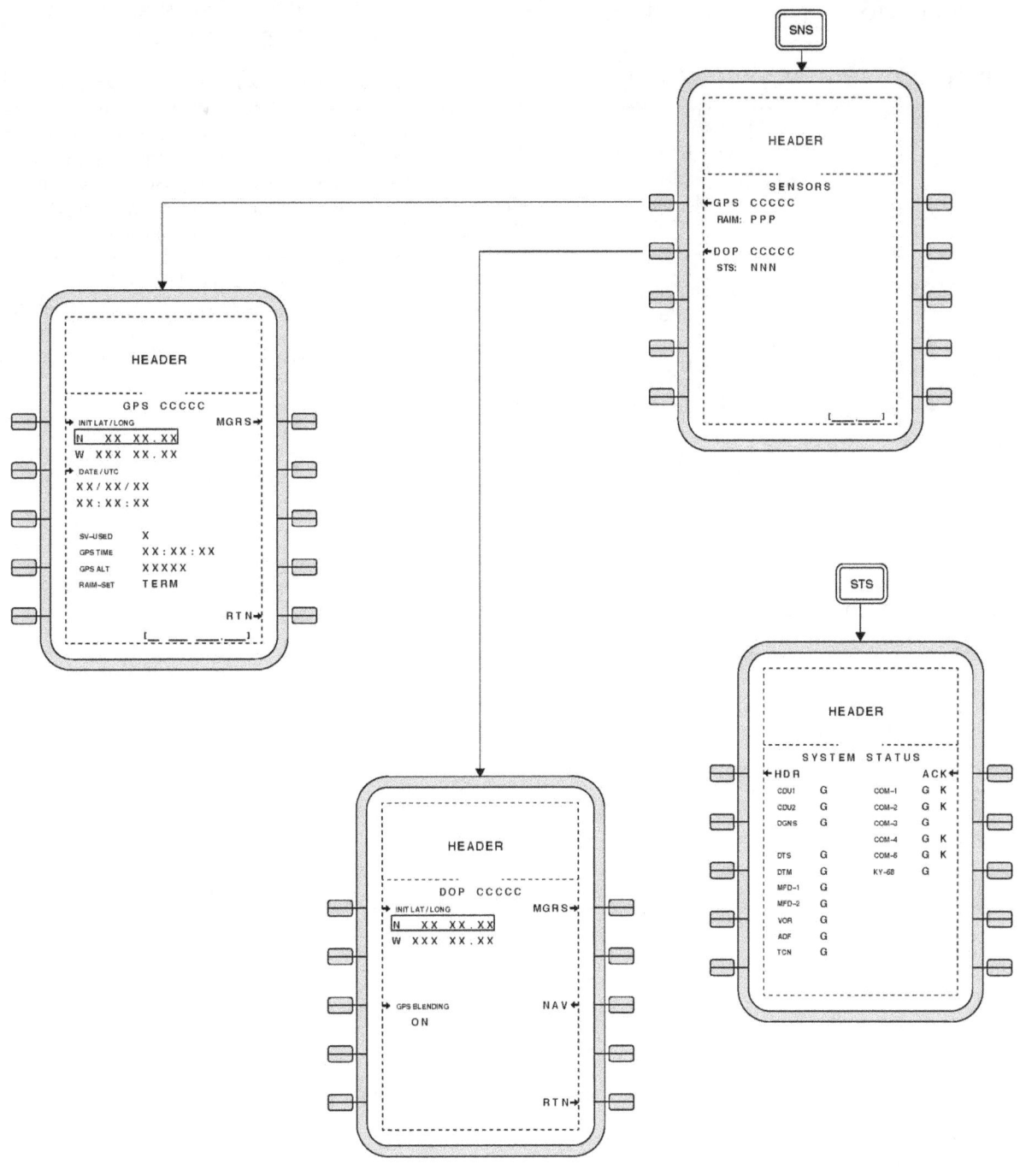

Figure 3-8. Status Screen Flow

3-13

INDICATION	FUNCTION
DTM	Displays status of DTM. **READY** indicates module in place and functional. **NOT HAWK** Module installed, but wrong format. **FAIL** Module inoperative. **NOT PRESENT** Module not installed in receptacle.
SAVE AS MSN	Shows mission name which will be used for the cartridge header on the next save.
LOAD	Commands the start of transferring mission data from the cartridge to the CDU.
LOAD-FILLS	Loads the DTM data fills for the AN/ARC-201Ds, AN/ARC-220 and IDM initialization.

3.4.3.7.2 System Status.

NOTE

Status of Doppler and GPS will flucutate from **GOOD** to **FAIL** if the magnetic variation is set to 0. This is normal and does not indicate a failed or degraded system.

System status screen is accessed by pressing the **STS** fixed function button (Figure 3-8). The status of each subsystem is displayed as either **G** (GOOD) or **F** (FAIL). If a subsystem has changed status since this screen was last exited, the status is displayed in inverse video and the **STS** annunciator on the CDU keyboard is lit. **KY-100**, **IDM** and **COM-5** status field will be blank if equipment is not installed. **K** following a **COM** signifies that crypto is configured. **K** will always follow **COM-1** and **COM-4** if a good status is received since the crypto is embedded in those radios. Press **ACK** to acknowledge present status, change text to normal video and extinguish **STS** annunciator. Acknowledgment is system wide (both CDUs).

3.4.3.7.3 Radio Offline Status. Bus failures, CDU failures, system zeroizing and emergency panel use will cause radios to go offline. After restoration of the failed system, allow 30 seconds for radios to return to online status, and then check all radios for proper frequency, band and mode settings.

Section II COMMUNICATIONS

3.5 Communications System Control (CSC) Panel.
The CSC panel provide audio interface and control for the communication radios, navigation radios, and intercommunication within the helicopter. Pilot's, copilot's, and crewchief stations continuously monitor ASE, IFF, radar altimeter and master warning tones. Hands free intercommunication is provided by hot mike and voice activated (VOX) features. An exterior jack is provided to the front of the main landing gear shock struts. When the walkaround cord is connected to it, the crewchief can communicate with the interior of the helicopter or with the other exterior jack through the medic's ICS stations. Pilot and copilot CSC panels are located on the lower console (Figure 2-4). Medic 1 CSC is located near the left cabin window. Medic 2 CSC located in cabin overhead. Crewchief's CSC is located by the right cabin window. Power for the system is provided by the 28 vdc essential bus through circuit breakers, marked **PLT ICS**, **CPLT ICS** and **ICS CABIN**.

3.5.1 CSC Controls and Functions. Controls for the intercom/radios are on the front panel (Figure 3-9). The function of each control is as follows:

CONTROL	FUNCTION
VOL Control Knob	Master volume control adjusts all **RADIO MON** and **NAV** volume levels simultaneously.
RADIO MON	Push to turn on and pull to turn off; rotate to adjust individual audio level.
1	Controls audio reception level for VHF/FM 1 radio.
2	Controls audio reception level for UHF radio.
3	Controls audio reception level for VHF/AM-FM radio.
4	Controls audio reception level for VHF/FM 2 radio.
5	Controls audio reception level for HF radio.
NAV	

CONTROL	FUNCTION
A	Controls audio reception level for VOR/ILS and marker beacon identification tones (Pilot, copilot and crewchief stations only).
B	Controls audio reception level for TACAN and ADF identification tones (Pilot, copilot and crewchief stations only).
VOX	Controls threshold for voice activation level when **VOX ON** microphone actuation is selected on by the function selector.
MIC Selector Switch	
Mode Selector Switch	
1	Select when using SPH-4 low impedance (5 ohm) microphone.
2	Select when using SPH-4B high impedance (150 ohm) microphone.
PVT	Selects private ICS between the pilots only or private ICS communications among the medic stations and crewchief.
ICS	Selects normal ICS operations.
1	Selects transmission/reception through the VHF/FM 1 radio.
2	Selects transmission/reception through the UHF-AM radio.
3	Selects transmission/reception through the VHF/AM-FM radio.
4	Selects transmission/reception through the VHF/FM 2 radio.
5	Selects transmission/reception through the HF radio.
RMT	Enables **RAD SEL** and **UP/DN** switches on the collective sticks for radio and frequency selections.

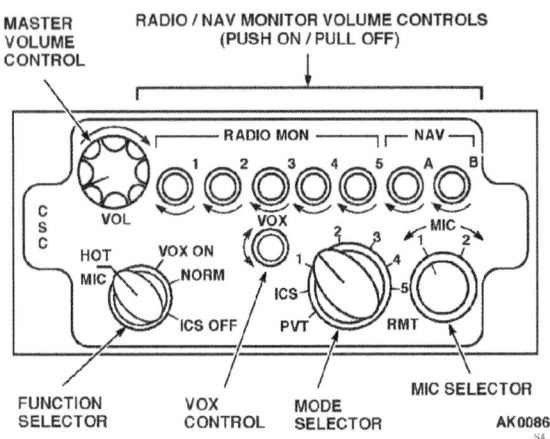

Figure 3-9. CSC Control Panel

CONTROL	FUNCTION
Function Selector Switch	
HOT MIC	Continuous ICS or radio communications without pressing a PTT switch.
VOX ON	ICS keys while operator is speaking. Not available when Mode Selector switch is to PVT.
NORM	Use press-to talk button for ICS and radio communications.
ICS OFF	Turns ICS off.

3.5.2 Intercommunication Keying System. Keying of the ICS system is done by the controls listed at the following stations:

3.5.2.1 Pilot or Copilot Station. An **ICS/RADIO** trigger switch on the top of each cyclic stick, or by a switch on the floor at the pilot's left and the copilot's right foot.

3.5.2.2 Exterior Jack (Maintenance Station). A pushbutton at the end of the exterior walkaround cord.

3.5.2.3 Medic 1, Medic 2, and Crewchief. A pushbutton at the end of the cord.

3.5.2.4 VOX Operation. For voice actuated intercom at all stations:

1. Function selector switch - **VOX ON**.

2. **VOX** knob - Adjust, until speaking into the microphone keys the intercom system.

3.5.3 Modes of Operation.

3.5.3.1 Primary Operation Check. There are several methods of intercommunication operation. In all cases, no operation action is required to receive intercom signals other than adjusting the **VOL** control for a comfortable level at the headset.

3.5.3.2 Intercommunication (Cockpit).

1. Transmitter selector switch, any position when using cyclic switch, ICS, or **PVT** for foot switches.

2. Function selector switch - **NORM**, or **VOX ON**, as desired.

3. Key switch - **ICS/RADIO** switch on pilot's or copilot's cyclic, or foot switch at pilot's and copilot's positions. Speak into the microphones in **VOX ON** mode.

3.5.3.3 Intercommunication (Cabin).

1. Transmitter selector switch - **ICS**, or **PVT**.

2. Function selector switch - **NORM**, or **VOX ON**, as desired.

3. Key switch - switch on pilot's or copilot's cyclic, or foot switch at pilot's and copilot's positions. Speak into the microphones in **VOX ON** mode.

3.5.3.4 External Radio Communication.

1. Transmitter selector - Desired position, **1** through **5**.

2. **ICS/RADIO** trigger switch on cyclic stick, or foot-operated push-to-talk switch - press; speak into microphone while holding switch; release to listen.

3.5.3.5 Receiver selection.

1. Receiver selection switch(es) - **RADIO MON** and **NAV** knobs - pull to monitor, push to turn

audio off. Rotate to adjust individual audio level.

2. Adjust master volume to comfortable listening level.

3.6 RADIO SET AN/ARC-201D (VHF-FM) (COM 1 AND 4).

Radio set AN/ARC-201 (Figure 3-10) is an airborne, very high frequency (VHF), frequency modulated (FM), radio receiving-transmitting set compatible with the Single Channel Ground Airborne Radio Sets (SINGCARS) Electronic Countermeasures (ECCM) mode of operation. The set provides communications of voice and data, secure or plain text, and homing over the frequency range of 30 to 87.975 MHz channelized in 25 Khz steps. A frequency offset tuning capability of -10 Khz, -5 Khz, +5 Khz and +10 Khz is provided in both transmit and receive mode; this capability is not used in ECCM mode. This set is used for receiving and transmitting clear-voice or X-mode communications. Secure voice capability is embedded in the radio. Each radio provides 6 preset channels, a manual channel and a cueing channel, for use in the frequency hopping (FH) mode. Each channel has the capability to select discrete frequencies in a single channel mode, or FH radio nets in the FH mode. The No. 1 AN/ARC-201 is referred to as COM 1, and the No. 2 AN/ARC -201 radio is referred to as COM 4, corresponding to their positions on the ICS mode select switch. Use of the homing capability of the No. 1 (COM 1) FM radio set provides a steering output to the VSI course deviation pointer for steering indications. COM 1 VHF-FM receives power from the dc essential bus through a circuit breaker marked **NO. 1 VHF-FM**. COM 4 VHF-FM receives power from the No. 1 dc primary bus through a circuit breaker marked **NO. 2 VHF-FM**.

3.6.1 Antennas.

a. The COM 1 VHF-FM communications antenna is on top of the tail rotor pylon (Figure 3-1). The COM 4 VHF-FM antenna is within the leading edge fairing of the tail pylon drive shaft cover. The FM homing antennas, one on each side of the fuselage, are used with FM No. 1 radio set.

3.6.2 Controls and Functions.
Both AN/ARC-201 radios are controlled by the AMS with the CDU (Figure 3-2). Control screens allow the pilot to choose frequency and mode of transmission (Figure 3-10). Operator functions are to change band, transmission frequency and mode, and edit and establish preset modes and frequencies. Bands associated with this radio are:

BAND FIELD	BAND NAME	FREQUENCY RANGE
FM 1, FM 4	FM Single channel	30.000 to 87.975 (Manual is preset 1)
FILL 1, FILL 4	FH- COLD	30.000 to 87.975
COLD 1, COLD 4	FH - COLD	30.000 to 87.975 (Always preset 0)
CUE 1,CUE 4	FH - CUE	30.000 to 87.975 (Always preset 0)
FH 1,FHM 1, FH 4, FHM 4	FREQ HOP	NET: 001 to NET:999 (SINCGARS NETS)
COM 1, COM 4		Indicates radio is inoperative.

3.6.2.1 COM Summary Screen.
The COM SUM screen allows the operator to perform all primary radio controls. SK1 selects COM 1, and SK4 selects COM 4 settings for editing

SOFT KEY	FUNCTION
SK-1	Selects and then toggles between COM 1 frequency and preset field for editing.
SK-4	Selects and then toggles between COM 4 frequency and preset field for editing.
LAST	Restores the last manually tuned frequency, while saving the current settings. This function saves one setting per band of operation.
EMERG	Swaps current frequency with the band based guard frequency for radio that has been selected for edit.
PT/CT	Toggles between plain mode (PT) and secure mode (CT) transmission for radio that has been selected for edit.
BAND	Access Band selection screen for radio that has been selected for edit.

TM 1-1520-253-10

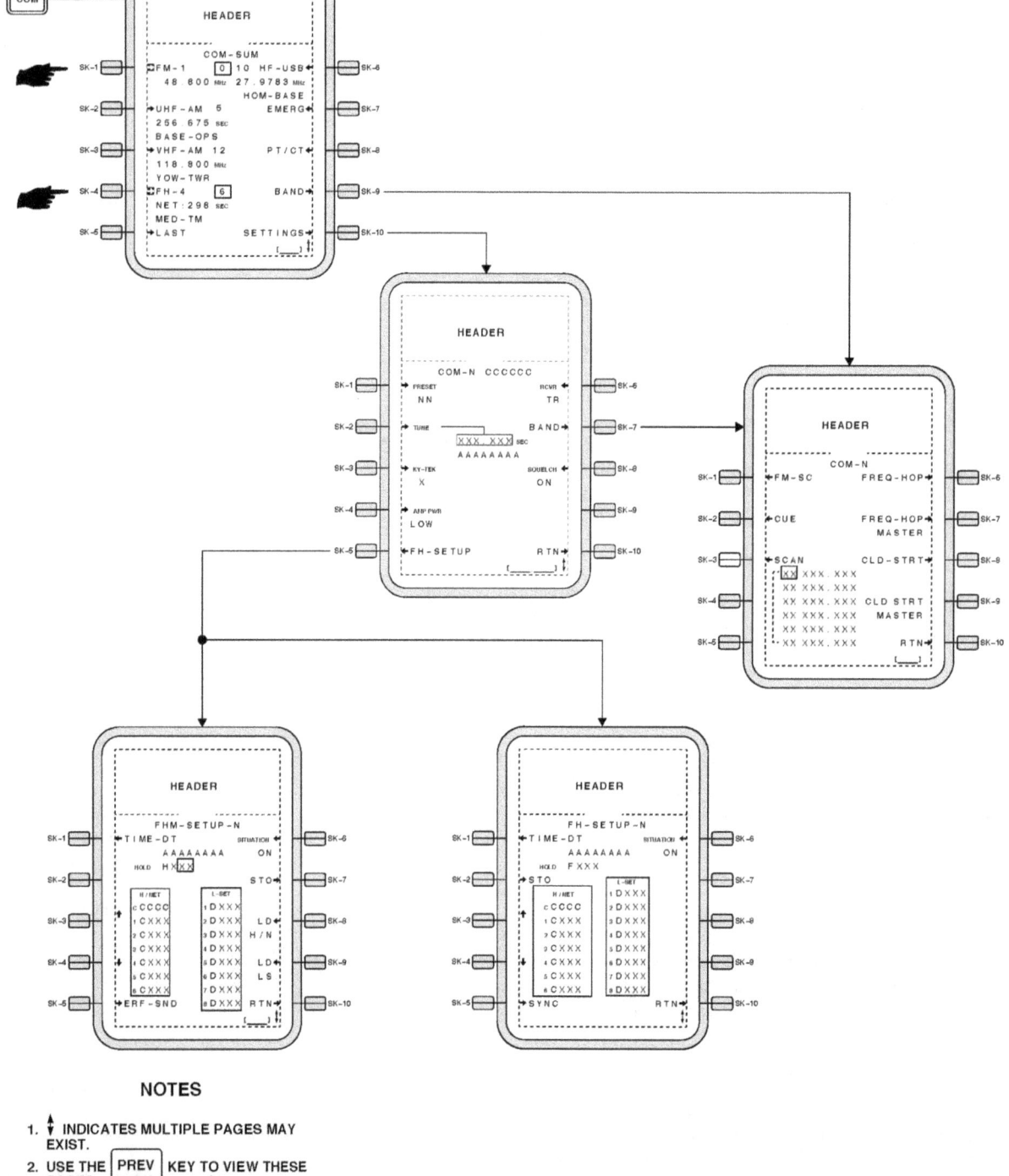

Figure 3-10. AN/ARC-201D (COM 1 and 4) Communication Screen Flow (Sheet 1 of 2)

3-18

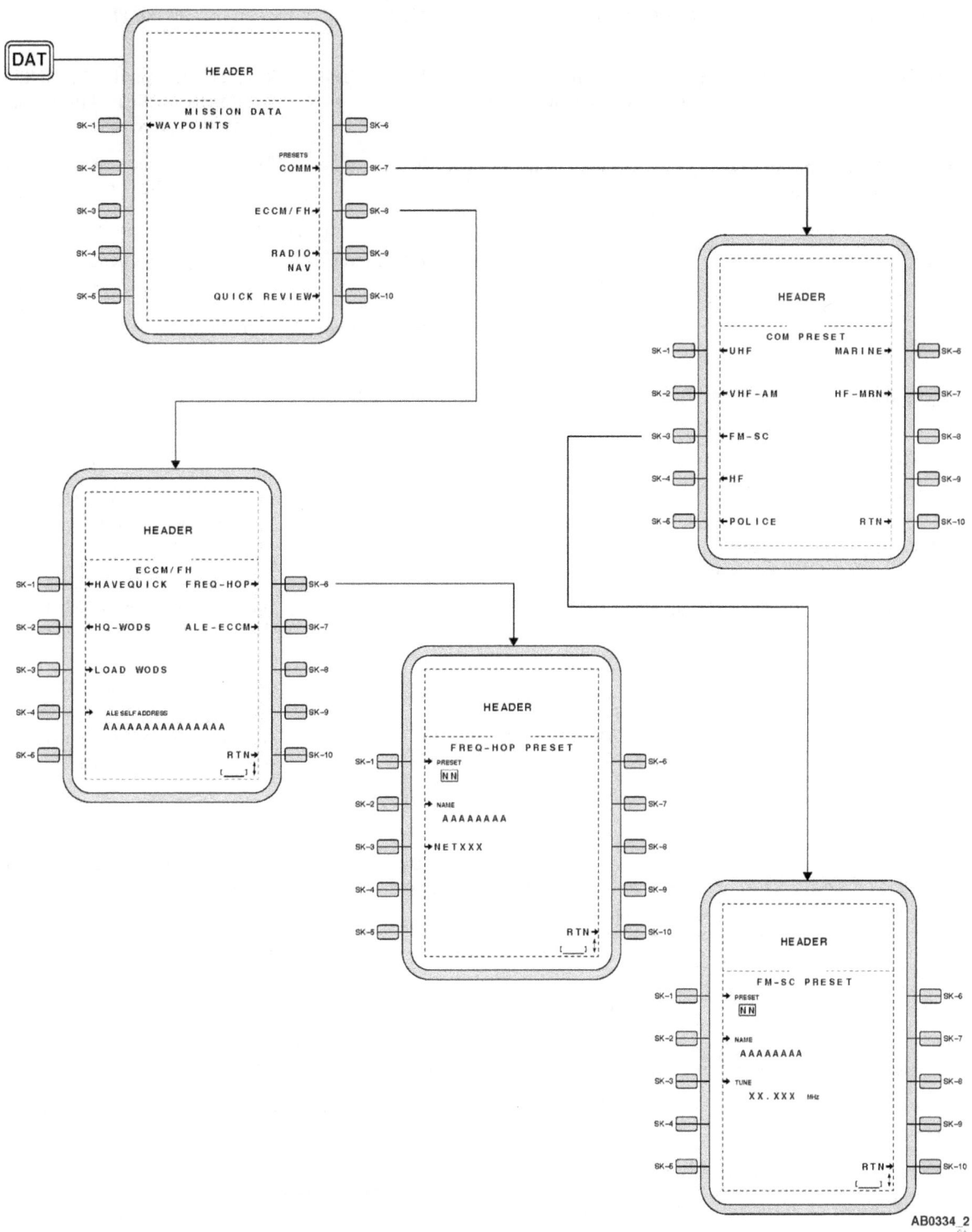

Figure 3-10. AN/ARC-201D (COM 1 and 4) Communication Screen Flow (Sheet 2 of 2)

SOFT KEY	FUNCTION
SETTING	Access Settings screen for radio that has been selected for edit.

3.6.2.2 Band Screen. The current operating band is shown in inverse video. When the pilot pushes a soft key for a new mode, that mode is selected, and the screen returns to either the COM summary screen or the Setting screen previously in use.

SOFT KEY	FUNCTION
♦FM-SC	Selects FM single channel, returns to previous screen.
♦CUE	Selects CUE frequency, returns to previous screen (preset marked to 0).
♦SCAN	Selects FM-SC (Scan) mode, returns to previous screen.
FREQ-HOP♦	Selects frequency hopping mode (FH), returns to previous screen.
FREQ-HOP MASTER♦	Selects frequency hopping - master, returns to previous screen.
CLD-STRT♦	Selects frequency hopping - cold start, returns to previous screen.
RTN♦	Returns to previous screen, without changing selected band.

3.6.2.3 Settings Screen. Setting screen allows setting of secondary radio controls, selection of a new preset, and gives access to frequency hopping set-up parameters.

SOFT KEY	FUNCTION
♦PRESET	Selects number in scratchpad as frequency preset number.
♦TUNE	Selects frequency field for editing.
♦KY TEK	Selects field for edit.
♦AMP PWR	Toggles radio transmit power outputs between **BYPS, LOW, MID, HI** (COM 1 only).

SOFT KEY	FUNCTION
♦FH-SETUP	Toggles between the **FH-SETUP** N and **FHM-SETUP N** (master and non-master) screens.
RCVR♦	Toggles between TR (transmit/receive) and **HOM** (COM 1 only).
BAND♦	Access Band screen for this radio.
SQUELCH♦	Toggles squelch **ON** or **OFF**.

3.6.2.4 Frequency Hop Setup.

SOFT KEY	FUNCTION
TIME-DT	Access FH-TIME/DATE-N screen.
STO	Stores hold memory contents into the selected Hopset or Lockout set as appropriate.
▲ (SK 3)	Toggle up through the radio stored frequency hopping fill sets from 8 through 1. Hop net stays on 6 while lockout set is either 7 or 8.
▼ (SK 4)	Toggle down through the radio stored frequency hopping fill sets from 1 through 8. Hop net stays on 6 while lockout set is either 7 or 8.
ERF-SND	Transmits ERF data from hold memory.
LD♦ HN	Loads hold memory contents with the selected Hopset.
LD♦ LS	Loads hold memory with the selected Lockout set.

3.6.2.5 Time and Date Screen. Frequency Hopping time and date screen is for information only, giving the internal clock status for either COM 1 or COM 4.

3.6.3 Mode of Operation. The radio set can be used for these modes of operations:

a. Single Channel Mode. In the single channel mode, the radio operates on one selected frequency. The scan feature for SINCGARS is dependent upon the scan channels that are selected from the SINCGARS band list. The sclected channels are monitored. The radio will notify the pilot with a tone when there is activity on the scanned channel(s).

b. Two-way secure voice utilizing embedded crypto.

c. Frequency Hopping Mode. The radios in a SINCGARS net simultaneously change frequencies up to 100 times per second in a pseudorandom fashion when transmitting and receiving which makes jamming and direction finding difficult. All radios in a frequency hopping net need common hopsets, lockout sets, transmission security key (TSK), and TOD (internal clock). The hopset contains the group of frequencies to be used in a particular channel. Lockout sets define the frequencies within the group that will not be used. The TSK determines the sequence of frequency hopping. The TOD synchronizes all the radios in the net. Hopsets are displayed in the **H/NET** column on the **FH SETUP** screen. There are 6 channels available for selection. Channel zero is not a full frequency hopping channel (cold channel) but is used to receive the electronic remote hopset, and lockout set fill. Each frequency hopping channel has its corresponding identifier, displayed next to its number. The receiver/transmitter maintains the TOD via GPS and provides the synchronization for SINCGARS frequency hopping mode. To operate in a net, all of the radios must be synchronized in time to the master, which is referencing the receiver/transmitter internal clock. Time of day may not be in synchronization with nets having radios not connected to GPS. Modifying and reading the TOD is available through the **FH-TIME/DATE** screen. If the pilot has a hopset, net entry, and lockout but the receivers/transmitters internal clock is less than or equal to 4 seconds off the master's net time, the net master must key the net master radio which will send out a preamble to the net members which synchronizes their receivers/transmitters internal clocks to the net master. If the clock's time is greater than 4 seconds but less than 1 minute off the net master's time, the pilot can get back into the net via the late net entry (SYNCH) function. Initial setup of an operating communications net using SINCGARS requires a net master. Only one net master can selected. Difference in net master and non master is ERF send and synchronization. There are five functions to enter frequency hopping: cue operation, cold hop operation, hopset/lockout loading, purging, and late net entry.

NOTE

To cue a SINCGARS radio which is in the frequency hopping mode, the pilot must keep the radio keyed for at least 4 seconds while tuned to the cue frequency while in single channel mode. This is needed because of the time factor that the radio monitors the cue channel which is once every 4 seconds.

(1) Cue Operation. This mode allows an pilot to prompt another SINCGARS radio who is working in the frequency hopping mode to come out of the frequency hopping mode and into single channel mode. When this is done, a 600-Hz tone is heard over the ICS system. When the member or master comes out of the frequency hopping mode to the single channel mode, they must be tuned to the cue band.

NOTE

If TSK do not match or are not loaded, cold hop operation will not be possible.

Due to the limited security of the cold channel of frequency hopping mode, it is recommended that only one hopset and lockout be sent in this mode.

(2) Cold Start Operation. Use cold start when radios in the net do not have matching hopset/lockout sets. Communication is established using the cold start frequency hopping set, which has only one frequency. When communication is established, the master station transmits a hopset/lockout set of choice to the net stations, who receive it, store and use them in the normal frequency hopping mode.

d. Homing (**HOM**)(COM 1 only).

3.6.4 Starting Procedure.

NOTE

Initial battery power on and/or initial APU ac power on may cause Com 1 AN/ARC-201 to go to **CT** mode - Via CDU Com 1 soft key select **PT** mode.

The radio is powered up when power is applied to helicopter's systems. As it will initialize faster than the GPS, updating its internal clock to GPS is the only start up procedure advisable.

3.6.4.1 Single Channel (SC) Mode.

1. **COM** fixed function key - Press, to access **COM SUM** screen.

2. SK 1 or SK 4 soft key - Press, to edit frequency or preset of desired radio (COM 1 or COM 4).

3-21

NOTE

If the radio is already in **FM-SC** mode, its preset and/or frequency desired is known, it may be edited on the **COM SUM** screen, and steps 4 thru 7 will be unnecessary. To edit preset or frequency, ensure that preset or frequency has edit box around it. Enter new number in scratchpad, then **ENT** - Press.

3. **BAND** soft key - Press.

4. **FM-SC** soft key - Press.

5. **SETTINGS** soft key - Press, to access Settings screen.

6. **TUNE** soft key - Press, if desired to change frequency. Enter new frequency in scratchpad. **ENT** fixed function key - Press to enter scratchpad frequency.

7. ICS transmitter selector - Position **1** (COM 1), or position **4** (COM 4).

8. Radio push-to-talk switch - Press to talk; release to listen.

3.6.4.2 Edit or Make Frequency Into PRESET.

1. **DAT** fixed function key - Press, to access **MISSION DATA** screen, then **COMM** soft key, to access **COM PRESET** screen.

2. **FM-SC**, or **ECCM-FH** soft key - Press, to access preset screen.

3. Use **PREV/NEXT** rocker switch to display preset to change. Select fields to edit with soft key, enter new values in scratchpad, and press **ENT** to change displayed values.

3.6.4.3 Frequency Hopping (FH or FH-M) Mode.

1. **COM** fixed function key - Press, to access **COM - SUM** screen.

NOTE

If the radio is already in FREQ-HOP mode, and its desired preset or channel is known, it may be edited on the **COM SUM** screen, and steps 4 thru 7 will be unnecessary.

2. SK 1 or SK 4 soft key - Press, to edit preset of desired radio (COM 1 or COM 4). To edit preset or channel, ensure that preset or channel has edit box around it. Enter new number in scratchpad, then **ENT** - Press.

3. **BAND** soft key - Press.

4. **FREQ HOP** soft key - Press. Screen returns to COM SUM screen.

5. **FH-SETUP** soft key - Press.

6. Select hopset and lockout set channels desired with SK 3 and SK 4. Return to COM SUM screen by **RTN** - Press.

7. ICS transmitter selector - Position **1** (COM 1), or position **4** (COM 4).

8. Radio push-to-talk switch - Press to talk; release to listen.

3.6.4.4 Transfer Hopset/Lockout Set (Cold Start).

1. **COM** fixed function key - Press, to access **COM - SUM** screen. Make sure the edit box is by the COM 1 or 4 radio.

2. **BAND** soft key - Press.

3. **COLD STRT MASTER** soft key - Press. Screen will revert to **COM - SUM** screen, with COLD START frequency and channel displayed. Establish communication with the rest of the net, arrange to transfer hopset/lockout sets. From SETTINGS screen, **FH - SETUP** - Press.

4. Select the hopset to download with SK 3 and SK 4. **LD H/N** soft key - Press, to enter hopset into memory.

5. **ERF-SND** soft key - Press, to send.

6. Select the lockout set to download with SK 3 and SK 4. **LD LS** soft key - Press, to enter lockout set into memory.

7. **ERF-SND** soft key - Press, to send.

8. As desired, change band **FREQ - HOP**, channel to the hopset and lockout set transmitted,

and establish normal frequency hopping communications (Refer to paragraph 3.6.4.3).

3.6.4.5 Receive Hopset/Lockout Set (Cold Start).

1. **COM** fixed function key - Press, to access **COM - SUM** screen. Make sure the edit box is by the COM 1 or 4 radio.

2. **BAND** soft key - Press.

3. **COLD STRT** soft key - Press. Screen will revert to **COM - SUM** screen, with COLD START frequency and channel displayed. Establish communication with the master station, arrange to receive hopset/lockout sets. From SETTINGS screen, **FH - SETUP** - Press.

4. When a hopset/lockout set is received, a tone will be heard in the headset. At the tone, **STO** soft key - Press, to enter hopset/lockout set into memory.

5. As desired, change band **FREQ - HOP**, channel to the hopset and lockout set transmitted, and establish normal frequency hopping communications (Refer to paragraph 3.6.4.3).

3.6.4.6 Homing (HOM) Mode (FM No. 1 only).

1. Using COM 1, establish single channel (**FM-SC**) communication with the station to home on (Refer to paragraph 3.6.4.1).

2. On COM 1 SETTING screen, **RCVR** soft key - Press, until **HOME** is displayed.

3. On CIS mode select panel, **NAV** button - Press.

4. On HSI/VSI mode select panel, **FM HOME** button - Press.

5. Observe homing indicators on vertical situation indicator (VSI) (Figure 3-28). These are:

   a. FM navigation (**NAV**) flag will move from view, and will come into view if the received signal is too weak.

   b. A steering (course indicator) pointer moves either left or right about 5° to indicate any deviation from the course to the transmitting station.

   c. Station passage will be indicated by course deviation change and **CIS MODE SEL** **NAV** switch light going out and **HDG** switch light going on.

3.7 UHF RADIO, AN/ARC-164(V) (COM 2).

Receiver-Transmitter Radio RT-1167C/ARC-164(V) is an airborne, ultra-high frequency (UHF), AM and FM, radio transmitting-receiving set. It contains a multi channel, electronically tunable main transmitter and receiver, and a fixed-tuned guard receiver. The main transceiver operates on any one of 7,000 channels, spaced in 0.025 MHz units in the 225.000 to 399.975 MHz UHF military band. The guard receiver is tunable in the 238.000 to 248.000 MHz frequency range with crystal replacement and realignment (usually 243.000 MHz). The radio set is primarily used for voice communications. HAVE QUICK is an antijamming mode which uses a frequency hopping scheme to change channels many times per second. Because the HQ mode depends on a precise time-of-day, both HQ radios must have synchronized clocks. The UHF radio is referred to as COM 2, corresponding to its position on the ICS mode select switch.

3.7.1 Antennas. The UHF antenna is under the fuselage transition section (Figure 3-1).

3.7.2 Controls and Functions. The UHF radio is controlled by AMS with the CDU (Figure 3-2). Control screens allow the pilot to choose frequency and mode of transmission (Figure 3-11). Operator functions are to change band, transmission frequency and mode, and edit and establish preset modes and frequencies. Bands associated with this radio are:

BAND FIELD	BAND NAME	FREQUENCY RANGE
UHF AM	UHF AM	225.000 - 395.975
HVQK	HAVEQUICK I	HQ1:001 to HQ1:999
HVQK	HAVEQUICK II	HQ2:001 to HQ2:999
HVQK	HAVEQUICK	HQn:001 to HQn:999(non NATO)
COM 2		Indicates radio is inoperative.

3.7.2.1 COM Summary Screen. The COM SUM screen allows the operator to perform all primary radio controls. SK-2 selects COM 2 (AN/ARC-164) settings for edit.

TM 1-1520-253-10

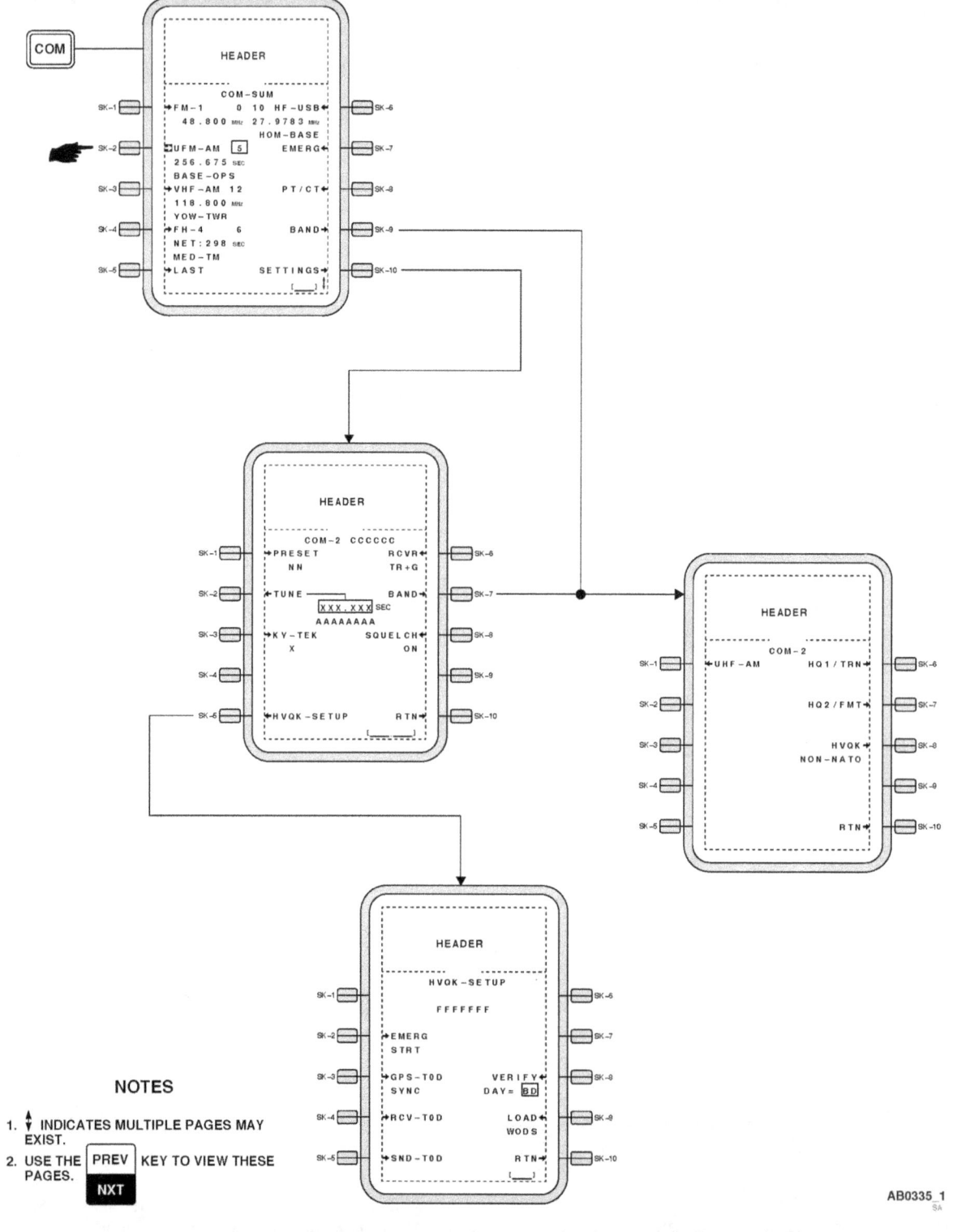

Figure 3-11. UHF (COM 2) Communication Screen Flow (Sheet 1 of 2)

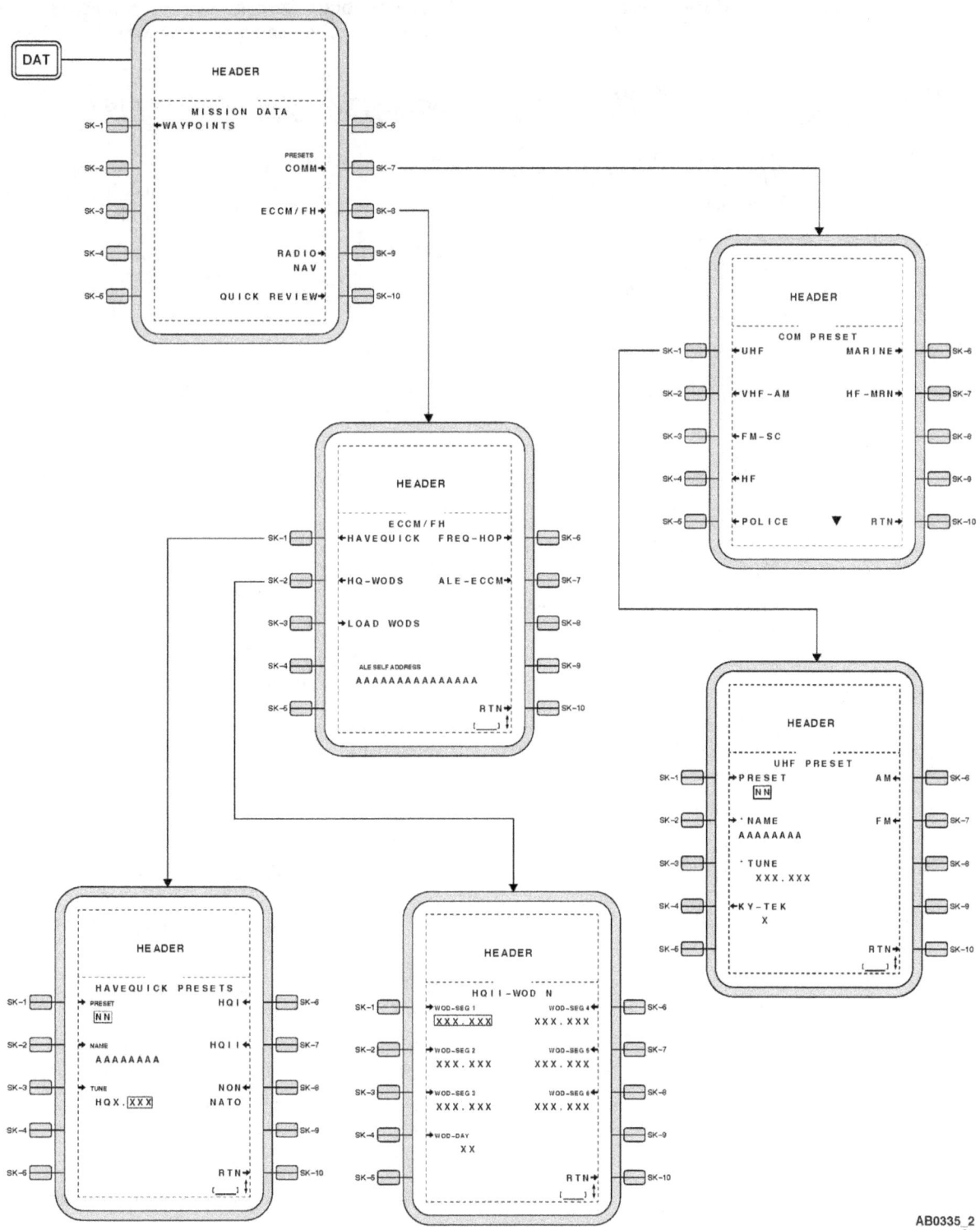

Figure 3-11. UHF (COM 2) Communication Screen Flow (Sheet 2 of 2)

Soft key labels and functions visible when SK-2 is selected are:

SOFT KEY	FUNCTION
SK-2	Selects and then toggles between COM 2 frequency and preset field for editing.
LAST	Restores the last manually tuned frequency, while saving the current settings. This function saves one setting per band of operation.
EMERG	Swaps current frequency with the band based guard frequency for radio that has been selected for edit.
PT/CT	Activates secure voice KY-58 associated with COM 2.
BAND	Access Band selection screen for radio that has been selected for edit.
SETTINGS	Access Settings screen for radio that has been selected for edit.

3.7.2.2 Band Screen. The current operating band is shown in inverse video. When the pilot pushes a soft key for a new mode, that mode is selected, and the screen returns to either the COM summary screen or the Setting screen previously in use.

SOFT KEY	FUNCTION
◆UHF - AM	Selects UHF - AM single channel, returns to previous screen.
HQ1/TRN◆	Selects HAVEQUICK I operation, returns to previous screen.
HQ2/FMT◆	Selects HAVEQUICK II operation, returns to previous screen.
HVQK NON-NATO◆	Selects HAVEQUICK non NATO operation, returns to previous screen.
RTN◆	Returns to previous screen without changing settings.

3.7.2.3 Settings Screen. Setting screen allows setting of secondary radio controls and selection of a new preset.

SOFT KEY	FUNCTION
COM 2 - ******	Screen header, giving COM selected, and band. If radio is not working, ***** is displayed.
◆PRESET	Selects number in scratchpad as frequency preset number.
◆TUNE	Selects frequency field for editing.
◆KY-TEK	
◆HVQK - SETUP	Access HVQK - SETUP screen.
RCVR◆	
BAND◆	Access Band screen for this radio.
SQUELCH◆	Toggles squelch ON or OFF.
RTN◆	Returns to previous screen without changing settings.

3.7.2.4 HVQK Setup Screen. The HVQK Setup screen allows control of frequency hopping modes.

SOFT KEY	FUNCTION
◆HVQK - SETUP	Title of screen.
Fill Status Line	Gives fill status of IN-PROG WOD load in progress. COMPLT WOD load complete. INVALID No WOD in memory.
◆EMERG START	Starts radio with internal clock, and sets the radio to HVQK I mode.
◆GPS-TOD SYNC	Synchronizes internal clock with GPS, and sets the radio to HVQK I mode.
◆RCV - TOD	Commands radio to receive external TOD.
◆SND - TOD	Commands radio to transmit TOD.

SOFT KEY	FUNCTION
VERIFY♦	Initiates a MWOD verify for the day information entered. If a valid MWOD is in the radio, the radio will respond with an audio tone.
LOAD WODS♦	Starts a WODS load from CDU data base mission memory to the radio. When loading is complete, erases MWOD data from data base mission memory, and sounds a confirming tone in the headset.

3.7.3 HAVE QUICK (HQ) System.

a. The HQ system provides a jam resistant capability through a frequency hopping technique. Frequency hopping is a technique in which the frequency being used for a given channel is automatically changed at some rate common to the transmitter and receiver. This is referred to as the normal mode, while frequency hopping operation is called the anti-jam (AJ) mode. Several ingredients are necessary for successful system operations. These are:

(1) Common frequency.

(2) Time synchronization.

(3) Common hopping pattern and rate.

(4) Common net number.

b. The common frequencies have been programmed into all HQ radios. Time synchronization is provided via UHF radio and/or hardware by external time distribution system. A time-of-day (TOD) signal must be received from the time distribution system for each time the system is powered up. GPS may be used for TOD, but needs to be updated upon power up, after the GPS initializes itself. The hopping pattern and hopping rate are determined by the operator inserted word-of-day (WOD). The WOD is a multi-digit code, common worldwide to all HAVE QUICK users. In the AJ mode, a communications channel is defined by a net number instead of a signal frequency as in the normal mode. Before operating in the AJ mode, the radio must be primed. This consists of setting the WOD, TOD, and net number. The anti jamming mode is a function of the band setting.

3.7.3.1 Time Of Day (TOD) Transmission.
The TOD entry is normally entered before flight, but it is possible to enter it in flight. Use the **HVQK - SETUP** screen to receive and transmit TOD information.

3.7.4 Modes of Operation.
The radio set can be used for these modes of operations:

3.7.4.1 UHF AM Clear Voice. UHF AM uncoded voice transmission and reception.

3.7.4.2 UHF AM Secure Voice. UHF AM encrypted voice transmission and reception through the attached KY-58.

3.7.4.3 HAVEQUICK anti jamming frequency hopping. Frequency hopping may be done in three submodes, HAVEQUICK I, HAVEQUICK II, and non NATO HAVEQUICK.

3.7.5 Normal Operation.

3.7.5.1 UHF AM Mode.

NOTE

Initial battery power on and/or initial APU ac power on may cause Com 2 AN/ARC-164 to go to **CT** mode - Via CDU Com 2 soft key, select **PT** mode.

1. **COM** fixed function key - Press, to access **COM SUM** screen.

2. SK 2 soft key - Press, to edit frequency or preset.

NOTE

If the radio is already in the desired band, and its preset and/or frequency desired is known, it may be edited on the **COM SUM** screen, and steps 4 thru 7 will be unnecessary. To edit preset or frequency, ensure that preset or frequency has edit box around it. Enter new number in scratchpad, then **ENT** - Press.

3. **BAND** soft key - Press.

4. **UHF AM** soft key - Press. The band will be selected, and screen will change to COM summary screen.

5. **SETTINGS** soft key - Press, to access Settings screen.

6. **TUNE** soft key - Press, if desired to edit frequency. Enter new frequency in scratchpad, and **ENT** fixed function key - Press.

7. ICS transmitter selector - Position **2**

8. Radio push-to-talk switch - Press to talk; release to listen.

3.7.5.2 Frequency Hopping Mode.

1. On initial start-up of radio, update TOD, and load WOD.

   a. **COM** fixed function key - Press, to access **COM SUM** screen.

   b. **SK 2** soft key - Press, to edit COM 2 settings.

   c. **SETTINGS** soft key - Press, to access Settings screen.

   d. **HVQK - SETUP** soft key - Press.

   e. Update TOD, with any one of the soft keys, depending on mission needs.

   f. **LOAD WODS** soft key - Press, to load WODS. The radio will emit a tone when WODS are loaded, and return to settings screen with band changed to **HVQCK I**.

2. On settings screen, select channel as desired.

3. ICS transmitter selector - Position **2**.

4. Radio push-to-talk switch - Press to talk; release to listen.

3.7.5.3 Receiving Time from Net Control Aircraft.

1. **COM** fixed function key - Press, to access **COM SUM** screen.

2. **SK 2** soft key - Press, to edit COM 2 settings.

3. **SETTINGS** soft key - Press, to access Settings screen.

4. **HVQK - SETUP** soft key - Press.

5. When net control announces TOD update, **RCV - TOD**.

3.7.5.4 Sending Time (Net Control Aircraft).

1. **COM** fixed function key - Press, to access **COM SUM** screen.

2. **SK 2** soft key - Press, to edit COM 2 settings.

3. **SETTINGS** soft key - Press, to access Settings screen.

4. **HVQK - SETUP** soft key - Press.

5. When net control requests TOD update, **SND - TOD**

3.7.5.5 Edit or Make Frequency Into PRESET.

1. **DAT** fixed function key - Press, to access **MISSION DATA** screen, then **COMM** soft key, to access **COM PRESET** screen.

2. **UHF** soft key - Press, to access preset screen.

3. Use **PREV/NEXT** rocker switch to display preset to change. Select fields to edit with soft key, enter new values in scratchpad and press **ENT** to change displayed values.

3.7.6 Emergency Operation.

NOTE

Placing **EMERG COMM** switch to **EMERG COMM** disables the CDUs and tunes COM 2 radios to Guard (243.0 MHz).

1. On emergency control panel, **EMERG COMM** switch - **EMERG COMM**.

2. **CSC** mode selector - **2**.

3. Radio push-to-talk switch - Press to talk; release to listen.

3.8 VHF RADIO SET AN/ARC-222 (COM 3).

The AN/ARC-222 VHF transceiver provides AM and FM communication on VHF frequencies between 30.00 MHz and 173.975 MHz. The set receives and transmits FM signals between 30.000 to 87.975 MHz, and 156.000 to 173.975 MHz. AM signals are receive only between 108.0 and 115.975, and receive and transmit between 116 and 155.975. The AN/ARC-222 is referred to as COM 3, which corresponds to its position on the ICS mode select switch. Power is supplied from the dc essential bus through a circuit breaker marked **VHF AM/FM**.

3.8.1 Antenna.
The antenna is located on the bottom of the cabin (Figure 3-1).

TM 1-1520-253-10

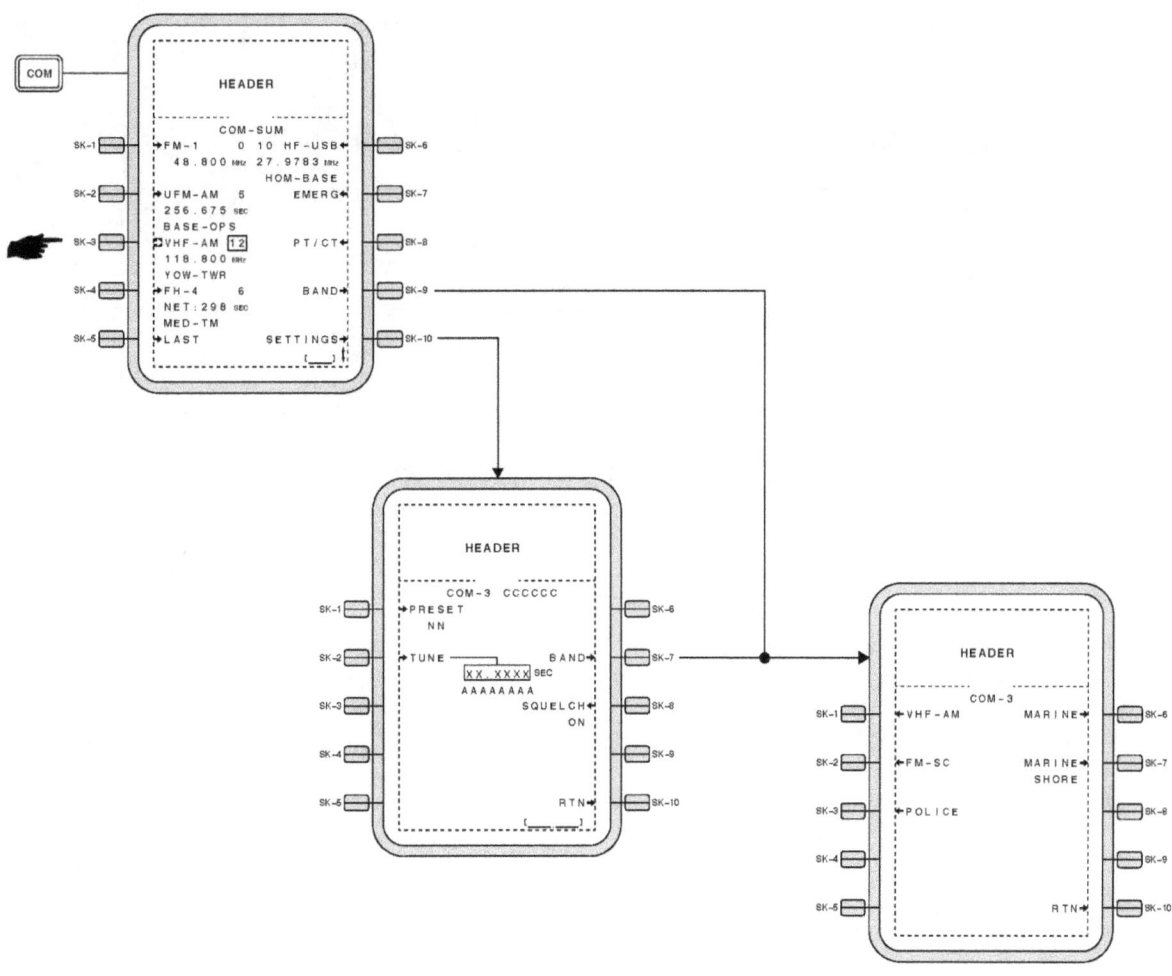

NOTE

↕ INDICATES MULTIPLE PAGES MAY EXIST.
USE THE PREV / NXT KEY TO VIEW THESE PAGES.

Figure 3-12. VHF (COM 3) Communication Screen Flow (Sheet 1 of 2)

3-29

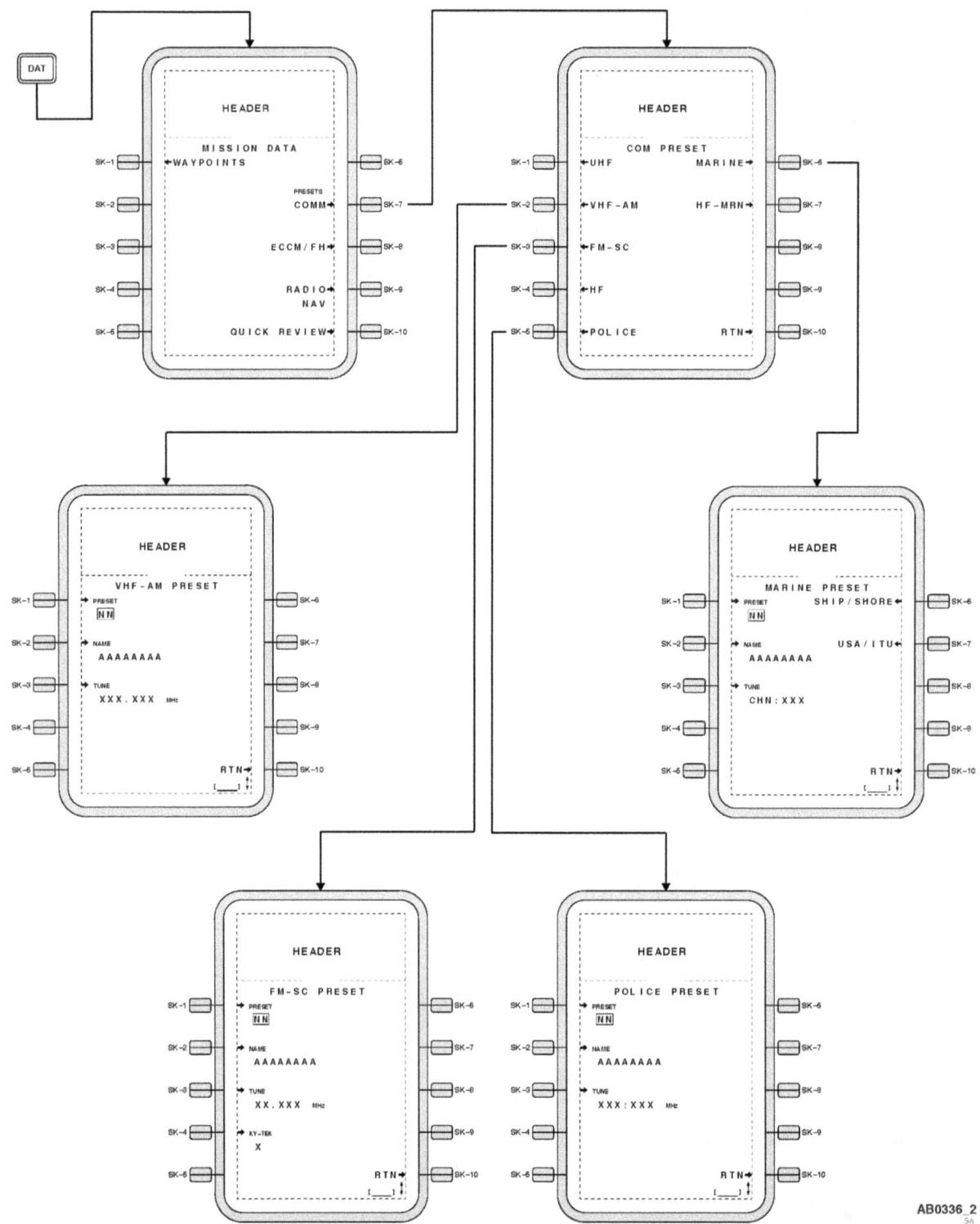

Figure 3-12. VHF (COM 3) Communication Screen Flow (Sheet 2 of 2)

3.8.2 Controls and Functions. The AN/ARC-222 radio is controlled by the AMS with the CDU (Figure 3-2), or in emergency by a control panel (Figure 3-13). Control screens allow the pilot to choose frequency and mode of transmission (Figure 3-12). Operator functions are to change band, transmission frequency and mode, and edit and establish preset modes and frequencies in normal mode. Bands associated with this radio are:

BAND FIELD	BAND NAME	FREQUENCY RANGE
FM-3	FM-SC	30.000 to 87.975
VHF-AM	VHF-AM	108.000 to 135.975
POLC	HF AM Police	136.000 to 173.995
MRN	Marine	CH:001 to CH:028 and CHN:060 to CH:088

3.8.2.1 COM Summary Screen. The COM SUM screen allows the operator to perform all primary radio controls. SK-3 selects COM 3 (AN/ARC-222) for edit. Soft key labels and functions visible when SK-3 is selected are:

SOFT KEY	FUNCTION
♦SK-3	Selects and then toggles between COM 3 frequency and preset field for editing.
♦LAST	Restores the last manually tuned frequency, while saving the current settings. This function saves one setting per band of operation.
EMERG♦	Swaps current frequency with the band based guard frequency for radio that has been selected for edit.
BAND♦	Access Band selection screen for radio that has been selected for edit.
SETTINGS♦	Access Settings screen for radio that has been selected for edit.

3.8.2.2 Band Screen. The current operating band is shown in inverse video. When the pilot pushes a soft key for a new mode, that mode is selected, and the screen returns to either the COM summary screen or the Setting screen previously in use.

SOFT KEY	FUNCTION
♦VHF - AM	Selects VHF - AM single channel, returns to previous screen.
♦FM - SC	Selects VHF - FM single channel, returns to previous screen.
♦POLICE	Selects Police band, returns to previous screen.
MARINE♦	Selects Marine band, returns to previous screen.
MARINE SHORE♦	Selects Marine shore band, returns to previous screen.
RTN♦	Returns to previous screen without changing selected band.

3.8.2.3 Settings Screen. Setting screen allows setting of secondary radio controls and selection of a new preset.

SOFT KEY	FUNCTION
COM 3 - ******	Screen header, giving COM selected, and band. If radio is not working, ***** is displayed.
♦PRESET	Selects number in scratchpad as frequency preset number.
♦TUNE	Selects frequency field for editing.
BAND♦	Access Band screen for this radio.
SQUELCH♦	Toggles squelch **ON** or **OFF**.
RTN♦	Returns to previous screen without changing settings.

3.8.3 Emergency Controls and Functions. The emergency control panel for the COM 3 VHF radio set is located on the lower console. Functions COM 3 in emergency operation are limited to FM single channel, VHF single channel, Marine and Police band. No crypto functions are available. Switch positions that have no function in this operation are listed as not connected. The function of each control is as follows:

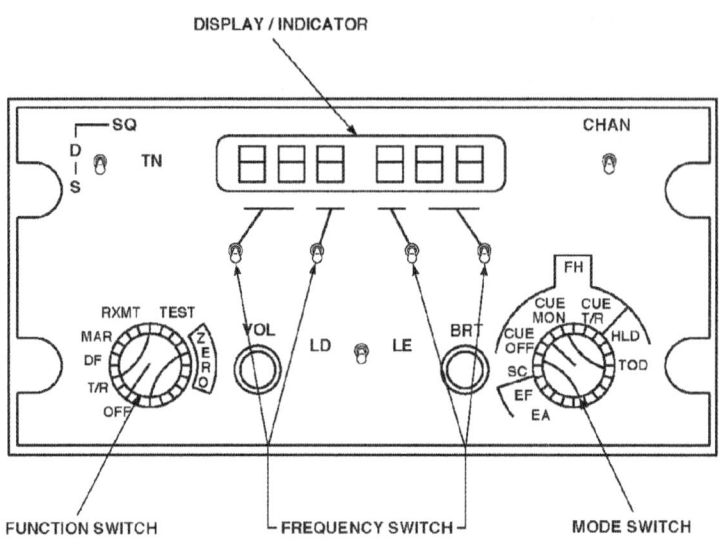

Figure 3-13. AN/ARC-222 Control Panel

CONTROL/ INDICATOR	FUNCTION
CHAN switch	Selects channels. Pressing the switch to rear momentarily will decrease the channel number by one. Pressing and holding the switch to rear more than two seconds will decrease the channel number by one, and then access **MN** channel. Pressing switch to front momentarily increases the channel number by one. Pressing switch to front and holding more than 2 seconds increases the channel number by one, and then access preset channel 20.
Display/indicator	Displays single channel preset numbers, frequencies, BIT status and other messages.
Frequency Adjustment switches	Push to front to increase frequency number by one, push to rear to decrease number by one.
Mode switch	
SC	Selects single channel mode of operation.

CONTROL/ INDICATOR	FUNCTION
MN	Selects manual channel mode of operation.
EA	Selects VHF AM guard channel for transmit and receive. (Monitor 121.5 MHz only when **SC AM**, **FM**, or maritime presets are selected).
EF	Selects VHF FM guard channel for transmit and receive. (Monitor 156.8 MHz, or 40.5 MHz only when **SC AM**, **FM**, or maritime presets are selected).
VOL	Adjusts volume of radio audio.
Function Switch	
OFF	Not connected.
T/R	Enables transmit and receive.
DF	Not connected.
MAR	Selects maritime preset channels.
RXMT	Not connected.
TEST	Initiates built in test (BIT).

CONTROL/ INDICATOR	FUNCTION
ZERO	Not connected.

3.8.4 Normal Operation.

3.8.4.1 Single Channel (SC) Mode.

NOTE

Initial battery power on and/or initial APU ac power on may cause COM 3 AN/ARC-222 to go squelch **OFF** mode - Via CDU Com 3 soft key and **SETTING** soft key, select **PT** mode.

Momentary loss of power, such as switching from external to internal power, may cause changes in radio settings, to include tuning, band and mode of operation.

1. **COM** fixed function key - Press, to access **COM SUM** screen.

2. **SK-3** soft key - Press, to edit frequency or preset.

NOTE

If the radio is already in the desired band, and its preset and/or frequency desired is known, it may be edited on the **COM SUM** screen, and steps 4 thru 7 will be unnecessary. To edit preset or frequency, ensure that preset or frequency has edit box around it. Enter new number in scratchpad, then **ENT** - Press.

3. **BAND** soft key - Press.

4. Choose desired band by pressing the adjacent soft key. The band will be selected, and screen will change to COM summary screen.

5. **SETTINGS** soft key - Press, to access Settings screen.

6. **TUNE** soft key - Press, if desired to edit frequency. Enter new frequency in scratchpad, and **ENT** fixed function key - Press.

7. ICS transmitter selector - Position **3**.

8. Radio push-to-talk switch - Press to talk; release to listen.

3.8.4.2 Edit or Make Frequency Into PRESET.

1. **DAT** fixed function key - Press, to access **MISSION DATA** screen, then **COMM** soft key, to access **COM PRESET** screen.

2. **VHF-AM**, **POLICE**, or **MARINE** soft key - Press, to access desired preset screen.

NOTE

When a **MARINE PRESET** is changed, all other Marine Preset's USA / ITU modes will be changed to current preset setting (for example, if the displayed preset mode is ITU, all Marine band presets will be changed to ITU when an edit is made to the displayed preset).

3. Use **PREV/NEXT** rocker switch to display preset to change. Select fields to edit with soft key, enter new values in scratchpad and press **ENT** to change displayed values.

3.8.5 Emergency Operation.

1. On emergency control panel, **EMERG COM** switch - **EMERG COM**.

2. Set mode switch on emergency control panel to band and channel desired.

3. ICS transmitter selector - Position **3**

4. Radio push-to-talk switch - Press to talk; release to listen.

3.9 HF RADIO SET AN/ARC-220 (COM 5).

WARNING

Make sure that no personnel are within 3 feet of the HF antenna when transmitting or performing radio checks. Do not touch the RF output terminal on the antenna coupler, the insulated feed through, or the antenna itself while the microphone is keyed (after the tuning cycle is complete) or while the system is in transmit self-test. Serious RF burns can result from direct contact with the above criteria.

a. The AN/ARC-220 HF transceiver provides long range communications. The HF radio receives and transmits on any one of 280,000 frequencies spaced at 100 Hz steps on the high frequency (HF) band. The HF radio has a frequency range of 2.0000 - 29.9999 MHz. Preset nets can be manually programmed by the pilot, or loaded with the Avionics Management System. The HF radio operates in the upper side band (USB) voice, lower side band (LSB) voice, amplitude modulation equivalent (AME), or continuous wave (CW) modes. Communication security is provided by a dedicated KY-100 COMSEC device. The HF radio provides either 10, 50, or 175 watts of power when transmitting. Transmit tune time is normally less than 1 second.

b. In addition to conventional HF communications the radio provides automatic link establishment (ALE). In this mode each station has an address that identifies it, instead of an assigned frequency. The radio automatically establishes a 2 way communications link between stations on the best available frequency, and then notifies the pilot that communications can begin. This raises the success rate for first try links to a distant station from 30 percent to 90 percent. This linking process may take up to 10 seconds, and will be performed after each pause in communications greater than 60 seconds. Electronic counter countermeasures (ECCM), in the form of frequency hopping requires that radios have the same keys and be synchronized to the same time source. This radio uses the helicopter's GPS as its time source. Both ALE protection and ECCM keys are loaded from the data transfer cartridge. ECCM keys control the frequency hopping pattern. ALE link protection keys encode station address information to prevent an unauthorized station entry in the net.

c. Power for the radio is provided from the No. 1 dc primary bus through a circuit breaker marked **HF**.

3.9.1 Antenna. The tubular antenna element is routed from the left side of the transition area to a point just forward of the hinged tailcone section, and is supported by four masts. RF energy is supplied to the antenna via the forward mast (Figure 3-1).

3.9.2 Controls and Functions. The AN/ARC-220 radio is controlled by the AMS with the CDU (Figure 3-2). Control screens allow the pilot to choose frequency and mode of transmission (Figure 3-14). The AN/ARC-220 is referred to as COM 5, which corresponding to its position on the ICS mode select switch. Operator functions are to change band, transmission frequency and mode, and edit and establish preset modes and frequencies. Bands associated with this radio are:

BAND FIELD	BAND NAME	FREQUENCY RANGE
HF-LSB	HF Lower Side Band	2.0000 to 29.9999
HF-USB	HF Upper Side Band	2.0000 to 29.9999
HF-AM	HF AM	2.0000 to 29.9999
HF-MRN	HF AM Marine	CHN:0401 to CHN:2510 with gaps.
ALE-ECM	ALE-ECCM	2.0000 to 29.9999

3.9.2.1 COM Summary Screen. The COM SUM screen allows the operator to perform all primary radio controls. SK-6 selects COM 5 settings for editing.

SOFT KEY	FUNCTION
SK-6♦	Selects and then toggles between COM 5 frequency and preset field for editing.
♦LAST	Restores the last manually tuned frequency, while saving the current settings. This function saves one setting per band of operation.
EMERG♦	Swaps current frequency with the band based guard frequency for radio that has been selected for edit.
KY-100♦	Access KY-100 screen.

SOFT KEY	FUNCTION
BAND♦	Access band selection screen for radio that has been selected for edit.
SETTINGS♦	Access settings screen for radio that has been selected for edit.

3.9.2.2 Band Screen. The current operating band is shown in inverse video. When the pilot pushes a soft key for a new mode, that mode is selected, and the screen returns to either the COM summary screen or the Setting screen previously in use.

SOFT KEY	FUNCTION
COM 5	Title of screen
◄USB	Selects upper side band mode, returns to previous screen.

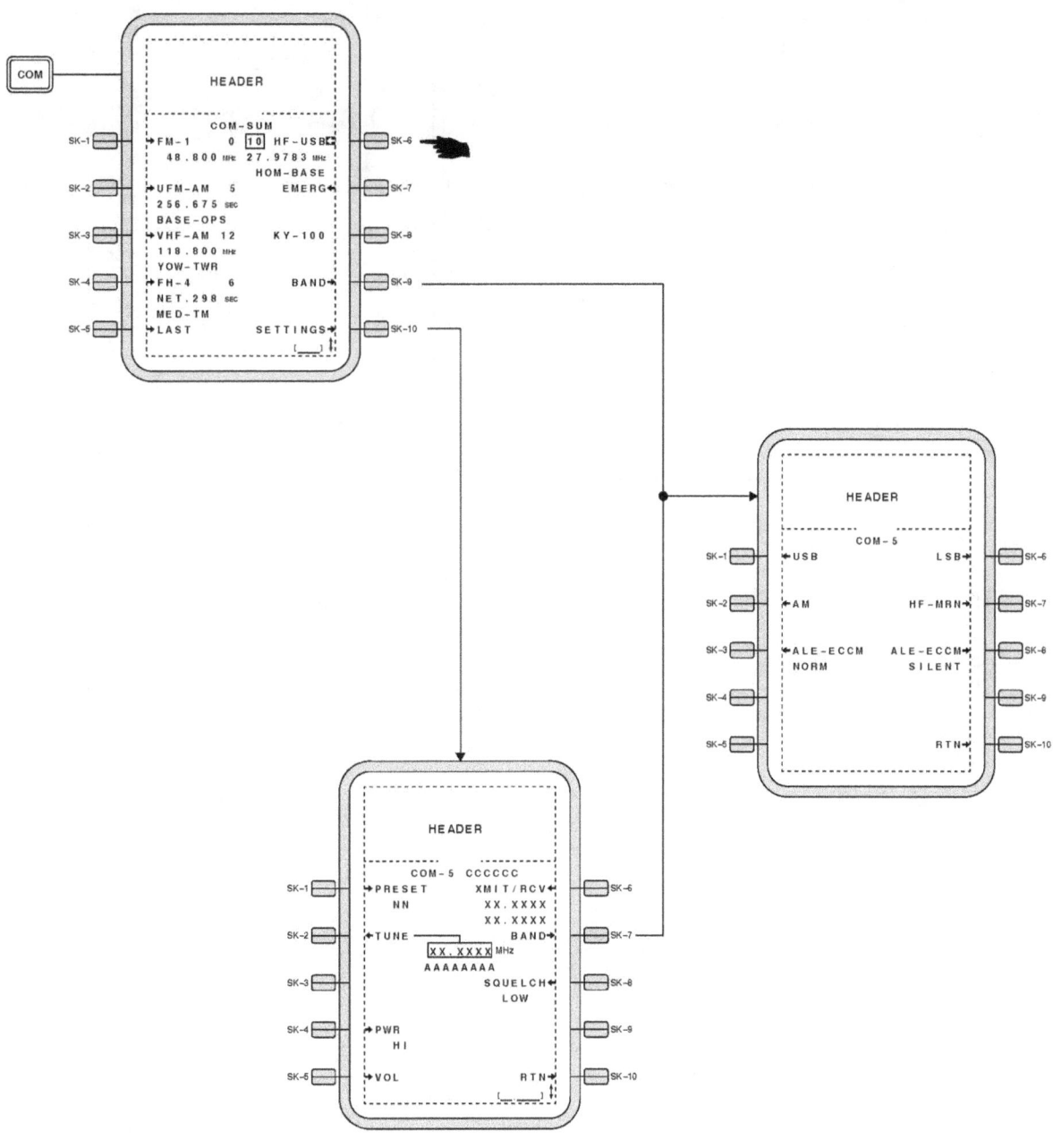

Figure 3-14. HF (COM 5) Communication Screen Flow (Sheet 1 of 2)

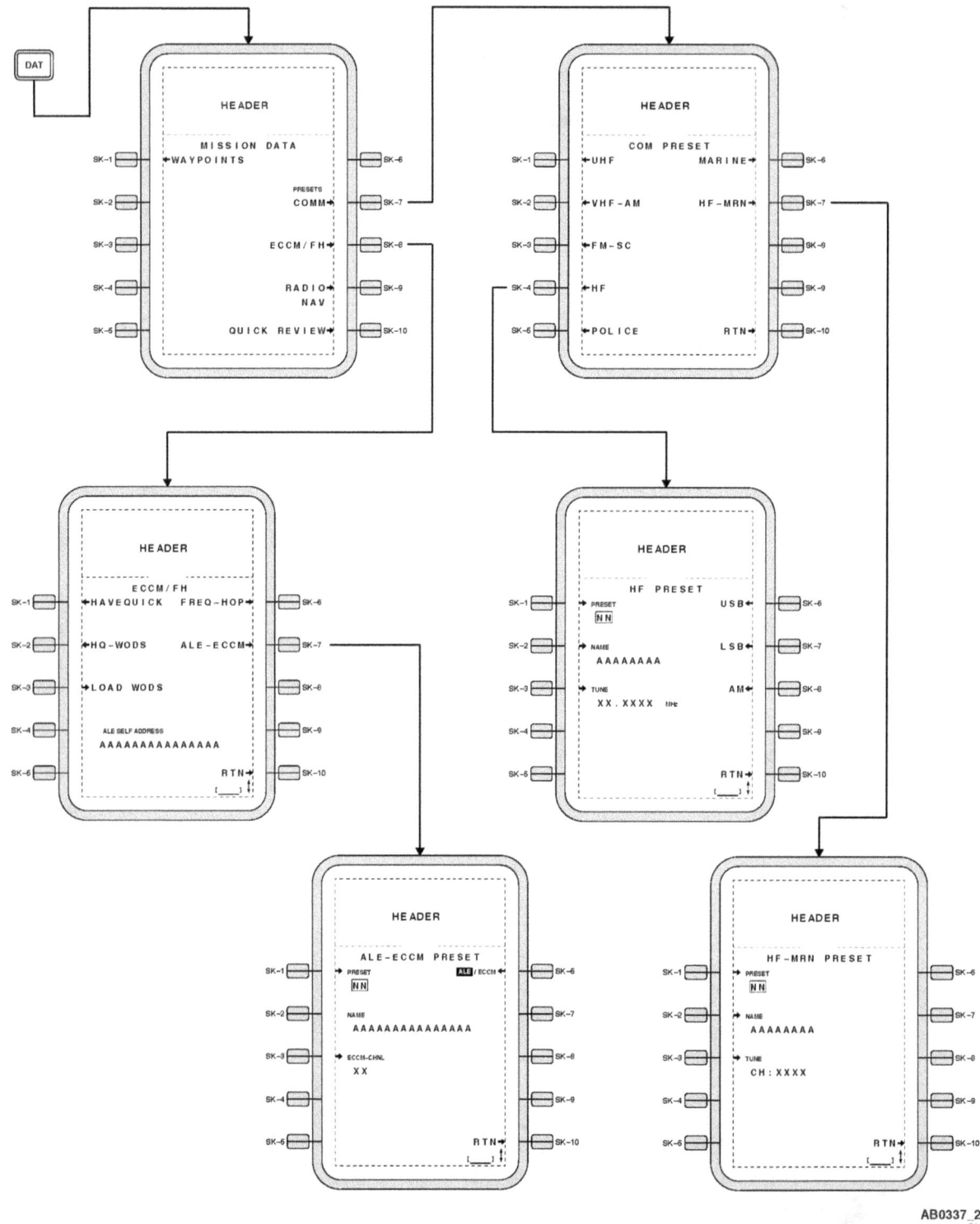

Figure 3-14. HF (COM 5) Communication Screen Flow (Sheet 2 of 2)

SOFT KEY	FUNCTION
♦AM	Selects AM (both sidebands) mode, returns to previous screen.
♦ALE - ECCM NORM	Selects **ALE - ECCM** mode, returns to previous screen.
LSB♦	Selects lower side band mode, returns to previous screen.
HF MRN♦	Selects ITU Marine channel band, returns to previous screen.
ALE - ECCM SILENT♦	Selects **ALE - ECCM** mode without automatic replies, returns to previous screen.
RTN♦	Returns to previous screen without changing existing band settings.

3.9.2.3 Settings Screen. Setting screen allows setting of secondary radio controls, selection of a new preset, and gives access to frequency hopping set-up parameters.

SOFT KEY	FUNCTION
COM 5 *****	Header identifying the radio and band selected.
♦PRESET	Selects number in scratchpad as frequency preset number.
♦TUNE	Selects frequency field for editing.
♦PWR	Toggles radio transmit power outputs between **LOW**, **MID**, **HI**.
♦VOL	Changes volume of radio in headset.
♦XMT/RCV	Shows current tuned frequencies for transmit and receive operation.
BAND♦	Access band screen for this radio.
SQUELCH♦	Toggles squelch **ON** or **OFF**.
RTN♦	Returns to previous screen without changing band, or settings.

3.9.2.4 ALE - ECCM Setup.

SOFT KEY	FUNCTION
ALE-ECCM SETUP	Title of screen.
♦SEND POS	Calls the selected station, sends GPS present position, and terminates the link.
♦ABORT	Cancels settings, ends established link.
♦SELF ADDRESS	Edit the current address for ALE operation.
♦CALL ADDRESS	Edit address of called stations.
♦APPLY	Applies address edits, if radio is in ALE-ECCM band.
GPS-TOD SYNC♦	Updates AN/ARC-220 internal clock with GPS time.
RTN♦	Returns to previous screen without changing edits.

3.9.3 Operation.

3.9.3.1 Starting Procedure.

    1. **BAND** and **FREQ** - Select.

    2. **CHAN** - Select.

3.9.3.2 Receive.

    1. **ICS VOL** control - As required.

    2. **SQL** control - As required.

3.9.3.3 Transmit.

    1. **ICS 5** transmitter selector switch - Set.

    2. Radio push-to-talk switch - Press-to-talk; release to listen.

3.9.3.4 ALE Operation. Initial setup to receive and transmit using ALE:

    1. **COM** fixed function button - Push.

    2. SK-6 soft key - Push, to highlight COM 5.

3. **BAND** soft key - Push.

4. Either **ALE-ECCM** soft key - Push.

5. On **COM SUM** screen, **SETTINGS** soft key - Push.

6. On **SETTINGS** screen, **ALE SETUP** soft key - Push.

7. On **ALE SETUP** screen, **SELF ADDRESS** soft key - Push. Select your address from the list. Scroll through addresses using **PREV NEXT** rocker switch.

NOTE

ALL is the last address entry on the list. Press **PREV** side of rocker switch to display this address quickly.

8. **CALL ADDRESS** soft key - Push. Select the other station's address from the list. Scroll through addresses using **PREV NEXT** rocker switch.

9. **APPLY** soft key - Push. Select your address from the list. The reference numbers next to **SELF ADDRESS** and **CALL ADDRESS** will return to **0**, but the addresses will remain as selected.

10. **RTN** soft key - Push, until **COM SUM** screen appears.

Communicate using ALE:

11. ICS transmitter selector - Position **5**, and radio push-to-talk switch - Press. **CALL** will appear under the COM 5 band annunciator, which will change to **LINK** when the ALE link is established.

12. Radio push-to-talk switch - Press to talk; release to listen.

Receive, using ALE:

13. After ALE is setup if another station calls, **INCM-CAL** will appear on CDU status line, a tone will sound in the headsets, and the annunciator under band for COM 5 will change to **LINK**.

14. ICS transmitter selector - Position **5**.

15. Radio push-to-talk switch - Press to talk; release to listen.

3.9.3.5 Edit or Make Frequency Into PRESET.

1. **DAT** fixed function key - Press, to access **MISSION DATA** screen, then **COMM** soft key, to access **COM PRESET** screen.

2. **HF**, or **HF-MRN** soft key - Press, to access desired preset screen.

3. Use **PREV/NEXT** rocker switch to display preset to change. Select fields to edit with soft key, enter new values in scratchpad and press **ENT** to change displayed values.

3.9.4 Messages. The following display advisory messages may appear during operation of the radio:

Table 3-2. AN/ARC-220 Messages

ERROR	MESSAGE	ACTION
ALE - NO DATA	ALE mission data not loaded.	Load mission data.
ALE - NO KEYS	ALE link protection keys not loaded.	
CALL FAIL	Radio failed to complete an outgoing call.	
CALLING	Radio is placing an ALE call to another address.	
CHANNEL BUSY	ALE or ECCM net is in use.	Wait or try another net.

Table 3-2. AN/ARC-220 Messages (Cont)

ERROR	MESSAGE	ACTION
CHANNEL INOP	ALE or ECCM keys are not loaded, or not correct.	
COPY COMPLETE	Copying process finished successfully.	
COPY FAIL	Copying process was unsuccessful.	
COPYING DATA	The radio is copying datafill contents from DTS.	
ECCM - NO DATA	ECCM data not installed.	
ECCM - NO KEYS	ECCM keys not installed.	
EMERG	Mode or net selected for emergency communication is inoperative.	
EMERG - NO KEYS	No keys available for net selected for emergency communication.	
EOM	End of message.	
EXT FAIL	Radio failed due to external device, such as antenna.	
GO DATA	Link quality analysis values too low for reliable voice communication; data transmissions recommended.	
GPS FAIL	Position report could not be issued.	
GPS TIME FAIL	Radio not receiving time signals from GPS.	
HELD	ALE call being held in specific frequency by operator.	
INCOMING CALL	Another radio is establishing an ALE link.	
INOP MODES EXIST	Warning to expect inoperative modes.	
LINKED	An ALE link is established.	
LOAD COMPLETE	Keys and data successfully loaded into radio.	
LOAD FAIL	Keys and data not successfully loaded into radio.	
LOADING DATA	Radio currently loading data.	
LOADING KEYS	Radio currently loading keys.	
MSG ABORT	Radio discontinuing sending of current message.	

Table 3-2. AN/ARC-220 Messages (Cont)

ERROR	MESSAGE	ACTION
NET INOP	Selected net contains no data, corrupted data, or hardware cannot support the selected mode of operation.	
NO AUTO XMT	Radio has been instructed not to make any automatic transmissions.	
NO DATA	Database is not filled with necessary data to perform requested operations.	
NO KEYS LOADED	Keys are not loaded for current selected mode or net.	
NO RCVD MSGS	No messages have been received.	
PAC FAIL	Failure radio in PA coupler.	
POSN RPT FAIL	Current location or GPS position report was not transmitted.	
PRE - NO DATA	Preset data not loaded.	
PTT FOR XMIT BIT	Instruction to press microphone PTT switch to enable transmission BIT.	
RCV BIT - GO	Receiver BIT functions completed without failure.	
RCV READY	Ready to receive ECCM transmissions.	
RCVG PREAMBLE	ECCM preamble being received.	
RCVG DATA	Radio currently receiving data.	
RT FAIL	Receiver Transmitter inoperative.	
RX-TX DEGRADED	Receive and transmit capabilities are degraded.	
RX-TX FAIL	Radio cannot receive or transmit.	
SENDING DATA	Radio currently sending data.	
SENDING POSN	Radio sending GPS position report.	
SOUND	Radio sending an ALE sound.	
SYNCING	Time synchronization being performed.	
TESTING	BIT in progress.	

TM 1-1520-253-10

Table 3-2. AN/ARC-220 Messages (Cont)

ERROR	MESSAGE	ACTION
TIME SYNC FAIL	Radio failed in attempt to synchronize.	
TRANSEC FAIL	BIT detected a failure that will not allow ECCM operation.	
TUNE XX%	Indicates percentage of ECCM frequencies tuned for current net.	
TUNING	Radio is currently tuning itself.	
TX DEGRADED	BIT detected a failure that is causing transmission capability to be degraded.	
TX FAIL	Radio cannot transmit.	
UNSYNC	ECCM is not synchronized.	
UNTUNED	An ECCM hop set is not tuned.	
XMT READY	Radio is ready to transmit in ECCM mode.	
ZEROIZED	All mission datafill and keys have been erased.	

3.10 TSEC/KY-100 SECURE COMMUNICATION SYSTEM.

The TSEC/KY-100 provides secure, half duplex voice, digital data, analog data and remote keying capabilities for transmission over the HF radio. It has six operational modes, and can store often used settings on presets. Power is supplied from the No. 1 dc primary bus through a circuit breaker marked **HF SCTY SET**.

3.10.1 Controls and Functions. The KY-100 is controlled by the AMS with the CDU (Figure 3-2). Pilot input is through a control screen (Figure 3-15), accessed by pressing **INI**, then **FILL** soft key, then **KY-100** soft key. Indications and soft key functions are as follows:

3.10.1.1 KY RTU Screen. Mode screen:

SOFT KEY	FUNCTION
♦**INIT KEY**	Selects operating modes.
♦**UP ARROW**	Acts as an up arrow key.
♦**RIGHT ARROW**	Acts as the right arrow key.

SOFT KEY	FUNCTION
♦**BOTH ARROWS**	Same function as pressing both arrow keys at the same time.
PT/CT♦	Toggles between plain text and cipher mode voice.
OFFLINE♦	Off line mode disables communications and accesses screens to select mode settings, test, and fill screens.
ZERO ALL♦	Erases all keys in the unit except the emergency backup key.

3.10.2 Starting Procedure.

3.10.2.1 Cold Start. A cold start is performed when there are no traffic keys in the KY-100 at start up.

1. Access KY-100 screen by **INI**, then **FILL** soft key, then **KY-100** soft key - Press.

2. **OFFLINE** soft key - Press. TEST will be displayed.

3-41

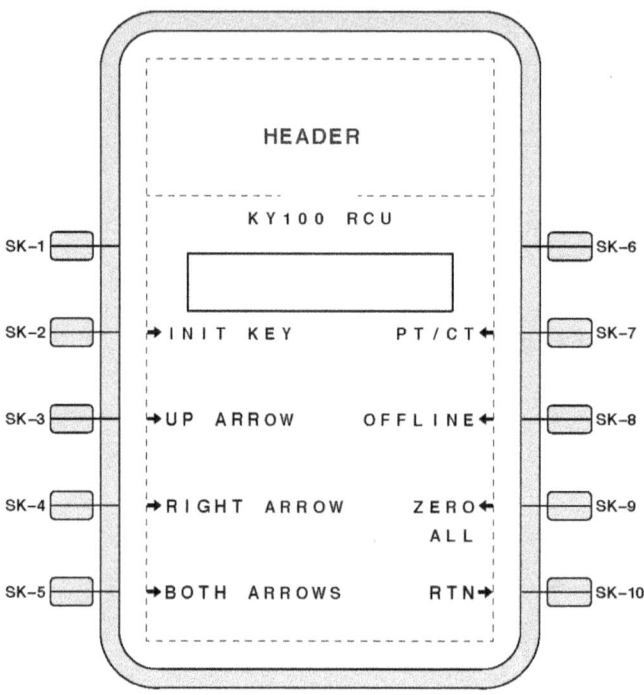

Figure 3-15. KY-100 Secure Communication Control Screen

3. **UP ARROW** soft key - Press. KEY OPS will be displayed.

4. Connect KYK-13 **KY-100** fill port on lower console.

5. On KYK-13:.

   a. Mode switch - **ON**

   b. Fill switch - Place to fill number (1-6) desired.

6. On CDU, **INIT** soft key - Press three times. **LOAD KEY**, then 1, then **LOAD 1** will be displayed.

7. On CDU, **INIT** soft key - Press again, to initiate load. **LOAD KEYS** will appear, then **KEY 1**(flashing), and **LOAD 1** with 1 flashing will appear. During load, 2 beeps will be heard in the headsets. The key that was loaded is stored in fill position 1.

8. On CDU, **UP ARROW** soft key - Press. **LOAD 2** (flashing) will be displayed.

9. On KYK-13, place Fill switch to next fill.

10. Repeat steps 6 through 9 for each key fill required for loading.

11. On CDU press **BOTH ARROWS** soft key twice.

12. Press **PT/CT** soft key.

13. Press **RTN** soft key.

14. Remove KYK-13 from fill port.

3.10.3 Normal Operation.

3.10.3.1 Change Mode.

1. To access KY-100 control screen, **COM** fixed function key, then SK-6 soft key, then **KY-100** soft key - Press.

2. On the KY-100 control screen, **PT/CT** soft key - Press, until either secure (**CT**) or clear voice (**PT**) appears in reverse video.

3.10.3.2 Zeroize All Keys.

1. On the KY-100 control screen, **ZERO ALL** soft key - Press. **ZEROED** will appear in the annunciator box, and a tone will be heard in the headset.

3.10.3.3 Zeroize Specific Keys.

1. On the KY-100 control screen, **OFFLINE** soft key - Press.

2. **UP ARROW**, or **RIGHT ARROW** soft key - Press, until **KEY OPS** appears in the annunciator box.

3. **INIT KEY** soft key - Press. **LOAD KEY** will be displayed in annunciator box.

4. **UP ARROW**, or **RIGHT ARROW** soft key - Press, until **ZERO** appears in the annunciator box.

5. **INIT KEY** soft key - Press. **ZERO**, with a flashing number appears. The flashing number indicates the currently selected key to be zeroized.

6. **UP ARROW**, or **RIGHT ARROW** soft key - Press, until key location to zeroize is displayed.

7. **INIT KEY** soft key - Press. The entire **ZERO N** will now flash.

8. **INIT KEY** soft key - Press again. The screen will blank while zeroizing process takes place. When zeroizing is complete, a tone will be heard in the headset, the display will briefly change to **ZEROED N**, and then revert to **ZERO N**.

9. Repeat steps 6 through 8 to zero other key positions, as desired.

10. When all desired key positions are zeroized, **PT/CT** - Press.

3.11 EMERGENCY CONTROL PANEL (ECP).

The emergency control panel contains switches that control emergency functions of the AMS. It provides a means of communications in the event of avionics management system (AMS) dual control display unit (CDU) failure. The

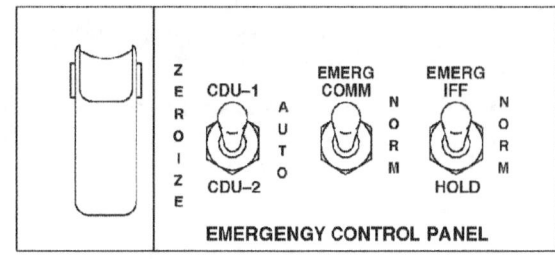

Figure 3-16. Emergency Control Panel (ECP)

zeroize switch will erase all sensitive data in the AMS, regardless of the status of the CDUs.

3.11.1 Controls and Functions. All emergency controls for the AMS are located on the control panel, mounted in the lower console (Figure 3-16). The function of each control is as follows:

CONTROL/INDICATOR	FUNCTION
ZEROIZE switch	Guarded switch. Placing in **ZEROIZE** erases all COMSEC data from the system.
CDU-1 AUTO CDU-2 switch	Designates bus controller
AUTO	Normal position. Bus controller is designated on startup automatically.
CDU-1 CDU-2	Manually designates either CDU 1 or CDU 2 as bus controller.
EMERG COMM switch	
NORM	Disables AN/ARC-222 control panel.
COMM	Activates AN/ARC-222 control panel, tunes UHF AN/ARC-164 radio to 243.0 MHz transmit and receive.
EMERG IFF switch	

CONTROL/ INDICATOR	FUNCTION
IFF	Causes the transponder to reply with code 7700 (emergency) in mode 3/A.
HOLD	Retains mode 4 code setting when power is removed from the transponder.

3.11.2 Modes of Operation.

3.11.2.1 Zeroize Mode. This mode provides centralized zeroization control for all secure information, including crypto codes, KIT-1C codes, flight plans and communications presets contained in AMS and the Data Transfer System, GPS almanac, and all information in DTS cartridge. After zeroizing, all radio settings may change and should be checked.

3.11.2.2 Emergency Comm Mode. This mode activates the AN/ARC-222 standby control panel, and tunes the AN/ARC-164 radio to 243.0 MHz. When this occurs, all radio settings in the AMS CDU may be changed and should be checked when **EMERG COMM** is placed in **NORM**.

Section III NAVIGATION

3.12 AREA NAVIGATION SYSTEM.

The area navigation system in the AMS receives inputs from navigation sensors and relates the helicopter's position to waypoints in flight plans to arrive at an output to the command instrument system and the navigation display (VSI and HSI, and the multifunction display) on the instrument panel. Area navigation maps, showing the flight plan waypoints and desired track between them, may be displayed on the MFD, while precise navigational guidance similar to VOR or ILS tracking is displayed on the VSI and HSI. Both horizontal and vertical navigation guidance is provided.

3.12.1 Flight Plans.

a. Three pilot defined flight plans are available in the AMS. Direct flight plans guide the helicopter in "direct to" flights, from any present position to a distant waypoint. Two other flight plans, labeled 1 and 2 are available.

b. Flight plans are an ordered series of waypoints. Each flight plan may contain up to 98 waypoints, which may be in any reference number sequence. Waypoints may also be repeated in a flight plan. Flight plan control screens are used to access, review and modify flight plans and waypoints.

3.12.1.1 Activating, Or Reactivating a Flight Plan. When the **ENGAGE** soft key is pressed on a flight plan for the first time, the first waypoint listed is made the TO waypoint, and the helicopter's present position becomes a phantom FROM waypoint. If the flight plan is partly navigated, and then left, it is suspended with the current TO waypoint remembered as the resume point. When the flight plan is re engaged it will navigate to the remembered TO waypoint. The helicopter's present position again becomes a phantom FROM waypoint, creating a leg that goes to the resume point of the flight plan.

3.12.1.2 Leg Sequencing. Leg sequencing in a flight plan may be automatic or manual. When manual sequencing is selected, arrival at the TO waypoint causes the header to display **WPT** on the status line and will flash the **WPT** or **MOB** label on the navigation header. The pilot must then press **NXT** key to sequence to the next leg. When automatic sequencing is selected, the **WPT** warning will flash for only a second prior to sequencing to the next leg. In the automatic mode, the exact time of leg sequencing changes with the selection of leg switching. When **EARLY** is selected, the helicopter will be guided to start the turn prior to the waypoint. For legs with course changes less than 120°, a standard rate turn will result in a roll out on the outbound course. When course changes direction greater than 120°, the turn will result in a teardrop pattern.

3.12.1.3 Flight Plan Sequencing. Flight plan legs may be advanced, re flown or skipped at the pilot's discretion. The **RVRS** soft key causes the flight plan sequence to reverse course, flying the helicopter back along the same route that it came. When this soft key is pressed, the displayed list is also changed to reflect the new routing. The **GO TO** function will give direction from the helicopter's present position to the designated TO waypoint, and continue sequencing from there through the balance of the flight plan. This allows the pilot to enter the flight plan from any position to any waypoint in the sequence.

3.12.1.4 Flight Plan Control Screens. The main control screen is **FPLN - N** (N is either 1 or 2), accessed by the **FPN** fixed function key (Figure 3-17). Soft key controls and their functions are as follows:

CONTROL/ INDICATOR	FUNCTION
▶AUTO/MAN	Toggles between automatic and manual leg changes.
WPT CAPTURE ▶EARLY/OVER	Toggles between turn anticipation and waypoint overfly turn command.
◀DIRECT	Accesses **PPOS-DIRECT** screen.
◀FPLN 1	Access **FPLN-1** screen.
◀FPLN 2	Access **FPLN-2** screen.
◀STOP	Deactivates the active flight plan, and ends steering commands.
◀SEQ-NXT	Manually advances flight plan to the next from-to pair, and changes leg change sequencing to **MANUAL**.
SEARCH CREEPLINE▶	Accesses **CREEPLINE** search pattern screen.
EXP-SQR▶	Accesses **EXPAND SQR** search pattern screen.

Change 3   3-45

TM 1-1520-253-10

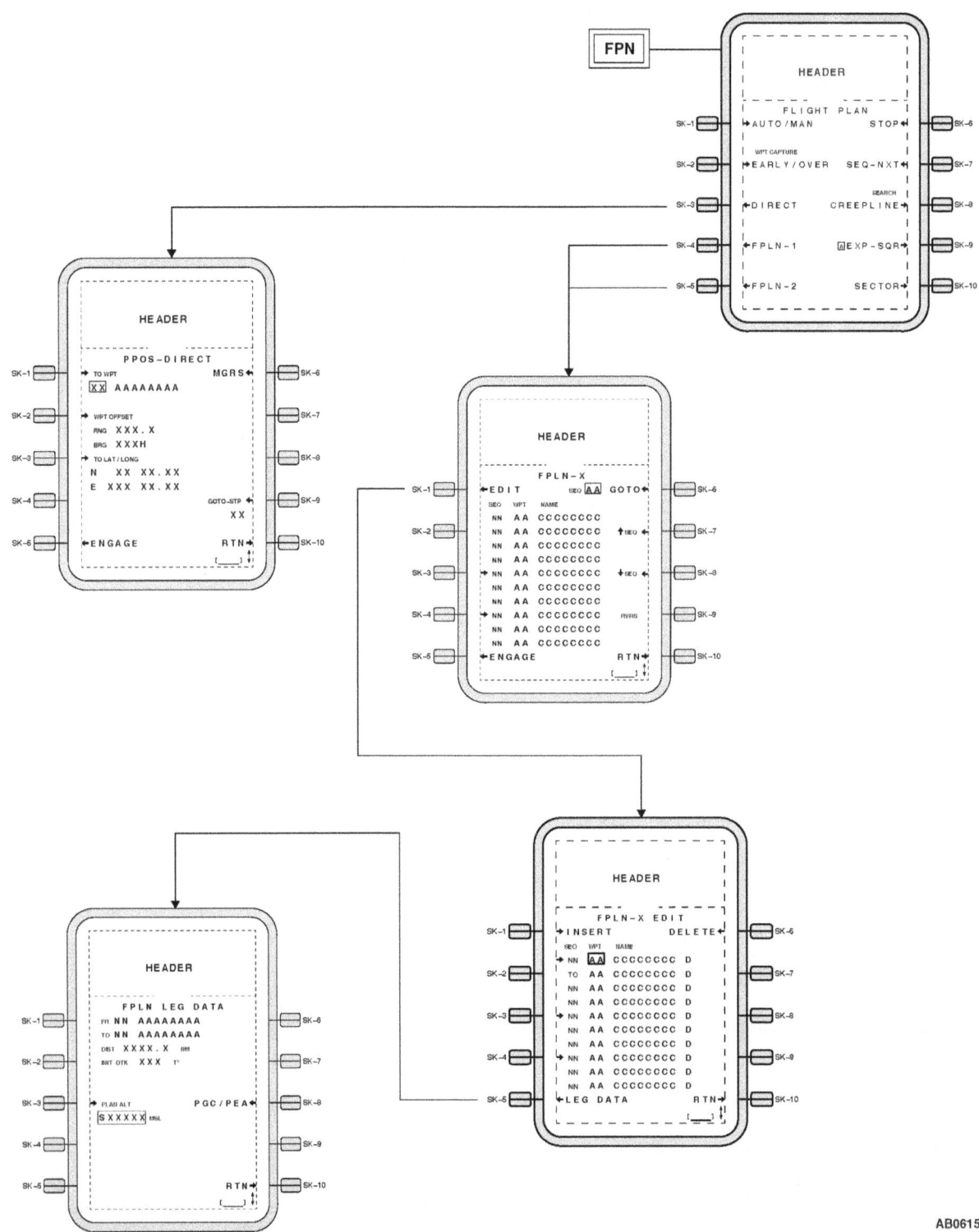

Figure 3-17. Flight Plan Control Screens

3-46

CONTROL/ INDICATOR	FUNCTION
SECTOR▶	Accesses **SECTOR** search pattern screen.

3.12.1.5 Present Position Direct Screen. Direct to flight planning is used to establish a track from the helicopter's present position to a selected waypoint. Use the screen to select the waypoint, and activate the flight plan.

CONTROL/ INDICATOR	FUNCTION
PPOS-DIRECT	Title of screen.
▶TO WPT	Enter or edit the direct - to waypoint by number or name.
▶WPT OFFSET	Selects offset range and bearing for entry and edit.
▶TO LAT/ LONG	Displays coordinates of TO destination.
◀ENGAGE	Activates Direct - To steering. When pressed, AMS marks the current position as the FROM waypoint and provides steering to fly to the TO destination. Repeated pressing of soft key re-marks and restarts the steering mode.
MGRS◀	Toggles between LAT/LONG and MGRS coordinates.
GOTO-STP◀	Makes the storepoint indicated below the TO waypoint.

3.12.1.6 FPLN - X Screen. FPLN - 1 or FPLN -2 screens review and modify the status of the flight plan.

CONTROL/ INDICATOR	FUNCTION
FPLN -N	Title of screen.
◀EDIT	Access **FPLN - N EDIT** screen.
FR TO	Selects offset range and bearing for entry and edit.
SK-3▶	Places adjacent waypoint number, then toggles the next two waypoint numbers in the **GOTO** field for selection.

CONTROL/ INDICATOR	FUNCTION
SK-4▶	Places adjacent waypoint number, then toggles the next two waypoint numbers in the GOTO field for selection.
◀ENGAGE	Activates flight plan. When first pressed, or resumed, waypoint **0 - P-POS** will be the FROM waypoint, and the first waypoint, or the last saved TO waypoint (if resumed) will be the TO waypoint.
GOTO◀	Skips directly to the specified sequence number in the flight plan list. The display list will shift to show the displayed number as the TO waypoint. The flight plan manager will fly a direct - to leg from the current position to that point, then resume normal sequencing.
←SEQ	Refly the previous leg. Entire waypoint list is shifted. This key is inactive when the flight plan is first activated, and the FROM waypoint is the marked present position.
→SEQ	Shifts flight plan forward one leg. Entire waypoint list is shifted. This key is inactive when the flight plan TO waypoint is the last waypoint in the flight plan.
RVRS◀	Reverse flight plan in AMS. Key is disabled on first leg of flight plan. Continued pressing will continue to reverse sequence.
RTN▶	Displays the previous screen with no change in status.

3.12.1.7 Edit FPLN - X Screen.

NOTE

Changes made on one CDU will not be seen on the other CDU until that CDU leaves **FLIGHT PLAN** screens, and returns.

Modify flight plans with this screen by inserting and deleting waypoints. AMS will compute leg data automatically.

TM 1-1520-253-10

CONTROL/ INDICATOR	FUNCTION
FPLN-X EDIT	Title of screen.
♦INSERT	When pressed, **INSERT** changes to reverse video. Enter the name or number of a waypoint to be inserted in the flight plan.
SK-2♦	Places edit selection on any one of the first four waypoint numbers on the screen.
SK-3♦	Places edit selection on the adjacent waypoint number, then the next two waypoint numbers on the screen.
SK-4♦	Places edit selection on the adjacent waypoint number, then the next two waypoint numbers on the screen.
♦LEG DATA	Access **LEG DATA** screen.
♦ENGAGE	Activates flight plan. When first pressed, or resumed, waypoint 0 P-POS will be the FROM waypoint, and the first waypoint, or the last saved TO waypoint (if resumed) will be the TO waypoint.
DELETE♦	Deletes the selected waypoint, moves the balance up one position.
♦SK-7	Places edit selection on any one of the first four waypoint names on the screen.
♦SK-8	Places edit selection on the adjacent waypoint name, then the next two waypoint names on the screen.
♦SK-9	Places edit selection on the adjacent waypoint name, then the next two waypoint names on the screen.
RTN♦	Displays the previous screen.

3.12.1.8 Flight Plan Leg Data Screen. The CDU performs a navigational calculation between the FROM and TO waypoints, computing a great circle distance, and desired track (DTK) for the leg. If the TO waypoint is the first in the flight plan, or a resumed flight plan, or a direct-to waypoint, the START waypoint will be used as the FROM

CONTROL/ INDICATOR	FUNCTION
FPLN LEG DATA	Title of screen.
FR TO	Displays number and name of the FROM and TO waypoints.
♦PLAN ALT	Enter planned altitude (-2000 to 29999 Ft)
♦PGC/PEA	Toggles between planned ground clearance and planned enroute altitude. Toggles planned altitude display between **MSL** and **AGL**.
RTN♦	Displays the previous screen.

3.12.2 Search Patterns. Predefined search patterns (Figure 3-18) are available for use in a flight plan, or on their own. These search patterns are creeping line, expanding square and sector search. A diagram of each appears on the CDU setup screen in order to illustrate the pilot entered values. All search patterns share a common trigger waypoint, so changing the waypoint on one search pattern page will change the display for all three. The last displayed search pattern will be considered the selected one, and will be armed if the trigger point is either the TO waypoint or is contained within the next eight waypoints of the flight plan. When the trigger point becomes the TO waypoint of a flight plan, the flight plan will be suspended, and the search pattern will be automatically engaged. Steering will continue direct to the trigger point and then through the pattern. Pattern setup screens are as follows:

3.12.2.1 Creepline Search Pattern. The suggested distance on this pattern generated from the FIND screen is limited to the along track (D-2). **DIR** sets the direction the pattern will expand towards. The controls and functions of the expanding square search pattern are as follows:

CONTROL/ INDICATOR	FUNCTION
CREEPLINE	Title of screen.
♦START AT	Selects trigger waypoint number and name for edit.
♦DIR	Enter direction of first leg.

3-48   Change 3

CONTROL/ INDICATOR	FUNCTION
▶**ORIENT**	Toggles direction of first turn between **LFT** and **RGT**.

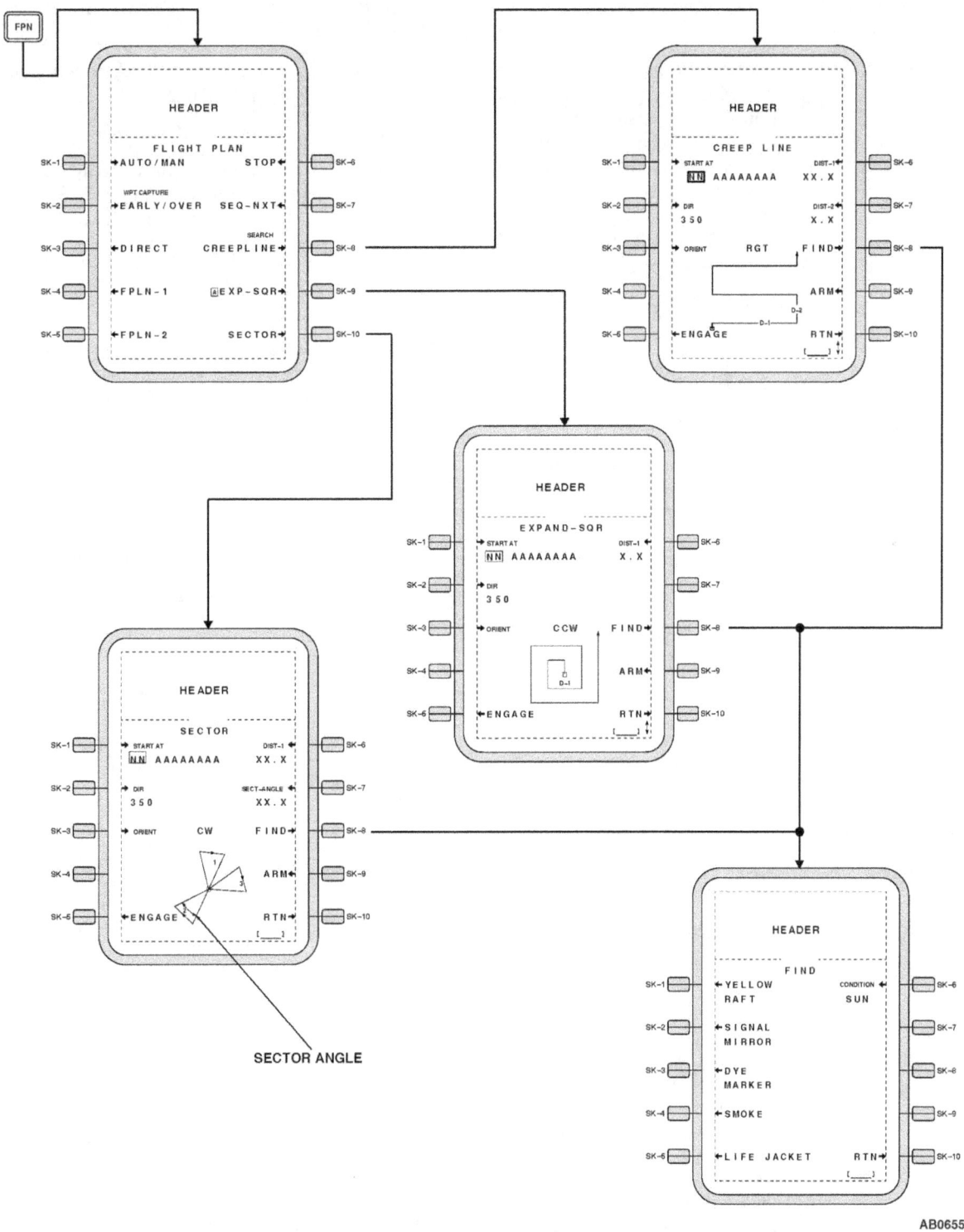

Figure 3-18. Search Pattern Control Screens.

CONTROL/INDICATOR	FUNCTION
◀ENGAGE	Activates the pattern immediately. If a trigger waypoint is specified, helicopter will fly a "direct-to" leg to the waypoint, and start the pattern. If 0 is entered as trigger waypoint, the pattern will start immediately. When pattern is active, **ENGAGE** is displayed in reverse video.
DIST-1◀	Enter cross track (**D-1**) distance in NM of pattern.
DIST-2◀	Enter along track (**D-2**) distance in NM of pattern.
FIND▶	Access **FIND** screen.
ARM▶	Arms pattern, for activation when trigger waypoint becomes the TO waypoint in an active flight pattern.
RTN▶	Return to previous displayed screen.

3.12.2.2 Expanding Square Search Pattern. The controls and functions of the expanding square search pattern are as follows:

CONTROL/INDICATOR	FUNCTION
EXPAND-SQR	Title of screen.
▶START AT	Selects trigger waypoint number and name for edit.
▶DIR	Enters direction of first leg.
▶ORIENT	Toggles direction of turn to give a clockwise or counter clockwise (**CW** or **CCW**) pattern orientation.
◀ENGAGE	Activates the pattern immediately. If a trigger waypoint is specified, helicopter will fly a "direct-to" leg to the waypoint, and start the pattern. If 0 is entered as trigger waypoint, the pattern will start immediately. When pattern is active, **ENGAGE** is displayed in inverse video.

CONTROL/INDICATOR	FUNCTION
DIST-1◀	Enter inter track (**D-1**) pattern spacing in NM.
FIND▶	Access **FIND** screen.
ARM▶	Arms pattern, for activation when trigger waypoint becomes the TO waypoint in an active flight pattern.
RTN▶	Return to previous displayed screen.

3.12.2.3 Sector Search Pattern. Sector angle and pattern radius are linked, so that changing one will change the other. The controls and functions of the expanding square search pattern are as follows:

CONTROL/INDICATOR	FUNCTION
SECTOR	Title of screen.
▶START AT	Selects trigger waypoint number and name for edit.
▶DIR	Enter direction of first leg.
▶ORIENT	Toggles direction of first turn between left or right to produce a clockwise or counter clockwise (**CW** and **CCW**) pattern.
◀ENGAGE	Activates the pattern immediately. If a trigger waypoint is specified, helicopter will fly a "direct-to" leg to the waypoint, and start the pattern. If 0 is entered as trigger waypoint, the pattern will start immediately. When pattern is active, **ENGAGE** is displayed in reverse video.
DIST-1◀	Enter sector radius (**D-1**) distance of pattern in NM.
SECT-ANGLE◀	Enter sector angle of pattern.
FIND▶	Access **FIND** screen.
ARM▶	Arms pattern, for activation when trigger waypoint becomes the TO waypoint in an active flight pattern.

CONTROL/INDICATOR	FUNCTION
RTN♦	Return to previous displayed screen.

3.12.2.4 Find Screen. Use the find screen to set suggested distances in the search patterns. These distances are based on a look up table embedded in AMS software. Pressing the soft key adjacent to the search object (yellow raft, smoke, hand held star) will cause the appropriate search distances to be entered in the pattern that was displayed when the **FIND** soft key was pressed. The controls and functions of this screen are as follows:

CONTROL/INDICATOR	FUNCTION
FIND	Title of screen.
SK-1♦YELLOW RAFT	Returns to previous screen with D-1, D-2, and sector angle (as applicable) set for conditions and objects displayed.
SK-2♦SIGNAL MIRROR SMOKE 2-CELL FLASHLIGHT	Returns to previous screen with D-1, D-2, and sector angle (as applicable) set for conditions and objects displayed.
SK-3♦DYE MARKER LIFE JACKET HAND HELD STAR	Returns to previous screen with D-1, D-2, and sector angle (as applicable) set for conditions and objects displayed.
SK-4♦SMOKE (BLANK) VERY CARTRIDGE	Returns to previous screen with D-1, D-2, and sector angle (as applicable) set for conditions and objects displayed.
SK-5♦LIFE JACKET (BLANK) (BLANK)	Returns to previous screen with D-1, D-2, and sector angle (as applicable) set for conditions and objects displayed.
CONDITION♦	Toggles between **SUN**, **OVRCAST**, and **NIGHT** condition, changing selection of search objects.

CONTROL/INDICATOR	FUNCTION
RTN♦	Return to previous displayed screen.

3.12.3 Waypoints. A waypoint is a geographic location. Waypoints are stored in the AMS data base with a unique navigation reference point (NRP) number and name. Waypoints may be part of the downloaded flight data, created or modified with the CDU, or automatically generated by the flight planning program. Waypoints generated to start flight plans, or as part of a search pattern are assigned special NRPs and names by the flight planning program. A flight plan engage start position will be labeled **START**. The helicopter's position when a direct-to function is activated is marked as **MAN-LL**. Search pattern waypoints will be marked **CR-NN**, **EX-NN**, or **SS-NN**. The pattern waypoints are also numbered from 1 to 99, and will reset to 1 if the pattern is flown long enough. A waypoint that is calculated as an offset of an existing waypoint will have * in front of its name.

3.12.3.1 Create and Modify Waypoints, and Storepoints. Waypoints are loaded in both CDUs by the data transfer system. Editing the waypoints changes both CDU files and DTS files as they are edited. Storepoints are created in the CDU by overflying a known point, establishing a GPS position, or marking a TACAN bearing and distance.

3.12.3.2 Create and Modify Waypoints. Use the **MISSION DATA** waypoint screens to create or modify waypoints originally loaded in the DTS. The mission data screen is accessed by pressing the **DAT** fixed function key.

CONTROL/INDICATOR	FUNCTION
♦MISSION DATA	Title of screen.
WAYPOINTS	Access the **WAYPOINT DATA** screen.
PRESETS COMM♦	Access the **COM PRESET** screen.
ECCM-FH♦	Access the **ECCM/FH** screen.
RADIO♦NAV	Access the **RADIO NAV PRESETS** screen.

Change 3   3-51

TM 1-1520-253-10

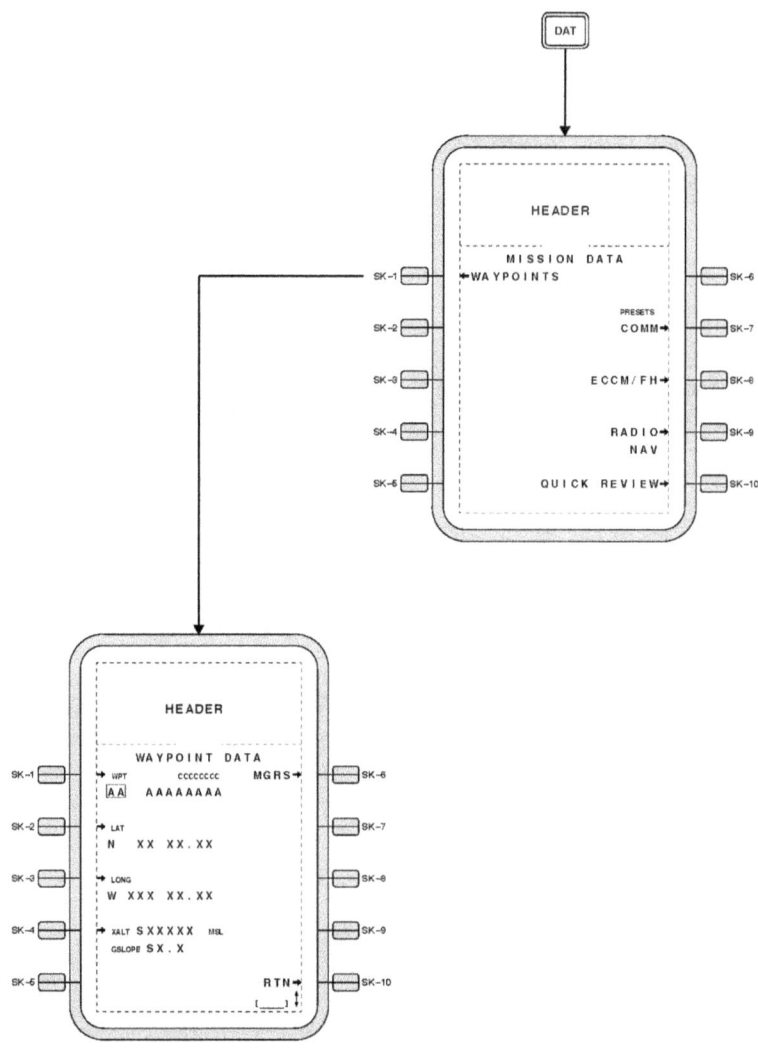

Figure 3-19. Waypoint Control Screens (Sheet 1 of 2)

3-52

TM 1-1520-253-10

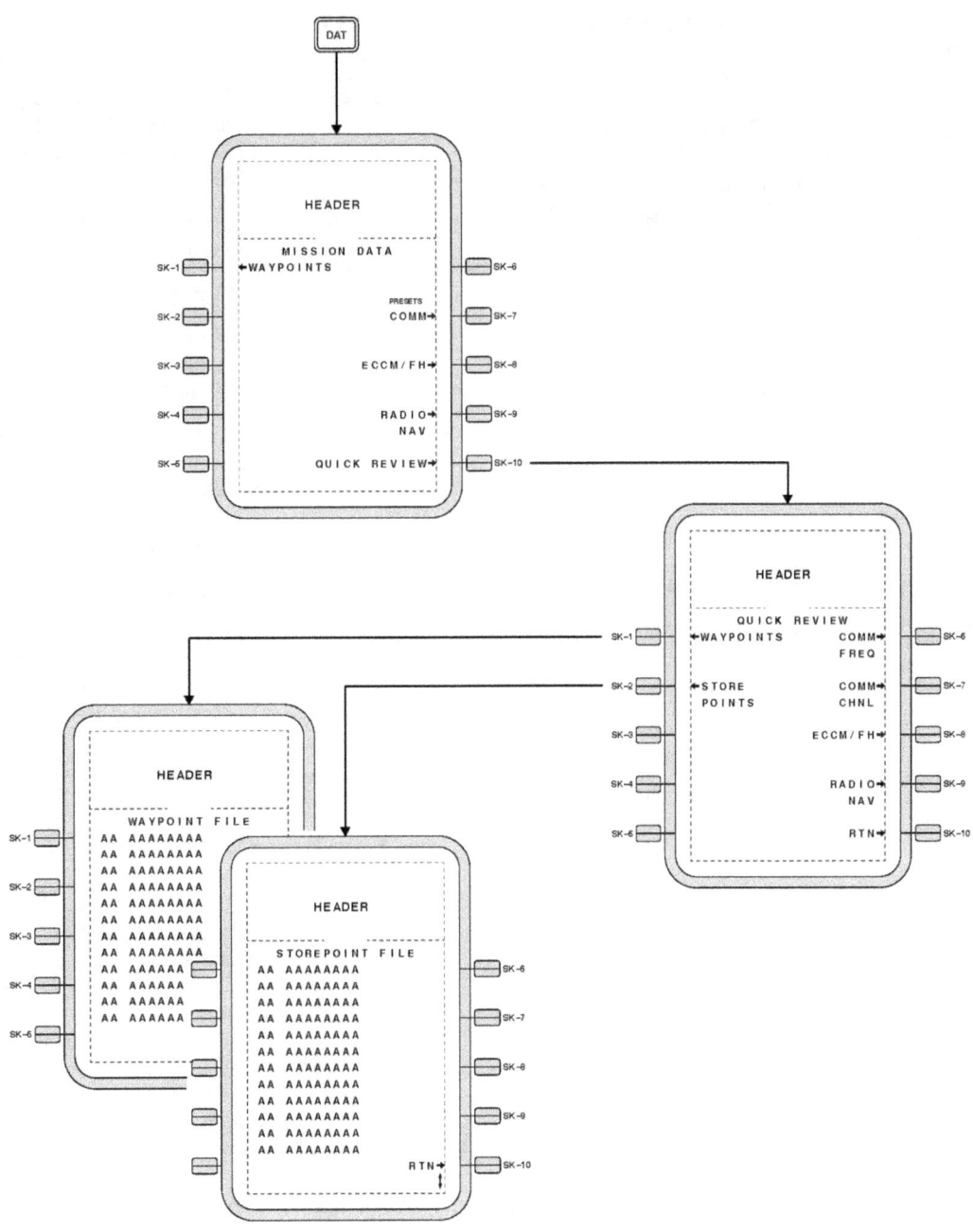

Figure 3-19. Waypoint Control Screens (Sheet 2 of 2)

3-53

CONTROL/ INDICATOR	FUNCTION
QUICK REVIEW♦	Access the **QUICK REVIEW** screen.

3.12.3.3 Waypoint Data Screen. The waypoint entry screen allows the pilot to edit, or define a waypoint. A waypoint is marked as used in the mission data base whenever there is any data in either the latitude or longitude or the waypoint name.

CONTROL/ INDICATOR	FUNCTION
WAYPOINT DATA	Title of screen.
♦WPT	Enter or edit waypoint number or name.
♦LAT	Enter or edit latitude coordinate.
♦LONG	Enter or edit longitude coordinate.
♦XALT	Toggles edit box between **XALT** and **GSLOPE**.
GSLOPE	With edit box around glideslope area, enter estimated glideslope angle (-9° to 9°), and press **ENT**.
MGRS♦	Toggles display between MGRS and LAT/LONG coordinate systems.
Deleted	
Deleted	

3.12.4 Create Storepoints. Storepoints are targets of opportunity, created "on the fly" which may be used later for navigation. Storepoints may be created by overflying a location and pressing **MARK**. As many as 25 storepoints may be created, and will be designated as A through Z less O.

3.12.4.1 Flyover Store Screen. Access this screen by pressing **FIX**, then **FLYOVER** SK-6 soft key. Functions of the soft keys are:

CONTROL/ INDICATOR	FUNCTION
FLYOVER STORE	Title of screen.
♦OFFSET	Edit box enables entry of range, and then bearing of helicopter's present position to the waypoint position.
LAT/LONG	Displays helicopter's current position.
WPT	Displays storepoint number.
AVAIL	Displays number of available unused storepoints (from 25 to 0), before overwrites must occur.
♦MARK	First press of soft key freezes position, display becomes reverse video. Second press of soft key resumes position updating and normal display.
MGRS♦	Toggles between **MGRS** and **LAT/LONG** coordinate format.
STORE♦	Stores the waypoint (either frozen, or, if free running, at the instant **STORE** soft key was pressed), and accesses **STORE-POINT DATA** screen.

3.12.5 Navigation Calculator.

NOTE

There is no connection between AMS and the helicopter's fuel measurement system. All fuel calculations are based on pilot inputs of fuel on board and estimated fuel flow. These calculations are estimates, and advisory only. They do not replace the primary fuel quantity system for fuel load and range planning.

AMS provides a navigational calculator to perform calculations based on the active flight plan and current conditions of groundspeed, position and time. It displays estimated time of arrival, estimated time enroute, range and fuel calculations. The CDU accesses the active flight plan for data used for the navigation calculator functions of estimated time of arrival, required groundspeed, and esti-

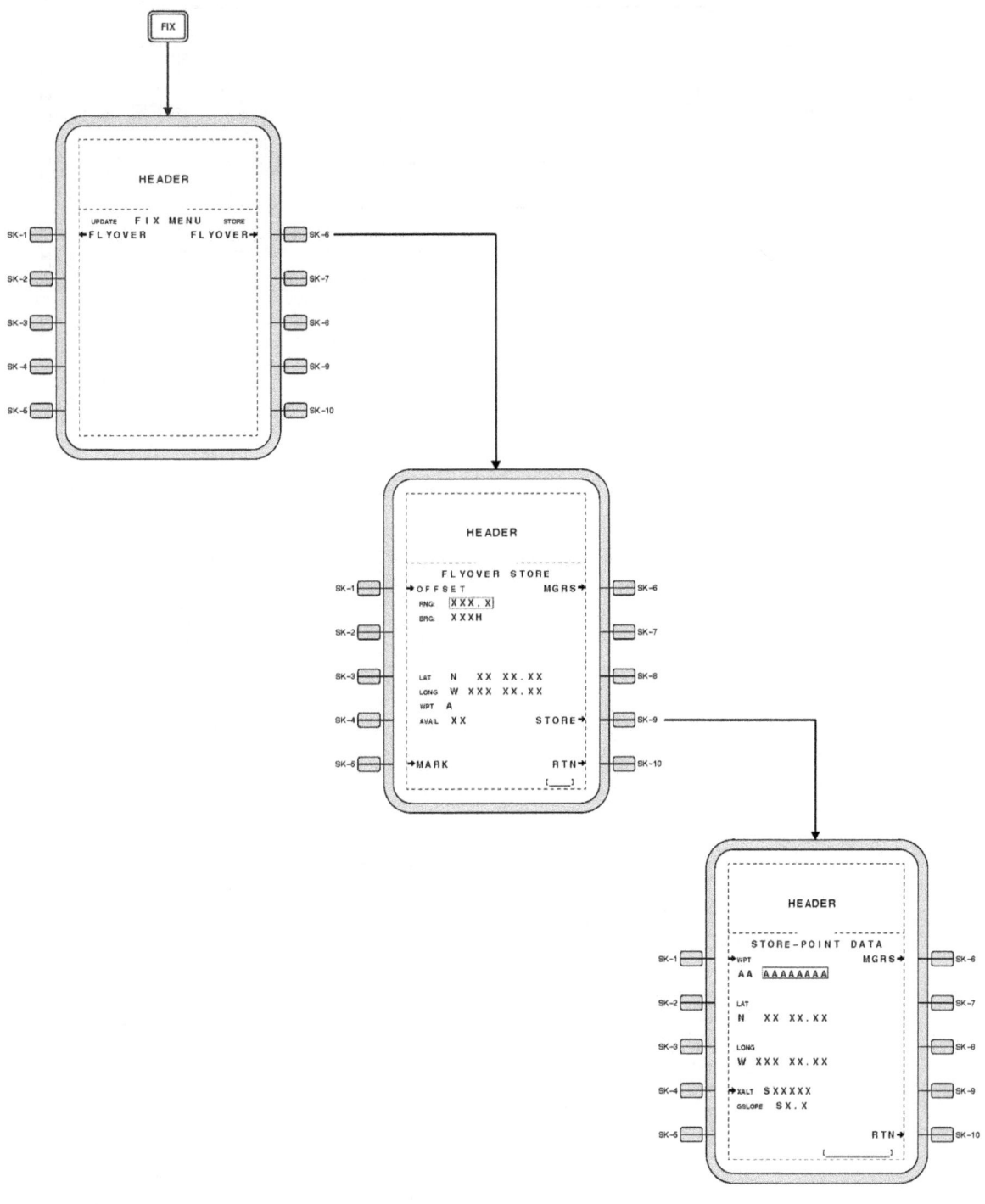

Figure 3-20. Storepoint Control Screens

TM 1-1520-253-10

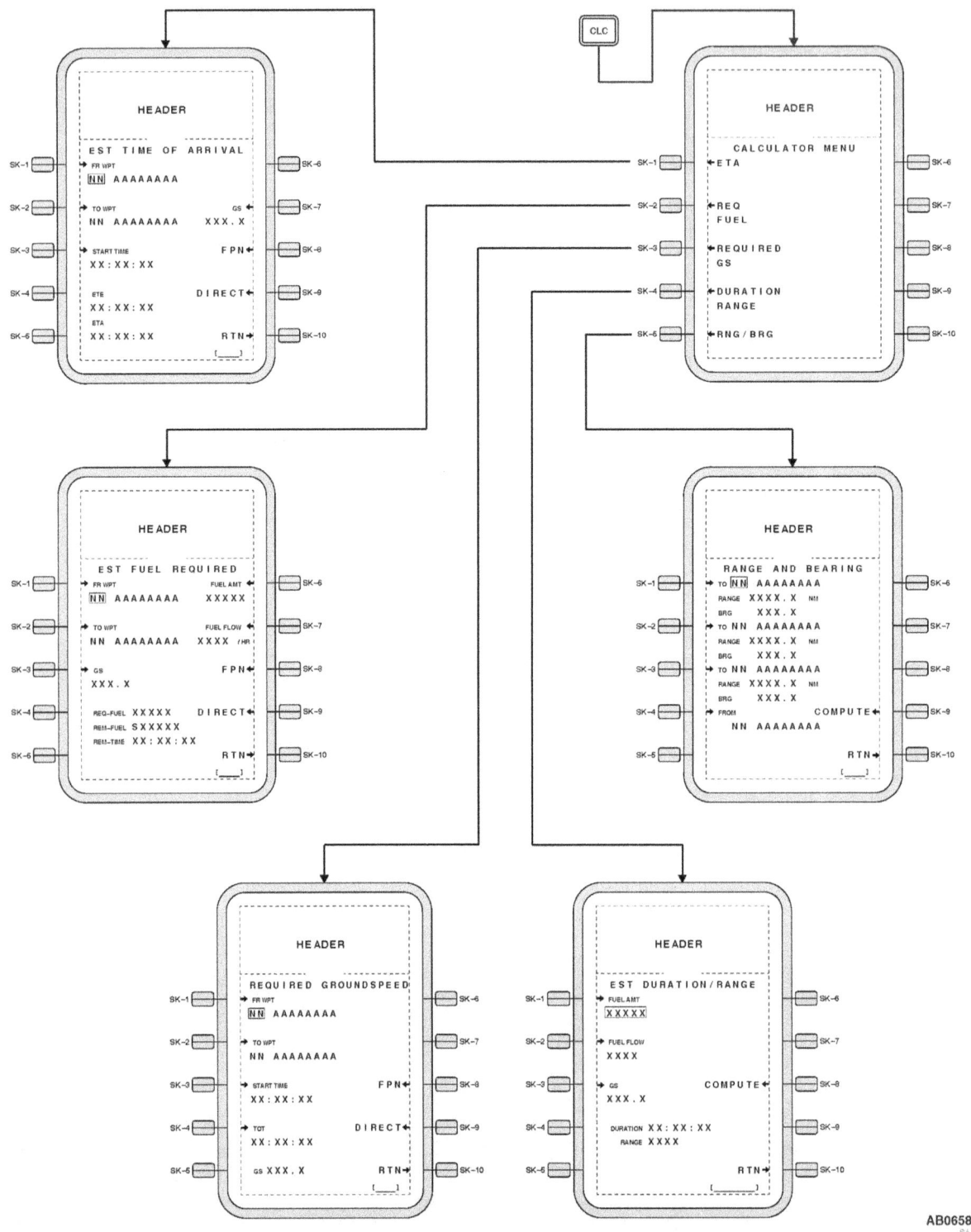

Figure 3-21. Navigation Calculator Control Screens

3-56

mated duration of flight. This data may be manually overwritten by the pilot, as desired. The navigation calculator screens are accessed through a main menu, accessed by the **CLC** fixed function key.

3.12.5.1 Calculator Menu Screen. The menu screen provides access to the display and data entry screens. It is accessed by **CLC** fixed function key. The displays and functions of active soft keys are as follows:

CONTROL/ INDICATOR	FUNCTION
♦ETA	Access **EST TIME OF ARRIVAL** screen.
♦REQ FUEL	Access **EST FUEL REQUIRED** screen.
♦REQ GS	Access **REQUIRED GROUNDSPEED** screen.
♦DURATION RANGE	Access **EST DURATION/ RANGE** screen.
♦RNG/BRG	Access **RANGE AND BEARING** screen.

3.12.5.2 Estimated Time of Arrival Screen. The CDU calculates and displays the ETA at any waypoint in the active flight plan. ETA is only displayed when all editable fields contain data, and either **FPN** or **DIRECT** soft key is pressed. The ETA calculations are preformed based on:

    a. Either current helicopter groundspeed, or a pilot entered groundspeed.

    b. Either present position and time, or a pilot entered start waypoint and expected start time.

    c. Either great circle route direct to destination, or along the active flight plan.

    d. The displays and functions of active soft keys are as follows:

CONTROL/ INDICATOR	FUNCTION
♦FR WPT	Enter FROM waypoint number and name. When soft key is pressed, present position is displayed.
♦TO WPT	Enter TO waypoint number or name.
♦START TIME	Displays system time. Press soft key to edit time to an expected start time.
ETE	Displays estimated time enroute when all edit fields contain data and **FPN** or **DIRECT** soft key is pressed.
ETA	Displays estimated time of arrival when all edit fields contain data and **FPN** or **DIRECT** soft key is pressed.
GS♦	Enter groundspeed. When soft key is pressed, current groundspeed is displayed.
FPN♦	Displays ETE and ETA based on flying the active flight plan. If either waypoint entered in **FR WPT** or **TO WPT** is not part of the flight plan, annunciation of **WPT NOT IN FPN** is displayed in scratchpad, and there will be no display in **ETE** or **ETA** fields.
DIRECT♦	Displays ETE and ETA as if flown as a direct to flight plan.
RTN♦	Returns to previously displayed screen.

3.12.5.3 Required Fuel Screen.

NOTE

There is no connection between AMS and the helicopter's fuel measurement system. All fuel calculations are based on pilot inputs of fuel on board and estimated fuel flow. These calculations are estimates, and advisory only. They do not replace the primary fuel quantity system for fuel load and range planning.

CDU calculates and displays the amount of fuel required and fuel remaining to reach any waypoint in the active flight plan. Calculations are performed using:

    a. Pilot entered fuel on board and fuel flow.

b. Either current helicopter groundspeed, or a pilot entered groundspeed.

c. Either present position and time, or a pilot entered start waypoint and expected start time.

d. Either great circle route direct to destination, or along the active flight plan.

e. The displays and functions of active soft keys are as follows:

CONTROL/ INDICATOR	FUNCTION
◆FR WPT	Enter FROM waypoint number and name. When soft key is pressed, present position is displayed.
◆TO WPT	Enter TO waypoint number or name.
GS◆	Enter groundspeed. When soft key is pressed, current groundspeed is displayed.
REQ-FUEL	Displays the calculated pounds of fuel required to fly between the FROM and TO waypoints, either by flight plan route, or direct between the two points.
REM-FUEL	Displays the difference between available and required fuel. Annotated S to indicate surplus fuel, or D to indicate insufficient fuel.
FUEL AMT	Enter initial pounds of fuel on board.
FUEL FLOW	Enter expected average fuel flow in lbs/hr.
FPN◆	Displays fuel calculations based on flying the active flight plan. If either waypoint entered in FR WPT or TO WPT is not part of the flight plan, annunciation of WPT NOT IN FPN is displayed in scratchpad, and there will be no display in REM-FUEL or REQ-FUEL fields.
DIRECT◆	Displays fuel calculation as if flown as a direct to flight plan.

CONTROL/ INDICATOR	FUNCTION
RTN◆	Returns to previously displayed screen.

3.12.5.4 Required Groundspeed Screen. This screen permits the pilot to determine the required groundspeed to achieve a desired time over target. The calculation is based on either a direct-to operation, or flying along the active flight plan. These calculations are performed using:

a. Pilot entered desired arrival time at the waypoint.

b. Either present position and time, or a pilot entered start waypoint and expected start time.

c. Either great circle route direct to destination, or along the active flight plan.

d. The displays and functions of active soft keys are as follows:

CONTROL/ INDICATOR	FUNCTION
◆FR WPT	Enter FROM waypoint number and name. When soft key is pressed, present position is displayed.
◆TO WPT	Enter TO waypoint number or name.
◆START TIME	Displays system time. Press soft key to edit time to an expected start time.
◆TOT	Used to enter the required time over target at the TO waypoint.
GS	Displays calculated groundspeed in knots when either FPN or DIRECT soft key is pressed.
FPN◆	Displays groundspeed based on flying the active flight plan. If either waypoint entered in FR WPT or TO WPT is not part of the flight plan, annunciation of WPT NOT IN FPN is displayed in scratchpad, and there will be no display in GS field.
DIRECT◆	Displays groundspeed as if flown as a direct to flight plan.

3-58   Change 3

CONTROL/ INDICATOR	FUNCTION
RTN◆	Returns to previously displayed screen.

3.12.5.5 Estimated Duration and Range Screen. This screen permits the pilot to estimate the duration and range available with a given amount of fuel. These calculations are performed after all editable fields have data in them, and **DIRECT** soft key is pressed. Editable soft fields contain:

a. The amount of fuel available and expected fuel flow, both entered by the pilot.

b. Either the current, or pilot entered groundspeed.

c. The displays and functions of active soft keys are as follows:

CONTROL/ INDICATOR	FUNCTION
◆FUEL AMT	Selects and displays pounds of fuel available, as previously calculated.
◆FUEL FLOW	Selects and displays fuel flow, as previously entered.
◆GS	Enter groundspeed for the duration calculation. Upon entry, the **FUEL AMT**, **FUEL FLOW**, and **GS** values set are the last entered values on any calculator screen.
DURATION	Displays the calculated flight time remaining based on available fuel.
RANGE	Displays the calculated range in nautical miles remaining based on groundspeed.
COMPUTE◆	Calculates duration and range, and displays results.
RTN◆	Returns to previously displayed screen.

3.12.5.6 Range and Bearing Screen. This screen calculates the range and bearing between a common waypoint and any three waypoints in the waypoint list when the **COMPUTE** soft key is pressed. Range and bearing to all TO waypoints is calculated using a great circle direct-to path between the FROM and each of the TO waypoints. The displays and functions of active soft keys are as follows:

CONTROL/ INDICATOR	FUNCTION
◆TO	Enter TO waypoint number or name.
RANGE	Displays great circle distance in nautical miles between the TO and FROM waypoints.
BRG	Displays magnetic bearing between the two waypoints measured from the FROM waypoint.
◆FR WPT	Enter FROM waypoint number and name. When soft key is pressed, present position is displayed.
COMPUTE◆	Commands CDU to compute the range and bearing between entered TO and FROM waypoints.
RTN◆	Returns to previously displayed screen.

3.12.6 Operation.

3.12.6.1 Navigate Flight Plan.

1. Access **FPLN 1**, or **FPLN 2** control screen. **ENGAGE** soft key - Press to activate the flight plan.

2. **BRG 1 DIST** switch - **DOPPLER/GPS**.

3. **MODE SEL DOP GPS** switch - **DOP GPS**.

4. **CIS MODE SEL NAV/ON** switch - As desired.

3.12.6.2 Direct To Operation.

1. Access **PPOS - DIRECT** control screen. Enter waypoint number, as desired. **ENGAGE** soft key - Press to activate the flight plan.

2. **BRG 1 DIST** switch - **DOPPLER/GPS**.

3. **MODE SEL DOP GPS** switch - **DOP GPS**.

3.12.6.3 Search Pattern Operation.

1. Access **CREEPLINE, EXPAND - SQR**, or **SECTOR** control screen. Enter waypoint number, as desired. **ARM** soft key - Press to activate the search pattern if there is an active flight plan that has the **START AT** waypoint in it, otherwise **ENGAGE** soft key - Press.

2. **BRG 1 DIST** switch - **DOPPLER/GPS**.

3. **MODE SEL DOP GPS** switch - **DOP GPS**.

3.13 DOPPLER/GPS NAVIGATION SET (DGNS) AN/ASN-128B.

The AN/ASN-128B DGNS is a Doppler navigation sensor, with an embedded GPS receiver. The AN/ASN-128B in conjunction with the aircraft's heading, vertical references, and position and velocity updates from its internal GPS, provides the Avionics Management system accurate aircraft position information from ground level to 10,000 feet. The sensor operates either as blended Doppler-GPS, or Doppler or GPS alone.

3.13.1 Antenna. The GPS antenna is located on the top aft section of the helicopter, and the Doppler antenna is on the underside of the cabin section (Figure 3-1).

3.13.2 Controls, Displays, and Function. The control and displays for the AN/ASN-128B are limited to selecting which position outputs are used for the area navigation and steering calculations performed within AMS, and position updating the Doppler sensor, when it is operating in the Doppler only mode.

3.13.2.1 Sensor Select Control Screen. The **NAV SELECT** control screen has the sensor select function. It is accessed by the **NAV** fixed function key (Figure 3-22):

CONTROL/ INDICATOR	FUNCTION
NAV SELECT	Title of screen.
RAIM	Gives GPS RAIM status: **P** = Pass. **F** = Fail. **P-B** = Pass with Baro. **F-B** = Fail with Baro. **NGP** = No GPS. **NA** = RAIM not available.
DOP	Gives Doppler status: **NAV** = Nav mode. **MEM** = In memory mode. **TST** = In test mode. **F** = Doppler inoperative.
DO-GPS◆	Provides blended GPS/Doppler position to navigation computer.
GPS◆	Provides GPS only position to navigation computer.
DOP◆	Provides Doppler only position to navigation computer.
VERT-NAV◆	Not available.

3.13.2.2 Present Position Update. Use present position update to correct for position error which builds up in the Doppler sensor when GPS coverage is not available. Updates may be accomplished by overflying a known position, fixing to GPS as a one time fix, or fixing to a TACAN position, after slant range is corrected using either radar or set point altitude. The screens used to accomplish a present position are accessed by the **FIX** fixed function key, and are described below (Figure 3-22). Doppler updates are done in two steps. The first step, performed by pressing the **MARK** soft key, tells the Doppler to prepare for the landmark update. Upon receipt of this message, the Doppler marks its internal position. The second step, performed by pressing the **ACC** soft key on the **DELTAS** screen, tells the Doppler the correct position at the time when the first message was sent. Doppler then calculates the difference between the correct position and its marked position, and then applies that correction to the Doppler current position.

3.13.2.2.1 Fix Menu Screen.

CONTROL/ INDICATOR	FUNCTION
FIX MENU	Title of screen.
UPDATE ◆FLYOVER	Access **FLYOVER UPDATE** screen.
STORE FLYOVER◆	Access **FLYOVER STORE** screen.

TM 1-1520-253-10

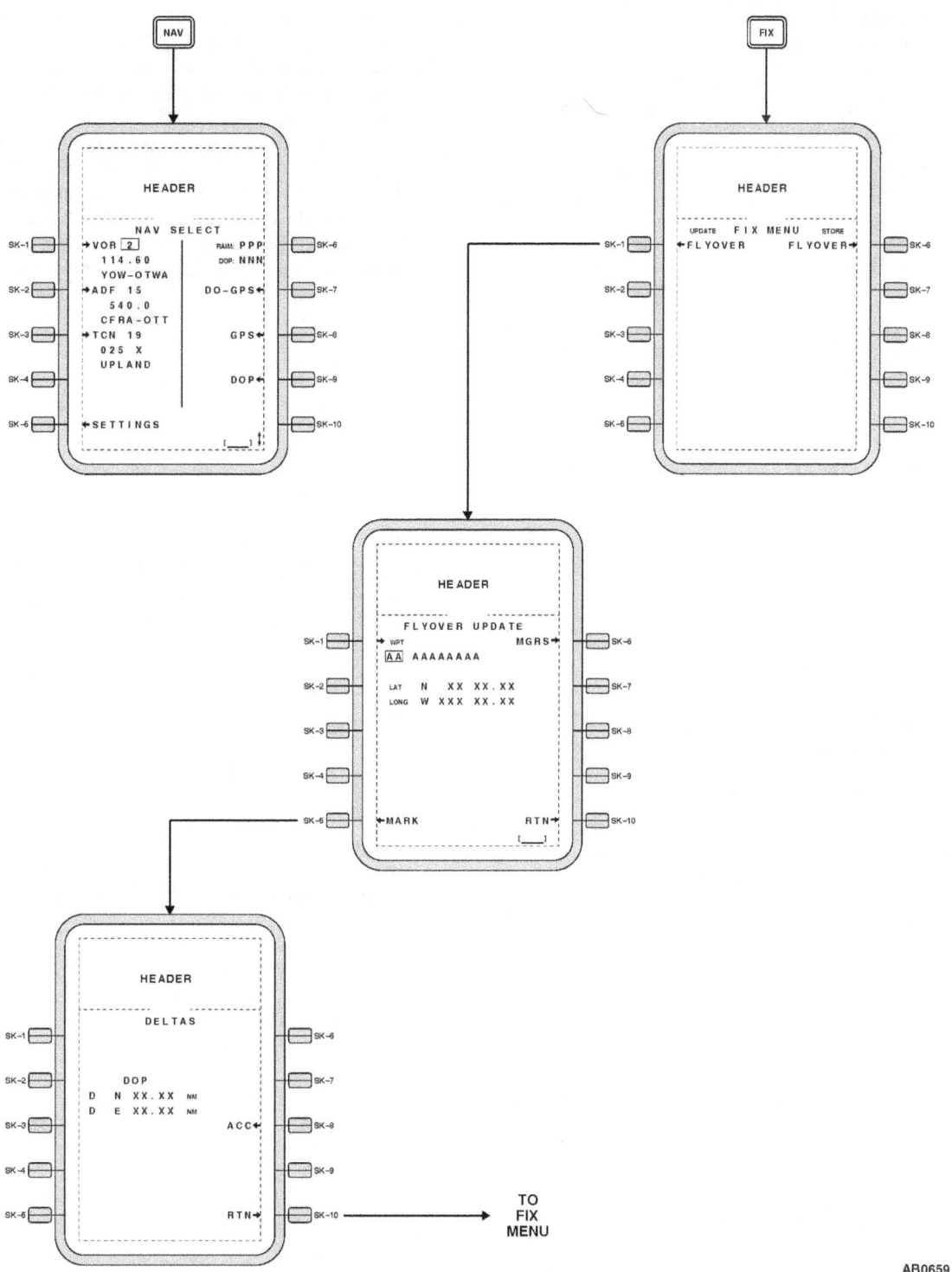

Figure 3-22. AN/ASN-128B DGNS Control Screens

3-61

3.13.2.2.2 Flyover Update Screen. Use this screen to designate a known position as a update waypoint, as the helicopter flies directly overhead.

CONTROL/ INDICATOR	FUNCTION
WPT	Used to enter the waypoint number. The name will be displayed automatically.
LAT/LONG	Displays coordinate of selected waypoint.
MARK	Initiates update, causes position to be transferred to **DELTAS** screen, where difference between the Flyover position and Doppler position is displayed.
MGRS	Toggles between **MGRS** and **LAT/LONG** coordinate format.
RTN	Access previously displayed screen.

3.13.2.2.3 DELTAS Screen. Use this screen to monitor and complete the Doppler update.

CONTROL/ INDICATOR	FUNCTION
DELTAS	Title of screen.
DOPP	Marks position differences between the **MARK** input and Doppler position in nautical miles.
ACC◆	Updates the Doppler's position.
RTN◆	Access **FIX MENU** screen.

3.14 RADIO RECEIVING SET AN/ARN-147(V)(VOR/ILS/MB).

Radio set AN/ARN-147(V) (Figure 3-23) is a very high frequency receiver, capable of operating from 108.0 to 126.95 MHz. Course information is presented by the vertical situation indicator deviation pointer and the selectable No. 2 bearing pointer on the horizontal situation indicator. The combination of the glide slope and localizer capabilities makes up the instrument landing system (ILS). The marker beacon portion of the receiver visually indicates on the vertical situation indicator **MB** advisory light, and aurally signals over the headphones helicopter passage over a transmitting marker beacon. The radio set may be used as a VHF omnirange (VOR) or ILS receiver. The desired type of operation is selected by tuning the receiving set to the frequency corresponding to that operation. ILS operation is selected by tuning to the odd tenth MHz frequencies from 108.0 to 111.95 MHz. VOR operation is selected by tuning from 108.0 to 126.95 MHz, except the odd tenth MHz from 108.0 to 111.95 MHz reserved for ILS operation. The three receiver sections do the intended functions independent of each other. Performance degradation within any one of the major sections will not affect performance of the others. Power for the AN/ARN-147 is provided from the dc essential bus through a circuit breaker, labeled **VOR/ILS**.

NOTE

Tuning to a localizer frequency will automatically tune to a glide slope frequency when available.

3.14.1 Antennas. The VOR/LOC antenna system (Figure 3-1) consists of two blade type collector elements, one on each side of the fuselage tail cone. The glide slope antenna is mounted under the avionics compartment in the nose. The antenna provides the glide slope receiver with a matched forward looking receiving antenna. The marker beacon antenna is flush-mounted under the center section of the fuselage.

3.14.2 Controls and Functions. The VOR/ILS/MB receiver is controlled by Avionics Management System (AMS). Operator functions are to choose frequency and sensitivity of marker beacon reception. A complete list of presets is displayed on **RADIO NAV REVIEW** screen, accessed through the **QUICK REVIEW** soft key on the **MISSION DATA** screen (Figure 3-23)

3.14.2.1 NAV SELECT Screen. The primary control screen is **NAV SELECT**, accessed by pressing **NAV** fixed function key (Figure 3-23). Displays on the screen and active soft keys for VOR/ILS/MB are as follows:

CONTROL	FUNCTION
NAV SELECT screen	
◆VOR soft key	Toggles between VOR preset channel and frequency for edit.

TM 1-1520-253-10

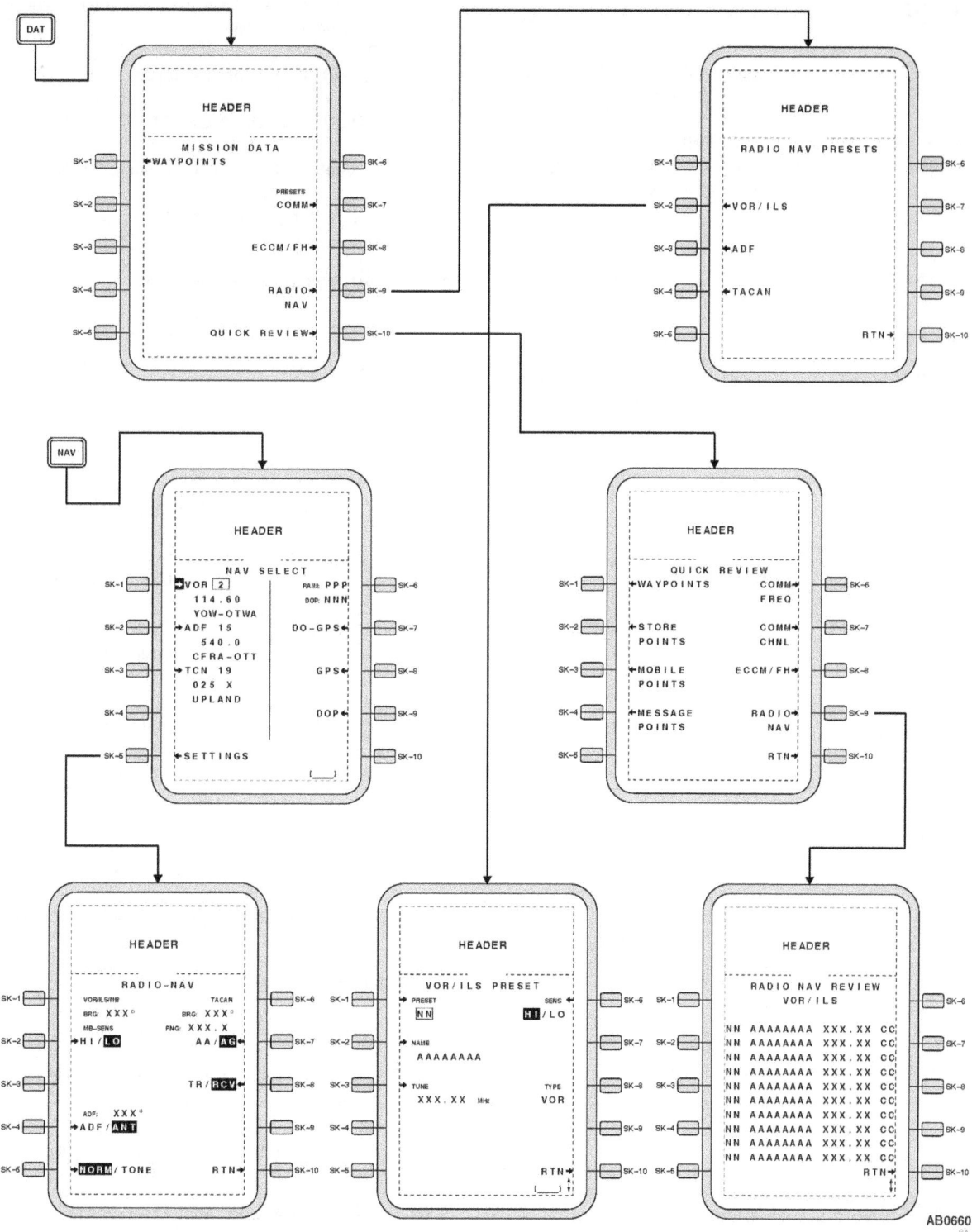

Figure 3-23. VOR/ILS/MB Control Screens AN/ARN-147(V)

3-63

CONTROL	FUNCTION
♦SETTINGS	Accesses **RADIO - NAV** screen.

3.14.2.2 RADIO - NAV Screen. The RADIO - NAV screen is accessed by SETTINGS soft key on the NAV SELECT screen. Current settings of the AN/ARN-147 are displayed as follows:

CONTROL	FUNCTION
RADIO - NAV	Title of screen.
VOR/ILS/MB	Display **O**, **I**, or **M** if Outer, Inner, or Middle marker is detected.
BRG	Displays bearing set on HSI.
♦MB - SENS	Toggles between **HI** and **LO** sensitivity. Selected sensitivity is displayed in inverse video.

3.14.2.3 VOR/ILS Preset Screen. See Figure 3-23 to access the VOR/ILS preset screen. Use this screen to edit or establish a preset. Displays on the screen and active soft keys are as follows:

CONTROL	FUNCTION
VOR/ILS PRESET	Title of screen.
♦PRESET	Edit the preset number.
♦NAME	Edit the preset name.
♦TUNE	Edit the preset frequency.
SENS♦ HI/LO	Toggles marker beacon receiver between high and low sensitiviy.
TYPE VOR	Displays frequency as VOR or ILS.
RTN♦	Access previously displayed screen.

3.14.3 Operation.

3.14.3.1 Normal Operation.

1. On **CSC** panel, **NAV A** monitor control - Press on, and adjust as desired.

2. On **NAV SELECT** control screen, frequency or preset - Select.

3. **NAV VOL** control - Adjust.

4. **VTAC** switch - **VOR/ILS**.

5. **MODE SEL VOR/ILS** switch - **VOR**.

6. **CIS MODE SEL NAV/ON** switch - As desired.

3.14.3.2 VOR/Marker Beacon Test.

NOTE

Test will not be valid if signal reception is invalid.

1. HSI **CRS** control (pilot and copilot) - Set 315° in course display.

2. Access **NAV TESTS** page by pressing TST fixed function key, then **NAV** soft key. To start test, **VOR/ILS** soft keys - Press, until **TEST** under VOR/ILS is displayed in inverse video.

3. All indications next to **PRI FAULT** and **SEC FAULT** under **TEST** should read **PASS**.

4. HSI VOR/LOC course arrow and VSI course deviator pointer - Centered (±1 dot).

5. No. 2 bearing pointer - 315° (±5°).

6. To-from arrow - **TO**.

7. On **NAV TESTS** screen, **RTN** soft key - Press.

3.14.3.3 VOR Operation. HSI CRS control - Course select.

3.14.3.4 ILS (LOC/GS) Operation.

1. ILS frequency or preset - Select.

2. On **CSC** panel, **NAV A** control - Press on, and adjust volume as desired.

3. **CIS MODE SEL NAV/ON** switch - As desired.

3.14.3.5 Marker Beacon (MB) Operation.

1. On **RADIO NAV** screen, **MB SENSE** soft key - Press, until **HI/LO** is as desired.

2. On **CSC** panel, **NAV A** control - Press on, and adjust volume as desired.

3.14.3.6 VOR Communications Receiving Operation.

1. Frequency or preset - Select.

2. On **CSC** panel, **NAV A** control - Press on, and adjust volume as desired.

3.15 DIRECTION FINDER SET AN/ARN -149 (LF/ADF).

The AN/ARN -149 (Figure 3-24) is a low frequency (LF), automatic direction finder (ADF) radio, providing compass bearing capability within the frequency range of 100 to 2199.5 kHz. The **ADF** has two functional modes of operation: **ANT** and **ADF**. The antenna (ANT) mode functions as an aural receiver, providing only an aural output of the received signal. The ADF mode functions as an automatic direction finder, providing a relative bearing-to-station signal to the horizontal situation indicator No. 2 bearing pointer and an aural output. A **TONE** submode of operation can be selected in either **ANT** or **ADF** mode, providing a 1000-Hz aural output to identify keyed unmodulated carrier wave (CW) signals. Power is provided to the LF/ADF system by the No. 1 dc primary bus through a circuit breaker labeled **ADF** and the ac essential bus through a circuit breaker, labeled **26 VAC INST**.

3.15.1 Antennas. The antenna system is a single combination antenna containing both loop and sense elements. The RF signal from one loop element is modulated with a reference sine signal while the other loop element is modulated with a reference cosine signal. The two modulated signals are combined, phase shifted 90°, and amplified. The resulting loop signal is summed with the sense antenna signal and sent to the ADF radio for visual and aural execution. The antenna configuration is flush mounted under the bottom cabin fuselage (Figure 3-1).

3.15.2 Controls and Functions. The ADF is controlled by the AMS with CDU control screens (Figure 3-24). Operator functions are to choose frequency and mode of reception. A complete list of presets is displayed on **RADIO NAV REVIEW** screen, accessed through the **QUICK REVIEW** soft key on the **MISSION DATA** screen (Figure 3-24). The function of each control screen is given below.

3.15.2.1 Nav Select Screen. The primary control screen is **NAV SELECT**, accessed by pressing **NAV** fixed function key (Figure 3-24). Displays on the screen and active soft keys for ADF are as follows:

SOFT KEY	FUNCTION
NAV SELECT	Title of screen.
♦**ADF**	Edits preset, or frequency.
SETTINGS	Access **RADIO NAV** screen.

3.15.2.2 Radio Nav Screen. Use Radio Nav screen to change modes of operation. This screen is accessed by pressing **SETTINGS** soft key on **NAV SELECT** screen. Displays on the screen and active soft keys are as follows:

SOFT KEY♦	FUNCTION
RADIO-NAV	Title of screen.
ADF	Displays bearing to radio beacon.
♦**ADF/ANT**	Toggles between direction finding and receive only.
♦**NORM/TONE**	Toggles between normal or tone mode of reception.

3.15.2.3 ADF Preset Screen. Use ADF preset screen to change frequency and mode settings of a preset. See Figure 3-24 for ways to access this screen. Displays on the screen and active soft keys are as follows:

SOFT KEY	FUNCTION
ADF PRESET	Title of screen.
♦**PRESET**	Change preset number.
♦**NAME**	Change name of preset.
♦**TUNE**	Change tune frequency.
NORM/TONE♦	Toggles between normal or tone mode of reception.
ADF/ANT♦	Toggles between direction finding or receive only mode.
RTN♦	Return to previously displayed screen.

TM 1-1520-253-10

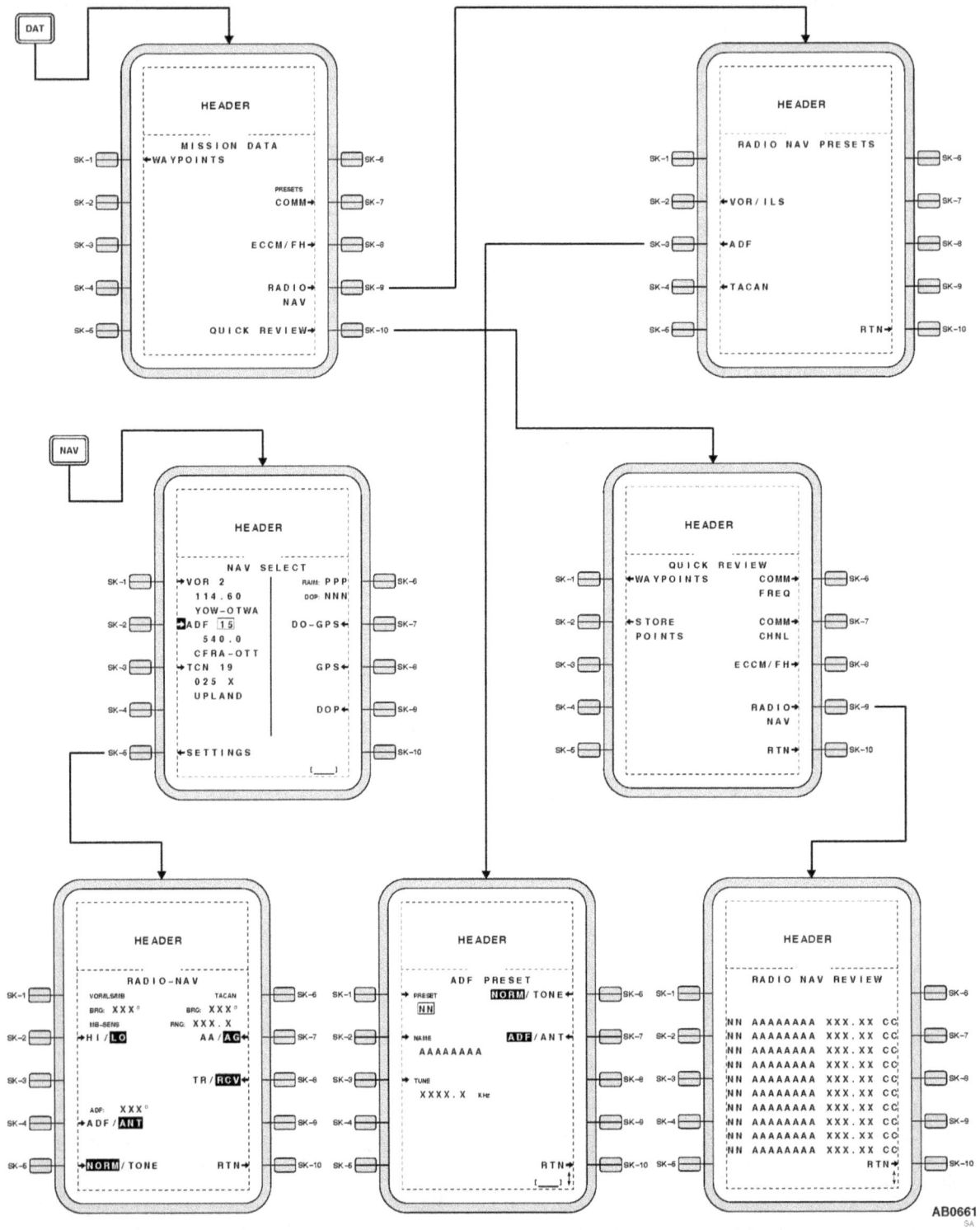

Figure 3-24. AN/ARN-149 Control Screens

3-66

3.15.3 Operation.

3.15.3.1 ANT (Aural Only) Operation.

1. On **CSC** panel, **NAV B** receiver selector switch - Push on.

2. Frequency or preset - As desired.

3. In either **RADIO-NAV**, or **ADF PRESET** screen, ensure **ANT** is in inverse video.

4. **NAV B** volume control - Adjust as desired.

3.15.3.2 ADF Operation.

1. On **CSC** panel, **NAV B** monitor control - Push on.

2. Frequency or preset - As desired.

3. In either **RADIO-NAV**, or **ADF PRESET** screen, ensure **ADF** is in inverse video.

If CW operation is desired:

4. **NORM/TONE** soft key - Press, until **TONE** is in inverse video.

5. On **CSC** panel, **NAV B** monitor control - Adjust as desired.

6. **MODE SEL BRG 2** switch - **ADF**.

7. Verify horizontal situation indicator (HSI) No. 2 bearing pointer displays appropriate relative bearing-to-the-station.

If self-test is required:

8. Access **NAV TESTS** page by pressing **TST** fixed function key, then **NAV** soft key. To start test, **ADF** soft key - Press, until **TEST** under ADF is displayed in inverse video.

9. All indications next to **TST VX, TST VY** and **TST VZ** should read **P**.

10. No. 2 bearing pointer deflects 90° away from original reading.

11. **RTN** soft key Press, to exit test screen.

12. Verify No. 2 bearing pointer returns to original reading.

3.16 RADIO RECEIVING SET AN/ASN-153 TACAN.

Radio set AN/ASN-153 is a TACAN receiver/transmitter. It measures the slant range distance and relative bearing to a selected ground station, or an airborne beacon, and computes speed that the helicopter is flying to or away from the from the ground station, and the time it will take to fly over the station. The system consists of a receiver transmitter, and two antennas. The TACAN is controlled by Avionics Management System (AMS). Signals are fed from the TACAN receiver transmitter to the command instrument system, and displayed on the HSI. Power for the AN/ASN-153 is provided from the No. 2 dc primary bus through a circuit breaker, marked **TACAN**.

3.16.1 Antennas. The upper TACAN antenna is on the nose avionics door. The lower antenna is located on the underside of the tailcone. See Figure 3-1 for exact antenna locations.

3.16.2 Primary Controls and Functions. The TACAN receiver/transmitter is controlled by the AMS with CDU control screens (Figure 3-25). Operator functions are to choose frequency and mode of operation. A complete list of presets is displayed on **RADIO NAV REVIEW** screen, accessed through the **QUICK REVIEW** soft key on the **MISSION DATA** screen. The function of each control screen is given below.

3.16.2.1 Nav Select Screen. The primary control screen is **NAV SELECT**, accessed by pressing **NAV** fixed function key (Figure 3-25). Displays on the screen and active soft keys for TACAN are as follows:

CONTROL/INDICATOR	FUNCTION
NAV SELECT	Title of screen.
TCN	Selects, and then toggles between TACAN channel or preset for edit.
SETTINGS	Accesses **RADIO - NAV** settings page.

3.16.2.2 Radio Nav Screen. Use Radio Nav screen to change modes of operation. This screen is accessed by

TM 1-1520-253-10

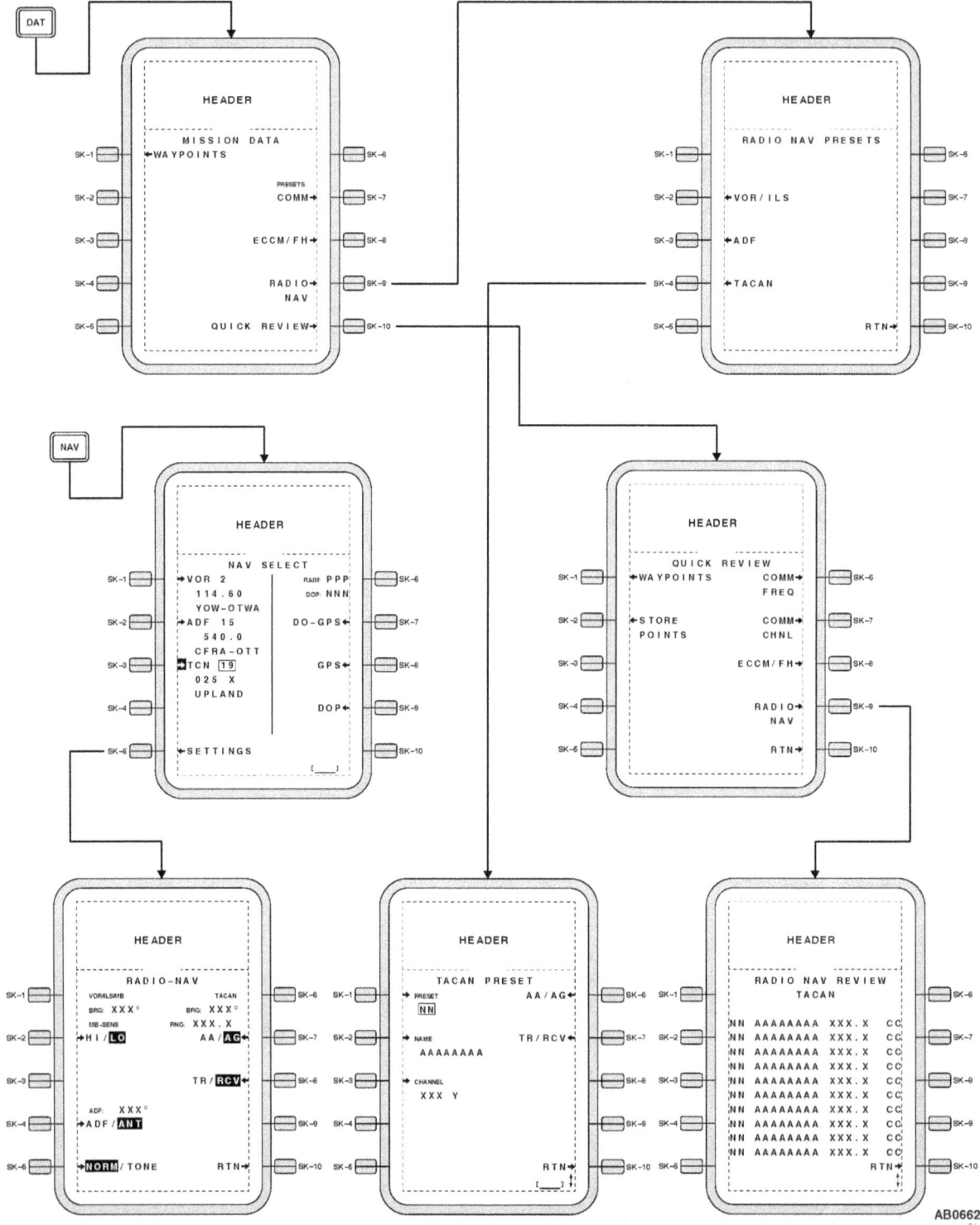

Figure 3-25. AN/ARN-153 TACAN Control Screens

3-68

pressing **SETTINGS** soft key on **NAV SELECT** screen. The function of each control is as follows:

CONTROL/ INDICATOR	FUNCTION
RADIO-NAV	Title of screen.
BRG:	Displays TACAN bearing to the selected station.
RNG:	Displays TACAN slant range to the selected station.
GS:	Displays TACAN computed groundspeed to the selected station.
TTG:	Displays TACAN computed time to the selected station at the calculated groundspeed.
AA/AG⭳	Toggles between air-to-air and air-to-ground mode. Selected mode is displayed in inverse video.
TR/RCV⭳	Toggles between transmit/receive and receive only mode. Selected mode is displayed in inverse video.
RTN⭳	Returns to previously selected screen.

3.16.2.3 TACAN Preset Screen. Use TACAN preset screen to change channel and mode settings of a preset. See Figure 3-25 for ways to access this screen. Displays on the screen and active soft keys are as follows:

CONTROL/ INDICATOR	FUNCTION
TACAN PRESET	Title of screen.
⭳PRESET	Change preset number.
⭳NAME	Change name of preset.
⭳CHANNEL	Change channel number.
A/A - A/G⭳	Toggles between air to air and air to ground mode of operation.
TR/RCV⭳	Toggles between transmit/receive and receive only or receive only mode.

3.16.3 Operation.

3.16.3.1 Test Procedure.

1. **VTAC** switch on instrument panel - **TACAN**.

2. HSI **CRS** control (pilot and copilot) - Set 180° in course display.

3. Access **NAV TESTS** page by pressing **TST** fixed function key, then **NAV** soft key. To start test, **TACAN** soft key - Press, until **TACAN** is displayed in inverse video.

4. All indications below **TACAN** should read **P**.

5. Indications on the HSI shall be as follows:

   a. Distance indicator shall read between 399.5 and 000.5 nmi.

   b. No. 2 bearing pointer shall read between 177° and 183°.

   c. Course deviation bar shall be centered within 1/2 dot, and To/From indicator shall indicate TO.

   d. TACAN indications on the HSI will be removed unless there is a station that the set is tuned to nearby.

3.16.3.2 Normal Operation Receive Mode.

1. Choose channel, or preset on **NAV SELECT** screen.

2. On **RADIO-NAV** screen, **AA/AG** and **TR/RCV** soft keys - Press, until **AG** and **RCV** is in inverse video.

3. Wait five seconds for signal acquisition and lock on.

4. On **CSC** panel, **NAV B** monitor control - Press.

5. Check for correct station identifier in earphones.

6. Navigation information will consist of bearing information only displayed on the HSI.

3-69

3.16.3.3 Normal Operation Transmit/Receive Mode.

1. Choose channel, or preset on **NAV SELECT** screen.

WARNING

TACAN is a transponder that emits radiation. Make sure no personnel are within 3 feet of either TACAN antenna when TACAN is used in Transmit/Receive mode.

2. On **RADIO-NAV** screen, **AA/AG** and **TR/RCV** soft keys - Press, until **AG** and **TR** is in inverse video.

3. Wait five seconds for signal acquisition and lock on.

4. On **CSC** panel, **NAV B** monitor control - Press.

5. Check for correct station identifier in earphones.

6. Navigation information shall consist of bearing, slant distance and groundspeed to station, displayed on HSI.

3.16.3.4 Normal Operation Air to Air Receive Mode.

1. Choose channel, or preset on **NAV SELECT** screen.

NOTE

Use channel pairings with a 63 channel separation between channels on the aircraft. For example, if the airborne beacon aircraft is operating on channel 15Y, the helicopter's control must be set to 78Y.

In all TACAN systems there is the possibility of interference from IFF, transponder, and DME signals when operating in the air to air modes. In order to minimize the possibility of interference, it is recommended that Y channels be used and that channels 1 through 11, 58 through 74, and 121 through 126 be avoided.

2. On **RADIO-NAV** screen, **AA/AG** and **TR/RCV** soft keys - Press, until **AA** and **RCV** is in inverse video.

3. Wait five seconds for signal acquisition and lock on.

4. On **CSC** panel, **NAV B** monitor control - Press.

5. Check for correct station identifier in earphones.

6. Navigation information will consist of bearing information only displayed on the HSI.

3.16.3.5 Normal Operation Air to Air Transmit/Receive Mode.

1. Choose channel, or preset on **NAV SELECT** screen.

NOTE

Use channel pairings with a 63 channel separation between channels on the aircraft. For example, if the airborne beacon aircraft is operating on channel 15Y, the helicopter's control must be set to 78Y.

In all TACAN systems there is the possibility of interference from IFF, transponder, and DME signals when operating in the air to air modes. In order to minimize the possibility of interference, it is recommended that Y channels be used and that channels 1 through 11, 58 through 74, and 121 through 126 be avoided.

When 2 aircraft are flying in close proximity, it is possible that a negative distance indication may be displayed due to the calibration of the TACAN systems in either aircraft. This information will cause the distance readings between 399.5 nmi, and 400.0 nmi, which correspond to distances between -0.4 nmi and -0.01 nmi, respectively.

2. On **RADIO-NAV** screen, **AA/AG** and **TR/RCV** soft keys - Press, until **AA** and **TR** is in inverse video.

3. Wait five seconds for signal acquisition and lock on.

4. On **CSC** panel, **NAV B** monitor control - Press.

5. Check for correct station identifier in earphones.

6. Navigation information shall consist of bearing, distance and closure speed to other aircraft, displayed on HSI.

3.17 PERSONNEL LOCATOR SYSTEM (PLS).

The ARS-6(V)3 personnel locator system (PLS) provides the pilot with heading and distance information to locate survivors with a transmitting AN/PRC-112A(V) survival radio set. The PLS consists of a receiver/transmitter, an antenna switching unit a control display unit, an instrument panel display, and two antennas. The two PLS antennas are mounted on the bottom of the fuselage. The PLS provides heading information to any source of continuous wave UHF signals within its operating range. The unit operates in the UHF frequency range between 225 and 300 MHz and is tunable in 25 KHz increments. If the ID codes in the survival radio match the ID codes being transmitted by the aircraft, a reply is transmitted from the survival radio. This reply is interpreted by the PLS, allowing calculation of the heading and slant range to the survival radio. The PLS can store up to 20 different survivor ID codes. The range error is less than 1% and the azimuth error is less than ±4 degrees with a final location accuracy within approximately 50 feet of the survivor transmitter. Angle to survivor information is displayed as a series of bars on either side of a bullseye, the bullseye indicating "straight ahead" to the survivor. The quantity of bars to the right or left of the bullseye indicates the approximate bearing to the survivor. 2 bars to the left or right of bullseye indicate a 5° to 10° turn is required to line up on the survivor. Full deflection of 8 bars indicates a turn of 45° to 90° is necessary. Power for the PLS is provided by the No. 2 dc primary bus through a circuit breaker labeled **PLS**.

3.17.1 Antenna. Two PLS blade antennas are located under the fuselage. See Figure 3-1 for exact locations.

3.17.2 Controls and Functions. All controls for the PLS are located on the control display unit, mounted in the lower console. The function of each control is as follows:

CONTROL/ INDICATOR	FUNCTION
CDU Display	Shows survivor number, mode, and frequency.
SVR	Identify the survivor number displayed next to it.
Alphanumeric Display	Indicate system mode of operation.
Frequency Display	Indicates frequency of operation in the **BRST**, **CONT**, and **HOME** modes, or 6 digit survivor ID code, or results of BIT.
Entry keypad	Used for survivor selection, survivor ID code entry, and channel A and B frequency selection.
CLR	Deletes indication on display.
ENT	Enters displayed value in memory.
T/R INTG	Controls radio interrogation operations.
MODE Select switch	Locked out in **OFF** position. Pull and turn to change from **OFF** to any other position.
OFF	Removes power from set.
BIT	Starts built in test.
FREQ	Enables entry of desired frequency.
CODE	Enables entry of codes for up to nine AN/PRC-112 radios.
BRST	Each interrogation is triggered with a manual command.
CONT	Interrogations are automatically transmitted by system.
HOME	Operates as direction finding receiver.
CHAN Selector	
A	Selects Channel A frequencies.
B	Selects Channel B frequencies.
243.0	Selects preset 243.0 MHz.
282.8	Selects preset 282.8 MHz.
VOL knob	Not connected.
Remote Display Unit (on instrument panel)	

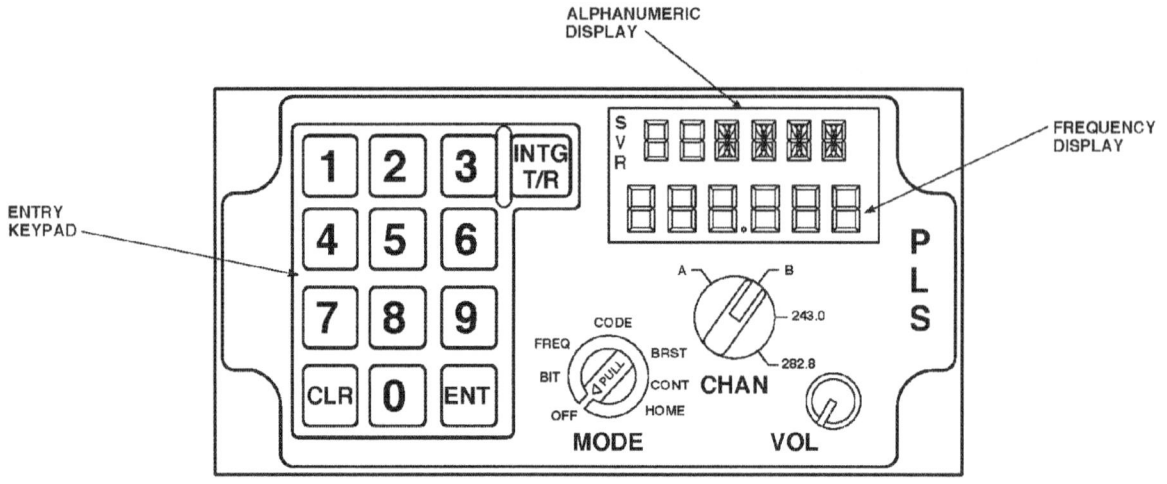

Figure 3-26. PLS Central Display Unit

CONTROL/ INDICATOR	FUNCTION
NO UPDT	In **BRST** mode, indicates no response to last interrogation. In **HOME** mode, indicates receive signal strength below receive threshold. If any data has been received, display retains the last valid reading until another survivor is selected.
FT NM	Indicate **FT** when distance is less than 9900 ft, and **NM** when range is greater than 9900 ft.
Distance display	Indicates distance from survivor.
Bargraph and Bullseye	Gives pilot visual steering directions to survivor. A solid bullseye is displayed when the helicopter in line with the survivor. As the helicopter turns away from the in line position, the bullseye extinguishes, and vertical bars light up indicating direction of turn needed to line up with the survivor. The bargraph will activate one bar on each side of the solid sphere if a steering command has not been received, or when the system is in **BRST**, **CONT**, or **HOME** mode.

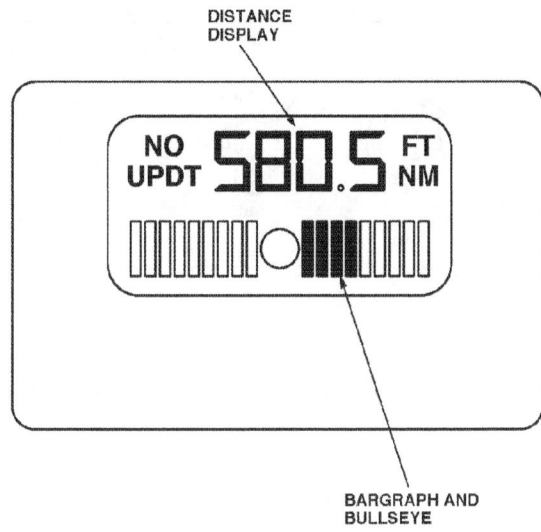

Figure 3-27. PLS Remote Display Unit

3.17.3 Modes of Operation.

3.17.3.1 Test Mode. Test mode is selected when the mode switch is in the **BIT** position. Built in test (BIT) takes approximately 5 seconds, and results in a display of **BIT PASS** or the name of the failed unit followed by **FAIL**.

3.17.3.2 Data Entry Mode. Data entry mode is selected when the mode switch is in the **FREQ** or **CODE** position. Use this mode to select and enter transponder codes and frequencies for the system to use.

3.17.3.3 Burst Mode. The burst mode allows the pilot to control the interrogation output of the PLS. When the **T/R INTG** key is pressed, the unit interrogates for less than 4 seconds. Data from the responses is then displayed on the instrument panel display.

3.17.3.4 Continuous Mode. This mode provides constant interrogations to the survivor's radio. Readouts from this mode include DME slant range distances in nautical miles for distances over 9900 ft, and in feet for distances under 9900 ft.

3.17.3.5 Homing Mode. PLS homing mode provides bearing information only from the source. Bearing indications greater than 25° off the nose of the helicopter should be used for turning direction only. The pilot must determine to or from direction of the radio source by signal strength/sound or the aid of the radio source operator. If constant transmissions from the radio source operator is not possible, request short transmissions as necessary to identify radio location.

3.17.4 Normal Operation.

3.17.4.1 Starting Procedure.

NOTE

The radio will transmit for approximately 1.5 seconds during BIT. If radio silence is required, turn **MODE** switch directly to **FREQ**.

1. **MODE** switch - **BIT**.

2. Observe display, as all segments light up, and **BIT PASS** or (**LRU**) **FAIL** is displayed.

3.17.4.2 Operation.

1. Set up PLS for survivor radio operation.

   a. **MODE** switch - **FREQ**.

   b. **CHAN** switch - **A** or **B**, as desired. Display reads **FREQ** followed by six dashes.

   c. **CLR** switch - Press, to clear the display. Flashing cursor display indicates that unit is ready for frequency selection.

   d. Select desired frequency with number keys. To enter frequency in memory, **ENT** key - Press.

   e. **MODE** switch - **CODE**. **SVR** display will indicate **1**, and CDU display indicates **CODE**, with six dashes.

   f. **CLR** switch - Press, to clear the display. Flashing cursor display indicates that unit is ready for code selection.

   g. Select desired code with number keys. To enter code in memory, **ENT** key - Press.

   h. To enter code for survivor No. 2, **2** - Press. Repeat Steps f. and g. to enter survivor codes in system.

i. Repeat Step h for each additional survivor code to be entered (up to 9), using numbers 3 through 9 in place of 2.

2. Normal Operation.

   a. Set **MODE** switch - As desired.

   b. Set **CHAN** switch - As desired.

   c. Select survivor code number with number keys.

   d. If **BRST** mode was selected, **TR/INTG** button - Press, to interrogate radio source. Display will briefly read **INTG**, when interrogation is taking place. RCU will then give distance and bearing to survivor, if interrogation was successful. If not, **NO UPDT** will appear.

   e. If **CONT** mode was selected, **TR/INTG** button - Press, to interrogate a beacon. Display will read **INTG**, indicating continuous interrogation. RCU will give distance and bearing to survivor, if interrogation was successful. If not, **NO UPDT** will appear when **TR/INTG** is pressed to end interrogation.

3.17.5 Stopping Procedure.

1. **MODE** switch - **OFF**.

3.18 GYRO MAGNETIC COMPASS SET AN/ASN-43.

Gyro Magnetic Compass Set AN/ASN-43 provides heading information by reference to a free directional gyro when operating in the **FREE** mode, or by being slaved to the earth's magnetic field when operated in the **SLAVED** mode. It provides heading information to the horizontal situation indicator. Power to operate the AN/ASN-43 is provided from the ac essential bus through circuit breakers, marked **COMP** and **AUTO XFMR** under the general heading **AC ESNTL BUS**.

3.18.1 Compass Control C-8021/ASN-75.
Control C-8021/ASN-75 (Figure 3-28) is required to synchronize (electrically and mechanically align) the AN/ASN-43 to the correct magnetic heading when used in the **SLAVED** mode of operation. The synchronizing knob on the control panel may be used as a set heading knob for operation in the **FREE** mode.

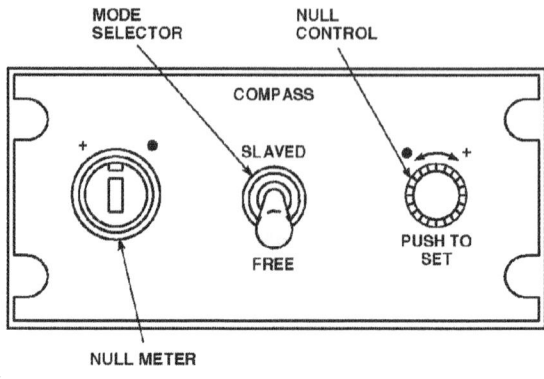

Figure 3-28. Compass Control Panel C-8021/ASN-75

3.18.2 Controls and Functions. Controls for the magnetic compass set are on the front panel of the unit. The function panel of each control is as follows:

CONTROL	FUNCTION
Null Meter	Moves left (+) or right (•) of center to indicate misalignment (synchronization) of the AN/ASN-43.
Mode Selector (SLAVED-FREE)	Selects either magnetically **SLAVED** or **FREE** gyro operation of the AN/ASN-43.
Null Control **PUSH-TO-SET**	Is manually pressed and turned to null the annunciator, thereby synchronizing (electrically and mechanically aligning) the AN/ASN-43. Turns compass card of HSI for alignment.

3.18.3 Operation.

3.18.4 Starting Procedure.

1. Mode selector - As desired.

2. Null control - Push, and turn in direction indicated by null meter (+ or •) until annunciator is centered. In **SLAVED** mode, during normal operation, the annunciator will oscillate slightly about the center position; however, during cer-

tain helicopter maneuvers the annunciator will move off center.

3. HSI - check to see that HSI heading agrees with a known magnetic heading.

3.19 ELECTRONIC NAVIGATION INSTRUMENT DISPLAY SYSTEM.

The instrument display system provides displays for navigation and command signals on a vertical situation indicator (VSI) and a horizontal situation indicator (HSI) for pilot visual reference. The system consists of the two VSIs and two HSIs on the instrument panel. The system has a common command instrument system processor (CISP), two HSI/VSI mode select panels, and one CIS mode select panel.

3.19.1 Vertical Situation Indicator. The VSI (Figure 3-29), provides a cockpit display of the helicopter's pitch, roll attitude, turn rate, slip or skid, and certain navigational information. It accepts command instrument system processor signals and displays the flight command information needed to arrive at a predetermined point. The system also monitors and displays warnings when selected navigation instrument readings lack reliability. The VSI is composed of a miniature airplane, four warning indicator flags **ATT**, **GS**, **NAV** and **CMD**, two trim knobs **ROLL** and **PITCH**, a bank angle scale, a bank angle index on the spheroid, a turn rate indicator and inclinometer, pitch and roll command bars, collective position pointer, a course deviation pointer, and a glide slope deviation pointer. Refer to Chapter 2, Section XIV for a description of the attitude indicating system, and turn and slip indicator. The gyro erect switch (Figure 2-7) supplies a fast erect signal to the pilot and copilot displacement gyros, thereby considerably reducing the time required for the gyros to reach full operating RPM. The pilot and copilot's displacement gyros supply pitch and roll attitude signals to the vertical situation indicators, automatic flight control system, and the Doppler/GPS navigation system. Power to operate the VSI is provided from the No. 2 ac primary bus through circuit breakers marked **VSI PLT**, **CPLT**.

3.19.1.1 Steering Command Bars and Pointer. The roll and pitch command bars and the collective position pointer operate in conjunction with the command instrument system processor (CISP) and the command instrument system/mode selector (**CIS MODE SEL**). Selection of **HDG** on the **CIS MODE SEL** panel provides a display of a roll signal by the roll command bar (Figure 3-29). The pitch command bar and the collective position pointer are out of view, and the **CMD** flag is held from view. Selecting the **CIS MODE SEL** switch **NAV** and the **MODE SEL** switch **VTAC ILS**, the roll command bar will display roll commands from the CISP. If an ILS (LOC) frequency is tuned in, the pitch command bar and the collective command pointer will also display CISP signals. If a VOR/TACAN frequency is tuned-in, the pitch command bar and collective position pointer will be held from view. The **CMD** warning flag will be held from view, indicating that the CISP functional integrity is being monitored. Refer to Figure 3-31 for VSI indications in other switch positions.

3.19.1.2 Command Warning Flag. The command warning flag marked **CMD** is at the top left of the VSI face (Figure 3-29). It is held from view when initial power is applied to the CIS processor. When any CIS mode selector switch is on, and that navigation system operating properly, the **CMD** flag is not in view. During operation, if the navigation signal becomes unreliable, or is lost, the **NAV** flag will become visible.

3.19.1.3 Glide Slope Warning Flag. A glide slope warning flag marked **GS** is on the right face of the indicator (Figure 3-29). The letters **GS** are black on a red/white stripe background. The warning flag will move out of view when the ILS receivers are operating and reliable signals are received.

3.19.1.4 Navigation Warning Flag. A navigation flag marked **NAV** is installed on both the VSIs and the HSIs (Figures 3-29 and 3-30) to indicate when navigation systems are operating and reliable signals are being received. The VSI **NAV** flag is marked **NAV** with a white background and red strips, and is on the lower left side of the indicator. The HSI **NAV** flag is within the compass card ring. Both instrument flags will retract from view whenever a navigation receiver is on and a reliable signal is being received.

3.19.1.5 Course Deviation Pointer. The course deviation pointer is on the VSI instrument (Figure 3-29). The pointer works with the course bar on the HSI to provide the pilot with an indication of the helicopter's position with respect to the course selected on the HSI. The scales represent right or left off course, each dot from center (on course) is 1.25° for ILS, 5° VOR ,TACAN, DPLR, and FM. The pilot must fly into the needle to regain on-course track.

3.19.1.6 Glide Slope Deviation Pointer. The glide slope pointer, on the right side of the VSI (Figure 3-29), is used with ILS. The pointer represents the glide slope position with respect to the helicopter. Each side of the on-glide slope (center) mark are dots, each dot representing .25° above or below the glide slope.

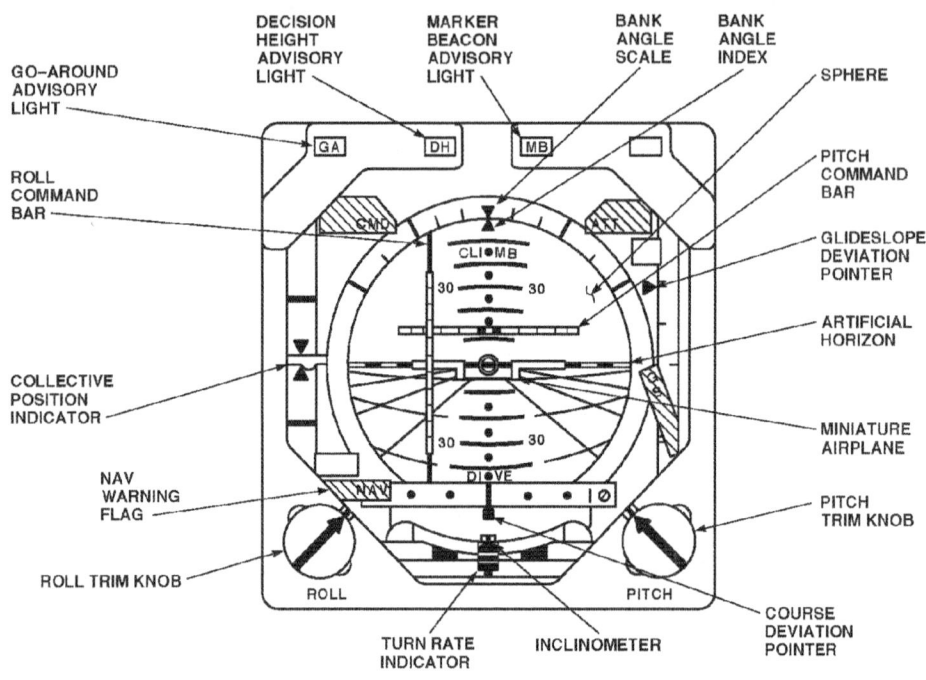

Figure 3-29. Vertical Situation Indicator

3.19.1.73.18.1.7 Controls and Indicators. Indicators of the VSI are on the face of the instrument. The function of each indicator is as follows:

CONTROL/ INDICATOR	FUNCTION
Miniature airplane/ horizon line	Provides reference to artificial horizon.
Bank angle scale	Right and left 0°, 10°, 20°, 30°, 45°, 60°, and 90° of bank.
Artificial horizon	Reference of helicopter's attitude to horizon.
Turn rate indicator	4-minute turn (one-needle width either side of center) 2-minute turn (two-needle width each side of center).
Pitch and roll command bars	Display to the pilot, control inputs he should make to arrive at a predetermined course, or glide slope.

CONTROL/ INDICATOR	FUNCTION
Collective position indicator	Display to the pilot the position of the collective relative to where it should be to arrive at a predetermined altitude.
GA	Go-around (**GA**) advisory light will go on whenever the **GA** switch on the pilot's or copilot's cyclic stick is pressed. The light will go off whenever the go-around mode is ended by engaging another mode on the CIS mode selector panel.
DH	Decision height (**DH**) advisory light will go on whenever the radar altimeter is operating and the altitude indicator is at or below the radar altitude L (low bug) setting.

CONTROL/INDICATOR	FUNCTION
MB	Marker beacon (**MB**) advisory light will go on and the associated marker beacon tone will be heard, depending upon volume control setting, when the helicopter is over the marker beacon transmitter.
Glide slope pointer	Displays to the pilot the position of the ILS glide slope relative to the helicopter. Pointer above center indicates helicopter is below glide path.
Course deviation pointer	Displays to the pilot the position of the course reference (VOR, LOC/TACAN, DPLR/GPS, FM HOME) relative to the helicopter.
ATT warning flag	Indicates loss of vertical gyro power or VSI malfunction.
NAV warning flag	Indicates loss, or unreliable signal indication.
GS warning flag	Indicates loss, or unreliable signal indicator.
PITCH trim knob	Adjust artificial horizon up (climb) from at least 4°, no more than 10° or down (dive) from at least 8°, no more than 20°.
ROLL trim knob	Adjust artificial horizon right or left from at least 8° to no more than 20°.

3.19.2 Horizontal Situation Indicator. Two HSIs (Figure 3-30) are installed on the instrument panel, one in front of each pilot. The HSI consists of a compass card, two bearing-to-station points with back-course markers, a course bar, a **KM** indicator, heading set (**HDG**) knob and marker, a course set (**CRS**) knob, a **COURSE** digital read-out, a to-from arrow, a **NAV** flag, and a compass **HDG** flag. The HSIs operating power is taken from the ac essential bus through a circuit breaker marked **HSI PLT/CPLT**.

3.19.3 Controls and Indicators. Controls of the horizontal situation indicators (Figure 3-30) are as follows:

CONTROL/INDICATOR	FUNCTION
Compass card	The compass card is a 360° scale that turns to display heading data obtained from the compass control. The helicopter headings are read at the upper lubber line.
COURSE set display	Displays course to nearest degree. Indicates same as course set pointer.
Bearing pointer No. 1	The pointer operates in conjunction with Doppler/GPS or TACAN. Indicates magnetic bearing to waypoint or TACAN station selected.
Bearing pointer No. 2	The pointer operates in conjunction with selected VOR, TACAN, or ADF receiver. The pointer is read against the compass card and indicates the magnetic bearing to the VOR or ADF station.
Course deviation bar	This bar indicates lateral deviation from a selected course. When the helicopter is flying the selected course, the course bar will be aligned with the course set pointer and will be centered on the fixed aircraft symbol.
CRS knob	Course set (**CRS**) knob and the course set counter operate in conjunction with the course pointer and allow the pilot to select any of 360 courses. Once set, the course pointer will turn with the compass card and will be centered on the upper lubber line when the helicopter is flying the selected course.
KM indicator	Digital distance display in kilometers (**KM**) to destination waypoint, or TACAN station.
HDG knob	Heading set (**HDG**) knob operates in conjunction with the heading select marker, allows the pilot to select any one of 360 headings. Seven full turns of the knob produces a 360° turn of the marker.

3-77

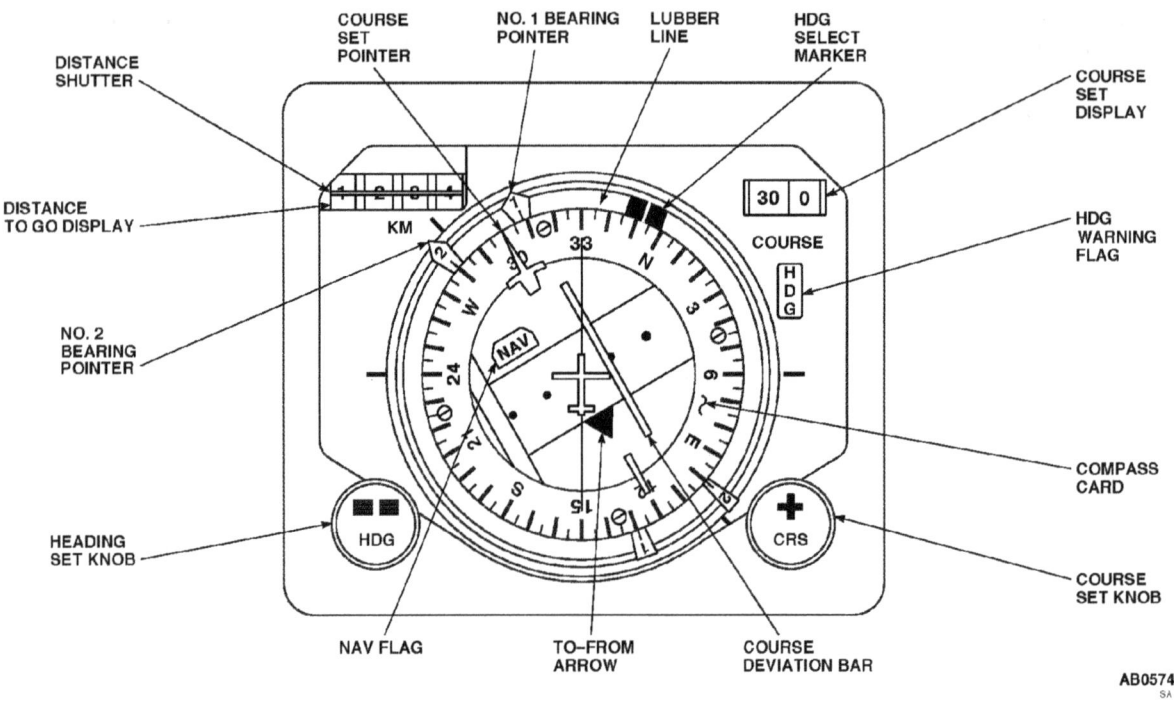

Figure 3-30. Horizontal Situation Indicator

CONTROL/ INDICATOR	FUNCTION
HDG warning flag	Visible when a failure occurs in the magnetic compass system.
To-From arrow	To-from arrow indicates that the helicopter is flying to or away from a selected VOR or TACAN.
NAV flag	The NAV flag at the top of the to indicator, turns with the compass card. The flag will retract from view when a reliable navigation signal is being applied to the instrument.

3.19.4 VSI/HSI and CIS Mode Selector Panels. The mode select panels (Figure 3-31) are integrally lighted, instrument panel mounted controls for the VSI, HSI, and CIS. The panels provide a means for selecting and displaying various navigation functions. Power to operate the pilot's **MODE SEL** is taken from the No. 2 dc primary bus through a circuit breaker, marked **PILOT MODE SELECT**. The copilot's **MODE SEL** takes power from the No. 1 dc primary bus through a circuit breaker, marked **CPLT MODE SELECT**.

NOTE

The switches on the VSI/HSI and CIS mode select panels may change state when the caution/advisory panel **BRT/DIM-TEST** switch is set to **TEST**. The original indications may be restored by pressing the applicable switches.

3.19.4.1 Controls and Functions. Controls of the mode selector panel (Figure 3-31) are as follows:

CONTROL	FUNCTION
DOP GPS	Directs long range NAV lateral deviation and NAV flag signals to VSIs and HSIs.
VOR ILS	Directs VOR or ILS signals to VSIs, and HSIs. Provides a signal to NAV flag.

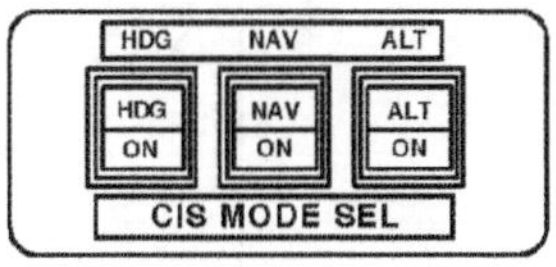

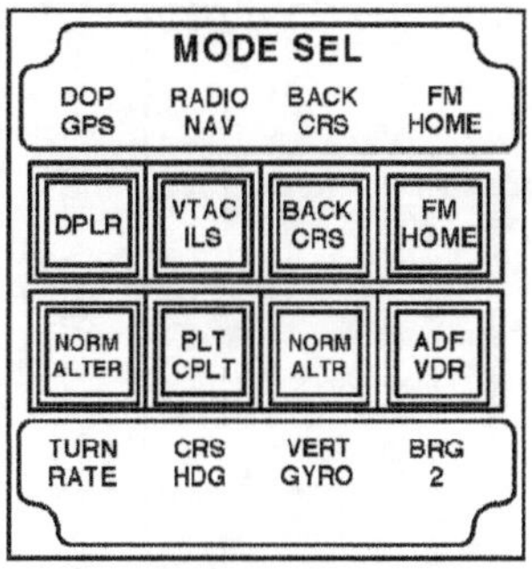

MODE OF OPERATIONS	CIS MODE SELECTOR	HSI / VSI MODE SELECTOR	VTAC SELECT
NONE	NONE	ANY	ANY
MANUAL HEADING	HDG	ANY	ANY
ALTITUDE HOLD	ALT	ANY	ANY
VOR NAVIGATION	NAV	VTAC	VOR
TACAN NAVIGATION	NAV	VTAC	TACAN
ILS NAVIGATION	NAV	ILS	VOR
ILS APPROACH	NAV	ILS	VOR
ILS BACK COURSE	NAV	BACK CRS	VOR
LEVEL OFF	NAV	VOR / ILS / BACK CRS	VOR
GO-AROUND	NAV	VOR / ILS	VOR
LONG RANGE NAV	NAV	DOP GPS	ANY
FM HOMING	NAV	FM HOME	ANY

Figure 3-31. CIS Modes of Operation (Sheet 1 of 2)

CYCLIC ROLL COMMAND BAR	CYCLIC PITCH COMMAND BAR	COLLECTIVE POSITION INDICATOR
OFF SCALE	OFF SCALE	OFF SCALE
PROCESSED CYCLIC ROLL COMMAND	OFF SCALE	OFF SCALE
OFF SCALE	OFF SCALE	PROCESSED COLLECTIVE POSITION
PROCESSED CYCLIC ROLL COMMAND	OFF SCALE	OFF SCALE
PROCESSED CYCLIC ROLL COMMAND	OFF SCALE	OFF SCALE
PROCESSED CYCLIC ROLL COMMAND	PROCESSED CYCLIC PITCH COMMAND	PROCESSED COLLECTIVE POSITION
PROCESSED CYCLIC ROLL COMMAND	PROCESSED CYCLIC PITCH COMMAND	PROCESSED COLLECTIVE POSITION
PROCESSED CYCLIC ROLL COMMAND	OFF SCALE	OFF SCALE
PROCESSED CYCLIC ROLL COMMAND	OFF SCALE OR PROCESSED CYCLIC PITCH COMMAND	PROCESSED COLLECTIVE POSITION
PROCESSED CYCLIC ROLL COMMAND	PROCESSED CYCLIC PITCH COMMAND	PROCESSED COLLECTIVE POSITION
PROCESSED CYCLIC ROLL COMMAND	OFF SCALE	OFF SCALE
PROCESSED CYCLIC ROLL COMMAND	OFF SCALE	OFF SCALE

Figure 3-31. CIS Modes of Operation (Sheet 2 of 2)

CONTROL	FUNCTION	CONTROL	FUNCTION
BACK CRS	Reverse polarity of back course signal to provide directional display for VSIs and HSIs. Provides a signal to **NAV** flag.	VOR	Allows pilot or copilot to select **VOR** on his No. 2 bearing pointer, each independent of the other.
FM HOME	Directs FM homing deviation and flag signals to VSIs.	CIS mode selector	Selects one of three modes of operation to direct navigational signals to the CISP for Command Signal display.
TURN RATE NORM	Provides pilot and copilot with his own turn rate gyro information displayed on his VSI.	HDG ON	Direct heading and roll signals to CIS processor for steering commands that will allow pilot to maintain a selected heading.
ALTER	Allows copilot's turn rate gyro information to be displayed on pilot's VSI, or pilot's gyro information to be displayed on copilot's VSI.	NAV ON	Gives heading commands to acquire and track a selected VOR, ILS,TACAN, DPLR/GPS, or FM intercept, or to acquire and track glide slope beam.
CRS HDG PLT	Provides for pilot's omni-bearing selector to be connected to navigation receiver and concurrent connection of pilot's HSI course datum and heading datum output to command instrument system processor.	ALT ON	Directs barometric pressure signals and collective stick position signals to CIS processor.
		INSTRUMENT PANEL	
CPLT	Provides for copilot's omni-bearing selector to be connected to navigation receiver and concurrent connection of copilot's HSI course datum and heading datum output to command instrument system processor.	VTAC	Allows pilot or copilot to select either VOR information or TACAN for display on individual HSI.
		BRG 1/ DIST	Selects either long range navigation (DPLR/GPS), or TACAN for display on both HSIs.
VERT GYRO NORM	Provides pilot and copilot with his own vertical gyro information displayed on his VSI.		
ALTR	Allows copilot's vertical gyro information to be displayed on pilot's VSI, or pilot's gyro information to be displayed on copilot's VSI.		
BRG2 ADF	Allows pilot or copilot to select ADF on his No. 2 bearing pointer, each independent of the other.		

3.19.4.2 Off Mode. The command instrument system off mode (no switch legends lit) causes the cyclic roll, cyclic pitch and collective command pointers on both vertical situation indicators to be stowed out of view and the command warning flag on both VSIs to be biased out of view. The CISP is in the off mode upon initial application of electrical power, before the pilot selects either **HDG**, **NAV** or **ALT** mode on the CIS mode selector. When **NAV** mode is selected, the CISP remains in the off mode unless the **DOP/GPS**, **VTAC ILS** or **FM HOME** navigation data has been selected on the pilot's VSI/HSI mode selector. The CISP will return to the off mode whenever the **HDG**, **NAV**, and **ALT** hold modes are disengaged, as indicated by the respective **ON** legends going off, or by turning off the associated navigation receiver. Separate modes are manually disengaged by pressing the mode switch when **ON** is lit.

3.19.4.3 Heading Mode. The heading mode processes the heading error and roll attitude signals to supply a limited cyclic roll command, which, when followed, causes the helicopter to acquire and track the heading manually selected on either pilot's HSI. The processed signal causes the VSI cyclic roll command bar to deflect in the direction of the required control response; i.e., bar deflection to the right indicates a coordinated right turn is required. When properly followed, the command results in not more than one overshoot in acquiring the selected heading and a tracking error of not more than 2°. The processor gain provides 1° of roll command for each degree of heading error up to a roll command limit of approximately 20°. The CISP heading mode is engaged by momentarily pressing the **HDG** switch on the pilot's CIS mode selector, or as described in paragraph 3.19.4.5.

3.19.4.4 Altitude Hold Mode. The altitude hold mode processes barometric pressure signals from the air data transducer in addition to the collective stick position signal. When the **ALT** switch on the pilot's CIS mode selector is pressed, the CISP provides collective command signals, which, when properly followed, cause the helicopter to maintain altitude to within plus or minus 50 feet. The altitude hold mode synchronizes on the engagement altitude for vertical rates up to 200 feet per minute and provides performance for altitude inputs between -1000 and +10,000 feet at airspeeds from 70 to 150 KIAS. It is possible to engage the altitude hold mode, regardless of whether the heading mode or navigation mode is engaged, except that the CISP logic prevents manual selection of the altitude hold mode whenever the **NAV** mode is engaged and an ILS frequency is selected. This prevents the operator from selecting altitude hold mode during an instrument approach. The altitude hold mode is manually engaged by pressing the **ALT** hold switch (subject to above restriction) or automatically engaged as described in paragraph 3.19.4.7. The altitude hold mode may be manually disengaged by pressing the **ALT** hold switch when the **ON** legend is lit. Altitude hold may be disengaged also by selecting any other mode which takes priority (e.g., Go Around).

NOTE

ALT hold mode should be manually disabled during localizer, localizer backcourse, VOR, and ADF approaches.

3.19.4.5 Navigation Mode. The CISP navigation mode is engaged by pressing the **NAV** switch on the CIS Mode Selector. This navigation mode causes the CISP to enter the **VOR NAV, TACAN NAV, ILS NAV, DOP NAV,** or **FM HOME** mode as selected on the pilot's VSI/HSI mode selector. The CISP provides steering commands based on the course selected on either the pilot's or copilot's HSI dependent on the mode select **CRS HDG** selection of **PLT** or **CPLT**.

3.19.4.6 VOR NAV Mode. The **VOR NAV** or **TACAN NAV** mode is established by selecting the **VTAC ILS** switch on the VSI/HSI mode selector and pressing the **NAV** switch on the CIS mode selector and selecting **VOR/ILS** switch on the instrument panel. The CISP processes the heading and course signals derived from either the pilot's or the copilot's HSI in addition to the lateral deviation and lateral flag signals applied to the pilot's VSI. The CISP provides a limited cyclic roll command, which, when followed, shall cause the helicopter to acquire and track the course setting manually selected on the HSI. Engagement of the **VOR NAV** or **TACAN NAV** mode when the helicopter position is in excess of 10° to 20° from the selected radial will cause the initial course intersection to be made in the heading mode as described in paragraph 3.19.4.3. The CISP logic will light the CIS mode selector **HDG** switch **ON** legend during the initial course intersection. When the helicopter is within 10° to 20° of the selected course, the CISP beam sensor will capture the VOR or TACAN lateral beam. The processor logic will turn off the **HDG** switch **ON** legend and the final course interception, about 45°, acquisition, and tracking will be based on the VOR or TACAN lateral deviation signals. The processor causes the roll command pointer to deflect in the direction of the required control response. When properly followed, the command will result in not more than one overshoot at a range of 10 NM at a cruise speed of 100 ± 10 knots, and not more than two overshoots at ranges between 5 and 40 NM at speeds from 70 to 140 knots. When passing over the VOR or TACAN station, the CISP reverts to a station passage submode and remains in this submode for 30 seconds. Cyclic roll commands during the station passage submode will be obtained from the HSI course datum signal. Outbound course changes may be implemented by the HSI **CRS** SET knob during the station passage submode. Course changes to a new radial, or identification of VOR or TACAN intersections may be made before station passage by setting the HSI **HDG** control to the present heading and actuating the **HDG** switch. This will disengage the **NAV** mode and allow the pilot to continue on the original radial in the heading mode. A VOR or TACAN intersection fix or selection of a new radial course may be made without affecting the CIS steering commands. Actuating the **NAV** switch re-engages the **VOR NAV** or **TACAN NAV** mode to either continue on the original VOR or TACAN radial or to initiate an intercept to the new selected radial.

3.19.4.7 ILS NAV Mode. The instrument landing system **NAV** mode is established by selecting the **VTAC/ILS** switch on the VSI/HSI mode selector, tuning a localizer frequency on the navigation receiver, and selecting **VOR/ILS** on the **VTAC** switch on the instrument panel and selecting the **NAV** switch on the pilot's **CIS MODE SEL** panel. During the **ILS NAV** mode the CISP processes the following signals in addition to those processed during the **VOR NAV** mode: 1. The vertical deviation and vertical flag signals, 2. the indicated airspeed (IAS) and barometric altitude signals, and 3. the collective stick position sensor and helicopter pitch attitude signals. The indicated airspeed and pitch attitude signals are processed to provide a limited cyclic pitch command, which, when properly followed, will result in maintaining an airspeed that should not deviate more than 5 knots from the IAS existing at the time the **ILS NAV** mode is engaged. The pitch command bar will deflect in the direction of the required aircraft response, i.e., an upward deflection of the pitch bar indicates a pitch up is required. The BAR ALT and collective stick position signals are processed to provide a limited collective position indication, which, when properly followed, will cause the helicopter to maintain the altitude existing at the time the **ILS NAV** mode is engaged. The collective position indicator will deflect in the opposite direction of the required control response, i.e., an upward deflection of the collective position indicator indicates a descent is required. The CISP will cause the **ALT** hold switch **ON** legend to light whenever the altitude hold mode is engaged. Actuating the **ALT** hold **ON** switch will disengage the altitude hold mode. Desired approach runway course must be set on the **CRS** window of the HSI selected by the **PLT/CPLT** indication of the **CRS HDG** switch. The initial course intersection and the localizer course interception, about 45°, acquisition, and tracking will be done as described for the **VOR NAV** mode except that not more than one overshoot at a range of 10 NM at 100 ± 10 KIAS, and not more than two overshoots at ranges between 5 and 20 NM should occur for airspeeds between 70 and 130 KIAS.

3.19.4.8 Approach Mode. The approach mode, a submode of the **ILS NAV** mode, will be automatically engaged when the helicopter captures the glide slope. During the approach mode, the CISP processes the vertical deviation, **GS** flag, and collective stick position signals to provide a limited collective position indicator, which, when properly followed, shall cause the helicopter to acquire and track the glide slope path during an approach to landing. When the glide slope is intercepted, the CISP logic disengages the altitude hold mode and causes the **ON** legend of the **ALT** hold switch to go off. The CISP will provide a down movement of the collective position indicator to advise the pilot of the transition from altitude hold to glide slope tracking, and to assist in acquiring the glide slope path. The cyclic roll commands are limited to ± 15° during the approach submode. When properly followed, the roll commands will result in the helicopter tracking the localizer to an approach. The collective position indicator, when properly followed, will result in not more than one overshoot in acquiring the glidepath and have a glidepath tracking free of oscillations. The cyclic roll and collective steering performance is applicable for approach airspeed from 130 KIAS down to 50 KIAS.

3.19.4.9 BACK CRS Mode. The back course mode is a submode of the **ILS NAV** mode and is engaged by concurrent **ILS ON** and **BACK CRS ON** signal from the pilot's HSI/VSI mode selector. The CISP monitors the localizer lateral deviation signals to provide cyclic roll commands, which, when properly followed, will allow the pilots to complete back course localizer approach in the same manner as the front course ILS. The desired final approach course should be set on the selected HSI **CRS** window.

3.19.4.10 Level-Off Mode. The level-off mode will be activated when either the **VOR NAV** or **ILS NAV** modes are engaged, and will be deactivated by selection of another mode or when a radar altitude valid signal is not present. The level-off mode is not a function of a VOR or ILS CIS approach. During ILS or VOR approaches, the barometric altimeter must be used to determine arrival at the minimum altitude. Radar altimeter setting shall not be used for level off commands in the **VOR NAV/ILS NAV** modes because variations in terrain cause erroneous altitude indications. The level-off mode provides the pilots with a selectable low altitude command. This mode is automatically engaged when the radar altitude goes below either the pilot's or copilot's radar altimeter low altitude warning bug setting, whichever is at the higher setting. A **DH** legend on the VSI and a **LO** light display on the radar altimeter indicator goes on whenever the radar altitude is less than the **LO** bug setting. The CISP monitors the radar altimeter and the collective stick position sensor to provide a collective pointer command, which, when properly followed, will cause the helicopter to maintain an altitude within 10 feet of the low altitude setting for settings below 250 feet, and 20 feet for settings above 250 feet. The CISP causes the **ALT** switch **ON** legend to light and the altitude hold mode to be engaged.

3.19.4.11 Go-Around Mode. The go-around mode processes roll and pitch attitude, altitude rate, collective stick position, and airspeed inputs in addition to internally generated airspeed and vertical speed command signals to provide cyclic roll, cyclic pitch and collective position indication. The go-around mode will engage when either pilot presses the **GA** (Go Around) switch on his cyclic control grip. When the go-around mode is engaged, the CISP immediately provides a collective position indication, which, when followed, will result in a 500 ± 50 fpm rate-of-climb at zero bank angle. Five seconds after the **GA** switch is pressed, the CISP will provide cyclic pitch bar commands, which, when followed, will result in an 80-KIAS for the climbout. The go-around mode is disengaged by changing to any other mode on the pilot's CIS mode selector.

3.19.4.12 Long Range Navigation (LRN) Mode. The LRN navigation mode is engaged by selecting the **DPLR/GPS** switch on the VSI/HSI mode selector and the **NAV** switch on the pilot's CIS mode selector. During the LRN navigation mode, the CISP processes LRN track angle error and the LRN **NAV** flag signals in addition to the roll angle input from the attitude gyro. The CISP provides cyclic roll bar commands, which, when followed, result in a straight line, wind-corrected, flight over distances greater than 0.1 nm from WPT The course deviation bar and course deviation pointer provide a visual display of where the initial course lies in relationship to the helicopter's position. The initial course is the course the LRN computes from the helicopter's position to the destination. To achieve a pictorially correct view of the course, rotate the course knob to the head of the No. 1 needle when the fly to destination is entered. The DPLR/GPS NAV logic detects the condition of station passover, and automatically switches to heading mode. The switch to heading mode will be indicated by the **HDG** switch **ON** legend being turned on, and the **NAV** switch **ON** legend being turned off. The Doppler/GPS navigation mode will not automatically re-engage, but will require manual re-engagement of the **NAV** switch on the CIS mode selector.

3.18.4.13 FM HOME Mode. The FM homing (Figure 3-31) is engaged by selecting the **FM HOME** switch on the pilot's VSI/HSI mode selector and the **NAV** switch on the pilot's CIS mode selector. Selecting FM homing on the VSI/HSI mode selector directs FM homing signals only to the VSI. Other **NAV** modes will be retained on the HSI if previously selected. During the **FM HOME** mode, the CISP processes the lateral deviation and flag signals displayed on the pilot's VSI in addition to the roll angle input from the attitude gyro. The CISP filters and dampens the FM homing deviation signals and provides cyclic roll commands to aid the pilot in homing on a radio station selected on the COM 1 communications receiver. When properly followed, the roll commands result in not more than two overshoot heading changes before maintaining a tracking error not to go over 3°. The CISP will revert to the heading mode whenever the lateral deviation rate is over 1.5°/sec for a period of over 1 second. The CISP will cause the CIS mode selector **HDG** switch **ON** legend to light, and remain in the heading mode until the **FM** mode or some other mode is manually selected. Concurrent VOR and FM, TACAN or concurrent DPLR and FM mode inputs will be considered an **FM** mode input to the CISP.

3.19.4.14 TURN RATE Select. The turn rate gyro selection provides each pilot the option of having his VSI display his own turn rate gyro signal (**NORM** operation) or of having the other pilot's turn rate gyro signal displayed (**ALTR** operation). The turn rate gyro selection is independent of the navigation modes selected by the top row of switches and is independent of which turn rate gyro the other pilot has selected. The **NORM** selection connects each pilot's VSI to his own turn rate gyro. The selection of **NORM** or **ALTR** operation is indicated by lighting the respective legend on the **TURN RATE** selector switch. The lamp power to the indicator legends is controlled through a relay so that the **NORM** legend is lit in case the mode selector logic or lamp drivers fail. Sequential operation of the **TURN RATE** switch alternates the rate gyro connected to the VSI.

3.18.4.15 CRS HDG Select. The **CRS HDG** switch on the mode selector provides for either the pilot's or the copilot's course selector (**CRS**) to be connected to the navigation receiver, and for concurrent connection of the same pilot's HSI course and heading information to the command instrument system processor. The CRS resolver is normally connected to the pilot's HSI until selected by the copilot on his mode selector. CRS HDG control is transferred by pressing the **CRS HDG** switch. The pilot having the **CRS HDG** control is indicated by lighting of either the **PLT** or the **CPLT** legend on each mode selector. When power is first applied to the mode selector, the pilot's position is automatically selected. The **CRS HDG** selection is independent of the navigation modes selected by the top row of switches.

3.19.4.16 VERT GYRO Select. The vertical gyro selection provides each pilot the option of having his VSI display his own vertical gyro attitude (**NORM** operation), or of having the other pilot's vertical gyro attitude displayed (**ALTR** operation). The vertical gyro selection is independent of the navigation modes selected by the top row of switches and is independent of which vertical gyro the other pilot has selected. Each pilot's VSI is normally connected to his own vertical gyro. The selection of **NORM** or **ALTR** operation is indicated by lighting the respective legend on the **VERT GYRO** selector switch. The lamp power to the indicator legends is controlled through a relay so that the **NORM** legend is lit in case the mode selector logic or lamp drivers fail. Sequential operation of the **VERT GYRO** switch alternates the vertical gyro connected to the VSI.

3.19.4.17 No. 2 Bearing Select. The HSI number 2 bearing pointer selection allows the option of either the LF/ADF bearing or the VOR bearing to a selected station. The **ADF/VOR** selection is independent of the navigation modes selected by the top row of switches, and either pilot selects **ADF** or **VOR**, independent of the other pilot's selection. The number 2 bearing pointer is normally connected to the LF/ADF bearing output. The selection of either ADF or either VOR or TACAN bearing is indicated by lighting of the respective legend on the selector switch. The lamp power to the indicator legends is controlled through a relay, so that the **ADF** legend is lit in case the mode selector logic or lamp drivers fail. Sequential operation of the **ADF/VOR** switch alternates the bearing source connected to the No. 2 bearing pointer between ADF and VOR or TACAN.

3.19.5 Operation.

a. Heading Hold.

   (1) **CIS MODE SEL** switch - **HDG**.

   (2) **HDG** set knob on HSI - Set as desired.

   (3) Selected heading is achieved by banking helicopter, to center roll command bar.

b. VOR Course Intercept.

   (1) Frequency - Set.

   (2) HSI **CRS** set knob - Set to desired course.

   (3) **CIS MODE SEL** switch - **NAV**.

   (4) Follow roll command bar to initially follow intercept heading and then follow command bar to intercept VOR course.

c. TACAN Course Intercept.

   (1) Channel or preset - Set.

   (2) **CIS MODE SEL** switch - **NAV**.

   (3) **CRS HDG PLT/CPLT** - As desired.

   (4) **VTAC** selector switch - **TACAN**.

   (5) **RADIO NAV** mode selector switch - **VTAC**.

   (6) HSI **CRS** set knob - Set to desired course.

d. ILS Approach.

   (1) Frequency - Set.

   (2) HSI **CRS** set knob - Set to desired course.

   (3) **CIS MODE SEL** switch - **NAV**.

   (4) **VTAC** switch - **VOR/ILS**.

   (5) **RADIO NAV** switch - **ILS**.

   (6) At two dots localizer deviation on HSI, follow roll command bar to intercept localizer.

   (7) As glide slope deviation pointer centers, follow collective position indications for glide slope tracking.

   (8) At decision height, press **GA** switch for go-around mode if breakout has not occurred.

e. Back Course Localizer Approach.

   (1) Frequency or preset - Set.

   (2) **LO** altitude bug - SET to missed approach point HAT.

   (3) HSI **CRS** set knob - Set to inbound back course.

   (4) **VTAC** switch - **VOR/ILS**.

   (5) **CIS MODE SEL** switch - **NAV**.

   (6) **MODE SEL** switch - **BACK CRS**.

   (7) Fly same as front course (paragraph 3.19.5d). Turn off **MODE SEL ALT** legend to stow collective position indicator before making manual descent on back course approach.

3.20 STORM SCOPE WEATHER MAPPING SYSTEM.

The storm scope, WX-1000, is a thunderstorm detection system. The system consists of an antenna, a receiver-computer, and a display screen. The receiver and antenna sections are continuously monitored by the built-in-test feature for proper operation. Electrical discharges associated with a storm cell are sensed by the antenna, processed by the receiver to determine range and azimuth, and displayed on the storm scope indicator as a plus (+) symbol. Power to the storm scope is provided by the No. 2 dc primary bus through a circuit breaker marked **STORM SCOPE**.

3.20.1 Antennas. The stormscope antenna is mounted on the bottom of the cabin (Figure 3-1).

3.20.2 Storm scope Controls, Functions, and Displays. All of the operating controls are located on the storm scope display, which is installed in the instrument panel (Figure 3-32). S1, S2, S3, and S4 selections are dependent upon which screen is currently being displayed. There are nine different screen displays for the storm scope (self-test, menu, 360 degree, 120 degree, time/date, options, error message, noise monitor, and test strikes). The following controls and functions are available for the storm scope:

3.20.2.1 Main Menu. Main menu. The main menu allows the pilots to select between the checklist, time/date, and options modes (Figure 3-32, Main Menu). The following controls and functions are available on the main menu:

CONTROL/LEGEND	FUNCTION
OFF BRT Knob	Turns system on/off and adjusts screen instensity.
CHECKLIST	Not functional.
TIME/DATE	Access **TIME/DATE** menu.
OPTIONS	Access **OPTIONS** menu.
NAVAID DISPLAY ON	Toggles NAVAID mode **ON** or **OFF**.
S1 **360°**	Selects 360-degree weather mapping mode.
S2 **NEXT**	Steps the highlight bar through the menu selections.
S3 **120°**	Selects 120-degree weather mapping mode.
S4 **GO**	Selects the mode indicated by the highlighted menu selection.

3.20.3 Modes of Operation.

3.20.3.1 360° Weather Mapping Mode. Three hundred sixty degrees. When the 360° weather mode is initially displayed, it will always be in the 200 nautical miles range (Figure 3-32, 360 Degree Presentation). At least two ranges are always labeled for reference. The 25 nautical miles range is always indicated by a solid ring. The following controls and functions are available for 360° weather mapping mode:

CONTROL/LEGEND	FUNCTION
OFF BRT switch	Turns system on/off and adjusts screen instensity.
S1 MENU	Displays the main menu.
S2 CLEAR	Clears strike memory and storm information from the screen.
S3 120°	Selects 120-degree weather mapping mode.
S4 NM	Starts at current nautical mile range, allows pilot to toggle through the range scales.

3.20.3.2 120° Weather Mapping Mode. The system shows weather in the 120° forward sector only (Figure 3-32, 120 Degree Presentation). When the 120° weather mode is initially selected, it will always be in the 200 nautical miles range. At least two ranges are always labeled for reference. The 25 nautical miles range is always indicated by a solid ring. The following controls and functions are available for 120° weather mapping mode:

CONTROL/LEGEND	FUNCTION
OFF BRT switch	Turns system on/off and adjusts screen instensity.
S1 MENU	Displays the main menu.
S2 CLEAR	Clears strike memory and storm information from the screen.
S3 360°	Selects 360-degree weather mapping mode.
S4 NM	Starts at current nautical mile range, allows pilot to steps down through the range scales.

3.20.3.3 Time and Date Mode.

NOTE

Date must be set before setting the time.

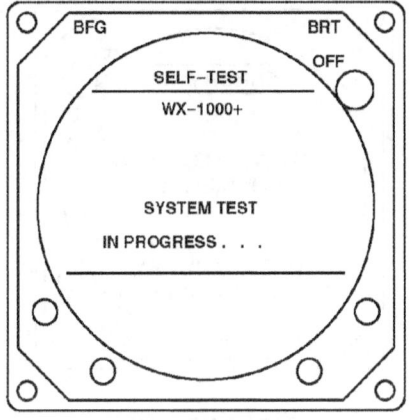
SELF-TEST PRESENTATION

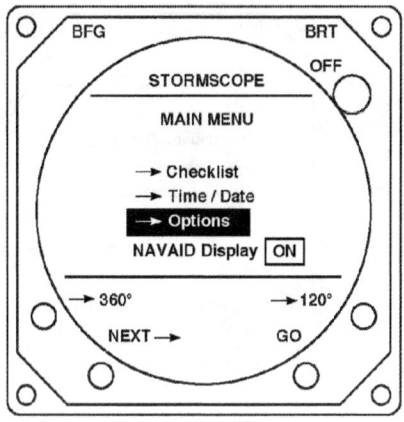
MAIN MENU

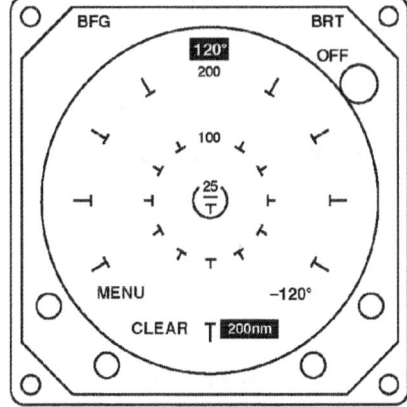
360 DEGREE PRESENTATION

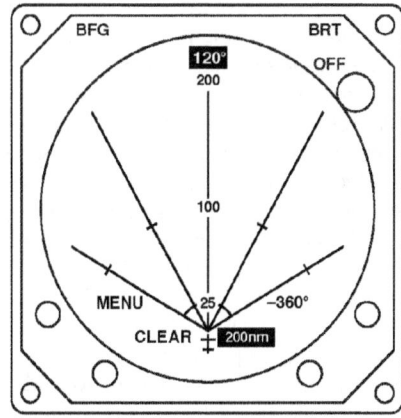
120 DEGREE PRESENTATION

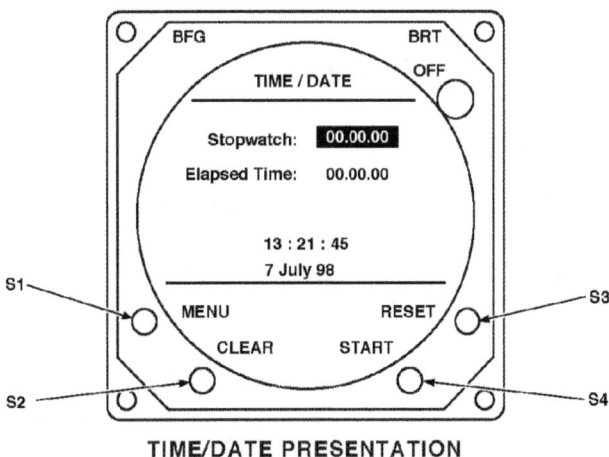
TIME/DATE PRESENTATION

Figure 3-32. Storm scope Displays (Sheet 1 of 2)

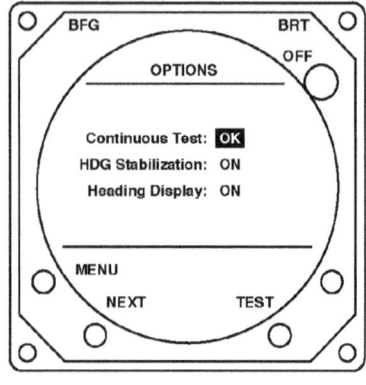
OPTIONS PRESENTATION

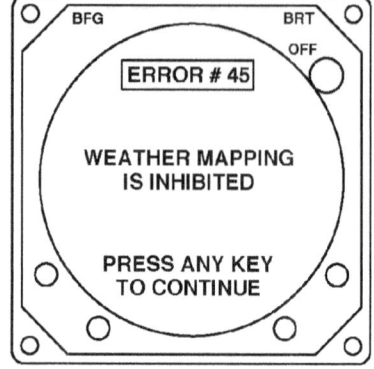
ERROR MESSAGE

Figure 3-32. Storm scope Displays (Sheet 2 of 2)

This mode allows the pilots to set the current time and date, and use the stopwatch and elapsed time features of the storm scope (Figure 3-32, Time/Date Presentation). Time and date are set by stepping the highlight bar through the date, month, year, hours, minutes, and seconds using the NEXT button. The UP and DOWN buttons are used to increment/decrement the highlighted time/date numeral. The stopwatch and elapsed time features count hours, minutes, and seconds up to 99.59.59. Removing power will stop the elapsed time counter, but will not reset the elapsed time counter to 00.00.00. This feature of the elapsed timer allows the pilots to press START to continue the elapsed timer counting. The following controls and functions are available for the time and date mode:

CONTROL/ LEGEND	FUNCTION
OFF BRT switch	Turns system on/off and adjusts screen instensity.
Time/Date Mode	
S1 MENU	Displays the main menu.
S2 NEXT	Steps the highlight bar through the stopwatch, elapsed time counter, and each portion of the time and date display.
Stopwatch Mode	
S1 MENU	Displays the main menu.
S2 NEXT	Selects other timing functions.

CONTROL/ LEGEND	FUNCTION
S3 RESET	Returns stopwatch digits to zeros.
S4 START or STOP	Starts or stops stopwatch time counting feature.
Elapsed Timer Mode	
S1 MENU	Displays the main menu.
S2 NEXT	Selects other timing functions.
S3 RESET	Returns elapse time digits to zeros.
S4 START or STOP	Starts or stops elapsed timer counting feature.
Set Current Time/Date Mode	
S1 MENU	Displays the main menu.
S2 NEXT	Highlights the digits to be changed.
S3 UP	Increments the highlighted number(s).
S4 DOWN	Decrement the highlighted number(s).

3.20.3.4 Options Mode. Displays the latest built-in-test result and allows the pilots to initiate a complete self test (Figure 3-32, Options Menu). OK indicates no faults detected during continuous self test. FAULT indicates a fault is detected (Table 3-3). The system will always power up with HDG Stabilization on. If the aircraft external heading source (gyro) fails, the HDG Stabilization feature should be turned off manually. Also, HDG Stabilization should be manually disabled if a compass failure occurs without causing a flag condition. When operating in the HDG Stabilization mode, the pilots may elect to have the Heading Display on or off in any weather mode. When Heading Display is on, the aircraft heading will appear as a digital readout at the top of the display. The following controls and functions are available on the options menu:

CONTROL/ LEGEND	FUNCTION
CONTINUOUS TEST	Displays status **ON** or **OFF** of built in test.
HDG Stabilization:	Displays status of heading stabilization **ON** or **OFF**.
Heading Display:	Displays status of heading display **ON** or **OFF**.
S1 **MENU**	Access the main menu.
S2 **NEXT**	Steps the highlight bar through the menu selections.
S4 **TEST**	Initiates the built-in-test when highlight bar is over Continuous Test, and toggle between ON and OFF for HDG Stabilization and Heading Display selections.

3.20.3.5 Navigation Display Mode. Weather mapping screen will also display course line to selected waypoints, a course deviation indicator and up to 6 additional data items provided by AMS. On initial start-up, the navaid mode will attempt to display range, ground speed, estimated time enroute, bearing, crosstrack error and estimated time of arrival. These additional items may be modified in the options mode.

3.20.4 Storm Scope Normal Operation. After the storm scope is turned on, a self test is automatically performed by internal diagnostics to verify system readiness. This test takes approximately 15 seconds. **SYSTEM TEST IN PROGRESS** should be displayed while test is being performed. Upon satisfactory completion of all tests, **ALL TESTS ARE OK** will be displayed for 3 seconds, then will be replaced by the main menu. If system is turned on cold, the test may be completed prior CRT start. In this case, the initial display will be the main menu.

Table 3-3. Storm Scope Error Messages.

ERROR	MESSAGE	ACTION
Bus Error Video Error Data Error Program Memory Video Memory	HARDWARE ERROR Continued operation is not possible	Turn the unit off
Real-Time Clock Real-Time Clock Battery	HARDWARE ERROR Time of day function not available	Press any key to continue operation without clock function
Antenna	ANTENNA ERROR Storm information is not available	Press any key to continue operation without thunderstorm data
Analog Processing	HARDWARE ERROR Storm information is not available	Press any key to continue operation without thunderstorm data
Heading Processing	HARDWARE ERROR Heading stabilization and display not available	Press any key to continue operation without heading information
Microphone Key Stuck	MIC KEY STUCK Strike processing is inhibited	Check mike key to correct problem.

Section IV TRANSPONDER AND RADAR

3.21 TRANSPONDER AN/APX-100(V)1 (IFF).

The transponder set (Figure 3-33) provides automatic radar identification of the helicopter to all suitably equipped challenging aircraft and surface or ground facilities within the operating range of the system. AN/APX-100(V) receives, decodes, and responds to the characteristic interrogations of operational modes 1, 2, 3/A, C, and 4. Specially coded identification of position (IP) and emergency signals may be transmitted to interrogating stations when conditions warrant. The transceiver can be operated in any one of four master modes, each of which may be selected by the operator at the control panel. Five independent coding modes are available to the operator. The first three modes may be used independently or in combination. Mode 1 provides 32 possible code combinations, any one of which may be selected in flight. Mode 2 provides 4096 possible code combinations, but only one is available and is normally preset before takeoff. Mode 3/A provides 4096 possible codes any one of which may be selected in flight. Mode C will indicate pressure altitude of the helicopter when interrogated. Mode C is only available if both mode 3/A and mode C switches are placed to the **ON** position. Mode 4 is the secure mode of cooperative combat identification, IFF operational codes are installed, the current period's code and either the previous or the next period's code. Power to operate the IFF system is provided from the No. 1 dc primary bus through a circuit breaker marked **IFF**. Refer to TM 11-5895-1199-12 and 11-5895-1037-12.

3.21.1 Antenna.

CAUTION

The transponder will **ignore** (and not respond to) interrogations received from the ground if the ANT switch is in the TOP position and will ignore interrogations received from above if the ANT switch is in the BOT position.

Antennas are installed on the top fairing between engine exhaust ports, (Figure 3-1) and under the transition section behind the UHF-AM antenna. They receive signals of interrogating stations and transmit reply signals. The AN/APX-100(V) is a diversity transponder, functioning to receive the rf interrogation from two antennas and transmit the reply via the antenna from which the stronger interrogation signal was received. If the **ANT** switch is in the **TOP** position and the stronger signal was received from the bottom antenna, no rf reply will be transmitted. If the **ANT** switch is in the **BOT** position and the stronger signal was received from the top antenna, no rf reply will be transmitted. Therefore the **ANT** switch must be in the **DIV** position to insure the IFF will reply to all valid interrogations.

3.21.2 Controls and Functions.
All operating and mode code select switches for transceiver operation are on Control Panel RT-1296/APX-100(V) (Figure 3-33).

CONTROL/INDICATOR	FUNCTION
TEST GO	Indicates successful BIT.
TEST/MON NO GO	Indicates unit malfunction.
ANT-DIV switch	Allows the pilot to select the **TOP** (upper antenna), **BOT** (bottom antenna), or **DIV** (diversity, both antennas) of the aircraft.

NOTE

The **ANT-DIV** switch shall be placed in the **DIV** position at all times.

TM 1-1520-253-10

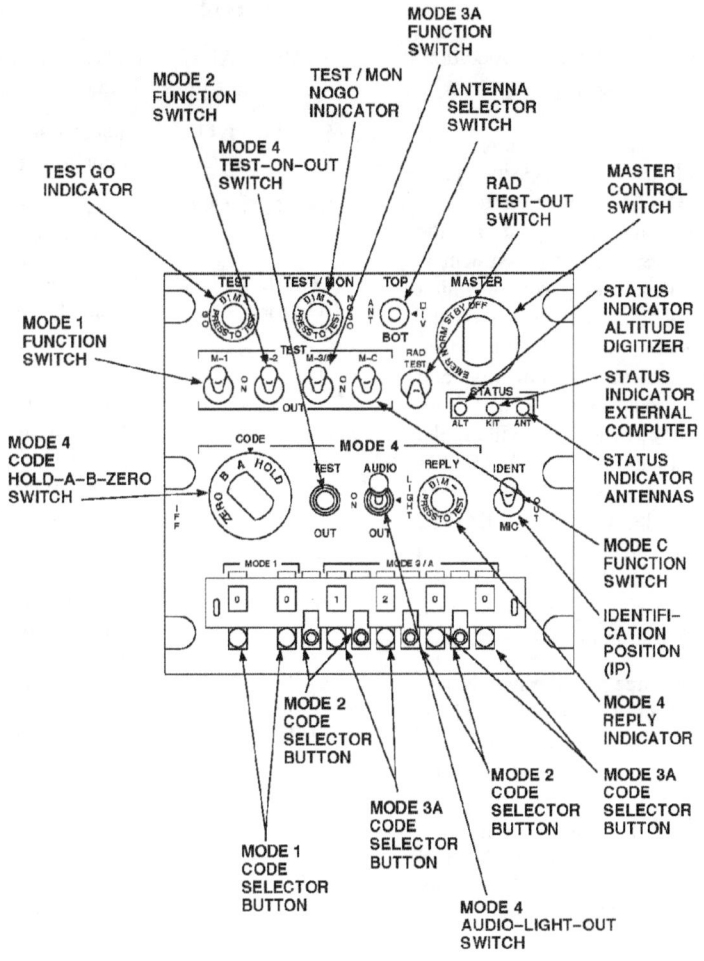

Figure 3-33. Control Panel RT-1296/APX-100(V)

3-91

CONTROL/INDICATOR	FUNCTION
MASTER/OFF/STBY/NORM/EMER	Selects operating condition. **NOTE** Emergency reply provisions. This mode of operation is possible when the **MASTER** switch on the IFF control panel is placed in the **EMER** position and the system is interrogated. Emergency operation results in four short dashes on the interrogating radar indicator, which indicates an aircraft in distress, and singles out the aircraft in emergency condition within the group of aircraft. (The **MASTER** switch must be in **NORM**, then lifted and turned to **EMER**, therefore preventing the switch from accidentally being in **EMER**.) The emergency reply consists of a code 7700 in mode 3/A.
M-1, M-2, M-3/A, M-C switches	The four, three position switches on the IFF control panel will enable or disable the system for modes **1, 2, 3/A**, or **C** operation. Mode 1, mode 2, mode 3/A, or mode C replies are possible only when their respective switches are placed in the **ON** positions. Mode C is available only if both mode 3/A and mode C are placed in the **ON** position. Mode 1 switches permit selection of a desired code from 00 through 73. Mode 2 and mode 3/A switches permit selection of a desired code from 0000 through 7777. The **OUT** position of each switch prevents a reply to the respective mode interrogations. The **TEST** position of each switch tests the respective mode operation.
RAD TEST/OUT	The **RAD** switch is used to allow the RT to reply to external test interrogation when held in the **RAD** position.
RAD TEST	Allows receiver transmitter to reply to external test interrogations.
OUT	Disables the **RAD TEST** features of the transponder.

CONTROL/INDICATOR	FUNCTION
STATUS ALT	Indicates that BIT or **MON** failure is due to altitude digitizer.
STATUS KIT	Indicates that BIT or **MON** failure is due to external computer.
STATUS ANT	Indicates that BIT or **MON** failure is due to cables or antenna.
MODE 4 CODE selector	When the IFF mode 4 computer is installed, mode 4 interrogations bypass the decoder in the RT and go directly to the crypto computer. In the crypto computer the mode 4 interrogation signal is decoded and applied to the mode 4 recognition circuit. When a mode 4 complete concurrence exists, the mode 4 recognition circuit generates a signal to the mode 4 computer which in turn generates a mode 4 reply. The **REPLY** light on the IFF control unit comes on to indicate a mode 4 reply is being transmitted.
ZERO	Zeroize code setting in computer.
A	Selects mode 4 code setting for previous, present, or next period, depending on which crypto period applies.
B	Selects mode 4 code setting for previous, present, or next period, depending on which crypto period applies.
HOLD	Retains mode 4 code setting when power is removed from transponder.
MODE 4 TEST/ON/OUT	
ON	Allows system to reply to mode 4 interrogations.
OUT	Prevents reply to mode 4 interrogations.
TEST	Provides self test for mode 4.
MODE 4 AUDIO/LIGHT/OUT	

CONTROL/ INDICATOR	FUNCTION
AUDIO	Enables aural and **REPLY** light monitoring of valid mode 4 interrogations and replies. (Preferred position)
LIGHT	Enables only **REPLY** light monitoring of valid mode 4 interrogations and replies.

WARNING

Placing the switch in the OUT position will disable mode 4 REPLY monitoring and IFF caution light.

OUT	Disables aural, **REPLY** light, and caution light monitoring of valid mode 4 interrogations and replies.
MODE 4 REPLY	Indicates that a mode 4 reply is transmitted.
IDENT/ OUT/MIC	The **IDENT/OUT/MIC** switch is spring loaded to the **OUT** position. If **IDENT** operation is desired, the switch must be moved to the **IDENT** position momentarily. The **IDENT** pulse trains will be transmitted for approximately 30 seconds. The **MIC** position is not connected in this installation.
MODE 1 selector buttons	Selects mode 1 reply code to be transmitted.
MODE 2 selector buttons	Selects four digit mode 2 reply code to be transmitted. (Located on the control panel or on the remote RT.)
MODE 3/A selector buttons	Selects four digit mode 3/A reply code to be transmitted.

3.21.3 Operation.

3.21.3.1 Starting Procedure.

CAUTION

When flying in a combat situation near friendly radar sites or in the vicinity of friendly fighter aircraft, the MODE 4 monitor switch must be in either the AUDIO or LIGHT position. This will enable the pilot to observe that the IFF is periodically responding to expected MODE 4 interrogations.

If the MODE 2 code has not been set previously, loosen two screws which hold MODE 2 numeral cover, and slide this cover upward to expose numerals of MODE 2 code switches (Figure 3-33). Set these switches to code assigned to helicopter. Slide numeral cover down and tighten screws.

1. **MASTER** switch - **STBY**. **NO-GO** light should be on.

2. Allow 2 minutes for warmup.

3. MODES 1 and **3A** CODE selector buttons - Press and release until desired code shows.

4. **TEST**, **TEST/MON**, and **REPLY** indicators -**PRESS-TO-TEST**. If **MODE 1** is to be used, check as follows:

5. **ANT** switch - **DIV**.

6. **MASTER** switch - **NORM**.

7. **M-1** switch - Hold at **TEST**, observe that only **TEST GO** indicator is on.

8. **M-1** switch - Return to **ON**. If modes **2**, **3A** or **M-C** are to be used, check as follows:

9. **M-2**, **M-3/A** and **M-C** switches - Repeat steps 7. and 8.

NOTE

Do not make any checks near a radar site or with **MASTER** control switch in **EMER**, nor with **M-3/A** codes 7500, 7600 or 7700, without first obtaining authorization from the interrogating station(s) within range of the transponder.

The following steps can be done only with KIT/1A computer transponder installed.

10. **MODE 4 CODE** switch - **A**.

    a. Set assigned test code in the KIT/1A computer transponder.

    b. **AUDIO-ON-OUT** switch - **OUT**.

    c. **MODE 4 TEST-ON-OUT** switch - Place to **TEST** and hold, then release.

    d. **TEST GO** light - **ON**, **MODE 4 REPLY** light off, **KIT STATUS** light off.

11. When possible, request cooperation from interrogating station to activate radar **TEST** mode.

    a. Verify from interrogating station that **MODE TEST** reply was received.

    b. **RAD TEST** switch - **RAD TEST** and hold.

    c. Verify from interrogating station that **TEST MODE** reply was received.

3.21.3.2 Normal Procedures. Completion of the starting procedure leaves the AN/APX-100(V) in operation. The following steps may be required, depending upon mission.

1. **MODE 4 CODE** selector switch - **A** or **B** as required.

    a. If code retention is desired, momentarily place the **MODE 4 CODE** selector switch to **HOLD** prior to turning the **MASTER** switch **OFF**.

    b. If code retention in external computer is not desired during transponder off mode, place **MODE 4 CODE** selector switch to **ZERO** to dump external computer code setting.

2. Mode **M-1**, **M-2**, **M-3/A**, **M-C**, or **MODE 4** switches - Select desired mode.

3. Identification of position (I/P) switch - **IDENT**, when required, to transmit identification of position pulses.

3.21.3.3 Emergency Operation.

NOTE

MASTER control switch must be lifted before it can be switched to **NORM** or **EMER**.

During a helicopter emergency or distress condition the AN/APX-100(V) may be used to transmit specially coded emergency signals on mode 1, 2, 3/A and 4 to all interrogating stations. Those emergency signals will be transmitted as long as the **MASTER** control switch on the control panel remains in **EMER** and the helicopter is interrogated. **MASTER** control switch - **EMER**.

3.21.4 Stopping Procedure. MASTER switch - **OFF**.

3.22 RADAR ALTIMETER SET AN/APN-209(V).

The radar altimeter set (Figure 3-34) provides instantaneous indication of actual terrain clearance height. Altitude, in feet, is displayed on two radar altimeter indicators on the instrument panel in front of the pilot and copilot. The radar altimeter indicators each contain a pointer that indicates altitude on a linear scale from 0 to 200 feet (10 feet per unit) and a second-linear scale from 200 to 1500 feet (100 feet per unit). An On/**OFF/LO** altitude bug set knob, on the lower left corner of each indicator, combines functions to serve as a low level warning bug set control, and an On/OFF power switch. The system is turned on by turning the **LO** control knob, marked **SET**, of either indicator, clockwise from **OFF**. Continued clockwise turning of the control knob will permit either pilot to select any desired low-altitude limit, as indicated by the LO altitude bug. Whenever the altitude pointer exceeds low-altitude set limit, the **LO** altitude warning light will go on. Pressing the **PUSH-TO-TEST HI SET** control provides a testing feature of the system at any time and altitude. When the **PUSH-TO-TEST** control knob is pressed, a reading between 900 feet and 1100 feet on the indicator, and a reading between 900 and 1100 feet on the digital display, and the **OFF** flag removed from view, indicates satisfactory system operation. Releasing the **PUSH-TO-TEST SET** control knob restores the system to normal operation. A low-altitude warning light, on the center left of the indicator,

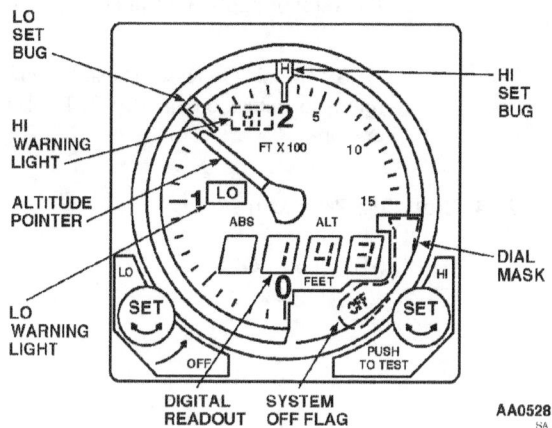

Figure 3-34. Radar Altimeter Set AN/APN-209(V)

will light to show the word **LO** any time the helicopter is at or below the altitude limit selected by the low altitude bug. Each pilot may individually select a low-altitude limit and only his **LO** light will go on when the low-altitude is reached or exceeded. Loss of system power will be indicated by the indicator pointer moving behind the dial mask and the **OFF** flag appearing in the center of the instrument. If the system should become unreliable, the flag will appear and the indicator pointer will go behind the dial mask, to prevent the pilot from obtaining erroneous readings. Flight operations above 1600 feet do not require that the system be turned off. The pointer will go behind the dial mask but the transmitter will be operating. Power to operate the AN/APN-209 is supplied from the No. 1 dc primary through circuit breakers, marked **RDR ALTM**.

3.22.1 Antennas. Two identical radar altimeter antennas (Figure 3-1) are on the cockpit section under the avionics compartment. One is for the transmitter and the other is for the receiver. The antennas are flush-mounted in the fuselage on the bottom of the helicopter.

3.22.2 Controls or Indicator Function. Control of the radar altimeter set is provided by the **LOW SET OFF** knob on the front of the height indicator. The knob, marked **HI SET**, also controls the **PUSH TO TEST** (Figure 3-34).

CONTROL/ INDICATOR	FUNCTION OR INDICATION
LO SET knob	Power control turned counterclockwise to **OFF**, clockwise to on.
L bug	Sets altitude trip point of **LO** warning light.
H bug	Sets altitude trip point of **HI** warning light.
HI SET knob	Pushing knob actuates built-in test system to self-test altimeter.
Altitude pointer	Provides an analog indication of absolute altitude from zero to 1500 feet.
Digital readout	Gives a direct-reading four digit indication of absolute altitude from zero to 1500 feet.
LO warning light	Lights whenever dial pointer goes below **L** altitude bug setting.
HI warning light	Lights whenever dial pointer goes above **H** altitude bug setting.
OFF flag	Moves into view whenever altimeter loses track while power is applied.

3.22.3 Operation.

1. Starting Procedure.

   a. **LO SET** knob - On.

   b. **L** bug - Set to 80 feet.

   c. **H** bug - Set to 800 feet.

   d. Indicator pointer - Behind mask above 1500 feet.

2. Track Operation. After about 2 minutes of warmup, the altimeter will go into track mode with these indications:

   a. **OFF** flag - Not in view.

   b. Altitude pointer - 0 ± 5 feet.

   c. Digital readout - 0 to +3 feet.

   d. **LO** warning light - Will light.

e. **HI** warning light - Will be off.

3. **HI SET** knob - Press and hold. The altimeter will indicate a track condition as follows:

    a. **OFF** flag - Not in view.

    b. Altitude pointer - 1000 ± 100 feet.

    c. Digital readout - 1000 ± 100 feet.

    d. **LO** warning light - Will be off.

e. **HI** warning light - Will light.

f. **HI SET** knob - Release. The altimeter will return to indications in step 2. Track Operation.

3.22.4 Stopping Procedure.

LO SET knob - **OFF**.

CHAPTER 4

MISSION EQUIPMENT

Section I MISSION AVIONICS

4.1 CHAFF AND FLARE DISPENSER M130.

4.1.1 Chaff Dispenser M130. The general purpose dispenser M130 (Figure 4-1) consists of a single system (dispenser assembly, payload module assembly, electronics module and dispenser control panels) and a **CHAFF DISPENSE** control button (on the lower console) designed to dispense decoy chaff, M-1 (Refer to TM 9-1095-206-13&P). The system provides effective survival countermeasures against radar guided weapon systems threats. The dispenser system, M130, has the capability of dispensing 30 chaff. Power to operate the chaff dispenser system is provided from the No. 1 dc primary bus through a circuit breaker, marked **CHAFF DISP**.

4.1.2 Controls and Function. The dispenser control panel (Figure 4-1) contains all necessary controls to operate the dispenser system from the cockpit. The control panel is on the lower console.

CONTROL/ INDICATOR	FUNCTION
CHAFF counter	Shows the number of chaff cartridges remaining in payload module.
Chaff counter setting knob	Adjusts counter to correspond to number of chaff cartridges remaining in payload module.
PUSH-RESET	When pushed, resets chaff counter to "00".

CONTROL/ INDICATOR	FUNCTION
ARM indicator light	Indicates that arming switch is at **ARM**, safety flag pin is removed, and payload module is armed.
ARM-SAFE switch	
ARM	Applies electrical power through safety flag switch to **CHAFF DISPENSE** button, and flare firing switch. Flare firing system is not used in this installation.
SAFE	Removes power from dispenser system.
FLARE counter	Not used in this installation.
Flare counter setting knob	Not used in this installation.
DISP CONT	Not used in this installation.
Mode selector	Selects type of chaff release operation.
MAN	Dispenses one chaff cartridge each time dispense button is pressed.
PGRM	Dispenses chaff according to predetermined burst/salvo and number of salvos automatically.
CHAFF DISPENSE	Ejects chaff cartridges from payload module.

TM 1-1520-253-10

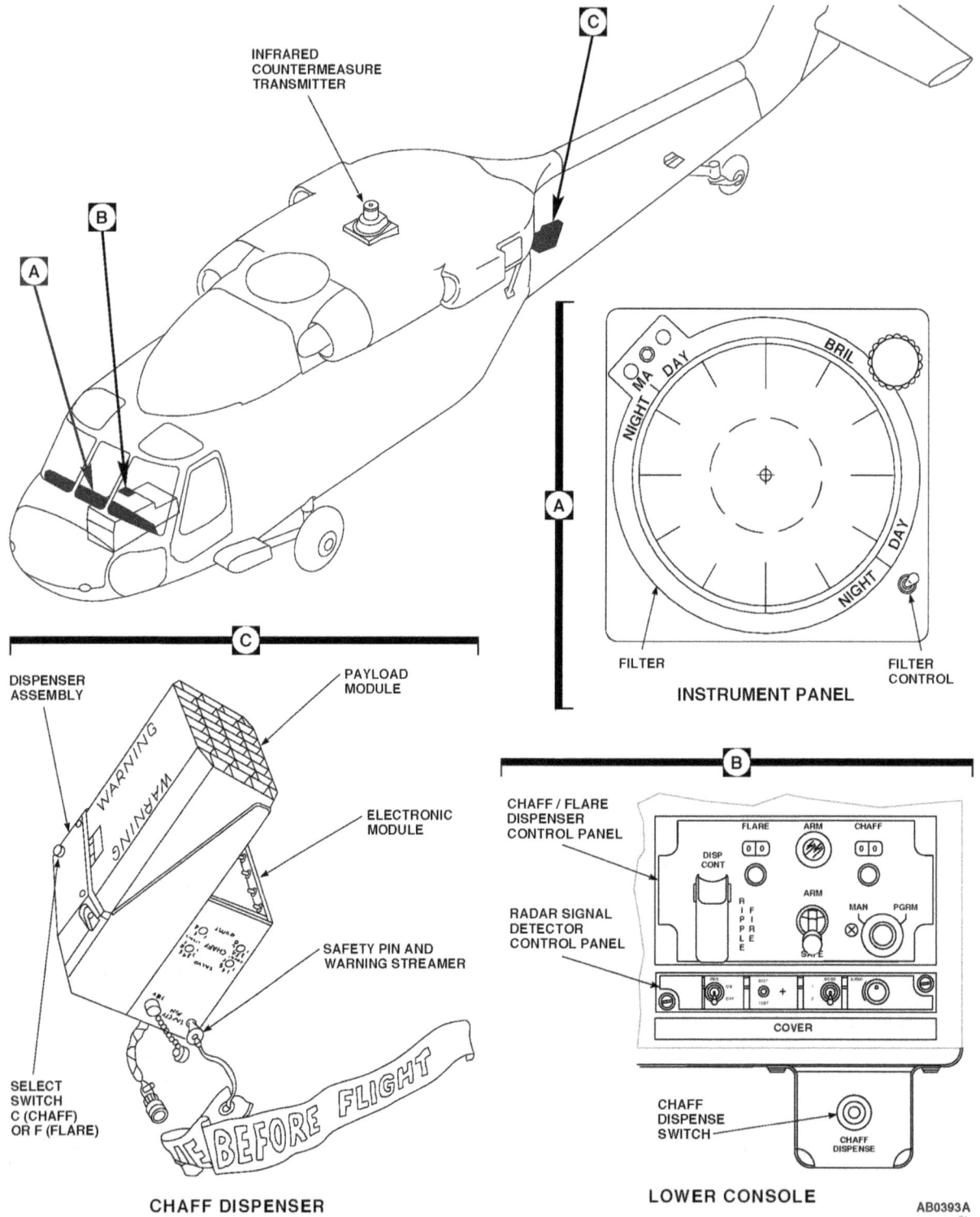

Figure 4-1. Mission Kits

4-2

4.1.3 Dispenser Assembly. The dispenser assembly (Figure 4-1) contains the breech assembly, C-F selector switch for either chaff or flares, a reset switch, and a housing containing the sequencer assembly. The sequencer assembly receives power through the firing switches circuit and furnishes pulses to each of the 30 contacts of the breech assembly, in sequential order 1 through 30, thus firing each of the impulse cartridges.

4.1.4 Payload Module Assembly. The payload module assembly (Figure 4-1) consists of the payload module and retaining plate assembly. The payload module has 30 chambers which will accept chaff. The chaff cartridges are loaded through the studded end of the module, one per chamber, and are held in place by the retaining assembly. The payload module assembly is assembled to the dispenser assembly.

4.1.5 Electronic Module Assembly (EM). The EM (Figure 4-1) contains a programmer and a cable assembly which includes a 28-volt supply receptacle and a safety switch, actuated by inserting the safety pin with streamer assembly. The programmer consists of a programming circuit which allows the setting of chaff burst number, chaff burst interval, chaff salvo number, and chaff salvo interval.

4.1.6 Electronics Module Controls. Controls on the electronic module are used to program the chaff dispenser for predetermined release of chaff cartridges. Controls on the electronic module are as follows: (Refer to TM 9-1095-206-13&P)

CONTROL	FUNCTION
SAFETY PIN	Safety switch to accept the safety pin with streamer, placing the dispenser in a safe condition when the helicopter is on the ground.
SALVO COUNT	Programs the number of salvos; 1, 2, 4, 8 or C (Continuous).
SALVO INTERVAL	Programs the time in seconds between salvos; 1, 2, 3, 4, 5, 8 or R (Random 2, 5, 3, 4, 3).
BURST COUNT	Programs the number of burst; 1, 2, 3, 4, 6 or 8.
BURST INTERVAL	Programs the time in seconds for burst intervals; 0.1, 0.2, 0.3 or 0.4.

4.1.7 Safety Procedures. The safety pin shall be installed in the safety switch when the helicopter is parked. Safety pin is removed immediately before takeoff.

4.1.8 Operation.

1. Counter(s) - Set for number of cartridges in payload module(s).

2. Mode switch - **MAN**.

NOTE

Mode switch should always be at **MAN** when the **ARM-SAFE** switch is moved to **ARM** to prevent inadvertent salvo of chaff.

3. **ARM SAFE** switch - **ARM**. **ARM** indicator light on.

4. Dispense button press or mode switch **PGRM**, as required.

4.1.9 Stopping Procedure. ARM SAFE switch - SAFE.

4.2 RADAR SIGNAL DETECTING SET AN/APR-39A(V)1.

Refer to TM 11-5841-294-12.

4.2.1 Controls and Functions. The operating controls of the AN/APR-39A(V)1 are as follows:

CONTROL	FUNCTION
POWER	Controls 28VDC from the No. 1 dc primary bus.
ON	Locks the switch in the **ON** position. System is fully operational after approximately one minute. On power up the synthetic voice will announce "APR-39 POWER UP". The plus (+) symbol will appear and be centered on the IP 1150A cathode ray tube (CRT) during system operation.
OFF	Turns system off. Switch must be pulled to unlock and turn system off.

CONTROL	FUNCTION
TEST	When momentarily depressed initiates self-test confidence check (except for antennas and antenna receiver cabling).
MODE	Selects synthetic voice message format only. **MODE ONE (UP)** selects normal voice message format. **MODE TWO (DOWN)** selects test/abbreviated voice message format.
AUDIO	Controls volume to the interphone system.
Direction/Display (Scope IP 1150A)	Shows alphanumeric symbology on a bearing for each processed emitter signal. Does not indicate any range data.
MA indicator	Not used.
MA switch	Not used.
BRIL control	Varies brilliance of CRT.

CAUTION

To prevent damage to the receiver detector crystals, assure that the AN/APR-39A(V)-1 antennas are at least **60 yards** from active ground radar antennas or **6 yards** from active airborne radar antennas. Allow an extra margin for new, unusual, or high power emitters.

Excessive indicator display brightness may damage CRT.

4.2.2 Modes of Operation.

a. Self test mode.

(1) After power up, the AN/APR-39A(V)1 synthetic voice will announce "APR-39 POWER UP" and the (+) symbol will stabilize in the center of the CRT. Self test should be initiated after approximately one minute. Self test can be performed in **MODE ONE** or **MODE TWO**. In **MODE ONE** the synthetic voice will announce "SELF TEST SET VOLUME, 1, 2, 3, 4, 5, 6, 7, 8, 9, 10, 11, 12,". In **MODE TWO** the synthetic voice will announce "SELF TEST SET VOLUME, 5, 4, 3, 2, 1".

(2) The CRT will display specific software version numbers i.e., operational flight program (OFP) at the 12 o'clock position and the emitter identification data (EID) at the 6 o'clock position.

(3) After the software version numbers have been displayed the test sequence checks the receivers. A good visual self test will show two triangles, one at the 6 o'clock and one at 12 o'clock position on the CRT. Snowflake symbols (*) will appear at the 2, 4, 8, and 10 o'clock positions and will flash if the AN/AVR-2 laser detecting set is not installed. This is a normal indication and does not effect system performance.

(4) A good self test (no faults detected) ends with the message "APR-39 OPERATIONAL". A bad self test (faults detected) ends with the "APR-39 FAILURE".

b. **MODE ONE** operation. Selecting **MODE ONE** the operator will hear all the normal synthetic voice audio when an emitter has been processed e. g., the AN/APR-39A(V)1 will announce; "SA, S-18 12 O'CLOCK TRACKING". Selection of this mode does not have any effect on emitters received, processed or displayed, it only affects synthetic voice audio.

c. **MODE TWO** operation. Selecting **MODE TWO** the operator will hear an abbreviated synthetic voice audio e. g., the AN/APR-39A(V)1 will announce; "MISSILE 12 O'CLOCK TRACKING".

4.2.3 Function.

a. The radar signal detecting set (RSDS) receives, processes and displays pulse type signals operating in the C-D and H-M radio frequency bands. The emitters that it processes and displays are derived from the EID contained in the user data module (UDM) that is inserted in the top of the digital processor. In normal circumstances the processor is classified confidential if a classified UDM is installed.

b. The UDM contains the electronic warfare threat data that makes up the specific library for a specific mission(s) or a geographical location (it is theaterized). When a match of the electronic warfare data occurs the processor generates the appropriate threat symbology and synthetic audio. It is important therefore that the correct theaterized EID and UDM are installed for the mission or geographic location.

c. Symbol generation and position relative to the center of the CRT shows the threat lethality, it does not show or represent any lethality of range, but of condition/mode of the emitter. Highest priority threats (most lethal) are shown nearest the center. Each symbol defines a generic threat type, symbols are modified to show change in the status of the emitter. The symbols are unclassified, the definitions of what the symbols mean are classified. The complete set of symbols and definitions are contained in TM 11-5841-294-30-2. Each theaterized library EID has a specific classified pilot kneeboard produced with it. The unit electronic warfare officer (EWO) should contact PM-ASE if sufficient cards are not available within his unit for the installed EID.

d. The RSDS on specific aircraft has been interfaced with other aircraft survivability equipment. The equipment includes the AN/AVR-2 laser detection set, AN/APR-44(V) continuous wave receiver and the AN/AAR-47 missile warning system.

4.3 INFRARED COUNTERMEASURE SET AN/ALQ-144(V).

Do not continuously look at the infrared countermeasure transmitter (Figure 4-1) during operation, or for a period of over 1 minute from a distance of less than 3 feet. Skin exposure to countermeasure radiation for longer than 10 seconds at a distance less than 4 inches shall be avoided.

Ensure the countermeasure set is cooled off before touching the unit.

CAUTION

Observe that the IRCM INOP caution legend illuminates when the OCU ON/OFF switch is set to OFF. After 60 seconds, observe that the IRCM INOP caution legend extinguishes.

The countermeasure system provides infrared countermeasure capability. The system transmits radiation modulated mechanically at high and low frequencies using an electrically-heated source. A built-in test feature monitors system operation and alerts the pilot should a malfunction occur. The system is made up of a control panel on the instrument panel and a transmitter on top of the main rotor pylon aft of the main rotor. The countermeasure system gets dc electrical power from the No. 2 dc primary circuit breaker panel and the No. 2 junction box. The 28 vdc is routed through the **IRCM PWR** circuit breaker in the No. 2 junction box to the transmitter. The No. 2 dc primary bus also supplies 28 vdc through the **IRCM CONTR** circuit breaker on the No. 2 dc primary circuit breaker panel to the control unit. Panel lighting of the control unit is controlled by the **INSTR LTS NON FLT** control on the upper console. The source begins to heat, the servo motor and drive circuits are energized, turning on the high and low speed modulators, and a signal is applied to stabilize system operations before energizing the built-in test function. After a warmup period the stabilizing signal is removed, and the system operates normally. Placing the **ON-OFF** control switch momentarily to **OFF** causes the power distribution and control circuits to de-energize the source and initiates a cooldown period. During the cooldown period, the servo motor drive circuits remain in operation, applying power to the motors that cause the modulators to continue turning. The **IRCM INOP** caution legend will be lit. After the cooldown period, the power distribution and control circuits de-energize, all system operating voltage is removed and the **IRCM INOP** caution legend will go off. If a system malfunction causes the **IRCM INOP** caution legend to appear, the **IRCM INOP** caution legend will remain until the control panel **ON-OFF** switch is momentarily placed **OFF**. The system can be returned to operating mode by momentarily placing **ON-OFF** switch **OFF**, then **ON**, provided the cause of the malfunction has cleared. For additional information, refer to TM 11-5865-200-12.

4.3.1 Infrared Countermeasure System Control Panel. Control of the countermeasure set is provided by the operator control panel on the helicopter lower console (Figure 2-7). Power to operate the countermeasure set is supplied from the No. 2 dc primary bus through a circuit breaker, marked **IRCM CONTR**.

4.3.2 Controls and Function. Controls for the AN/ALQ-144 are on the front panel of the control unit. The function of each control is as follows:

CONTROL	FUNCTION
ON-OFF switch	Turns set on and off.
IRCM INOP caution legend	Indicates malfunction has occurred or the countermeasure system is in cooldown cycle.

4.3.3 Operation.

1. **ON-OFF** switch - **ON** momentarily, then release (Switch will return to center position when released).

NOTE

If the **IRCM INOP** caution legend appears, place the power switch **OFF**.

4.3.4 Stopping Procedure. ON-OFF switch - **OFF**. The transmitter will continue to operate for about 60 seconds during the cooldown cycle. **IRCM INOP** caution legend should appear during cooldown cycle.

4.4 HEADS UP DISPLAY AN/AVS-7.

Heads up display (HUD) AN/AVS-7; (Figure 4-2) consists of signal data converter CV-4229/AVS-7 (SDC) located in the avionics compartment, the converter control C-12293/AVS-7 (CCU) located on the lower console, and the display, SU-180/AVS-7 (DU) consisting of the optical unit (OU) and power supply calibration unit (PSCU). Two thermocouple amplifiers are located in the avionics compartment and two **HUD** control switches are located on the pilot's collective sticks. The HUD system serves as an aid to pilots using the AN/AVS-6 (ANVIS) during night flight operations by providing operational symbology information about the aircraft. There are two programming modes and one operational mode which allow both pilots to independently select the symbology for their respective display modes from a master set of symbols in the signal data converter. Power to operate the HUD system is provided by the No. 1 ac primary bus and the No. 1 dc primary bus through circuit breakers marked **HUD REF** and **HUD SYS**.

4.4.1 Basic Principles of Operation. The pilots can independently select from four normal symbology modes and four declutter modes that were pre-programmed. Declutter mode has four vital symbols that will always be displayed: Airspeed, Altitude (MSL), Attitude (pitch and roll), and Engine Torque(s). An adjust mode, during operation, is used to adjust barometric altitude, pitch, and roll. If the HUD system loses operating power after adjustments have been made, the brightness, mode, barometric altitude, pitch, and roll must be adjusted as necessary. The system self test is divided into power-up or operator initialized built-in-test (BIT) and in-flight BIT. The system BIT is initialized during power-up or selected by the operator. Part of the BIT is a periodic test that is performed automatically along with normal system operation. A failure of the SDC, or the pilot's DU will illuminate the CCU **FAIL** light and display a **FAIL** message on the display unit. When a **FAIL** message is displayed on the DU, the operator should acknowledge the failure and re-run BIT to confirm the fault.

4.4.2 Controls and Functions. The CCU, located on the lower console, (Figures 2-8 and 4-2), and the control switches on the pilot's collective stick (Figure 2-11) are controls and indicators necessary for HUD operation. The **EYE SELECT L/R** position is set when display units are connected prior to operation. A focus ring on the OU provides control for focusing the display. The OU is adjusted by the manufacturer and under normal conditions adjustment is not required.

a. The converter control is described below:

CONTROL/ INDICATOR	FUNCTION
CPLT	
BRT/DIM	Copilot's control for display brightness.
DSPL POS D/U/ L/R	Copilot's control for display position down/up (outer knob) and left/right (inner knob).
MODE 1-4/ DCLT	Copilot's mode select 1-4 and declutter switch.
PLT	
BRT/DIM	Pilot's control for display brightness.
DSPL POS D/U/ L/R	Pilot's control for display position down/up (outer knob) and left/right (inner knob).
MODE 1-4/ DCLT	Pilot's mode select 1-4 and declutter switch.
FAIL	Indicates a system failure.
ON	Indicates system ON.
ADJ/ON/OFF	Selects adjust mode, enabling the **INC/DEC** switch to adjust altitude, pitch, or roll. Turns power on or off to HUD system.
P-PGM/OP/CP-PGM	Selects pilot program mode, operational mode, or copilot program mode. Used with the **PGM NXT/SEL** switch.
BIT/ACK	Selects built-in-test or used to acknowledge a displayed fault, completion of an adjustment, or completion of a programming sequence.

CONTROL/ INDICATOR	FUNCTION
ALT/P/R DEC/ INC	Active when adjust mode is selected to decrease/increase altitude/pitch roll. When adjusting altitude (MSL) a momentary movement of the **INC/DEC** switch will change data in 5 feet increments. When the **INC/DEC** switch is held for one second data will change 10 foot increments. Pitch and roll change in increments of one degree.

TM 1-1520-253-10

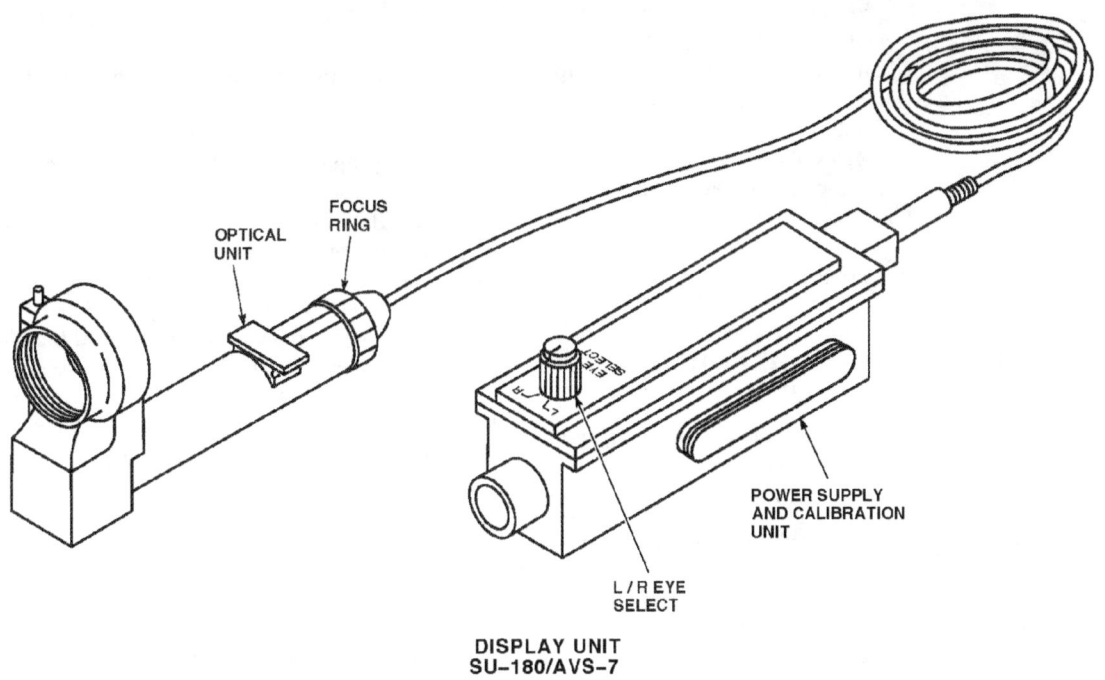

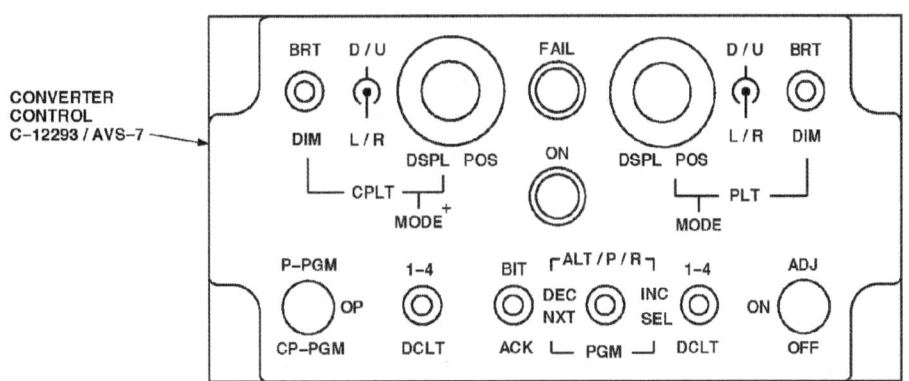

Figure 4-2. Heads Up Display AN/AVS-7

4-7

CONTROL/ INDICATOR	FUNCTION
PGM NXT/SEL	Active when program mode is selected. Allows operator to preprogram the four normal modes and four declutter modes. Operator can select a flashing symbol for display and/or go to the next symbol. Once complete, operator toggles the **ACK** switch to save programmed display.

b. Pilot's collective controls are described as follows:

CONTROL	FUNCTION
BRT/DIM	Allows pilot's to control brightness of their respective displays.
MODE/DCLT	Allows pilot's to select respective display modes or declutter modes.

c. Attach optic unit to either ANVIS monocular housing. Set **EYE SELECT** switch on **PSCU** to **L** or **R**.

4.4.3 Modes of Operation. There are two programming modes and one operational mode for the HUD system selected by the programming switch on the CCU. The adjust mode is a submode under the operational mode.

1. Pilot programming switch - Set to **P-PGM**.

2. Copilot programming switch - Set to **CP-PGM**.

3. Operation (flight mode) switch - Set to **OP**. (Adjust - **ADJ/ON/OFF** switch to **ADJ**).

4.4.4 Display Modes. Symbology display modes are programmable by the pilots via the converter control located on the lower console. Modes are defined by selecting from a master symbology menu (Figure 4-3 and Table 4-1). Up to eight display modes, four normal and four declutter, can by programmed for each user and can be selected for display using the display mode selection switch on the pilot's collective control or on the CCU. The default declutter mode has a minimum symbology display of:

- Airspeed - No. 25.
- Altitude (MSL) - No. 7.
- Attitude (pitch and roll) - No. 1, 5, 6, 20, 26.
- Engine Torque(s) - No. 22, 23.

Table 4-1. Master Mode Symbology Display (HUD)

No.	Symbol	Source	Range/Description
1	Angle of Pitch Scale	HUD System	± 30° (10° units, tic marks flash when angle of pitch is > ± 30°).
2	Bearing to Waypoint - Pointer	Doppler	0 - 359° (cursor will invert "V" when aircraft is moving away from waypoint).
3	Compass Reference Scale	HUD System	0 - 359° (10° units).
4	Aircraft Heading Fix Index	HUD System	Fixed Reference Mark.
5	Angle of Roll - Pointer	Copilot's Vertical Gyro	± 30° (right turn moves pointer to right, pointer flashes > ± 30°).
6	Angle of Roll - Scale	HUD System	± 30° (10° units).
7	Barometric Altitude (MSL)	Air Data System	-1000 to 20,000 feet (set during adjustment mode).
8	Adjust/Program Mode Message	HUD System	**ADJ** or **PROG**.
9	**OK/FAIL**	HUD System	**OK** or **FAIL**.
10	Velocity Vector	Doppler	0 - 15 knots/15 kilometers, 0 - 359°.

Table 4-1. Master Mode Symbology Display (HUD) (Cont)

No.	Symbol	Source	Range/Description
11	Rate of Climb Pointer	Air Data System	± 2000 feet-per-minute (used with vertical speed scale, No. 15).
12	Radar Altitude (AGL) - Numeric	Pilot's Radar Altimeter	0 - 1000 feet (0 - 200 feet, 1 foot units; 200 - 1000 feet, 10 foot units; disappears above 999 feet, and reappears below 950 feet).
13	Minimum Altitude Warning	Pilot's Radar Altimeter	Blinking square around symbol - No. 12, (set on pilot's low warning bug).
14	Radar Altitude (AGL) Analog Bar	Pilot's Radar Altimeter	0 - 250 feet (disappears at 250 feet, reappears at 230 feet; digital readout symbol, No. 12).
15	AGL, Vertical Speed - Scale	HUD System	0 - 200 feet/± 2000 feet-per-minute.
16	HUD Fail Message	HUD System	**CPM, SDR, SDA, PS, PDU, CPDU, NAV, PGM**; can be cleared from the display by selecting **ACK** (see note).
17	Trim (Slide Ball)	SAS/FPS Computer	± 2 balls (left/right).
18	**MST, MEM, HOOK** Messages	Caution annunciation	**MST, MEM, HOOK** cannot be cleared from the display by selecting **ACK**.
19	Sensor, Engine, Fire, RPM Warnings	Master Warning Panel	**ATT, ENG 1** or **2, FIRE, RPM**; **ATT** can be cleared from the display by selecting **ACK** (see note). **ENG, FIRE**, and **RPM** cannot be cleared.
20	Horizon Line (pitch, roll)	Copilot's Vertical Gyro	Pitch: ± 30° Roll: 0 - 359°.
21	Display Mode Number	HUD System	**1N - 4N** for normal modes, **1D - 4D** for declutter modes.
22	Torque Limits	Torque Transducer	0 - 150% Yellow (>100%), (solid box) Red (>110%) Thresholds (solid box flashes).
23	Torque - Numerics	Torque Transducer	0 - 150% (flashes when engine torque separation is greater than 5% threshold) Maximum % torque split between cockpit panel and HUD is 3%.
24	Ground Speed	Doppler	0 - 999 knots/0 - 530 km/h (dependent on doppler).
25	Indicated Airspeed	SAS/FPS Computer	30 - 180 knots (no symbol 30 knots and below, reappears at 32 knots).
26	Attitude Reference Indicator	HUD System	Represents helicopter.
27	Engines Temperature	Thermocouple Amplifers	0 - 999°C (0 - 755°C - 999°C, 1° units) Maximum split between cockpit and HUD is ± 15°.
28	Distance to Waypoint	Doppler	0 - 999.9 km.
29	Bearing to Waypoint - Numeric	Doppler	0 - 359°

Table 4-1. Master Mode Symbology Display (HUD) (Cont)

No.	Symbol	Source	Range/Description

NOTE: After **ACK** is used to acknowledge a fault, the fault will not reappear until BIT is selected or power is cycled off and on.

4.4.5 Operation.

4.4.5.1 Starting Procedure.

1. **ADJ/ON/OFF** switch - **OFF**.

2. Optical unit support clamps - Installed on ANVIS. Verify clamps can by rotated.

NOTE

Check surface of lens for cleanliness. Clean in accordance with TM 11-5855-300-10.

3. DU lens - Check.

WARNING

Failure to remove the ANVIS neck cord prior to operation of the HUD may prevent egress from the aircraft in an emergency.

4. ANVIS neck cord - Removed.

5. Optical unit - Install on ANVIS. Attach optical unit to either monocular housing. Do not tighten OU clamp completely with thumbscrew at this time. The OU (display) may have to be rotated to horizon after the system is operating.

NOTE

The helmet may now have to be rebalanced.

6. **EYE SELECT** switch on PSCU - **L** or **R**.

CCU ADJ/ON/OFF switch must by OFF before connecting or disconnecting quick-release connector.

The AN/AVS-7 system should not be used if the quick-release connector is not in working order.

7. PSCU - Connect. Connect PSCU to quick-release connector by rotating the connector engagement ring.

CAUTION

Keep the protective caps on the ANVIS whenever it is not in use. Operate the ANVIS only under darkened conditions.

NOTE

Ensure ANVIS operator procedures have been completed.

8. **P-PGM/OP/CP-PGM** switch -**OP**.

9. **ADJ/ON/OFF** switch - **ON**. System **ON** and **FAIL** lights illuminate and BIT will initiate automatically.

10. **FAIL** light - Check. Light should go out after ten seconds. BIT is complete.

NOTE

Allow one minute for display warm-up. Display intensity is preset to low each time **ADJ/ON/OFF** switch is set from **OFF** on **ON**.

If a fault is displayed in the DU, acknowledge fault and re-run BIT to confirm fault.

11. **BRT/DIM** switch - As desired.

12. **DSPL POS** control - As required. Center display in field of view.

13. Display aligned to horizon - Check. Tighten OU clamp.

4.4.5.2 Operator Self Test (BIT).

1. **BIT/ACK** switch - Press to **BIT** and hold. The **ON** and **FAIL** light will illuminate. At end of BIT, **FAIL** indicator will extinguish.

2. **BIT/ACK** switch - Release.

4.4.5.3 Displayed System Faults. The system self test is divided into power-up or operator initialized built-in-test (BIT) and inflight BIT. The faults result as warnings and messages that blink at a rate of two per second in the display units. Part of the BIT is a periodic test that is performed automatically along with normal system operation. This BIT monitors and/or tests SDC functions and/or signals. A failure of the SDC, NAV signals pilot's DU, will illuminate the converter control **FAIL** light and display a FAIL message **CPM, SDR, SDA, PS, NAV, PDU** or **CPDU** on the display unit. An attitude (ATT) sensor indication will be displayed when a gyro invalid condition exits. **ATT, NAV, PDU, CPDU,** and all SDC faults can be cleared by setting **BIT/ACK** switch to **ACK**. The following helicopter status messages are also displayed.

1. The caption **MST** (first priority) indicates operation of the master caution warning lamp. This message will disappear during the rest of the main warning lamp operation.

2. The caption **MEM** (second priority indicates that the doppler data is not updated. a previous computed data is available. This message will appear simultaneously with the **MEM** lamp on the doppler operating panel.

3. The caption **HOOK** (third priority) indicates the cargo hook is open. The message will appear simultaneously with the indication lamp in the cockpit.

Setting **BIT/ACK** switch to **ACK** will not clear **MST, MEM,** or **HOOK** status messages from the DU. Engine, **FIRE** and **RPM** warnings cannot be cleared from the DU. The faulty unit or warning must be removed from the aircraft. When both engines fail at the same time, engine priority is: **ENG 1** then **ENG 2.**

4.4.5.4 Programming Procedure.

NOTE

The programming procedure for the pilot and copilot is identical except for the location of controls on the CCU.

1. Select mode to be programmed (**1N-4N**). The first mode that will appear is 1N (normal mode 1).

2. **P-PGM/CP-PGM/OP** switch - **P-PGM** or **CP-PGM**.

3. **PROG** blinking in display - Check. Verify that a complete set of symbology is displayed and attitude reference symbol is blinking. Verify **PGM** is displayed in the **HUD FAIL** message location for the DU not being programmed.

4. **BIT/ACK** switch - **ACK** to program the full display or go to step 5 and select desired symbols.

5. **PGM SEL/NXT** control - **SEL** to select symbol. Selected symbol stops blinking. If symbol is not desired, toggle switch to **NXT** and the symbol will disappear.

NOTE

All symbols have been programmed when the **PROG** annunciator is the only symbol flashing.

6. **BIT/ACK** switch - **ACK**. (Hold switch to **ACK** for one second.)

7. **OK** displayed - Check. (**OK** will be displayed for two seconds.)

NOTE

If programming is not accepted, **FAIL** will be displayed. If a **FAIL** message is displayed, attempt to reprogram the same mode, if **FAIL** reappears notify maintenance.

Declutter mode is recognized by flashing ground speed indicator in lieu of attitude reference symbology.

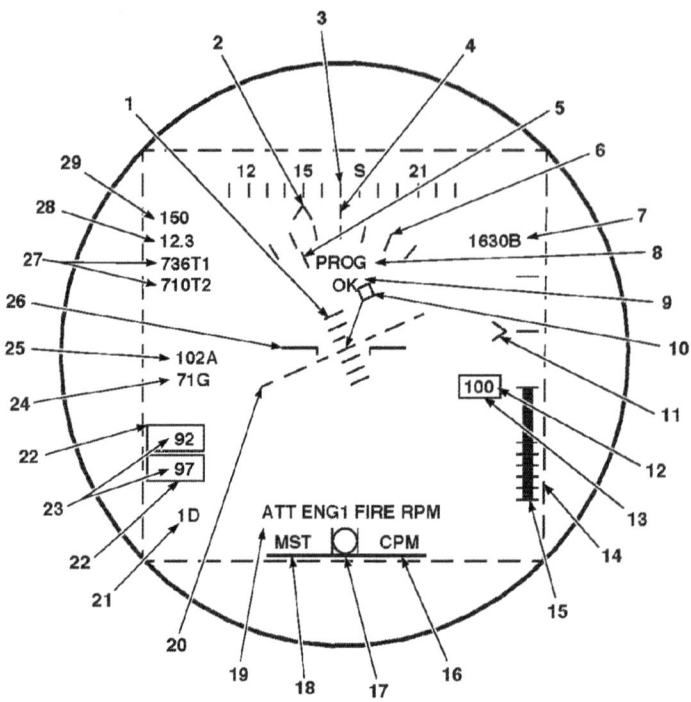

Figure 4-3. Master Mode Display

8. **MODE 1-4/DCLT** - **DCLT (1D-4D)**. The first **DCLT** mode that will appear is **1D** (declutter mode 1).

NOTE

If **MODE 1-4/DCLT** switch is toggled to **DCLT** a second time the display will cycle back to the **DCLT's** normal mode (**1N-4N**). The **MODE 1-4/DCLT** switch must be set to **MODE 1-4** to advance to another normal mode.

9. Repeat steps 4 through 7, for declutter.

10. **MODE 1-4/DCLT** switch - As required.

11. Repeat steps 4 through 10 until all desired modes are programmed.

12. **P-PGM/CP-PGM/OP** switch - **OP**.

4.4.5.5 Adjustment of Barometric Altitude, Pitch, and Roll.

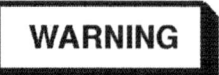

An improperly adjusted barometric altimeter will result in an improperly set HUD barometric altitude display.

NOTE

Barometric altimeter should be set to the most current altimeter settings, field elevation.

1. Ensure **P-PGM/CP-PGM/OP** switch is in the **OP** position.

2. **ADJ/ON/OFF** switch - Pull and set to **ADJ**.

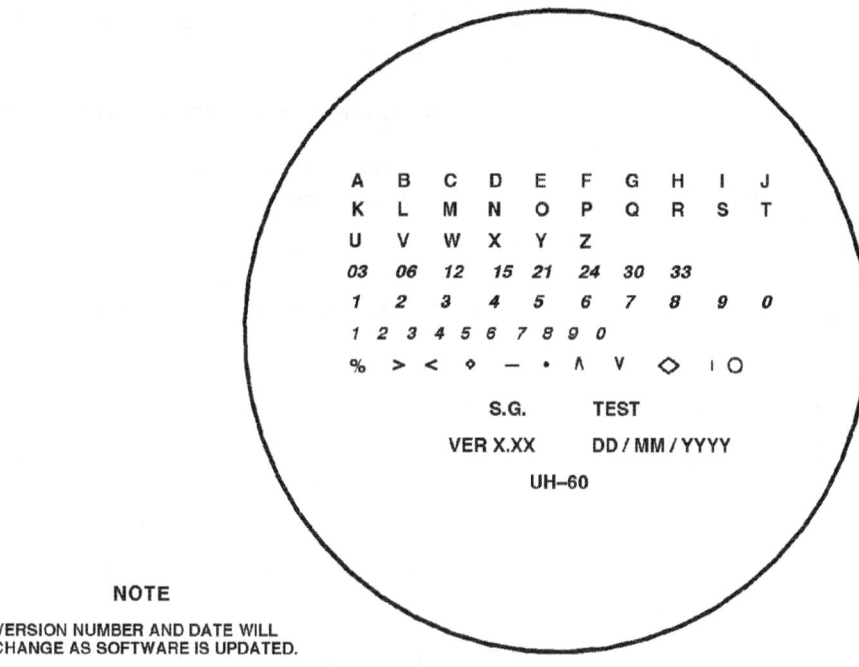

NOTE

VERSION NUMBER AND DATE WILL CHANGE AS SOFTWARE IS UPDATED.

Figure 4-4. Symbol Generator Test Mode

3. **ADJ** blinking in display - Check.

NOTE

Changes to barometric altimeter settings require a corresponding change to the HUD barometric altitude. Each .01 inch change in pressure equals 10 feet.

4. **INC/DEC** switch - As required.

5. **BIT/ACK** switch - ACK.

6. Repeat steps 3 through 5 for pitch and roll.

7. **ADJ/ON/OFF** switch - ON.

4.4.5.6 In-flight Operation.

Whenever the symbology displayed in the DU is suspected of being incorrect the pilot's will compare the data with the aircraft instrument indicator and take the appropriate action.

Excessive brightness of the symbology display may impair vision outside the cockpit.

Interruption of electrical power, such as change over from APU generator to NO. 1 and NO. 2 generators and vice versa, will cause DU to default to dim and MODE 1N. Any adjustments made to the barometric altitude, pitch and roll prior to flight will be lost, thereby decreasing the accuracy of the barometric altitude, pitch and roll.

1. **BRT/DIM** switch - As desired.

NOTE

Whenever the symbology is interfering with the outside visibility, decluttering may be selected to remove symbology.

2. **MODE 1-4/DCLT** switch - As desired.

4-13

4.4.5.7 System Shutdown Procedure.

1. **ADJ/ON/OFF** switch - **OFF**.

2. Turn off ANVIS.

CCU ADJ/ON/OFF switch must be OFF before connecting or disconnecting quick-release connector.

Do not disconnect DU by pulling on the cable connected to the PSCU. The DU could be damaged or the cable may separate from the PSCU creating an explosive atmosphere hazard.

Do not attempt to egress the aircraft without performing disconnect as this may result in neck injury.

Do not disconnect DU by pulling on the cable. To do so may damage the DU.

3. Display unit - Disconnect. Disconnect DU by grasping the PSCU and rotating the quick-release connector engagement ring and pull downward. Remove OU and remove from the ANVIS and place into storage case.

4. Reattach neck cord to ANVIS.

4.4.5.8 Emergency Egress.
The quick-release feature allows you to exit quickly from the aircraft in an emergency without:

a. Damaging or turning the unit off.

b. Getting tangled in cords.

c. Being restrained in the cockpit by hardwired connections.

d. Removing ANVIS.

It is up to the operator to determine the desired mode of disconnect based upon his evaluation of the emergency condition and whether or not the ANVIS goggles will be needed following egress. The available means of disconnect are as follows:

a. Release the ANVIS goggles from the helmet.

b. Disconnect the OU from the ANVIS goggles via the thumbscrew.

c. Grasp PSCU and pull down.

4.5 MULTI FUNCTION DISPLAY (MFD).

Each MFD displays flight and communications data, caution and advisory legends, and FLIR video independently of each other. Displays may be overlayed on each other, such as attitude information presented with FLIR video. Caution legends appear automatically as they are generated in a pop up window, or displayed in a caution advisory grid. Power for the MFDs is from the dc essential bus through circuit breakers marked **PLT MFD** and **COPLT MFD** respectively.

4.5.1 Controls and Functions.
All controls for the MFD are on the bezel of the MFD (Figure 4-5). Marked keys on top and bottom keys are fixed function, while the unmarked keys function is dependent on the adjacent display. Controls are as described below:

CONTROL/INDICATOR	FUNCTION
COMM	Toggles communications header on or off.
NAV	Toggles navigation information header on or off.
DAY NGT OFF switch	Adjust brightness of display for either day or night operation, turns MFD off.
FLT	Toggles digital flight data on or off. On **FLT** data page, **TAS/IAS** soft key appears.
TAS IAS	Toggles display between true airspeed and indicated airspeed.
ATT	Toggles heading, pitch, roll, and course deviation information on or off.
HOV	Toggles hover information on or off.

TM 1-1520-253-10

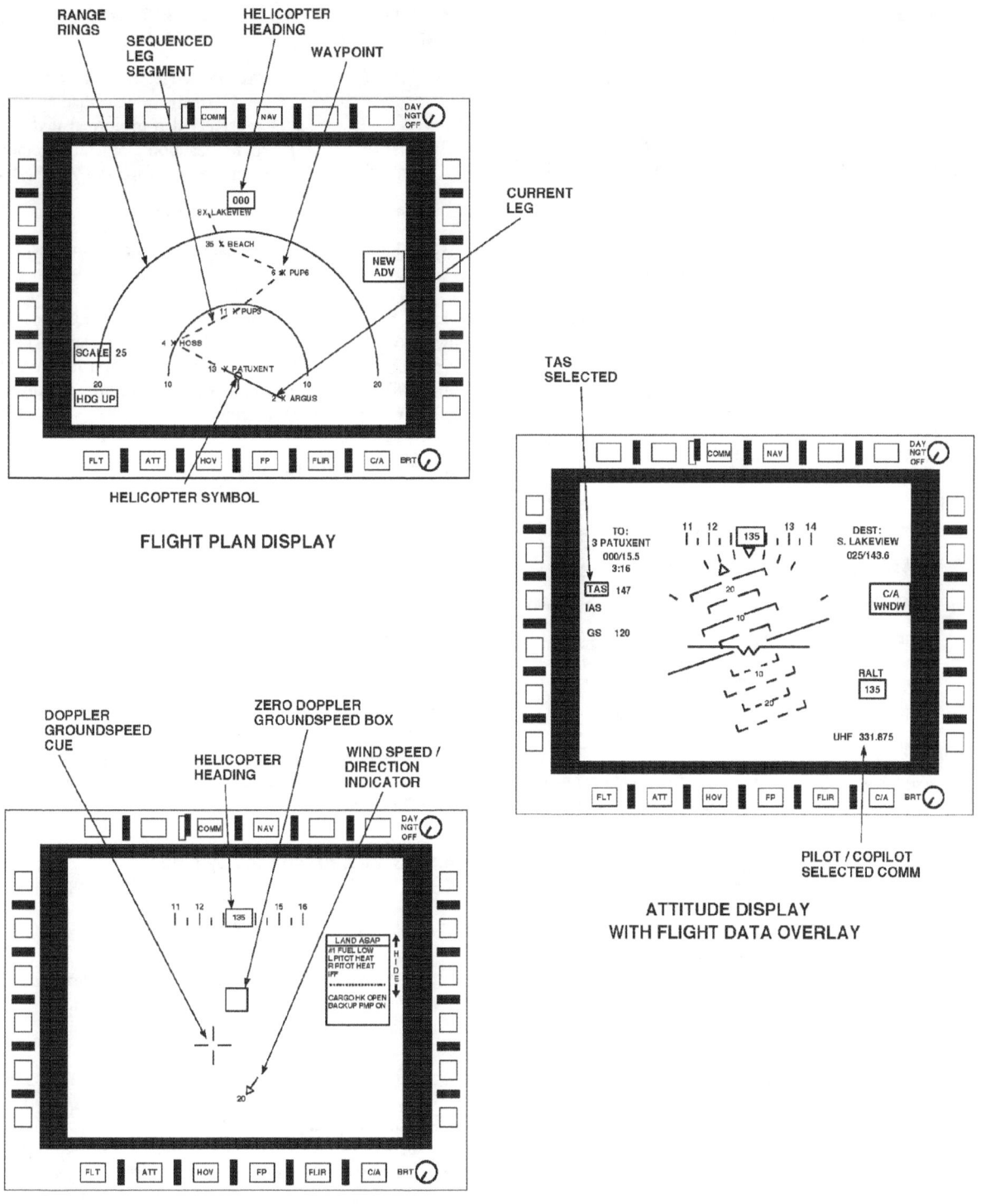

Figure 4-5. Multi Function Display (MFD)

4-15

CONTROL/ INDICATOR	FUNCTION
Windspeed/Direction indicator	Gives windspeed and direction.
Zero Doppler groundspeed box	When Doppler groundspeed cue is in the box, Doppler groundspeed is 0, and helicopter is hovering.
Doppler groundspeed cue	Shows Doppler groundspeed in relation to the zero doppler groundspeed cue. Full scale displacement on from box on MFD in all directions represents 25 knots groundspeed. At full displacement, Doppler groundspeed cue will be displayed approximately 1/2 the distance between zero doppler groundspeed box and edge of MFD.
FP	Toggles active flight plan from AMS on or off.
SCALE	Cycles through display scales.
HDG UP	Access heading up map display.
N UP	Access north up map display.
Range rings	Shows scale of display.
Sequenced leg segment	Future legs of the active flight plan.
Waypoint	Gives waypoint number, name and symbolizes the location of the waypoint.
Current leg	Indicates the active from to leg of the flight plan.
Helicopter symbol	Shows current location of helicopter.
FLIR	Toggles FLIR information on or off.
C/A	Toggles between caution advisory grid and **C/A WNDW** icon.
C/A WNDW	Activates caution adivsory pop up window.
Soft keys when caution advisory window is activated	
▲	Scrolls list up.

CONTROL/ INDICATOR	FUNCTION
HIDE	Acknowledges new caution legend and changes its display from reverse video to normal text. If no new caution legend, removes window and displays **C/A WNDW**.
▼	Scrolls list down.
BRT knob	Variable brightness adjustment.

4.5.2 Stand Alone Display Modes. Display modes are divided into stand alone displays, and overlay displays. Pressing the associated fixed function button displays the mode. Pressing the button a second time turns the display off, reverting to a blank screen.

4.5.2.1 Attitude Display Mode.

NOTE

Attitude information is for reference only, and not to be used in place of primary flight instruments.

Displays an attitude indicator, giving pitch, roll, heading and course deviation.

4.5.2.2 Hover Display Mode. Displays helicopter's ground speed and direction, radar altitude, and wind speed and direction.

4.5.2.3 Flight Plan Display Mode.

NOTE

Navigation information is for situational awareness, and is not to be used a primary means of navigation.

Gives graphic display of avionics management system (AMS) active flight plan. The scale of display is variable, and marked by range rings. The heading up display orients the display to the helicopter's heading, The north up display orients the display to magnetic north.

4.5.3 Overlay Display Modes. Overlay displays may be either shown alone, or overlaid on the three stand alone displays described above.

4.5.3.1 FLIR Display Mode.

NOTE

Selecting **FLIR** mode when FLIR is not installed will cause MFD to flicker or cycle. To cleaar this condition, press **FLIR** again.

Displays FLIR video and command menus. See paragraph 4.6 for displays and indications.

4.5.3.2 C/A Popup Display Mode. Displays active caution and advisory legends. Caution legends are separated from advisories by a row of white asterisks.

4.5.3.3 Flight Display Mode.

NOTE

Navigation information is for situational awareness, and is not to be used a primary means of navigation.

Displays waypoint and destination data with magnetic heading and estimated time enroute (ETE), true or indicated airspeed, groundspeed and radar altitude.

4.5.3.4 Communications Display Mode. Displays pilot and copilot selected COMM radio preset, band, frequency, and call sign. If COMM is pressed when flight data screen is displayed, radar altitude is removed, and radio setting is displayed in its place.

4.5.3.5 Navigation Display Mode. Displays digital navigation information as a header, giving current active flight plan information, as well as ground speed, time to go, and wind speed and direction.

4.5.4 Operation.

4.5.4.1 Starting Procedure.

1. **OFF NGT DAY** switch - As desired

2. **BRT** switch - Full clockwise.

3. **ILLUM ALL** soft key - Press. Check caution advisory grid for complete display.

4. Operational mode(s) - As desired

4.5.4.2 Shutdown Procedure.

1. **OFF NGT DAY** switch - **OFF**.

4.6 FORWARD LOOKING INFRARED SYSTEM AN/AAQ-22.

WARNING

The FLIR shall not be used for pilotage.

The forward looking infrared (FLIR) system (Figure 4-6) detects infrared radiation. The system consists of a Turret-FLIR unit (TFU), central electronics unit (CEU), and a hand control unit (HCU). The system uses the HCU for TFU movement, target cursor movement, and automatic video tracking. The FLIR can operate during night, day, and adverse weather conditions. The system shall only be used for target recognition and surveillance. The FLIR sensor converts infrared (IR) radiation patterns within its field of view to a video format, which can be viewed on the multi function displays (MFD). The system generates visible and thermal video of the area within the field of view and displays it on the MFDs. System status information is displayed above and below the imagery. Symbology is overlaid on the imagery and may be suppressed or decluttered. Power for the FLIR system is provided from the No.1 dc primary bus through a circuit breaker marked **FLIR VCR** and from the No. 2 dc primary bus through a circuit breaker marked **FLIR**.

4.6.1 Turret.

CAUTION

Optical lens of FLIR is easily scratched. To avoid damage, use cleaning procedures and supplies referenced in the maintenance manual.

The FLIR turret (Figure 3-1) is three axis, and gyro stabilized in outer azimuth, inner azimuth, and elevation. The turret provides the remote movement of the FLIR line of sight, corresponding to the center of the imaged scene, to any position within the field of regard (FOR). The FOR is +30° to -120° in elevation and a continuous 360° in azimuth from the look ahead position.

4.6.2 Controls and Function. The controls for the FLIR system are on the front of the HCU (Figure 4-6). The function of each is as follows:

TM 1-1520-253-10

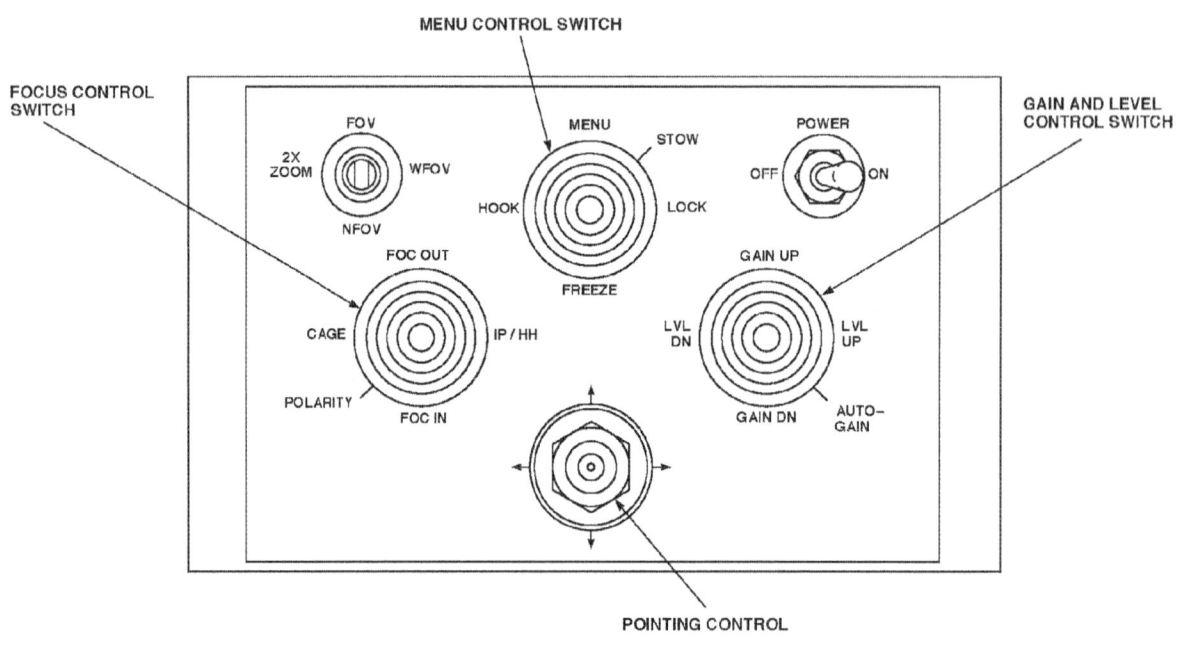

Figure 4-6 FLIR System

CONTROL	FUNCTION	CONTROL	FUNCTION
PWR switch		**STOW**	For stowing the TFU prior to turning the power **OFF**. In the **STOW** position the TFU is rotated to the 180° azimuth, +130° elevation to protect the windows. This mode is activated by the pilot as part of the normal power off sequence.
OFF	OFF is the normal power down for the system.		
ON	Power is applied to the system and on completion of the start-up BIT sequence system status is reported.		
Menu control	Used to display and activate menu controlled functions.	**LOCK**	Used to execute a change or selection in menus and to close the menus.
MENU	Activates the menu page by momentarily toggling the switch. The menu page is displayed on the left side of the MFD overlaid on the imagery.	**FREEZE**	Provides the ability to freeze the IR video image at any time. To freeze the image toggle the **FREEZE** switch. To return to live video toggle the **FREEZE** switch again.
		HOOK	Used to select menus or change parameters and to open sub-menus within the menu pages.
		FOV switch	Three position switch used to alter field of view.

4-18   Change 4

CONTROL	FUNCTION	CONTROL	FUNCTION
WFOV	Sets display to 28° horizontal, 17° vertical field of view.	**2X ZOOM**	Sets narrow field display to 2X magnification.
NFOV	Sets display to 5° horizontal, 3° vertical field of view.		

CONTROL	FUNCTION
Focus Control	Used to manually set focus.
CAGE	Commands the TFU to a particular pointing angle with respect to the aircraft centerline.
POLARITY	Toggles thermal image polarity from white-hot or black-hot, representing hot scene objects. White-hot is the recommended polarity.
FOC IN	Acts only on the IR sensor. Manually adjusts the focus for operational work.
FOC OUT	Acts only on the IR sensor. Manually adjusts the focus for operational work.
IP/HH	Toggles between inertial pointing mode and heading hold mode.
Gain and level control	Gain sets system sensitivity, while level is used to position a selected span of temperatures relative to all temperatures in the scene.
GAIN UP	Higher gains represent narrower spans of temperatures.
GAIN DN	Lower gains represent wider spans of temperatures.
LVL UP	In the recommended white-hot mode, higher levels settings are needed to view detail in darker (cold) areas.
LVL DOWN	In the recommended white-hot mode, lower level settings are needed to view detail in brighter (hot) areas.
AUTO-GAIN	Selects automatic control of system gain and level (temperature offset). The system automatically adjusts the FLIR image with near optimum scene contrast for general purpose viewing, and as a starting point for manual adjustment.
Pointing Control	Used to manually control TFU movement.

4.6.3 Starting Procedure.

1. FLIR **PWR** switch - **ON**.

2. MFD **FLIR** switch - Press.

NOTE

The start-up BIT is performed at power up and the RDY indicator should be displayed in the right end of the upper status bar. If FAULT is displayed the system has detected a problem and should be checked by maintenance personnel.

Allow three to five minutes for system to reach operating temperature. Do not move controls until **RDY** is displayed.

3. Adjust MFD **BRT** knob.

4. Use the pointing control to confirm up/down and left/right operation of the TFU. As soon as inputs are received from the pointing control the system will switch from cage mode to inertial pointing mode.

5. Any mode can now be selected and controls can be adjusted to suit operational needs.

4.6.4 Modes of Operation.

4.6.4.1 BIT Mode. The start up BIT is performed at power up and the **READY** indication should be displayed in the right end of the upper status bar (Figure 4-7). If **FAULT** is displayed the system has detected a problem. See the appropriate maintenance manual.

4.6.4.2 Menu Operation. Menus are accessed and manipulated with the **MENU**, **HOOK**, and **LOCK** switch and the pointing control located on the HCU. The menus are organized into two basic pages (Figure 4-8), with additional sub-menus that are presented at the appropriate time by a ">" to indicate that a sub-menu exists. The menus contain one or more labels, the labels are highlighted one at a time. If a label can not be highlighted or does not appear, then that function is not currently available. The **HOOK** function is used to select or change parameters and to open sub-menus. The **LOCK** function is used to execute a change or selection and close the menus.

To activate the menu page:

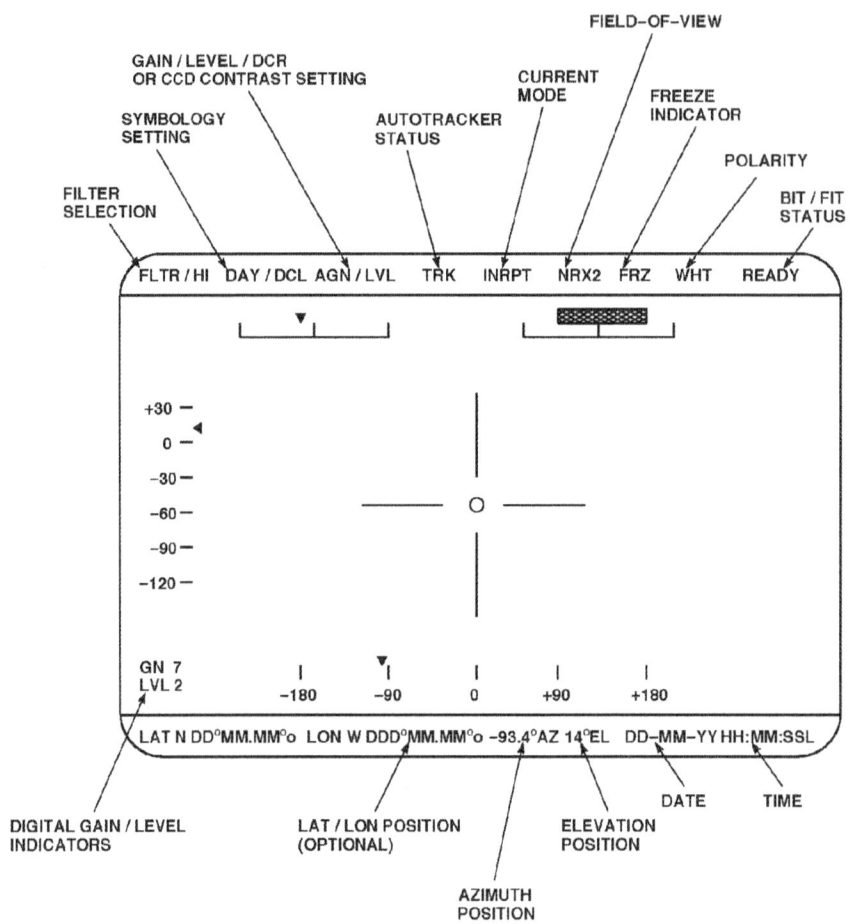

Figure 4-7 FLIR System Status Display

1. Toggle the **MENU** switch. Page one is displayed down the left side of the VDU overlaid on the imagery.

   NOTE

   In order to escape the menus at any time either momentarily toggle the **MENU** switch or **HOOK** the **EXIT** label.

2. Use pointing control to scroll the menu bar.

3. Once the desired label is highlighted, toggle the **HOOK** switch. This hooks the label. If the function is an on/off function, the change will be immediately seen. The function can be toggled back and forth by repeatedly toggling the **HOOK** switch.

4. Once the desired label is selected toggle the **MENU** switch, this locks in the selection, turns the menus off and returns the system to it's previous mode of operation.

5. Toggle the **MENU** switch again before making another adjustment.

Some functions utilize sub-menus or analog scales for adjustment of parameters, if a sub-menu appears:

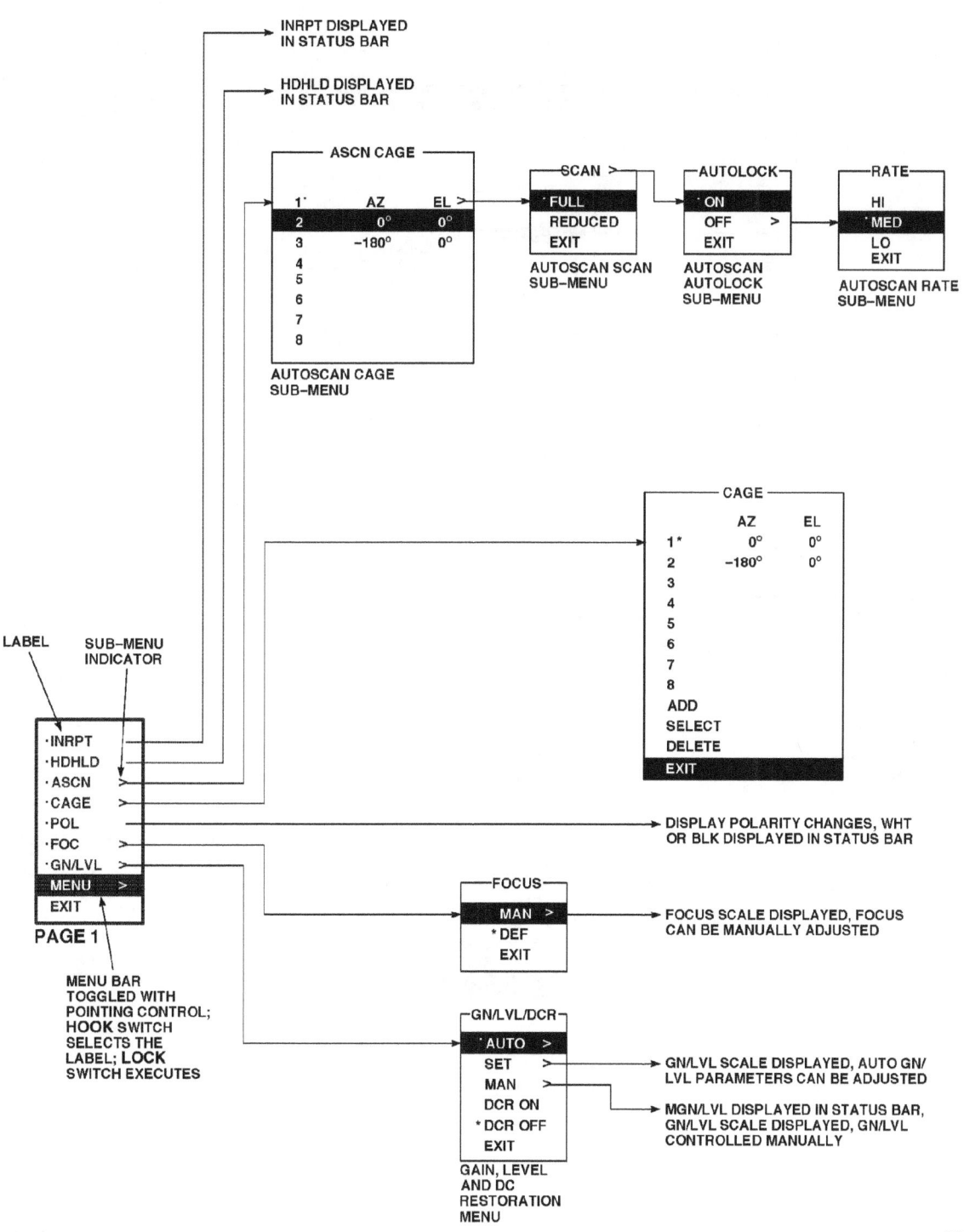

Figure 4-8. FLIR Menus (Sheet 1 or 2)

TM 1-1520-253-10

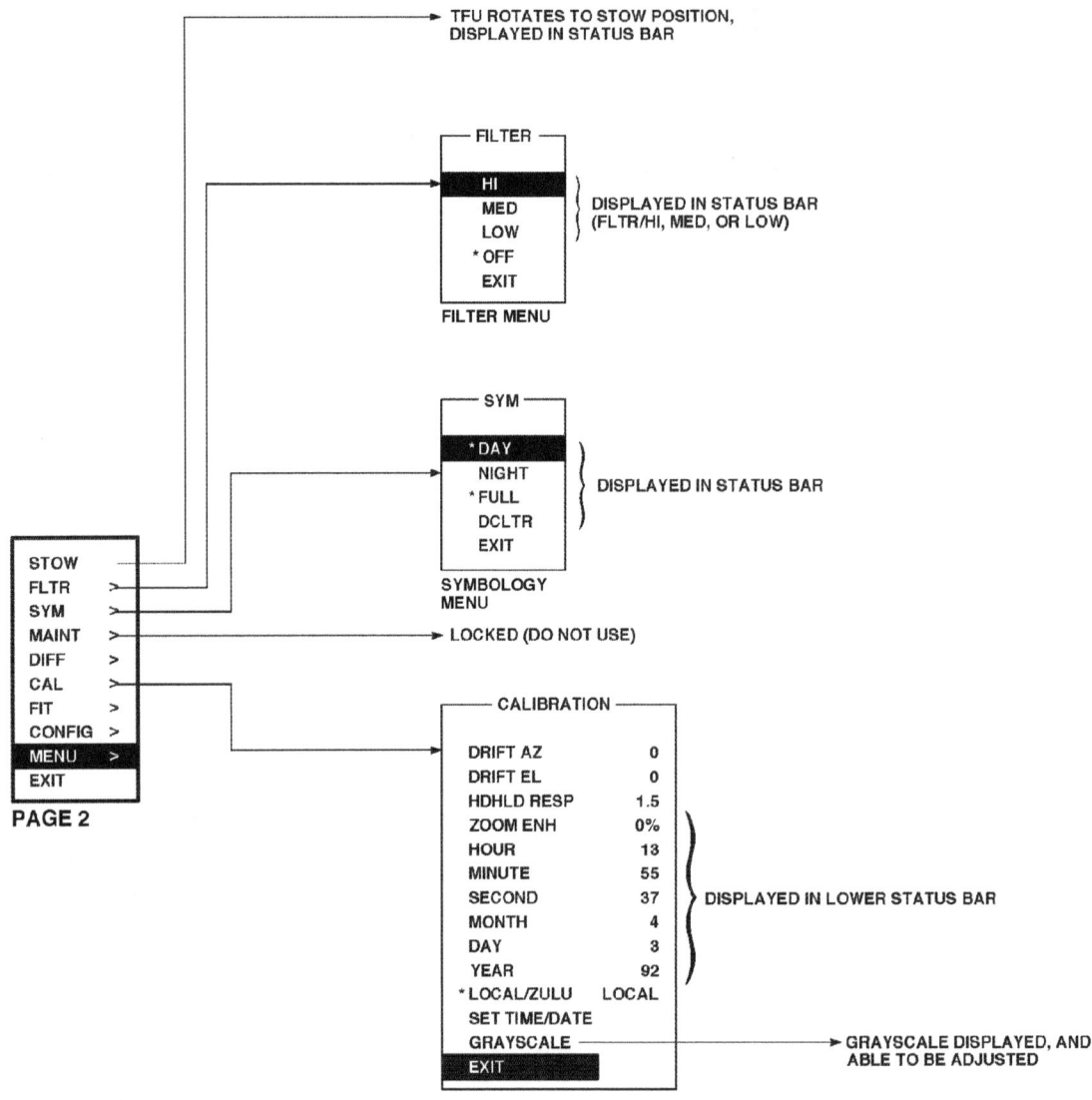

Figure 4-8. FLIR Menus (Sheet 2 of 2)

4-22   Change 4

1. Highlight the desired sub-menu choice, and push the **LOCK** button to lock in the sub-menu change.

2. This allows the possibility of selecting a particular control value as the current value. The current value is indicated by an asterisk to the left of the label. If the current function provides analog adjustment, such as **GAIN/LVL**, then a second level of control adjustment is performed using the pointing control.

3. Activating the **LOCK** switch activates the selected mode and exits the menus.

4.6.4.3 Inertial Pointing Mode. The inertial pointing mode controls the line of sight of the TFU manually by commands generated from the HCU pointing control. If no commands are generated from the pointing control, the TFU gyros cause the TFU to maintain its inertial bearing and elevation, thus compensating for small disturbances due to aircraft vibration and any changes in the direction of the aircraft. The inertial pointing mode is selected, from heading hold mode by activating the **IP/HH** toggle control once and is selected from any other mode by activating the **IP/HH** toggle control twice. The mode can also be selected by enabling menu, moving the highlight bar to the **INRPT** label, and toggling the **LOCK** switch. When the mode is selected **INRPT** will be displayed in the mode position of the status bar.

The inertial pointing mode consists of:

a. Manual pointing phase. In this phase the TFU line of sight is controlled by the pointing control commands. The larger the output from the pointing control the higher the slew rate. When no command is received from the pointing control, the turret line of sight is controlled by the gyro-servo mechanism.

4.6.4.4 Heading Hold Mode. In the heading hold mode the TFU is controlled manually by commands generated from the pointing control. If no commands are generated from the pointing control, the TFU maintains its relative bearing and elevation with respect to the aircraft. The heading hold mode is selected by toggling the **IP/HH** toggle control. The mode can also be selected by enabling the menu , moving the highlight bar to the **HDHLD** label, and toggling the **LOCK** switch. The system then switches to the heading hold mode and **HDHLD** is displayed in the mode position of the status bar.

The heading hold mode consists of two phases.

a. In the first phase the TFU is controlled by the pointing control commands. This phase is identical to the inertial pointing mode.

b. The second phase commences whenever the pointing control outputs return to zero. In this phase the TFU is caged to the last commanded position. It remains caged to this position until a new pointing control command is received or a different mode is selected that changes the line of sight.

4.6.4.5 Autoscan Mode. When the **ASCN** label is hooked, the **CAGE** sub-menu appears (Figure 4-8). When the desired **CAGE** value label is highlighted and hooked, the **SCAN** sub-menu appears. The scan pattern is selected by moving the highlight bar to the desired label and toggling the **HOOK** switch. When the desired scan label is hooked, the **AUTOLOCK** sub-menu appears. The autolock feature is then enabled or disabled. If autolock is disabled the **RATE** sub-menu appears. The rate is selected by hooking the desired label. The rate and scan pattern are reprogrammable in the configuration menu. At anytime during this process the **ASCN** function can be activated by toggling the **LOCK** switch. The previous sub-menu can be returned to by hooking on the **EXIT** label at the bottom of any sub-menu. The system performs **ASCN** until the pointing control is depressed or another mode is selected.

4.6.4.6 Cage Mode. In CAGE mode the TFU is commanded to a particular pointing angle with respect to the aircraft center line. The default cage position is 0° azimuth, and 0° elevation and this is the position the TFU will cage to when the system is powered on. The default cage position and one other position are stored in nonvolatile memory and can be reprogrammed in the configuration menu (Figure 4-8). The secondary default cage position is preprogrammed at 180° azimuth, and 0° elevation. Up to six additional **CAGE** positions are programmable by selecting the current gimbal as the cage position. The system reverts from **CAGE** to **HH** mode if a rate command is issued by depressing the pointing control.

a. When **CAGE** is hooked in the main menu, the **CAGE** sub-menu appears with control labels provided to add, select, or delete cage values. The **ADD** function allows the pilot to add the current TFU position as an additional cage position. Up to eight cage positions can be stored (including the two default cage positions). **CAGE** positions are deleted with the **DELETE** command. A specific cage position is selected with the **SELECT** command.

To add a cage position.

(1) Position the TFU to the desired position.

Change 4   4-22.1

(2) Activate the menus and hook the **CAGE** label. The **CAGE** menu will appear on the right side of the screen.

(3) Move the highlight bar to the **ADD** label and activate **HOOK**. The new cage position will be added in the first available slot on the list.

(4) To exit the **CAGE** menu move the highlight bar to the **EXIT** label and activate **HOOK**.

To select a cage position.

(1) Hook the **SELECT** label in the **CAGE** menu.

(2) Move the highlight bar to the desired **CAGE** position and **HOOK** to select the position and remain in the menus or **LOCK** to select the position, place the system in the **CAGE** mode.

(3) Exit the menus.

To delete one or more cage positions.

(1) Hook the **DELETE** label in the **CAGE** menu. The highlight bar should appear over position 3 in the list. Positions 1 and 2 are permanently stored in nonvolatile memory and can only be changed in the configuration menu. Move the highlight bar to the desired cage position to be deleted and activate **LOCK** to delete the position. Repeat this procedure until all desired positions are deleted.

b. To cage the currently selected position depress the **CAGE** switch or activate the menus and **LOCK** on the **CAGE** label. The TFU will cage to the selected position and the **CAGE** indicator appears in the mode position of the status bar.

4.6.4.7 Stow Mode. The stow mode is for storing the TFU prior to turning the power **OFF**. In stow mode the TFU is rotated to 180° azimuth, and +130° elevation to protect the windows. This mode is activated by the pilot as part of the normal power off sequence. To stow the TFU activate the menus and **LOCK** on the **STOW** label, or toggle the menu control switch to **STOW**. The system will rotate to the stow position, the azimuth and elevation rotations will be locked, and the **STOW** indicator is displayed in the mode position of the status bar.

4.6.5 MFD Adjustments. Adjustment of the MFD image is accomplished by first hooking the calibration (**CAL**) menu, moving the highlight bar to the **GRAY-**

SCALE label, and **LOCK** to turn the grayscale on. This displays the varied grayscale across the top of the MFD screen. Turn the MFD**BRT** control until the bar on the far left is white and the bar on the far right is black, with intermediate bars being various shades of gray.

4.6.5.1 Image Filtering Operation. The image filtering control activates the image filtering function and adjusts it to a high, medium, or low setting. After hooking on the **FLTR** label on menu page 2, a sub-menu appears containing **HI, MED, LOW, OFF,** and **EXIT** labels. Move the highlight bar to the desired label and toggle the **HOOK** switch to change the filter setting. The setting is indicated in the status bar at the top to the screen. To exit the menus toggle the **LOCK** switch. To return to the main menu hook the **EXIT** label.

4.6.5.2 Symbology Controls. The **SYM** label when hooked displays a sub-menu with **DAY, NIGHT, FULL,** and **DCLTR** choices.

4.6.5.2.1 Daytime/ Nighttime Symbology. This allows the pilot to select a configuration of displayed symbology at brightness levels suitable for daytime or nighttime ambient light conditions. Day and night configurations are reprogrammable in the configuration menu. These configurations are accessed by hooking the **SYM** label on menu page 2. The selections are **DAY** and **NIGHT**. The current symbology selection is indicated by an asterisk next to the current label and the symbology indicator in the status bar. To change the current selection, move the highlight bar to the desired selection and toggle the **HOOK** or **LOCK** switch. **HOOK** leaves the symbology menu open and displays the results on the screen. **LOCK** closes the menus and activates the selection.

4.6.5.2.2 Full/Decluttered Symbology. The **FULL/DCLTR** symbology control allows the pilot to select a decluttered symbology configuration which displays only the most essential symbology. The decluttered configuration is reprogrammable by the pilot in the configuration menu.

4.6.5.3 Video Difference Control. Video difference displays the difference between the live video and the frozen image. This allows the pilot to detect motion in the scene. To enable the video difference function move the highlight bar to the **DIFF** label in menu page 2 and **HOOK** it. The **DIFF** sub-menu appears, **LOCK** on the **ON** label and the difference function will be enabled. Toggling the **FREEZE** initiates the **DIFF** function. Toggling the **FREEZE** a second time returns the system to normal operation.

4.6.5.4 Calibration Controls. The calibration label when hooked activates a sub-menu (Figure 4-8) containing labels for setting azimuth and elevation gyro drift compensation, date/time, and for turning the display grayscale on and off.

4.6.5.4.1 HDHLD Response. HDHLD response is the response speed of the TFU position to aircraft movements. The response speed has a range from 0.0 to 3.0. This parameter needs to be adjusted to match the characteristics of the aircraft and mission requirements. When set low, image vibration is reduced, but the TFU responds slower to intentional aircraft movements. When set high, the TFU responds faster to intentional aircraft movements, but image vibration is increased.

4.6.5.4.2 Date/Time. The **HOUR, MINUTE, SECOND, MONTH, DAY, YEAR, LOCAL/ZULU,** and **SET TIME/DATE** labels are used to change the date and time displayed in the lower status bar on the VDU. Adjustment of all time/date parameters is accomplished by highlighting the label, hooking, adjusting and hooking to return. The new date and time is locked in by hooking the **SET TIME/DATE** label. The **LOCAL/ZULU** label is highlighted and hooked to switch between local and zulu time indicators next to the time display in the lower status bar. If the pilot selects the local time, an "L" will appear next to the time to indicate that the time is set to local time. If the pilot selects the zulu time, a "Z" will appear next to the time to indicate that the time is set to zulu time.

4.6.5.4.3 Grayscale. The **GRAYSCALE** can be turned on and off by toggling the **LOCK** switch when the highlight bar is on the **GRAYSCALE** label.

4.6.5.4.4 Focus Control Operation. The focus control is set to default which is adjusted to the hyperfocal distance which is the setting where all objects beyond a certain distance will be in focus. Through the focus menu (Figure 4-8) the pilot can select **MAN**, which allows manual adjustment of the FLIR. To manually adjust the focus, hook the **FOC** label, move the highlight bar to the **MAN** label, and toggle the **HOOK** switch. Use the HCU pointing control (left/right) to adjust the system focus. Toggle the **LOCK** switch to lock in the change and exit the menus.

4.6.6 System Status / Symbology. System status/symbology information is displayed on the screen of the MFD (Figures 4-7 and 4-14) on an upper and a lower status bar. System status/symbology are overlaid on the imagery. Status/Symbology are as follows:

TM 1-1520-253-10

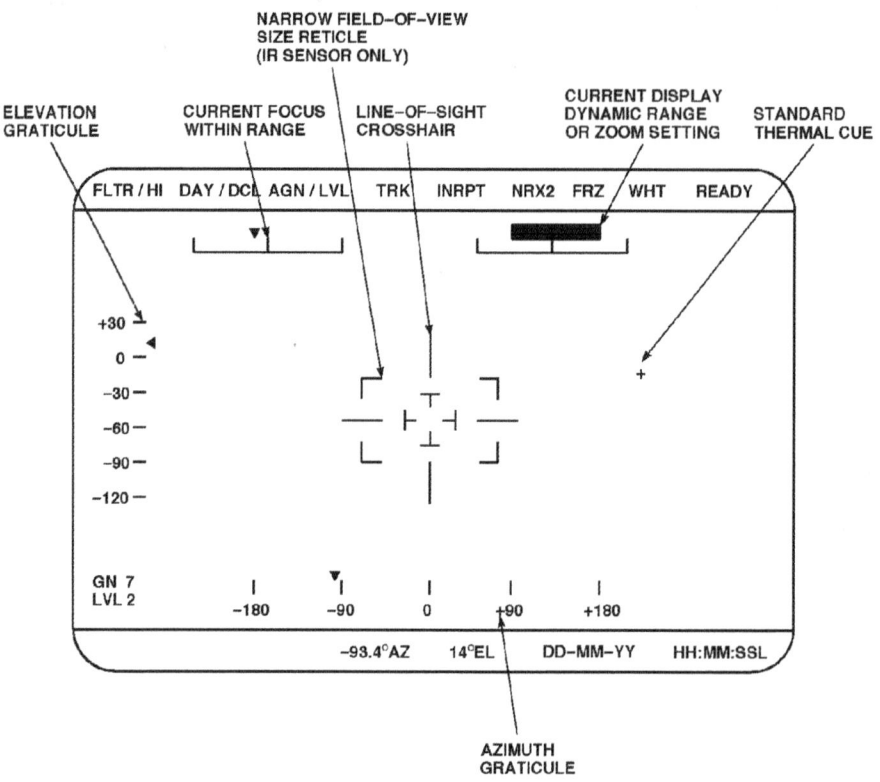

Figure 4-14. FLIR System Symbology Display

STATUS/ SYMBOLOGY	FUNCTION	STATUS/ SYMBOLOGY	FUNCTION
Filter selection	Indicates the current setting of the adaptive filter. If the adaptive filtering is off, the filter status is blank. If the filter is active, the status item will reflect the current setting by displaying **FLTR/LO**, **FLTR/MD**, or **FLTR/HI**.	Symbology setting	Indicates the current selection for the symbology display. The different symbology display selections include: **DAY**, **DAY/DCLT**, **NIT**, or **NIT/DCLT**.

4-24   Change 4

STATUS/ SYMBOLOGY	FUNCTION	STATUS/ SYMBOLOGY	FUNCTION
Gain/Level/DCR or CCD contrast setting	Indicates the current setting of the gain, level, an DC restoration controls for the IR sensor or the current setting of the contrast enhancement mode of the TV sensor. The current gain, level, DC restoration setting is indicated by one of the following: **AGN/LVL**, **AGN/DCR**, **MGN/LVL**, **MGN/DCR**, **SGN/LVL**, or **SGN/DCR**. The current contrast enhancement mode setting is indicated by one of the following: Blank (no enhancement), x4, x4/C, x10, x10/C, x40, or x40/C.	Azimuth position	Displays the current azimuth position, in degrees, relative to the look-ahead position of the system.
		Elevation position	Displays the current elevation position, in degrees, relative to the look-ahead position of system.
		Digital gain and level indicators	Displays the current gain and level settings in digital format.
		Date	Displays the current date in month-day-year format.
		Time	Displays the current time and indicates whether the time is set to zulu (**Z**) or local (**L**) time.
Autotracker status		Elevation graticule	Provides a graphical representation of the present elevation position within the field of regard.
Current mode	Indicates the current mode of the system. The mode indicators are as follows: **INT** (initialization), **INRPT** (inertial pointing), **HDHLD** (heading hold), **ASCN** (autoscan), **CAGE**, **STOW**, and **FIT**.	Azimuth graticule	Provides a graphical representation of the present azimuth position within the field of regard.
		Highest priority thermal cue	Provides a graphical indication of the location of the target that will be tracked if the autotrack is activated.
Field of view	Indicates the current field of view selection and appears only for the IR sensor. **WIDE** is displayed when the system is in wide field of view. **NRW** is displayed when in narrow field of view. **NRX2** is displayed when in narrow field of view with **2X** electronic zoom.	Standard thermal cue	Provide graphical indications of the locations within the field of view that the autotracker detects a potential target.
		Narrow field of view size reticle	Indicates the size and location of the narrow field of view relative to the wide field of view.
Polarity selection	Indicates the current polarity of the displayed imagery for the IR sensor. **WHT** is displayed when white-hot polarity is selected and **BLK** is displayed when black-hot polarity is selected.	Line of sight crosshair	Indicates the center of the field of view. The line of sight crosshair can also be used to estimate range to an object.
BIT/FIT status	Indicator is displayed in the status bar indicating the current BIT/FIT status. **READY** is displayed if no error is detected and indicates that the system is ready for operation. The **READY** indicator is displayed only for a few seconds after start up BIT and FIT report no errors. **TEST** is displayed while the system is performing FIT. **FAULT** is displayed if an error is detected.	Current focus	Displays the current focus position within the available focus range. The left end of the scale indicates near focus and the right end of the scale indicates infinity focus.

Pages 4-26 through 4-28 deleted.

Figures 4-9 though 4-13 deleted.

STATUS/ SYMBOLOGY	FUNCTION
Current dynamic display range or zoom setting	Indicates the dynamic display range and the level offset derived from the Gain/Level/DC restoration settings for the IR sensor or the current zoom position of the TV sensor. For the IR sensor the width of the highlighted bar indicates the dynamic range. The position of the highlighted bar within the scale indicates the level offset.

4.6.7 POWER UP AND MODE SET Operation.

1. Cycle FLIR control panel **POWER** switch - **ON**.

2. Allow approximately 3 minutes for FLIR to complete the auto self-test BIT cycle, cool up period and auto cage.

3. Gain as desired or press **AUTO GAIN** button.

4. Polarity as desired, press **POLARITY** button.

NOTE

Focusing the FLIR initially in the 2X ZOOM field of view automatically sets focus for the NFOV and WFOV modes.

5. FOV set to 2X ZOOM and adjust focus **FOC OUT/IN**.

6. FOV - **WFOV**.

7. **MENU** button press.

8. Menu SYM hook, set day or night mode, exit **HOOK**.

9. Hook menu **CONFIG**, day/night symbology hook - Set as desired to change bright/dim indications of status bar, reticle, and misc. symbology.

10. Exit **MENU**.

4.6.8 Stopping Procedure. Using the menus place the system in **STOW**. The TFU will slew to the **STOW** position and the system is ready for shutdown. To shutdown the system turn **OFF** the system **PWR** switch.

Section II ARMAMENT

Not Used.

Section III CARGO HANDLING SYSTEMS

4.7 CARGO HOOK SYSTEM.

The system consists of a hook assembly (Figure 4-15) mounted on the lower fuselage, a control panel on the upper console (Figure 2-6), a normal release button on each cyclic stick grip, one emergency release switch on each collective stick grip, and a firing key in the cabin for use by the crew chief. The hook capacity is limited to a maximum of 8,000 pounds for UH-60Q aircraft. The system incorporates three modes of load release, an electrical circuit actuated from the cockpit, a manual release worked by the crewmember through a covered hatch in the cabin floor, and an emergency release system using an electrically-activated explosive charge.

4.7.1 Cargo Hook Stowage. The cargo hook shall be maintained in the stowed position during periods of non-use. The cargo hook can be placed in a stowed position (Figure 4-15) by opening the cargo hook access cover in the cabin floor, and pulling the hook to the right and up. When the hook is in the stowed position, the load beam rests on a spring-loaded latch assembly and is prevented from vibrating by a teflon bumper applying downward pressure on the load beam. To release the hook from its stowed position, downward pressure is placed on the latch assembly lever, retracting the latch from beneath the load beam, allowing the cargo hook to swing into operating position.

4.7.2 Cargo Hook Control Panel. The **CARGO HOOK** control panel (Figure 4-15), on the upper console, consists of an **EMERG REL NORM, OPEN, SHORT** test switch, a **TEST** light, **CONTR CKPT** or **ALL** station selector switch and an **ARMING, SAFE, ARMED** switch. Before the normal release (electrical) can operate, the **ARMING** switch must be at **ARMED** to provide electrical power to the release switches. The pilot and copilot **CARGO REL** switches, on the cyclics, will release the load when the **CONTR** switch is at **CKPT** or **ALL**. The crewmember's **NORMAL RLSE** switch will release the load when the **CONTR** switch is at **ALL**. The **EMERG REL** switch and **TEST** light permits checking the emergency release circuit when at **SHORT** or **OPEN**. In both cases of testing, if the release circuit is good, the **TEST** light will go on when the **HOOK EMER REL** switch on pilot's or copilot's collective, or the **EMER RLSE** switch on the crewmember's pendant, is pressed.

4.7.3 Crewmember's Cargo Hook Control Pendant. The crewmember's cargo hook control pendant (Figure 4-16), in the aft cabin, provides the crew chief with an electrical release and jettison of an external load when the **CARGO HOOK CONTR** switch is placed to **ALL**. The **NORMAL RLSE** and **EMER RLSE** switches are covered by guards to prevent accidental activation. When the cover is raised the switch can be pressed. When not in use, the pendant is stowed in the stowage bag at the back of the pilot's seat. Electrical power to operate the pendant is provided from the No. 2 dc primary bus through a circuit breaker, marked **CARGO HOOK CONTR**.

4.7.3.1 Normal Release. Normal release of external cargo is done by pressing the **CARGO REL** switch on either cyclic stick grip or the **CARGO HOOK NORMAL RLSE** on the crewmember's cargo hook pendant, after placing the **CARGO HOOK ARMING** switch to **ARMED**. A legend on the MFD will go on, indicating **HOOK ARMED**. This informs the pilot that electrical power is applied to the control circuit; the actuation of any of the release switches will release the load. When the **CARGO REL** switch is pressed and the release solenoid begins to move, a switch closes, lighting the **CARGO HOOK OPEN** advisory legend. The load arm will swing open, releasing the cargo. When the sling is detached from the load beam, spring tension on the arm will cause it to close and relatch, putting out the **CARGO HOOK OPEN** advisory legend. The normal release system is a one-shot cycle; once the solenoid travel begins and the load arm relatches, the release cycle can again be initiated. Power to operate the normal release system is supplied from the No. 2 dc primary bus through circuit breakers marked **CARGO HOOK CONTR** and **PWR**.

4.7.3.2 Operational Check - Normal Release Mode.

1. **CARGO HOOK CONTR** switch - As required. **CKPT** for pilot and copilot check, or **ALL** for crewmember check.

2. **CARGO HOOK ARMING** switch - **ARMED**.

3. **HOOK ARMED** advisory legend - Check on.

4. Place about 20 pounds downward pressure on load beam.

5. **CARGO REL** switch (pilot and copilot); **NORMAL RLSE** (crewmember) - Press and release.

6. **CARGO HOOK OPEN** advisory legend - Check on.

TM 1-1520-253-10

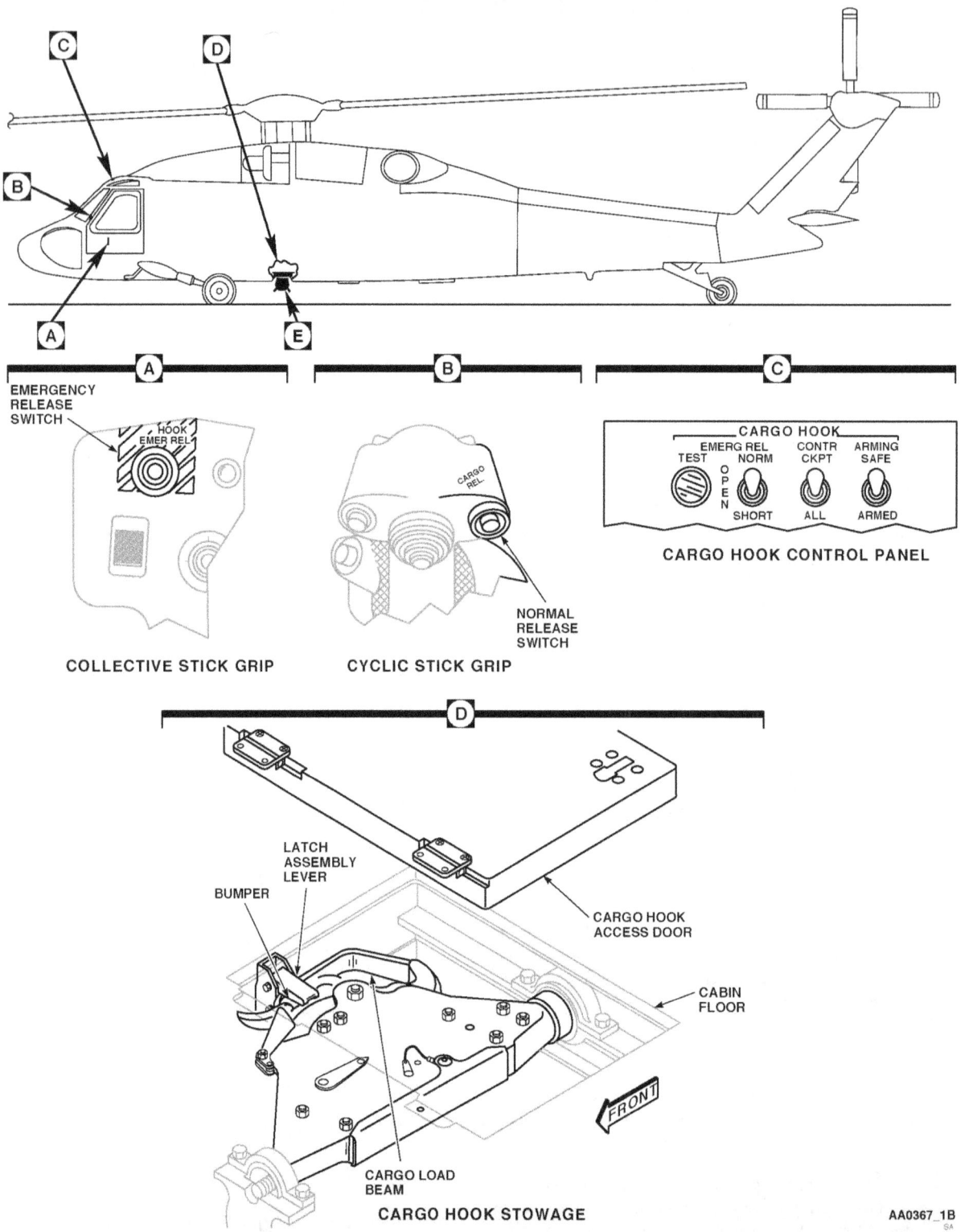

Figure 4-15. Cargo Hook System (Sheet 1 of 2)

4-32

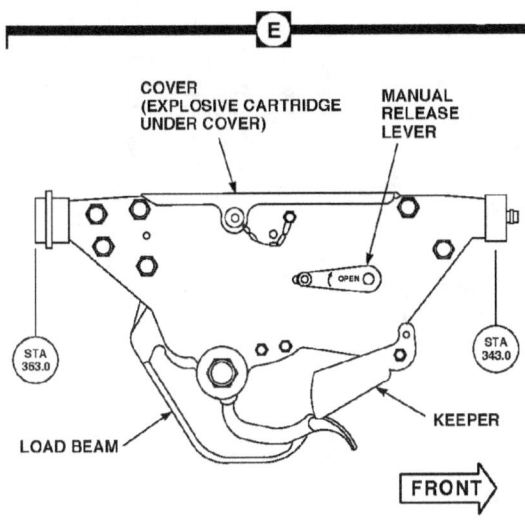

Figure 4-15. Cargo Hook System
(Sheet 2 of 2)

7. **CARGO HOOK OPEN** advisory legend - Check off when hook closes.

8. Repeat steps 4. through 7. for copilot and crewmember position.

4.7.3.3 Manual Release. Manual release of external cargo can be done from the cabin, through a covered port in the floor, or by ground personnel from outside the helicopter, with power on or off. Turning the release control on the right side of the hook (Figure 4-15) clockwise, causes the latching mechanism to release the load beam. The load beam will not move unless a downward pressure is exerted to cause opening. With power applied to the helicopter and the **CARGO HOOK ARMING** switch at **ARMED**, the **CARGO HOOK OPEN** advisory legend will go on at the start of release control turning, and will go off at the end of release control rotation.

4.7.3.4 Operational Check - Manual Release Mode.

1. Manual release lever spring - Installed. Check that spring is straight and provides positive pressure on the lever.

2. Place about 20 pounds downward pressure on load beam.

3. Manual release lever - Pull up/turn fully clockwise and release.

4. Load beam - Check open.

5. **CARGO HOOK OPEN** advisory legend - On.

6. When downward pressure is released, load beam will close and latch.

7. **CARGO HOOK OPEN** advisory legend - Off when hook closes.

4.7.4 Emergency Release Circuit Tester. The cargo hook emergency release circuit tester (Figure 2-6) marked **CARGO HOOK EMERG REL** on the upper console, contains a test light and switch. The test light, marked **TEST**, goes on during circuit testing to indicate the system is functioning properly. The switch, with marked positions **NORM, OPEN,** and **SHORT**, is normally at **NORM**. When the switch is placed to **OPEN** or **SHORT** and the cargo **HOOK EMER REL** switch on the pilot's or copilot's collective, or **EMER RLSE** switch on the crewmember's cargo hook control pendant is pressed, the circuit tester light will go on if the circuit is good.

4.7.4.1 Cargo Hook Emergency Release Circuit Check.

1. **EMERG REL TEST** light - Press. Light should be on.

NOTE

To prevent unintentional discharge of the cargo hook explosive cartridge, the pilot shall call off each procedural step of the emergency release circuit test before that step is done. Station being checked shall reply to pilot's command.

2. Pilot's release - Check.

   a. Short test.

   (1) **CARGO HOOK EMERG REL** switch - **SHORT**.

   (2) Pilot's **HOOK EMER REL** button - Press and hold.

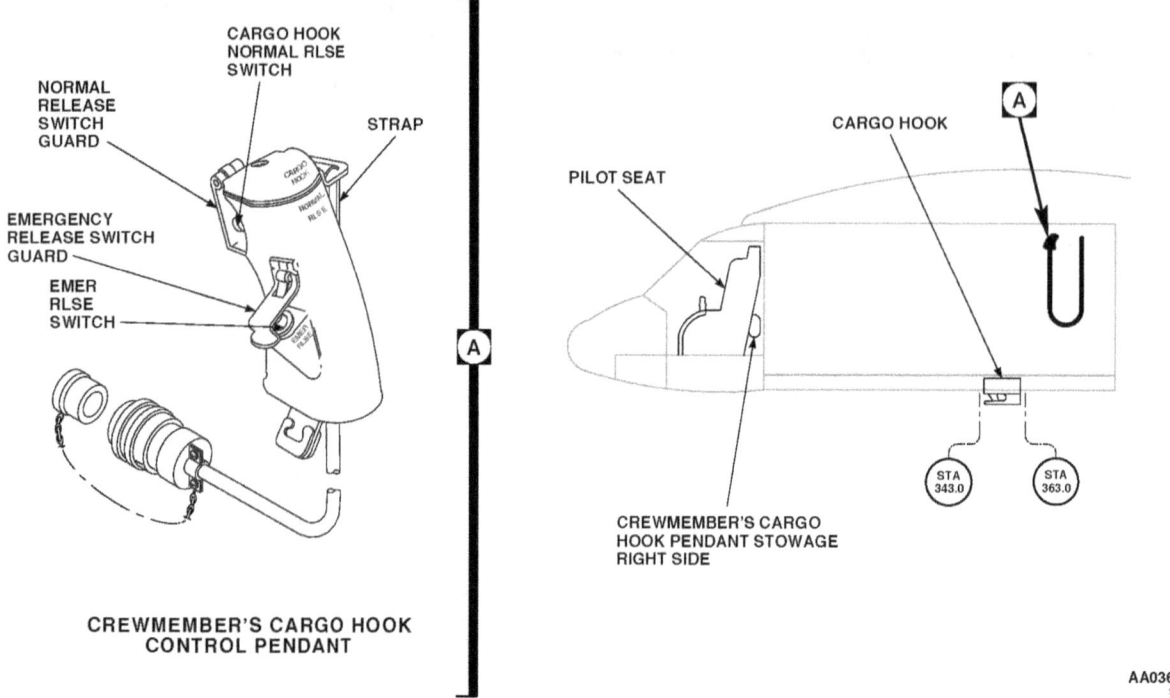

Figure 4-16. Crewmember's Cargo Hook Control Pendant

(3) **CARGO HOOK TEST** light - On.

(4) **HOOK EMER REL** button - Release. **TEST** light off.

(5) Repeat steps (2) through (4) for copilot's **HOOK EMER REL** button, and crewmember's cargo hook control pendant **EMER RLSE** button.

b. Open test.

(1) **CARGO HOOK EMERG REL** switch - **OPEN**.

(2) Pilot's **HOOK EMER REL** button - Press and hold.

(3) **CARGO HOOK TEST** light - On.

(4) **HOOK EMER REL** button - Release. **TEST** light off.

(5) Repeat steps (2) through (4) for copilot's **HOOK EMER REL** button, and crewmember's cargo hook control pendant **EMER RLSE** button.

3. **CARGO HOOK EMERG REL** switch **NORM**. If the cargo hook is not to be used immediately after completing the circuit test check, the **EMERG REL** switch shall remain at **OPEN** until ready for load pickup.

4.7.4.2 Emergency Release.

NOTE

When the emergency hook release has been used and a replacement squib (explosive cartridge) is not available, the hook can not be used until the explosive device is replaced, since the hook load beam will not close and lock.

Emergency release of an external cargo load is done by an electrically-fired explosive cartridge, initiated from either of the collective stick grip switches, marked **HOOK EMER REL**, or the crewman's cargo hook control pendant, marked **EMER RLSE**. The emergency release is used when the electrical and manual releases are inoperative, and the load must be jettisoned. With the **CARGO HOOK EMERG REL** switch at **NORM**, power will be applied to the emergency release switch. Pressing the switch applies 28 vdc to the explosive cartridge, producing a high gas pressure to drive a piston in the lock assembly, releasing the load arm lock. The weight of the load will cause the load arm to open. Once the emergency release is used, the hook will remain open and the **CARGO HOOK OPEN** advisory legend will remain on until the explosive cartridge device is replaced. When the explosive cartridge device is replaced the load arm will close, the light will go off, and the emergency release mode is returned to operation. Power to operate the emergency release system is from the dc essential bus through a circuit breaker, marked **CARGO HOOK EMER**.

4.7.5 Preflight. When cargo hook loads are to be carried, checks within this paragraph and procedures of paragraphs 4.7.6, 4.7.7, 4.7.8 and 4.7.9 apply.

1. Cargo hook - Check condition, security and explosive cartridge installed.

2. Emergency release system - Check. (Go to paragraph 4.7.4.)

3. Manual release - Check. (Go to paragraph 4.7.3.3.)

4.7.6 Before Takeoff.

1. **CARGO HOOK EMERG REL** switch - **NORM**.

2. **CARGO HOOK ARMING** switch - **ARMED**.

4.7.7 Emergency Release Procedure.

Pilot or copilot **HOOK EMER REL** or crewman's control pendant **EMER RLSE** - Press.

4.7.8 In-flight Procedures.

Cargo suspended from the cargo hook should not be over a 30° cone angle. To prevent damage to the cargo hook keeper, the pilot shall use extreme care to prevent placing load pressure on the keeper.

CARGO HOOK ARMING switch - As required. **ARMED** for low altitude/low airspeed. **SAFE** at cruise altitude and airspeed.

4.7.9 Before Landing. CARGO HOOK ARMING switch - **ARMED**.

Section IV MISSION FLEXIBLE SYSTEMS

4.8 MISSION READINESS CIRCUIT BREAKER PANEL.

The mission readiness circuit breaker panel (Figure 2-18) is on the No. 1 electrical junction box in the cabin, and contains all required circuit breakers for mission equipment.

4.9 RESCUE HOIST.

The rescue hoist system (Figure 4-17) consists of a hoist assembly, control section, relays, circuit breakers, and necessary electrical wiring. The hoist has a capacity of 600 pounds, is electrically powered from the No. 1 ac and dc primary buses through circuit breakers labeled **HOIST PWR**, and speed is variable from zero to 350 fpm. It is supported by a fixed tubular strut above the cabin door which is bolted to a support fitting on the fuselage. The hoist contains 290 usable feet of cable and has a guillotine-type cable cutter and an automatic cable brake. The rescue hoist system receives power through the No. 1 ac and dc primary buses through circuit breakers labeled **HOIST PWR**, and controlled from the No. 1 dc primary bus through a circuit breaker labeled **HOIST CONTR**.

4.9.1 Hoist Control Panel. There are two control panels (Figure 4-17.), one is located in the cockpit on the rear of the lower console and the other is in the right cabin aft of the cabin door. The **HOIST POWER** switch is located on the pilot's hoist control panel. The control panel also contains a **PILOT OVERRIDE-UP-DOWN** switch which allows the pilot to override any crew hoist command and operate the hoist at a fixed speed. The hoist cable can be cut from the cockpit via the **CABLE CUT** switch. The **CABLE CUT** switch is covered to avoid accidental firing of the cable cutter. The crew control panel located in the cabin, contains a **ARM-TEST** switch, **SQUIB TEST** light, **SEARCH LIGHT** switch, and a covered **CABLE CUT** switch.

4.9.2 Rescue Hoist Pendant. The crewmember's rescue hoist control pendant (Figure 4-17.), in the aft cabin, contains three lighted indicators labeled, **FULL IN**, **FULL OUT**, and **MTR HOT**. The pendant also contains a direction and speed thumbwheel labeled **UP-OFF-DN**, cable speed is directly proportional the amount of thumbwheel deflection. The search light control switch labeled **SCHLT-FWD-AFT-LEFT-RIGHT** allows control of the search light from the cabin. A cable length indicator labeled **CABLE-FEET**, indicates the amount of cable that is paid out.

> **CAUTION**
>
> The cable pay out reading is for reference only, cable stretch varies with the load attached to the end of it and also varies with the amount of cable paid out.

4.9.3 Controls and Function. The rescue hoist control system (Figure 4-17.) has all the necessary controls for operating the hoist from the cockpit or the cabin. The function of each control is as follows:

CONTROL/ INDICATOR	FUNCTION
HOIST POWER ON-OFF switch	Turns on power to the hoist when in the **ON** position. Turns off power to the hoist when in the **OFF** position.
PILOT OVERRIDE UP-DOWN switch	Provides the pilot with the capability to override any hoist command and operate the hoist up or down at a fixed speed.
CABLE CUT switch (cockpit/ cabin)	Controls cable cutter firing circuit.
SEARCH LIGHT switch	
ON/NORMAL position	Turns on power to the searchlight.
ON/NVG position	Turns on power to the NVG compatible searchlight.
OFF position	Turns power off to both searchlight modes.
ARM-TEST switch	Tests the cable cut squib circuit.
ARM position	Arms the cable cut circuit.
TEST position	Tests the cable cut squib circuit.
SQUIB TEST light	**PRESS TO TEST**, tests the light only.
FULL IN light	Illuminates when the hoist cable is in the full in position.

TM 1-1520-253-10

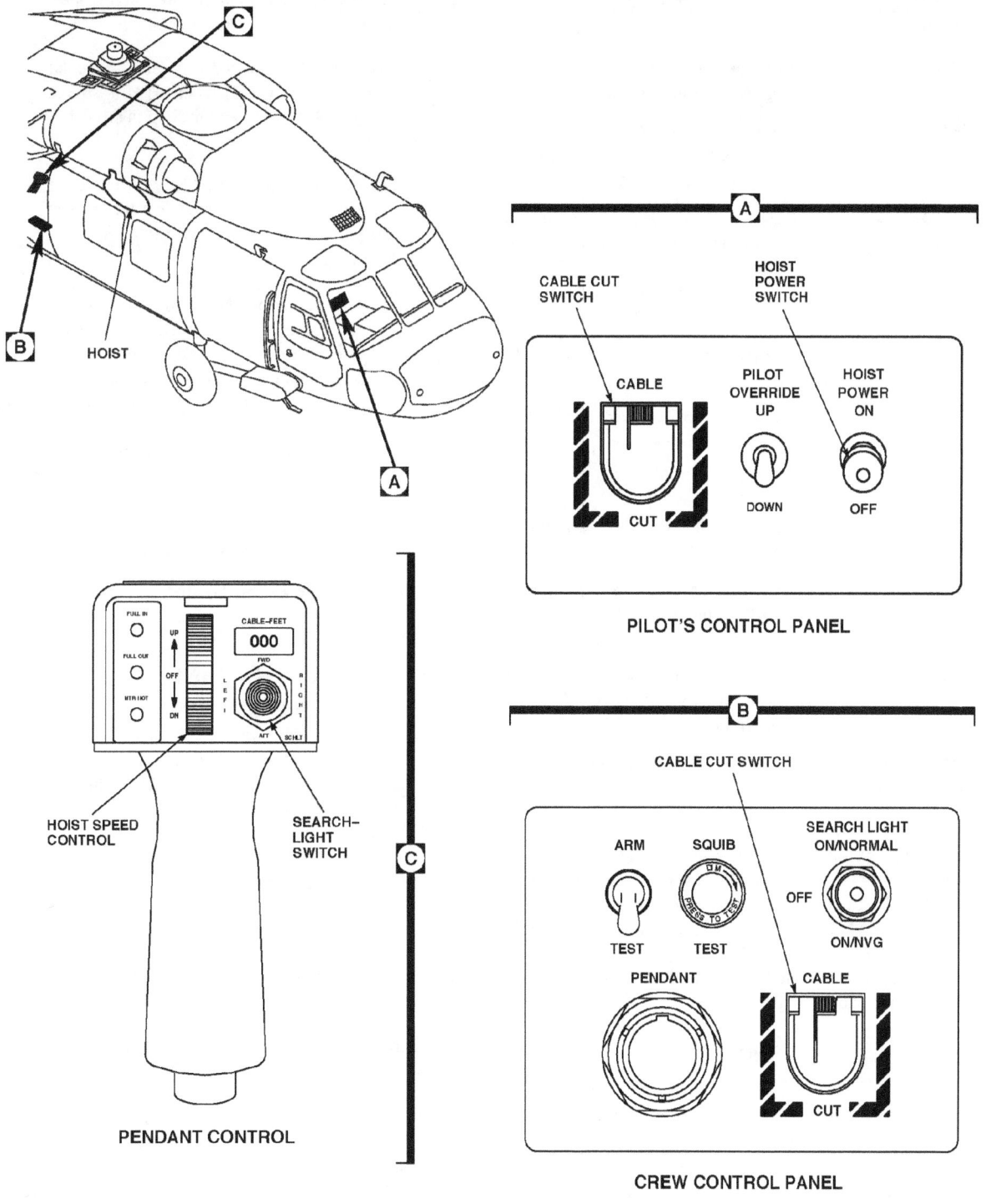

Figure 4-17. Rescue Hoist System

CONTROL/ INDICATOR	FUNCTION
FULL OUT light	Illuminates when the hoist cable is in the full out position.
MTR HOT light	Indicates that the hoist motor is hot. The hoist will operate at a reduced rate to permit cool down.
UP-OFF-DN thumbwheel	Hoist speed and direction are controlled via the amount and direction of thumbwheel deflection. The thumbwheel is spring loaded to the center **OFF** position.
SCHLT switch	Controls the direction of the search light.
FWD	Pressing switch to the **FWD** position moves hoist searchlight forward.
AFT	Pressing switch to the **AFT** position moves hoist searchlight rearward.
LEFT	Pressing switch to the **LEFT** position moves hoist searchlight to the left.
RIGHT	Pressing switch to the **RIGHT** position moves hoist searchlight to the right.
CABLE-FEET length indicator	Indicates the amount of cable that has been reeled out.

4.9.4 Hoist Operation. The rescue hoist system may be operated from controls located in the cabin or in the cockpit. The pilot can override the crewmember's controls. The **HOIST POWER** switch in cockpit must be in the **ON** position in order to operate the rescue hoist. Operation of the rescue hoist system is controlled through the rescue hoist control panel in either of two ways:

NOTE

All controls have automatic slow speed prior to the automatic stop at the cable extremes.

Power will be removed from environmental control system (ECS) when **HOIST POWER** switch is placed **ON**. Do not operate the rescue hoist while operating the ECS.

Power will be removed from environmental control system (ECS) when APU is source of helicopter power and backup pump is operating.

Rescue hoist operational daily checks prior to use and after use require that the backup pump be off to facilitate use with APU power.

1. The primary method is from the cabin by means of the crewmember's pendant, which can control the hoist in either direction at any speed up to 350 fpm, depending on the thumbwheel position, it is spring-loaded to the **OFF** position.

2. The secondary method is from the cockpit by means of the **PILOT OVERRIDE** switch which controls the hoist in either direction at a fixed speed. The pilot's controls have priority over the crewmember's pendant.

4.9.5 Hoist Cable Shear System.

Cable cut will not work from any station unless hoist power is on, and crew ARM - TEST switch is placed to ARM. There is no pilot override function for the ARM - TEST switch.

CAUTION

The rescue hoist shear capability is active on the ground.

The rescue hoist shear relay can be energized either from the cabin rescue hoist panel **CABLE CUT** switch or the **CABLE CUT** switch from the cockpit. Activating either switch fires an explosive cartridge that shears the hoist cable. If the lower console **HOIST POWER** switch is at **OFF**, neither **CABLE CUT** switches are operative. Power is provided from the dc essential bus through a circuit breaker marked **HOIST CABLE SHEAR**.

4.9.6 Rescue Hoist Operational Check.

WARNING

It is the hoist operator's responsibility to assure that the hoist cable does not contact any portion of the aircraft. The rescue hoist cable must be kept clear of all parts of the aircraft and free from other external obstacles when operating the hoist. Cable abrasion during hoist operations can lead to cable failure. If cable contact or snagging occurs, interrupt hoist operations and inspect the cable for damage in accordance with applicable procedures. If any broken wires, unraveling, or kinks are observed, hoisting operations should be discontinued and the cable replaced.

Reeling a kinked/damaged cable into the hoist may cause a hoist jam condition when reel-out is attempted, rendering hoist inoperative.

The hoist operator is responsible to maintain stability of the hoisted load by use of hoist controls, ICS calls to pilot, and physical control of cable (hand or foot). For minor oscillation (linear or circular swing), stop reel-in, apply hand motion to cable in direction opposite to oscillation. For significant oscillation, stop reel-in, start reel-out or call for pilot to lower aircraft.

WARNING

Rescue hoist cable is stiff and abrasive. Broken cable strands are sharp, therefore leather work gloves must be worn whenever handling rescue hoist cables.

If the oscillation is not quickly stopped, it may become unmanageable. Reeling in an oscillating load will only aggravate the motion.

All crew should watch for shock loads, jerks, or snaps that impart high loads on cable. If observed, hoisting should be interrupted and cable inspection undertaken to verify integrity (no broken wires, unraveling, or kinks) before resuming operations.

1. **HOIST POWER** switch - **ON**.

2. **ARM-TEST** switch - **ARM**.

3. Pilot lower hoist using **PILOT OVERRIDE UP-DOWN** switch - Observe cable lowers.

4. Pilot raise hoist to full up position.

5. Crewman - Perform hoist check.

    a. Crewman lower hoist using rescue hoist pendant thumbwheel (check variable speeds). Cable should lower. Pilot verify override capability using **PILOT OVERRIDE UP-DOWN** switch.

    b. Verify **UP** and **DOWN** control using thumbwheel switch.

    c. Raise rescue hoist hook to full up.

6. **ARM** switch - Off.

7. **HOIST POWER** switch - **OFF**.

4.10 EXTERNAL EXTENDED RANGE FUEL SYSTEM KIT ERFS.

The external extended range fuel system is supported by the external stores support system extending horizontally from each side of the fuselage aft of the cockpit doors (Figure 4-18). The 230-gallon jettisonable tanks are suspended from the vertical stores pylons (VSP). Removable fuel lines, bleed-air lines, valves, and electrical connectors are within the horizontal stores supports (HSS). A tank pressurizing system, using bleed-air, transfers fuel to the main tanks. Fuel lines carrying fuel to the No. 1 and No. 2 main fuel tanks contain check valves to prevent backflow. The extended range system does not supply fuel directly to the engines but is used to replenish the main tanks. Servicing of the external tanks can be done only through fueling ports on the tanks. Control of the system is provided by a control panel on the lower console. Power to operate the fuel transfer system is provided from the No. 1 dc primary bus through circuit breakers marked **EXT FUEL LH**, and **NO. 1 XFER CONTROL** and from the No. 2 dc primary bus through circuit breakers marked **EXT FUEL RH** and **NO. 2 XFER CONTROL** and from the No. 2 ac primary bus through a circuit breaker marked **AUX FUEL QTY** on the mission readiness circuit breaker panel.

4.10.1 External Extended Range Fuel Transfer Modes.
Fuel can be transferred from external tanks to main tanks in either of two modes, **AUTO MODE** or

MANUAL. **AUTO** (primary) transfers fuel automatically after switches are manipulated. Fuel transfer will be managed by the microprocessor as described in paragraph 4.10.6. The pilot need only occasionally monitor the **AUXILIARY FUEL MANAGEMENT** panel to ensure that during **AUTO MODE** of fuel transfer, fuel in external tanks is decreasing as it should. The second mode of transfer is the **MANUAL XFR** (secondary) mode. In the **MANUAL** mode the pilot may replenish main tank fuel in any quantity or frequency desired. Transfer must be initiated by the pilot. The pilot must constantly monitor the fuel quantity indicator in order to start and terminate transfer to remain within CG limits. It is possible to transfer fuel from any one tank while in **MANUAL** mode. Transfer is shut off by the pilot when the external tank low-level sensor signals that the tank is empty. During manual transfer, at the illumination of a tank **EMPTY** light, immediately switch from **OUTBD** to **INBD** or to manual transfer **MODE OFF**. Do not wait for the **NO FLOW** light to illuminate. This will preclude air from entering the fuel line and entering the main tank. At the illumination of the **TANK EMPTY** capsule, 2.5 to 4.0 gallons of fuel remain in the tank. Sloshing of the fuel will cause frequent illumination of the **TANK EMPTY**, **NO FLOW**, and **AUX FUEL** lights when the tank is in this condition.

4.10.2 External Extended Range Fuel System Tanks. External extended range system contains two or four tanks suspended from supports outboard of the fuselage. The tanks contain baffles to prevent fuel sloshing. Quick-disconnect valves are provided in external fuel and bleed-air lines to provide seals when tanks are jettisoned or removed. If tanks are not installed cccc will be displayed in the **AUX FUEL QTY POUNDS** display when **OUTBD** or **INBD** is selected on the rotary fuel quantity selector. The preferred location of the External Extended Range Fuel System (External ERFS) auxiliary fuel tank is the outboard pylon. This facilitates ingress and egress of troops and loading of cargo.

4.10.3 Auxiliary Fuel Management Control Panel. The **AUXILIARY FUEL MANAGEMENT** control panel (Figure 4-18) contains all controls for operating the external extended range fuel system. Controls description is as follows:

CONTROL/INDICATOR	FUNCTION
FUEL XFR	Controls fuel management of external extended range system.
PRESS	
OUTBD ON	Opens bleed-air valves to outboard tanks for pressurization.
OFF	Closes bleed-air valves to tanks.
INBD ON	Not used.
OFF	Closes bleed-air valves to tanks.
TANKS INBD	Not used.
TANKS OUTBD	Selects fuel transfer valves from outboard tanks for fuel transfer to main tanks; deselects inboard valves.
MODE	Selects **AUTO-OFF-MANUAL** mode of fuel transfer from external fuel tanks.
AUTO	Automatically transfers fuel to main tanks from selected external tanks, until empty sensor in each tank interrupts transfer. Transfer occurs in levels as shown under fuel transfer sequence. When tanks are empty, **NO FLOW** and **EMPTY** indicators and **AUX FUEL** caution light will be turned on.
OFF	Interrupts automatic or manual transfer mode of operation.
MANUAL	Provides electrical path to **MANUAL XFR** switch(es), which allows transfer from selected tank(s) until switch is moved to off.
MANUAL XFR	
RIGHT ON	Transfers from right tank used in conjunction with **MODE** switch in **MANUAL** position of the pair selected by **TANKS** select switch.
OFF	Interrupts transfer operation.

CONTROL/INDICATOR	FUNCTION
LEFT ON	Transfers from left tank of the pair selected by **TANKS** select switch.
OFF	Interrupts transfer operation.
AUX FUEL QTY POUNDS	Indicates pounds of external fuel remaining in symmetrical pair of tanks total of auxiliary tanks, self-test indication or failure codes. Displays K factors of flow meter.

NOTE

Fuel tanks selector and quantity indicators are also used in conjunction with **INCR-DECR** switch when initializing fuel quantity of tanks.

CONTROL/INDICATOR	FUNCTION
OUTBD	Total pounds of fuel remaining in outboard pair of tanks.
INBD	Not used.
TOTAL	Pounds of fuel remaining in all external extended range tanks.
CAL	Adjusts K factor of flow switch on **AUXILIARY FUEL MANAGEMENT** panel.
INCR switch position	Increases setting of digital readout to adjust for fuel remaining in tanks selected by fuel tank selector.
DECR switch position	Decreases setting of digital readout to adjust for fuel remaining in tanks selected by fuel tank selector.
STATUS button	Resets **AUX FUEL** caution light and stores condition of **NO FLOW** and **EMPTY** indicators.

CONTROL/INDICATOR	FUNCTION
TEST	Checks display and indicator lights. Performs memory checksum, displays 8 sequentially in each digital display. Verifies that temperature probe is connected; verifies that flow meter is connected; performs trial calculation based on a known temperature and flow meter input, compares it with a known good value, and displays setting of fuel density switch. At completion of test, **GOOD** or error code will be displayed (Table 4-2).
DEGRADED light	Error in critical function has occurred. Error code will be displayed as shown under **TEST**. Only E02 error will allow microprocessor to clear failure code and regain fuel remaining information by doing two self-tests.
EXTERNAL	
*RIGHT NO FLOW light	Fuel flow does not exit from selected right tank.
*INBD EMPTY light	Not used.
*OUTBD EMPTY light	Right outboard tank fuel exhausted.
*LEFT NO FLOW light	Fuel flow does not exit from selected left tank.
*INBD EMPTY light	Not used.
*OUTBD EMPTY light	Left outboard tank fuel exhausted.
VENT SENSOR	Detects the presence of fuel on the vent thermistor.
*OVFL	Indicates fuel venting overboard.

TM 1-1520-253-10

CONTROL/ INDICATOR	FUNCTION

NOTE

Illumination of this capsule on the Fuel Management Panel will cause illumination of the **AUX FUEL** caution legend and the **MASTER CAUTION** light. Pushing the **STATUS** button will reset the **NO FLOW**, **AUX FUEL** and the **MASTER CAUTION** lights, but does not correct the no flow condition.

FAIL   Open in vent sensor line.

4.10.4 External Extended Range Fuel Quantity Indicating System.

The **AUX FUEL QTY POUNDS** digital readout (Figure 4-18) displays the amount of fuel remaining. Fuel type is preset by switches in the **AUXILIARY FUEL MANAGEMENT** panel. Preset can only be done when the helicopter weight is on the wheels. When measuring quantity, the readout is used in conjunction with the rotary selector switch to select tank pair subtotal, or **TOTAL** remaining in all tanks. Fuel used is sensed from a common flow transmitter within the fuel line to the main tanks. This amount is subtracted from the preset fuel quantity input and is displayed on the digital readout as pounds remaining. A **DEGRADED** light will go on, when a complete failure has occurred in the microprocessor, or an error condition is detected by the microprocessor, or when the temperature sensor has failed. Power for the fuel quantity subsystem is provided from the No. 2 ac primary bus through a circuit breaker marked **AUX FUEL QTY**, on the mission readiness circuit breaker panel.

4.10.5 Auxiliary Fuel Management Control Panel Test.

1. **TEST** button - Press. Digits should display 8's and **DEGRADED** and **VENT SENSOR** (**FAIL** and **OVFL**) lights should illuminate.

2. **TEST** button - Release. Digits should display 8's in sequence from left to right three times; 5 seconds later, display GOOD or EO failure code; 3 seconds later, display type fuel density, then fuel **TOTAL**.

3. Auxiliary fuel quantity switch - **CAL**.

NOTE

CAL is the calibration value marked on the fuel flow transmitter. Enter the four digit number, disregarding the numbers to the right of the decimal point.

4. **INCR/DECR** switch - Set calibration.

5. Auxiliary fuel quantity switch - **OUTBD**.

6. **INCR/DECR** switch - Set outboard fuel quantity.

7. Auxiliary fuel quantity switch move to **TOTAL** - Check.

8. **PRESS OUTBD** switch - As desired.

4.10.6 Fuel Transfer Sequence.

WARNING

FUEL BOOST PUMP CONTROL switches shall remain on during external range fuel transfer and remain on for 10 minutes after PRESS switches are moved to OFF. Failure to observe this warning may cause engine flameout.

CAUTION

Fuel transfer sequence must be carefully planned and executed in order to maintain CG within limits.

Fuel transfer sequence shall be based on mission requirement and center of gravity limitations. Automatic transfer is started when the proper switches are manipulated and fuel level is as shown below and external range tanks internal pressure is increased enough to force fuel to the main tanks. Transfer will continue until the main tank signal conditioner provides a signal through the microprocessor to stop fuel transfer. This cycle is done as required until interrupted by placing the **MODE** switch to **OFF** or **MANUAL** or placing the **PRESS** switch OFF. Manual transfer will be started on selection of **MANUAL** and appropriate switches, and external fuel tanks are bleed-air pressurized to start fuel transfer from external tank(s) to

Pages 4-42.1 through 4-42.2 deleted.

4-42   Change 3

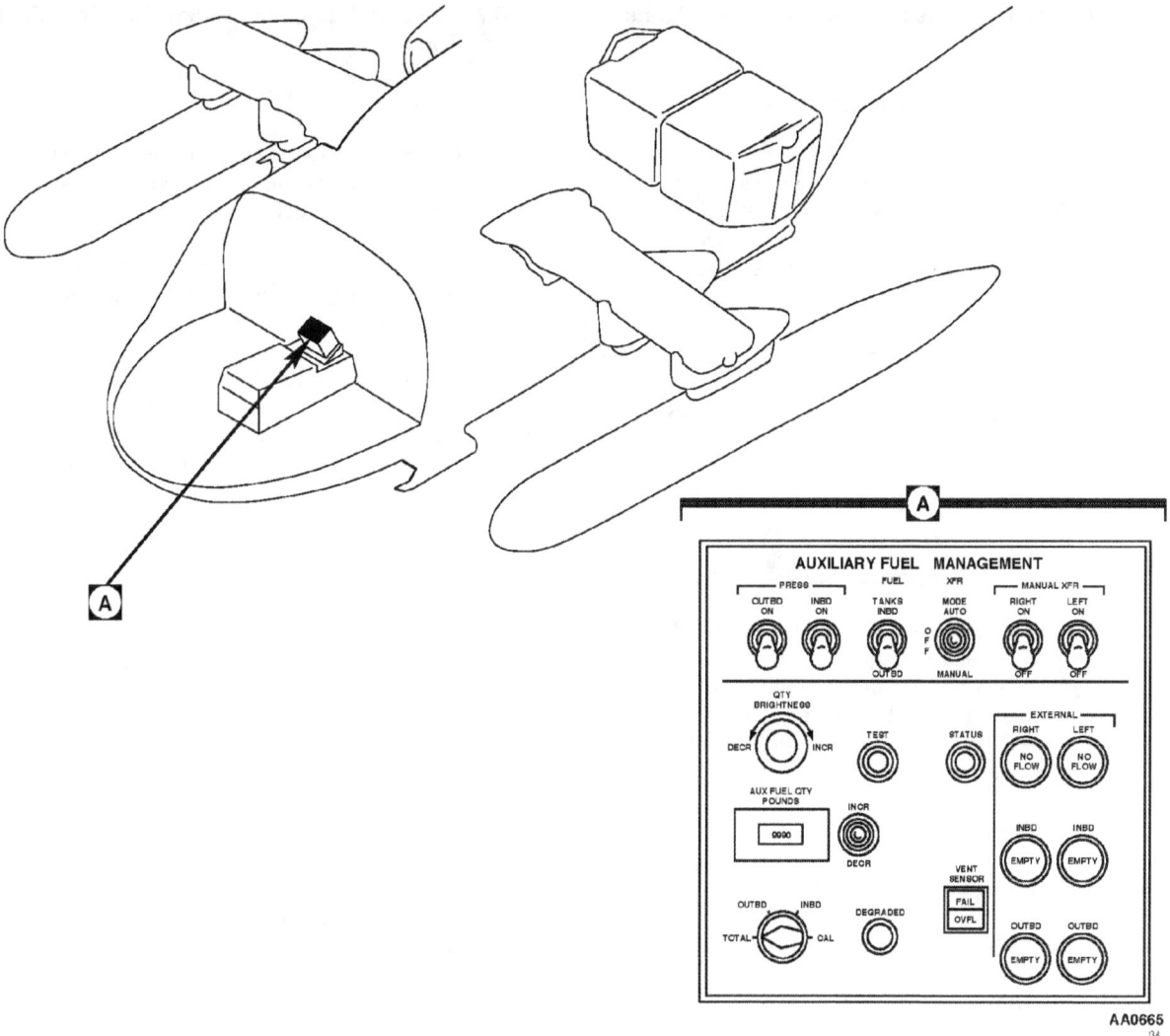

Figure 4-18. Auxiliary Fuel Management Control Panel

main tanks. Transfer will continue until tanks are full. They will remain full as long as the manual mode remains engaged. Manual transfer requires close monitoring of fuel level to initiate and stop transfer to remain within CG limits. The automatic transfer sequence is as follows:

TOTAL AUXILIARY FUEL REMAINING (BASED ON JP-4 DENSITY)	TRANSFER START WHEN ONE MAIN FUEL TANK QUANTITY LESS THAN	TRANSFER STOP WHEN EACH MAIN FUEL TANK QUANTITY MORE THAN
8840-7041 lbs	950 lbs	1000 lbs
7040-5001 lbs	750 lbs	1000 lbs
5000-0 lbs	600 lbs	1000 lbs

4.10.7 External Extended Range Fuel Transfer Check.

NOTE

When ambient temperature is below 4°C (40°F), ESSS/ERFS shall not be turned off after transfer check has been completed to avoid potential for freeze-up of the pressure regulator.

1. **AIR SOURCE HEAT/START** switch - **ENG**.
2. **FUEL BOOST PUMP CONTROL** switches - Check **ON**.

WARNING

FUEL BOOST PUMP CONTROL switches shall remain on during external range fuel transfer and remain on for 10 minutes after PRESS switches are moved to OFF. Failure to observe this warning may cause engine flameout.

3. **PRESS OUTBD** switch - **ON**.
4. Fuel quantity switch - **TOTAL**.
5. **TANKS** switch - As desired.
6. **MODE** switch - **MANUAL**.
7. **MANUAL XFR RIGHT** switch - **ON**.
8. Main **FUEL QTY TOTAL FUEL** readout - Check for increase of about 20 pounds.
9. **TANKS** switch - Repeat for other position.
10. **MANUAL XFR RIGHT** switch - **OFF**.
11. **MANUAL XFR LEFT** switch - **ON**.
12. Repeat steps 8. and 9. for **MANUAL XFR LEFT**.
13. **MANUAL XFR** switches - **OFF**.
14. External extended range fuel system - Set as desired.

4.10.7.1 External Extended Range Fuel Transfer In AUTO Mode.

NOTE

If either main fuel quantity is below 1,000 lbs., selecting the automatic mode may initiate a transfer sequence.

Allow sufficient time for tank pressurization (approximately 10 minutes for a half full 230-gallon tank).

During transfer, periodically verify that **AUXILIARY FUEL MANAGEMENT** panel quantity is decreasing at a minimum of 40 pounds per minute, per tank pair. Fuel transfer rate of less than 40 pounds per minute may indicate reduced flow from one or both tanks.

1. **AIR SOURCE HEAT/START** switch - **ENG**.
2. **FUEL BOOST PUMP CONTROL** switches - **ON**.
3. **PRESS OUTBD** switch - **ON**.
4. **MODE** switch - **AUTO**.
5. **TANKS** switch - **OUTBD**.

4.10.7.2 External Extended Range Fuel Transfer In MANUAL Mode.

If **AUTO** mode is inoperative, transfer in **MANUAL** mode as follows:

CAUTION

Monitor fuel transfer to remain within CG limits and avoid asymmetric loading.

1. **AIR SOURCE HEAT/START** switch - **ENG**.
2. **FUEL BOOST PUMP CONTROL** switches - **ON**.
3. **PRESS OUTBD** switch - **ON**.
4. **MODE** switch - **MANUAL**.
5. **TANKS** switch - **OUTBD**.

6. **MANUAL XFR** switches **RIGHT** and **LEFT** - **ON**.

4.10.7.3 External Extended Range Fuel Flow Verification In Manual Mode. If extended range without landing is required and the aircraft is not equipped with an ERFS fuel indicating system, verify fuel flow from each tank as follows:

NOTE

Ensure main fuel tanks are not completely full.

1. **AIR SOURCE HEAT/START** switch - **ENG**.

2. **FUEL BOOST PUMP CONTROL** switches - **ON**.

3. **PRESS OUTBD** switch - **ON**.

4. **MODE** switch - **MANUAL**.

5. **TANKS** switch - **OUTBD**.

6. **MANUAL XFR RIGHT** switch - **ON**. Note the rate of decrease of the **AUX FUEL QTY POUNDS** indicator. The normal transfer fuel flow rate per tank should be between 20 to 38 pounds per minute.

7. **MANUAL XFR RIGHT** switch - **OFF**.

8. Repeat steps 6. and 7. for left tank.

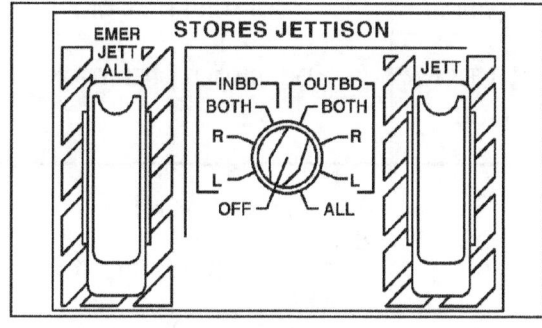

Figure 4-19. Stores Jettison Control Panel ES

4.11 EXTERNAL STORES SUPPORT SYSTEM (ESSS). ES

ESSS provides a means of carrying a variety of external stores, including external extended range fuel tanks. The ESSS consists of fixed and removable provisions.

4.11.1 External Stores Fixed Provisions. Fixed provisions are: upper fuselage fixed fittings for attaching the horizontal stores support (HSS) subsystem, and lower fuselage strut support fittings for attaching two struts for each HSS. In addition to exterior components, fixed provisions are: interior helicopter provisions, including electrical harnesses, fuel lines, bleed-air lines, and circuit breakers.

4.11.2 External Stores Removable Provisions. The external stores removable subsystem extends horizontally from each side of the helicopter at station 301.5, buttline 42.0. Extending below each horizontal stores support (HSS) are two vertical stores pylons (VSP) and attaching ejector racks. The racks are used to attach fuel tanks or other external stores dispensers.

4.11.3 ESSS Side Position Lights. A position light is on each outboard end of HSS. Those lights use the power source provided to operate the standard installed position lights, colors are the same. Upon installation of the HSS, the electrical connectors connected to the jumper plugs, providing power for the standard position lights, are removed and reconnected to the connectors from the HSS position lights. Operation and power source for the ESSS position lights are the same as for the standard installed position lights.

4.11.4 External Stores Jettison Control Panel. The jettison control panel (Figure 4-19) provides the capability of phase jettison of all external stores or symmetrical jettison of fuel tanks. Interlock circuitry prevents jettison of fuel tanks other than in pairs. Emergency jettison is completely independent of the primary jettison subsystem.

WARNING

The ejector rack CARTRIDGES are explosive devices and must not be exposed to heat, stray voltage or static electricity. Refer to TM 9-1300-206 for information concerning handling and storage of ammunition.

The jettison control panel (Figure 4-19) contains all controls for jettisoning external stores. Jettison controls are as follows:

CONTROL	FUNCTION
EMER JETT ALL	Applies 28 volts from essential dc bus to all stores stations when the helicopter weight is off the wheels, regardless of the rotary selector switch. A 1-second time delay permits the outboard stations to jettison before the inboard stations.
Rotary selector switch	Determines which station receives primary jettison signal.
OFF	Prevents jettison signal from going to any stores station.
INBD	
L	*Directs jettison signal to inboard left station.
R	*Directs jettison signal to inboard right station.
BOTH	Directs jettison signal to inboard left and right stores stations.
OUTBD	
L	*Directs jettison signal to outboard left station.
R	*Direct jettison signal to outboard right station.

Table 4-2. Extended Range Fuel System Degraded Operation Chart ERFS

SYSTEM FAILURE CODES AND INDICATIONS	DEGRADED LIGHT	AUX FUEL CAUTION LIGHT	DESCRIPTION OF DEGRADED OPERATION
E01 MICROPROCESSOR ERROR E03 FLOWMETER DISCONNECTED E04 ERROR FUEL FLOW CIRCUITS E05 ERROR FUEL FLOW COMPUTATION E06 MEMORY ERROR	ON	ON	1. AUTO XFR CAPABILITIES REMAIN 2. DEFAULTS TO CURRENT XFR SCHEDULE 3. PILOT MUST COMPUTE FUEL USAGE

E02 TEMPERATURE SENSOR NOT CONNECTED OR OUT OF RANGE	ON	ON	1. AUTO XFR CAPABILITIES REMAIN
			2. PERFORMING TWO SELF-TESTS WILL:
			  A. CLEAR FAILURE CODE AND REGAIN FUEL REMAINING INFO
			  B. RESET AUX FUEL LIGHT
			  C. DEFAULT TO PRESELECTED TEMP VALUE

LOSS OF DIGITAL READOUT	ON	ON	1. AUTO XFR CAPABILITIES REMAIN 2. NO FLOW AND EMPTY MONITORING INDICATIONS REMAIN 3. PILOT MUST COMPUTE FUEL USAGE
LOSS OF ONE MAIN TANK LEVEL QUANTITY SENSOR OR LOSS OF ONE SIGNAL CONDITIONER INPUT	OFF	OFF	NO DEGRADATION
FAILED AUX TANK EMPTY SENSOR PROVIDES FALSE EMPTY SIGNAL	OFF	ON-IF FUEL TRANSFER SELECTED	AUX TANK FUEL TRANSFER SHUTOFF VALVE CLOSES. PILOT SELECTING MANUAL MODE REOPENS VALVE.

CONTROL	FUNCTION	CONTROL	FUNCTION
BOTH	Directs jettison signal to outboard left and right stores stations.		**NOTE**
ALL	Directs primary jettison signal to all stores stations. Outboard stores will jettison and 1 second later inboard stores will jettison.		*If fuel tanks are connected to the left, right, or both stores stations, the **BOTH** mode of jettison is automatically selected even if the selector switch is at **L** or **R**.

CONTROL	FUNCTION
JETT	Applies 28 volts from primary dc bus through the rotary selector switch to the selected stores station if the weight is off the wheels and the selector switch is not **OFF**.

4.11.5 Stores Jettison Control Operation.

To prevent unintentional jettison of external stores when the helicopter weight is on the wheels, do not actuate any jettison switch.

The jettison system provides two modes of jettisoning external stores, primary and emergency. The primary subsystem uses the rotary selector switch and the **JETT** toggle switch. The emergency jettison subsystem uses only the **EMER JETT ALL** toggle switch. Primary jettison is used when selective jettison is desired. The rotary switch is used to select the stores point for release, and the **JETT** toggle switch is used to actuate the release. Emergency jettison is used to release all external stores through one actuation of the **EMER JETT ALL** toggle switch, regardless of rotary switch position. During primary (rotary switch **ALL** selected) and emergency jettison, a 1-second delay is provided after the outboard stores are released, before the inboard stores will be released. When one pair of tanks is jettisoned in a four tank system, **cccc** will appear on the **AUX FUEL QTY POUNDS** digital readout when the corresponding fuel quantity position is selected. The fuel remaining in the tanks jettisoned will be subtracted from the total displayed when **TOTAL** is selected. Power to operate the primary jettison subsystem is from the No. 1 dc primary bus through circuit breakers marked **ESSS JTSN INBD** and **OUTBD**. The emergency jettison subsystem is powered from the dc essential bus through circuit breakers marked **ESSS JTSN INBD** and **OUTBD**.

4.12 MEDICAL EVACUATION (MEDEVAC) SYSTEM.

The MEDEVAC System (Figure 4-20) includes two medical stations positioned longitudinally on each side of the forward cabin. Each station includes two electromechanical litter lifts that support two litter platforms. The platforms are positioned to accommodate up to four primary litter patients or six ambulatory (seated) patients. When the situation requires multiple patient evacuation, two Standardization Agreement (STANAG) litters can be placed on the floor under the forward lifts for a total of six litter patients. Litter lighting is provided for each patient. Provisions to support intravenous (IV) fluid bags, are mounted overhead in the cabin and along the face of the doorpost panels. A modular medical cabinet containing oxygen system indicators and controls, provisions for carry-on medical equipment, and storage of medical supplies is installed at the aft bulkhead between the two troop seats. Three crew seats are provided in the cabin for the crew chief/medical attendants. The medical life support equipment includes an oxygen system, suction system, and outlets for 28 VDC and 115 VAC 60-cycle electrical power. Controls for the medical stations are located on the doorpost panels, one panel for each station. Blackout curtains are provided between the cockpit and cabin and for the cabin windows.

4.12.1 Medical Stations. Each station (Figure 4-21) provides accommodations for two primary patients and one secondary patient or three ambulatory patients. The stations include the dual electromechanical litter lifts which support the litter platforms, ambulatory patient/litter platforms, and the adjacent doorpost control panel.

4.12.2 Litter Lift System. The litter lift system consists of left and right litter platforms stations to provide transport of six littered patients, six seated patients, or cargo or a combination of these. The dual station system supports and controls the positioning of two litter platforms. Both platforms may be moved to the ceiling to accommodate cargo on the floor or moved to the floor to accommodate ambulatory (seated) patients. The top side of the upper platform is configured with the attaching brackets for the ambulatory seats. The litter platforms are moved by medical attendants to change the level or tilt. Loading is simplified by allowing patients to be loaded at floor level and moved up to their flight position. The system utilizes electromechanical non hydraulic motor mechanisms that are shielded from the cabin with a steel curtain for the protection of both personnel and equipment. In the event of a power failure, a manual mechanical back-up system is provided to actuate the lift mechanism. The litter lift system is designed to quickly and easily:

1. Load and unload patients.

2. Adjust height and tilt to accommodate patient size and needs.

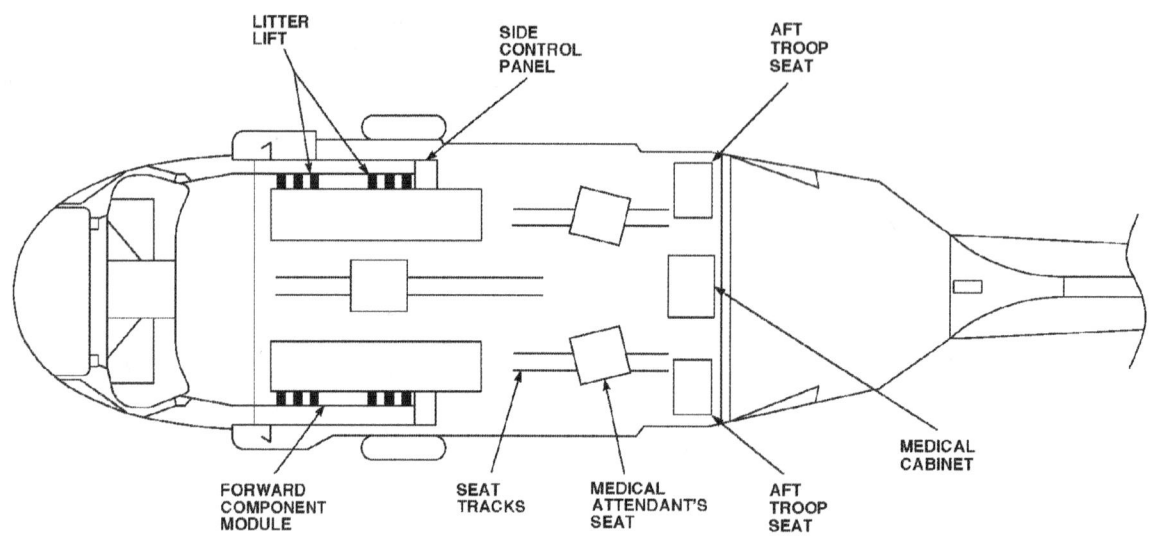

Figure 4-20. MEDEVAC System

3. Change between ambulatory patient, littered patient and cargo configurations.

Each station operates independently of the other to permit several loading variations. Variations include:

1. One to three littered patients on one side and one to three seated patients on the other.

2. One to three littered patients on one side and cargo on the other.

3. One to three seated patients on one side and cargo on the other.

4.12.3 Ambulatory Patient Configuration. The two medical stations can be reconfigured to seat six ambulatory patients (Figure 4-22). An additional two ambulatory patients may be seated on the two aft troop seats for a total of eight patients. Seating for the patients is contained in the upper patient litter platform. The lower platform must be positioned to the floor position and the upper platform to the seat position. When the platforms are in place, the upper portion of the ambulatory platform is raised to act as a backrest. Restraints, consisting of seatbelts and shoulder harnesses, are built into the platform and headrests for the three ambulatory patients. Headrests, stored in the ceiling, are lowered in position and secured to the backrest by locking pins.

NOTE

Ensure the backrest and headrests are secured in place.

4.12.4 Litter Platforms. There are a total of four platforms installed in the aircraft, two at each station (Figure 4-23). The platforms provide a loading surface for a patient strapped to a litter. The litter is secured to the platform by means of a locking device mounted in the end of the platform and two restraint belts. The platforms attach to the support rods and are raised, lowered, or tilted by the lift mechanism. The platforms are similar in construction, with the exception that the upper platform may be reconfigured to provide seating for three ambulatory patients.

4.12.5 MEDEVAC Seats Installation. Three crew seats, two located in the aft cabin area and one located in the center between the forward medical stations, are provided for the crew chief/medical attendants. Each seat swivels 360 degrees and is T track mounted, which allows the seats to move fore and aft for better access to the pa-

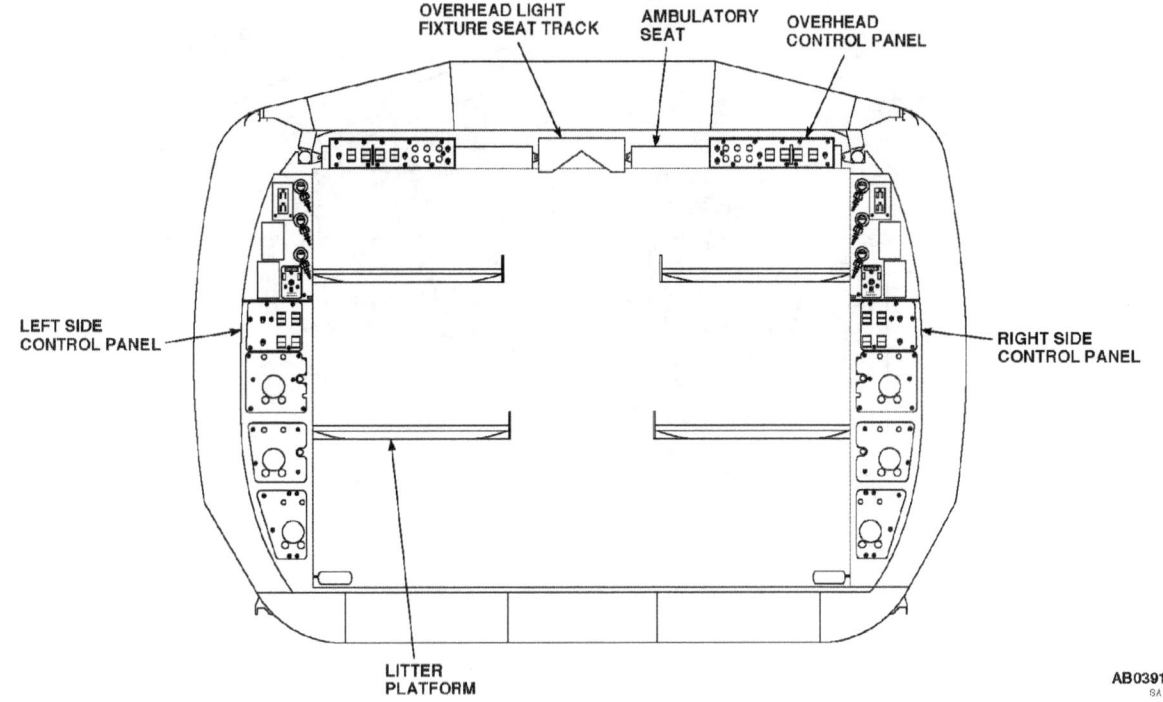

Figure 4-21. Medical Stations

tients. Each seat contains a headrest, which attendant restraints provided by a lap safety belt which connects to a shoulder harness. Lift forward (upper) knob to swivel, aft (lower) knob to move fore and aft.

4.12.6 Medical Control Panels. The Medical Control Panels are located on each side of the aircraft (doorpost panels), and on the ceiling (overhead panel) (Figure 4-24) to provide full access to medical controls by medical personnel. The side control panels contain covered 115 VAC 60 Hz electrical outlets and controls for the litter lifts, suction systems, and oxygen system. Lighted Indicators are ANVIS (Aviators Night Vision Imaging System) compatible and have the ability to be dimmed. Control and functions are further defined:

CONTROLS/ INDICATORS	FUNCTION
OXYGEN	
Regulator Control	Regulates oxygen flow.
DISS/Barbed outlet	Connection for oxygen outlet hose.
Quick Disconnect Oxygen Outlet	Quick disconnect connection for the Chemetron compatible oxygen hose.
LITTER LIFTS switches	
UPPER PLATFORM FWD UP DOWN and **AFT UP DOWN**	Moves the forward and aft end of the upper litter platform up or down.
LOWER PLATFORM FWD UP DOWN and **AFT UP DOWN**	Moves the forward and aft end of the lower litter platform up or down.
EMERGENCY STOP	

TM 1-1520-253-10

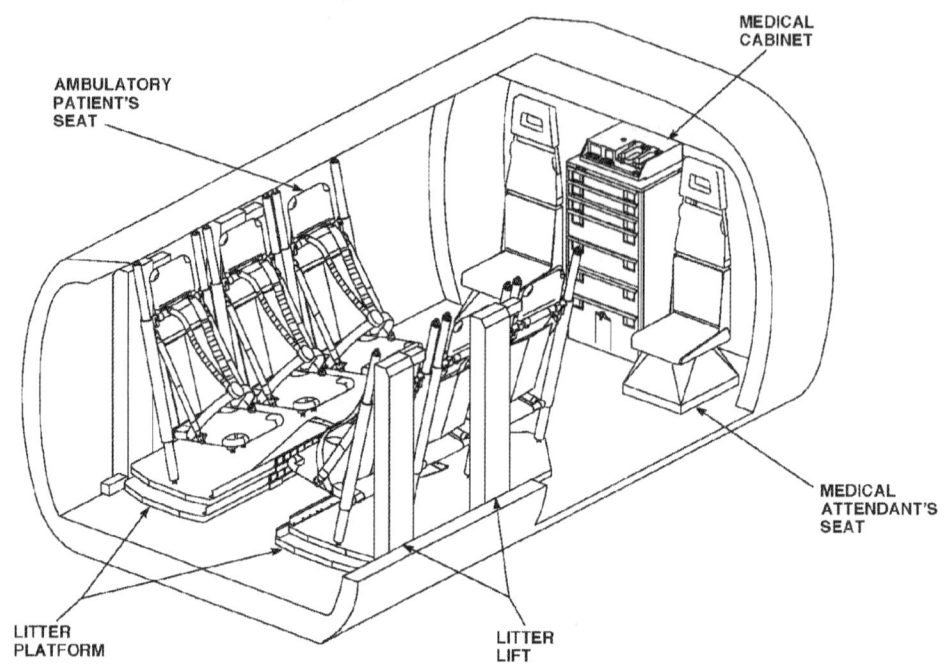

Figure 4-22. Ambulatory Seat Arrangement

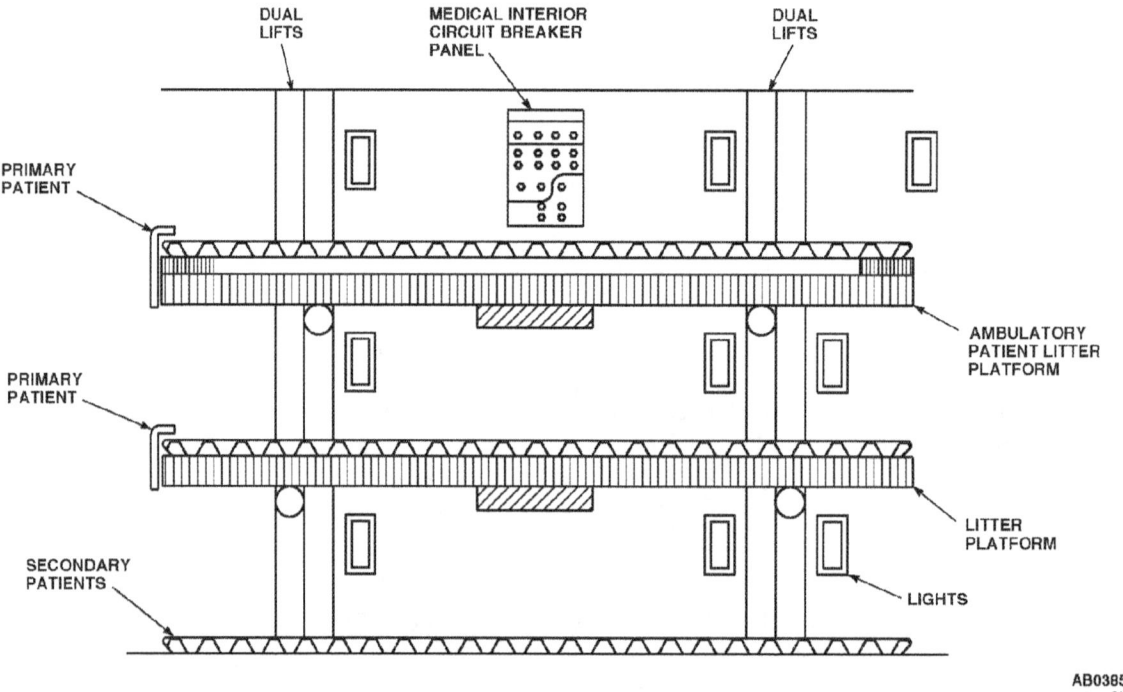

Figure 4-23. Litter Platform

4-50

CONTROLS/ INDICATORS	FUNCTION
STOP	Stops motion of all litter platforms.
RUN	Allows normal platform operation.
SEAT OVERRIDE DISABLE ON OFF	When **ON** disables the **LITTER LIFTS** switches on the overhead console. When OFF, LITTER LIFTS switches on overhead console are enabled.
Upper lift reference mark	Provides reference for positioning upper litter.
Lower lift reference mark	Provides reference for positioning lower litter.
SUCTION	
Power mode knob	Selects **CONTINUOUS**, **INTERMITTENT**, or **NONE**.
REGULATOR knob	Increases or decreases the amount of suction.
INCREASE OFF TIME	Changes the off cycle times.
INCREASE ON TIME	Changes the on cycle times.
Suction gauge	Displays actual suction level.
ELECTRICAL	
115 VAC 60Hz (2)	Provides power source for commercial medical equipment (three each side).
28 VDC	Provides 28 VDC power source for medical equipment.

4.12.7 Overhead Control Panel. Two overhead control panels (Figure 4-24) are provided (one for each side of the aircraft) to control of the lighting and suction systems and master lift controls. Except for the **EMERGENCY STOP** switch, the controls only affect the systems on one side of the aircraft. The suction, lighting, and lift controls on the left control panel affect the associated systems on the left side only, likewise the right control panel controls the right side only. The **EMERGENCY STOP** switches stop all litter lifts. Control and functions are further defined:

CONTROLS/ INDICATORS	FUNCTION
EMERGENCY STOP switch	
STOP	Stops motion of all litter platforms.
RUN	Allows normal platform operation.
LITTER LIFTS switches	
UPPER PLATFORM FWD UP DOWN and AFT UP DOWN	Moves the forward and aft end of the upper litter platform up or down.
LOWER PLATFORM FWD UP DOWN and AFT UP DOWN	Moves the forward and aft end of the lower litter platform up or down.

NOTE

When operating the lifts from this panel, the side control panel lift controls are disabled.

SUCTION ON OFF	Turns the suction pump **ON** or **OFF** on the side associated with the control panel.
LIGHTING	Controls the brightness of the associated lights.
CEILING ON OFF	Turns overhead lights **ON** or **OFF**.
SIDE ON OFF	Turns side panel lights **ON** or **OFF**.

4.12.8 Medical Cabinet. A modular medical cabinet (Figure 4-25) is located between the troop seats at the aft bulkhead. The cabinet contains provisions for twelve three inch medical equipment storage drawers or a mix of three inch and six inch drawers. The top drawer may be locked for storage of controlled items. The bottom drawer is dedicated for disposal of Waste and BioHazard material. A quick access hold down door is located in the center of the

TM 1-1520-253-10

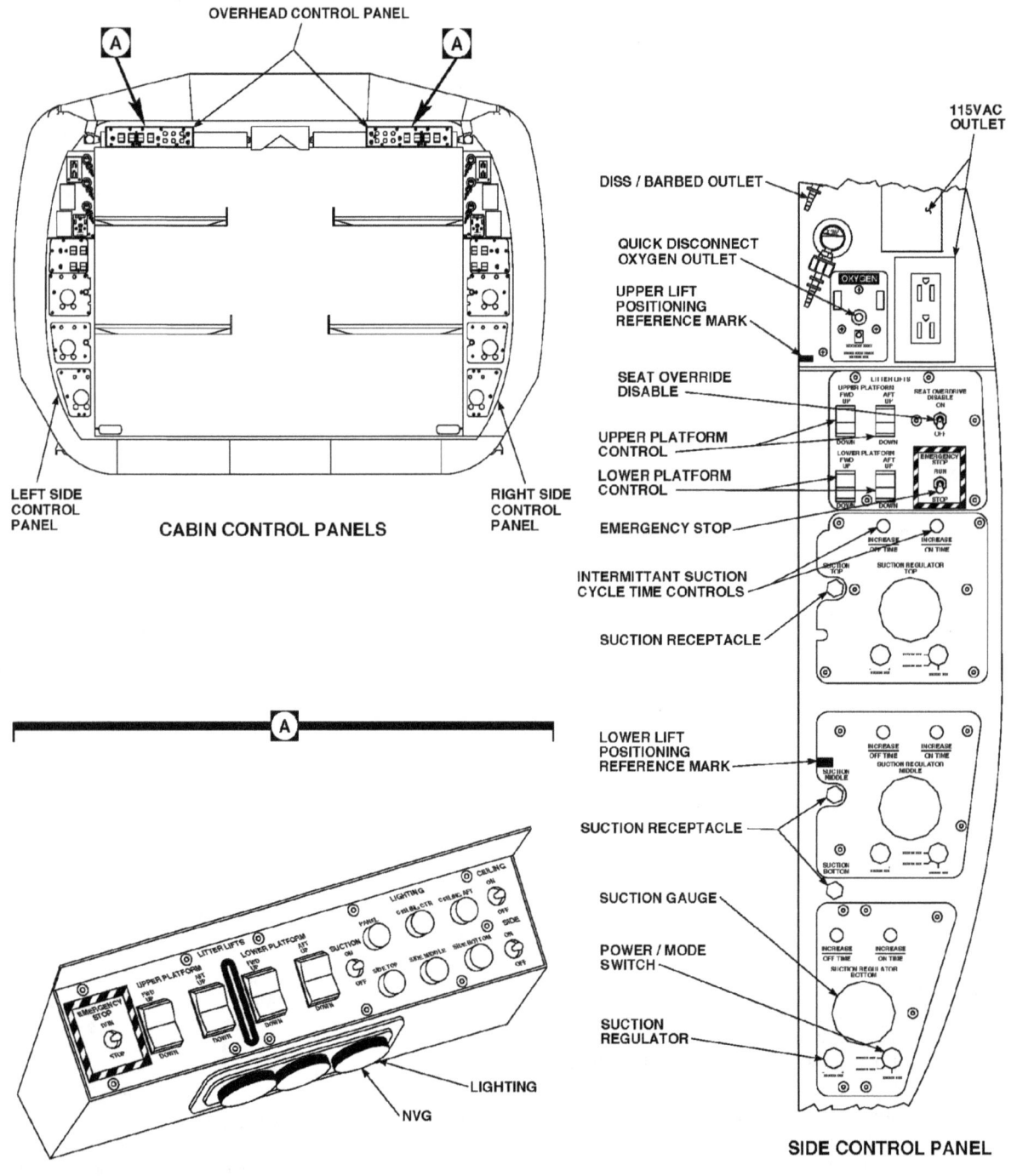

Figure 4-24. Medical Control Panels

4-52

4.12.9 Medical IV Bags. Provisions for IV bags are installed on the cabin ceiling. Flow adjustment and IV bag replacement are accomplished by the medical attendants.

4.12.10 Interior Lighting System. Lighting controls are located on the left and right overhead control panels (Figure 4-24). The controls on each panel affect the lighting system for that side of the aircraft only. The lighting system is interlocked through the pilot's **CABIN DOME LT** switch. When the pilot selects **BLUE** on the pilots **CABIN DOME LT** switch, the medical cabin overhead and panel lighting changes to blue/green and is controllable from the cabin, dimmer controls are still functional. Side lighting is turned off. If the pilot places the **CABIN DOME LT** switch to **WHITE**, the medical cabin lighting control is enabled in **WHITE** light and is controlled from the cabin, dimmer controls are still functional. If the pilot places the **CABIN LIGHTING** switch to **OFF** the medical cabin lighting is disabled.

4.12.10.1 Panel Overlay Lighting. Panel lighting is turned on with the **CEILING** lights **ON-OFF** switch on the right side of the overhead control panel. Both ceiling lights and panel overlay lighting are turned on and off together. Brightness is controlled separately. The **CEILING CTR** and **CEILING AFT** knobs control the brightness of the ceiling lights and the **PANEL** knob controls the brightness of the panel overlay lighting.

1. Place the **CEILING ON-OFF** switch to **ON**. The ceiling and panel overlay lights illuminate.

2. Turn the **PANEL** knob clockwise to increase panel light brightness, counter clockwise to decrease panel light brightness.

3. Place the **CEILING ON-OFF** switch to **OFF**. The ceiling and panel overlay lights turn off.

4.12.10.2 Ceiling Lighting. The **CABIN DOME LT** switch must be in the **WHITE** position to operate the overhead lights in the white light mode. If the **CABIN DOME LT** switch is in the **BLUE** position, the overhead lights will be blue/green. If the pilots lighting control switch is **OFF** the overhead lights will not operate.

1. Place the **CEILING ON-OFF** switches to **ON**.

2. Adjust the **CEILING CTR** and **CEILING AFT** knobs on the left and right overhead control panels to obtain desired intensity. Turn

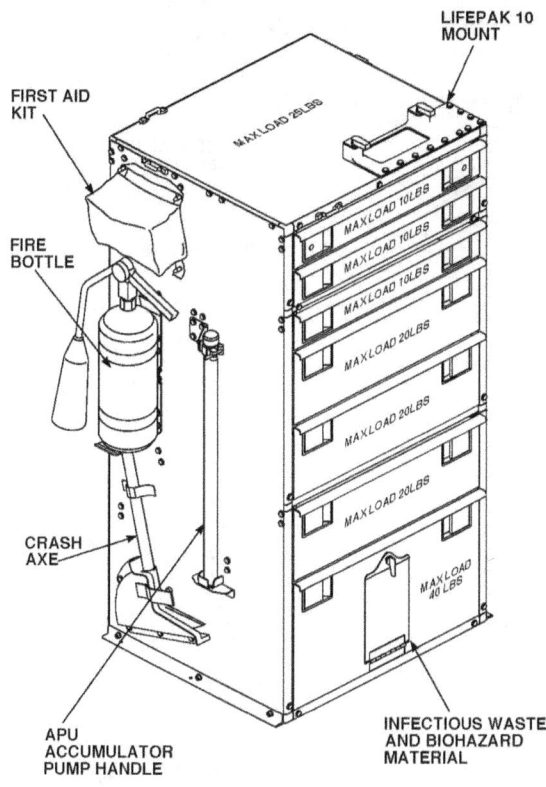

Figure 4-25. Medical Cabinet

drawer for convenient disposal of materials. Electrical power (115 VAC 60Hz) and space provisions for PROPAQ portable patient monitors and LIFEPAK 10 defibrillator monitors are included. The upper cabinet also includes the status panel for the molecular sieve oxygen generating system (MSOGS). Hooks are provided on the side of the cabinet to stow a fire extinguisher, first aid kit, crash axe and a accumulator pump (APU) handle. An access plate in the base of the medical cabinet can be removed to provide access to the aircraft computers. Circuit breakers for the AC-DC converter and oxygen panel displays are located on the underside of the oxygen status panel.

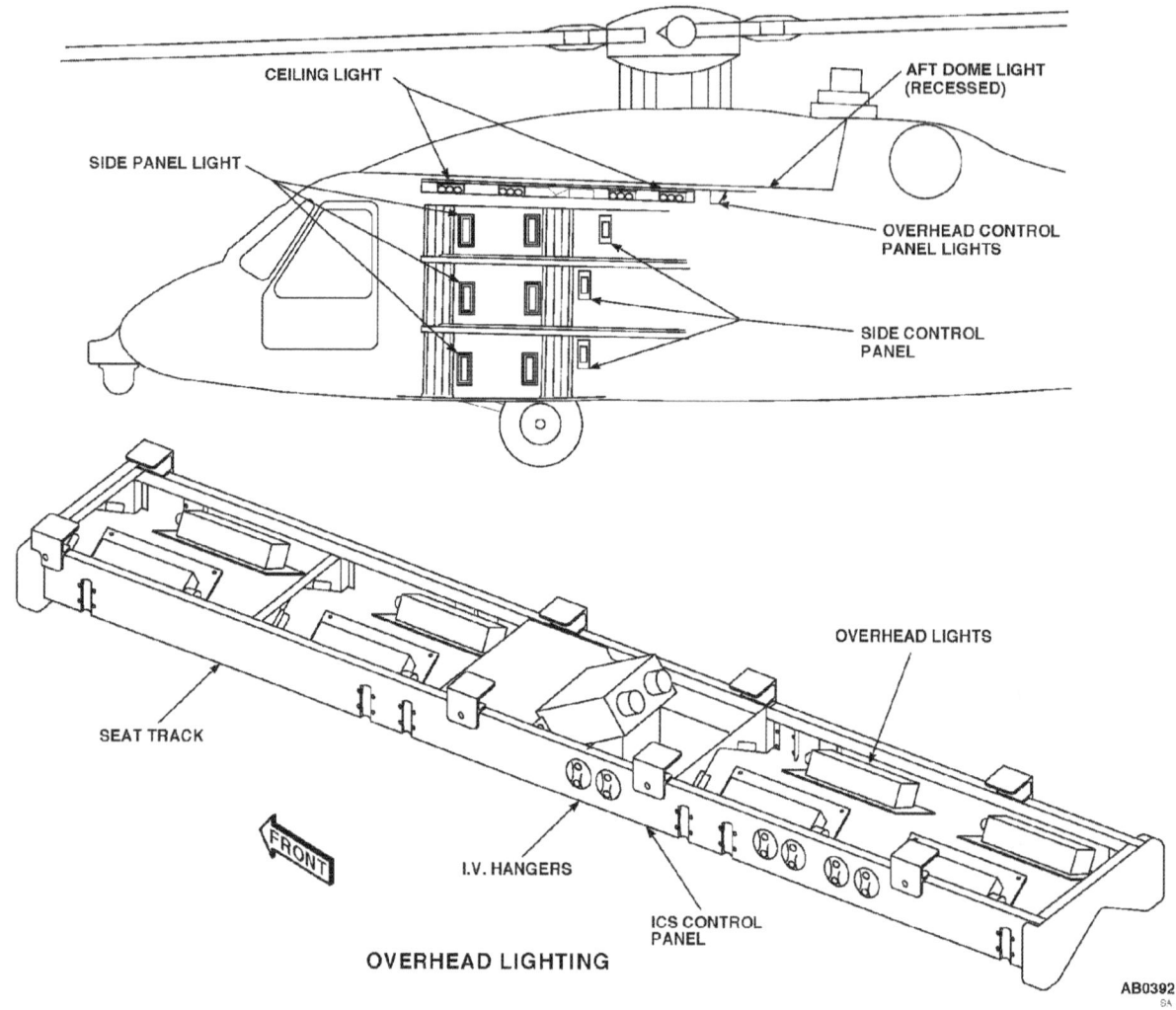

Figure 4-26. Overhead Lighting

clockwise to increase intensity and counter clockwise to decrease intensity.

3. Place the **CEILING ON-OFF** switches on the left and right overhead control panels to **OFF**. All ceiling lights and panel overlay lighting turns off.

4.12.10.3 Side Panel Lighting. Side panel lights are located on the cabin walls at each litter platform location. A **SIDE ON-OFF** switch on each overhead control panel controls the side panel lights for the side associated with that panel. Each platform (top, middle, and bottom) is provided with individual brightness controls.

1. Place the **SIDE ON-OFF** switches to **ON**. The side lights illuminate.

2. Adjust the intensity of the side lights with the **SIDE TOP**, **SIDE MIDDLE**, and **SIDE BOTTOM** knobs. Turn clockwise to increase intensity and counter clockwise to decrease intensity.

3. Place the **SIDE ON-OFF** switches to **OFF**. The side lights turn off.

4.12.11 Medical Suction System. The medical suction system (Figure 4-27) provides regulated airway and gastric suction to each litter platform location. The system is capable of supporting six patients simultaneously. A single suction pump and three regulators serve each side of the aircraft. The suction regulator consists of an adjustable regulator for continuous or intermittent operation, a suction gauge, and selector switches. The regulators provide adjustable, regulated suction from 0 to 300 mmHg. The gauge is divided into color coded ranges of low, medium, high, and full suction. The system is capable of continuous and intermittent operation at all suction levels. There are two independent suction systems located in the component modules at each of the forward medical stations. Each system consists of a vacuum pump, vents, and a vent solenoid. Each station contains a manifold, three vacuum regulators, and three collection canisters. There are six suction outlets available, one at each litter station. A vacuum regulator is provided at each outlet and is capable of continuous or intermittent operation. Operation of the system will be by the medical attendant.

4.12.11.1 Normal Operation.

1. Place **SUCTION** switch located on the overhead control panel to **ON**.

2. To turn the regulator on, position the **CONTINUOUS-NONE-INTERMITTENT** knob to **CONTINUOUS** or **INTERMITTENT**.

3. To adjust the regulator vacuum level, turn the **REGULATOR** knob towards **+** to increase the vacuum or **−** to decrease the vacuum.

4. INTERMITTENT operation can be adjusted using the timing controls labeled **INCREASE OFF TIME** or **INCREASE ON TIME**. To increase or decrease the **ON** and **OFF** cycle time, turn the appropriate timing control clockwise to increase the time or counterclockwise to decrease the time.

5. Six collection canisters are included within the vacuum system. Three canisters are located in each of the two medical stations.

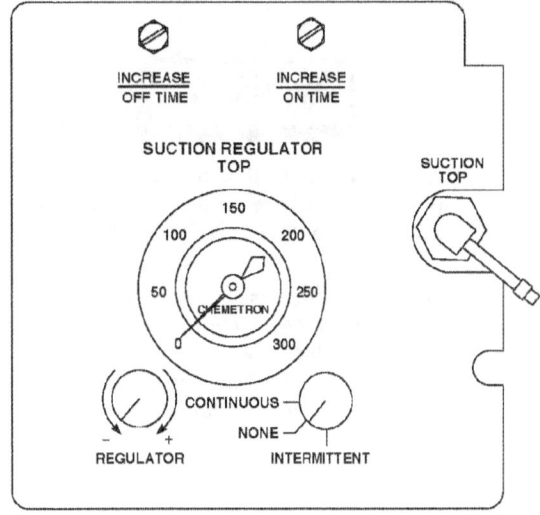

SUCTION CONTROL PANEL

NOTE

THE INTERMITTENT TIME ON AND OFF CONTROLS ARE NORMALLY PRESET TO VALUES OF 15 SECONDS ON AND 8 SECONDS OFF AT SELECTED SUCTION LEVELS. IF THESE SETTINGS NEED TO BE CHANGED, REMOVE THE PROTECTIVE PLASTIC CAP AND USE A SCREWDRIVER TO TURN THE SCREW-LIKE ADJUSTMENTS.

Figure 4-27. Medical Suction Controls

4.12.11.2 Shut Down.

1. All suction control panel power mode switches - **NONE**.

2. Left and right overhead medical control panel **SUCTION** switches - **OFF**.

4.12.12 Oxygen Delivery System.

WARNING

The pilot must be advised when oxygen is on board and its use must be per the Surgeon Generals directives.

When operating the oxygen system during extremely cold cabin conditions, ice may form in the lines blocking the flow of oxygen and possibly causing death or serious injury to the patient.

1. The oxygen system consists of a On - Board Oxygen Generating System (OBOGS) and associated delivery system. The delivery system includes oxygen regulators, hoses, outlets, and outlet controls and status displays.

2. Oxygen is supplied from the OBOGS described in paragraph 4.12.13. On each medical doorpost panel there are three patient regulators, a quick disconnect outlet, and one crew outlet. Oxygen content indicators and on/off indicators are located on the control/status panel at the top of the medical cabinet.

3. The OBOGS's Backup Oxygen System (BOS) has a capacity of 260 liters of oxygen.

4. Adjustment of oxygen regulators will be accomplished by the medical attendant.

5. The OBOGS control/status panel, located at the top of the medical cabinet is described in paragraph 4.12.13.2.

4.12.13 Oxygen Generating System.
A OBOGS (Figure 4-28) powered by bleed air is installed in the transition section. The system will charge from empty in 30 minutes with either APU or engine bleed air power. It is fully operational with either APU power, or when engines apply greater than 30% torque. Each regulated station has the capability to provide oxygen up to 10 liters / minute. The quick disconnect oxygen outlet has the capability of 36 liters / minute. Maximum system output is 36 liters / minute. The OBOGS utilizes engine bleed air and electrical power from the aircraft to provide oxygen enriched breathing gas for MEDEVAC operations. Bleed air is conditioned by a heat exchanger and filter assembly and then routed to a concentrator. The concentrator utilizes pressure swing absorption technology to produce oxygen enriched breathing gas. When bleed air is removed from the system, a self contained backup oxygen supply (BOS) with a capacity of 260 liters, provides 15 minutes of oxygen to six litter patients at 3 liters / minute. The backup system will be operational when O2 requirements exceed the flow rate. The pilot has control of the system and must activate the OBOGS prior to attendants using the oxygen delivery system. The attendants can monitor the flow of oxygen by observing the **OXY FLOW** dial on the OBOGS panel. When the purity of the oxygen falls below 91 percent the OBOGS unit will switch to backup oxygen supply (BOS) breathing gas and trip the **BIT FAULT** indicator on the status panel.

4.12.13.1 Controls and Functions. Controls and indicators are located on a panel above the medical cabinet. The pilot has the capability to disable the OBOGS if required.

CONTROLS/ INDICATORS	FUNCTION
OXY FLOW	Indicates rate (lpm) of oxygen being delivered.
BOS QTY	Indicates level (liters) of oxygen.
PWR ON Light	Indicates flow of oxygen.
BOS Light	Indicates backup oxygen is being supplied.
BIT FAULT Light	Indicates system fault.

4.12.13.2 Normal Operation.

NOTE

Built in test (BIT) will be initiated on initial start up of OBOGS, and will last 3 to 5 minutes. BIT light on monitor panel will be lit during BIT.

1. **AIR SOURCE HEAT/START** switch -**APU** or **ENGINE** .

2. **AUX SW** panel **OBOGS** switch - **ON** Check that **BIT/FAULT** light goes out within 5 minutes.

3. The medical attendant determines the oxygen system is available after the **PWR ON** light is illuminated.

4. Determine which patients need oxygen and obtain an oxygen hose and mask from the medical cabinet.

5. Attach the patients oxygen hose to the patient and to the corresponding oxygen regulator on the side medical control panel.

6. Select the desired oxygen rate on the regulator.

NOTE

Oxygen flow from the OBOGS is degraded with increased altitude or ambient temperature. Up to 10,000 feet, the flow can be up to 10% below the selected rate. Between 10,000 and 15,000 feet the flow rate can be 15% below the selected rate. To achieve a specific minimum flow rate above 10,000 feet, the next higher rate may be needed.

To prevent depleting oxygen levels, ensure unused oxygen regulators are turned to **OFF**.

Puritan Bennet outlets are provided, but connection plates may be changed to others: i.e. Ohio, Chemetron, etc, as required.

4.12.13.3 Back Up System Operation.

1. Check BOS quantity gage on O2 status indicator panel for charge.

2. Determine which patients need oxygen and obtain an oxygen hose and mask from the medical cabinet.

3. Attach the patients oxygen hose to the patient and to the corresponding oxygen regulator on the side medical control panel.

4. Select the desired oxygen rate on the regulator.

5. Make sure unused oxygen regulators are turned to **OFF**.

4.12.14 Electrical Power. A frequency converter located over the left fuel cell and in the aft transition section provides 115 VAC 60 Hz power. Electrical outlets for 115 VAC are provided at the bottom of the medical doorpost panels. A 28 VDC outlet is provided at the top of each doorpost panel.

4.12.15 Litter Lift System Operation.

WARNING

To prevent injury to patient or damage to equipment, do not press the litter platform switches on the overhead control panel and the side control panel at the same time. This could cause sudden and unpredictable motion of the platform when releasing the switches on the overhead control panel.

The litter lift system is designed with limit switches that assist in preventing mechanical damage. The litter lift for the upper platform contains a limit switch that prevents the platform from going higher than the mechanical limits of the lift columns. This switch stops the platform about three inches from the fold down seats attached to the ceiling. This switch does not prevent the patient from being raised high enough to cause injury.

The litter lift for the upper platform has no limit switch to stop its downward motion. The operator must release the control switch to stop the platform before it comes in contact with the lower platform or the patient on that platform.

The litter lift for the lower platform contains a limit switch that prevents the platform from coming in contact with he floor. This switch stops the platform about three inches from the floor. This switch does not prevent the platform from going low enough to cause injury to the patient on the bottom of the litter platform. The litter lift for the lower platform has no limit switch to stop its upward motion. The operator must be release the control switch to stop the platform before it or the patient on that platform comes in contact with the upper platform.

CAUTION

Due to mechanical limits, the platform must not be tilted, from its horizontal position, more that 17 degrees (seven inches difference between vertical position of the forward and aft litter lift pins).

When operating the litter lift system the **LITTER LIFTS** switches on the overhead control panel have priority over the switches on the side control panel. The controls and functions are as follows:

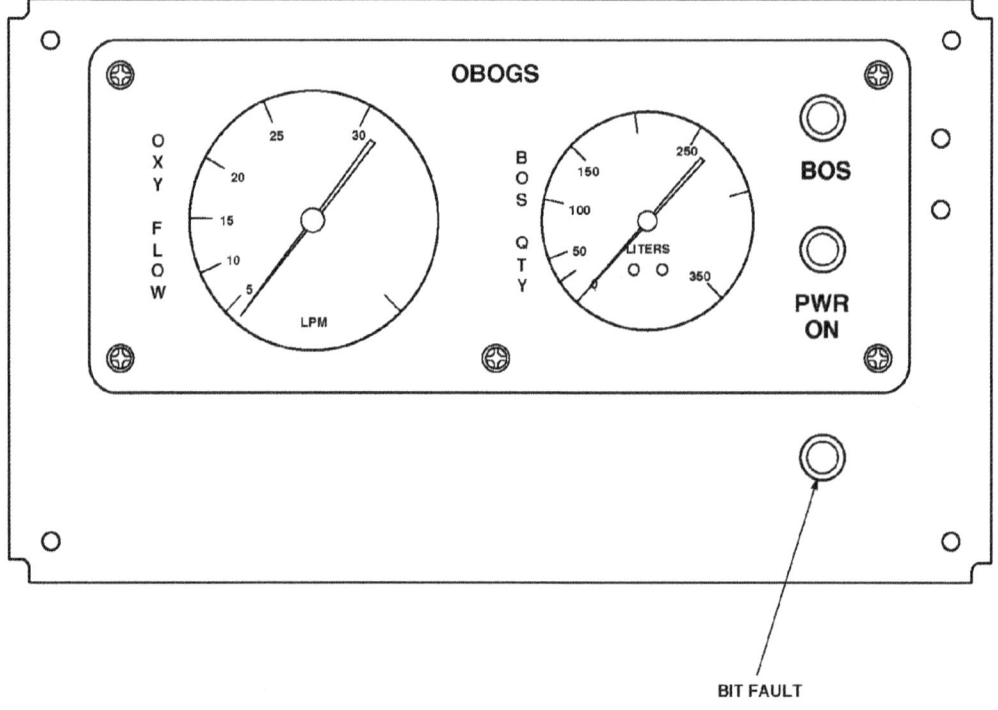

Figure 4-28. OBOGS Panel

CONTROLS/ INDICATORS	FUNCTION
UPPER PLATFORM	
FWD UP DOWN	Moves the forward end of the upper litter platform up or down.
AFT UP DOWN	Moves the aft end of the upper litter platform up or down.
LOWER PLATFORM	
FWD UP DOWN	Moves the forward end of the lower litter platform up or down. Upper platform must be positioned to the flight position prior to moving the lower platform. For loading ambulatory patients, the lower platform must be in the floor position before moving the upper litter platform.
AFT UP DOWN	Moves the aft end of the lower litter platform up or down. Upper platform must be positioned to the flight position prior to moving the lower platform. For loading ambulatory patients, the lower platform must be in the floor position before moving the upper litter platform.
EMERGENCY STOP	
STOP	Stops motion of all litter platforms. The switch resets in two seconds.
RUN	Allows normal platform operation.
SEAT OVERRIDE DISABLE	
ON	Disables the litter platform override feature of the overhead console.
OFF	Allows normal platform operation.

4.12.16 Preparation for Littered Patient Loading.

Use the litter lift controls on the overhead control panel or the side control panel for the following procedures.

1. Simultaneously, press and hold the **LOWER PLATFORM, FWD** and **AFT** controls to the **DOWN** position. The lower litter platform moves down. Hold the switches until the platform stops moving, releasing and pressing the **FWD** or **AFT** switches as necessary to ensure the platform maintains a level position. The platform should stop about 3 inches above the floor.

2. Simultaneously, press and hold the **UPPER PLATFORM, FWD** and **AFT** controls to the **DOWN** position until upper platform moves down to the desired level. Press and release the **FWD** or **AFT** switches as necessary to ensure the platform maintains a level position while moving.

4.12.17 Litter Lift System Patient Loading and Unloading.

WARNING

To prevent patient injury or death, or damage to equipment or cargo, ensure the patients platforms do not come in contact with the patient, each other, cargo, or the aircraft.

CAUTION

Do not operate the litter lift mechanism continuously for more than one minute or damage to drive mechanism may occur.

Patient restraints are secured prior to loading the helicopter. Up to a maximum of four patients can be carried on the platforms. To load litter patients:

4.12.17.1 Load First Patient.

1. **AUX SW** panel **MED INT** switch - **ON**.

2. All four cabin medical control panel **EMERGENCY STOP** switches placed - **RUN**.

3. Ensure associated medical station control panel **SEAT OVERRIDE** switch - **ON**.

4. Position and secure the first patient on the litter platform using the platform restraint belts. If injuries permit, the belt closest to the head is placed under the arms and over the chest and

tightened. The other two belts are placed over the entire body and tightened.

NOTE

EMERGENCY STOP switches are provided on each control panel to stop lift motion if necessary. To stop all lifts from operating, place any of the four **EMERGENCY STOP** switches to the **STOP** position. To resume lift operations, pull the switch outwards, past the raised notch and move it up to the **RUN** position.

5. Simultaneously, press the **UPPER PLATFORM**, **FWD** and **AFT** controls to the **UP** position. The upper litter platform moves up.

6. As the platform approaches the desired flight position, release the switches. The platform stops. For three patient configurations, use the upper lift positioning reference mark on the side control panel to determine approximate position of the top patient. (Figure 4-23).

7. Use individual **FWD** or **AFT** controls to adjust the platform to the necessary tilt being careful to avoid patient to aircraft contact.

4.12.17.2 Load Second Patient.

1. Position and secure the second patient on the litter platform using the platform restraint belts.

2. Simultaneously, press the **LOWER PLATFORM**, **FWD** and **AFT** controls to the **UP** position.

3. As the platform approaches the desired flight position, release the switches. The platform stops. For three patient configurations, use the lower lift positioning reference mark on the side control panel to determine approximate position of the middle patient. (Figure 4-23).

4. Use individual **FWD** or **AFT** controls to adjust the platform to the necessary tilt being careful to avoid patient to aircraft contact.

4.12.17.3 Load Third Patient.

1. Position the patient under the lower litter platform.

2. Position and fasten the patient restraints.

3. Once litter(s) are positioned, place one or all four cabin medical control panel **EMERGENCY STOP** switches - **STOP**.

4.12.17.4 Unload the Third Patient.

1. Unfasten the patient restraints.

2. Reverse the loading procedure and carefully unload the patient.

4.12.17.5 Unload the Second Patient.

1. Use individual **FWD** or **AFT** controls to level the platform as much as possible.

2. Simultaneously press the **LOWER PLATFORM**, **FWD**, and **AFT** controls to the **DOWN** position.

3. As the platform approaches the floor position, release the switches. The platform stops.

4. Reverse the loading procedure and slide the litter platform out of the aircraft.

4.12.17.6 Unload the First Patient.

1. Use individual **FWD** or **AFT** controls to level the platform as much as possible.

2. Simultaneously press the **UPPER PLATFORM**, **FWD**, and **AFT** controls to the **DOWN** position. The upper litter platform moves down.

3. As the upper platform approaches the lower platform, release the switches. The platform stops.

4. Reverse the loading procedure and slide the litter platform out of the aircraft.

4.12.18 Ambulatory (Seated) Patient Configuration.
The upper platform of each medical station is used for seating up to three ambulatory patients. The upper half of the platform is raised to provide a backrest for the patients. Up to a maximum of six ambulatory patients can be carried on the platforms. Two additional ambulatory patients can be seated on the aft troop seats.

NOTE

Use of the MEDEVAC ambulatory configuration for transport of personnel other then patients or essential medical personnel is prohibited.

1. Simultaneously press and hold the **LOWER PLATFORM**, **FWD**, and **AFT** controls to the **DOWN** position. The lower litter platform moves down. Hold the switches until the platform stops moving. The platform stops about 3 inches above the floor.

2. Simultaneously press and hold the **UPPER PLATFORM**, **FWD**, and **AFT** controls to the **DOWN** position until the upper litter platform moves down to just above the lower platform.

CAUTION

To prevent damage to the platforms, stop the upper platform motion prior to reaching the lower platform.

3. Unlock and release the forward and aft seat tracks fittings from the seat tracks in the overhead lighting fixture (Figure 4-26) by pulling out, with a firm pull, on the circular clip at the end of the seat track fitting.

4. Fold down the ambulatory seats from the top of the compartment and extend the telescoping guide tubes to the top of the upper litter platform.

5. Remove the quick release pins from their stowed position in the seat pan and install them in the telescoping guide tubes next to the headrest.

6. Lock the seat track fittings into the tracks on the litter platform.

7. Rotate the seat pan down and headrest up into position.

4.12.19 Stow Ambulatory Patient Seats.

1. Rotate the seat pan up and headrest down to the stowed positions.

2. Locate the seat track fittings holding the seat legs to the upper litter platform and pull up on the circular clip at the end of the seat track fitting.

3. Slide each seat rack fitting into the open slot and remove it from the upper litter platform.

4. Remove the quick release pins from the telescoping guide tubes next to the head rest and install them in their stowed position in the seat pan.

5. Fold the seat to the ceiling and insert the seat rack fittings, on the bottom of the legs, into the stowage tracks of the overhead light fixture.

6. Slide the track fittings toward the end of the slot to align the circular clip lock to the bottom circular slot.

7. Press the circular clip lock into the slot until it clicks into place.

4.12.20 Cargo Configuration. In the event the aircraft is to be used to carry cargo the litter platforms must be positioned to the highest point on the lift near the ceiling to clear the floor space for cargo.

NOTE

The upper platform must be in the upper position before moving the lower platform to the upper position.

1. Ensure the ambulatory patient seats are stowed in the ceiling.

2. Use the litter lift control switches and move both litter platforms to the top of the litter lift columns.

3. Load and secure cargo.

CHAPTER 5

OPERATING LIMITS AND RESTRICTIONS

Section I GENERAL

5.1 PURPOSE.

This chapter identifies or refers to all important operating limits and restrictions that shall be observed during ground and flight operations.

5.2 GENERAL.

The operating limitations set forth in this chapter are the direct results of design analysis, tests, and operating experiences. Compliance with these limits will allow the pilot to safely perform the assigned missions and to derive maximum use from the aircraft.

5.3 EXCEEDING OPERATIONAL LIMITS.

Any time an operational limit is exceeded an appropriate entry shall be made on DA Form 2408-13-1. Entry shall state what limit or limits were exceeded, range, time beyond limits, and any additional data that would aid maintenance personnel in the maintenance action that may be required. The helicopter shall not be flown until corrective action is taken.

5.4 MINIMUM CREW REQUIREMENTS.

The minimum crew required to fly the helicopter is two pilots. Additional crewmembers as required will be added at the discretion of the commander, in accordance with pertinent Department of the Army regulations.

Section II SYSTEM LIMITS

5.5 INSTRUMENT MARKING COLOR CODES.

NOTE

Instrument/color markings may differ from actual limits.

Operating limitations are shown as side arrows or colored strips on the instrument face plate of engine, flight and utility system instruments (Figures 5-1 and 5-2). Those readings are shown by ascending and descending columns of multicolor lights (red, yellow and green) measured against vertical scales. RED markings indicate the limit above or below which continued operation is likely to cause damage or shorten component life. GREEN markings indicate the safe or normal range of operation. YELLOW markings indicate the range when special attention should be given to the operation covered by the instrument.

5.6 ROTOR LIMITATIONS.

It is not abnormal to observe a % **RPM 1** and **2** speed split during autorotational descent when the engines are fully decoupled from the main rotor. A speed increase of one engine from 100% reference to 103% maximum can be expected. During power recovery, it is normal for the engine operating above 100% RPM to lead the other engine. Refer to Figure 5-1 for limitations.

5.6.1 Rotor Start and Stop Limits. Maximum wind velocity for rotor start or stop is 45 knots from any direction.

5.6.2 Rotor Speed Limitations. Refer to Figure 5-1 for rotor limitations. Power off (autorotation) rotor speeds up to **120% RPM R** are authorized for use by maintenance test flight pilots during autorotational RPM checks.

5.7 MAIN TRANSMISSION MODULE LIMITATIONS.

a. Oil pressure should remain steady during steady state forward flight or in level hover. Momentary fluctuations in oil pressure may occur during transient maneuvers (i.e. hovering in gusty wind conditions), or when flying with pitch attitudes above +6°. These types of oil pressure fluctuations are acceptable, even when oil pressure drops into the yellow range (below 30 psi). Oil pressure should remain steady and should be in the 45 to 55 psi range to ensure that when fluctuations occur they remain in the acceptable range as defined above. If oil pressure is not steady during steady state forward flight or in a level hover, or if oil pressure is steady but under 45 psi, make an entry on Form 2408-13-1. Sudden pressure drop (more than 10 PSI) without fluctuation requires an entry on Form 2408-13-1.

b. A demand for maximum power from engines with different engine torque factors (ETF) will cause a torque split when the low ETF engine reaches TGT limiting. This torque split is normal. Under these circumstances, the high power engine may exceed the dual engine limit. (Example: #1 TRQ = 96% at TGT limiting, #2 TRQ is allowed to go up to 104%. Total aircraft torque = (96%+104%)/2 = 100%).

c. With transmission oil temperature operation in the precautionary range, an entry should be made on DA Form 2408-13-1 except when hovering in adverse conditions described in Chapter 8 Desert and Hot Weather Operations.

MAIN ROTOR OVERSPEED

* ▒ 127%
** ▒ 137%
*** ▒ 142%

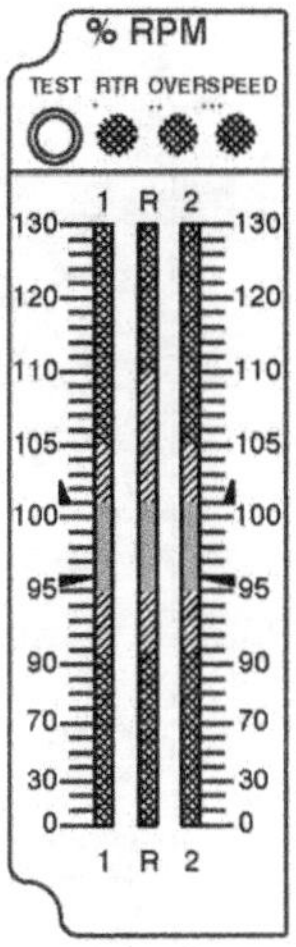

ENGINE % RPM 1-2

12-SECOND TRANSIENT	105% – 107%
TRANSIENT	101% – 105%
CONTINUOUS	95% – 101%
MINIMUM EXCEPT FOR IDLE AND TRANSIENT	91%

AVOID OPERATIONS IN 20% – 40% AND 60% – 90% RANGE EXCEPT DURING START AND SHUTDOWN

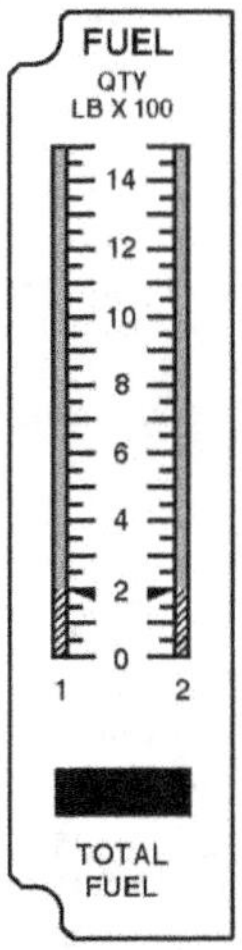

MAIN ROTOR % RPM R

POWER ON

TRANSIENT	101% – 107%
CONTINUOUS	95% – 101%
MINIMUM EXCEPT FOR IDLE AND TRANSIENT	91%

POWER OFF (AUTOROTATION)

MAXIMUM	110%
TRANSIENT	105% – 110%
NORMAL	90% – 105%

FUEL QUANTITY

NORMAL	200 – 1500 LBS
PRECAUTIONARY	0 – 200 LBS

LEGEND

- ▒ RED
- ▓ YELLOW
- ░ GREEN
- ■ DIGITAL READOUT

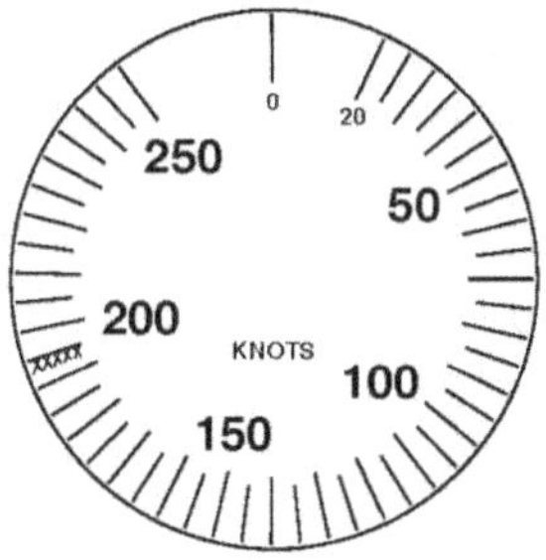

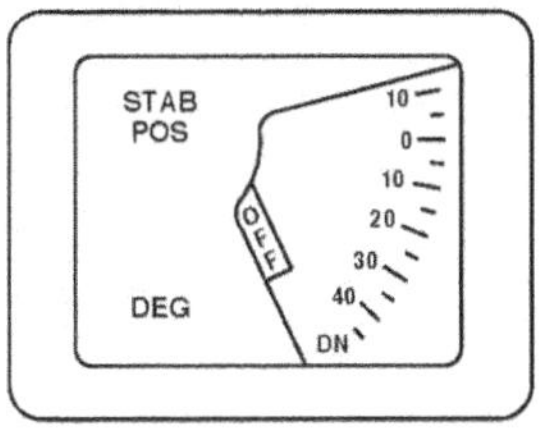

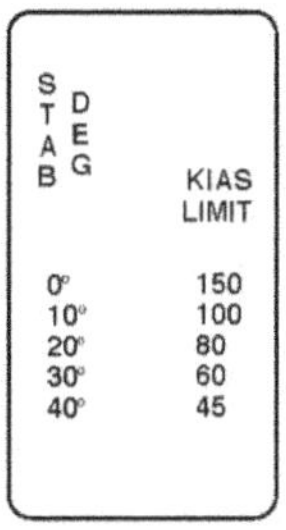

AIRSPEED

MAXIMUM	193 KNOTS

REFER TO SECTION V FOR ADDITIONAL AIRSPEED LIMITATIONS

STAB DEG	KIAS LIMIT
0°	150
10°	100
20°	80
30°	60
40°	45

Figure 5-1. Instrument Markings (Sheet 1 of 3)

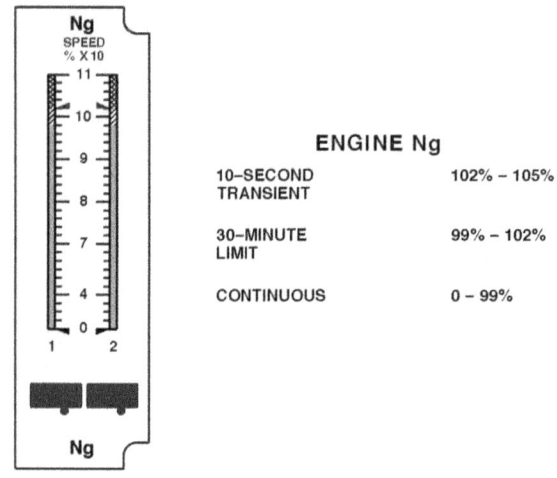

ENGINE Ng

10-SECOND TRANSIENT	102% – 105%
30-MINUTE LIMIT	99% – 102%
CONTINUOUS	0 – 99%

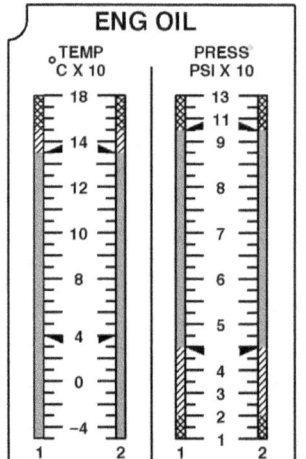

ENGINE OIL TEMPERATURE

MAXIMUM	150 °C
30-MINUTE LIMIT	135 – 150°C
CONTINUOUS	–50 – 135°C

ENGINE OIL PRESSURE

MAXIMUM	100 PSI
CONTINUOUS	20 – 100 PSI*

* 35 PSI MINIMUM AT 90% Ng AND ABOVE

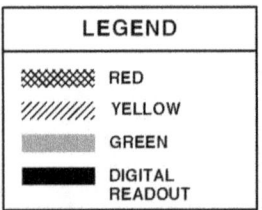

Figure 5-1. Instrument Markings (Sheet 2 of 3)

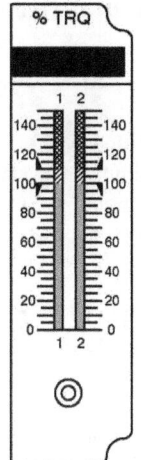

ENGINE % TRQ

10-SECOND TRANSIENT	
DUAL-ENGINE	100% – 125%
SINGLE-ENGINE	110% – 135%
CONTINUOUS SINGLE-ENGINE ONLY	0% – 110%
CONTINUOUS DUAL-ENGINE	0% – 100%

TURBINE GAS TEMPERATURE

10-SECOND TRANSIENT	850 – 886°C
START ABORT LIMIT	850°C
30-MINUTE LIMIT	775 – 850°C
NORMAL	0 – 775°C

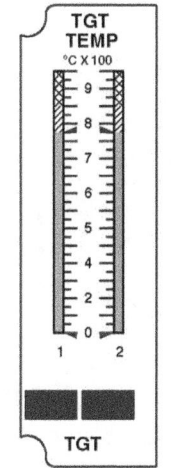

MAIN TRANSMISSION OIL TEMPERATURE

MAXIMUM	120°C
PRECAUTIONARY	105 – 120°C
CONTINUOUS	–50 – 105°C

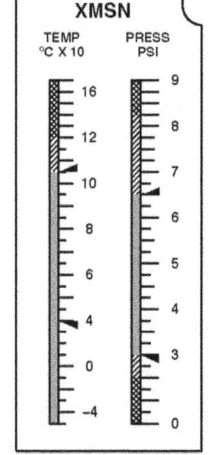

MAIN TRANSMISSION OIL PRESSURE

MAXIMUM	130 PSI
PRECAUTIONARY	65 – 130 PSI
CONTINUOUS	30 – 65 PSI
IDLE AND TRANSIENT	20 – 30 PSI
MINIMUM	20 PSI

Figure 5-1. Instrument Markings (Sheet 3 of 3)

Section III POWER LIMITS

5.8 ENGINE LIMITATIONS.

5.8.1 Engine Power Limitations. The limitations which are presented in Figure 5-2, present absolute limitations, regardless of atmospheric conditions. For variations in power available with temperature and pressure altitude, refer to the TORQUE AVAILABLE charts in Chapter 7.

5.8.2 Engine % RPM Limitations. Transient % RPM 1 or 2 operation in yellow range (101% to 105%) is not recommended as good operating practice. However no damage to either engine or drive train is incurred by operation within this range. Momentary transients above 107% Np are authorized for use by maintenance test pilots during autorotational rpm checks.

5.8.3 Engine Starter Limits.

a. The pneumatic starter is capable of making the number of consecutive start cycles listed below, when exposed to the environmental conditions specified, with an interval of at least 60 seconds between the completion of one cycle and the beginning of the next cycle. A starting cycle is the interval from start initiation and acceleration of the compressor, from zero rpm, to starter dropout. The 60-second delay between start attempts applies when the first attempt is aborted for any reason, and it applies regardless of the duration of the first attempt. If motoring is required for an emergency, the 60-second delay does not apply.

b. At ambient temperatures of 15°C (59°F) and below, two consecutive start cycles may be made, followed by a 3-minute rest period, followed by two additional consecutive start cycles. A 30-minute rest period is then required before any additional starts.

c. At ambient temperatures above 15° up to 52°C (59° up to 126°F), two consecutive start cycles may be made. A 30-minute rest period is then required before any additional start cycles.

5.9 PNEUMATIC SOURCE INLET LIMITS.

The minimum ground-air source (pneumatic) required to start the helicopter engines is 40 psig and 30 ppm at 149°C (300°F). The maximum ground-air source to be applied to the helicopter is 50 psig at 249°C (480°F), measured at the external air connector on the fuselage.

5.10 ENGINE START LIMITS.

CAUTION

Engine start attempts at or above a pressure altitude of 20,000 feet could result in a Hot Start.

Crossbleed starts shall not be attempted unless the anti-ice light is off, and operating engine must be at 90% **Ng SPEED** or above and rotor speed at 100% **RPM R**. When attempting single-engine starts at pressure altitudes above 14,000 feet, press the start switch with the **ENG POWER CONT** lever **OFF**, until the maximum motoring speed (about 24%) is reached, before going to **IDLE**. Engine starts using APU source may be attempted when within the range of FAT and pressure altitude of Figure 5-2.

5.11 ENGINE OVERSPEED CHECK LIMITATIONS.

Engine overspeed check in flight is prohibited. Engine overspeed checks, on the ground, are authorized by designated maintenance personnel only.

5.12 FUEL LIMITATIONS.

When using all fuel types, both fuel boost pumps shall be on and operational, otherwise engine flameout may result.

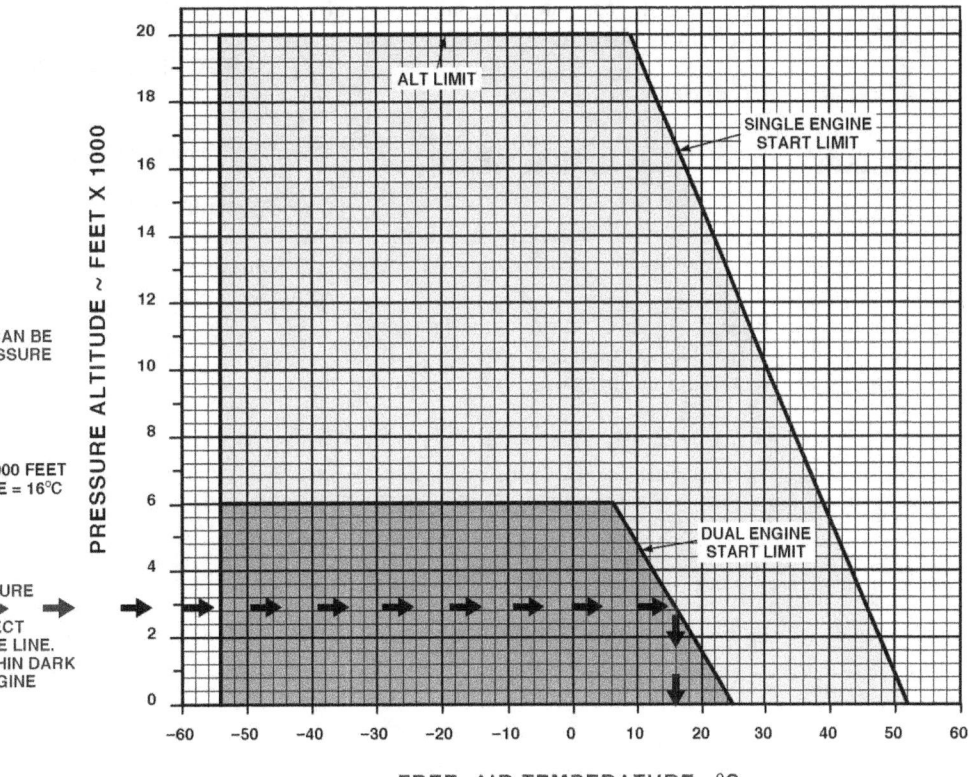

Figure 5-2. Engine Start Envelope

Section IV LOADING LIMITS

5.13 CENTER OF GRAVITY LIMITATIONS.

Center of gravity limits for the aircraft to which this manual applies and instructions for computation of the center of gravity are contained in Chapter 6.

5.14 WEIGHT LIMITATIONS.

AIRCRAFT	MAXIMUM WEIGHT
UH-60Q	22,000

In addition to the above limits, maximum weight is further limited by cargo floor maximum capacity of 300 pounds per square foot. Refer to Chapter 6.

5.15 CABIN CEILING TIEDOWN FITTINGS.

The four cabin ceiling tiedown fittings have a limited load capability of 4,000 pounds.

5.16 CARGO HOOK WEIGHT LIMITATION.

For UH-60Q aircraft, the maximum weight that may be suspended from the cargo hook is limited to 8,000 pounds.

5.17 RESCUE HOIST WEIGHT LIMITATIONS.

The maximum weight that may be suspended from the rescue hoist is 600 pounds.

Section V AIRSPEED LIMITS

5.18 AIRSPEED OPERATING LIMITS.

The airspeed operating limits charts (Figures 5-3 and 5-4) define velocity never exceed (Vne) as a function of altitude, temperature, and gross weight. The dashed lines represent the Mach limited airspeeds due to compressibility effects. Additional airspeed limits not shown on the charts are:

a. Maximum airspeed for one engine inoperative is 130 KIAS.

b. Maximum airspeed for autorotation at a gross weight of 16,825 pounds or less is 150 KIAS.

c. Maximum airspeed for autorotation at a gross weight of greater than 16,825 pounds is 130 KIAS.

d. Sideward/rearward flight limits. Hovering in winds greater than 45 knots (35 knots with external ERFS) from the sides or rear is prohibited. Sideward/rearward flight into the wind, when combined with windspeed, shall not exceed 45 knots (35 knots with external ERFS). .

e. SAS inoperative airspeed limits:

(1) One SAS inoperative - 170 KIAS.

(2) Two SAS inoperative - 150 KIAS.

(3) Two SAS inoperative in IMC - 140 KIAS.

f. Hydraulic system inoperative limits:

(1) One hydraulic system inoperative - 170 KIAS.

(2) Two hydraulic systems inoperative - 150 KIAS.

(3) Two hydraulic systems inoperative in IMC - 140 KIAS.

g. Searchlight and landing light airspeed limits.

(1) Landing light. If use is required, the landing light must be extended prior to reaching a maximum forward airspeed of 130 KIAS. With landing light extended, airspeed is limited to 180 KIAS.

(2) Searchlight(s). If use is required, searchlight(s) must be extended prior to reaching a maximum forward airspeed of 100 KIAS. With searchlight extended, airspeed is limited to 180 KIAS.

5.19 FLIGHT WITH CABIN DOOR(S)/WINDOW(S) OPEN.

The following airspeed limitations are for operating the helicopter in forward flight with the cabin doors/window open:

a. Cabin doors

(1) Cabin doors may be fully open up to 100 KIAS with soundproofing installed aft of station 379.

(2) Cabin doors may be fully open up to 145 KIAS with soundproofing removed aft of station 379 or with soundproofing secured properly.

(3) The doors will not be intentionally moved from the fully open or closed position in flight. The cabin doors may be opened or closed during hovering flight. The cabin doors must be closed or fully opened and latched before forward flight. Should the door inadvertently open in flight, it may be secured fully open or closed.

b. Flight with cockpit door(s) removed is prohibited.

5.20 AIRSPEED LIMITATIONS FOLLOWING FAILURE OF THE AUTOMATIC STABILATOR CONTROL SYSTEM.

a. Manual control available. If the automatic stabilator control system fails in flight and operation cannot be restored:

(1) The stabilator shall be set full down at speeds below 40 KIAS.

(2) The stabilator shall be set at zero degrees at speeds above 40 KIAS.

(3) Autorotation airspeed shall be limited to 120 KIAS at all gross weights.

b. Manual control not available. The placard airspeed limits shall be observed as not-to-exceed speed (powered flight and autorotation), except in no case shall the autorotation limit exceed 120 KIAS.

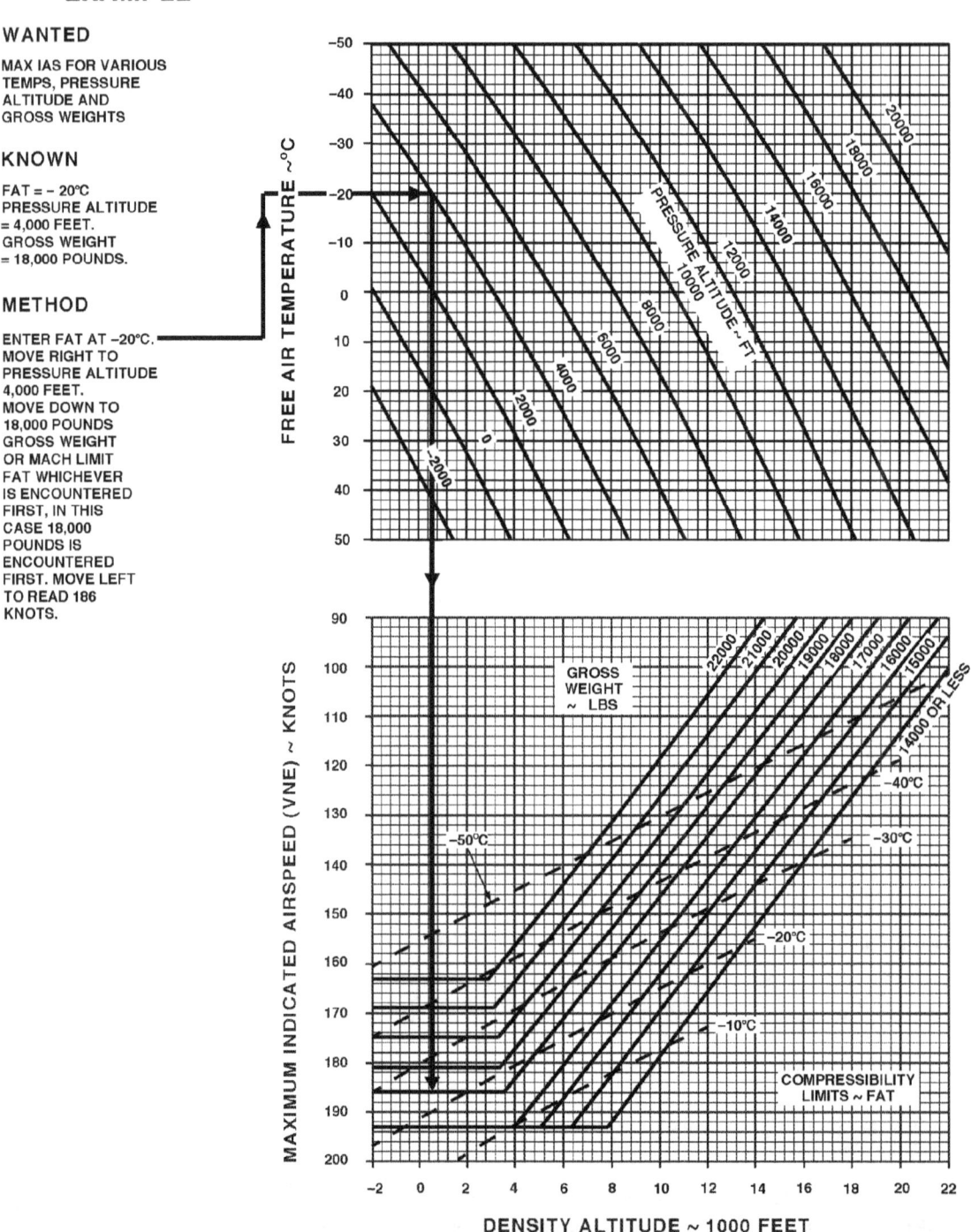

Figure 5-3. Airspeed Operating Limits

AIRSPEED OPERATING LIMITATIONS
AIRCRAFT WITH EXTERNAL STORES SUPPORT SYSTEM INSTALLED
100% RPM R

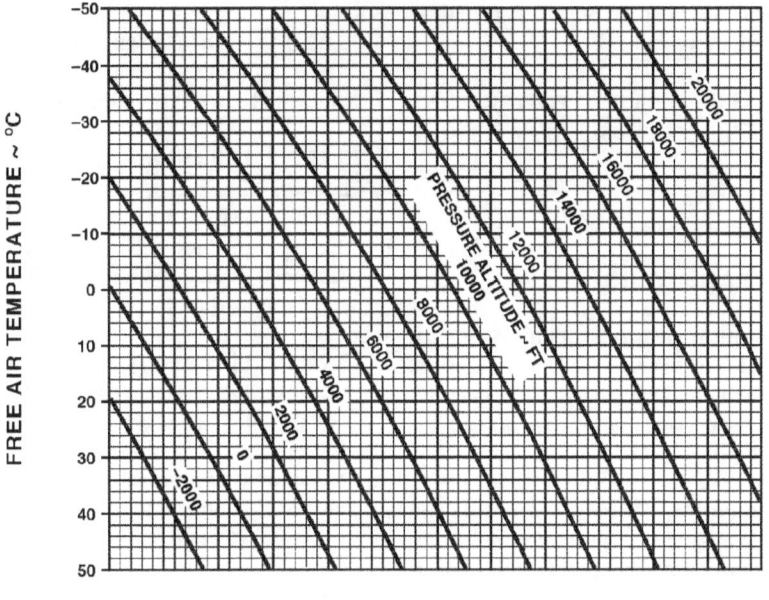
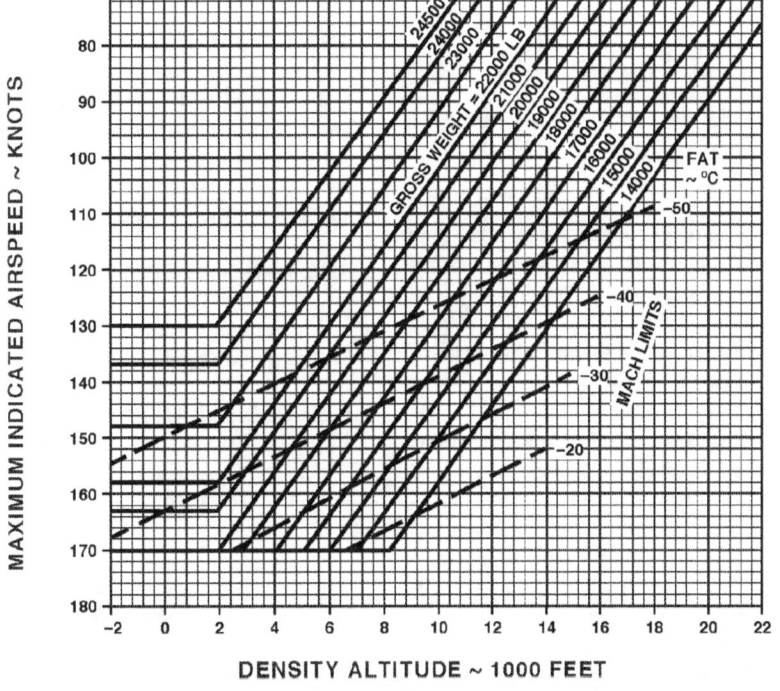

Figure 5-4. Airspeed Operating Limits

Section VI MANEUVERING LIMITS

5.21 PROHIBITED MANEUVERS.

a. Hovering turns greater than 30° per second are prohibited. Intentional maneuvers beyond attitudes of ±30° in pitch or over 60° in roll are prohibited.

b. Simultaneous moving of both **ENG POWER CONT** levers to **IDLE** or **OFF** (throttle chop) in flight is prohibited.

c. Rearward ground taxi is prohibited.

5.22 RESTRICTED MANEUVERS.

5.22.1 Manual Operation of the Stabilator. Manual operation of the stabilator in flight is prohibited except as required by formal training and maintenance test flight requirements, or as alternate stabilator control in case the **AUTO** mode malfunctions.

5.22.2 Downwind Hovering. Prolonged rearward flight and downwind hovering are to be avoided to prevent accumulation of exhaust fumes in the helicopter and heat damage to windows on open cargo doors.

5.22.3 Maneuvering Limitations.

NOTE

Maneuvers entered from a low power setting may result in transient droop of 5% **RPM R** or greater.

a. The maneuvering limits of the helicopter, other than as limited by other paragraphs within this section, are always defined by main rotor blade stall. Stall has not been encountered in one G flight up to the airspeeds shown in Figure chart Figure 5-3 for aircraft without ESSS installed and 5-4 for aircraft with ESSS installed.

b. The blade stall chart (Figure 5-5) while not an aircraft limitation, provides the level flight angle of bank at which blade stall will begin to occur as a function of airspeed, gross weight, pressure altitude and temperature. When operating near blade stall, any increase in airspeed, load factor (bank angle), turbulence, or abrupt control inputs will increase the severity of the stall. Fully developed stall will be accompanied by heavy four per rev vibration, increasing torque, and loss of altitude. Recovery is always accomplished by reducing the severity of the maneuver, that is by reducing collective, reducing airspeed, and/or reducing the angle of bank. Maneuvering flight which results in severe blade stall and significant increase in 4 per rev vibration is prohibited.

5.22.3.1 High Speed Yaw Maneuver Limitation. Above 80 KIAS avoid abrupt, full pedal inputs to prevent excess tail rotor system loading.

5.22.3.2 Limitations for Maneuvering With Sling Loads. Maneuvering limitations with a sling load is limited to a maximum of 30° angle of bank in forward flight (Figure 5-6). Side flight is limited by bank angle and is decreased as airspeed increases. Rearward flight with sling load is limited to 35 knots.

5.22.3.3 Limitations for Maneuvering With Rescue Hoist Loads. Maneuvering limitations with a rescue hoist load is limited to maximum of 30° angle of bank in forward flight (Figure 5-6). Side flight is limited by bank angle and is decreased as airspeed is increased. Rearward flight with hoist load is limited to 35 knots. Rate of descent is limited to 1,000 feet-per-minute.

5.22.3.4 Bank Angle Limitation. Bank angles shall be limited to 30° when a **PRI SERVO PRESS** caution light is on.

5.23 LANDING GEAR LIMITATIONS.

Do not exceed a touchdown sink rate of 540 feet-per-minute on level terrain and 360 feet-per-minute on slopes with gross weights of up to 16,825 pounds; above 16,825 pounds gross weight 300 feet-per-minute on level terrain and 180 feet-per-minute on slopes.

5.24 LANDING SPEED LIMITATIONS.

Maximum forward touchdown speed is limited to 60 knots ground speed on level terrain.

5.25 SLOPE LANDING LIMITATIONS.

The following slope limitations apply regardless of gross weight or CG, with or without ESSS/ERFS.

When performing slope landings with External Extended Range Fuel System Tanks, ensure tank to ground clearance.

AIRSPEED FOR ONSET OF BLADE STALL
LEVEL FLIGHT 100% RPM R

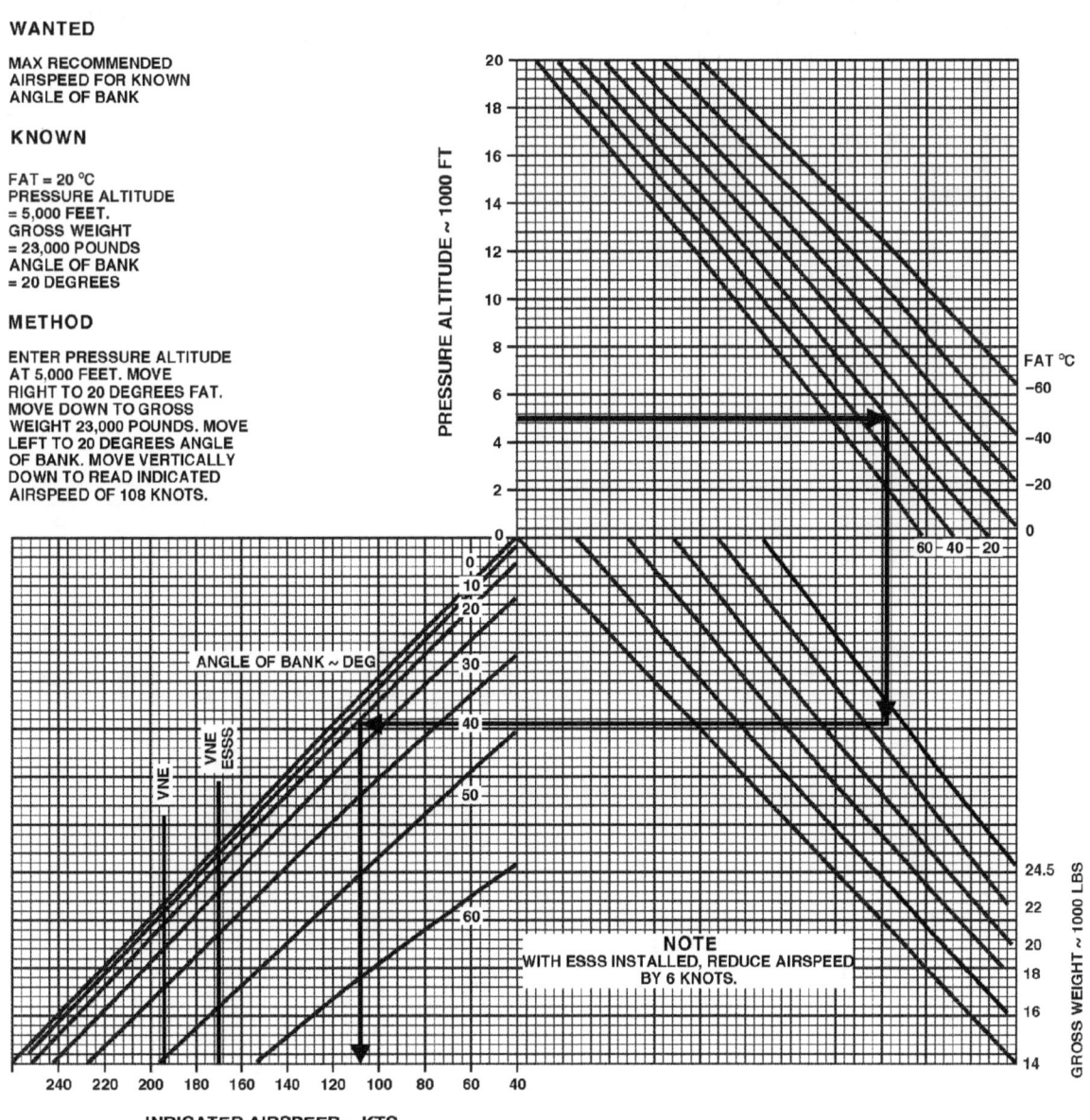

Figure 5-5. Airspeed for Onset of Blade Stall

NOTE

Because of the flat profile of the main transmission and forward location of both transmission oil pumps, transmission oil pressure will drop during nose-up slope operations. At slope angle of 10° an indicated oil pressure of 30 to 35 psi is normal, and at a 15° slope angle a pressure in the range of 10 to 15 psi is normal, due to pitching of the helicopter.

a. 15° nose-up, right wheel up or left wheel upslope. The slope limitations shall be further reduced by 2° for every 5 knots of wind.

b. 6° nose downslope. Landing in downslope conditions with tail winds greater than 15 knots shall not be conducted. A low-frequency oscillation may occur when landing nose-down on a slope with the cyclic near the aft stop.

c. The main gearbox may be operated up to 30 minutes at a time with pressure fluctuations when the helicopter is known to be at a nose-up attitude (i.e., slope landings or hover with extreme aft CG).

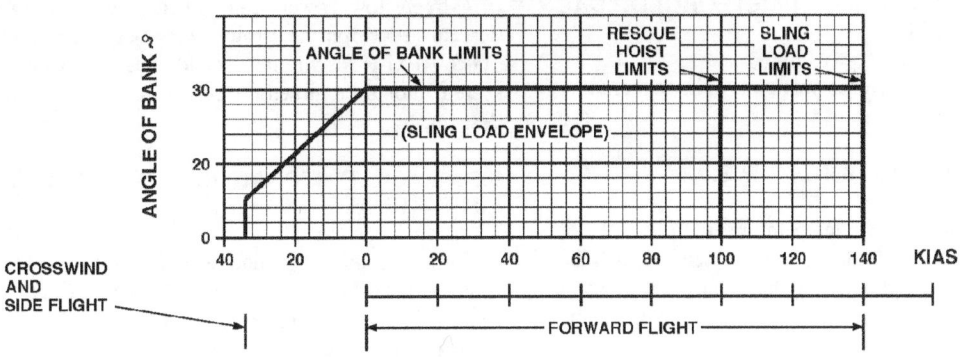

Figure 5-6. Sling/Hoist Load Maneuvering Limitations

Section VII ENVIRONMENTAL RESTRICTIONS

5.26 FLIGHT IN INSTRUMENT METEOROLOGICAL CONDITIONS (IMC).

This aircraft is qualified for operation in instrument meteorological conditions.

5.27 FLIGHT IN ICING CONDITIONS.

a. When the ambient air temperature is 4°C (39°F) or below and visible liquid moisture is present, icing may occur. Icing severity is defined by the liquid water content (LWC) of the outside air and measured in grams per cubic meter (g/m3).

(1) Trace   :LWC 0 to 0.25 g/m3
(2) Light   :LWC 0.25 to 0.5 g/m3
(3) Moderate   :LWC 0.5 to 1.0 g/m3
(4) Heavy   :LWC greater than 1.0 g/m3

b. Helicopters with the following equipment installed and operational are permitted to fly into trace or light icing conditions. Flight into light icing is not recommended without the blade deice kit. Flight into moderate icing shall comply with paragraph 5.27 c.

(1) Windshield Anti-ice.

(2) Pitot Heat.

(3) Engine Anti-ice.

(4) Engine Inlet Anti-ice Modulating Valve.

(5) Insulated Ambient Air Sensing Tube.

c. For flight into moderate icing conditions, all equipment in paragraph 5.27 b. and blade deice kit must be installed and operational. Flight into heavy or severe icing is prohibited.

d. Helicopters equipped with blade erosion kit are prohibited from flight into icing conditions.

5.28 ENGINE AND ENGINE INLET ANTI-ICE LIMITATIONS.

At engine power levels of 10% TRQ per engine and below, full anti-ice capability cannot be provided, due to engine bleed limitations. Avoid operation under conditions of extreme low power requirements such as high rate of descent (1900 fpm or greater), or ground operation below 100% RPM R, during icing conditions. The cabin heating system should be turned off before initiating a high rate of descent.

5.29 BACKUP HYDRAULIC PUMP HOT WEATHER LIMITATIONS.

During prolonged ground operation of the backup pump using MIL-H-83282 or MIL-H-5606 with the rotor system static, the backup pump is limited to the following temperature/time/cooldown limits because of hydraulic fluid overheating.

FAT °C (°F)	Operating Time (Minutes)	Cooldown Time (Pump Off) (Minutes)
-54° - 32° (-65° - 90°)	Unlimited	- -
33° - 38° (91° - 100°)	24	72
39° - 52° (102° - 126°)	16	48

5.30 APU OPERATING LIMITATIONS.

To prevent APU overheating, APU operation at ambient temperature of 43°C (109°F) and above with engine and rotor operating, is limited to 30 minutes. With engine and rotor not operating, the APU may be operated continuously up to an ambient temperature of 51°C (124°F).

5.31 WINDSHIELD ANTI-ICE LIMITATIONS.

Windshield anti-ice check shall not be done when FAT is over 21°C (70°F).

5.32 TURBULENCE AND THUNDERSTORM OPERATION.

a. Intentional flight into severe turbulence is prohibited.

b. Intentional flight into thunderstorms is prohibited.

c. Intentional flight into turbulence with a sling load attached and an inoperative collective pitch control friction is prohibited.

Section VIII OTHER LIMITATIONS

5.33 EXTERNAL EXTENDED RANGE FUEL SYSTEM KIT CONFIGURATIONS.

The ERFS kit shall only be utilized with a 230-gallon tank installed on each outboard vertical stores pylon.

5.34 JETTISON LIMITS.

a. **ES** The jettisoning of fuel tanks in other than an emergency is prohibited.

b. **ES** The recommended external fuel tank jettison envelope is shown in Table 5-1.

5.35 GUST LOCK LIMITATIONS.

NOTE

Before engine operations can be performed with the gust lock engaged, all main rotor tie downs shall be removed.

a. Dual-engine operation with gust lock engaged is prohibited.

b. Single-engine operation with gust lock engaged will be performed by authorized pilot(s) at **IDLE** only. Gust lock shall not be disengaged with engine running.

5.36 RESCUE HOIST LIMITATIONS.

Refer to Airworthiness Release from U. S. Army Aviation and Missile Commend for limitations.

5.37 CARRY ON MEDICAL EQUIPMENT LIMITATIONS.

Refer to Airworthiness Release from U. S. Army Aviation and Missile Commend for limitations.

5.38 MAINTENANCE OPERATIONAL CHECKS (MOC).

Whenever a MOC requires that engines be started, pilots performing the MOCs must be authorized by the commander, trained and qualified in accordance with aircrew training manual (ATM), (TM 55-1500-328-23), DA PAM 738-751, and local standard operating procedures (SOP). The MOCs must be performed with checks enumerated in the maintenance test flight manual (MTF) or the -23 series maintenance manuals.

Table 5-1. Recommended Emergency External Fuel Tank Jettison Envelope

RECOMMENDED EMERGENCY JETTISON ENVELOPE							
	AIRSPEED KIAS						
	0 TO 120						120 TO Vh
LEVEL FLIGHT	SLIP INDICATOR DISPLACED NO MORE THAN ONE BALL WIDTH LEFT OR RIGHT						NO SIDESLIP BALL CENTERED
DESCENT	*JETTISON BELOW 80 KIAS NOT RECOMMENDED	AIRSPEED KIAS					*JETTISON ABOVE 120 KIAS NOT RECOMMENDED
		80	90	100	110	120	
		1000	875	750	625	500	
		MAX RATE OF DESCENT FT/MIN					
*Not recommended because safe jettison at these conditions has not been verified by tests.							

CHAPTER 6

WEIGHT/BALANCE AND LOADING

Section I GENERAL

6.1 INTRODUCTION.

This chapter contains instructions and data to compute any combination of weight and balance for this helicopter, if basic weight and moment are known.

6.2 CLASS.

Army helicopters defined in this manual are in Class 2. Additional directives governing weight and balance of Class 2 aircraft forms and records are contained in AR 95 series, TM 55-1500-342-23, and DA PAM 738-751.

6.3 HELICOPTER COMPARTMENT AND STATION DIAGRAM.

Figure 6-1 shows the reference datum line that is 341.2 inches forward of the centroid of the main rotor, the fuselage stations, waterlines and buttlines. The fuselage is divided into compartments A through F. The equipment in each compartment is listed on DD Form 365-1 (Chart A) in the individual aircraft weight and balance file.

TM 1-1520-253-10

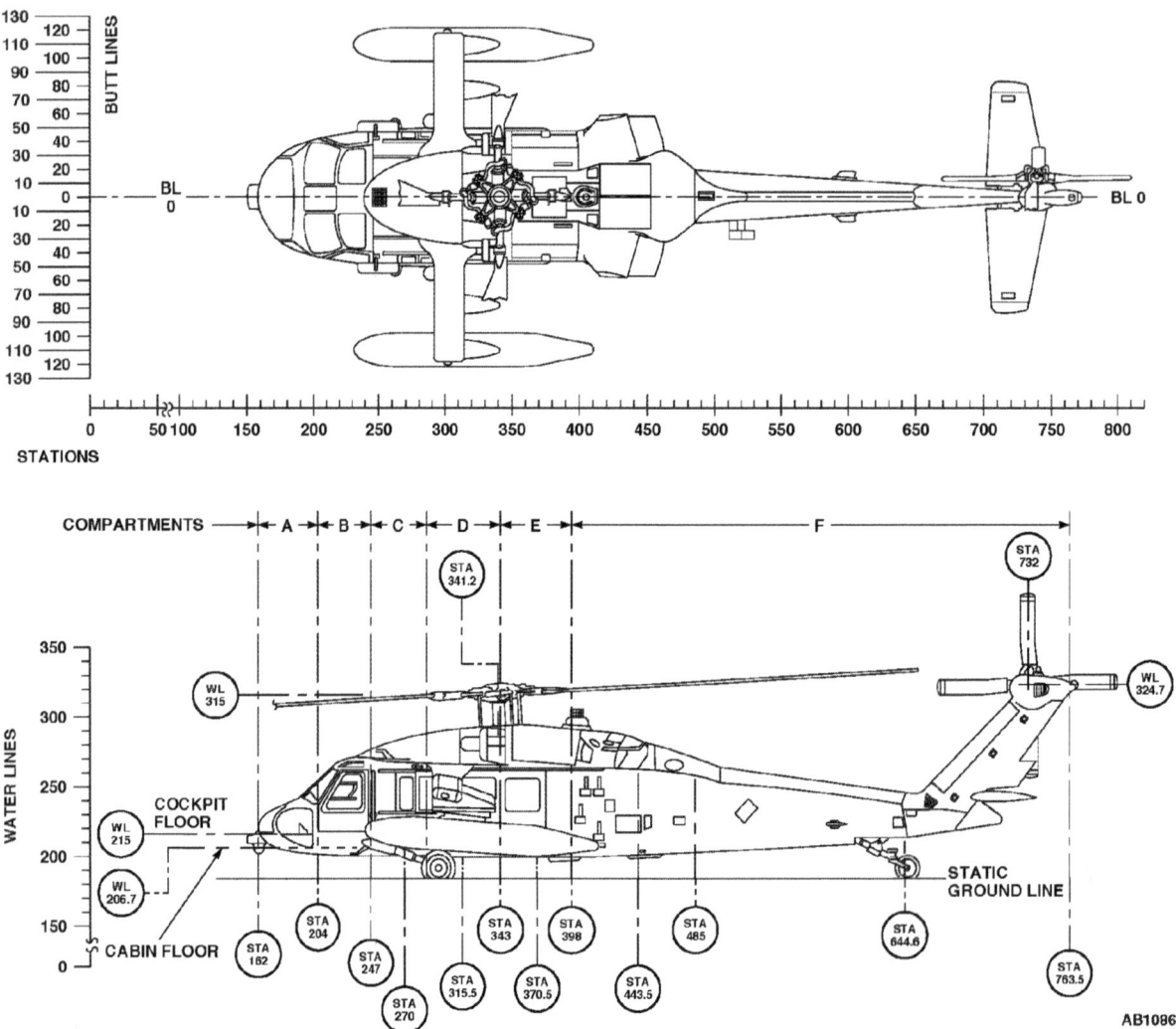

Figure 6-1. Helicopter Compartment and Station Diagram

Section II WEIGHT AND BALANCE

6.4 SCOPE.

This section provides appropriate information required for the computation of weight and balance for loading an individual helicopter. The forms currently in use are the DD Form 365 series. The crewmember has available the current basic weight and moment which is obtained from DD Form 365-3 (Chart C) for the individual helicopter. This chapter contains weight and balance definitions; explanation of, and figures showing weights and moments of variable load items.

6.5 WEIGHT DEFINITIONS.

a. Basic Weight. Basic weight of an aircraft is that weight which includes all hydraulic systems and oil systems full, trapped and unusable fuel, and all fixed equipment, to which it is only necessary to add the crew, fuel, cargo, passengers and patients to determine the gross weight for the aircraft. The basic weight varies with structural modifications and changes of fixed aircraft equipment.

b. Operating Weight. Operating weight includes the basic weight plus aircrew, the aircrew's baggage, and emergency and other equipment that may be required. Operating weight does not include the weight of fuel, ammunition, cargo, passengers or external auxiliary fuel tanks if such tanks are to be disposed of during flight.

c. Gross Weight. Gross weight is the total weight of an aircraft and its contents.

6.6 BALANCE DEFINITIONS.

6.6.1 Horizontal Reference Datum. The horizontal reference datum line is an imaginary vertical plane at or forward of the nose of the helicopter from which all horizontal distances are measured for balance purposes. Diagrams of each helicopter show this reference datum line as balance station zero.

6.6.2 Arm. Arm, for balance purposes, is the horizontal distance in inches from the reference datum line to the CG of the item. Arm may be determined from the helicopter diagram in Figure 6-1.

6.6.3 Moment. Moment is the weight of an item multiplied by its arm. Moment divided by a constant is generally used to simplify balance calculations by reducing the number of digits. For this helicopter, moment/1000 has been used.

6.6.4 Average Arm. Average arm is the arm obtained by adding the weights and moments of a number of items, and dividing the total moment by the total weight.

6.6.5 Basic Moment. Basic moment is the sum of the moments for all items making up the basic weight. When using data from an actual weighing of a helicopter, the basic moment is the total of the basic helicopter with respect to the reference datum. Basic moment used for computing DD Form 365-4 is the last entry on DD Form 365-3 for the specific helicopter. Cargo Hook Moments and Rescue Hoist Moments are shown in Figures 6-4 and 6-5, respectively.

6.6.6 Center of Gravity (CG). Center of gravity is the point about which a helicopter would balance if suspended. Its distance from the reference datum line is found by dividing the total moment by the gross weight of the helicopter.

6.6.7 CG Limits. CG limits (Figures 6-9 and 6-10) defines the permissible range for CG stations. The CG of the loaded helicopter must be within these limits at takeoff, in the air, and on landing.

6.7 DD FORM 365-3 (CHART C) WEIGHT AND BALANCE RECORDS.

DD Form 365-3 (Chart C) is a continuous history of the basic weight, moment, and balance, resulting from structural and equipment changes in service. At all times the last weight, moment/constant, is considered the current weight and balance status of the basic helicopter.

6.8 LOADING DATA.

The loading data in this chapter is intended to provide information necessary to work a loading problem for the helicopter. From the figures, weight and moment are obtained for all variable load items and are added arithmetically to the current basic weight and moment from DD Form 365-3 (Chart C) to obtain the gross weight and moment. If the helicopter is loaded within the forward and aft CG limits, the moment figure will fall numerically between the limiting moments. The effect on the CG of the expenditures in flight of such items as fuel and passengers may be checked by subtracting the weights and moments of such items from the takeoff gross weight and moment, and checking the new moment, with the CG limits chart. This check should be made to determine whether or not the CG will remain within limits during the entire flight.

6.9 DD FORM 365-4 (FORM F).

There are two versions of DD Form 365-4. Refer to TM 55-1500-342-23 for completing the form.

Section III FUEL/OIL

6.10 FUEL MOMENTS.

Fuel transfer sequence must be carefully planned and executed in order to maintain CG within limits.

When operating with a light cabin load or no load, it may be necessary to adjust fuel load to remain within aft CG limits. Fuel loading is likely to be more restricted on those aircraft with the HIRSS installed.

For a given weight of fuel there is only a very small variation in fuel moment with change in fuel specific weight. Fuel moments should be determined from the line on Figure 6-2 which represents the specific weight closest to that of the fuel being used. The full tank usable fuel weight will vary depending upon fuel specific weight. The aircraft fuel gage system was designed for use with JP-4, but does tend to compensate for other fuels and provide acceptable readings. When possible the weight of fuel onboard should be determined by direct reference to the aircraft fuel gages. The following information is provided to show the general range of fuel specific weights to be expected. Specific weight of fuel will vary depending on fuel temperature. Specific weight will decrease as fuel temperature rises and increases as fuel temperature decreases at the rate of approximately 0.1 lb/gal for each 15°C change. Specific weight may also vary between lots of the same type fuel at the same temperature by as much as 0.5 lb/gal. The following approximate fuel weights at 15°C may be used for most mission planning:

Fuel Type	Specific Weight
JP-4	6.5 lb/gal.
JP-5	6.8 lb/gal.
JP-8	6.7 lb/gal.
Jet A	6.8 lb/gal.
Jet B	6.3 lb/gal.

TM 1-1520-253-10

EXAMPLE

WANTED

FUEL MOMENT

KNOWN

FUEL QUANTITY
MAIN 1700 POUNDS

ITEM	STA	WEIGHT LBS	MOM/1000
230-GALLON TANK	321	150	48

METHOD

FOR MAIN TANK ENTER
AT 1700 POUNDS AND
MOVE RIGHT TO MAIN LINE.
MOVE DOWN READ
MOMENT / 1000 = 710

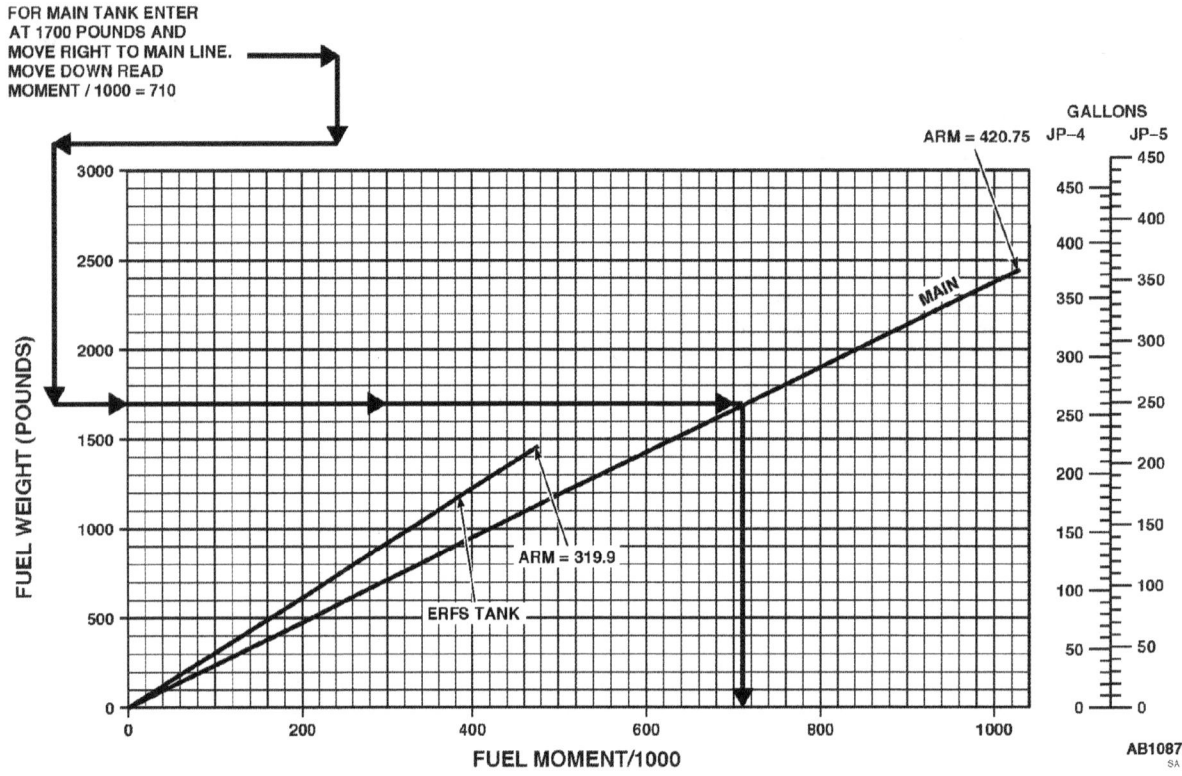

Figure 6-2. Fuel Moments

6-6

Section IV PERSONNEL

6.11 PERSONNEL MOMENTS.

When aircraft are operated at critical gross weights, the exact weight of each individual occupant plus equipment should be used. Personnel stations are shown on Figure 6-3. If weighing facilities are not available, or if the tactical situation dictates otherwise, loads shall be computed as follows:

a. Combat equipped soldiers: 240 pounds per individual.

b. Crew and passengers with no equipment: compute weight according to each individual's estimate.

6.12 MEDEVAC EQUIPMENT MOMENTS.

a. Litter moments are in Figure 6-4.

b. Medevac system (excluding litters) weight and moments are included in the helicopter basic weight and moments Form 365-3 when installed.

c. Litter weight is estimated to 25 pounds which includes litter, splints, and blankets.

d. Medical equipment and supplies should be stored per unit loading plan and considered in weight and balance computations.

TM 1-1520-253-10

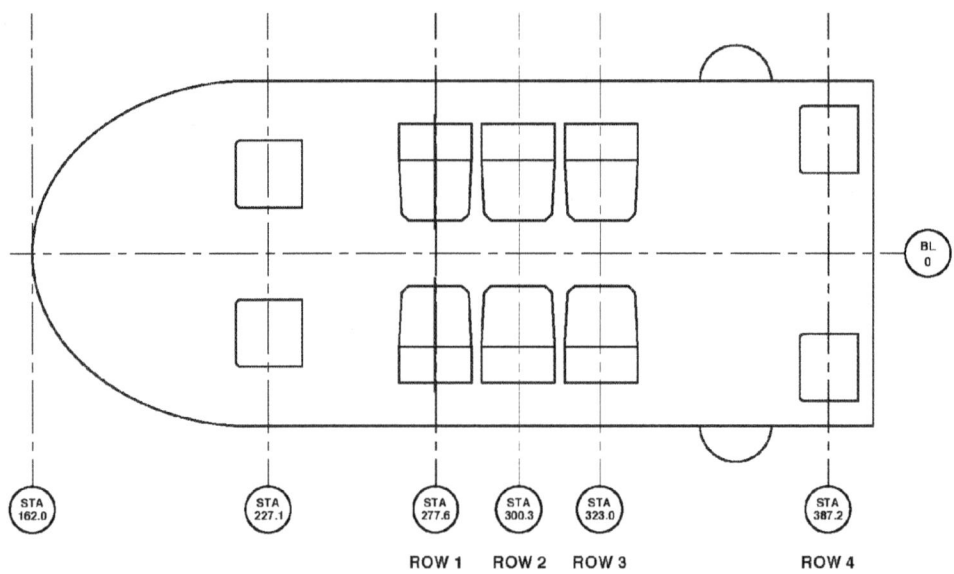

PILOT, COPILOT AND AMBULATORY SEATING POSITION DIAGRAM

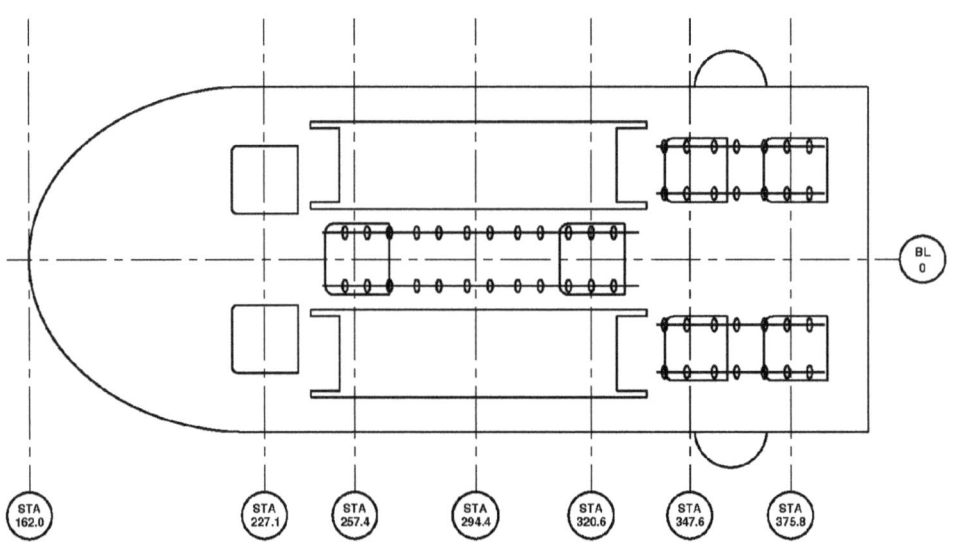

PILOT, COPILOT, TRACKABLE SWIVAL SEATS AND LITTER POSITION DIAGRAM

AB0571

Figure 6-3. Personnel Stations

6-8

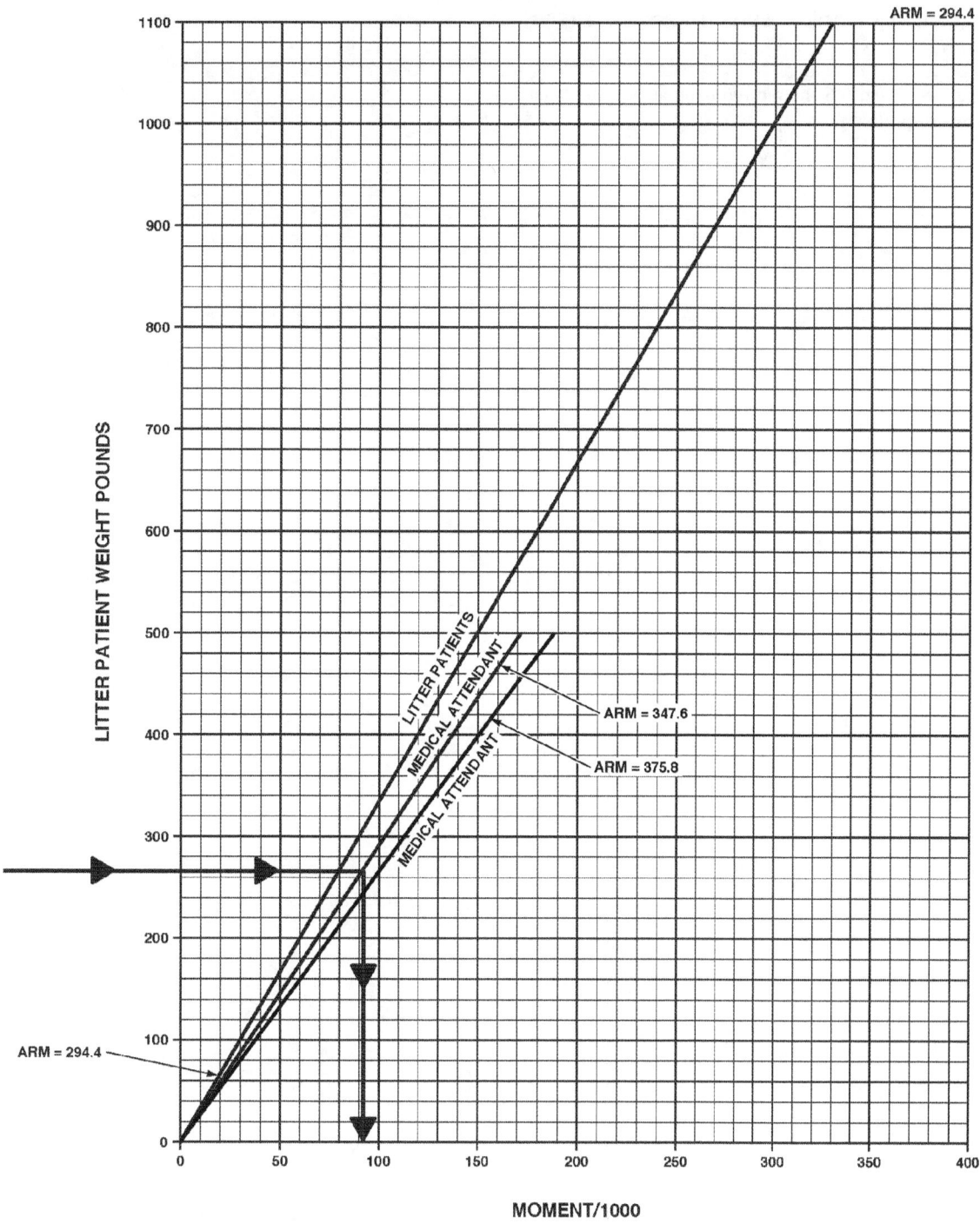

Figure 6-4. Litter Moments

Section V MISSION EQUIPMENT

6.13 CARGO HOOK AND RESCUE HOIST MOMENTS.

Figures 6-5 and 6-6 show cargo hook and rescue hoist moments respectively.

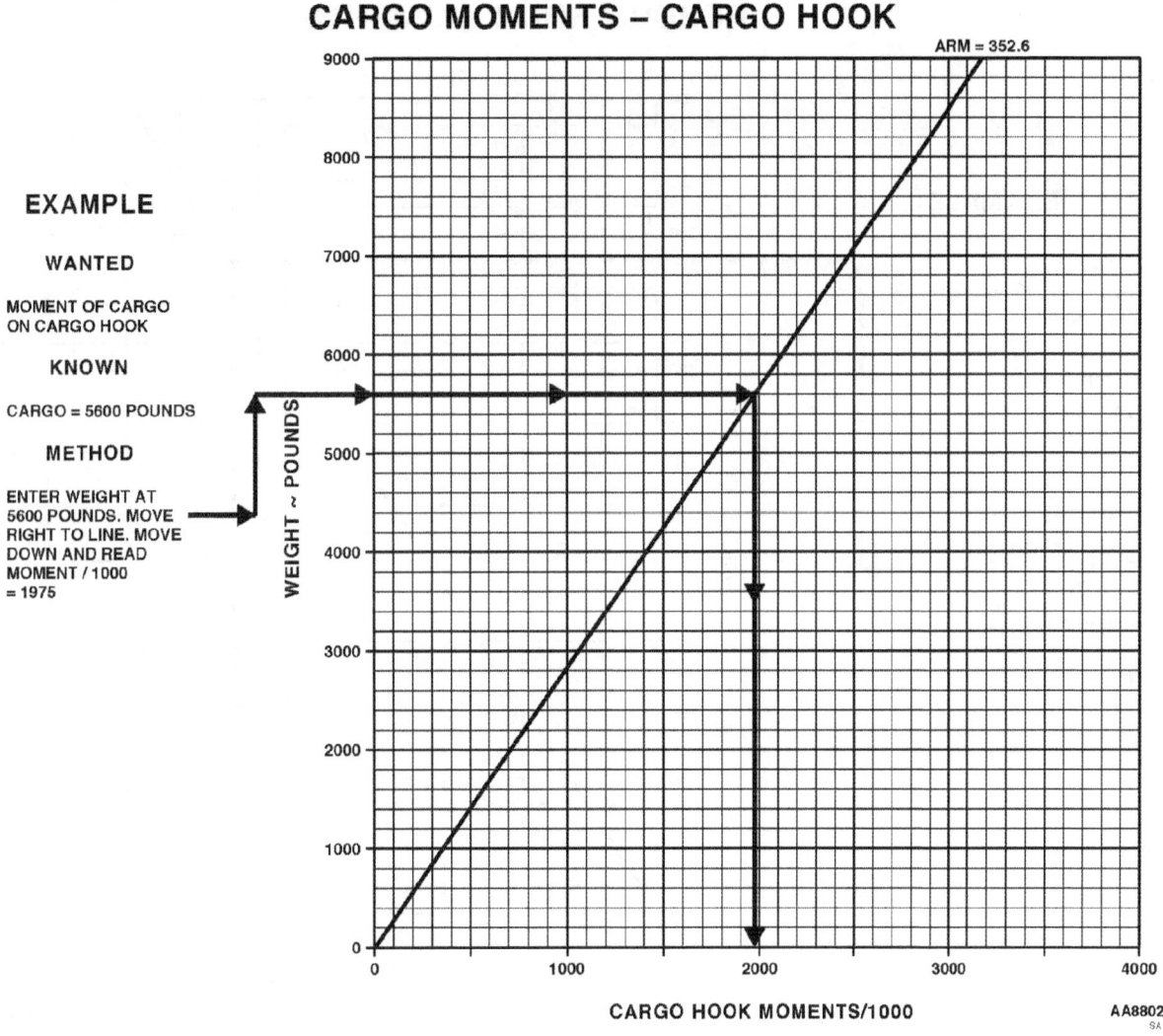

Figure 6-5. Cargo Hook Moments

TM 1-1520-253-10

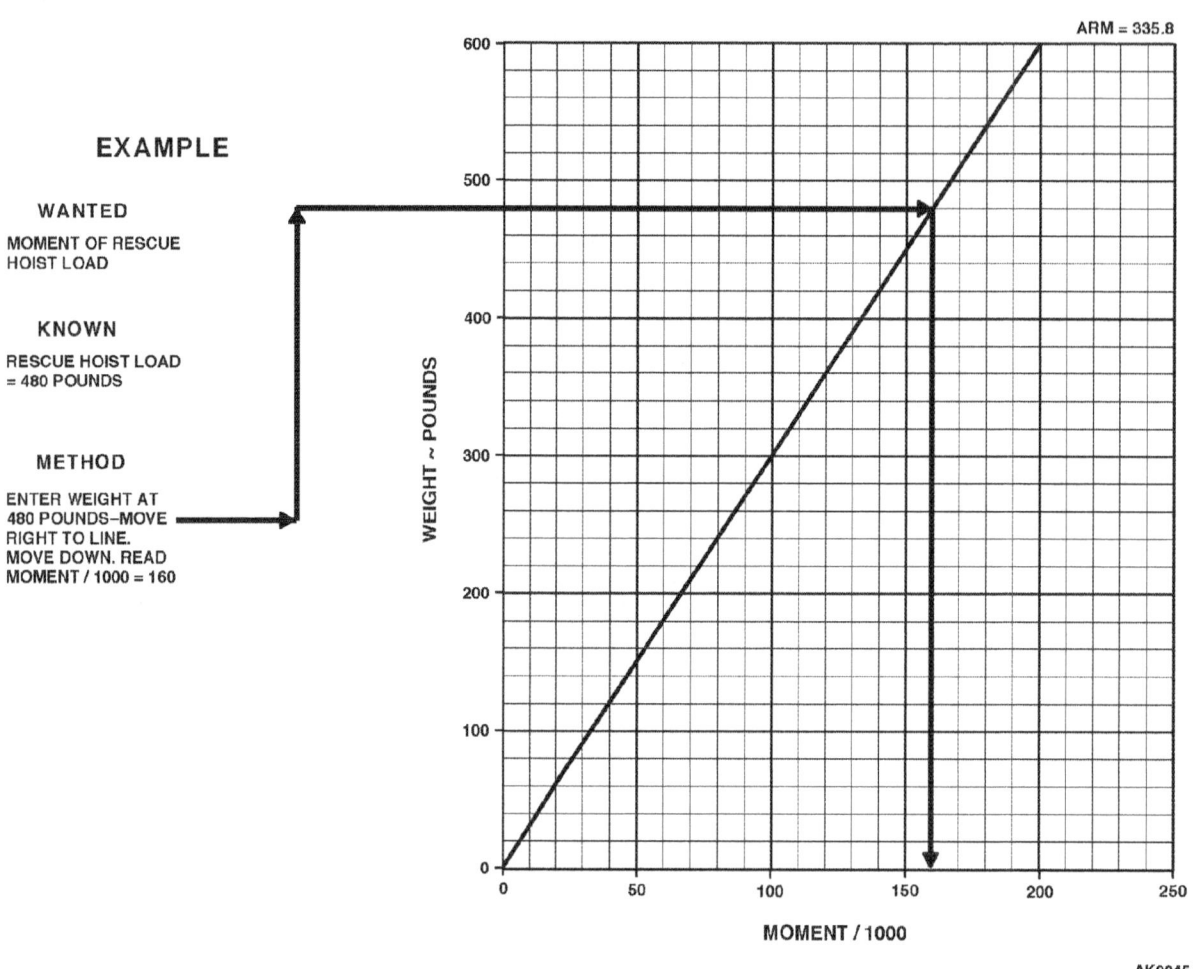

Figure 6-6. Rescue Hoist Moments

Section VI CARGO LOADING

6.14 CABIN DIMENSIONS.

Refer to Figure 6-7 for dimensions. For loading, and weight and balance purposes, the helicopter fuselage is divided into five compartments, labeled A through E, three of which are in the cabin, C, D, and E (Figure 6-7). Tiedown fittings are rated at 5,000 pounds each. Cargo carrier restraint rings are at stations 308 and 379, to cover the 71 inches of longitudinal space.

6.15 CABIN DOORS.

Cabin doors are at the rear of the cabin on each side of the fuselage. The door openings are 54.5 inches high and 69 inches wide; maximum package sizes accommodated by the openings are 54 inches high by 68 inches wide.

6.16 MAXIMUM CARGO SIZE DIAGRAM FOR LOADING THROUGH CABIN DOORS.

Figure 6-7 shows the largest size of cargo of various shapes that can be loaded into the cabin through the cabin doors.

6.17 TIEDOWN FITTINGS AND RESTRAINT RINGS.

The tiedown fittings (Figure 6-7) installed on the cargo floor can restrain a 5,000-pound load in any direction. All tiedown fittings incorporate studs that are used to install the troop seats. Eight net restraint rings in the cargo compartment prevent cargo from hitting the bulkhead at station 398, or entering the crew area. Each restraint ring is rated at 3500-pound capacity in any direction.

6.18 EQUIPMENT LOADING AND UNLOADING.

6.18.1 Data Prior to Loading. The following data should be assembled or gathered by the loading crew before loading (Refer to FM 55-450-2, Army Helicopter Internal Load Operations):

a. Weight of the individual items of cargo.

b. Overall dimensions of each item of cargo (in inches).

c. The helicopter's center of gravity.

d. Floor loads for each item of cargo.

e. Any shoring that may be required.

f. When required, the location of the center of gravity of an individual item of cargo.

6.18.2 Cargo Center of Gravity Planning. The detail planning procedure consists of four steps, as follows:

a. Determine ALLOWABLE LOAD from LIMITATIONS section of DD Form 365-4.

b. Plan the location in the helicopter for the individual items of cargo. Since the CG of the load is determined by the station method, then specific locations must be assigned to each item of cargo.

c. Determine the CG of the cargo load as planned. Regardless of the quantity, type, or size of cargo, use the station method.

d. Determine the CG of the fully-loaded helicopter from Figures 6-9 and 6-10, and if the CG of the helicopter falls within allowable limits. If it does, the cargo can be loaded. If not, the planned location of the individual items must be changed until an acceptable loading plan is obtained. When cargo loads consists of more than one item, the heavier items of cargo should be placed so that their CG is about in the center of the cabin, and the lighter items of cargo are forward and rear of them.

6.18.3 Restraint Criteria. The amount of restraint that must be used to keep the cargo from moving in any direction is called the "restraint criteria" and is usually expressed in units of the force of gravity, of Gs. Following are the units of the force of gravity or Gs needed to restrain cargo in four directions:

	Cargo
Forward	12 Gs
Rear	3 Gs
Lateral	8 Gs
Vertical	3 Gs (Up)
	3 Gs (Down)

TM 1-1520-253-10

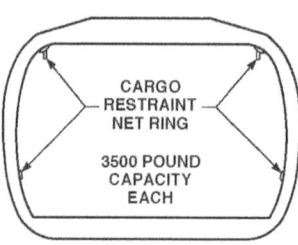

STA 379.0
LOOKING TO THE FRONT

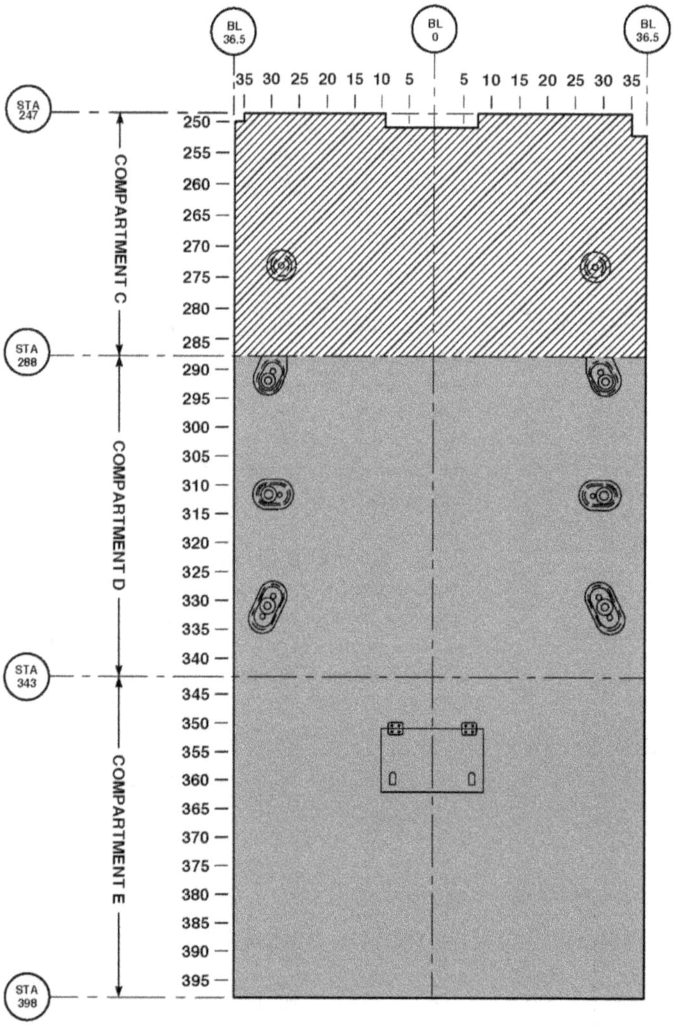

Figure 6-7. Cargo Tiedown Arrangement

	MAXIMUM COMPARTMENT CAPACITY IN POUNDS	FLOOR CAPACITY POUNDS PER SQUARE FOOT
▨	5460	300
▒	8370	300

◎ TIEDOWN FITTING
5000 POUNDS CAPACITY

6-14

Section VII CENTER OF GRAVITY

6.20 CENTER OF GRAVITY LIMITS CHART.

The CG limit charts (Figures 6-8 and 6-9) allow the center of gravity (inches) to be determined when the total weight and total moment are known.

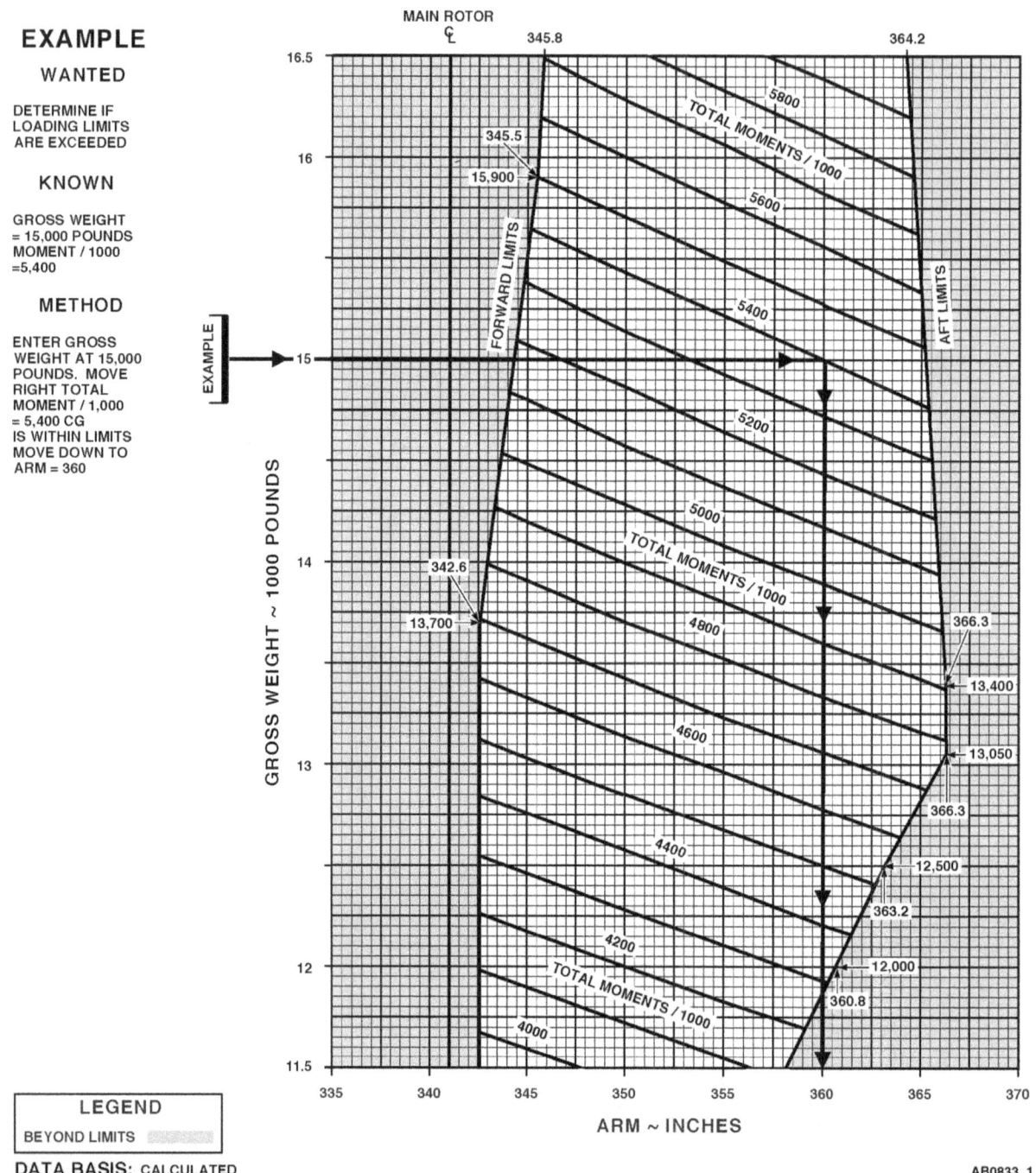

Figure 6-8. Center of Gravity Limits Chart (Sheet 1 of 2)

CENTER OF GRAVITY

WITHOUT EXTERNAL STORES SUPPORT SYSTEM
16,000 TO 22,000 POUNDS GROSS WEIGHT
CENTER OF GRAVITY LIMITS

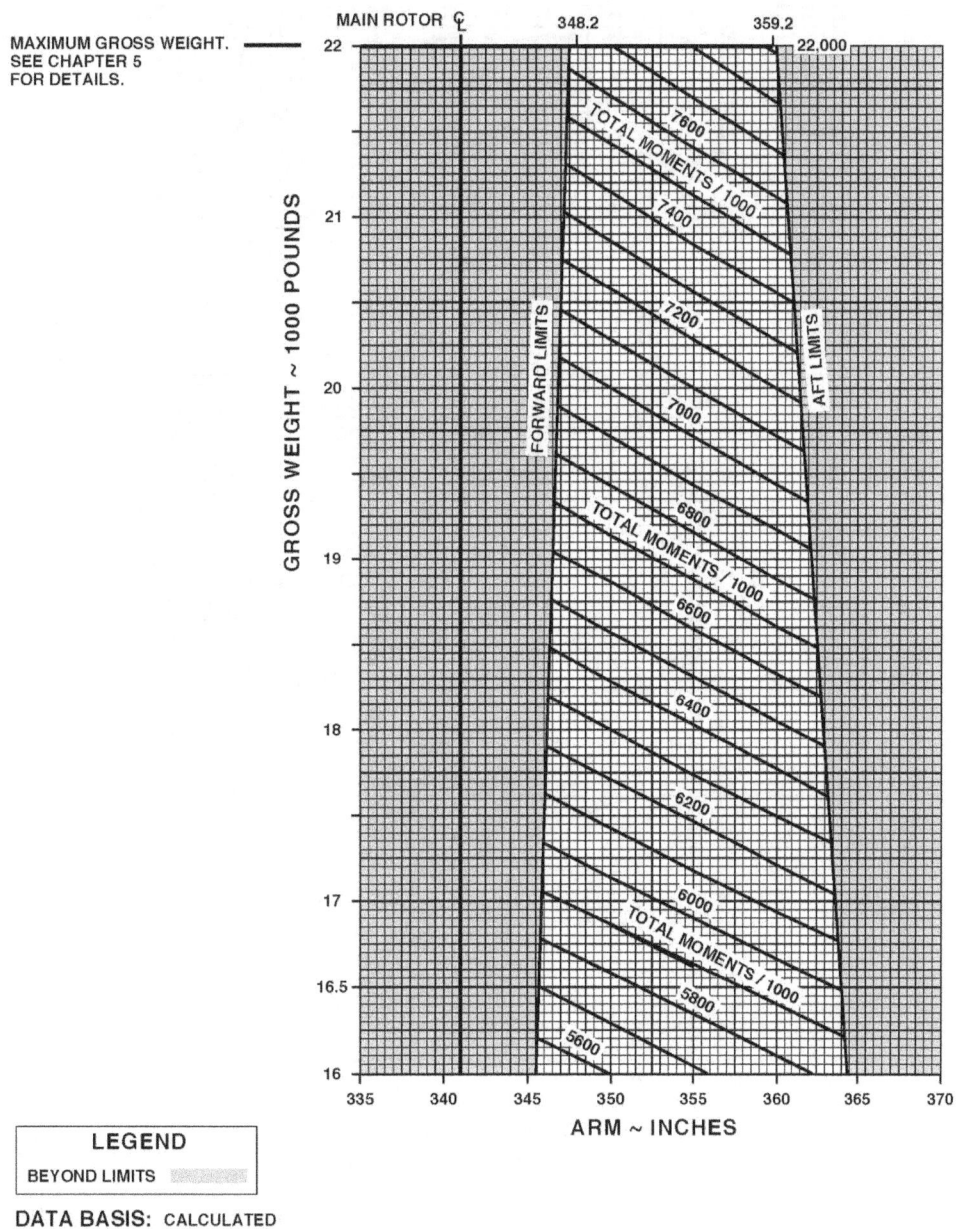

DATA BASIS: CALCULATED

Figure 6-8. Center of Gravity Limits Chart (Sheet 2 of 2)

CENTER OF GRAVITY

WITH EXTERNAL STORES SUPPORT SYSTEM INSTALLED
11,500 TO 16,500 POUNDS GROSS WEIGHT
CENTER OF GRAVITY LIMITS

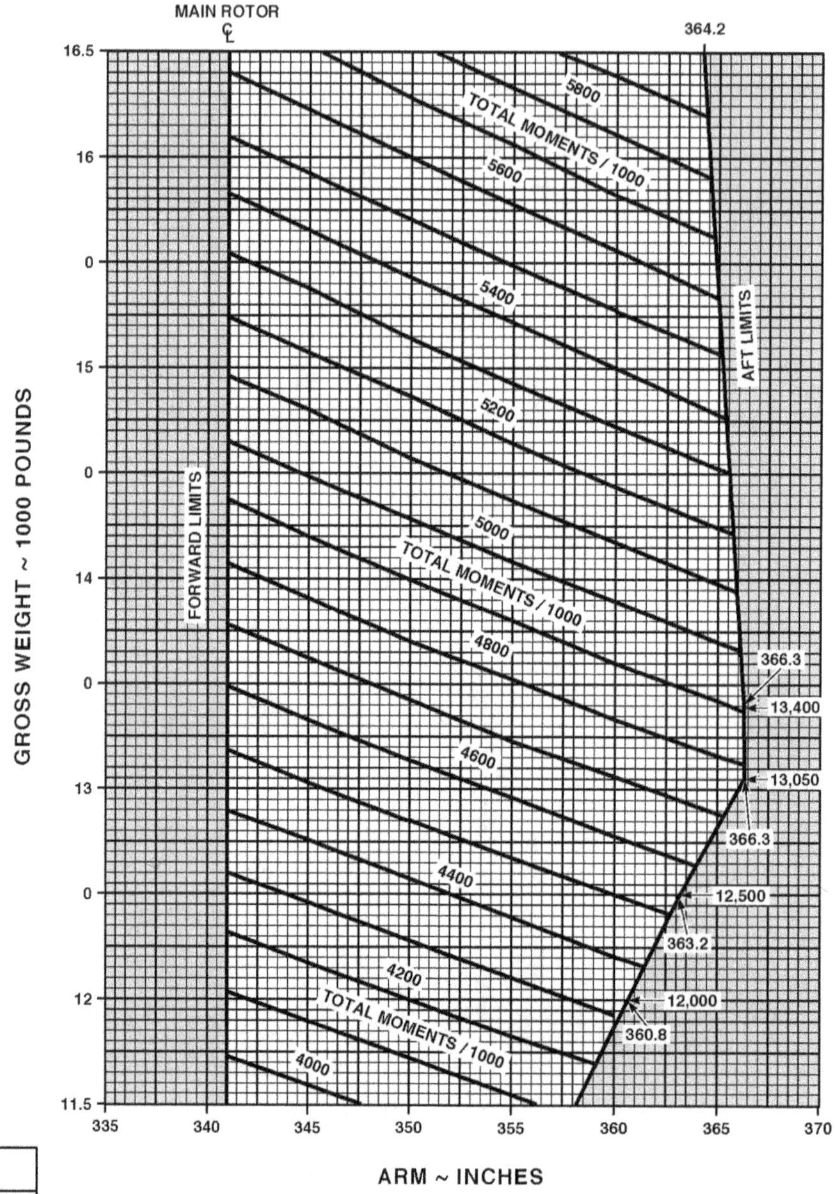

DATA BASIS: CALCULATED

AA1254_1A

Figure 6-9. Center of Gravity Limits Chart (Sheet 1 of 2)

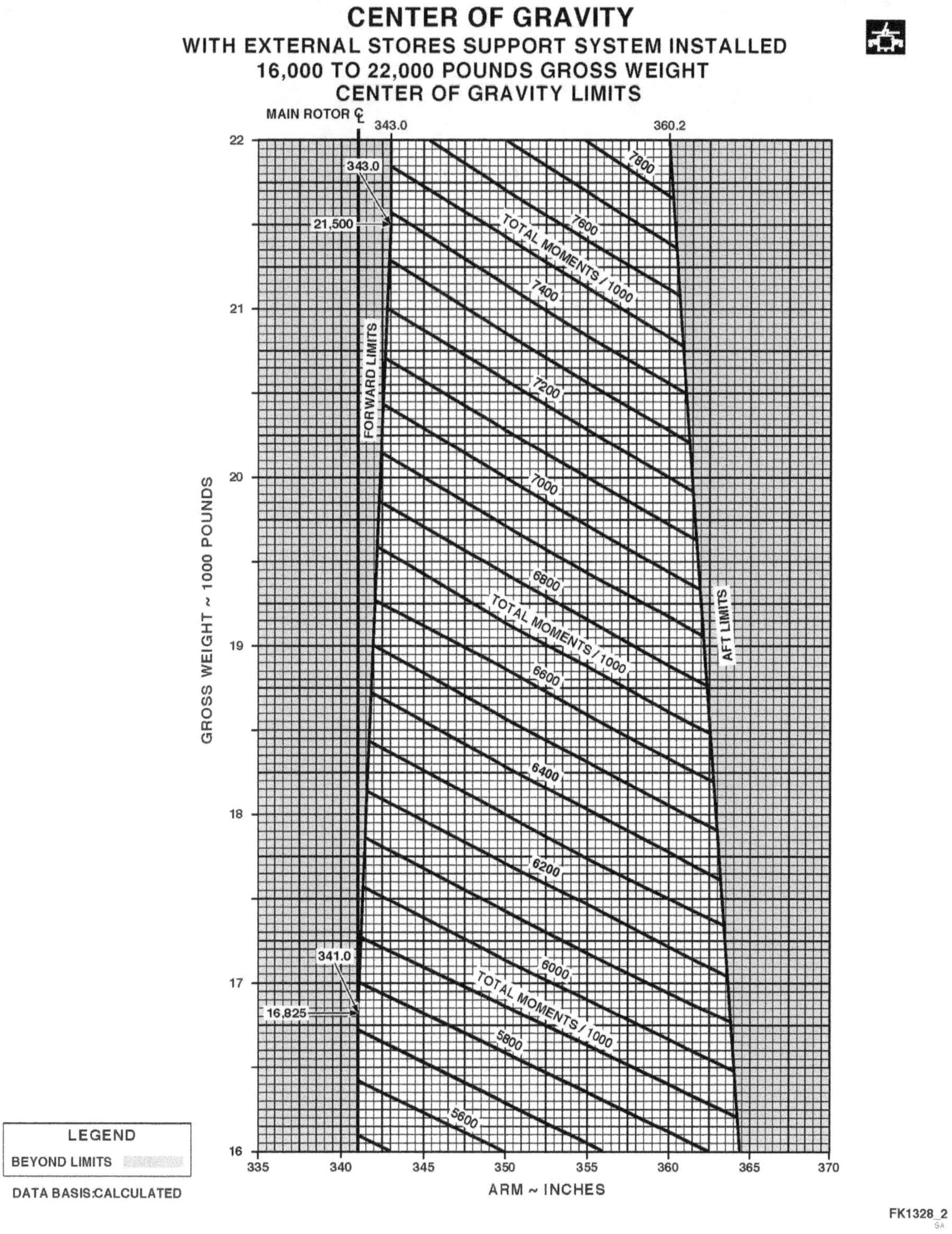

Figure 6-9. Center of Gravity Limits Chart (Sheet 2 of 2)

CHAPTER 7
PERFORMANCE DATA

Section I INTRODUCTION

NOTE

Tabular performance data is presented in the checklist (TM 1-1520-253-CL) and may be used in lieu of Figures 7-3 and 7-4 to obtain "Maximum Hover Weight", "Torque Required to Hover" and "Maximum Torque Available".

7.1 PURPOSE.

a. The purpose of this chapter is to provide the best available performance data. Regular use of this information will enable you to receive maximum safe utilization of the helicopter. Although maximum performance is not always required, regular use of this chapter is recommended for these reasons:

(1) Knowledge of your performance margin will allow you to make better decisions when unexpected conditions or alternate missions are encountered.

(2) Situations requiring maximum performance will be more readily recognized.

(3) Familiarity with the data will allow performance to be computed more easily and quickly.

(4) Experience will be gained in accurately estimating the effects of variables for which data are not presented.

b. The information is primarily intended for mission planning and is most useful when planning operations in unfamiliar areas or at extreme conditions. The data may also be used in flight, to establish unit or area standard operating procedures, and to inform ground commanders of performance/risk trade-offs.

7.2 CHAPTER 7 INDEX.

The following index contains a list of the sections, titles, figure numbers, subjects and page numbers of each performance data chart contained in this chapter.

Section and Figure Number	Title	Page
I	INTRODUCTION	7-1
7-1	Temperature Conversion Chart	7-4
II	MAXIMUM TORQUE AVAILABLE	7-5
7-2	Aircraft Torque Factor (ATF)	7-6
7-3	Maximum Torque Available - 30-Minute Limit	7-7
III	HOVER	7-8
7-4	Hover - Clean Configuration	7-9
7-5	Hover - High Drag	7-11
IV	CRUISE	7-12
7-6	Sample Cruise Chart - Clean	7-14
7-7	Cruise - Pressure Altitude Sea Level	7-15
7-8	Cruise High Drag - Pressure Altitude Sea Level	7-21
7-9	Cruise - Pressure Altitude 2,000 Feet	7-27
7-10	Cruise High Drag - Pressure Altitude 2,000 Feet	7-33
7-11	Cruise - Pressure Altitude 4,000 Feet	7-39
7-12	Cruise High Drag - Pressure Altitude 4,000 Feet	7-45
7-13	Cruise - Pressure Altitude 6,000 Feet	7-51

Section and Figure Number	Title	Page
7-14	Cruise High Drag - Pressure Altitude 6,000 Feet	7-57
7-15	Cruise - Pressure Altitude 8,000 Feet	7-63
7-16	Cruise High Drag - Pressure Altitude 8,000 Feet	7-69
7-17	Cruise - Pressure Altitude 10,000 Feet	7-75
7-18	Cruise High Drag - Pressure Altitude 10,000 Feet	7-80
7-19	Cruise - Pressure Altitude 12,000 Feet	7-85
7-20	Cruise High Drag - Pressure Altitude 12,000 Feet	7-90
7-21	Cruise - Pressure Altitude 14,000 Feet	7-95
7-22	Cruise High Drag - Pressure Altitude 14,000 Feet	7-100
7-23	Cruise - Pressure Altitude 16,000 Feet	7-105
7-24	Cruise High Drag - Pressure Altitude 16,000 Feet	7-110
7-25	Cruise - Pressure Altitude 18,000 Feet	7-114
7-26	Cruise High Drag - Pressure Altitude 18,000 Feet	7-119
7-27	Cruise - Pressure Altitude 20,000 Feet	7-123
7-28	Cruise High Drag - Pressure Altitude 20,000 Feet	7-127
V	OPTIMUM CRUISE	7-131
7-29	Optimum Altitude for Maximum Range	7-132
VI	DRAG	7-134
7-30	External Load Drag	7-135
VII	CLIMB - DESCENT	7-137
7-31	Climb/Descent	7-138
7-32	Climb/Descent - High Drag	7-139
VIII	FUEL FLOW	7-140
7-33	Single/Dual-Engine Fuel Flow	7-141
IX	AIRSPEED SYSTEM CHARACTERISTICS	7-142
7-34	Airspeed Correction Chart - Clean	7-143
7-35	Airspeed Correction Chart - High Drag	7-144
X	SPECIAL MISSION PERFORMANCE	7-145
7-36	Special Mission Profile (2 - 230 Gallon Tanks)	7-147

7.3 GENERAL.

The data presented covers the maximum range of conditions and performance that can reasonably be expected. In each area of performance, the effects of altitude, temperature, gross weight, and other parameters relating to that phase of flight are presented. In addition to the presented data, your judgment and experience will be necessary to accurately obtain performance under a given set of circumstances. The conditions for the data are listed under the title of each chart. The effects of different conditions are discussed in the text accompanying each phase of performance. Where practical, data are presented at conservative conditions. However, NO GENERAL CONSERVATISM HAS BEEN APPLIED. All performance data presented are within the applicable limits of the helicopter. All flight performance data are based on JP-4 fuel. The change in fuel flow and torque available, when using JP-5 or JP-8 aviation fuel, or any other approved fuels, is insignificant.

7.4 LIMITS.

CAUTION

Exceeding operating limits can cause permanent damage to critical components. Overlimit operation can decrease performance, cause early failure, or failure on a subsequent flight.

Applicable limits are shown on the charts. Performance generally deteriorates rapidly beyond limits. If limits are exceeded, minimize the amount and time. Enter the maximum value and time above limits on DA Form 2408-13-1, so proper maintenance action can be taken.

7.5 USE OF CHARTS.

7.5.1 Dashed Line Data. Weights above 22,000 pounds are limited to ferry missions for which an Airworthiness Release is required. On some charts dashed line data are shown for gross weights greater than 22,000 pounds.

7.5.2 Data Basis. The type of data used is indicated at the bottom of each performance chart under DATA BASIS. The data provided generally is based on one of three categories:

 a. Flight test data. Data obtained by flight test of the helicopter by experienced flight test personnel at precise conditions using sensitive calibrated instruments.

 b. Calculated data. Data based on tests, but not on flight test of the complete helicopter.

 c. Estimated data. Data based on estimates using aerodynamic theory or other means but not verified by flight test.

7.5.3 Specific Conditions. The data presented is accurate only for specific conditions listed under the title of each chart. Variables for which data is not presented, but which may affect that phase of performance, are discussed in the text. Where data is available or reasonable estimates can be made, the amount that each variable affects performance will be given.

7.6 PERFORMANCE DISCREPANCIES.

Regular use of this chapter will allow you to monitor instrument and other helicopter systems for malfunction, by comparing actual performance with planned performance. Knowledge will also be gained concerning the effects of variables for which data is not provided, thereby increasing the accuracy of performance predictions.

7.7 PERFORMANCE DATA BASIS - CLEAN.

The data presented in the performance charts are primarily derived for a clean UH-60A aircraft and are based on U. S. Army test data. The clean configuration assumes all doors and windows are closed and includes the following external configuration:

 a. Fixed provisions for the External Stores Support System (ESSS).

 b. Main and tail rotor deice system.

 c. Mounting brackets for IR jammer and chaff dispenser.

 d. The Hover Infrared Suppressor System (HIRSS) with baffles installed.

 e. Includes wire strike protection system.

NOTE

Aircraft which have an external configuration which differs from the clean configuration may be corrected for drag differences on cruise performance as discussed in Section VI DRAG.

7.8 PERFORMANCE DATA BASIS - HIGH DRAG.

The data presented in the high drag performance charts are primarily derived for the UH-60A with the ESSS system installed and the 230-gallon tanks mounted on the outboard pylons, and are based on U. S. Army test data. The high drag configuration assumes all doors and windows are closed and includes the following external configuration:

 a. External stores support system installed.

 b. Two 230-gallon tanks mounted on the outboard pylons.

 c. Inboard vertical pylons empty.

 d. IR jammer and chaff dispenser installed.

 e. Hover Infrared Suppressor System (HIRSS) with baffles are installed.

 f. Main and tail rotor deice and wire strike protection systems are installed.

NOTE

Aircraft with an external configuration that differs from the high drag configuration baseline may be corrected for differences in cruise performance as discussed in Section VI DRAG.

7.9 FREE AIR TEMPERATURES.

A temperature conversion chart (Figure 7-1) is included for the purpose of converting Fahrenheit temperature to Celsius.

TEMPERATURE CONVERSION

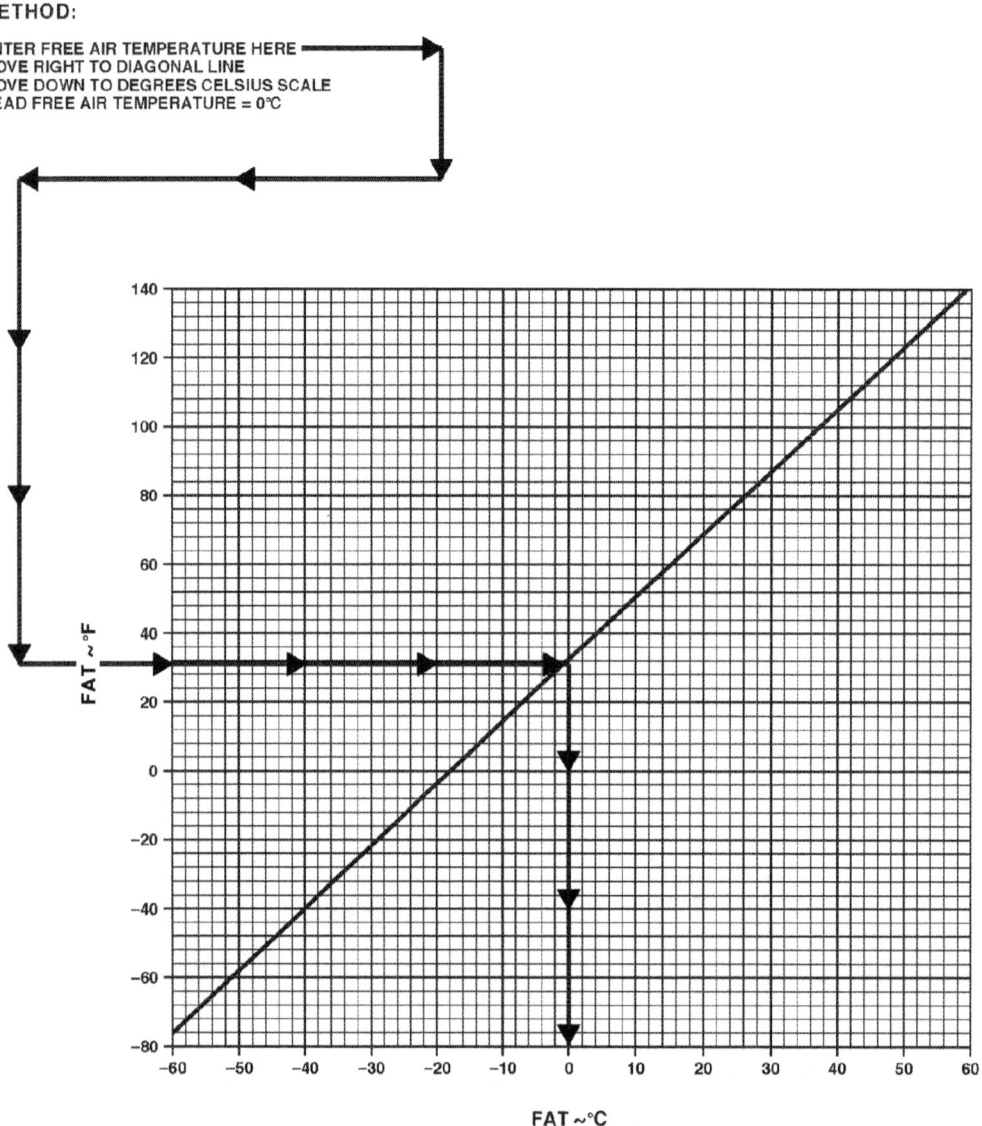

Figure 7-1. Temperature Conversion Chart

Section II MAXIMUM TORQUE AVAILABLE

7.10 TORQUE FACTOR METHOD.

The torque factor method provides an accurate indication of available power by incorporating ambient temperature effects on degraded engine performance. This section presents the procedure to determine the maximum dual- or single-engine torque available for the T700-GE-700 engine as installed in each individual aircraft. Specification power is defined for a newly delivered low time engine. The aircraft HIT log forms for each engine, provide the engine and aircraft torque factors which are obtained from the maximum power check and recorded to be used in calculating maximum torque available.

7.10.1 Torque Factor Terms. The following terms are used when determining the maximum torque available for an individual aircraft:

a. Torque Ratio (TR). The ratio of torque available to specification torque at the desired ambient temperature.

b. Engine Torque Factor (ETF). The ratio of an individual engine torque available to specification torque at reference temperature of 35°C. The ETF is allowed to range from 0.85 to 1.0.

c. Aircraft Torque Factor (ATF). The ratio of an individual aircraft's power available to specification power at a reference temperature of 35°C. The ATF is the average of the ETF's of both engines and its value is allowed to range from 0.9 to 1.0.

7.10.2 Torque Factor Procedure. The use of the ATF or ETF to obtain the TR from Figure 7-2 for ambient temperatures between -15°C and 35°C is shown by the example. The ATF and ETF values for an individual aircraft are found on the engine HIT Log. The TR always equals 1.0 for ambient temperatures of -15°C and below, and the TR equals the ATF or ETF for temperatures of 35°C and above. For these cases, and for an ATF or ETF value of 1.0, Figure 7-2 need not be used.

7.11 MAXIMUM TORQUE AVAILABLE CHART.

This chart (Figure 7-3) presents the maximum specification torque available at zero airspeed and 100% RPM R for the operational range of pressure altitude and FAT. The single- and dual-engine transmission limits for continuous operation are shown and should not be exceeded. The engine torque available data above the single-engine transmission limit is presented as dashed lines and is required for determining torque available when TR values are below 1.0. When the TR equals 1.0, the maximum torque available may be read from the horizontal specification torque available per engine scale. When the TR value is less than 1.0, the maximum torque available is determined by multiplying the TR by the specification torque available. The lower portion of Figure 7-3 presents TR correction lines which may be used in place of multiplication to read torque available per engine directly from the vertical scale. Reduce torque by 2% with OBOGS on.

7.12 ENGINE BLEED AIR.

With engine bleed air turned on, the maximum available torque is reduced as follows:

a. Engine Anti-Ice On: Reduce torque determined from Figure 7-3 by a constant 16% TRQ. Example: (90% TRQ - 16% TRQ) = 74% TRQ.

b. Cockpit Heater On: Reduce torque available by 4% TRQ.

c. Both On: Reduce torque available by 20% TRQ.

d. OBOGS On: Reduce torque available by 2% TRQ.

7.13 INFRARED SUPPRESSOR SYSTEM.

When the hover IR suppressor system is installed and operating in the benign mode exhaust (baffles removed) the maximum torque available is increased about 1% TRQ. When an IR suppressor system is not installed, maximum torque available is also increased about 1%.

TORQUE FACTOR

TORQUE FACTOR ~ ATF OR ETF

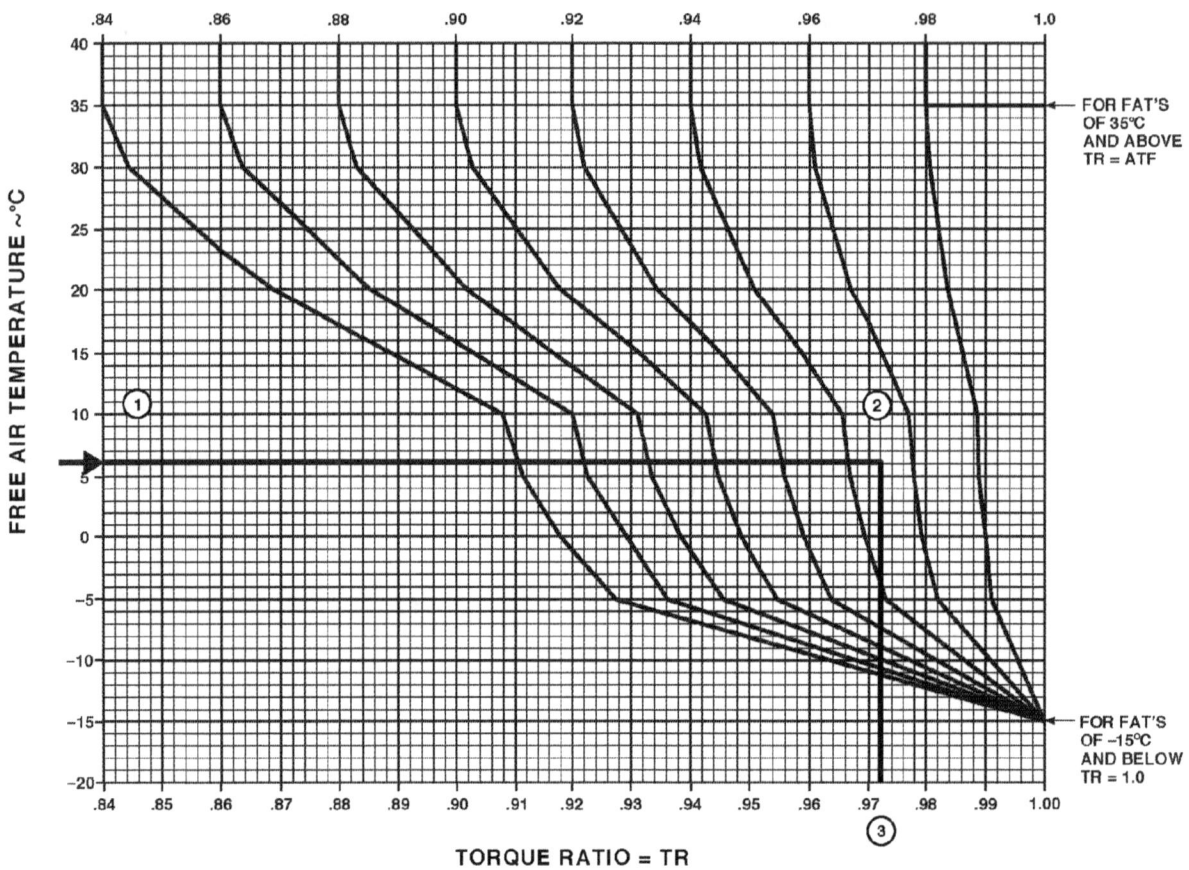

EXAMPLE

WANTED:
TORQUE RATIO AND MAXIMUM TORQUE AVAILABLE

KNOWN:
ATF = .95
PRESSURE ALTITUDE = 6000 FT
FAT = 6°C

METHOD:

TO OBTAIN TORQUE RATIO:

1. ENTER TORQUE FACTOR CHART AT KNOWN FAT
2. MOVE RIGHT TO THE ATF VALUE
3. MOVE DOWN, READ TORQUE RATIO = .972

TO CALCULATE MAXIMUM TORQUE AVAILABLE:

4. ENTER MAXIMUM TORQUE AVAILABLE CHART AT KNOWN FAT (FIGURE 7-3)
5. MOVE RIGHT TO KNOWN PRESSURE ALTITUDE
6. MOVE DOWN, READ SPECIFICATION TORQUE = 97.2%

TO OBTAIN VALUE FROM CHART:

7. MOVE DOWN TO TORQUE RATIO OBTAINED FROM FIGURE 7-2
8. MOVE LEFT, READ MAXIMUM TORQUE AVAILABLE = 93.0%

DATA BASIS: CALCULATED

Figure 7-2. Aircraft Torque Factor (ATF)

MAXIMUM TORQUE AVAILABLE
30 MIN LIMIT 100% RPM R HIRSS (BAFFLES INSTALLED)
ZERO AIRSPEED BLEED AIR OFF

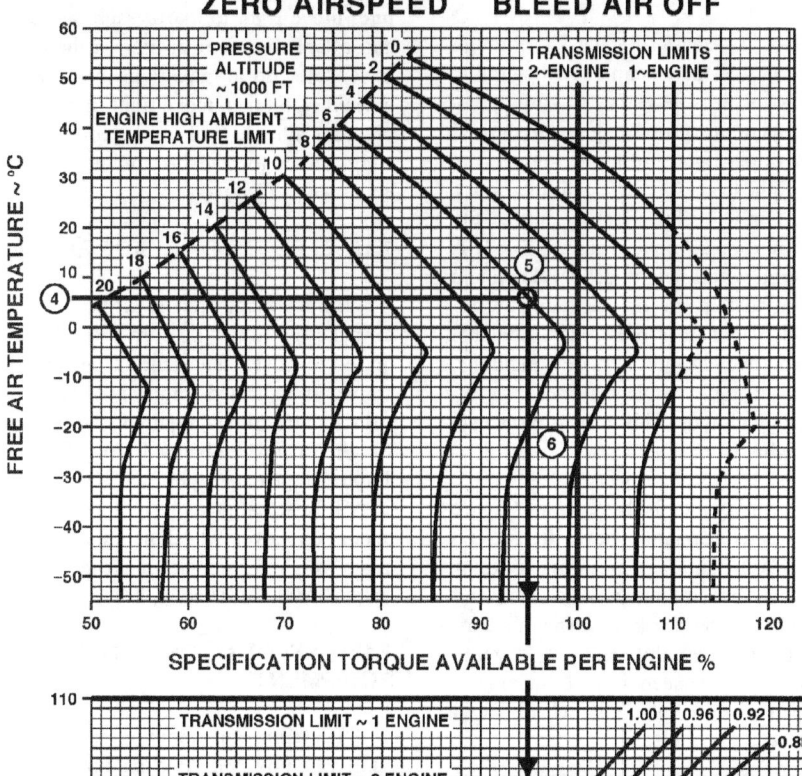
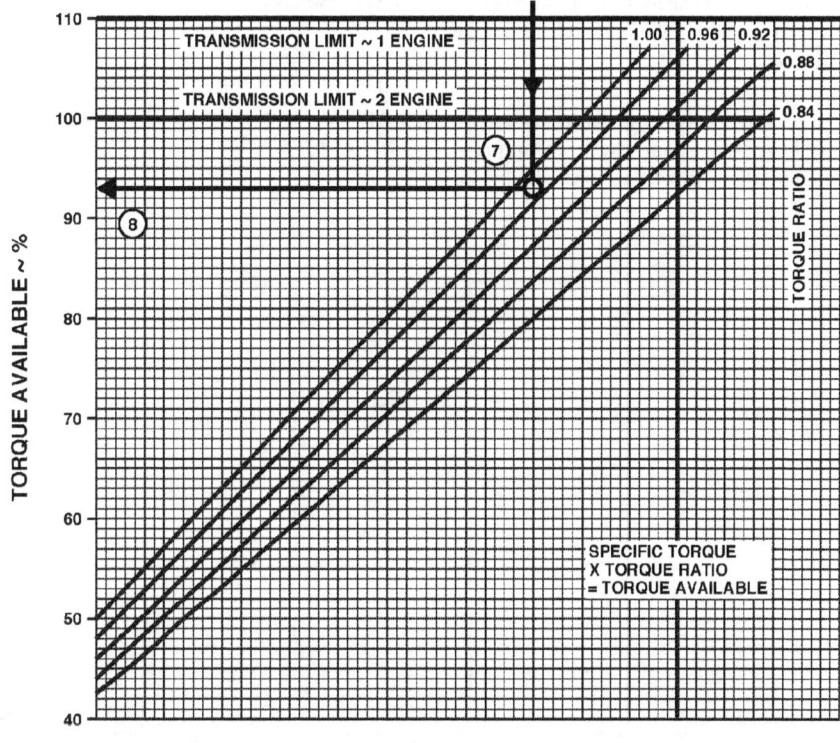

DATA BASIS: FLIGHT TEST

Figure 7-3. Maximum Torque Available - 30-Minute Limit

Section III HOVER

7.14 HOVER CHART.

a. The primary use of the chart (Figures 7-4 through 7-5) is illustrated by part A of the example. To determine the torque required to hover, it is necessary to know pressure altitude, free air temperature, gross weight, and desired wheel height. Enter the upper right grid at the known free air temperature, move right to the pressure altitude, move down to gross weight. For OGE hover, move left to the torque per engine scale and read torque required. For IGE hover, move left to desired wheel height, deflect down and read torque required for dual-engine or single-engine operation. The IGE wheel height lines represent a compromise for all possible gross weights and altitude conditions. A small torque error up to ±3% torque may occur at extreme temperature and high altitude. This error is more evident at lower wheel heights.

b. In addition to the primary use, the hover chart (Figure 7-4) may be used to predict maximum hover height. To determine maximum hover height, it is necessary to know pressure altitude, free air temperature, gross weight, and maximum torque available. Enter the known free air temperature move right to the pressure altitude, move down to gross weight, move left to intersection with maximum torque available and read wheel height. This wheel height is the maximum hover height.

c. The hover chart may also be used to determine maximum gross weight for hover at a given wheel height, pressure altitude, and temperature as illustrated in method B of the example (Figure 7-4). Enter at known free air temperature, move right to the pressure altitude, then move down and establish a vertical line on the lower grid. Now enter lower left grid at maximum torque available. Move up to wheel height, then move right to intersect vertical line from pressure altitude/FAT intersection. Interpolate from gross weight lines to read maximum gross weight at which the helicopter will hover.

7.15 EFFECTS OF BLADE EROSION KIT.

With the blade erosion kit installed, it will be necessary to make the following corrections. Multiply the torque required to hover determined from the charts by 1.02. (Example: If indicated torque is 90%, multiply 90 x 1.02 = 91.8% actual torque required.) Multiply the maximum gross weight to hover obtained from the charts by 0.98. (Example: If gross weight is 22,000 lb, multiply by 0.98 = 21,560 lb actual gross weight to hover.) When determining maximum hover wheel height, enter the chart at 1.02 x gross weight. (Example: If gross weight is 20,000 lb, multiply 20,000 x 1.02 = 20,400 lb).

7.16 EFFECTS OF ADDITIONAL INSTALLED EQUIPMENT.

To determine maximum gross weight to hover, multiply chart value by .995. For maximum hover height or torque required to hover, enter chart at a value of 1.005 multiplied by the gross weight.

EXAMPLE A

WANTED:

    TORQUE REQUIRED TO HOVER OGE AND AT A 10-FOOT WHEEL HEIGHT

KNOWN:

    FAT = 30°C
    PRESSURE ALTITUDE = 2,000 FEET
    GROSS WEIGHT = 19,500 POUNDS

METHOD:

    ENTER HOVER CHART AT KNOWN FAT. MOVE RIGHT TO PRESSURE ALTITUDE, MOVE DOWN THROUGH GROSS WEIGHT LINES TO DESIRED GROSS WEIGHT. MOVE LEFT TO INDICATE TORQUE/ENGINE % (OGE) SCALE AND READ OGE HOVER TORQUE (94%). MOVE DOWN FROM INTERSECTION OF 10-FOOT HOVER LINE AND HORIZONTAL LINE TO READ TORQUE REQUIRED TO HOVER 10 FEET (80%).

EXAMPLE B

WANTED:

    MAXIMUM GROSS WEIGHT TO HOVER OGE

KNOWN:

    ATF = 1.0
    FAT = 15°C
    PRESSURE ALTITUDE = 8,000 FEET
    MAXIMUM TORQUE AVAILABLE = 96%

METHOD:

    ENTER INDICATED TORQUE/ENGINE (IGE) SCALE AT MAXIMUM TORQUE AVAILABLE (96%), MOVE UP TO OGE LINE. ENTER CHART AT KNOWN FAT (15°C). MOVE RIGHT TO PRESSURE ALTITUDE LINE (8,000 FT). MOVE DOWN FROM PRESSURE ALTITUDE LINE AND MOVE RIGHT FROM OGE LINE. WHERE LINES INTERSECT, READ MAXIMUM GROSS WEIGHT TO HOVER OGE.

Figure 7-4. Hover - Clean Configuration (Sheet 1 of 2)

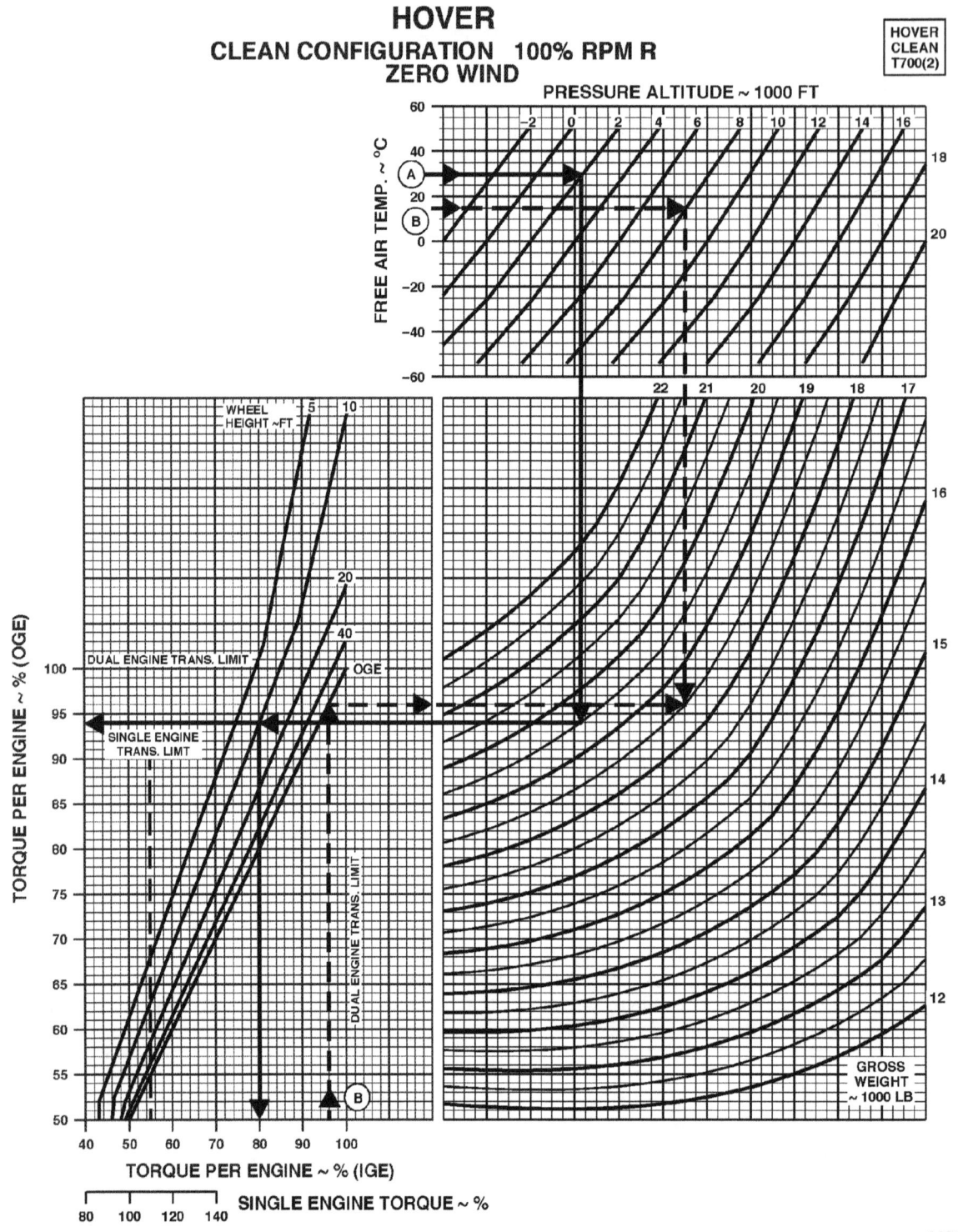

Figure 7-4. Hover - Clean Configuration (Sheet 2 of 2)

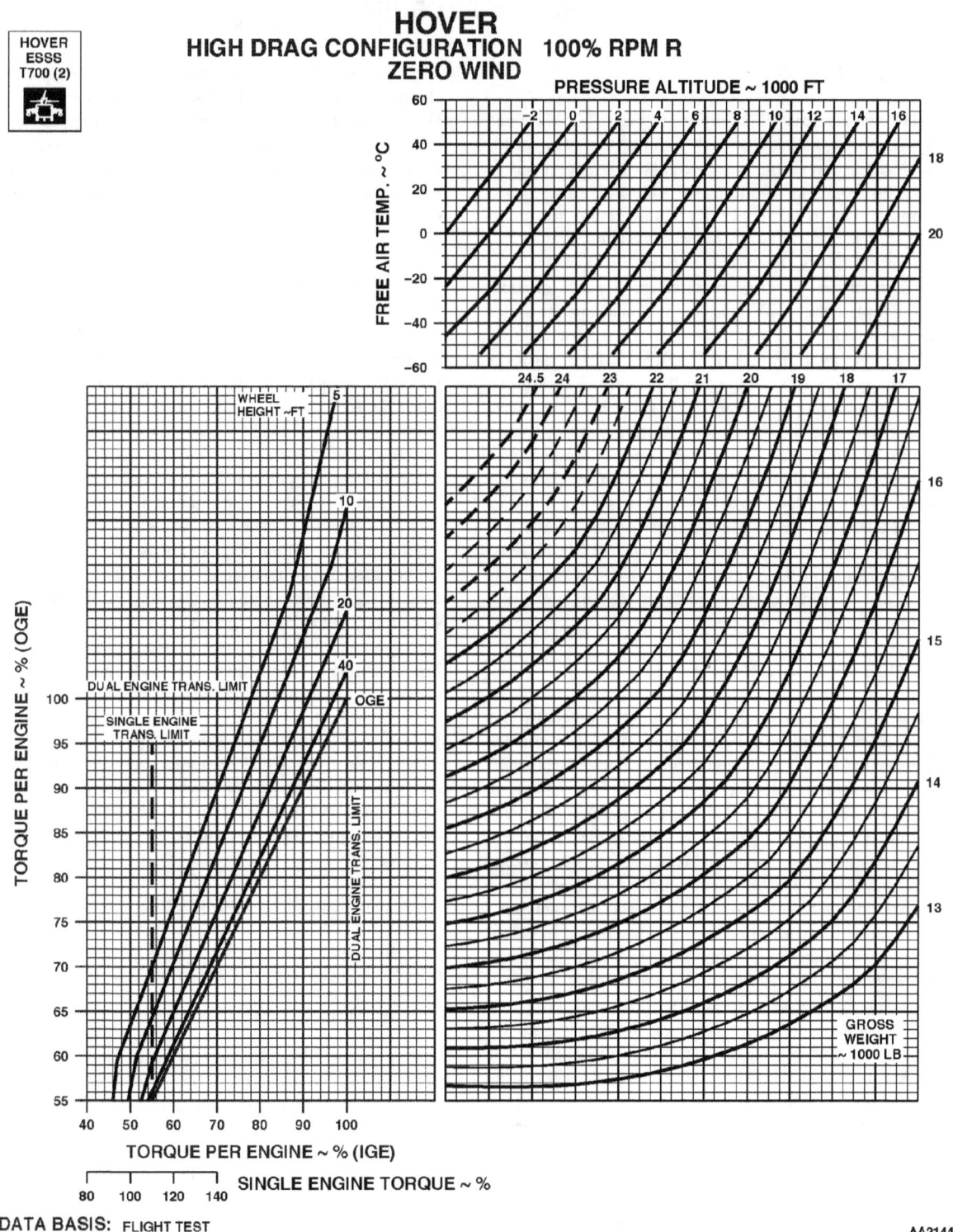

Figure 7-5. Hover - High Drag

Section IV CRUISE

7.17 DESCRIPTION.

The cruise charts (Figures 7-6 through 7-28) present torque required and total fuel flow as a function of airspeed, altitude, temperature, and gross weight at 100% rotor speed. Scales for both true airspeed and indicated airspeed are presented. The baseline aircraft configuration for these charts was the "clean and high drag" configuration as defined in Section I. Each cruise chart also presents the change in torque (Δ TRQ) required for 10 sq. ft. of additional flat plate drag with a dashed line on a separate scale. This line is utilized to correct torque required for external loads as discussed in Section VI DRAG. Maximum level flight airspeed (Vh) is obtained at the intersection of gross weight arc and torque available - 30 minutes or the transmission torque limit, whichever is lower. Airspeeds that will produce maximum range, maximum endurance, and maximum rate of climb are also shown. Cruise charts are provided from sea level to 20,000 feet pressure altitude in units of 2,000 feet. Each figure number represents a different altitude. The charts provide cruise data for free air temperatures from -50° to +60°C, in units of 10°. Charts with FAT's that exceed the engine ambient temperature limits by more than 10°C are deleted.

7.18 USE OF CHARTS.

The primary uses of the charts are illustrated by the examples of Figure 7-6. To use the charts, it is usually necessary to know the planned pressure altitude, estimated free air temperature, planned cruise speed, TAS, and gross weight. First, select the proper chart on the basis of pressure altitude and FAT. Enter the chart at the cruise airspeed, IAS, move horizontal and read TAS, move horizontal to the gross weight, move down and read torque required, and then move up and read associated fuel flow. Maximum performance conditions are determined by entering the chart where the maximum range line or the maximum endurance and rate of climb line intersects the gross weight line; then read airspeed, fuel flow, and torque required. Normally, sufficient accuracy can be obtained by selecting the chart nearest the planned cruising altitude and FAT or, more conservatively, by selecting the chart with the next higher altitude and FAT. If greater accuracy is required, interpolation between altitudes and/or temperatures is permissible. To be conservative, use the gross weight at the beginning of the cruise flight. For greater accuracy on long flights, however, it is preferable to determine cruise information for several flight segments to allow for the decreasing gross weight.

a. Airspeed. True and indicated airspeeds are presented at opposite sides of each chart. On any chart, indicated airspeed can be directly converted to true airspeed (or vice versa) by reading directly across the chart without regard for the other chart information. The level flight airspeed calibration for aircraft with wedge mounted pitot static probes (hard points only) was used to convert indicated to true airspeed.

b. Torque. Since pressure altitude and temperature are fixed for each chart, torque required varies according to gross weight and airspeed. The torque and torque limits shown on these charts are for dual-engine operation. The maximum torque available is presented on each chart as either the transmission torque limit or torque available - 30 minute for both ATF-1.0 and 0.9 values. The maximum torque available for aircraft with an ATF value between these shall be interpolated. The continuous torque available values shown represent the minimum torque available for ATF's of 0.95 or greater. For ATF's less than 0.95 maximum continuous torque available may be slightly reduced. Higher torque than that represented by these lines may be used if it is available without exceeding the limitations presented in Chapter 5. An increase or decrease in torque required because of a drag area change is calculated by adding or subtracting the change in torque from the torque on the curve, and then reading the new fuel flow total.

c. Fuel Flow. Fuel flow scales are provided opposite the torque scales. On any chart, torque may be converted directly to fuel flow without regard to other chart information. Data shown in this section is for two-engine operation. For one-engine fuel flow, refer to Section VIII FUEL FLOW.

(1) With bleed-air extracted, fuel flow increases:

(a) Engine anti-ice on -About 60 lbs/hr Example: (760 lbs/hr + 60 lbs/hr = 820 lbs/hr.)

(b) Heater on - About 20 lbs/hr.

(c) Both on - About 80 lbs/hr.

(2) When the cruise IR suppressors are removed or hover IR suppressor system is installed and operating in the benign mode (exhaust baffles removed), the dual-engine fuel flow will decrease about 16 lbs/hr.

d. Maximum Range. The maximum range lines (MAX RANGE) indicate the combinations of gross weight and airspeed that will produce the greatest flight range per pound of fuel under zero wind conditions. When maximum range airspeed line is above the maximum torque available, the resulting maximum airspeed should be used for maximum range. A method of estimating maximum range speed in winds is to increase IAS by 2.5 knots per each 10 knots of effective headwind (which reduces flight time and minimizes loss in range) and decrease IAS by 2.5 knots per 10 knots of effective tailwind for economy.

c. Maximum Endurance and Rate of Climb. The maximum endurance and rate of climb lines (MAX END and R/C) indicate the combinations of gross weight and airspeed that will produce the maximum endurance and the maximum rate of climb. The torque required for level flight at this condition is a minimum, providing a minimum fuel flow (maximum endurance) and a maximum torque change available for climb (maximum rate of climb).

f. Change in Frontal Area. Since the cruise information is given for the "clean configuration," adjustments to torque should be made when operating with external sling loads or aircraft external configuration changes. To determine the change in torque, first obtain the appropriate multiplying factor from the drag load chart (Figure 7-30), then enter the cruise chart at the planned cruise speed TAS, move right to the broken ΔTRQ line, and move up and read Δ TRQ. Multiply ΔTRQ by the multiplying factor to obtain change in torque, then add or subtract change in torque from torque required for the primary mission configuration. Enter the cruise chart at resulting torque required, move up, and read fuel flow. If the resulting torque required exceeds the governing torque limit, the torque required must be reduced to the limit. The resulting reduction in airspeed may be found by subtracting the change in torque from the limit torque; then enter the cruise chart at the reduced torque, and move up to the gross weight. Move left or right to read TAS or IAS. The engine torque setting for maximum range obtained from the clean configuration cruise chart will generally result in cruise at best range airspeed for the higher drag configuration. To determine the approximate airspeed for maximum range for alternative or external load configurations, reduce the value from the cruise chart by 6 knots for each 10 square foot increase in drag area, ΔF. For example, if both cabin doors are open the ΔF increases 6 ft^2 and the maximum range airspeed would be reduced by approximately 4 knots (6 Kts/10 ft$^2 \times$6 ft^2 = 3.6 Kts).

g. Additional Uses. The low speed end of the cruise chart (below 40 knots) is shown primarily to familiarize you with the low speed power requirements of the helicopter. It shows the power margin available for climb or acceleration during maneuvers, such as NOE flight. At zero airspeed, the torque represents the torque required to hover out of ground effect. In general, mission planning for low speed flight should be based on hover out of ground effect.

7.19 SINGLE-ENGINE.

a. The minimum or maximum single-engine speeds can be determined by using a combination of the 700 torque available and cruise charts. To calculate single-engine speeds, first determine the torque available from Section II at the TGT limit desired and divide by 2. (Example: 90% TRQ$\div$2 = 45% TRQ.)

b. Select the appropriate cruise chart for the desired flight condition and enter the torque scale with the torque value derived above. Move up to the intersection of torque available and the mission gross weight arc, and read across for minimum single-engine airspeed. Move up to the second intersection of torque and weight, and read across to determine the maximum single-engine speed. If no intersections occur, there is no single-engine level flight capability for the conditions. Single-engine fuel flow at the desired 10 minute, 30 minute, continuous conditions may be obtained by doubling the torque required from the cruise chart and referring to Figure 7-33.

CRUISE EXAMPLE
CLEAN CONFIGURATION
100% RPM R

EXAMPLE

WANTED:

A. CRUISE CONDITIONS FOR MAXIMUM RANGE
B. CONDITIONS FOR MAXIMUM ENDURANCE
C. MAXIMUM AIRSPEED IN LEVEL FLIGHT
D. DETERMINE TORQUE AND FUEL FLOW REQUIRED TO CRUISE AT THE CONDITIONS OF EXAMPLE A WITH CABIN DOORS OPEN

KNOWN:

FAT = +30°C
PRESSURE ALTITUDE = 6000 FT
GW = 17000 LBS
ATF = 0.95

METHOD:

A. TURN TO CRUISE CHARTS NEAREST KNOWN FLIGHT CONDITIONS, AT INTERSECTION OF MAX RANGE LINE AND KNOWN VALUE OF GROSS WEIGHT:
  MOVE LEFT, READ TAS = 135 KTS
  MOVE RIGHT, READ IAS = 119 KTS
  MOVE DOWN, READ TORQUE = 62% TRQ
  MOVE UP, READ TOTAL FUEL FLOW = 900 LBS / HR

B. AT INTERSECTION OF MAX END. / AND R / C LINE AND KNOWN VALUE OF GROSS WEIGHT:
  MOVE LEFT, READ TAS = 82 KTS
  MOVE RIGHT, READ IAS = 67 KTS
  MOVE DOWN, READ TORQUE = 41% TRQ
  MOVE UP, READ TOTAL FUEL FLOW = 700 LBS / HR

C. AT INTERSECTION OF 30-MINUTE TORQUE AVAILABLE AS INTERPOLATED FOR THE ATF VALUE AT THE KNOWN GROSS WEIGHT:
  MOVE LEFT, READ MAXIMUM TAS = 153 KTS
  MOVE RIGHT, READ MAXIMUM IAS = 135 KTS
  MOVE DOWN, READ MAXIMUM TORQUE = 82% TRQ
  MOVE UP, READ TOTAL FUEL FLOW = 1125 LBS / HR

D. ENTER Δ TRQ% PER 10 SQ FT SCALE AT 135 KTAS MOVE UP READ Δ TRQ = 8.0%
  TURN TO DRAG TABLE IN SECTION VII
  NOTE CABIN DOORS OPEN = 6.0 SQ FT Δ F
  AND HAS A DRAG MULTIPLYING FACTOR VALUE OF 0.60, CALCULATE TOTAL TORQUE REQUIRED:

62% + (0.6 X 8.0%) = 66.8% TRQ

READ FUEL FLOW AT–TOTAL TORQUE = 950 LBS / HR

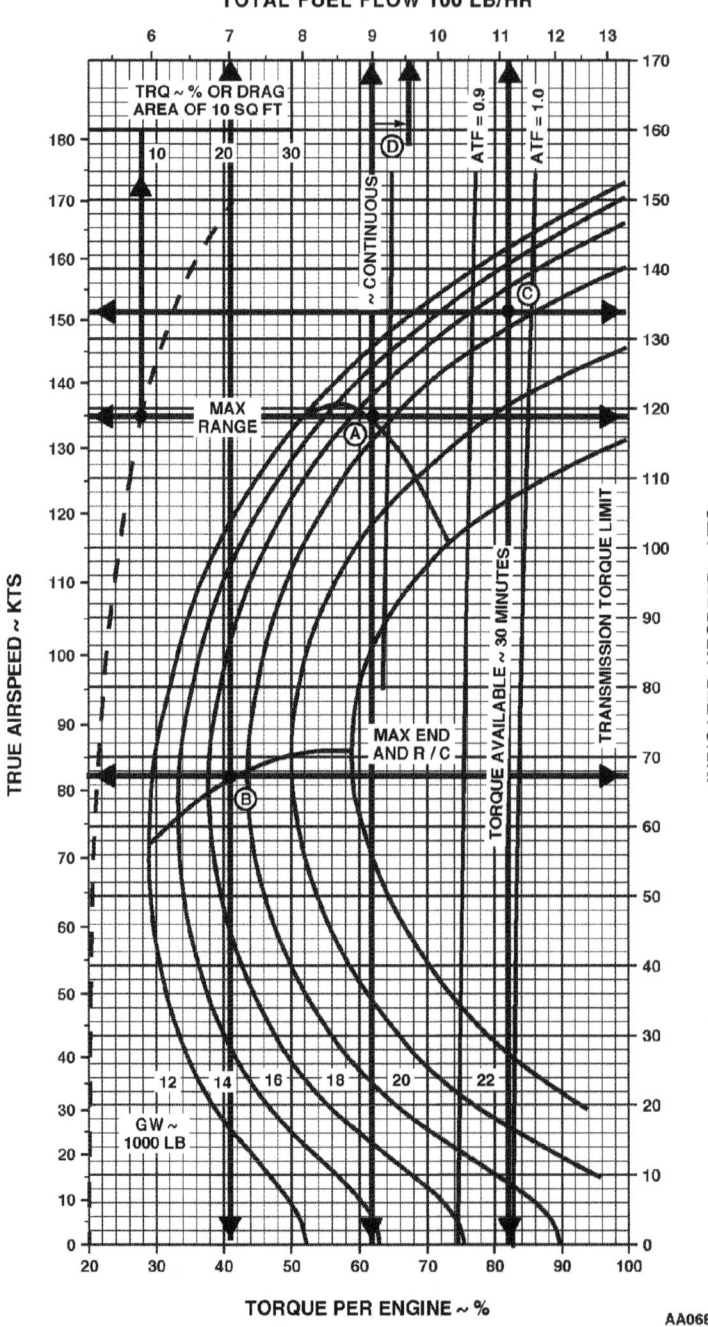

Figure 7-6. Sample Cruise Chart - Clean

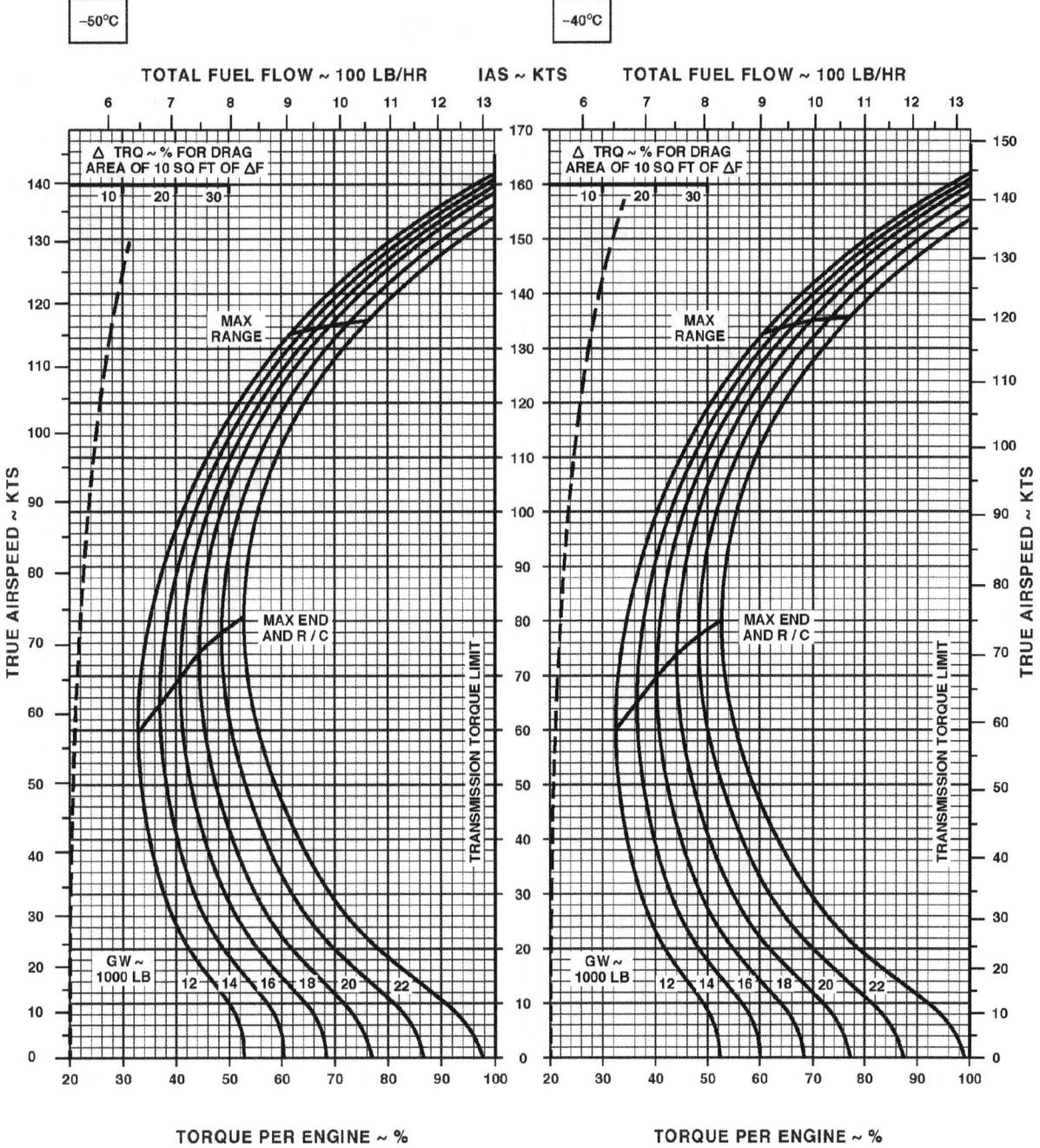

Figure 7-7. Cruise - Pressure Altitude Sea Level (Sheet 1 of 6)

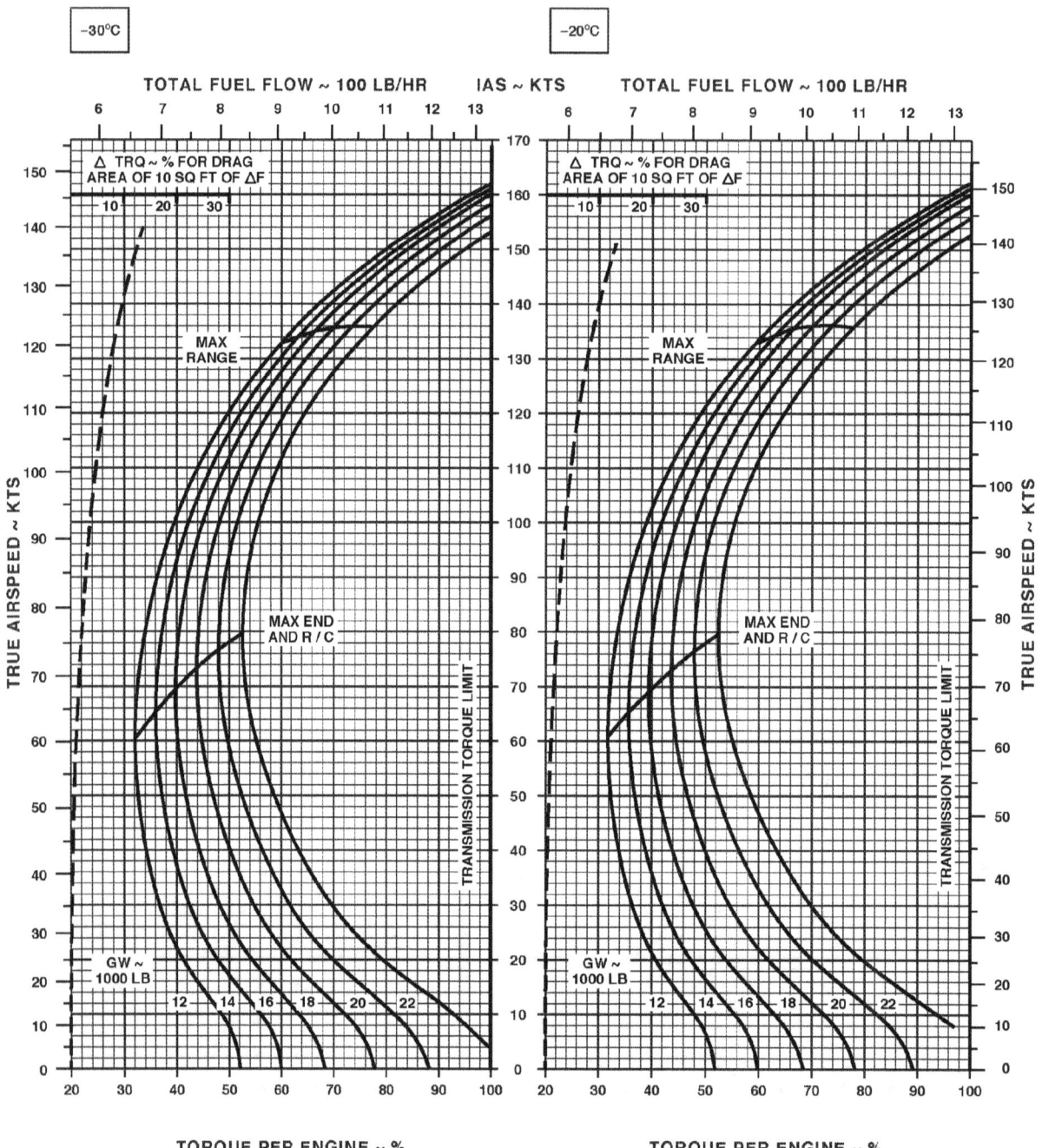

Figure 7-7. Cruise - Pressure Altitude Sea Level (Sheet 2 of 6)

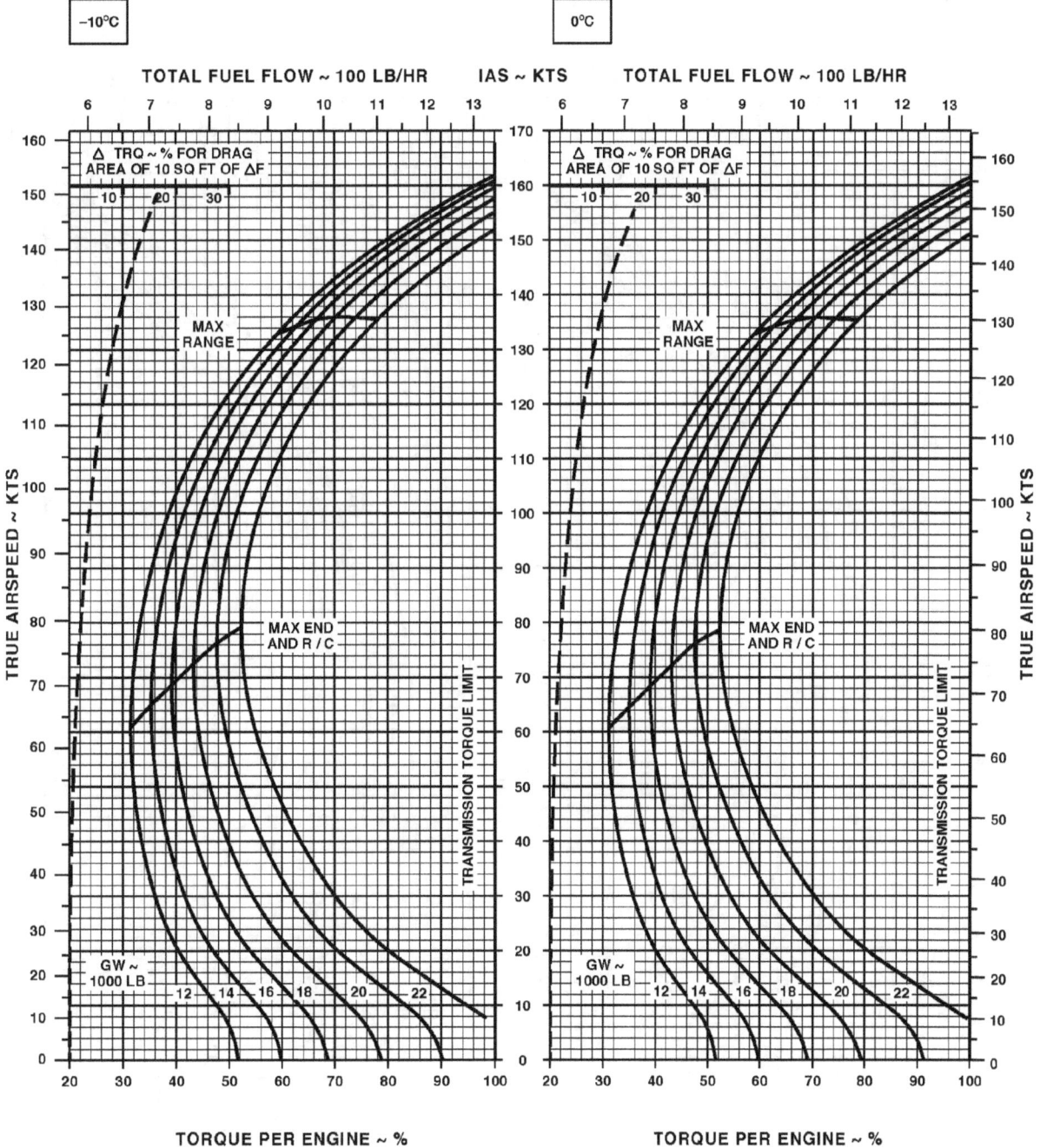

Figure 7-7. Cruise - Pressure Altitude Sea Level (Sheet 3 of 6)

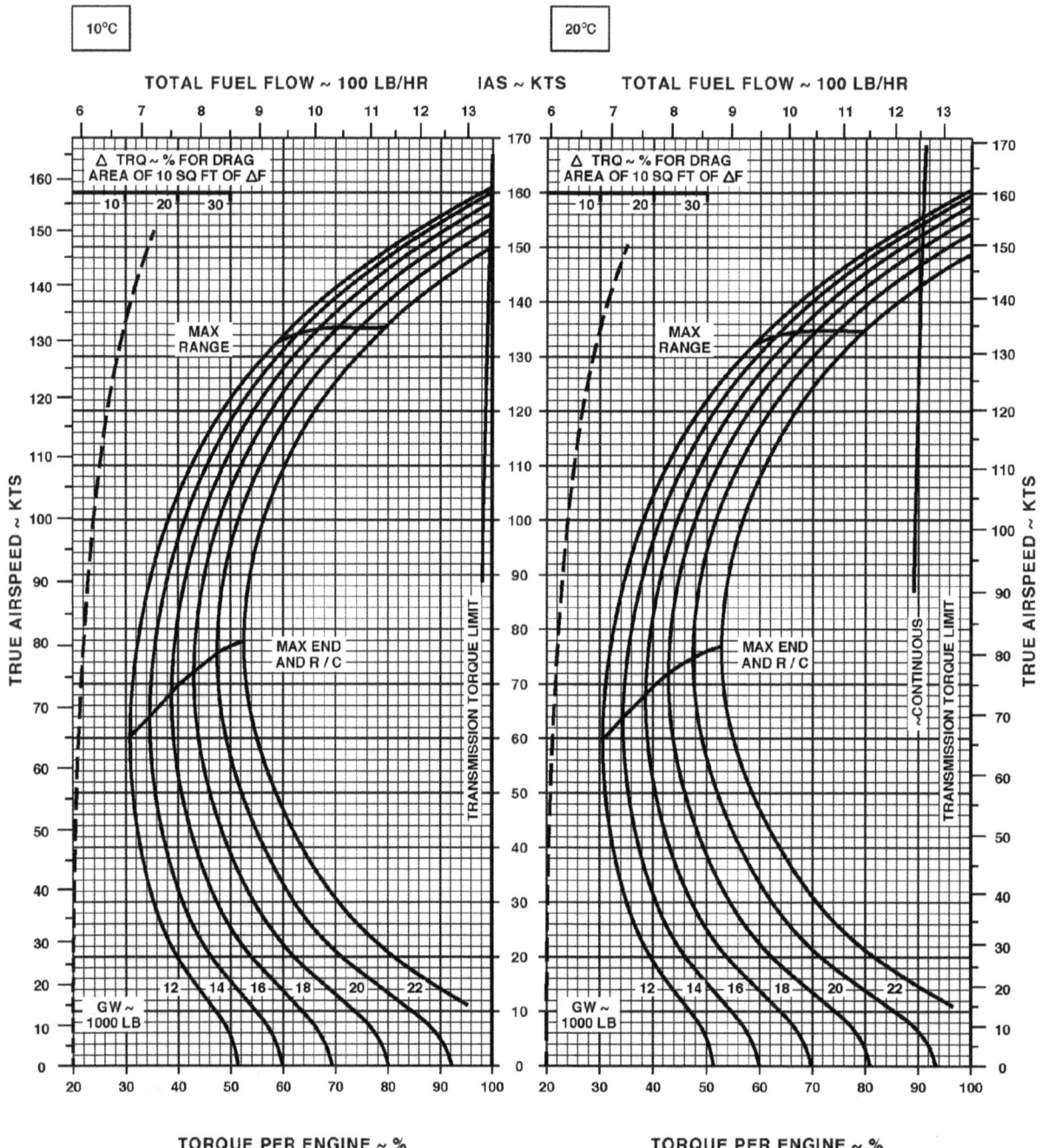

Figure 7-7. Cruise - Pressure Altitude Sea Level (Sheet 4 of 6)

CRUISE
CLEAN CONFIGURATION
PRESS ALT: 0 FT

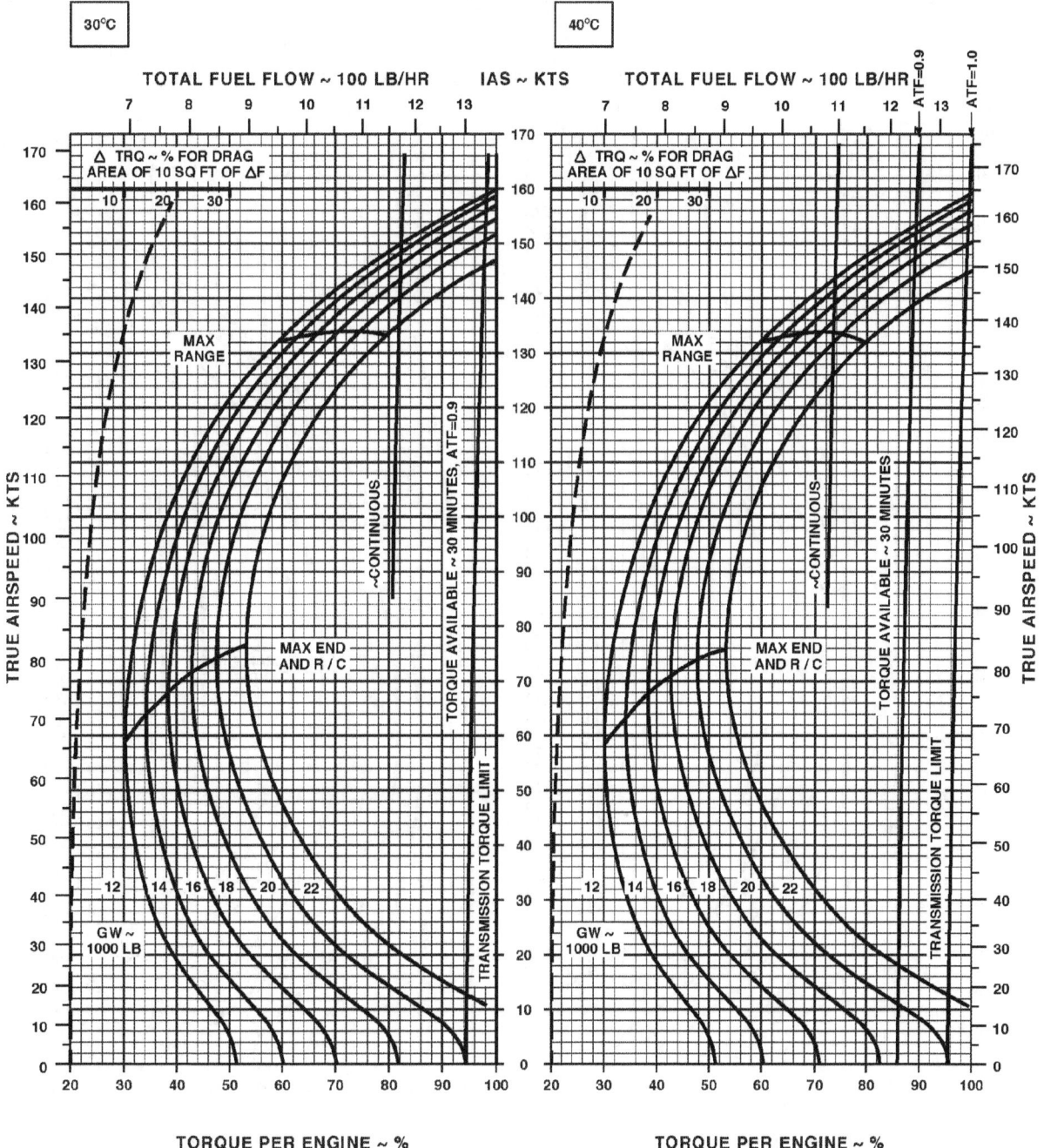

Figure 7-7. Cruise - Pressure Altitude Sea Level (Sheet 5 of 6)

CRUISE
CLEAN CONFIGURATION
PRESS ALT: 0 FT

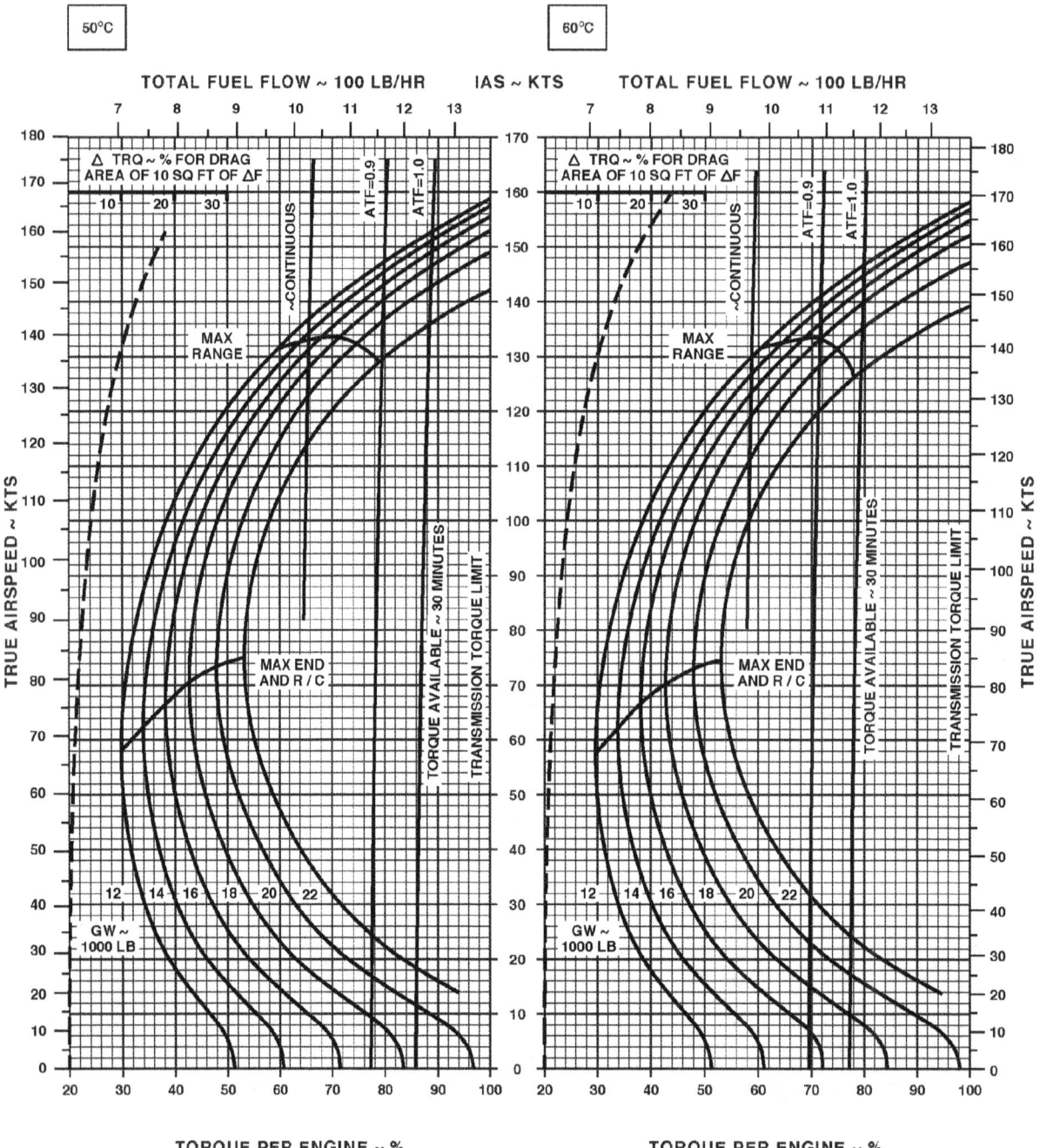

Figure 7-7. Cruise - Pressure Altitude Sea Level (Sheet 6 of 6)

CRUISE

PRESS ALT: 0 FT

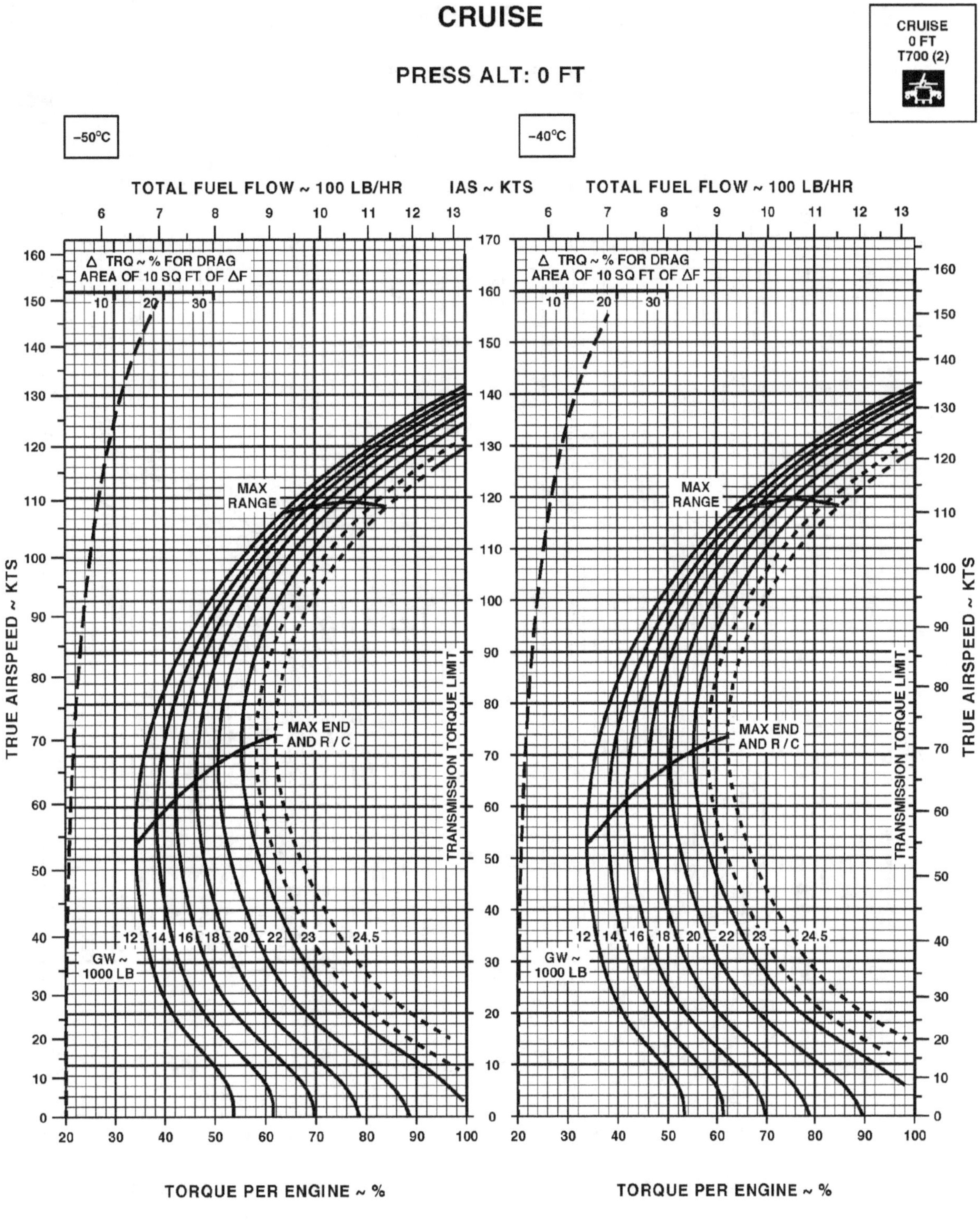

Figure 7-8. Cruise High Drag - Pressure Altitude Sea Level (Sheet 1 of 6)

CRUISE

PRESS ALT: 0 FT

Figure 7-8. Cruise High Drag - Pressure Altitude Sea Level (Sheet 2 of 6)

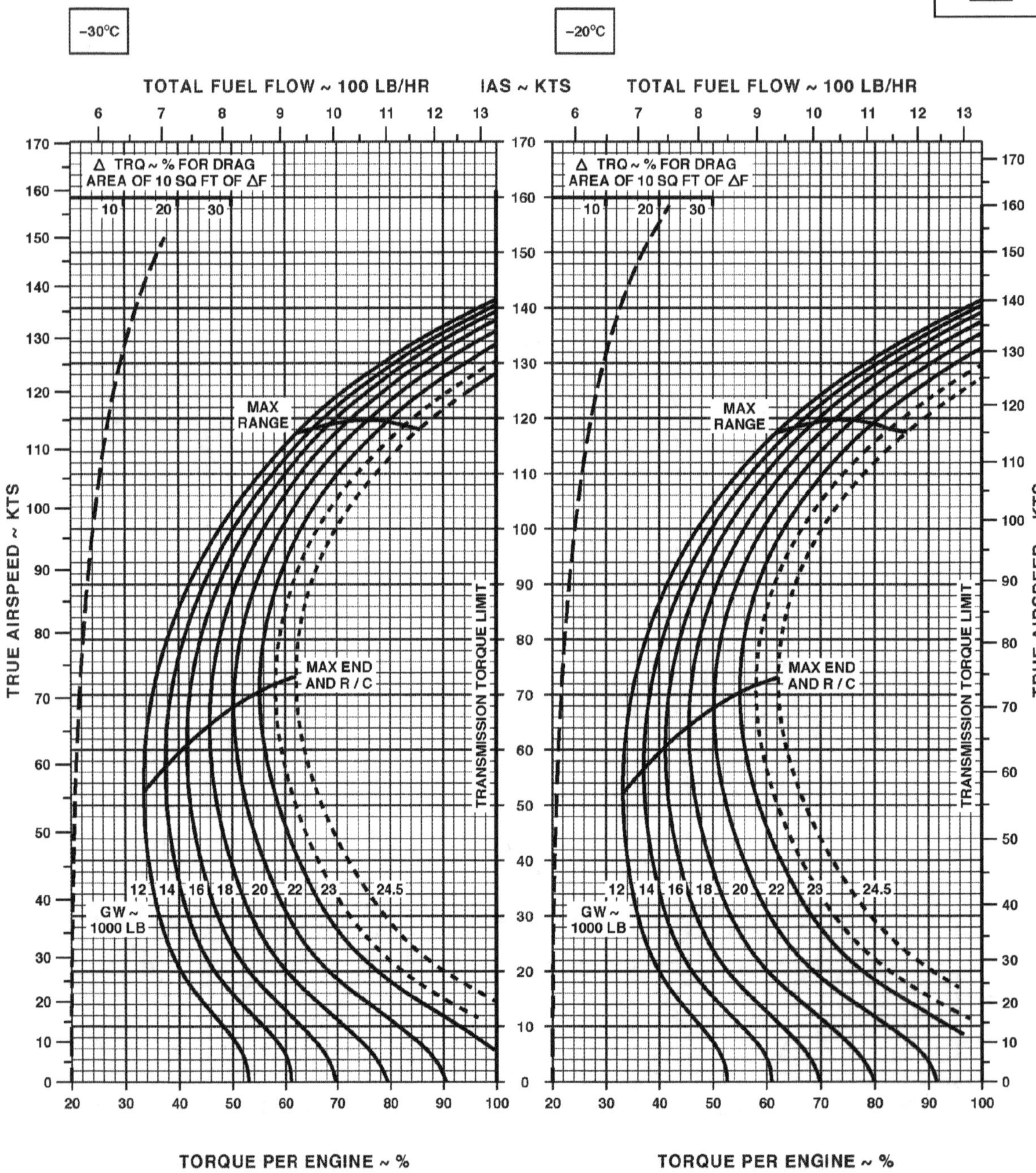

CRUISE

PRESS ALT: 0 FT

CRUISE
0 FT
T700 (2)

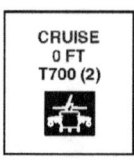

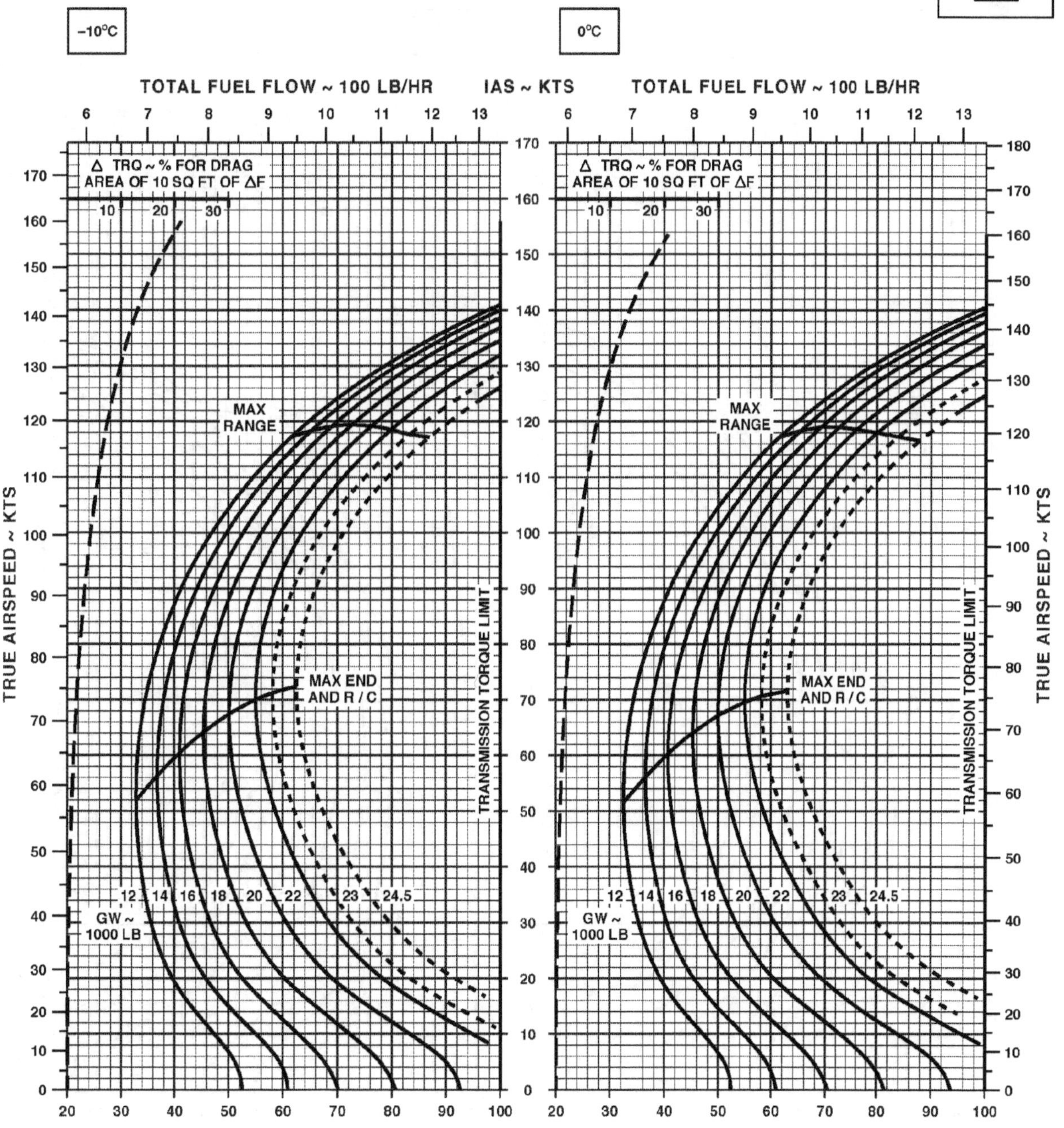

DATA BASE: FLIGHT TEST

AA0536
SA

Figure 7-8. Cruise High Drag - Pressure Altitude Sea Level (Sheet 3 of 6)

CRUISE

PRESS ALT: 0 FT

CRUISE
0 FT
T700 (2)

DATA BASE: FLIGHT TEST

AA0537
SA

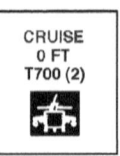

Figure 7-8. Cruise High Drag - Pressure Altitude Sea Level (Sheet 4 of 6)

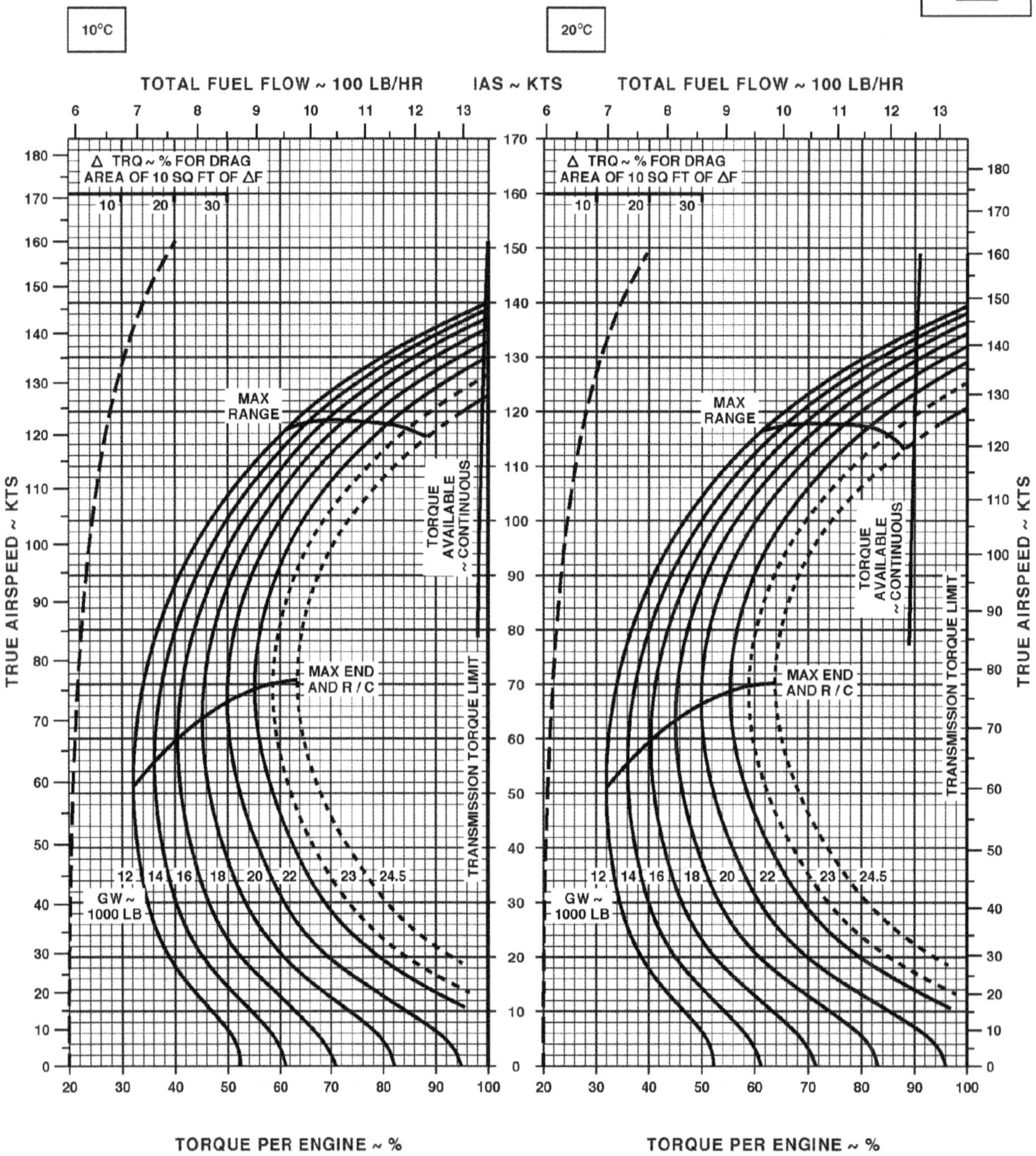

CRUISE

PRESS ALT: 0 FT

CRUISE
0 FT
T700 (2)

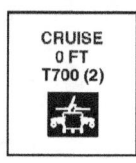

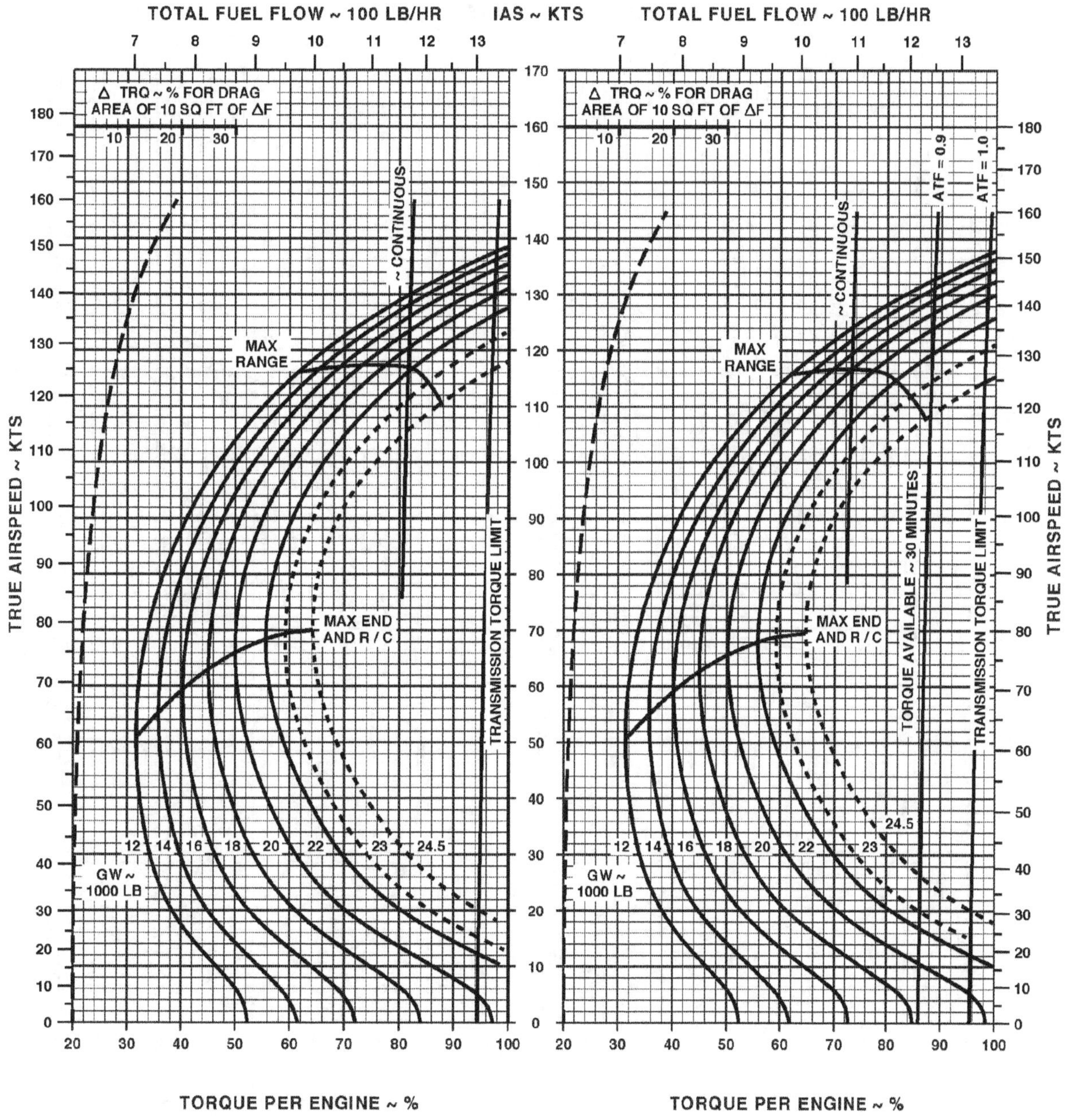

DATA BASE: FLIGHT TEST

AA0538
SA

Figure 7-8. Cruise High Drag - Pressure Altitude Sea Level (Sheet 5 of 6)

CRUISE

PRESS ALT: 0 FT

Figure 7-8. Cruise High Drag - Pressure Altitude Sea Level (Sheet 6 of 6)

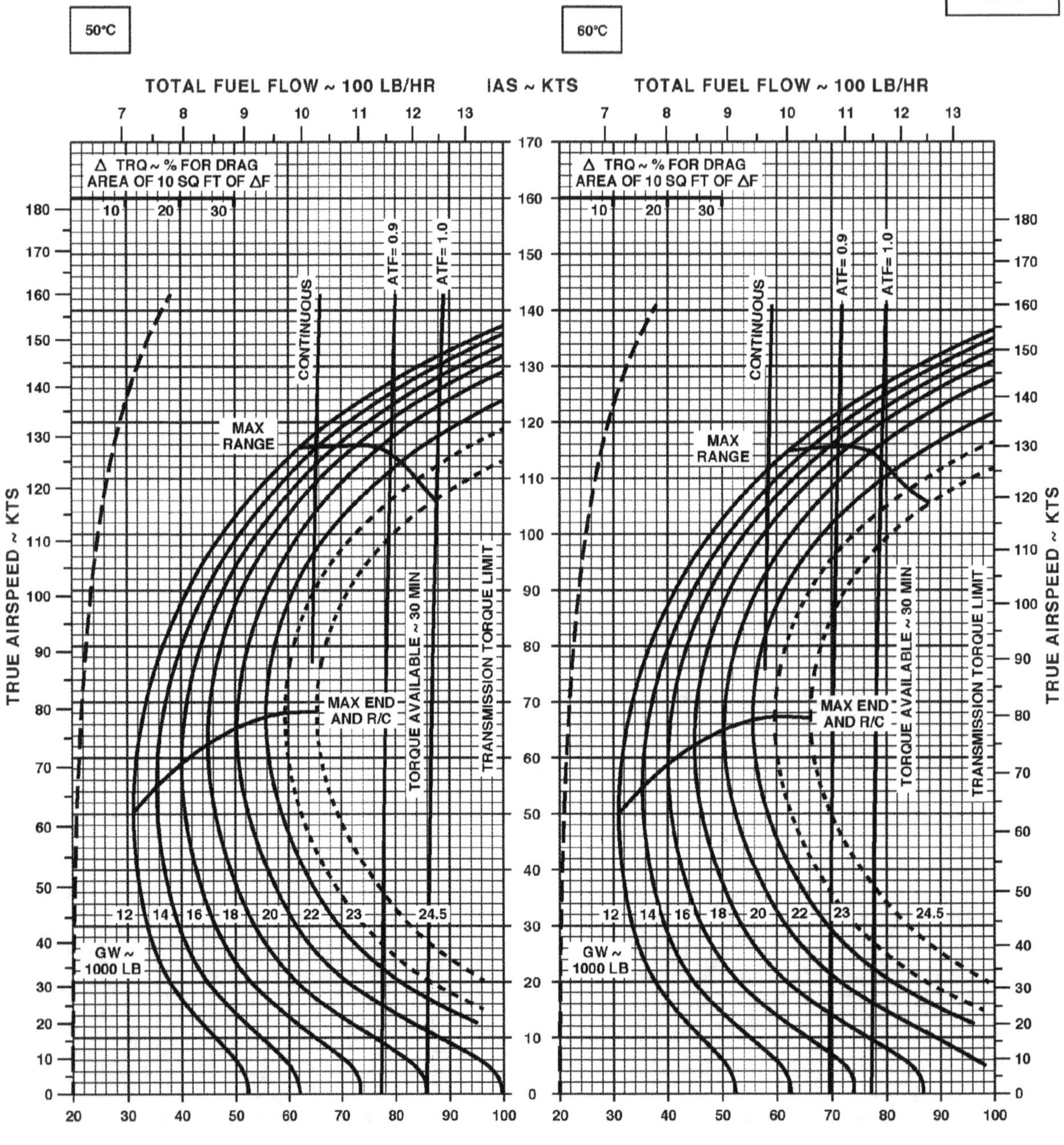

DATA BASE: FLIGHT TEST

CRUISE
CLEAN CONFIGURATION
PRESS ALT: 2000 FT

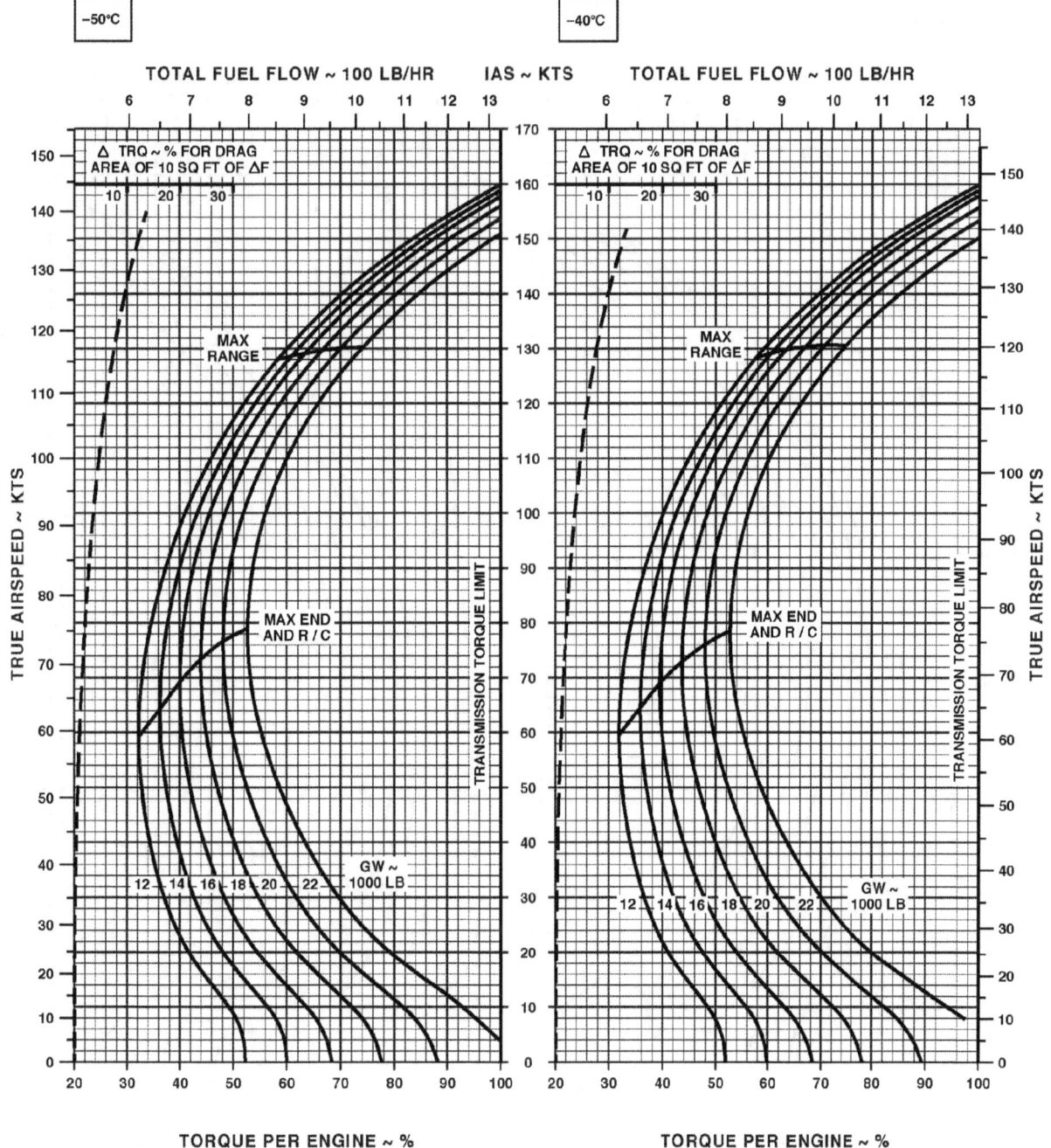

Figure 7-9. Cruise - Pressure Altitude 2,000 Feet (Sheet 1 of 6)

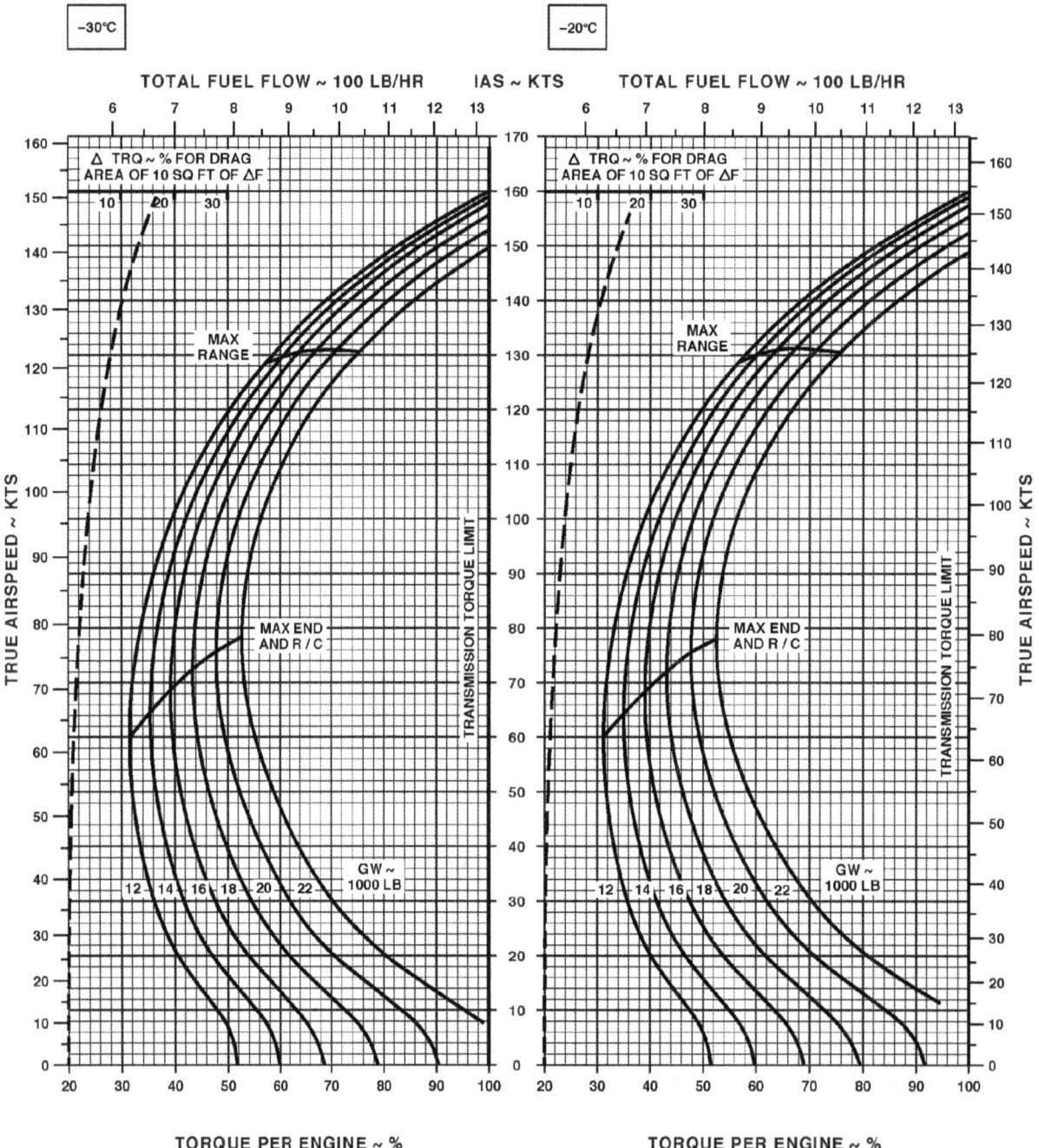

Figure 7-9. Cruise - Pressure Altitude 2,000 Feet (Sheet 2 of 6)

CRUISE
CLEAN CONFIGURATION
PRESS ALT: 2000 FT

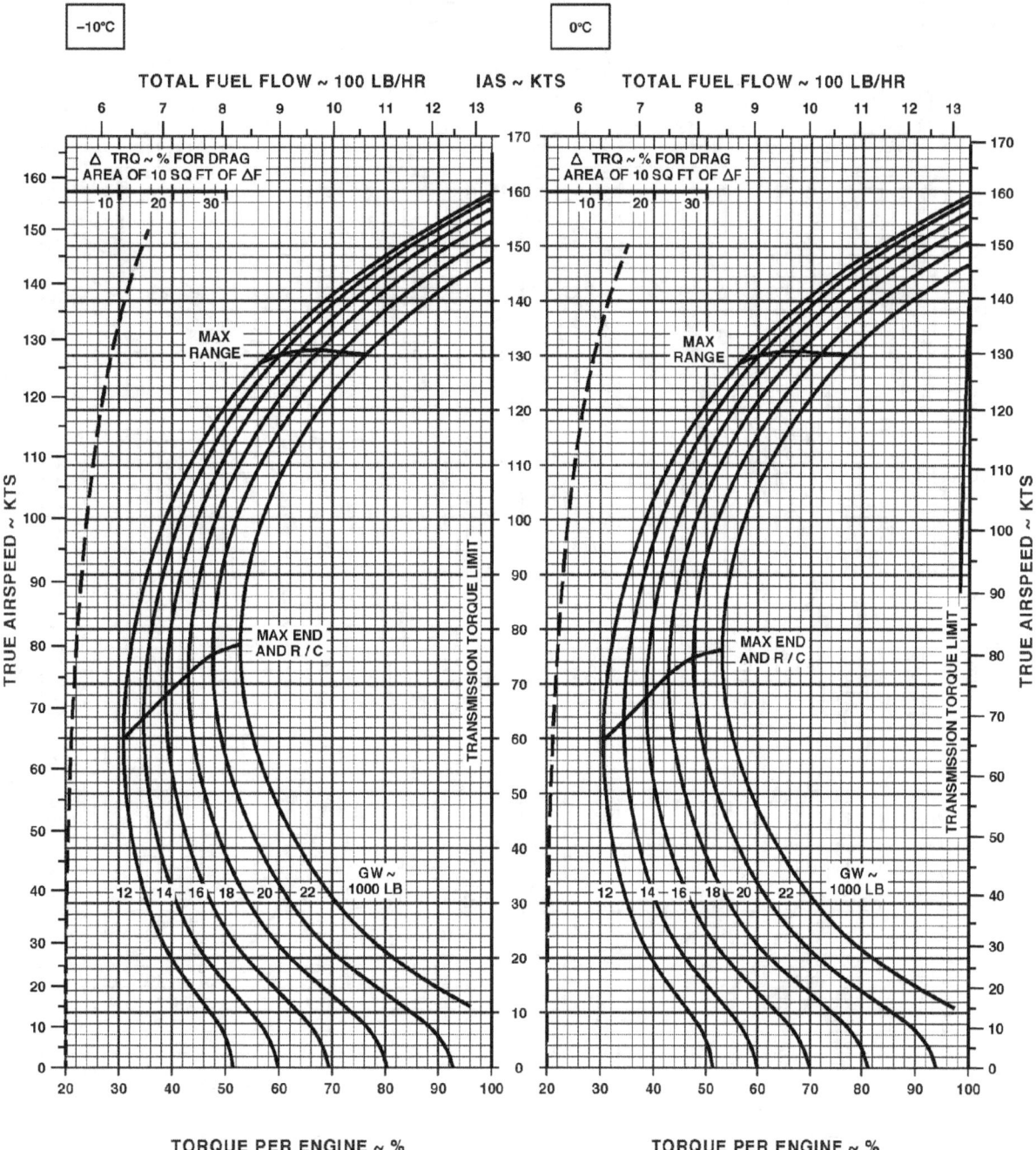

Figure 7-9. Cruise - Pressure Altitude 2,000 Feet (Sheet 3 of 6)

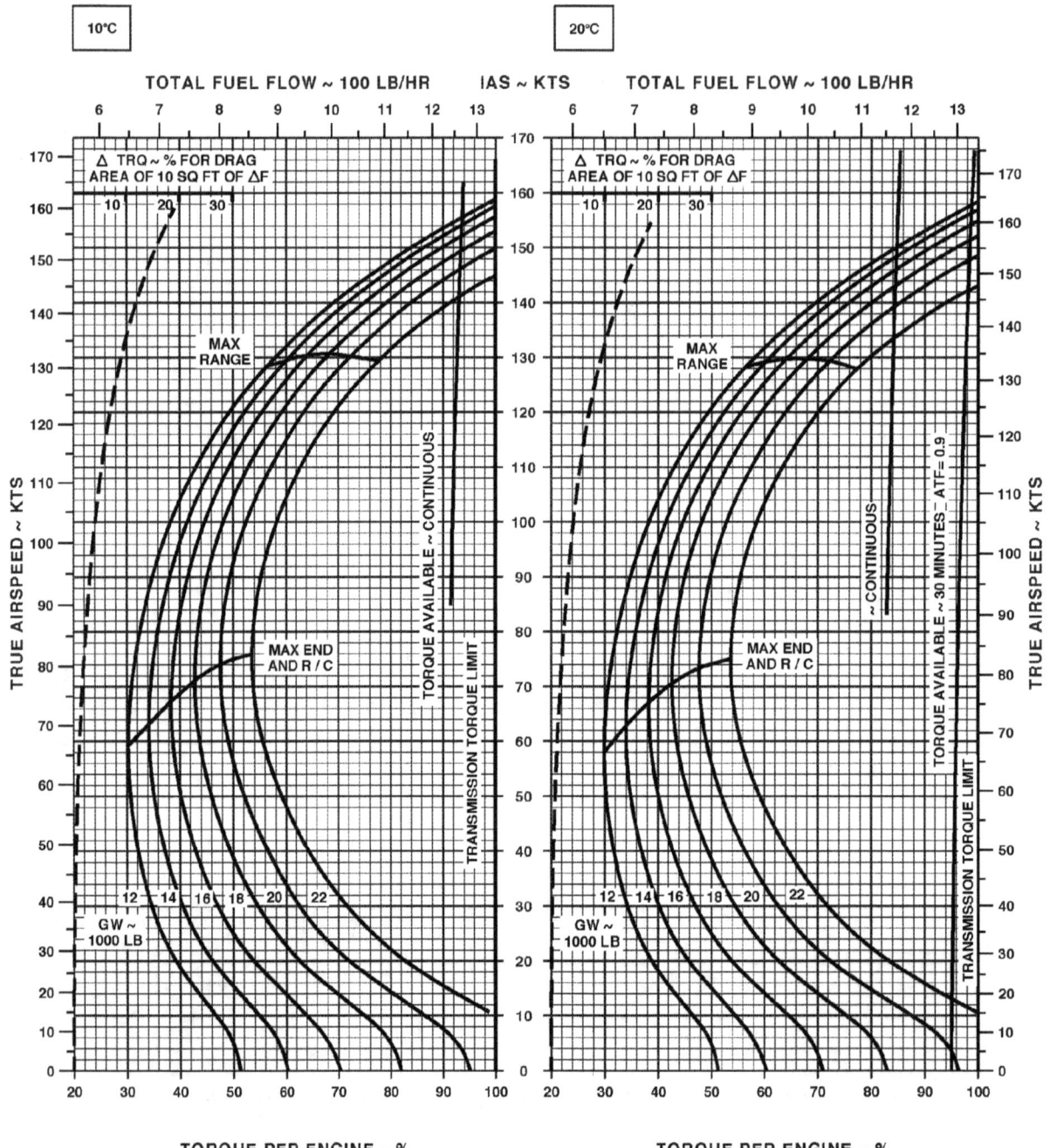

Figure 7-9. Cruise - Pressure Altitude 2,000 Feet (Sheet 4 of 6)

CRUISE
CLEAN CONFIGURATION
PRESS ALT: 2000 FT

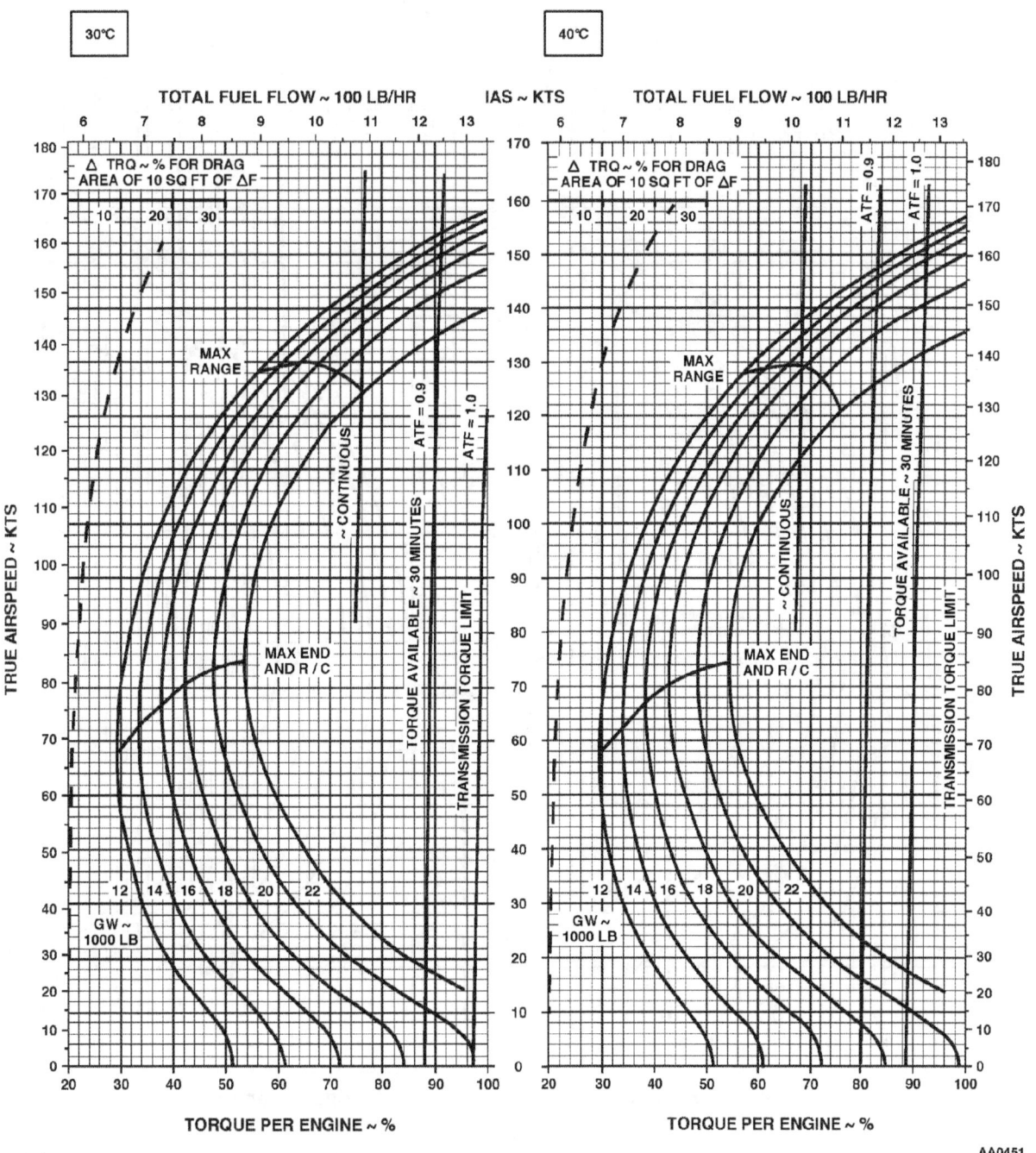

Figure 7-9. Cruise - Pressure Altitude 2,000 Feet (Sheet 5 of 6)

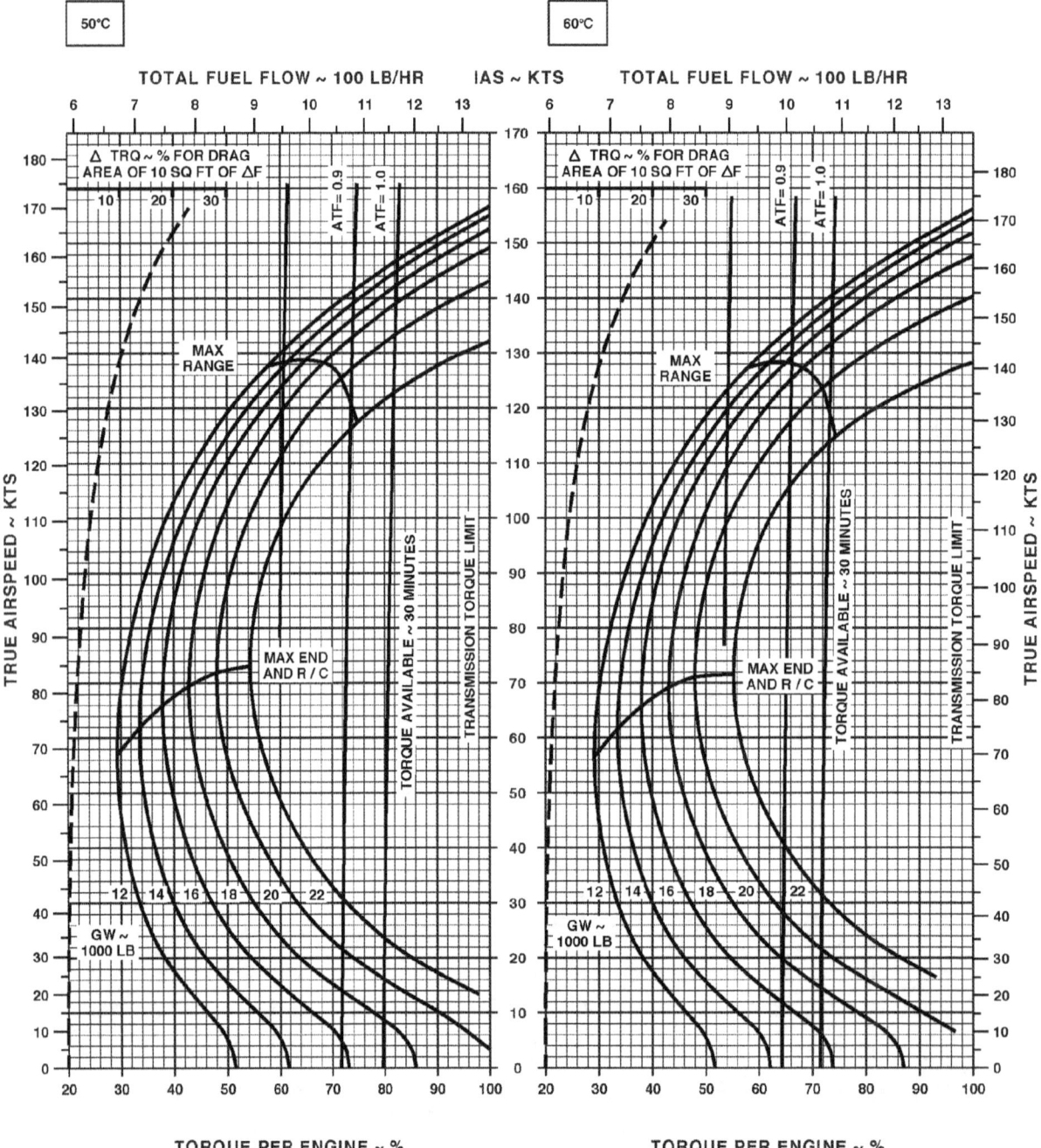

Figure 7-9. Cruise - Pressure Altitude 2,000 Feet (Sheet 6 of 6)

CRUISE

PRESS ALT: 2000 FT

CRUISE
2000 FT
T700 (2)

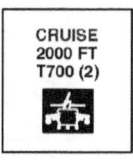

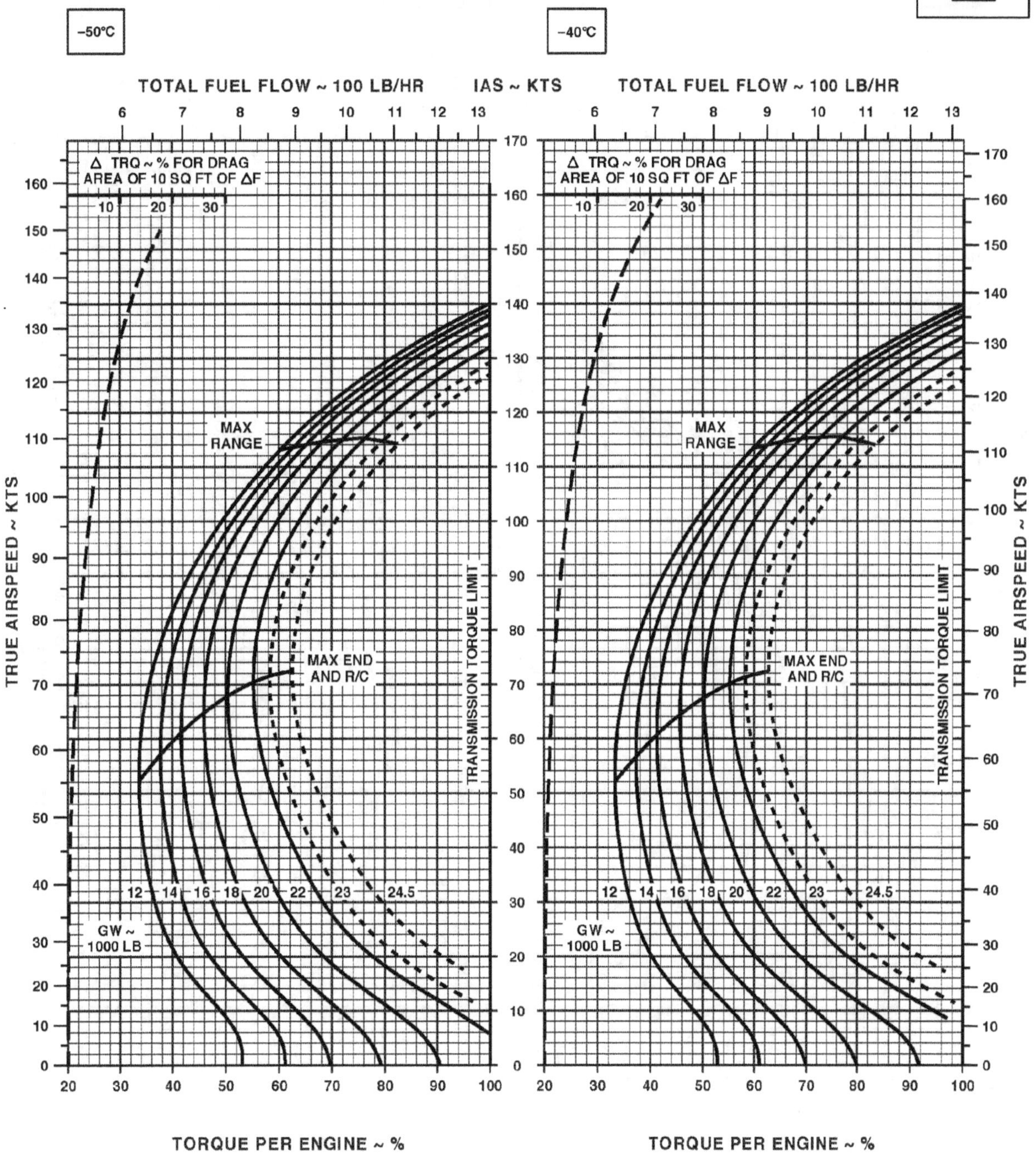

DATA BASE: FLIGHT TEST

AA0540

Figure 7-10. Cruise High Drag - Pressure Altitude 2,000 Feet (Sheet 1 of 6)

CRUISE

PRESS ALT: 2000 FT

CRUISE
2000 FT
T700 (2)

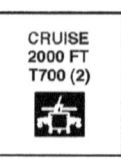

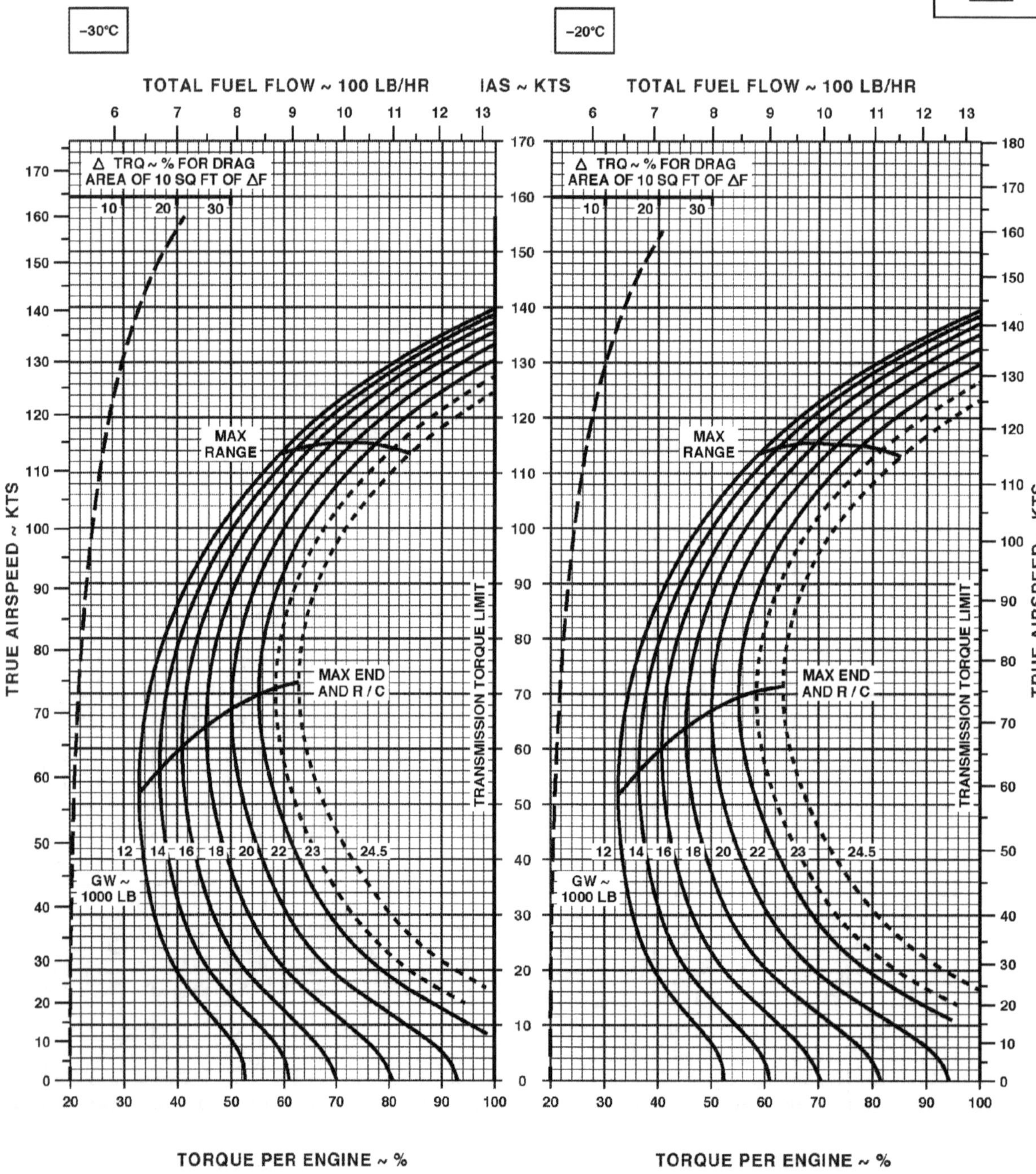

DATA BASE: FLIGHT TEST

AA0541

Figure 7-10. Cruise High Drag - Pressure Altitude 2,000 Feet (Sheet 2 of 6)

CRUISE

PRESS ALT: 2000 FT

Figure 7-10. Cruise High Drag - Pressure Altitude 2,000 Feet (Sheet 3 of 6)

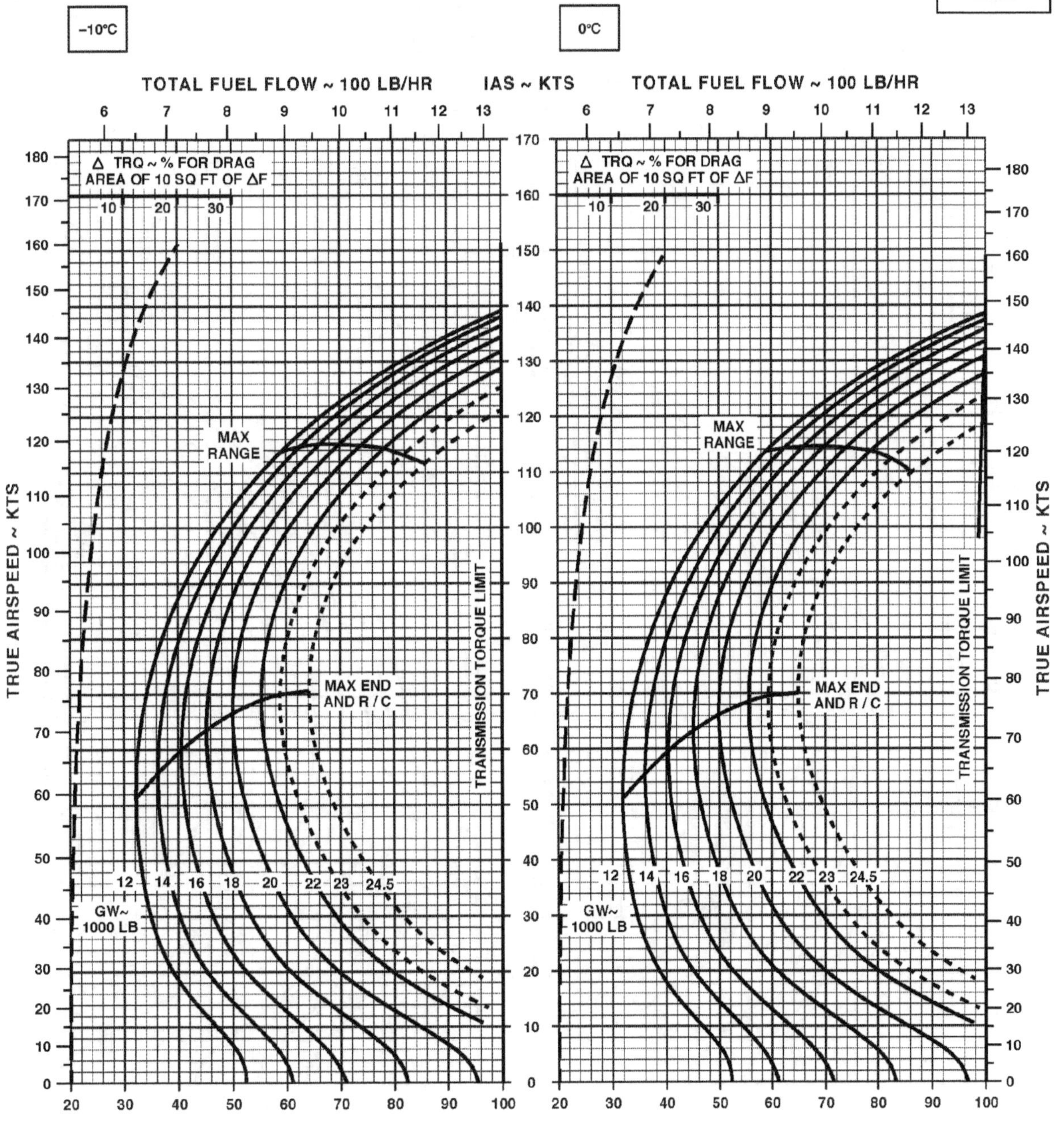

DATA BASE: FLIGHT TEST

CRUISE

PRESS ALT: 2000 FT

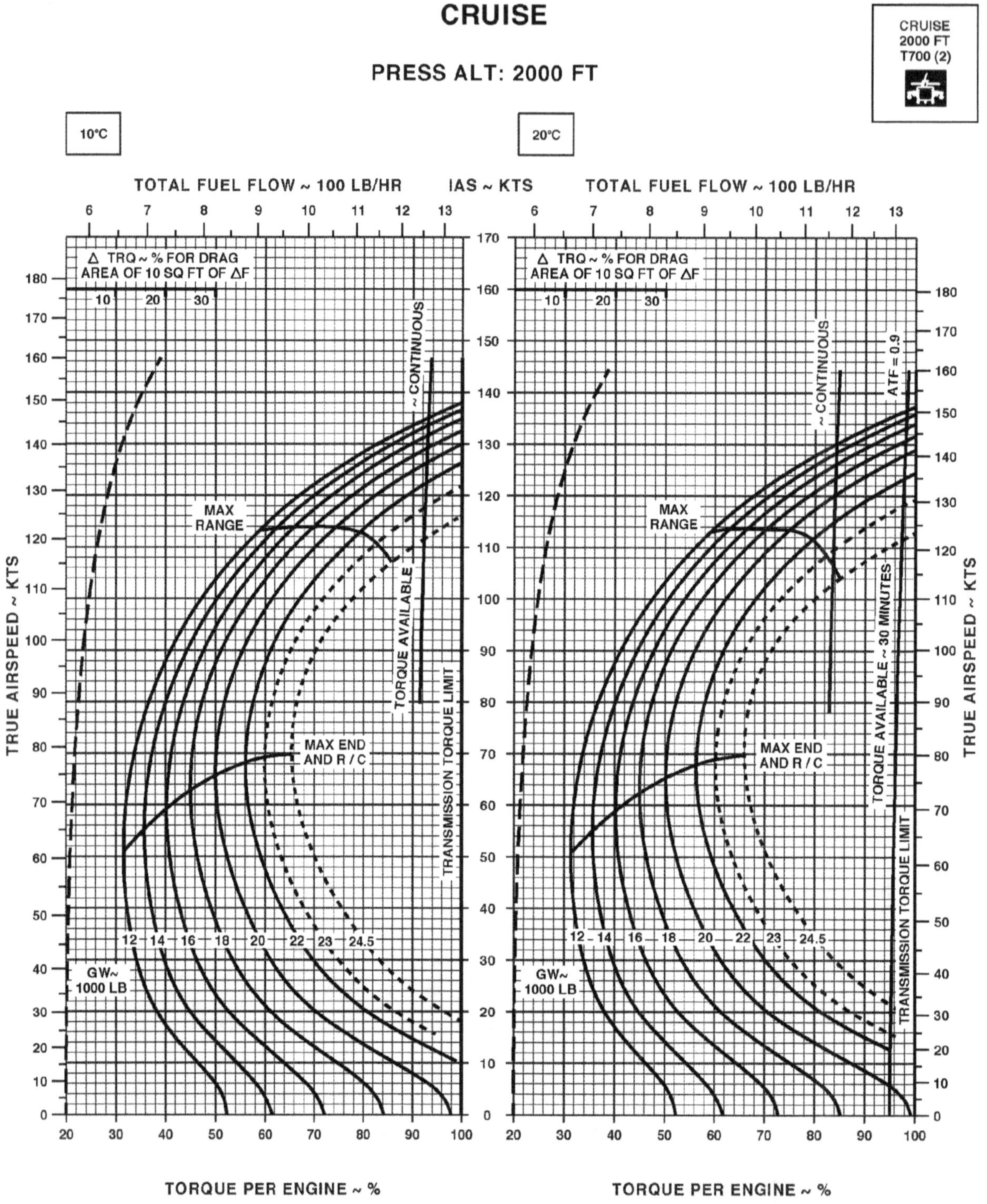

DATA BASE: FLIGHT TEST

AA0543
SA

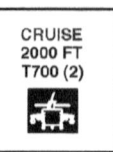

Figure 7-10. Cruise High Drag - Pressure Altitude 2,000 Feet (Sheet 4 of 6)

CRUISE

PRESS ALT: 2000 FT

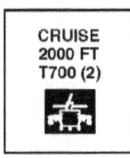

Figure 7-10. Cruise High Drag - Pressure Altitude 2,000 Feet (Sheet 5 of 6)

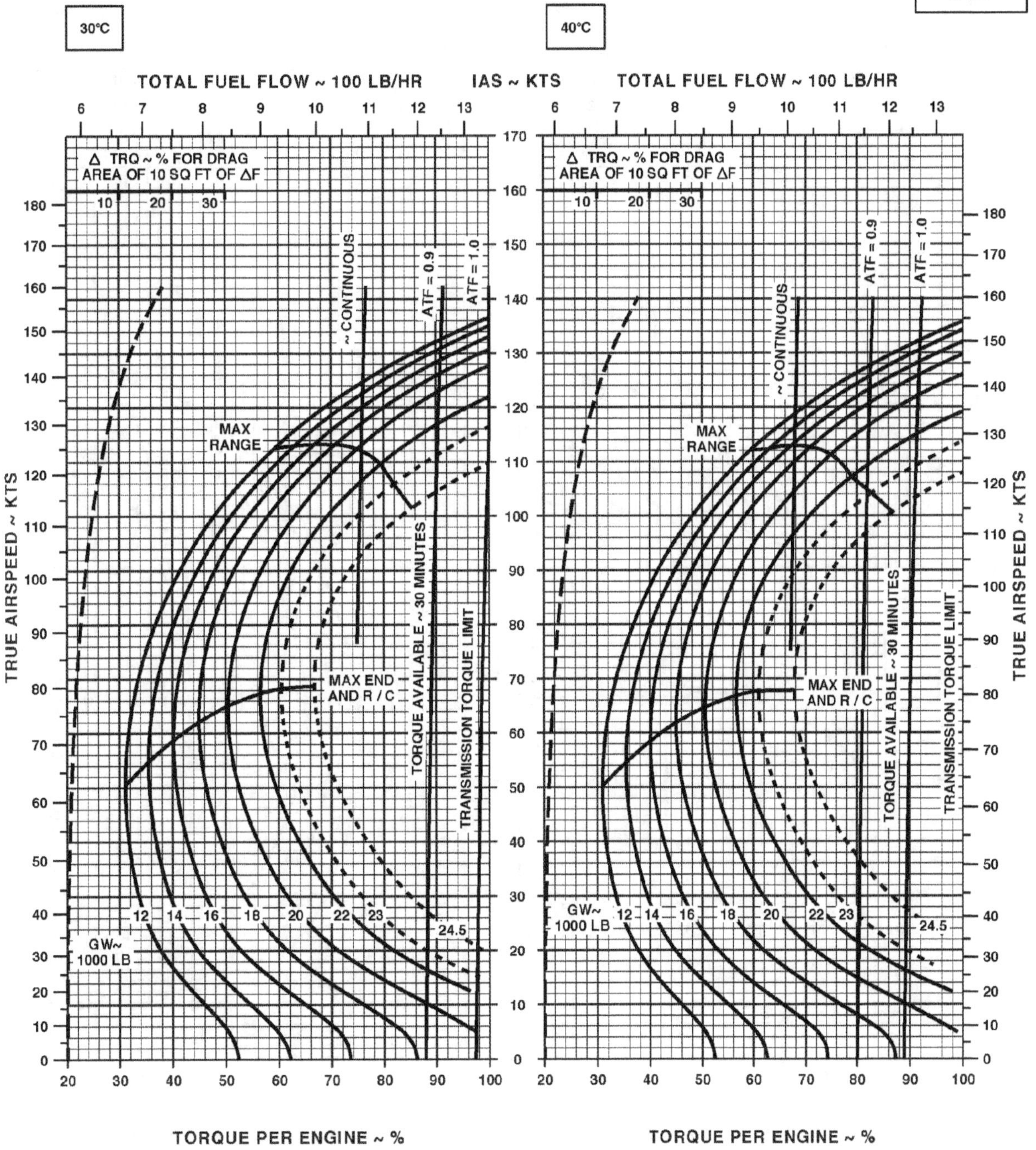

DATA BASE: FLIGHT TEST

CRUISE

PRESS ALT: 2000 FT

Figure 7-10. Cruise High Drag - Pressure Altitude 2,000 Feet (Sheet 6 of 6)

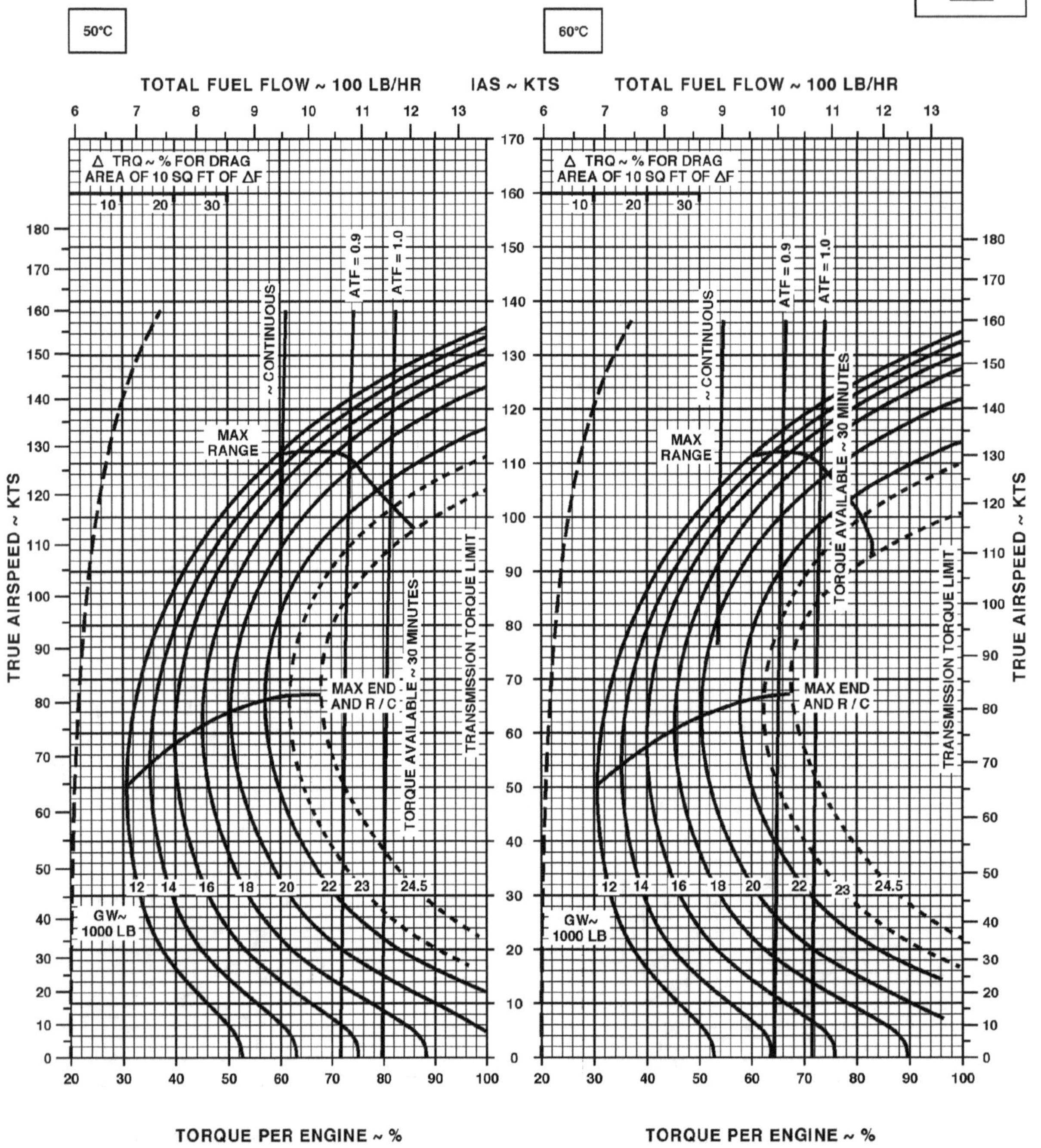

DATA BASE: FLIGHT TEST

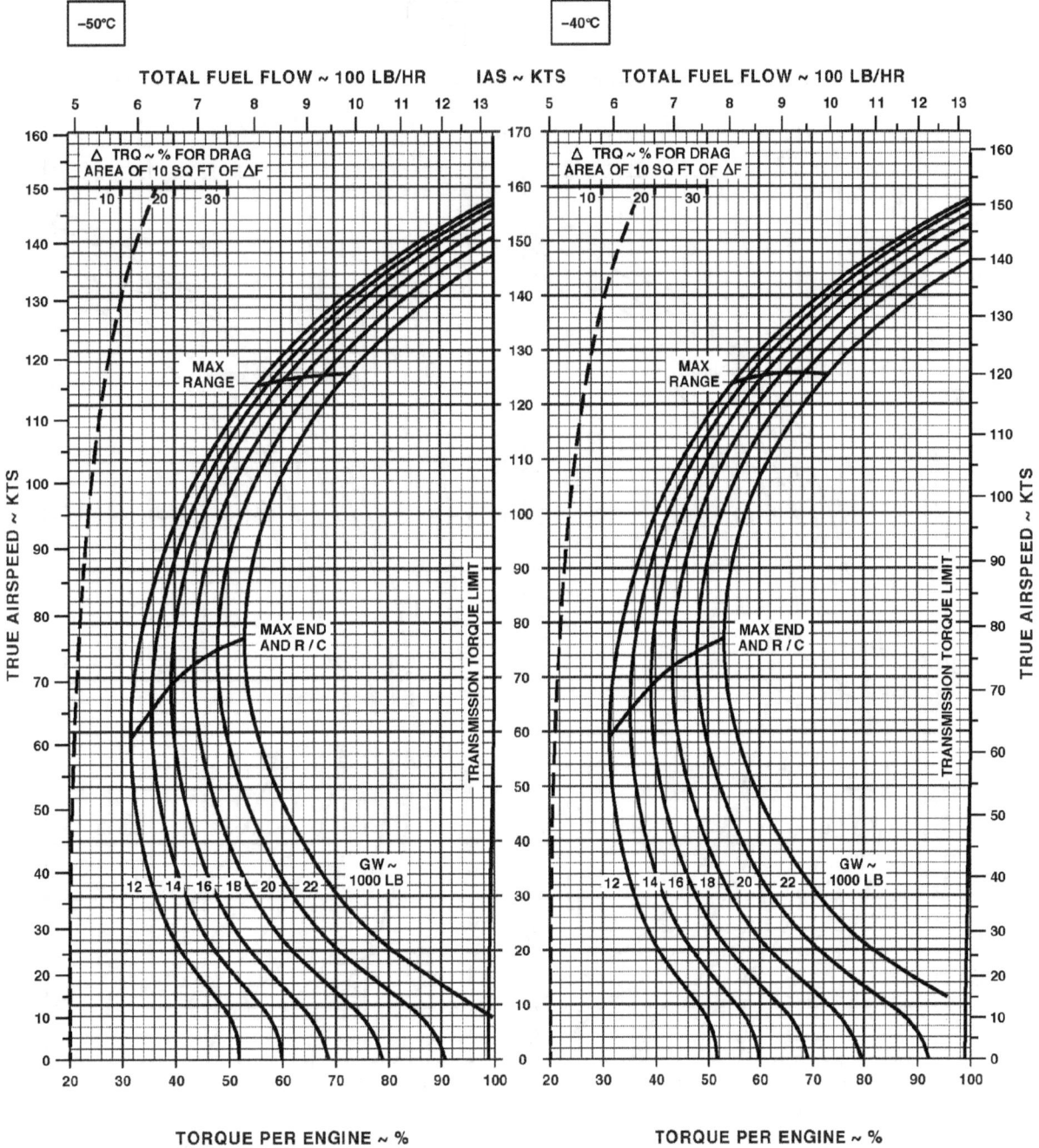

Figure 7-11. Cruise - Pressure Altitude 4,000 Feet (Sheet 1 of 6)

CRUISE
CLEAN CONFIGURATION
PRESS ALT: 4000 FT

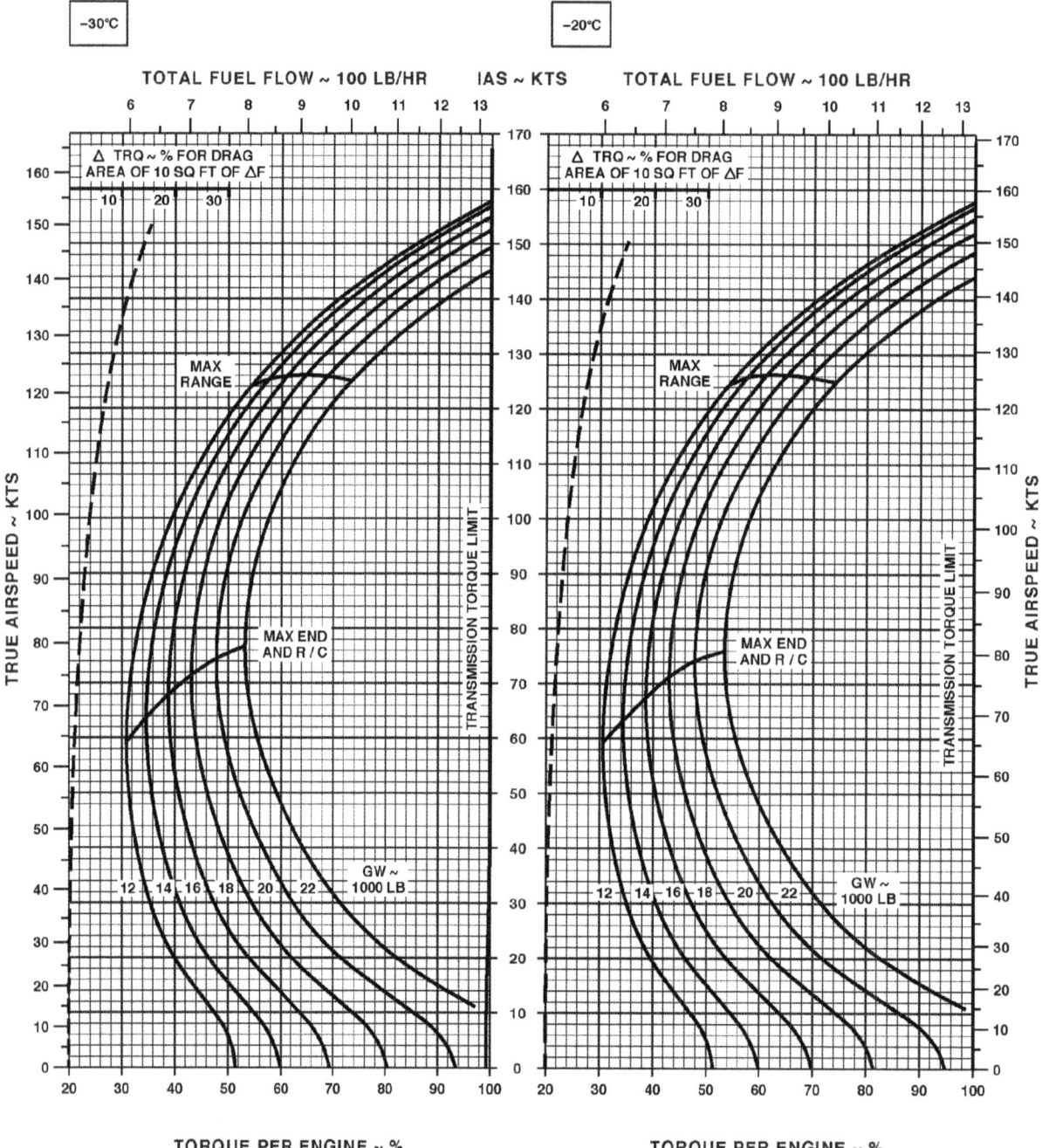

Figure 7-11. Cruise - Pressure Altitude 4,000 Feet (Sheet 2 of 6)

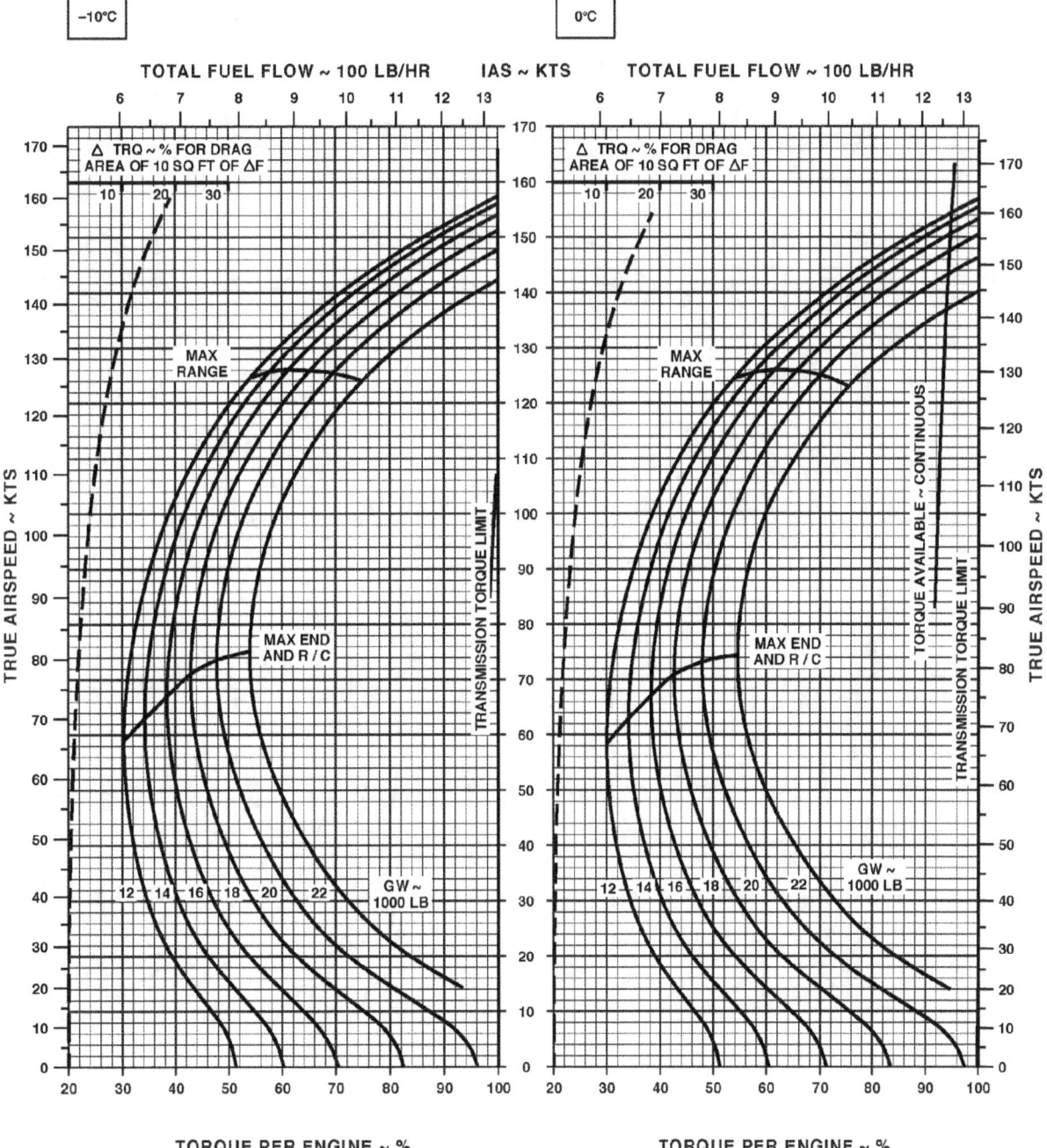

Figure 7-11. Cruise - Pressure Altitude 4,000 Feet (Sheet 3 of 6)

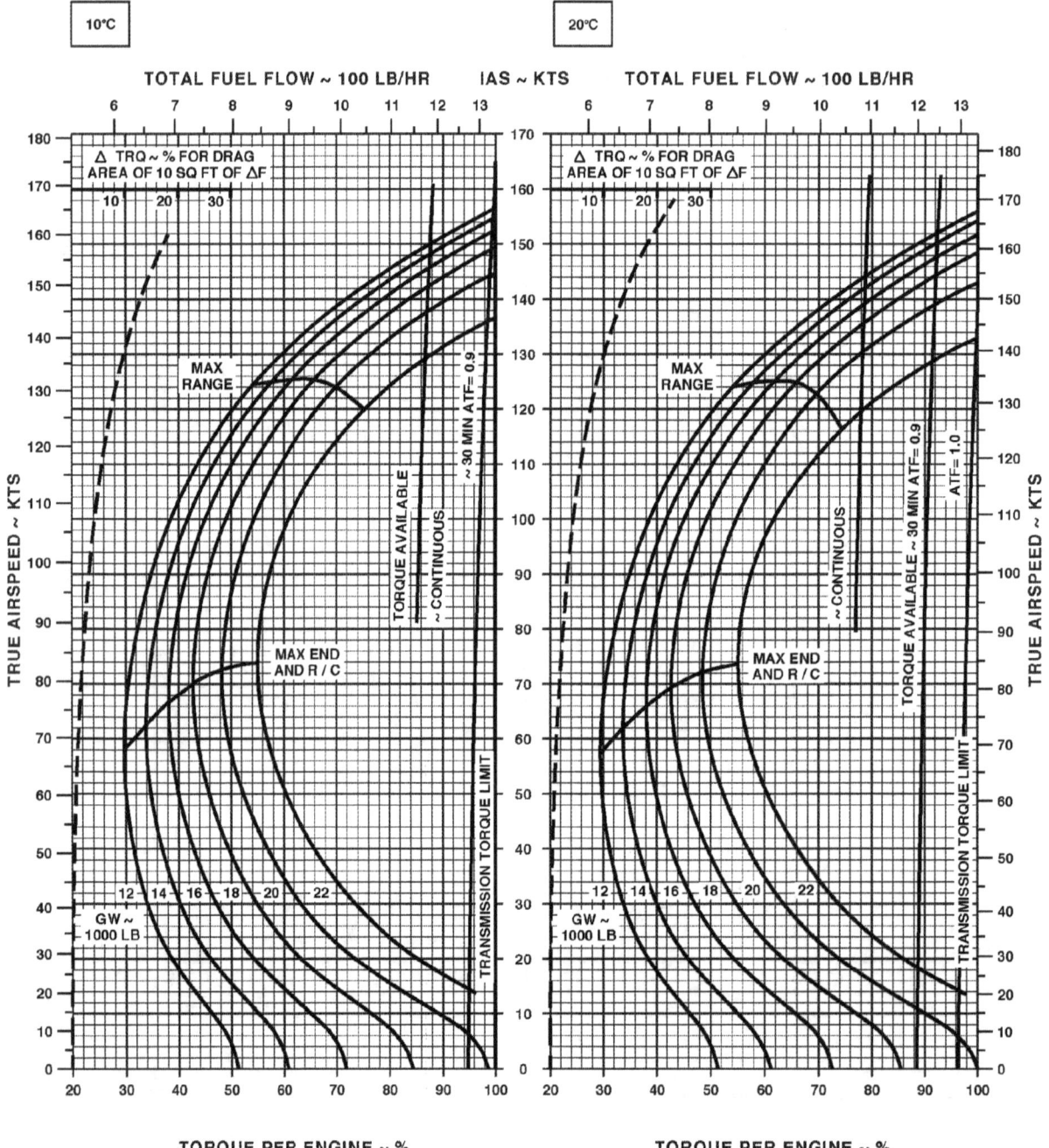

Figure 7-11. Cruise - Pressure Altitude 4,000 Feet (Sheet 4 of 6)

CRUISE
CLEAN CONFIGURATION
PRESS ALT: 4000 FT

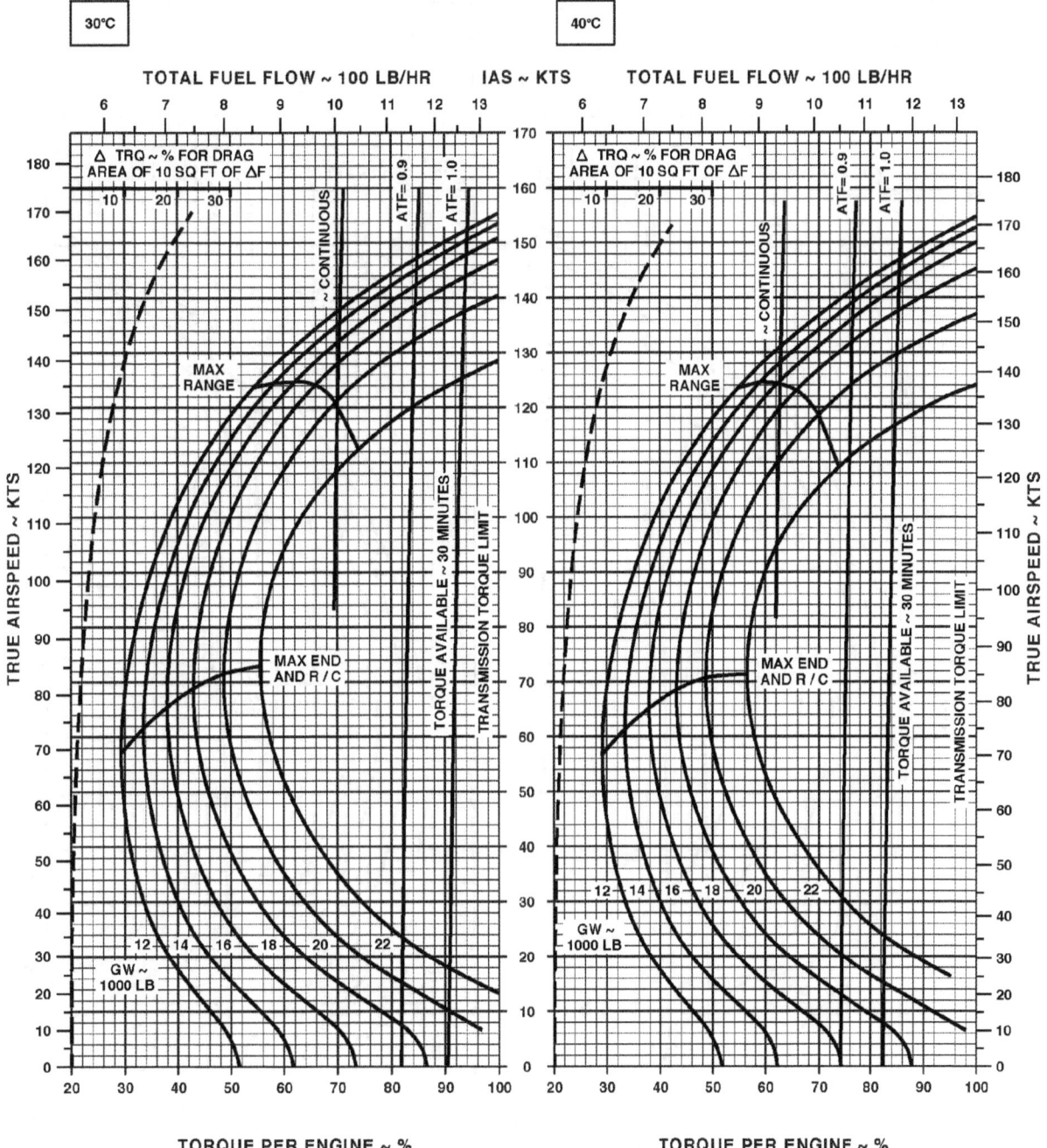

Figure 7-11. Cruise - Pressure Altitude 4,000 Feet (Sheet 5 of 6)

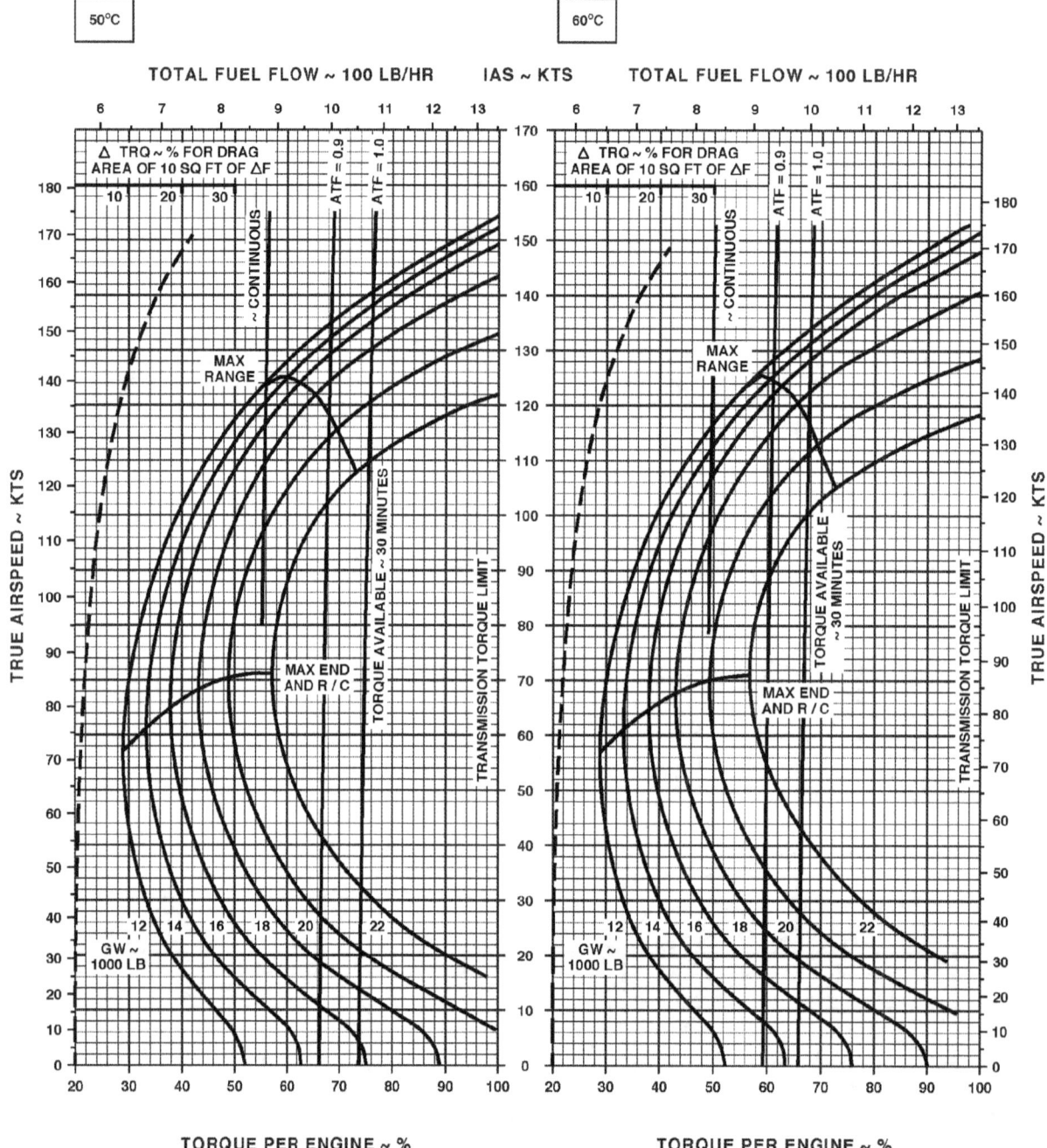

Figure 7-11. Cruise - Pressure Altitude 4,000 Feet (Sheet 6 of 6)

CRUISE

PRESS ALT: 4000 FT

CRUISE
4000 FT
T700 (2)

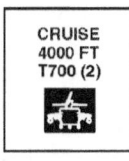

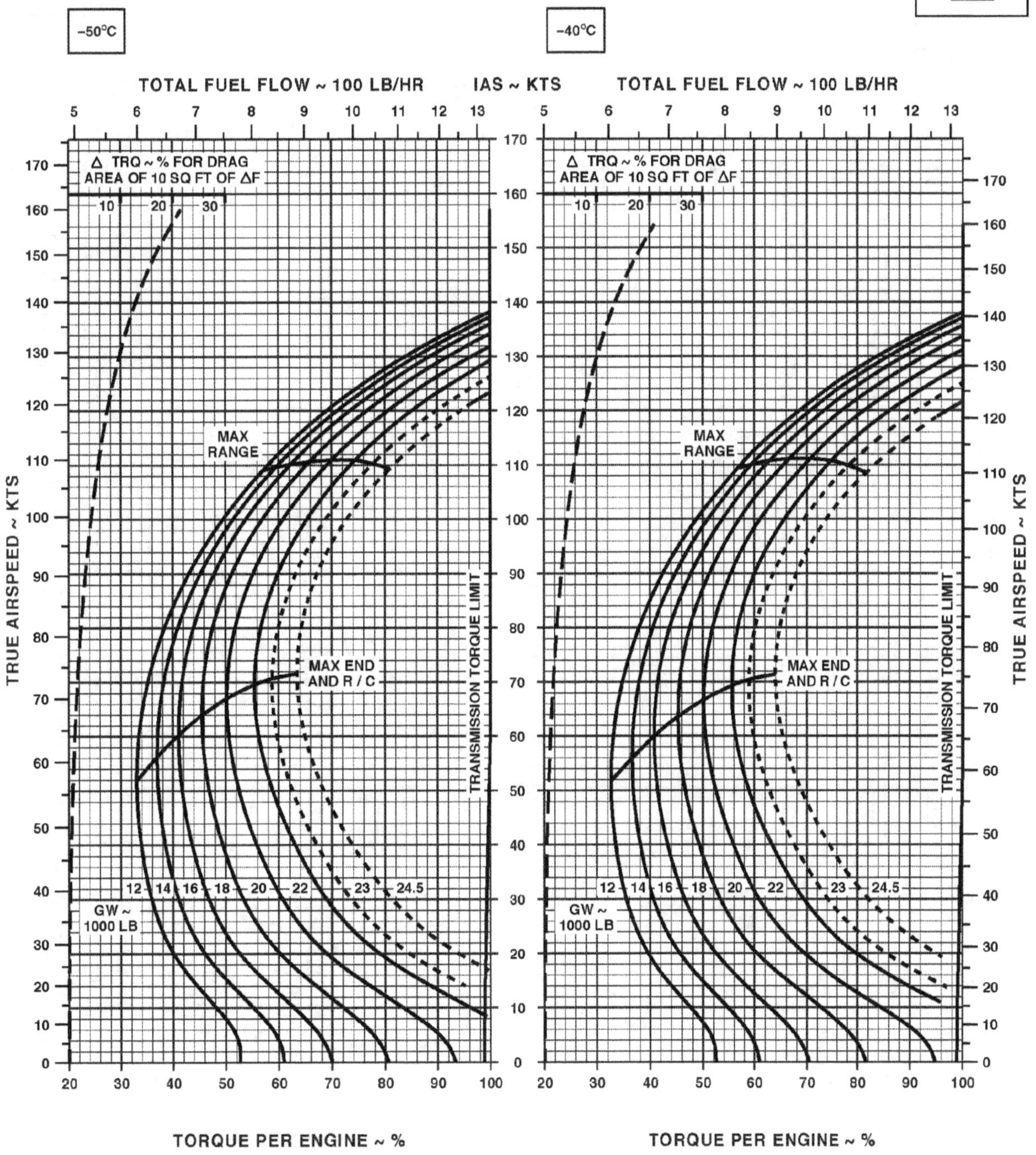

DATA BASE: FLIGHT TEST

AA0546
SA

Figure 7-12. Cruise High Drag - Pressure Altitude 4,000 Feet (Sheet 1 of 6)

CRUISE

PRESS ALT: 4000 FT

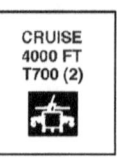

Figure 7-12. Cruise High Drag - Pressure Altitude 4,000 Feet (Sheet 2 of 6)

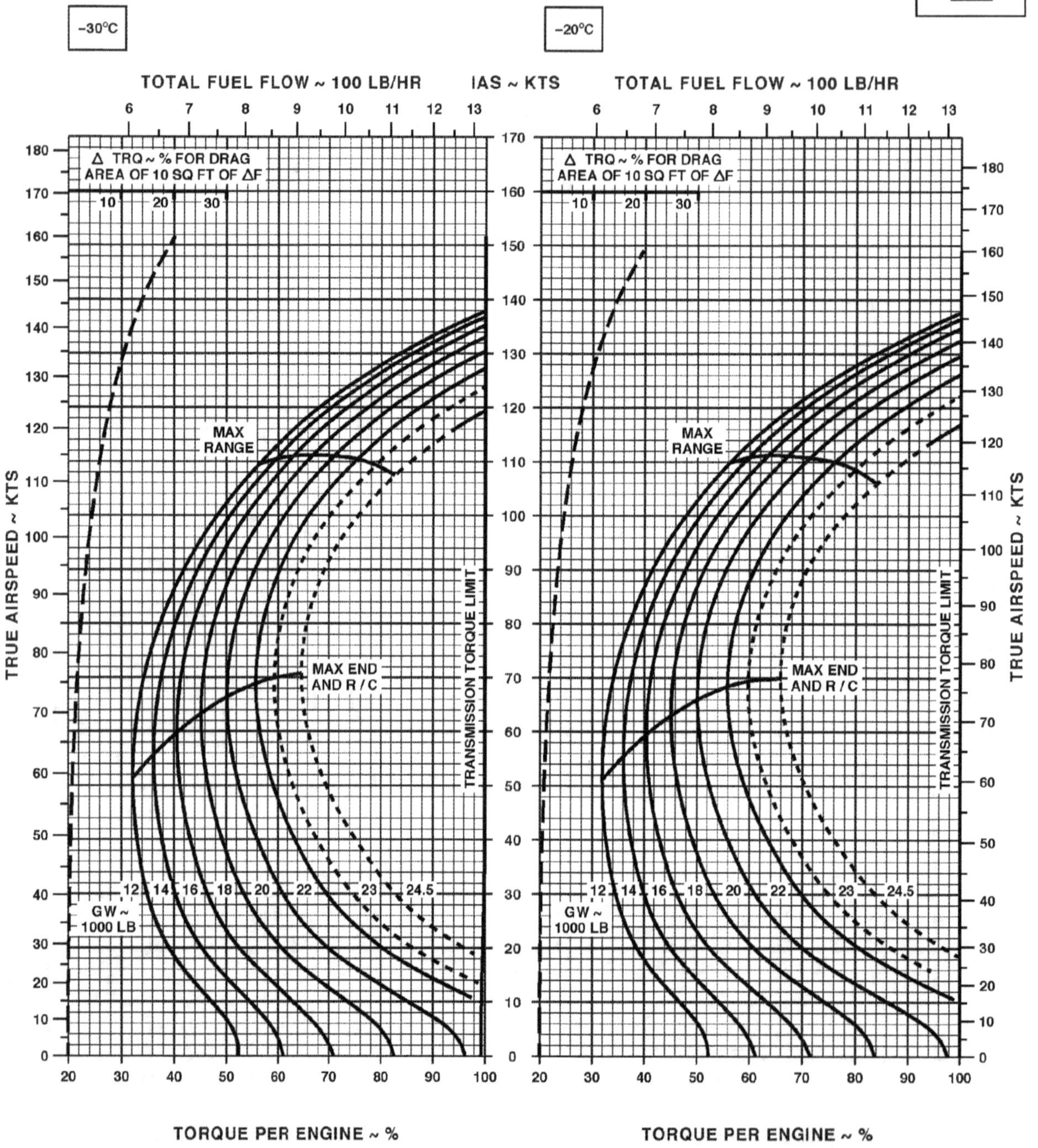

DATA BASE: FLIGHT TEST

CRUISE

PRESS ALT: 4000 FT

DATA BASE: FLIGHT TEST

AA0548
SA

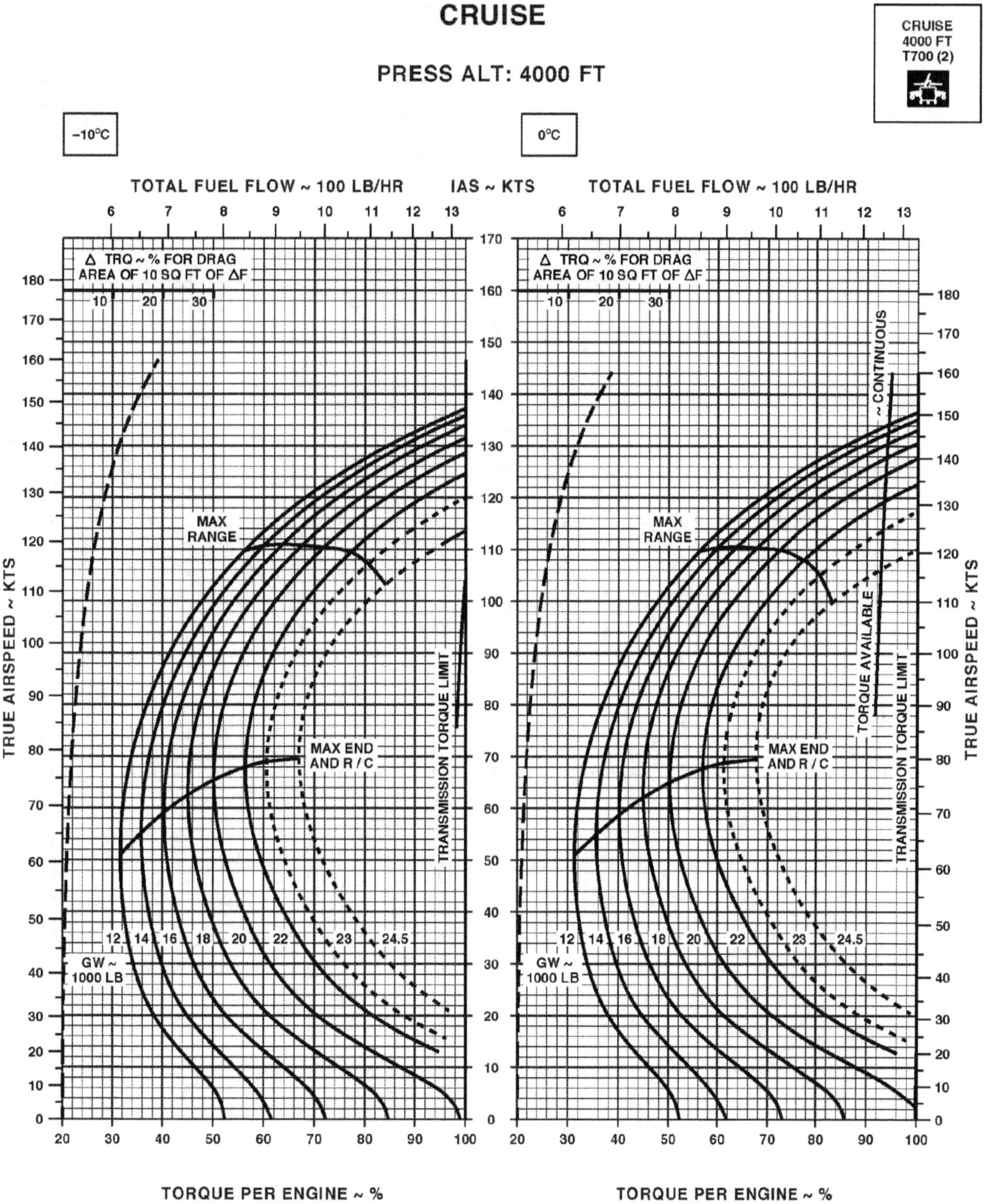

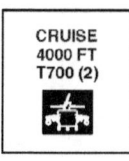

Figure 7-12. Cruise High Drag - Pressure Altitude 4,000 Feet (Sheet 3 of 6)

CRUISE

PRESS ALT: 4000 FT

Figure 7-12. Cruise High Drag - Pressure Altitude 4,000 Feet (Sheet 4 of 6)

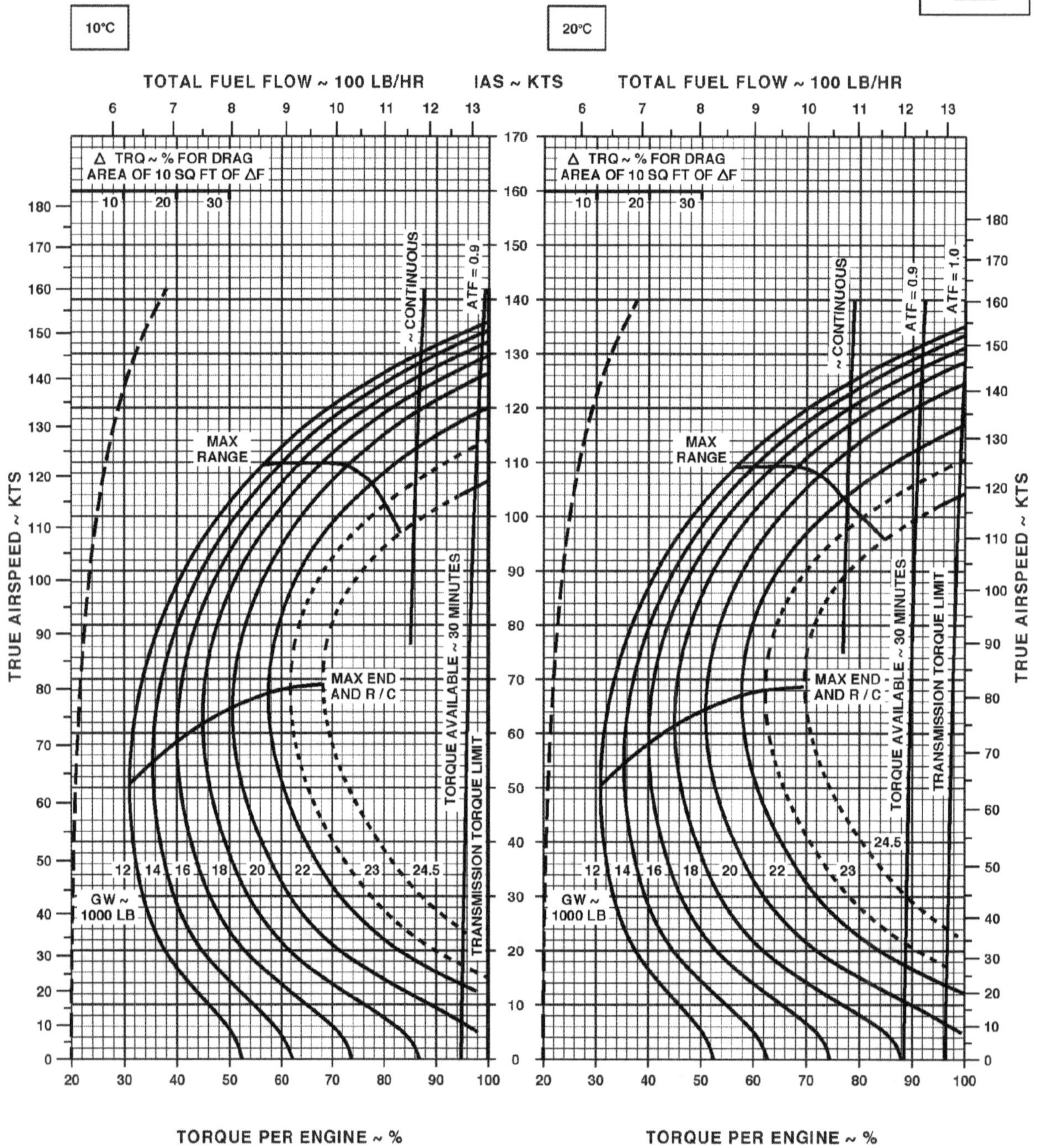

DATA BASE: FLIGHT TEST

CRUISE

PRESS ALT: 4000 FT

CRUISE
4000 FT
T700 (2)

DATA BASE: FLIGHT TEST

AA0550

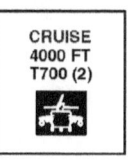

Figure 7-12. Cruise High Drag - Pressure Altitude 4,000 Feet (Sheet 5 of 6)

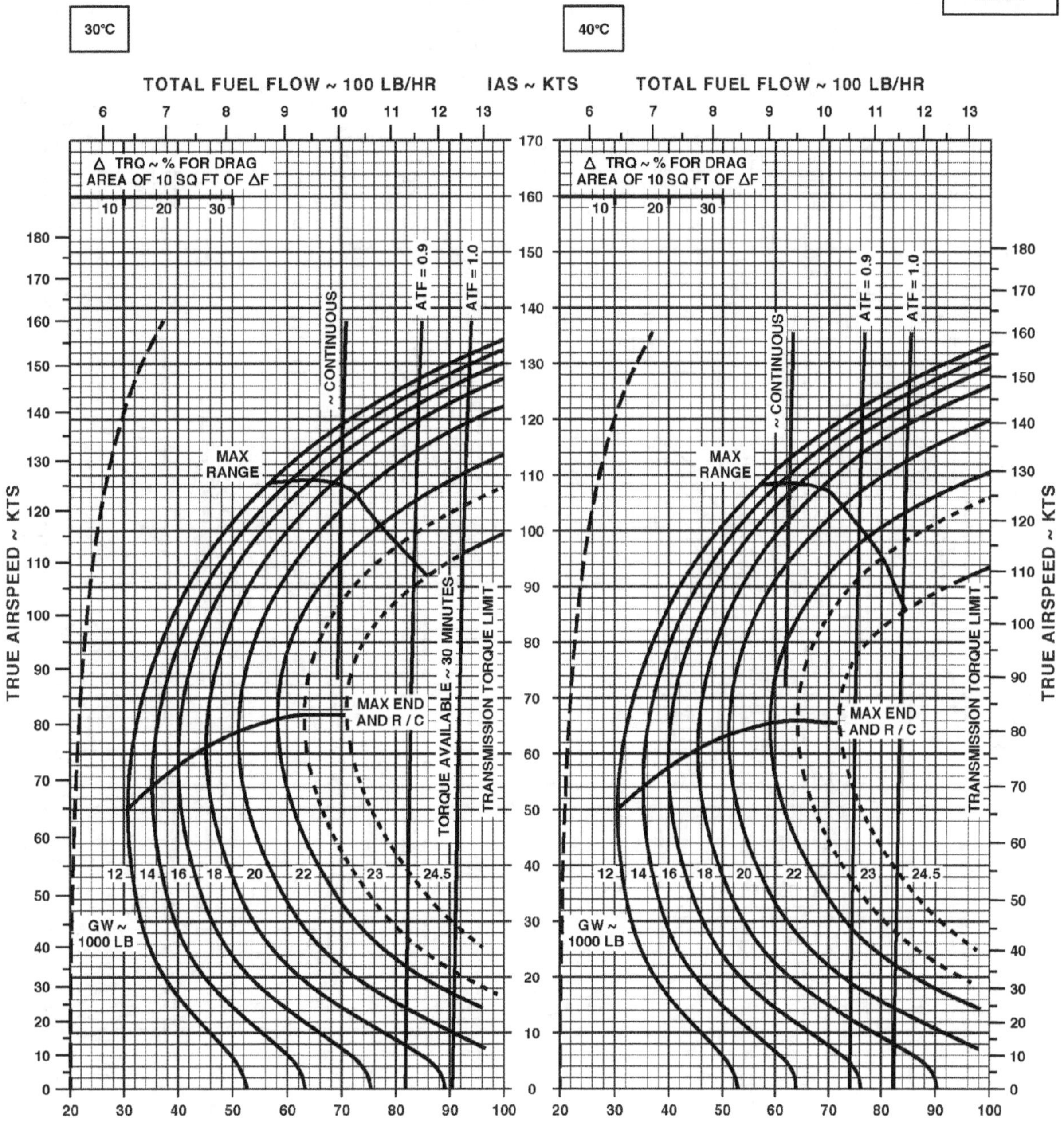

CRUISE

PRESS ALT: 4000 FT

CRUISE
4000 FT
T700 (2)

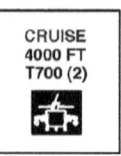

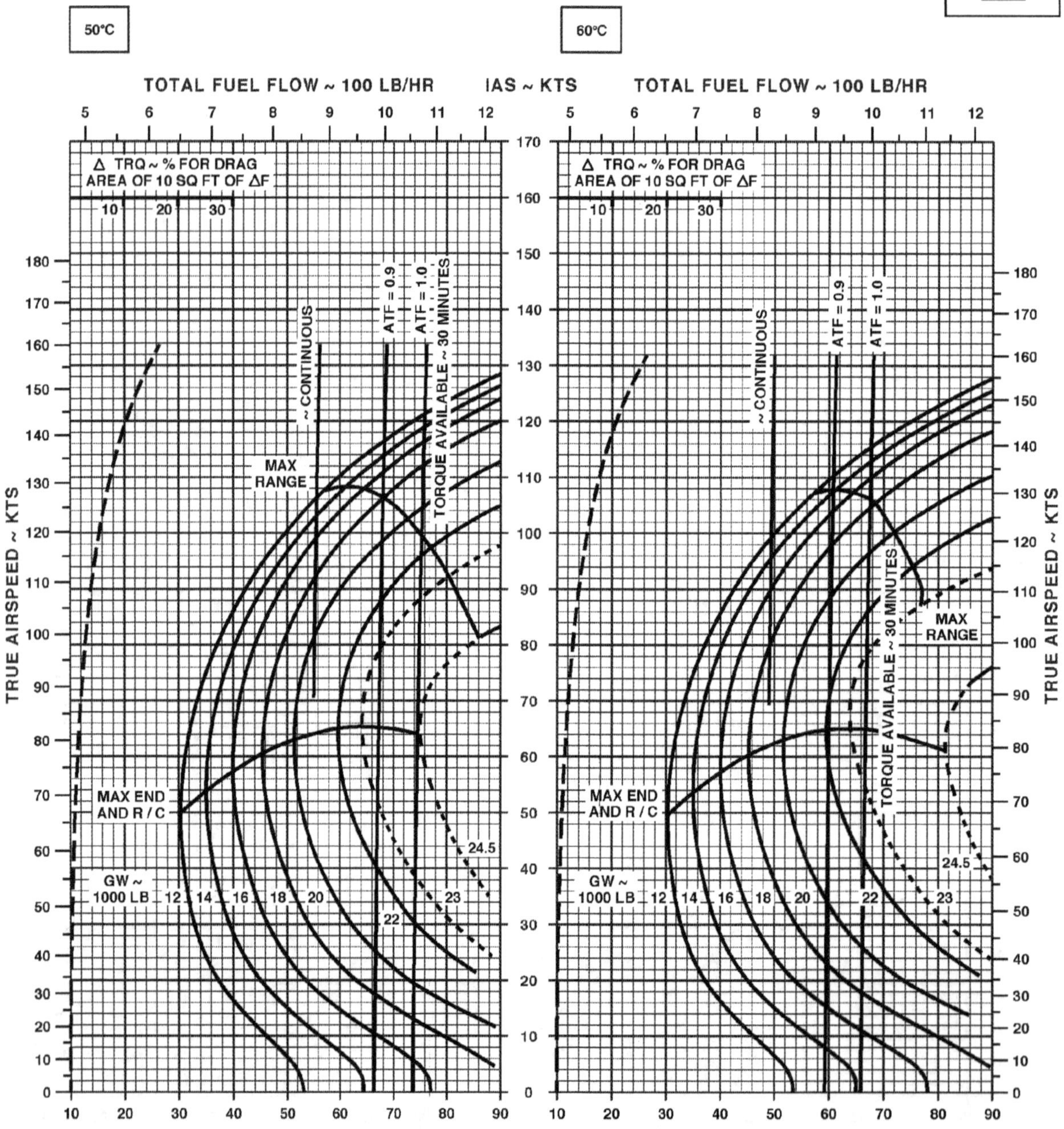

DATA BASE: FLIGHT TEST

AA0551

Figure 7-12. Cruise High Drag - Pressure Altitude 4,000 Feet (Sheet 6 of 6)

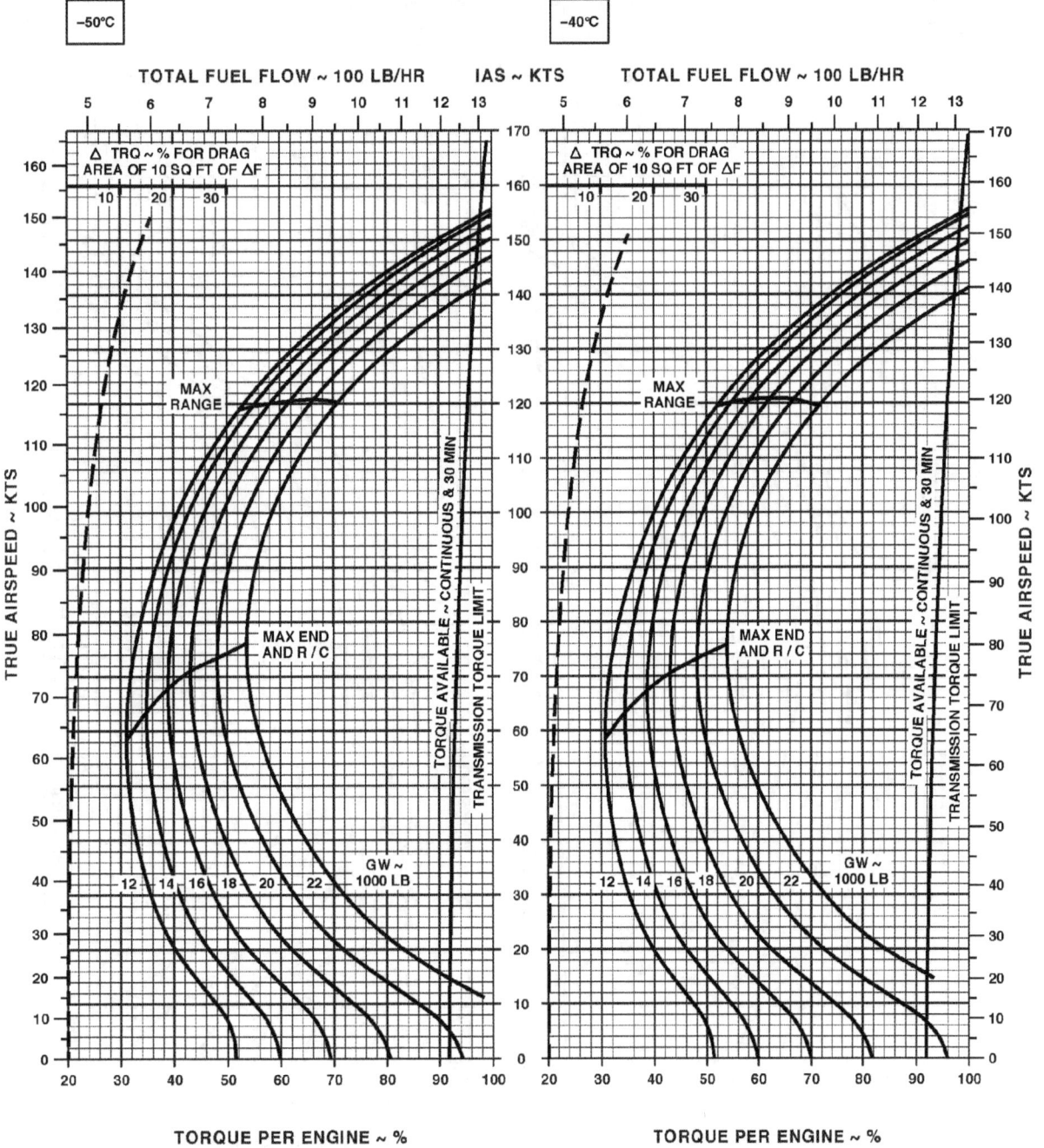

Figure 7-13. Cruise - Pressure Altitude 6,000 Feet (Sheet 1 of 6)

CRUISE
CLEAN CONFIGURATION
PRESS ALT: 6000 FT

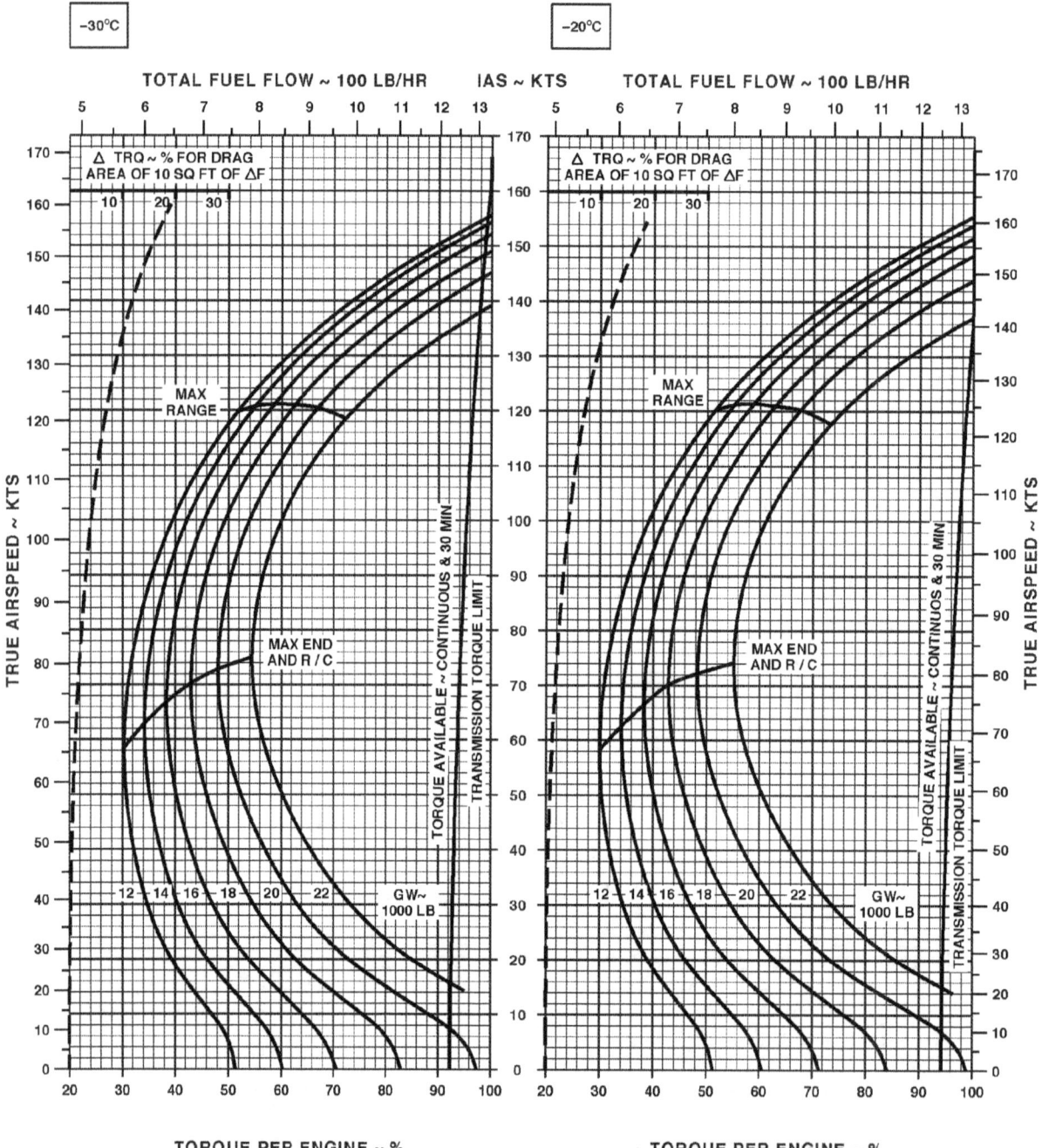

Figure 7-13. Cruise - Pressure Altitude 6,000 Feet (Sheet 2 of 6)

CRUISE
CLEAN CONFIGURATION
PRESS ALT: 6000 FT

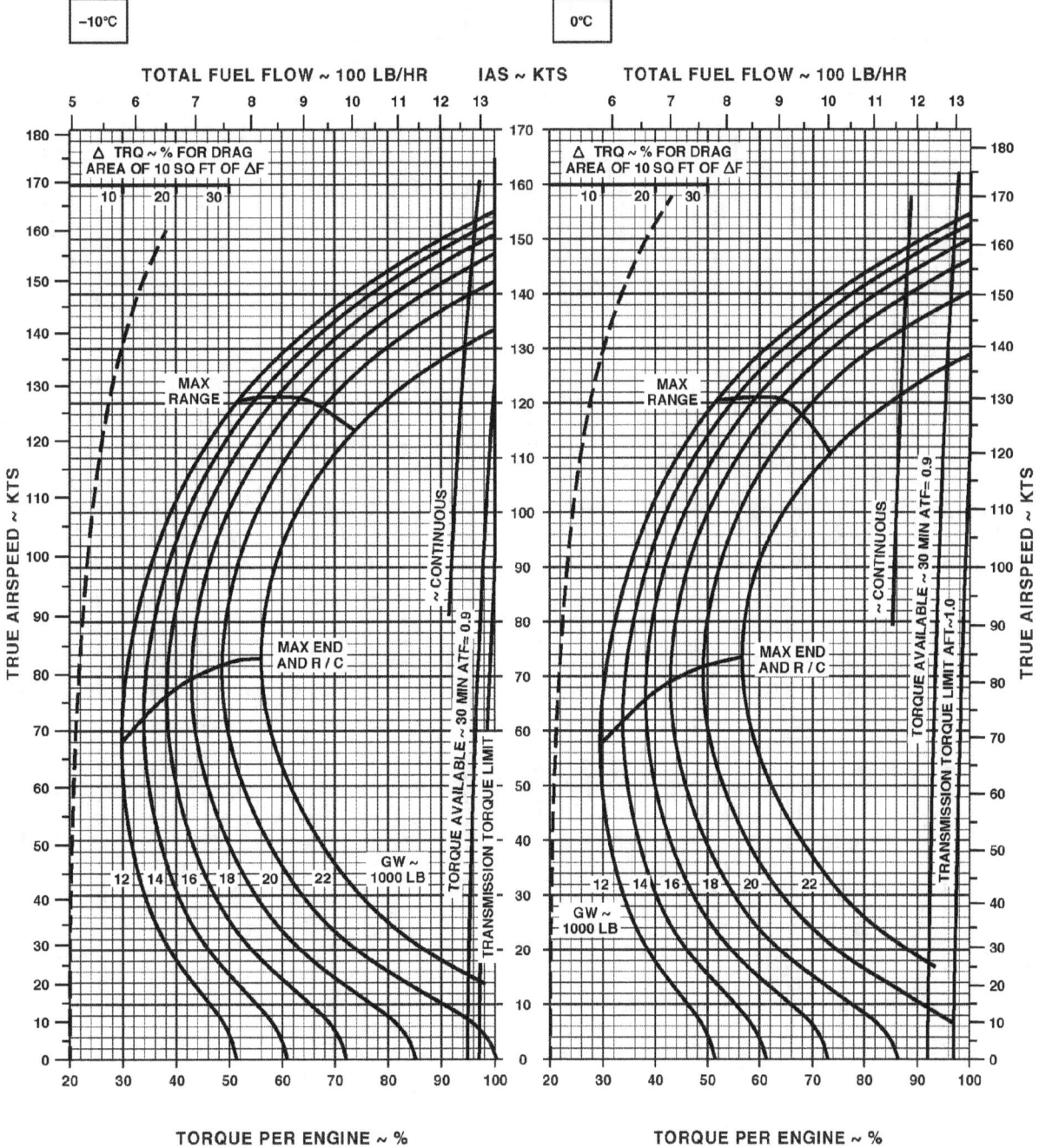

Figure 7-13. Cruise - Pressure Altitude 6,000 Feet (Sheet 3 of 6)

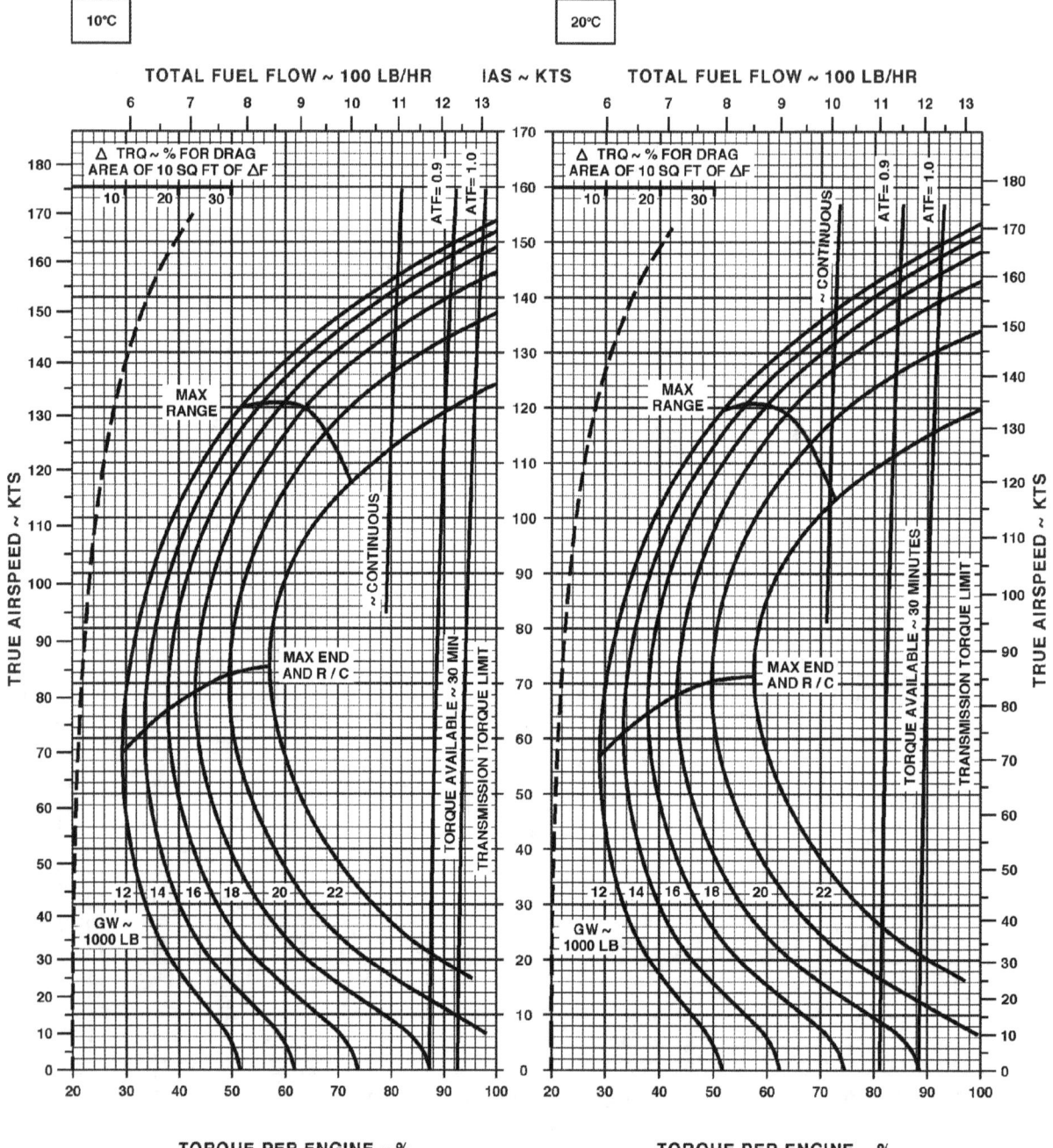

Figure 7-13. Cruise - Pressure Altitude 6,000 Feet (Sheet 4 of 6)

CRUISE
CLEAN CONFIGURATION
PRESS ALT: 6000 FT

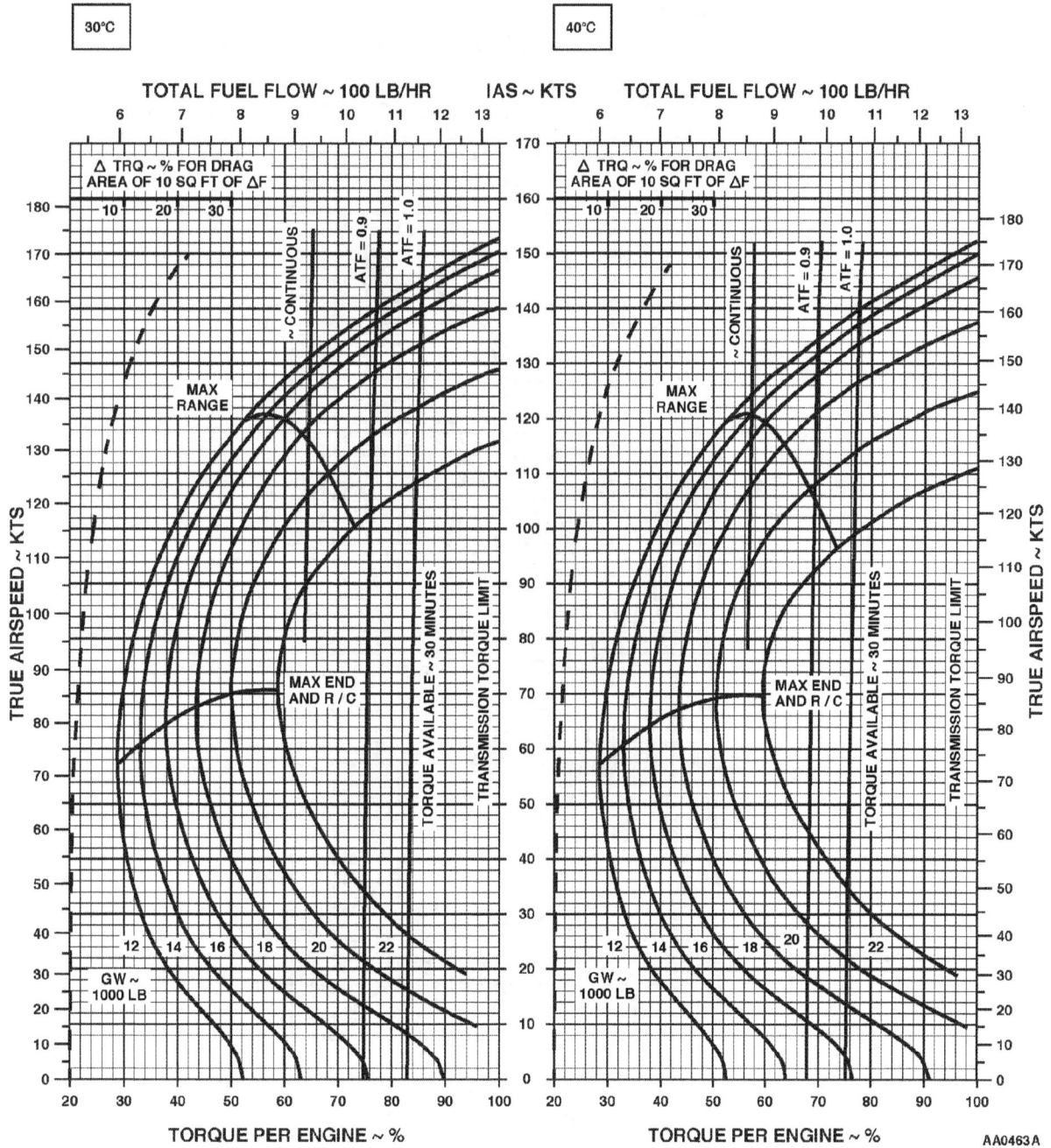

Figure 7-13. Cruise - Pressure Altitude 6,000 Feet (Sheet 5 of 6)

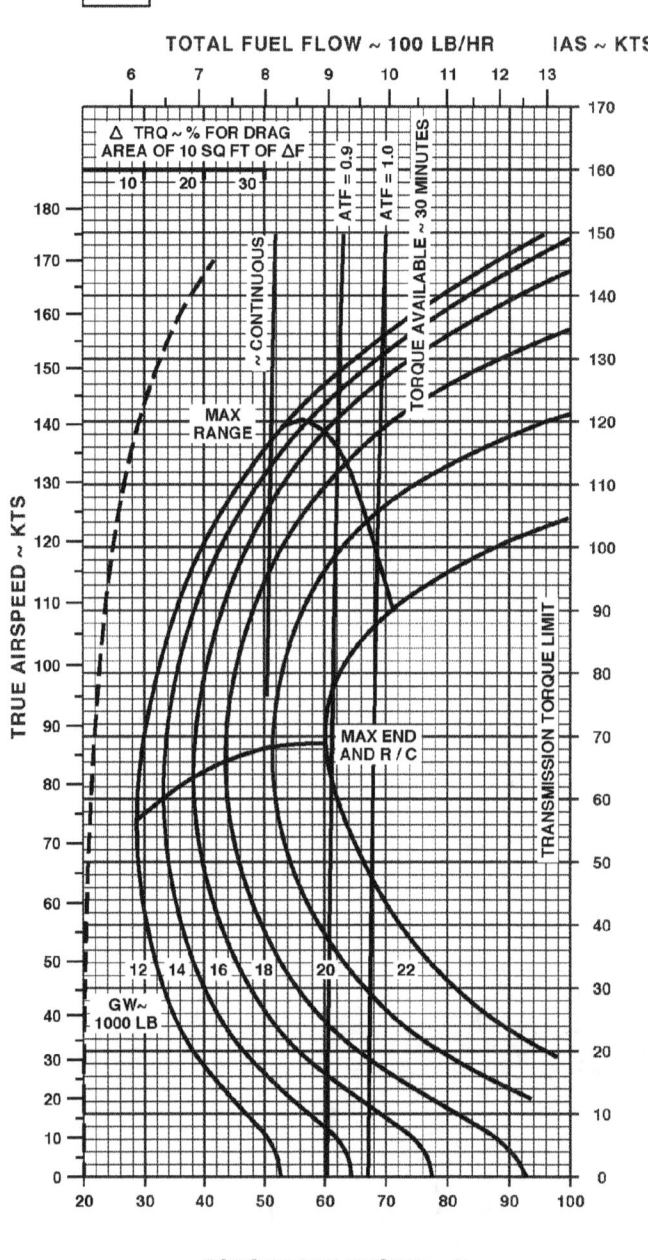

Figure 7-13. Cruise - Pressure Altitude 6,000 Feet (Sheet 6 of 6)

CRUISE

PRESS ALT: 6000 FT

CRUISE
6000 FT
T700 (2)

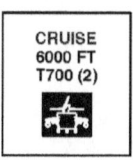

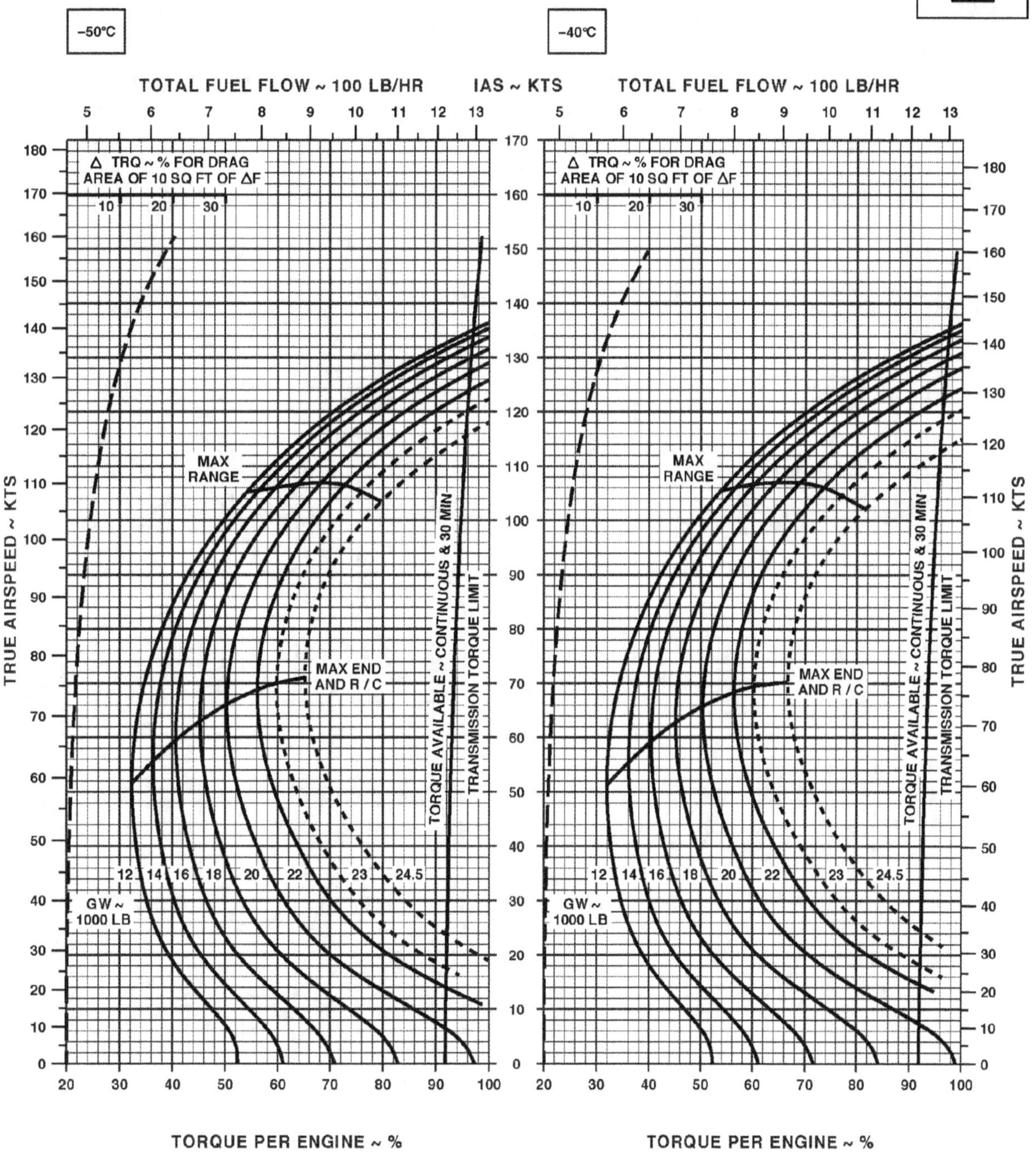

DATA BASE: FLIGHT TEST

AA0552
SA

Figure 7-14. Cruise High Drag - Pressure Altitude 6,000 Feet (Sheet 1 of 6)

CRUISE

PRESS ALT: 6000 FT

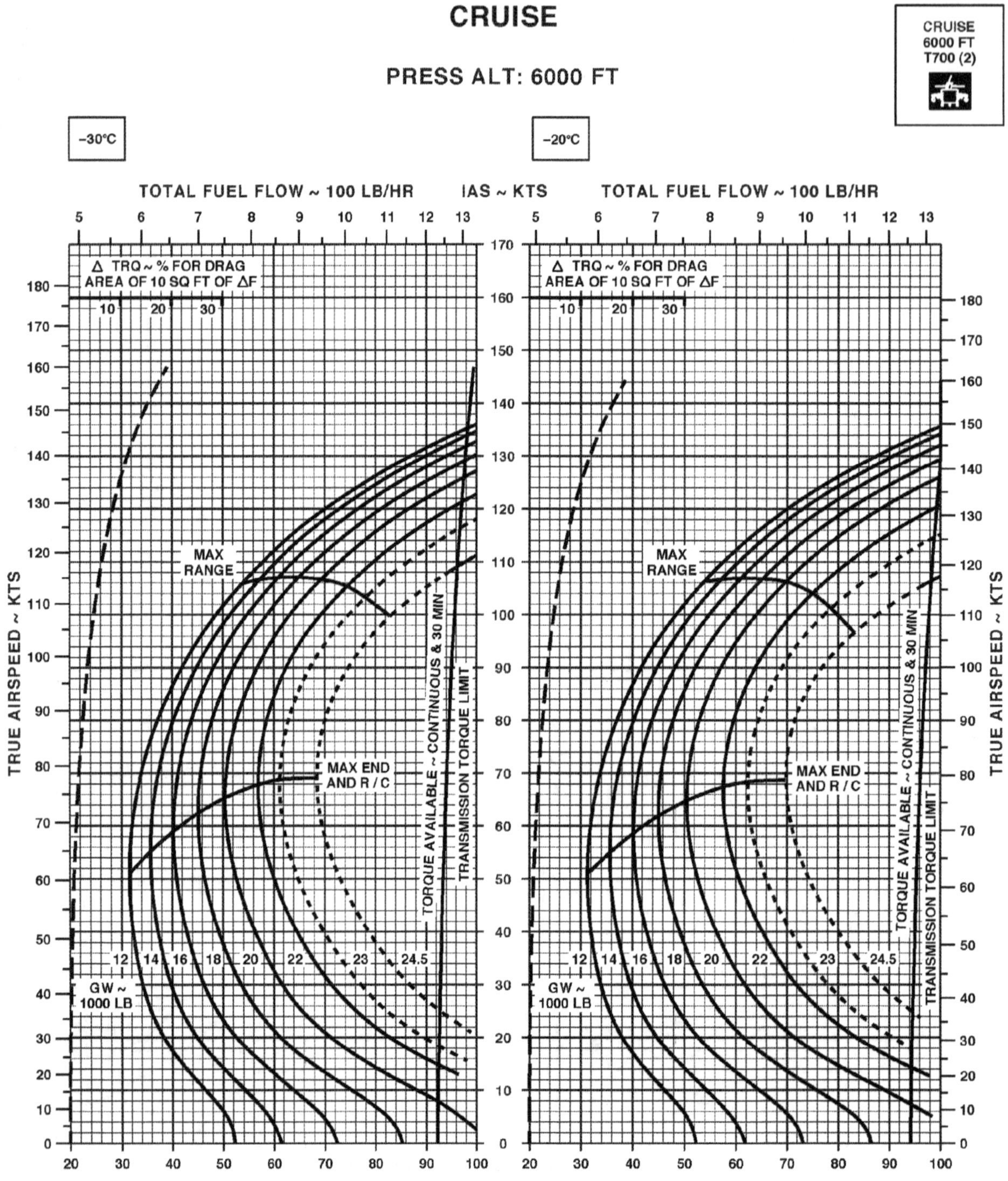

Figure 7-14. Cruise High Drag - Pressure Altitude 6,000 Feet (Sheet 2 of 6)

CRUISE

PRESS ALT: 6000 FT

Figure 7-14. Cruise High Drag - Pressure Altitude 6,000 Feet (Sheet 3 of 6)

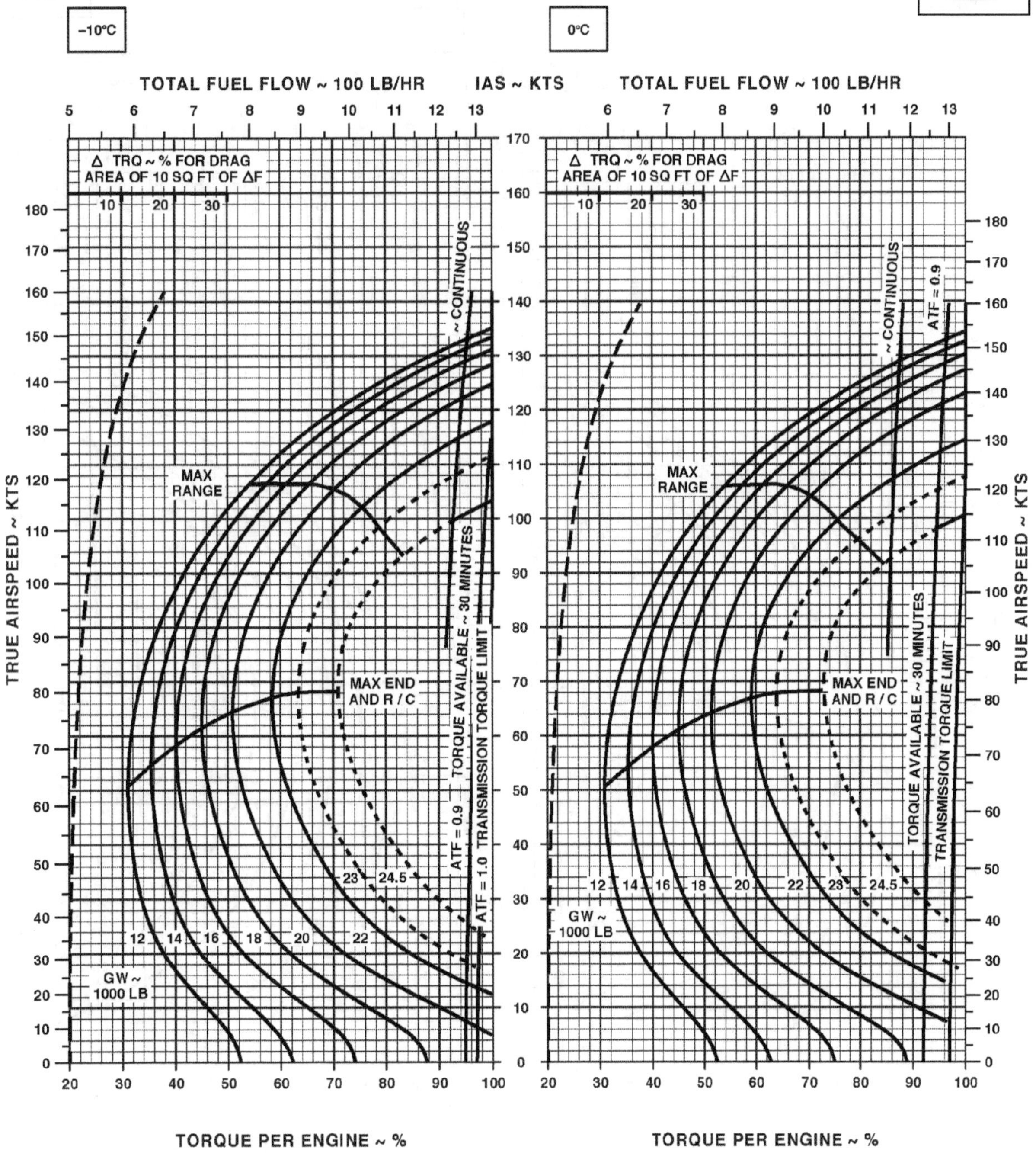

DATA BASE: FLIGHT TEST

CRUISE

PRESS ALT: 6000 FT

CRUISE
6000 FT
T700 (2)

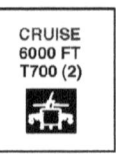

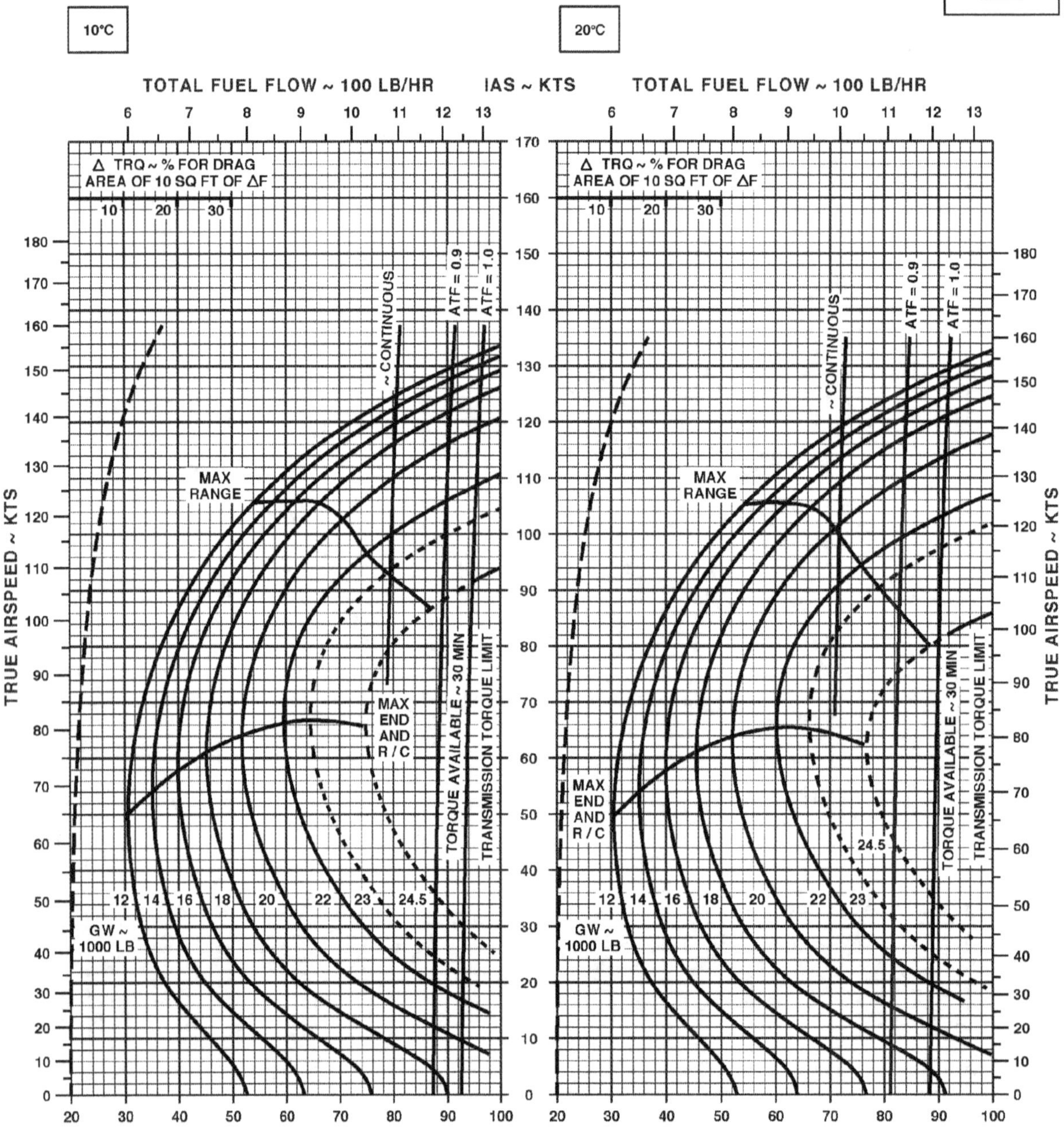

DATA BASE: FLIGHT TEST

AA0555

Figure 7-14. Cruise High Drag - Pressure Altitude 6,000 Feet (Sheet 4 of 6)

CRUISE

PRESS ALT: 6000 FT

Figure 7-14. Cruise High Drag - Pressure Altitude 6,000 Feet (Sheet 5 of 6)

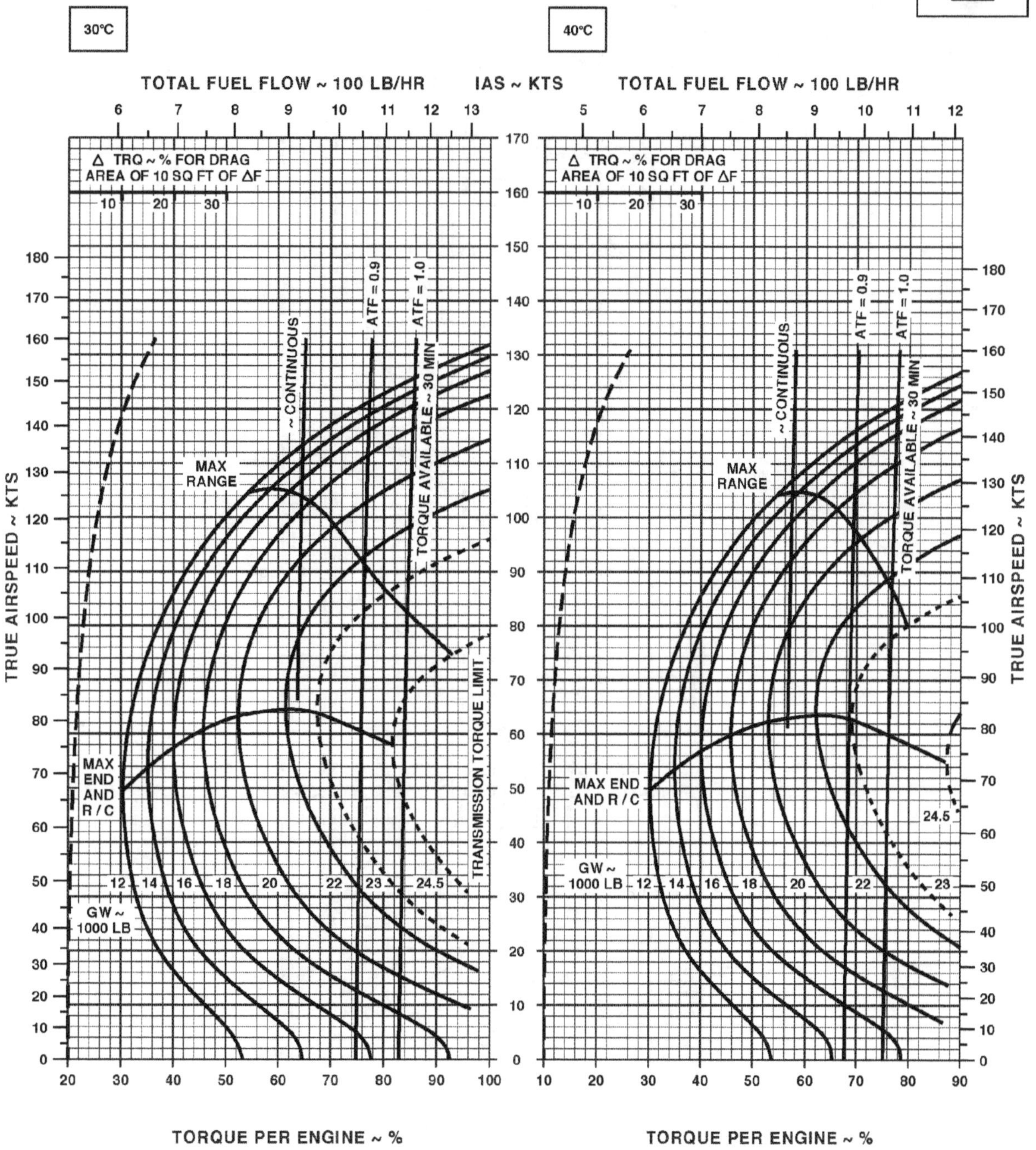

CRUISE

PRESS ALT: 6000 FT

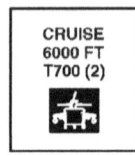
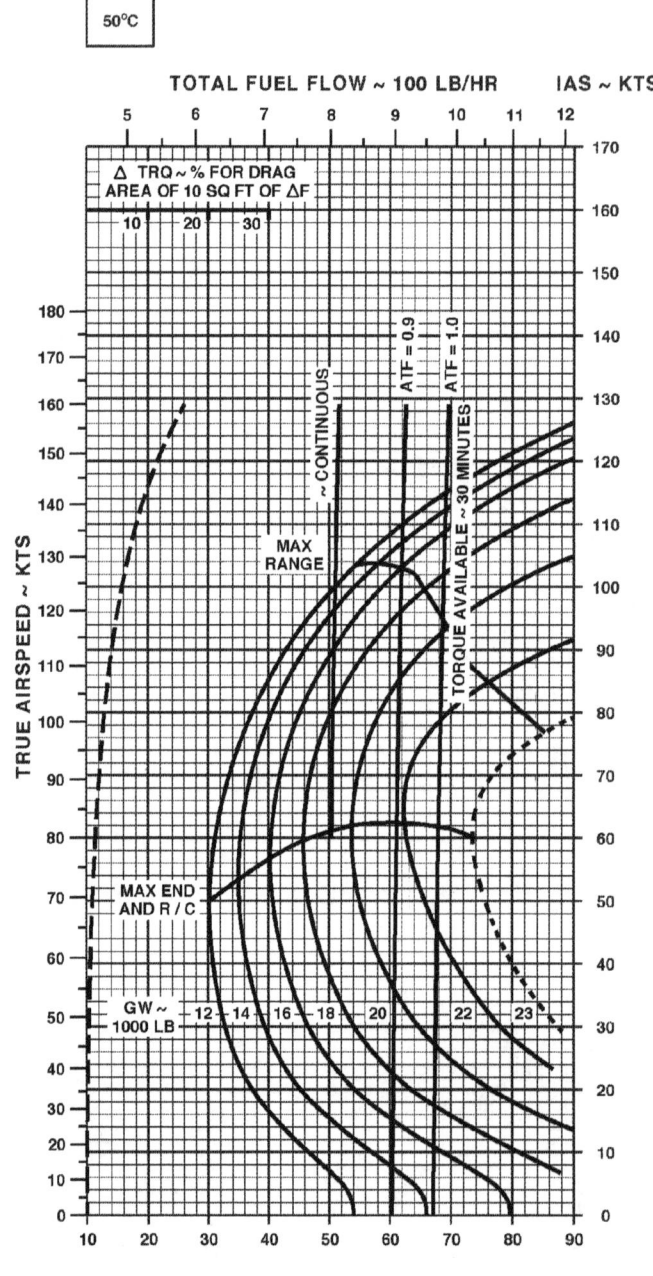

Figure 7-14. Cruise High Drag - Pressure Altitude 6,000 Feet (Sheet 6 of 6)

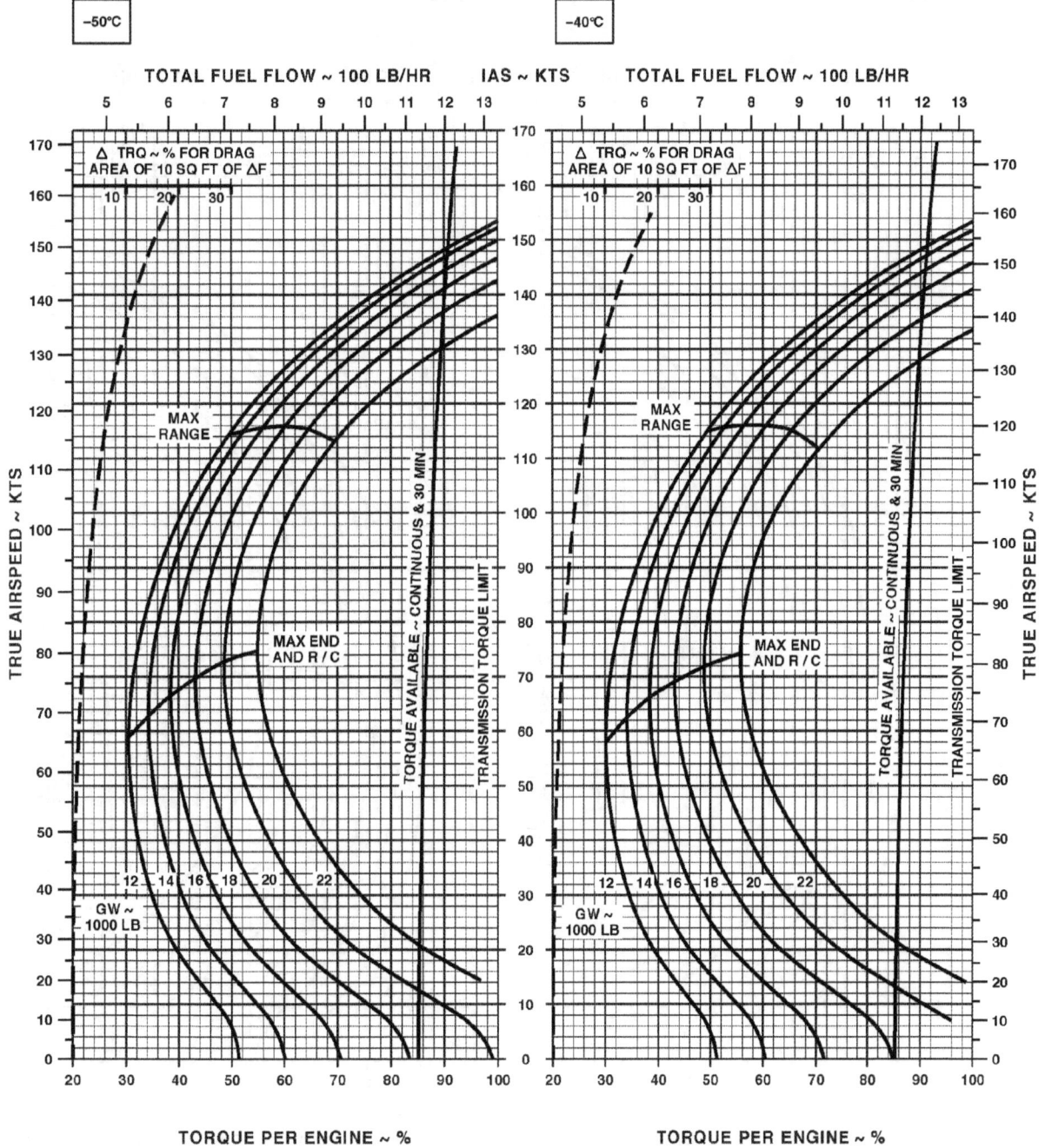

Figure 7-15. Cruise - Pressure Altitude 8,000 Feet (Sheet 1 of 6)

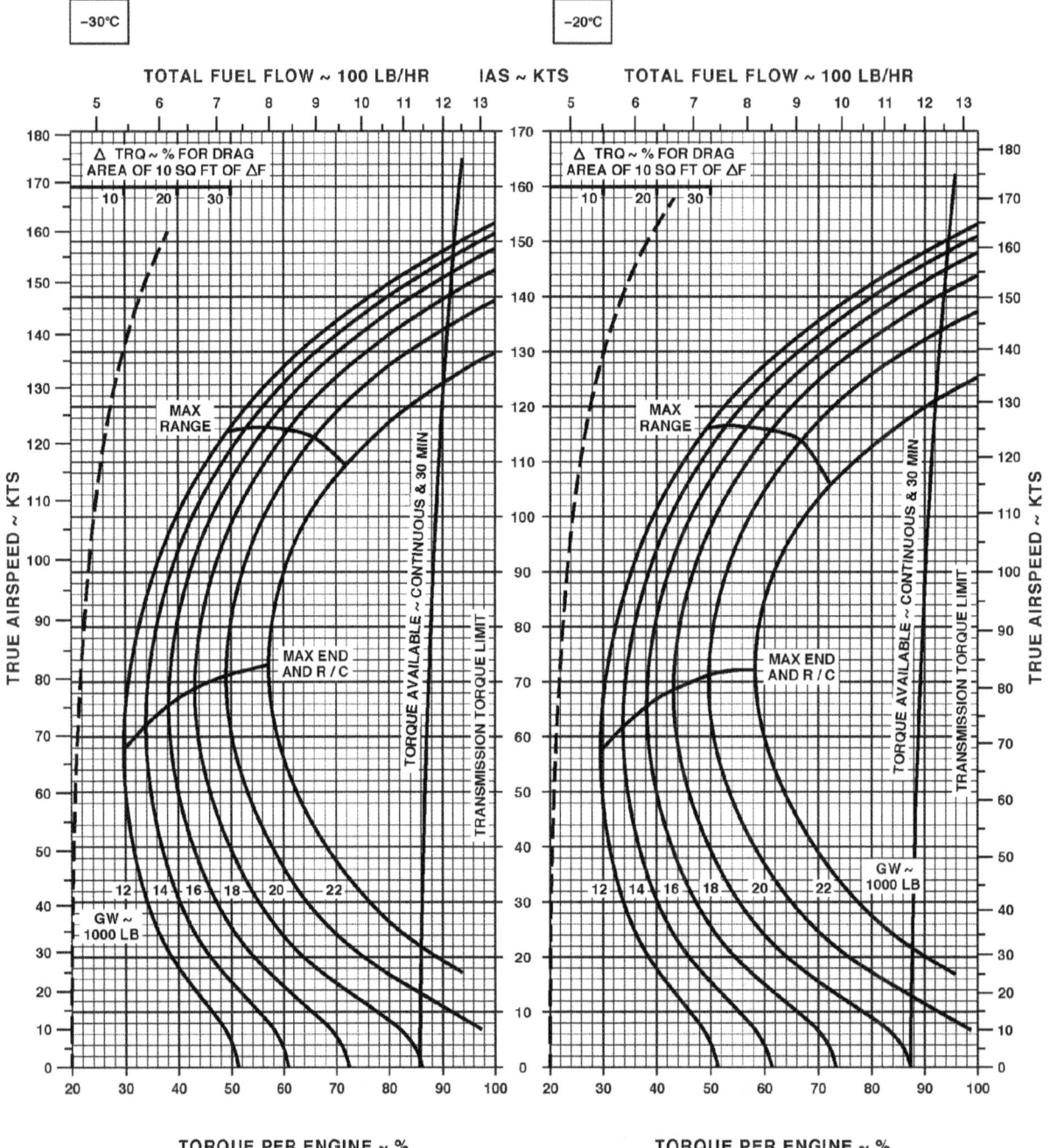

Figure 7-15. Cruise - Pressure Altitude 8,000 Feet (Sheet 2 of 6)

CRUISE
CLEAN CONFIGURATION
PRESS ALT: 8000 FT

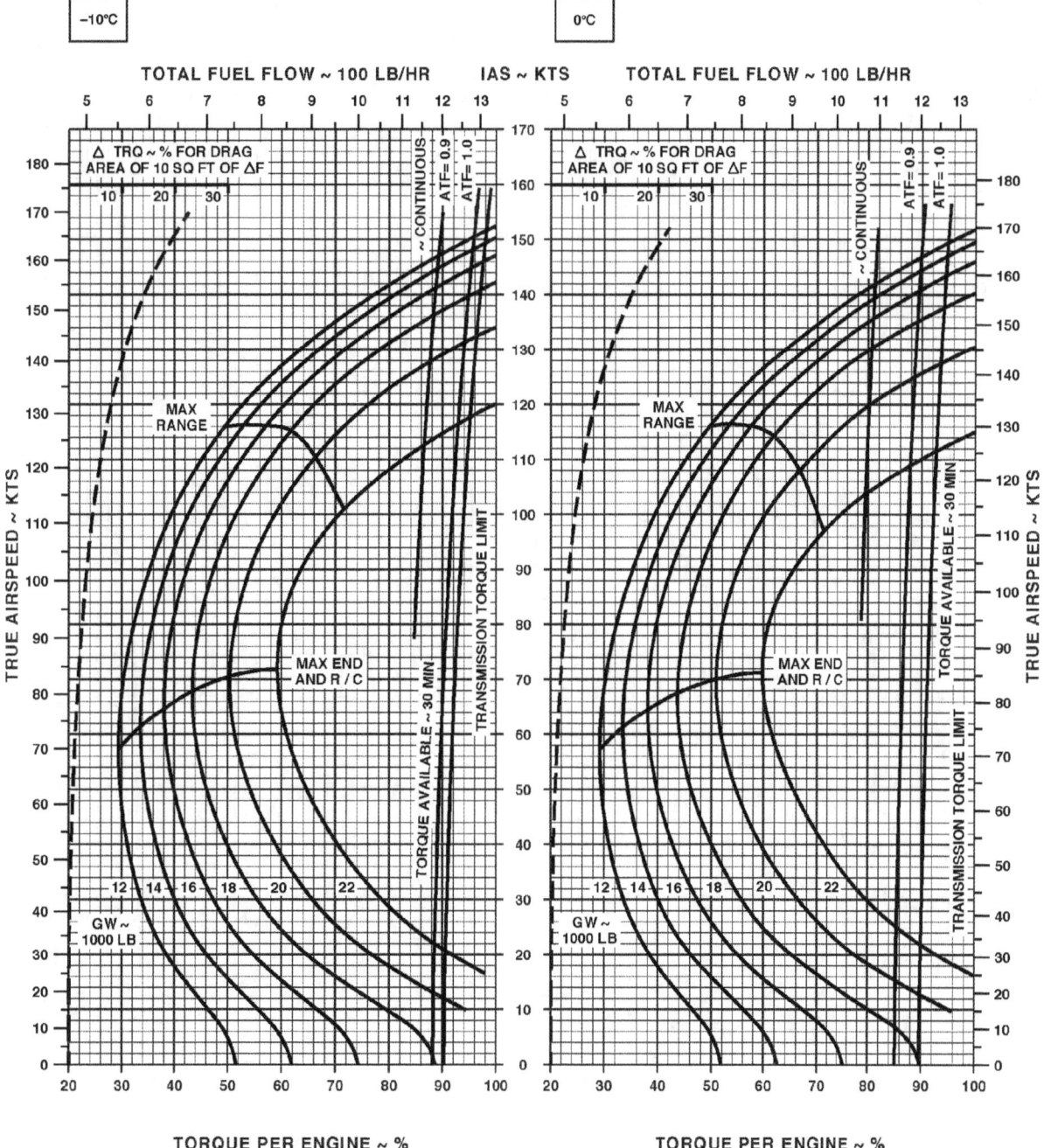

Figure 7-15. Cruise - Pressure Altitude 8,000 Feet (Sheet 3 of 6)

CRUISE
CLEAN CONFIGURATION
PRESS ALT: 8000 FT

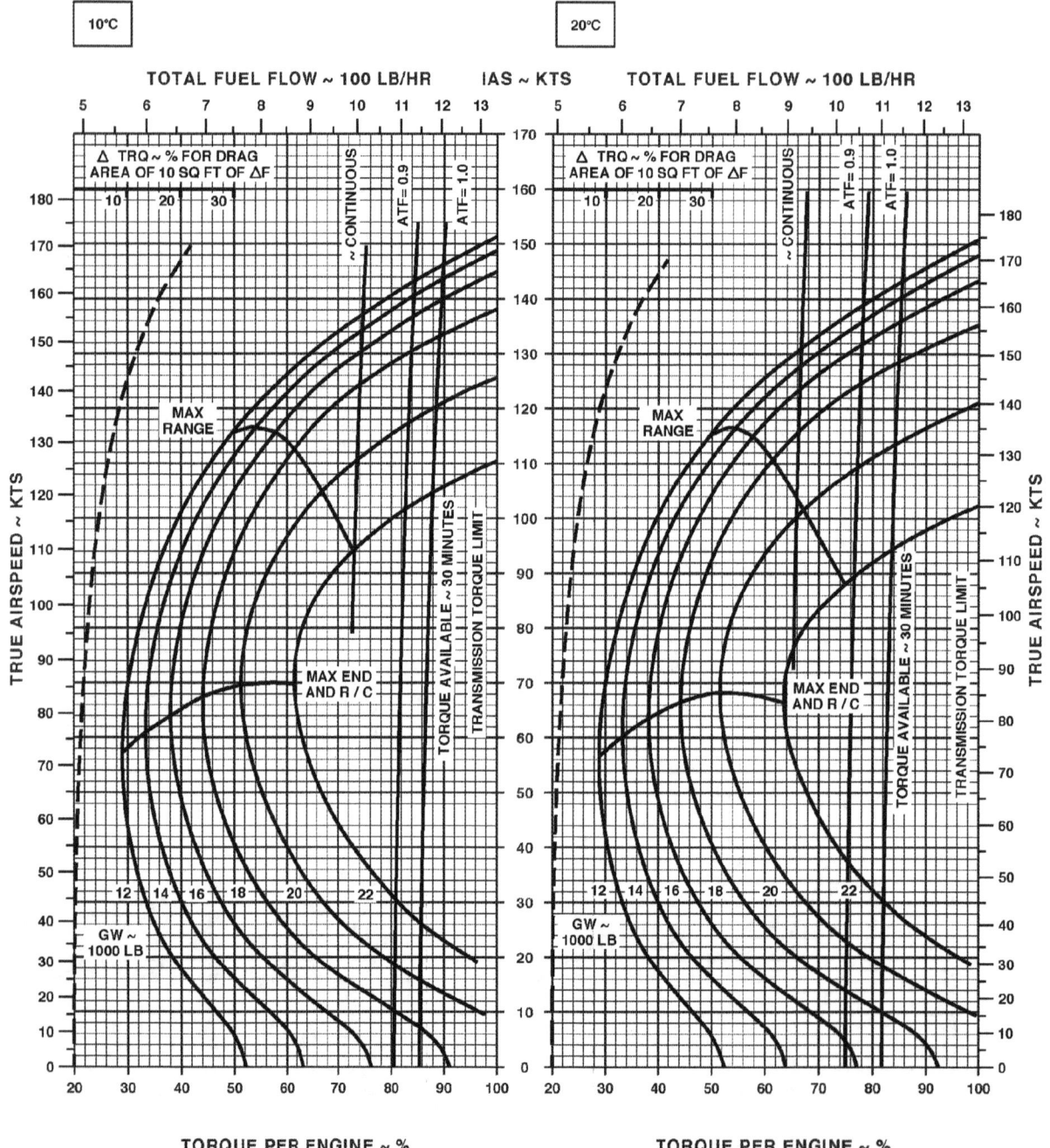

Figure 7-15. Cruise - Pressure Altitude 8,000 Feet (Sheet 4 of 6)

CRUISE
CLEAN CONFIGURATION
PRESS ALT: 8000 FT

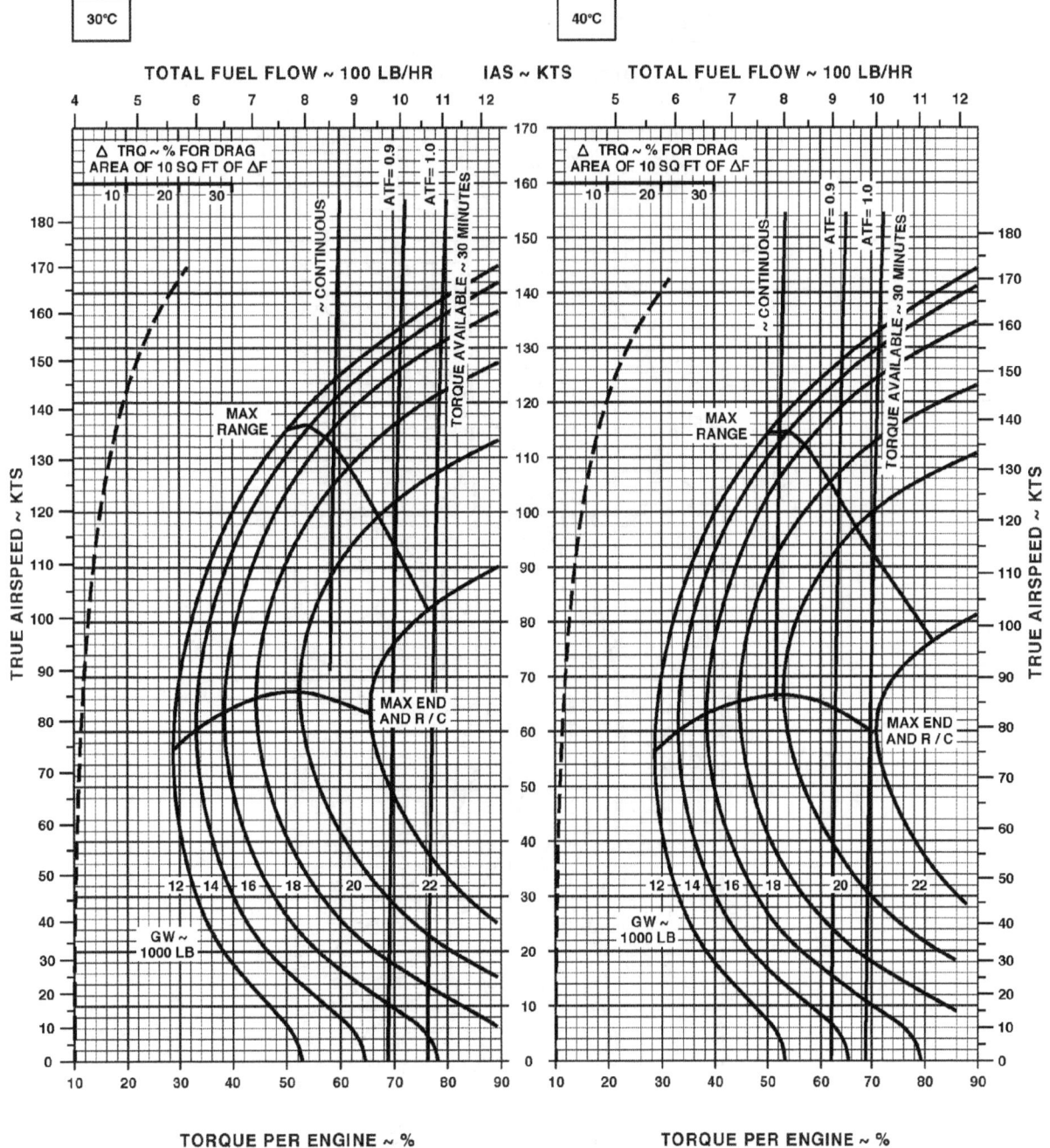

Figure 7-15. Cruise - Pressure Altitude 8,000 Feet (Sheet 5 of 6)

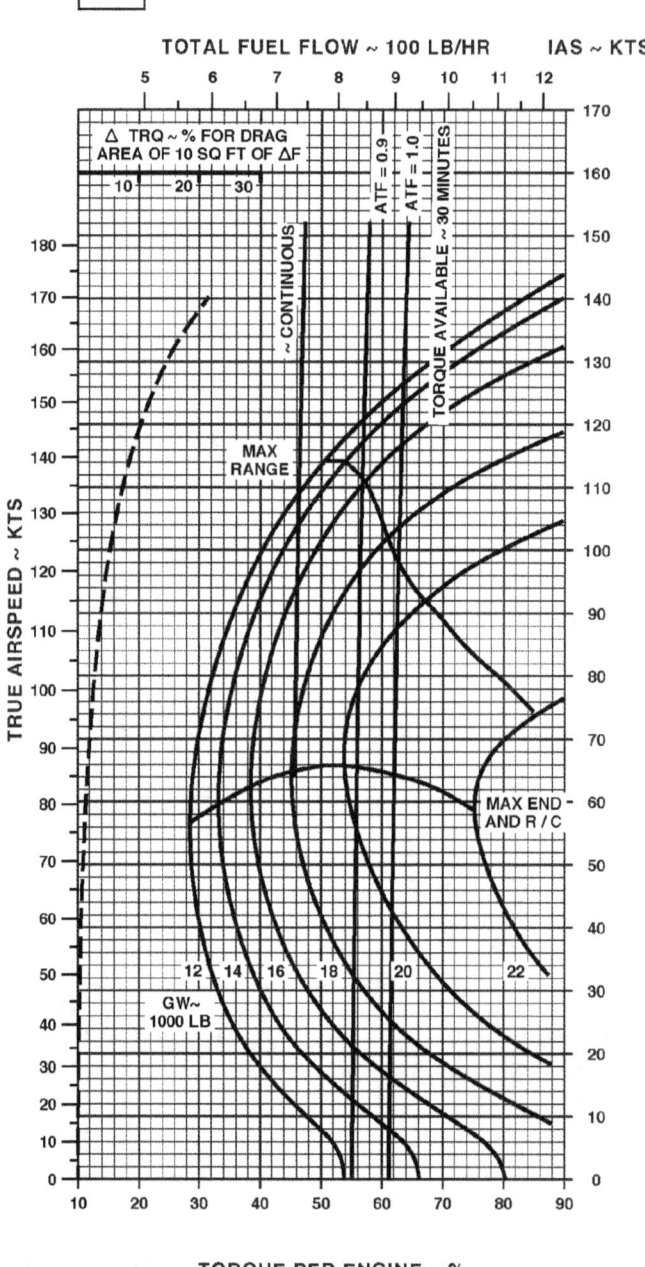

Figure 7-15. Cruise - Pressure Altitude 8,000 Feet (Sheet 6 of 6)

CRUISE

PRESS ALT: 8000 FT

CRUISE
8000 FT
T700 (2)

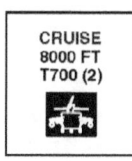

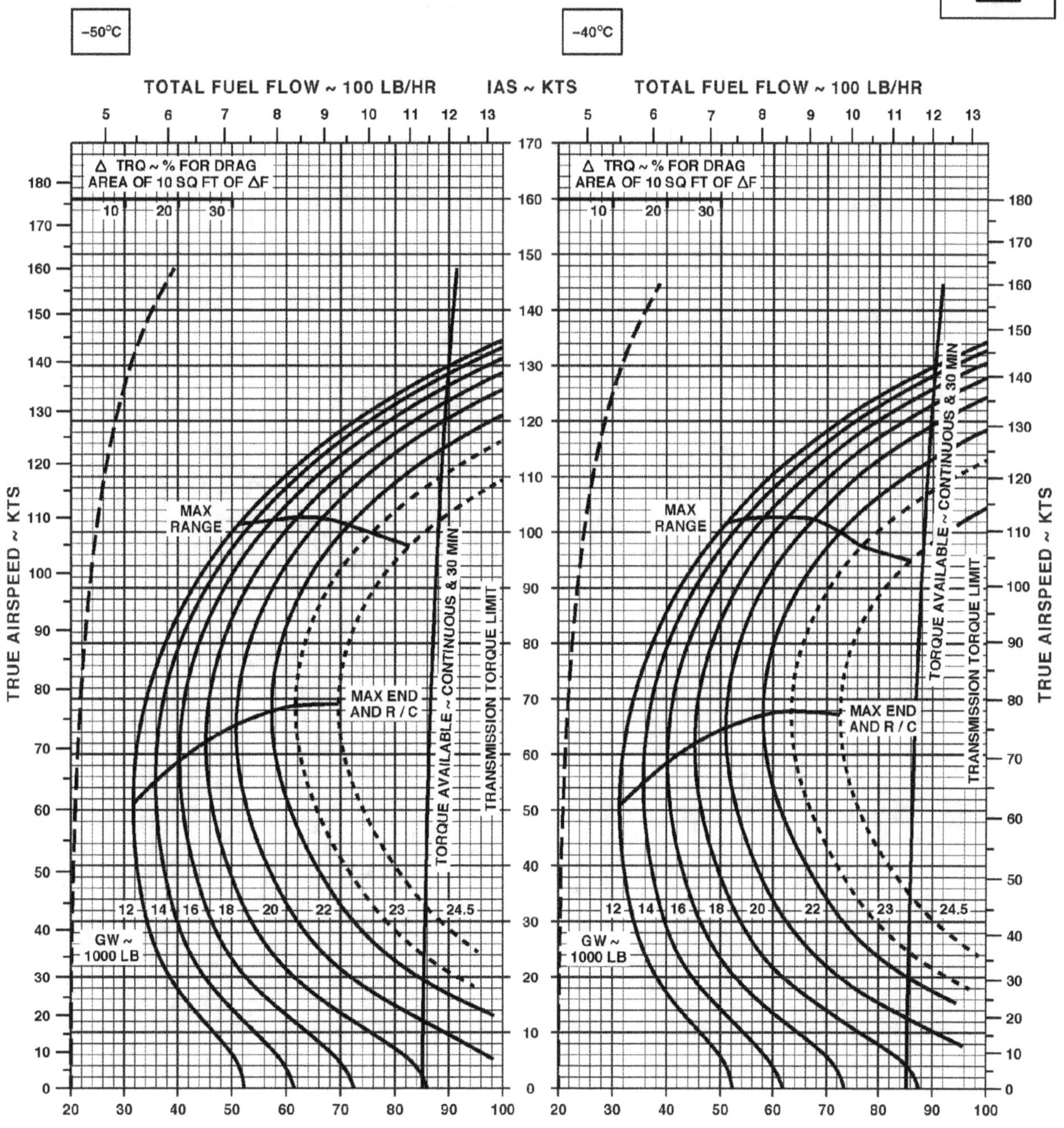

DATA BASE: FLIGHT TEST

AA0558

Figure 7-16. Cruise High Drag - Pressure Altitude 8,000 Feet (Sheet 1 of 6)

CRUISE

PRESS ALT: 8000 FT

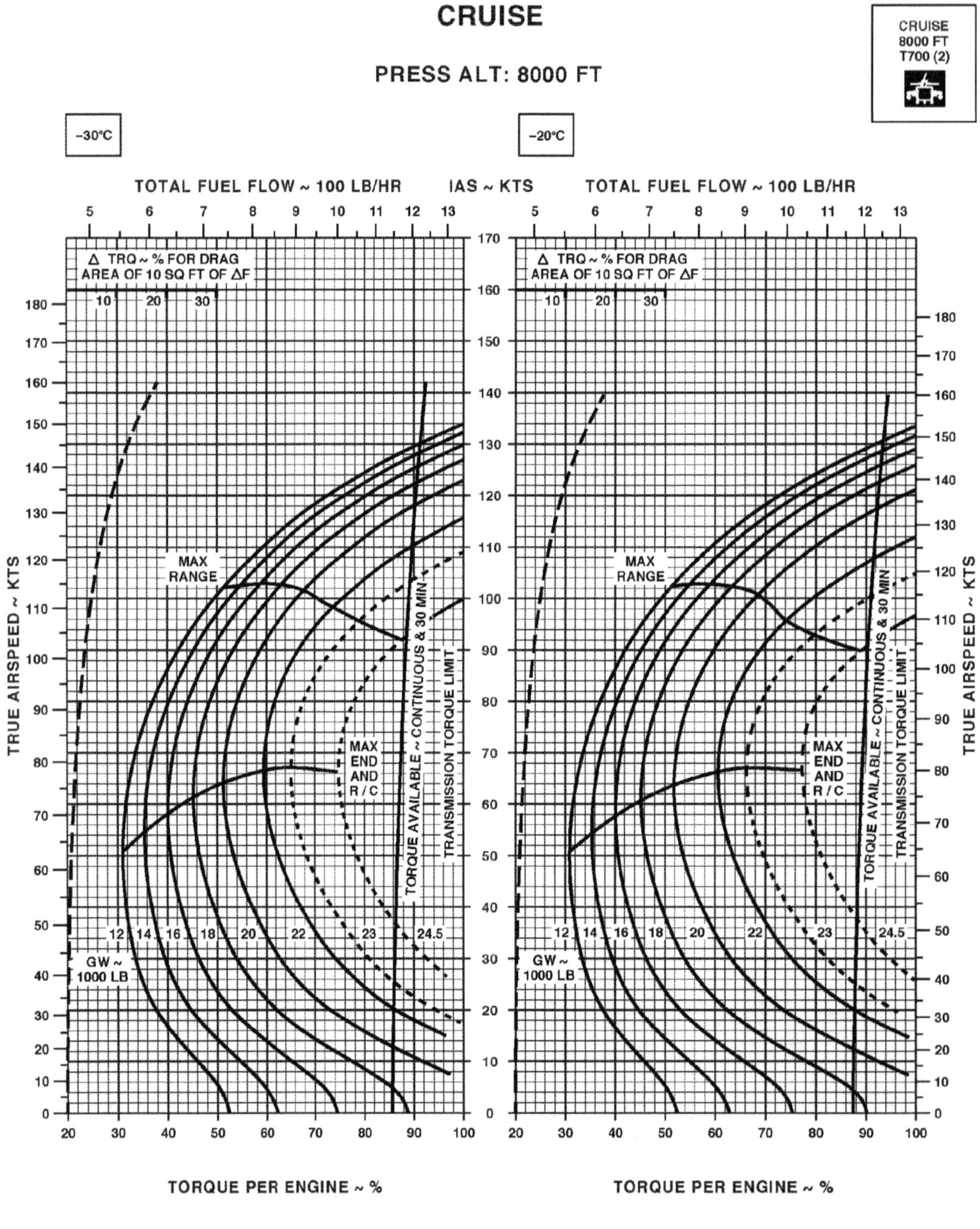

Figure 7-16. Cruise High Drag - Pressure Altitude 8,000 Feet (Sheet 2 of 6)

DATA BASE: FLIGHT TEST

CRUISE

PRESS ALT: 8000 FT

CRUISE
8000 FT
T700 (2)

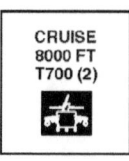

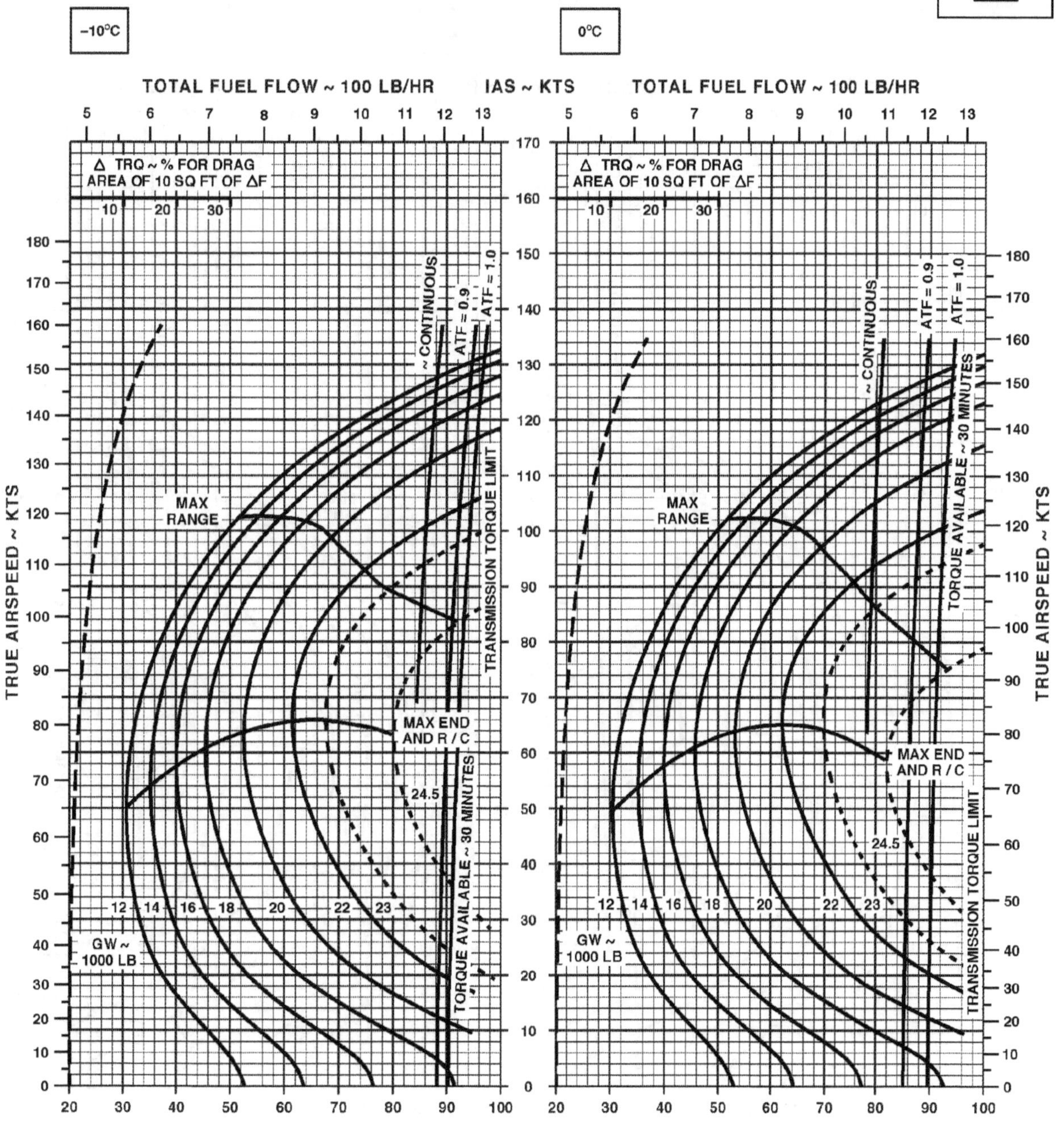

DATA BASE: FLIGHT TEST

AA0560

Figure 7-16. Cruise High Drag - Pressure Altitude 8,000 Feet (Sheet 3 of 6)

CRUISE

CRUISE
8000 FT
T700 (2)

PRESS ALT: 8000 FT

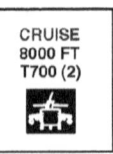

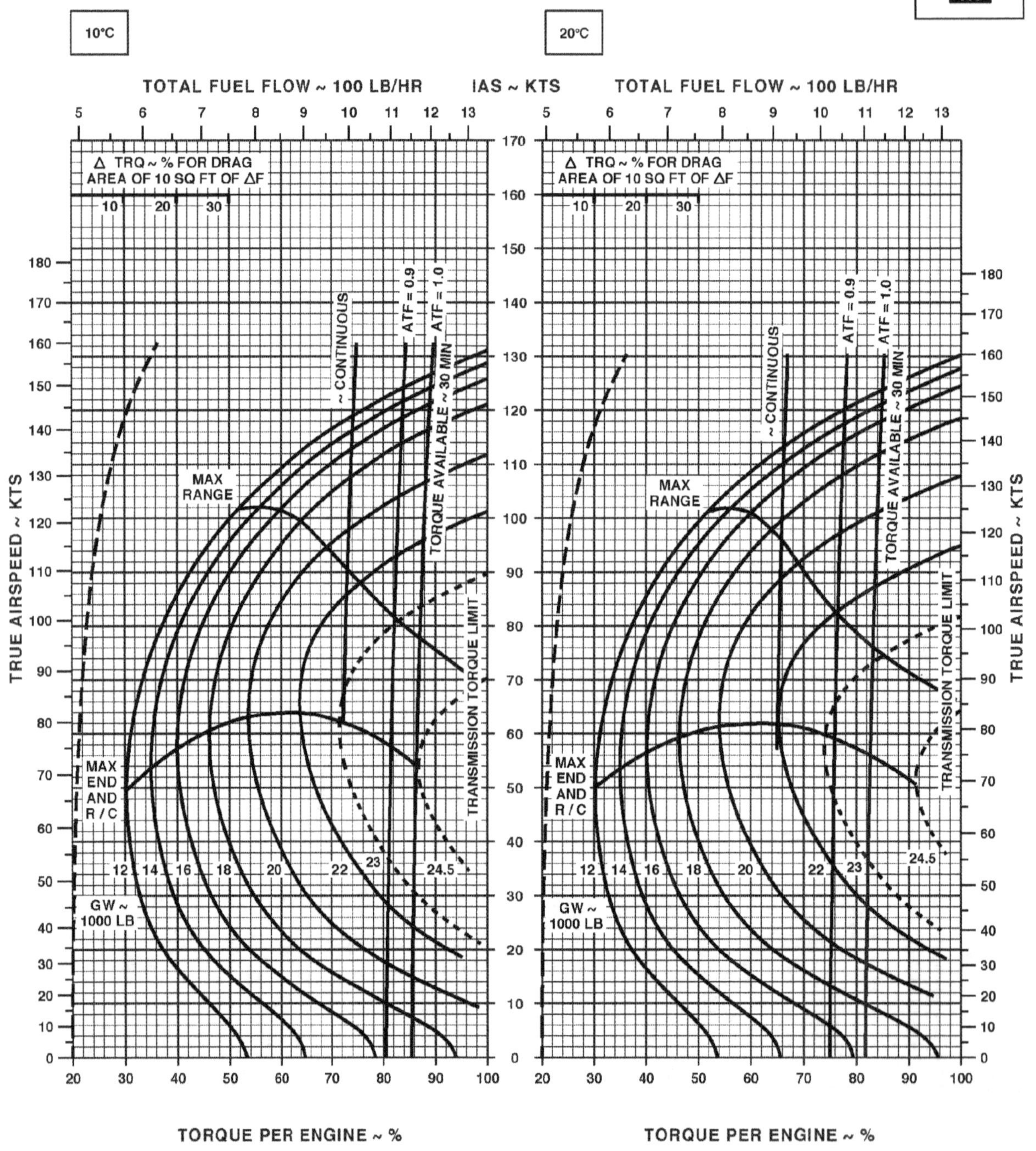

DATA BASE: FLIGHT TEST

AA0561

Figure 7-16. Cruise High Drag - Pressure Altitude 8,000 Feet (Sheet 4 of 6)

CRUISE

PRESS ALT: 8000 FT

CRUISE
8000 FT
T700 (2)

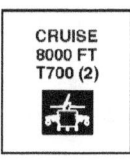

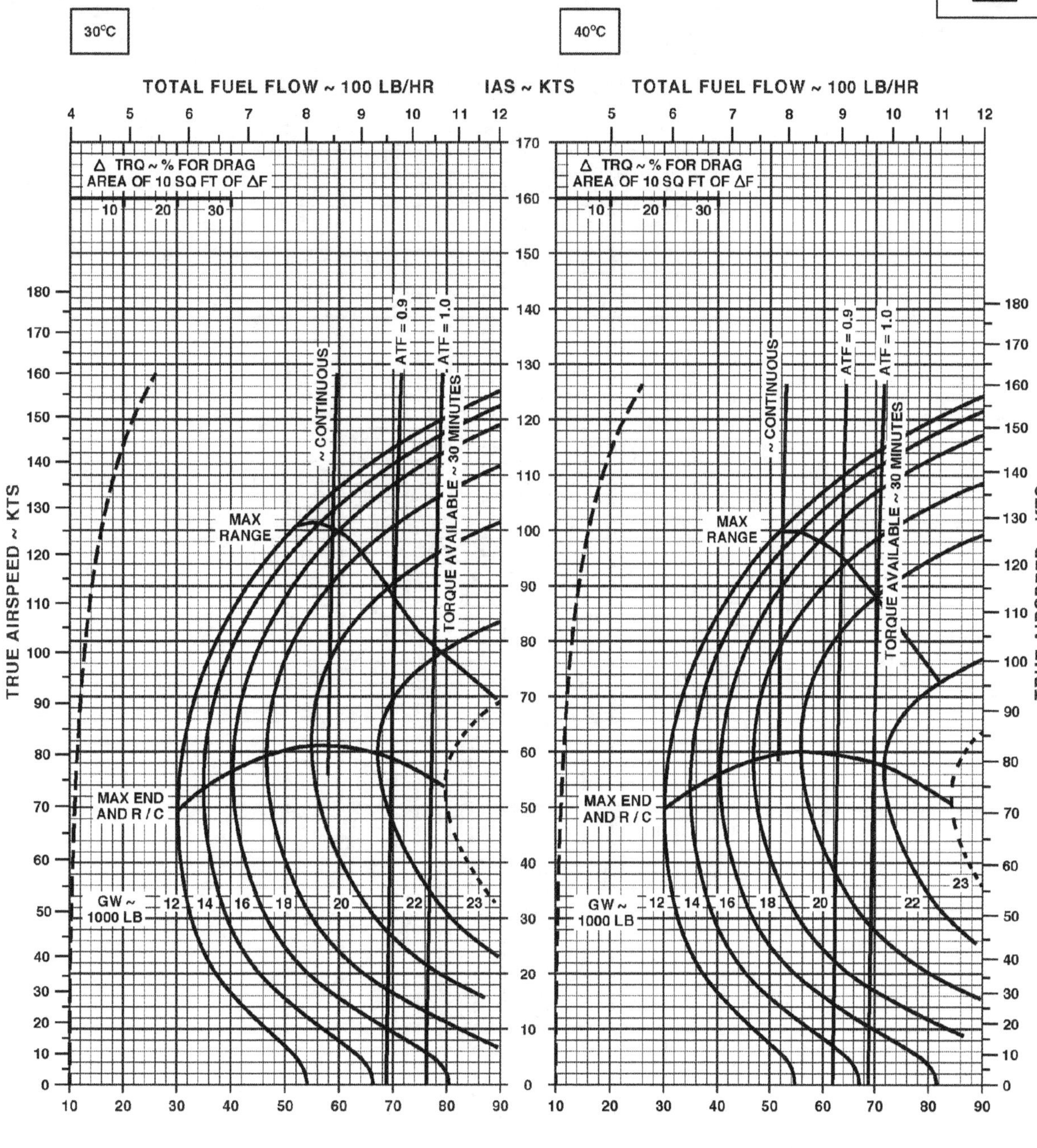

DATA BASE: FLIGHT TEST

AA0562
SA

Figure 7-16. Cruise High Drag - Pressure Altitude 8,000 Feet (Sheet 5 of 6)

CRUISE

PRESS ALT: 8000 FT

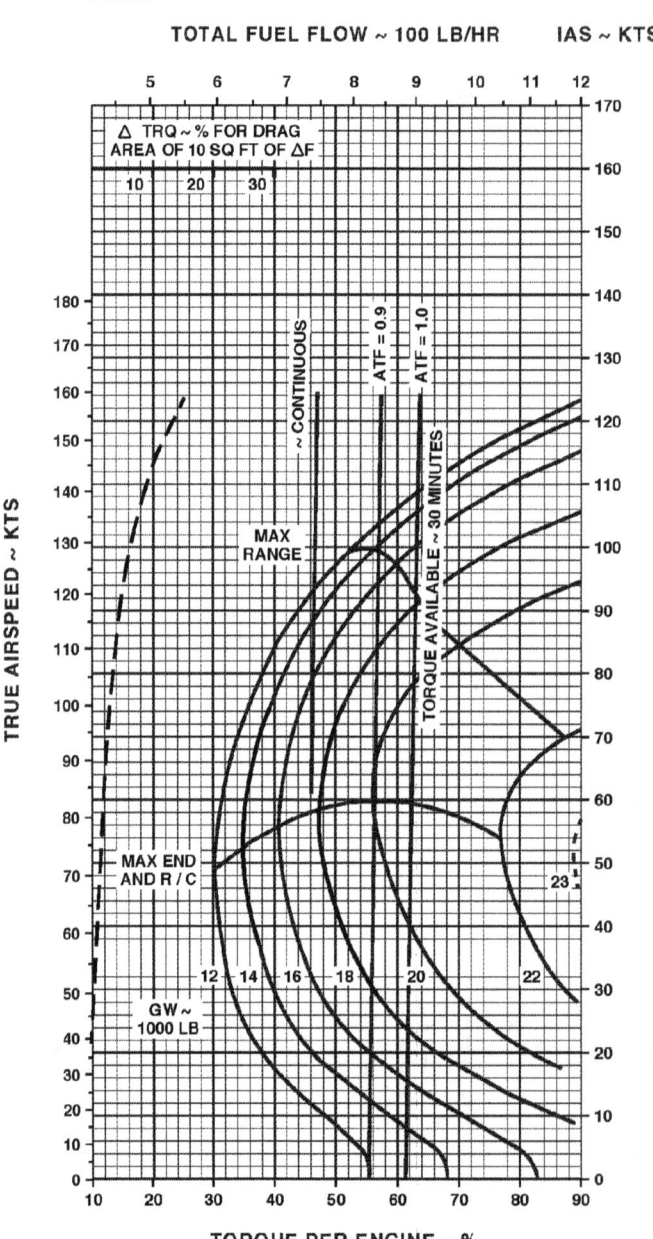

Figure 7-16. Cruise High Drag - Pressure Altitude 8,000 Feet (Sheet 6 of 6)

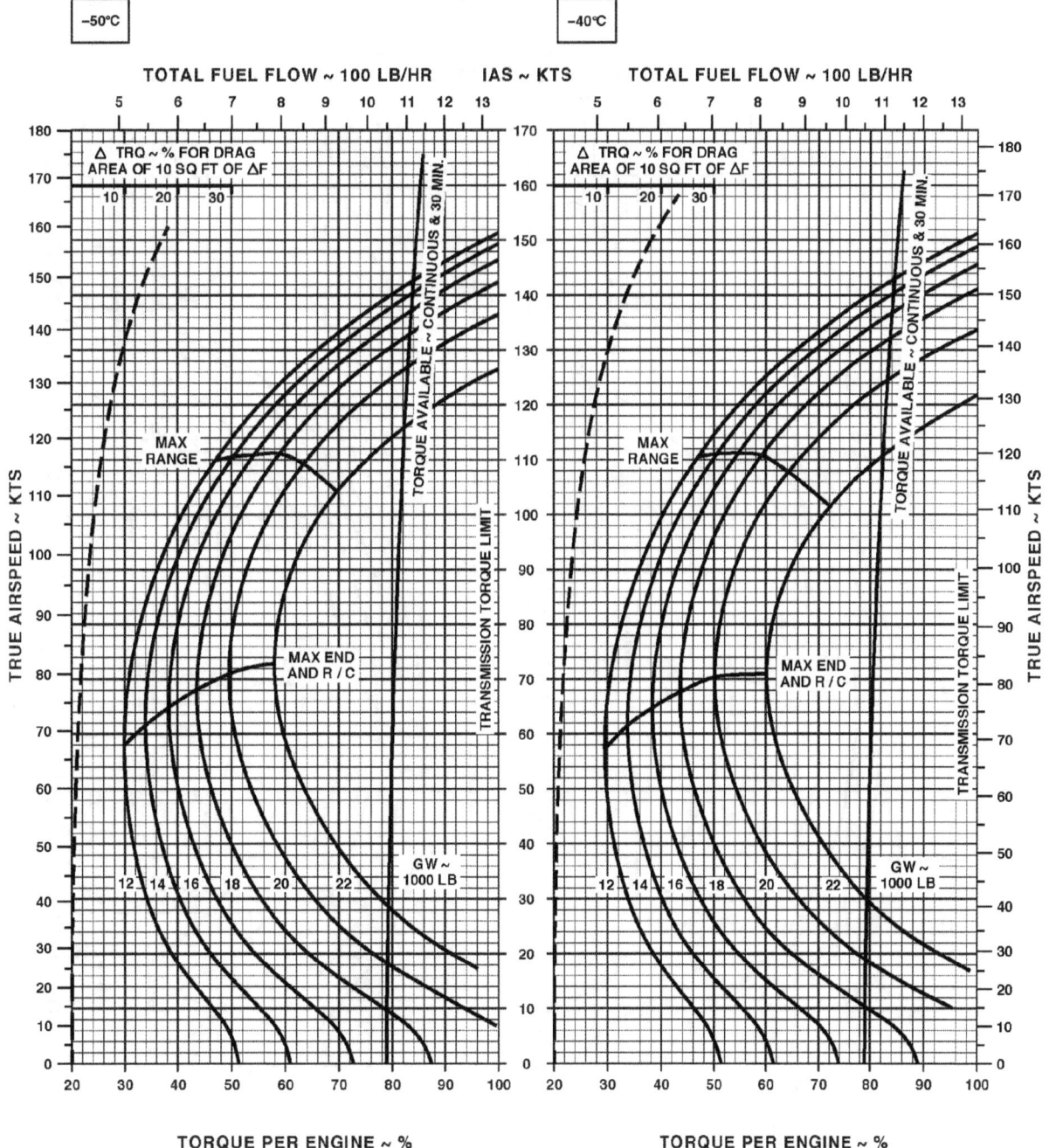

Figure 7-17. Cruise - Pressure Altitude 10,000 Feet (Sheet 1 of 5)

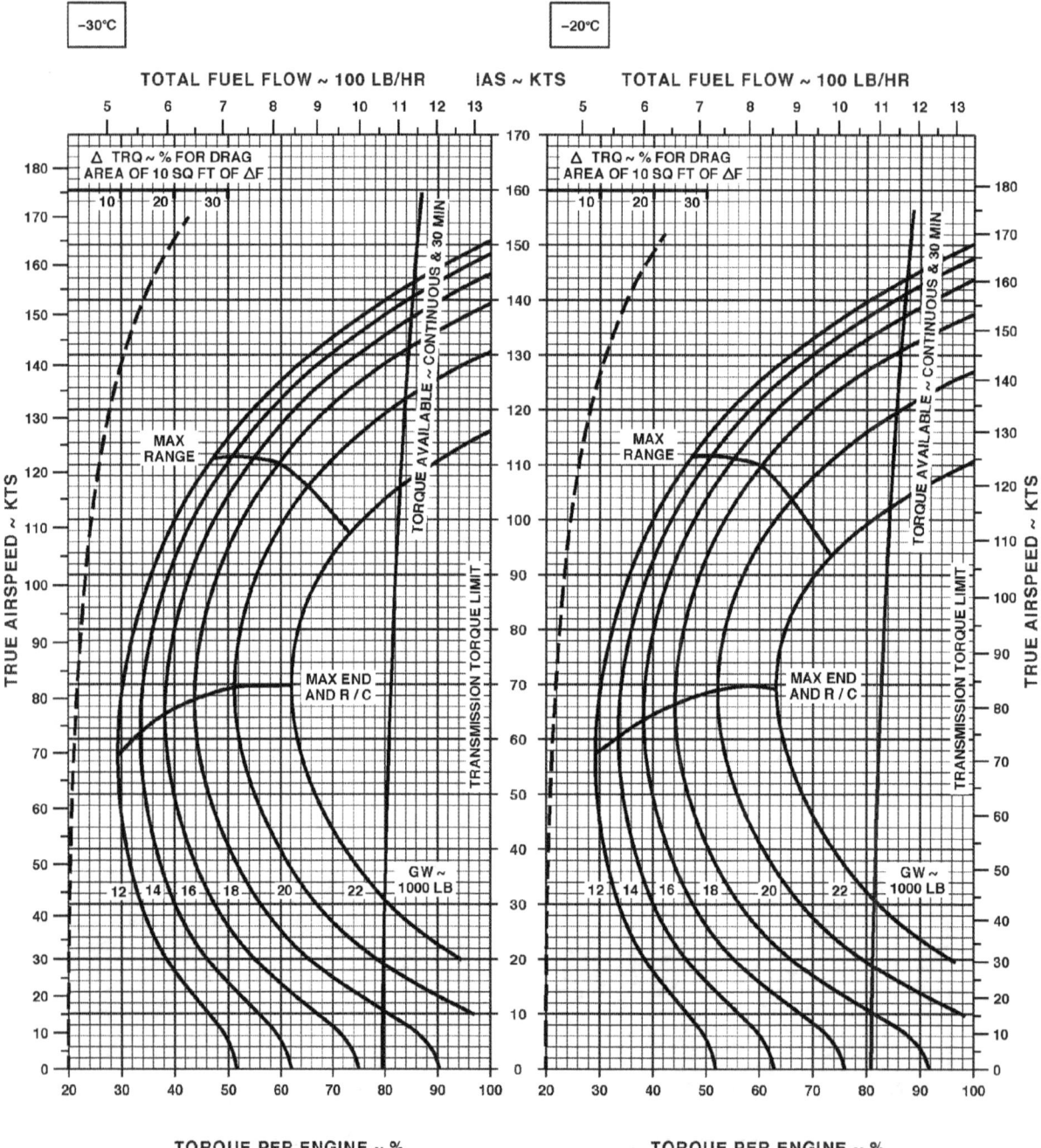

Figure 7-17. Cruise - Pressure Altitude 10,000 Feet (Sheet 2 of 5)

CRUISE
CLEAN CONFIGURATION
PRESS ALT: 10000 FT

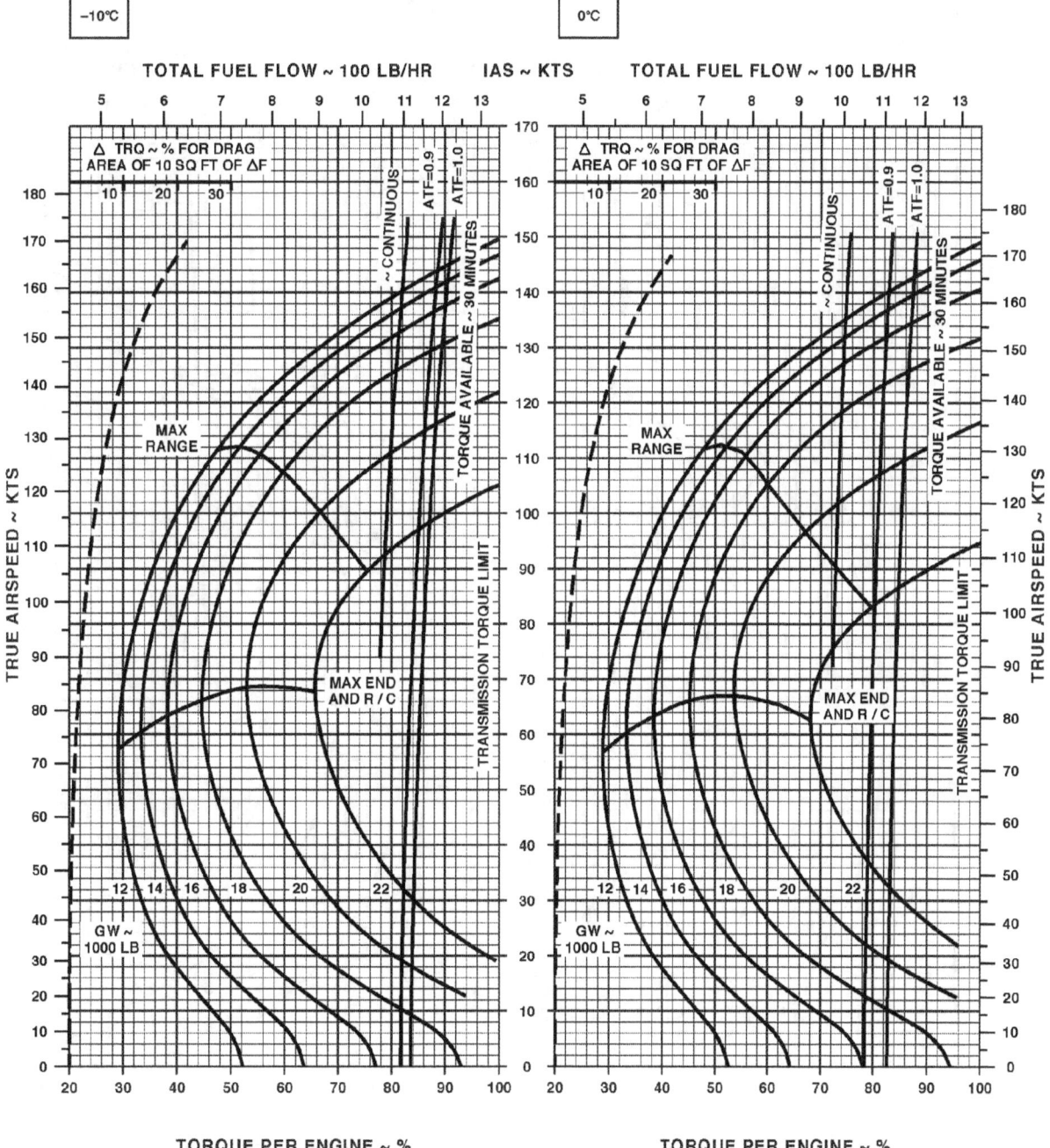

Figure 7-17. Cruise - Pressure Altitude 10,000 Feet (Sheet 3 of 5)

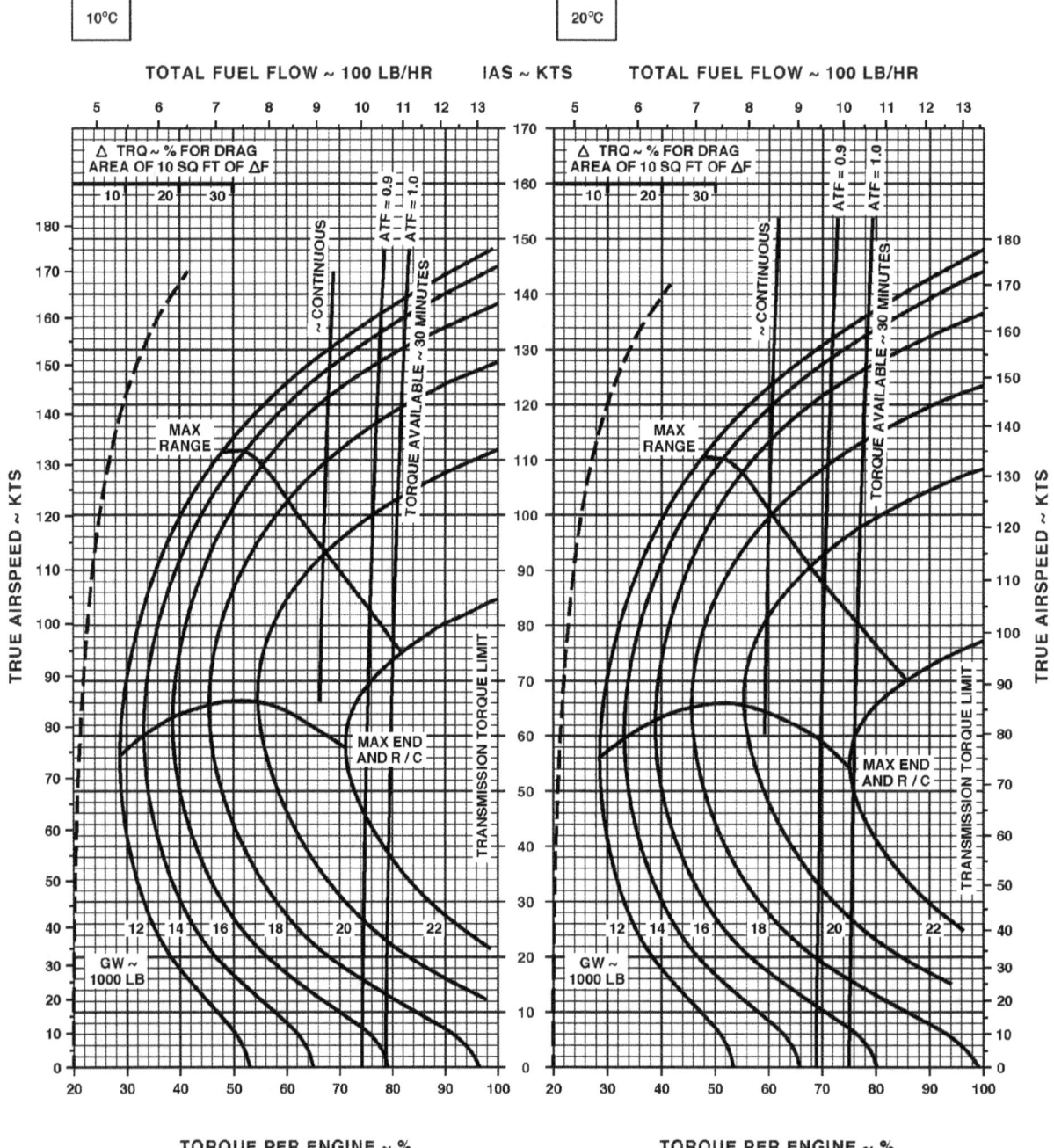

Figure 7-17. Cruise - Pressure Altitude 10,000 Feet (Sheet 4 of 5)

CRUISE
CLEAN CONFIGURATION
PRESS ALT: 10000 FT

CRUISE
10000 FT
T700 (2)

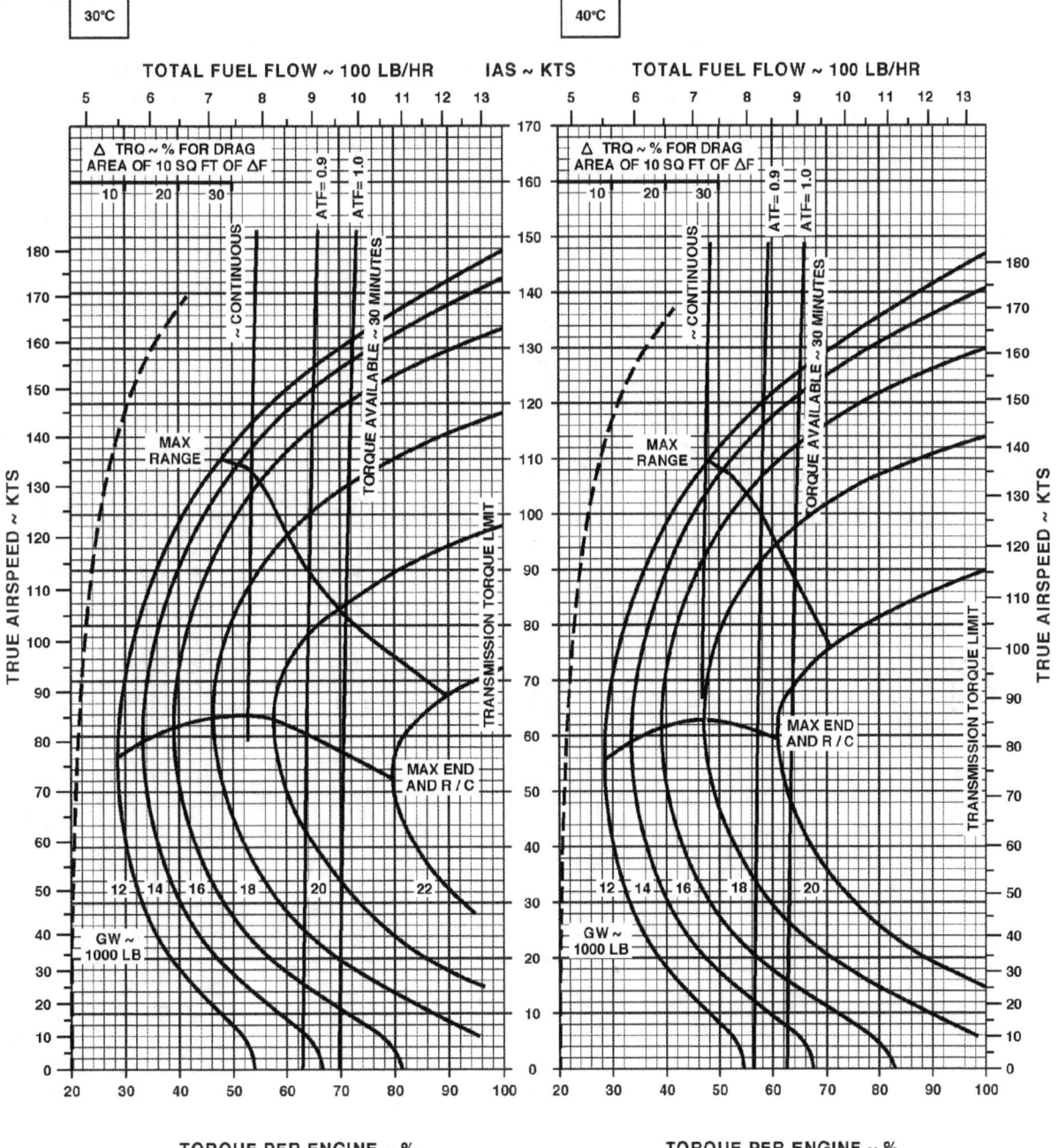

DATA BASE: FLIGHT TEST

Figure 7-17. Cruise - Pressure Altitude 10,000 Feet (Sheet 5 of 5)

CRUISE

PRESS ALT: 10000 FT

CRUISE
10000 FT
T700 (2)

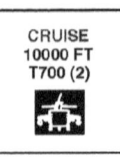

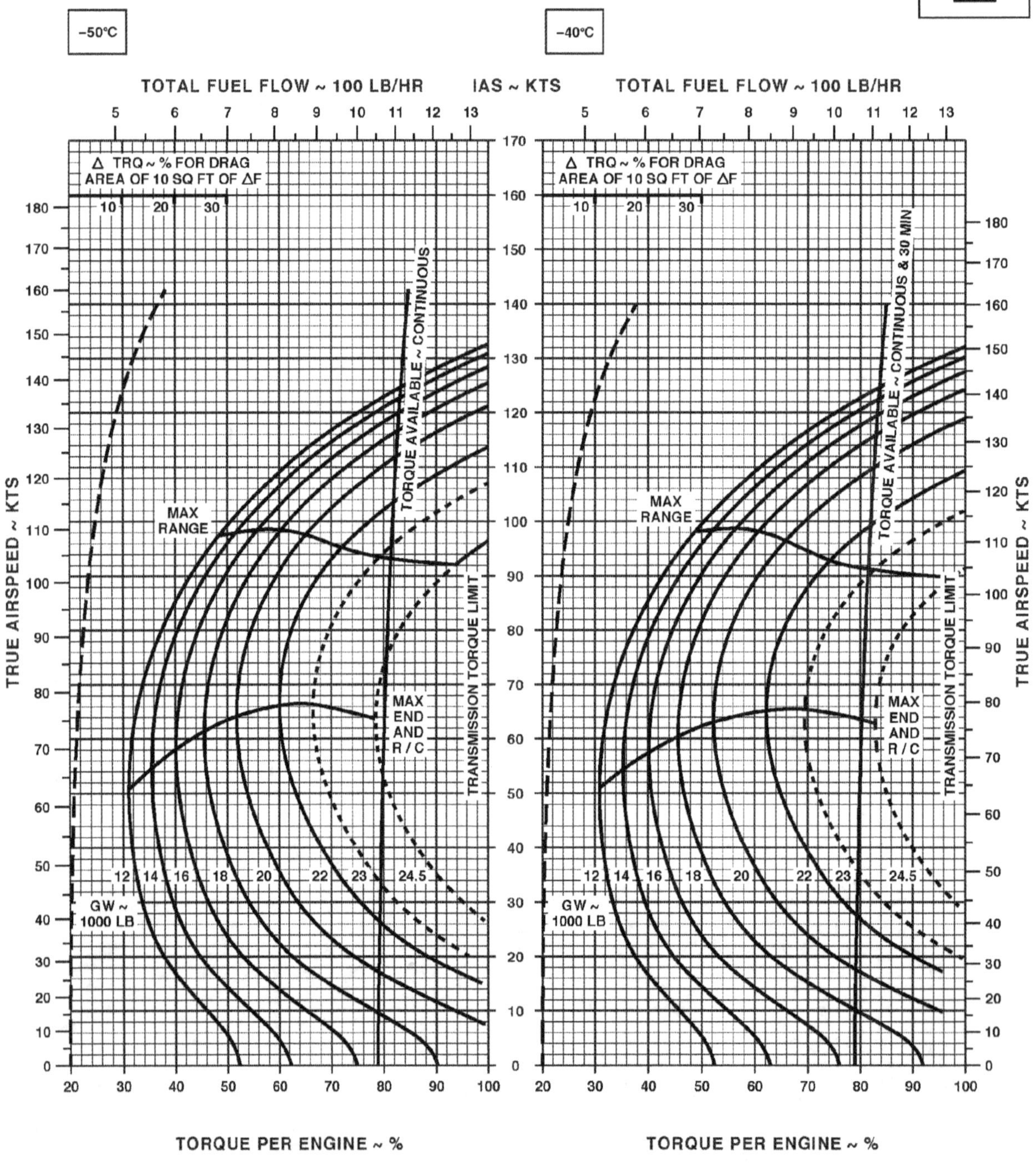

DATA BASE: FLIGHT TEST

AA0564

Figure 7-18. Cruise High Drag - Pressure Altitude 10,000 Feet (Sheet 1 of 5)

CRUISE

PRESS ALT: 10000 FT

CRUISE
10000 FT
T700 (2)

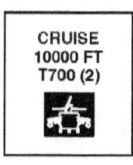

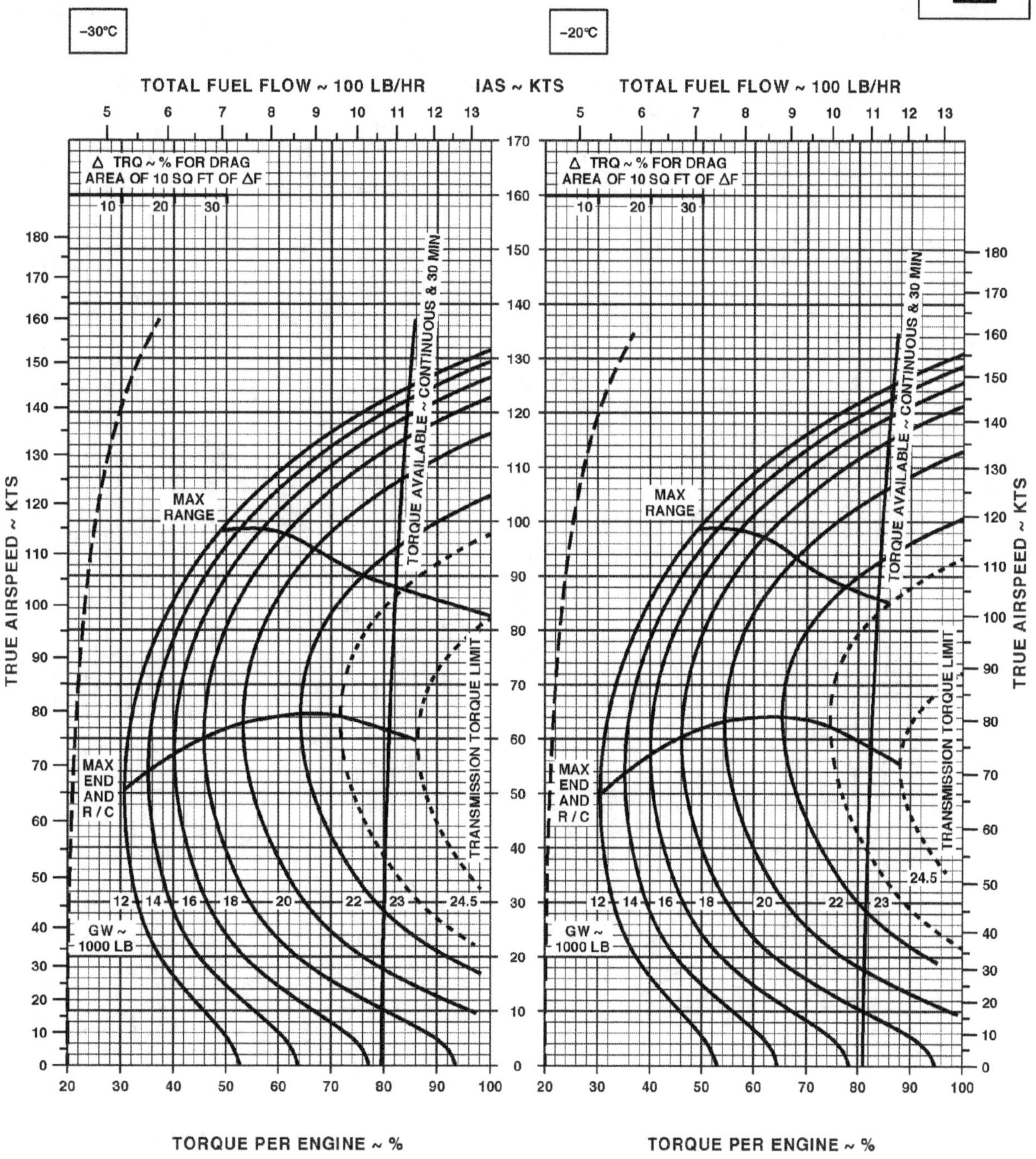

DATA BASE: FLIGHT TEST

AA0565
SA

Figure 7-18. Cruise High Drag - Pressure Altitude 10,000 Feet (Sheet 2 of 5)

CRUISE

PRESS ALT: 10000 FT

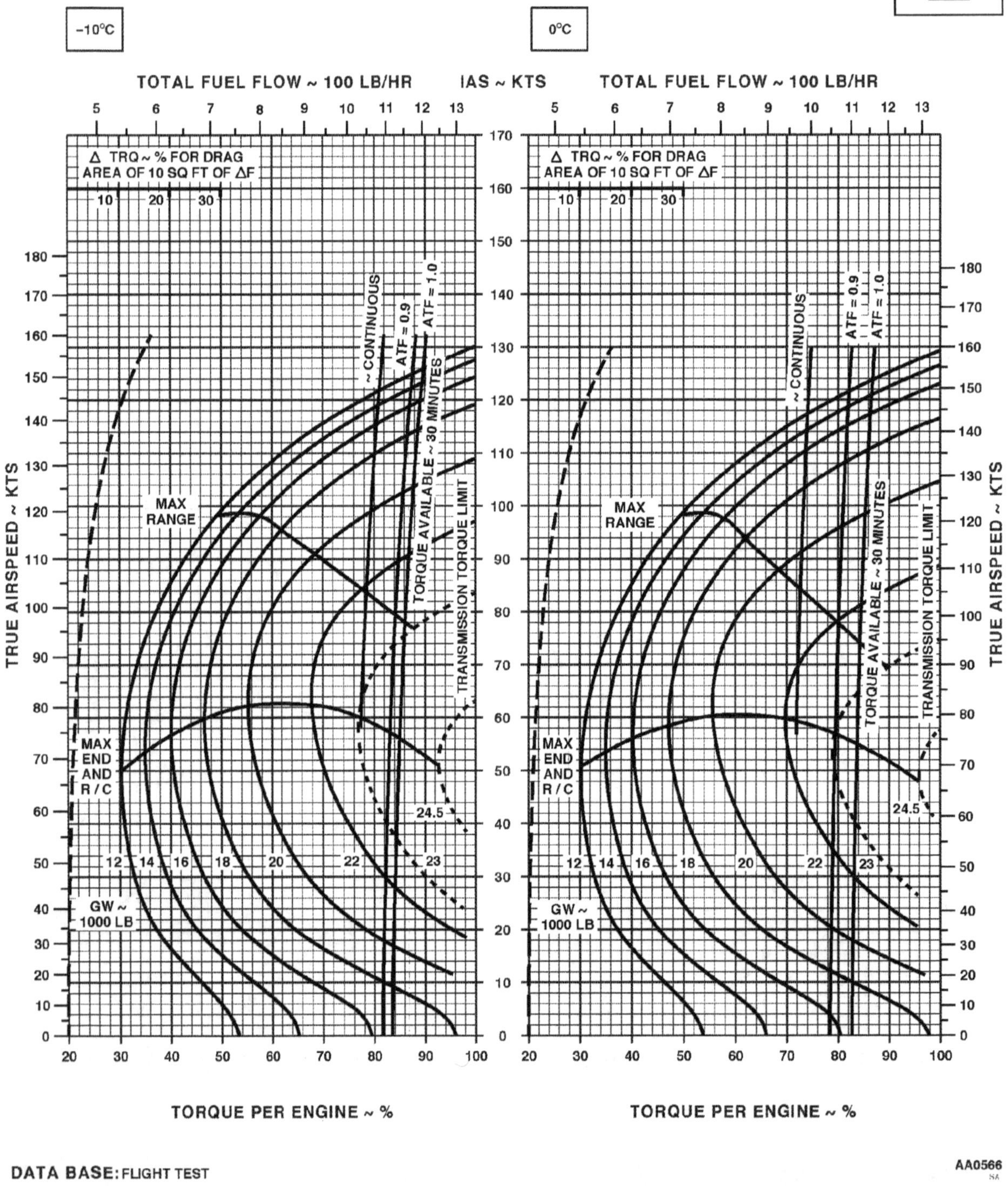

Figure 7-18. Cruise High Drag - Pressure Altitude 10,000 Feet (Sheet 3 of 5)

CRUISE

PRESS ALT: 10000 FT

Figure 7-18. Cruise High Drag - Pressure Altitude 10,000 Feet (Sheet 4 of 5)

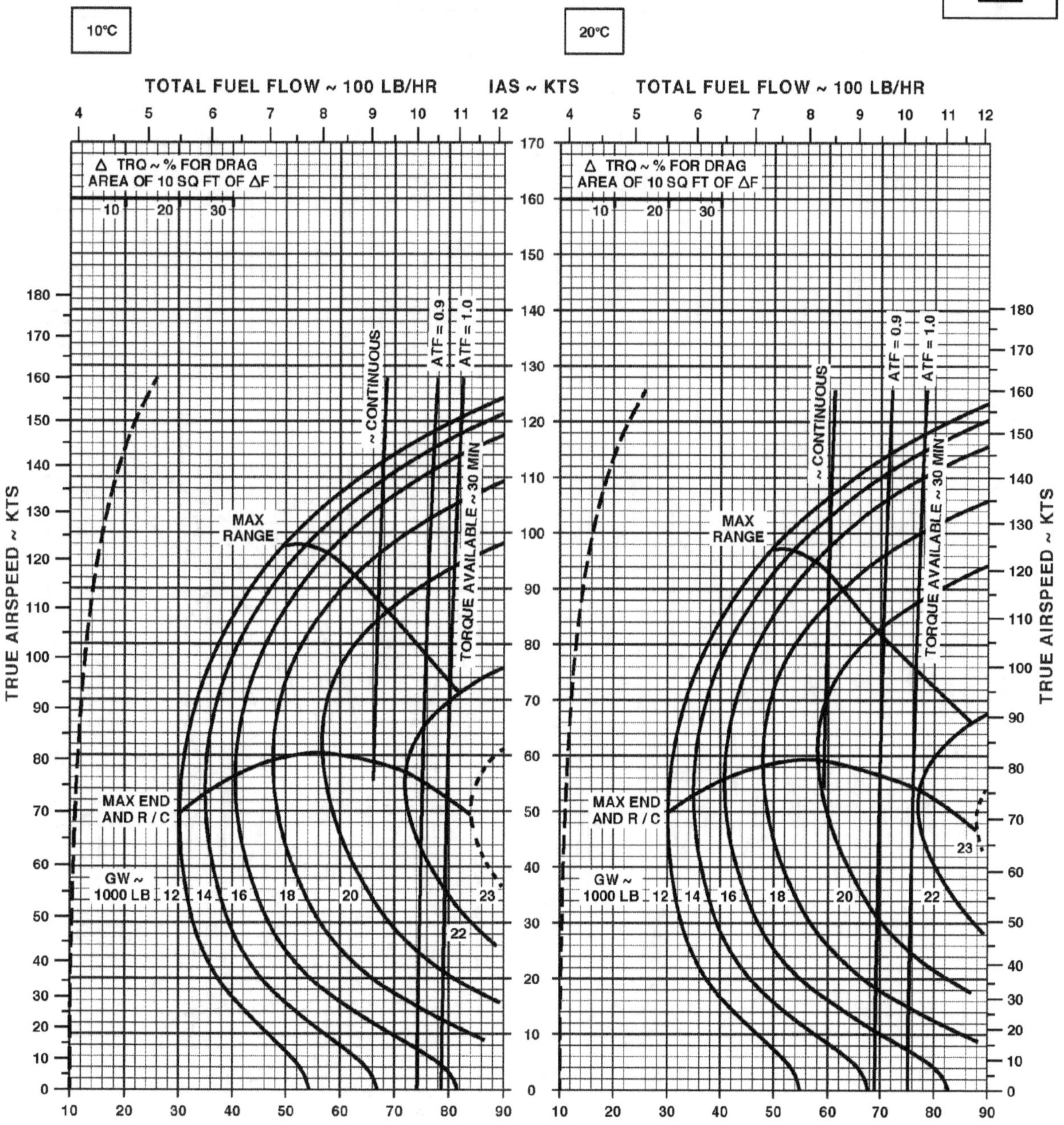

CRUISE

PRESS ALT: 10000 FT

CRUISE
10000 FT
T700 (2)

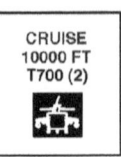

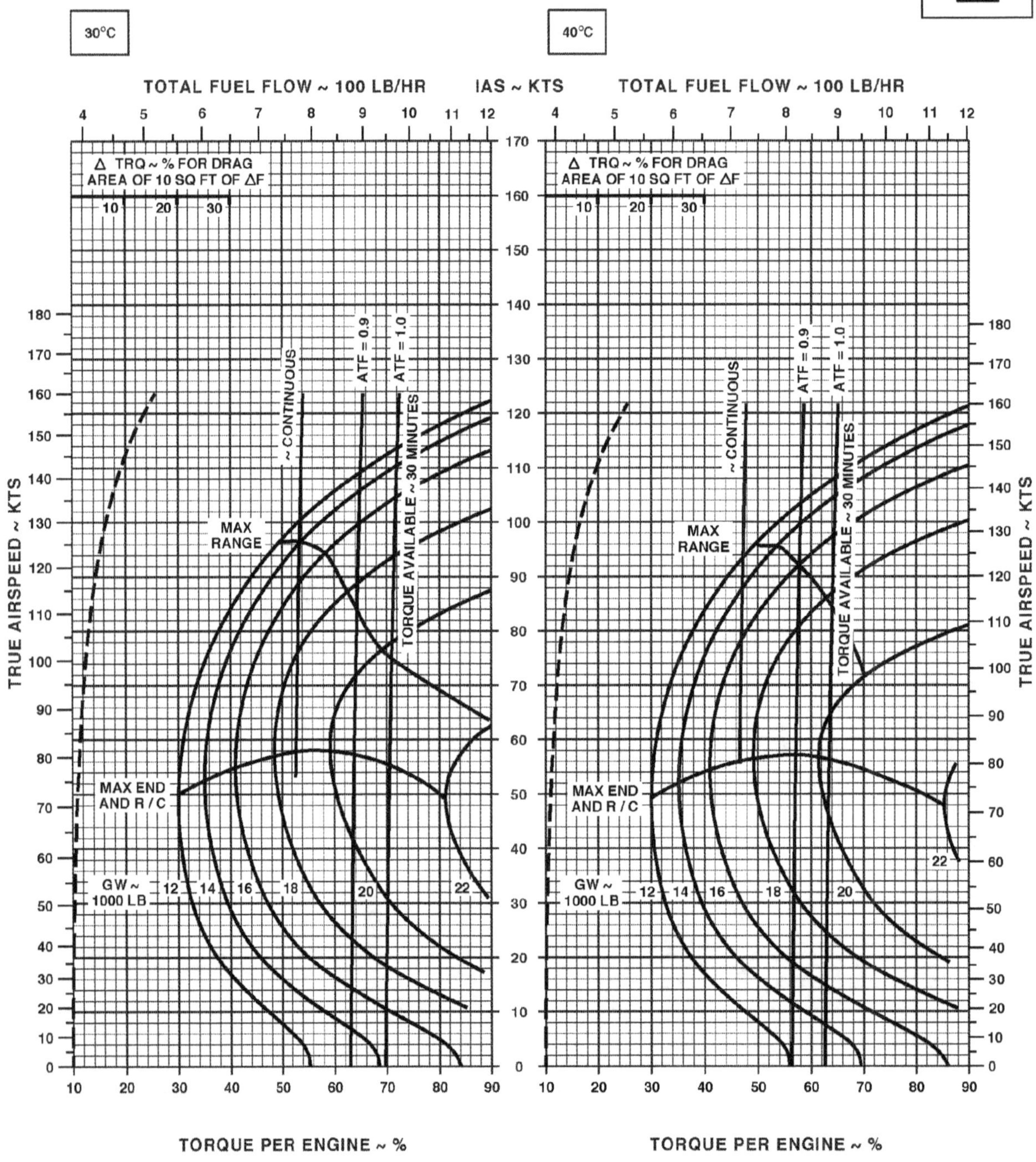

DATA BASE: FLIGHT TEST

AA0568

Figure 7-18. Cruise High Drag - Pressure Altitude 10,000 Feet (Sheet 5 of 5)

CRUISE
CLEAN CONFIGURATION
PRESS ALT: 12000 FT

CRUISE 12000 FT T700 (2)

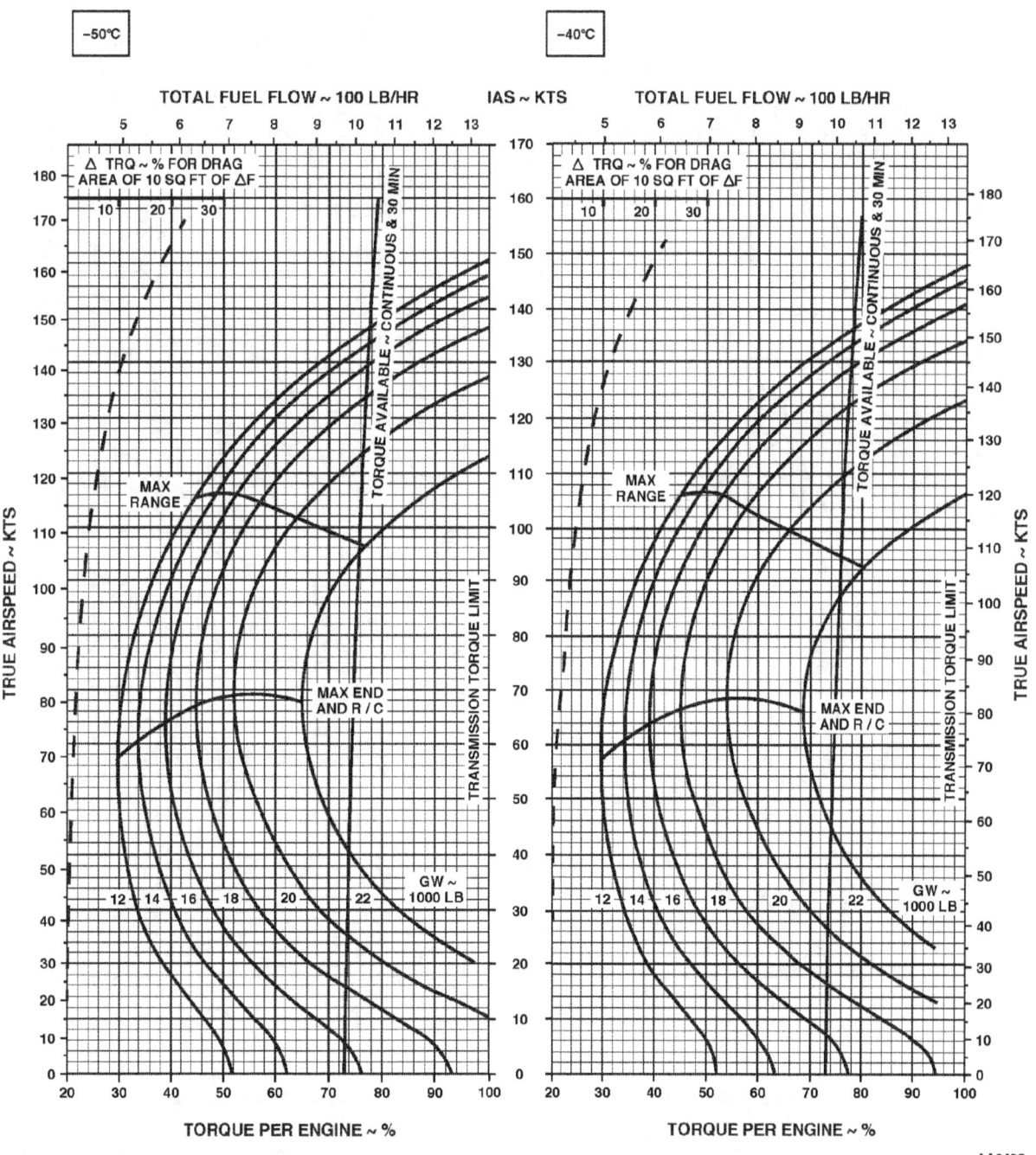

Figure 7-19. Cruise - Pressure Altitude 12,000 Feet (Sheet 1 of 5)

CRUISE
CLEAN CONFIGURATION
PRESS ALT: 12000 FT

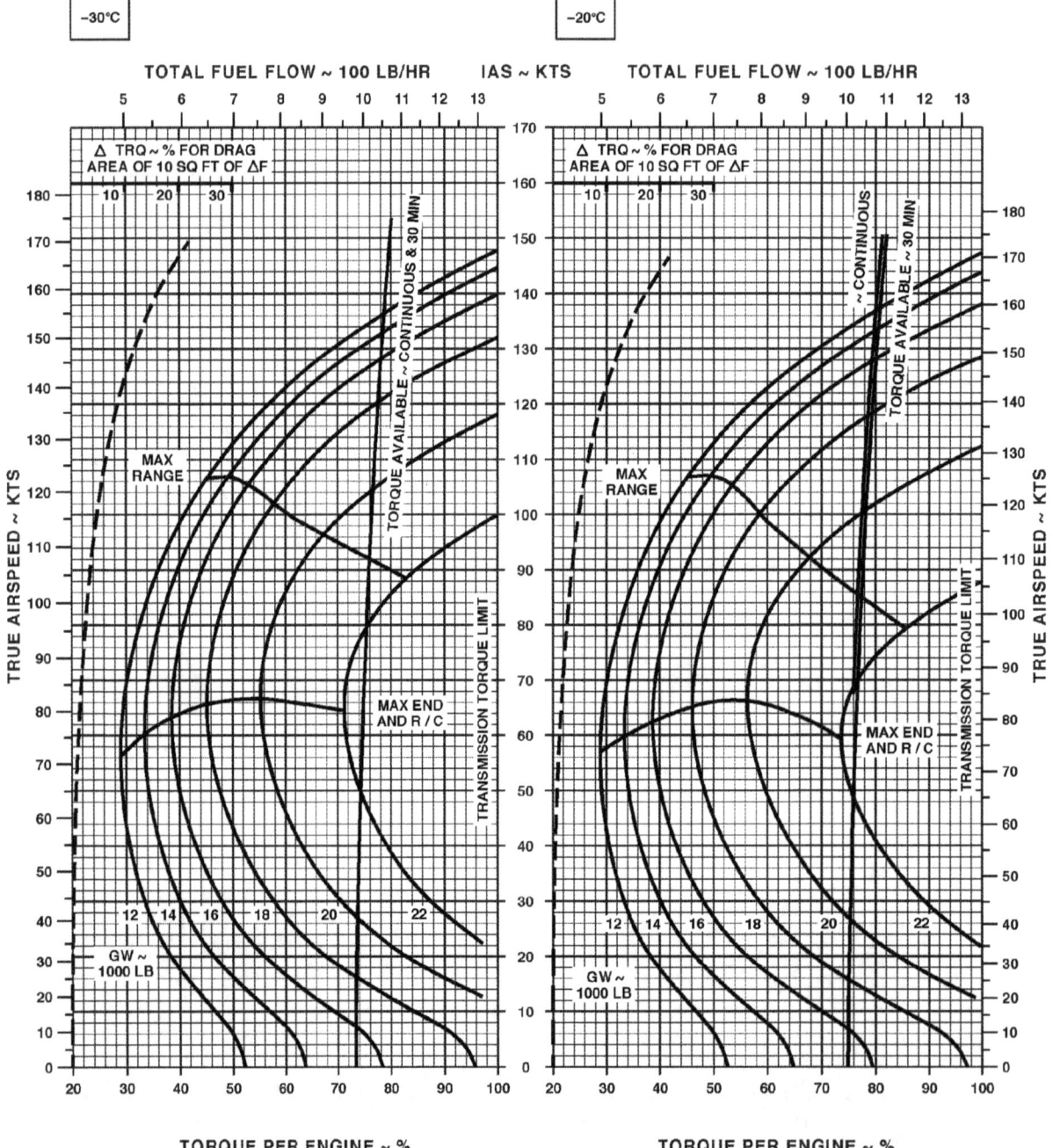

Figure 7-19. Cruise - Pressure Altitude 12,000 Feet (Sheet 2 of 5)

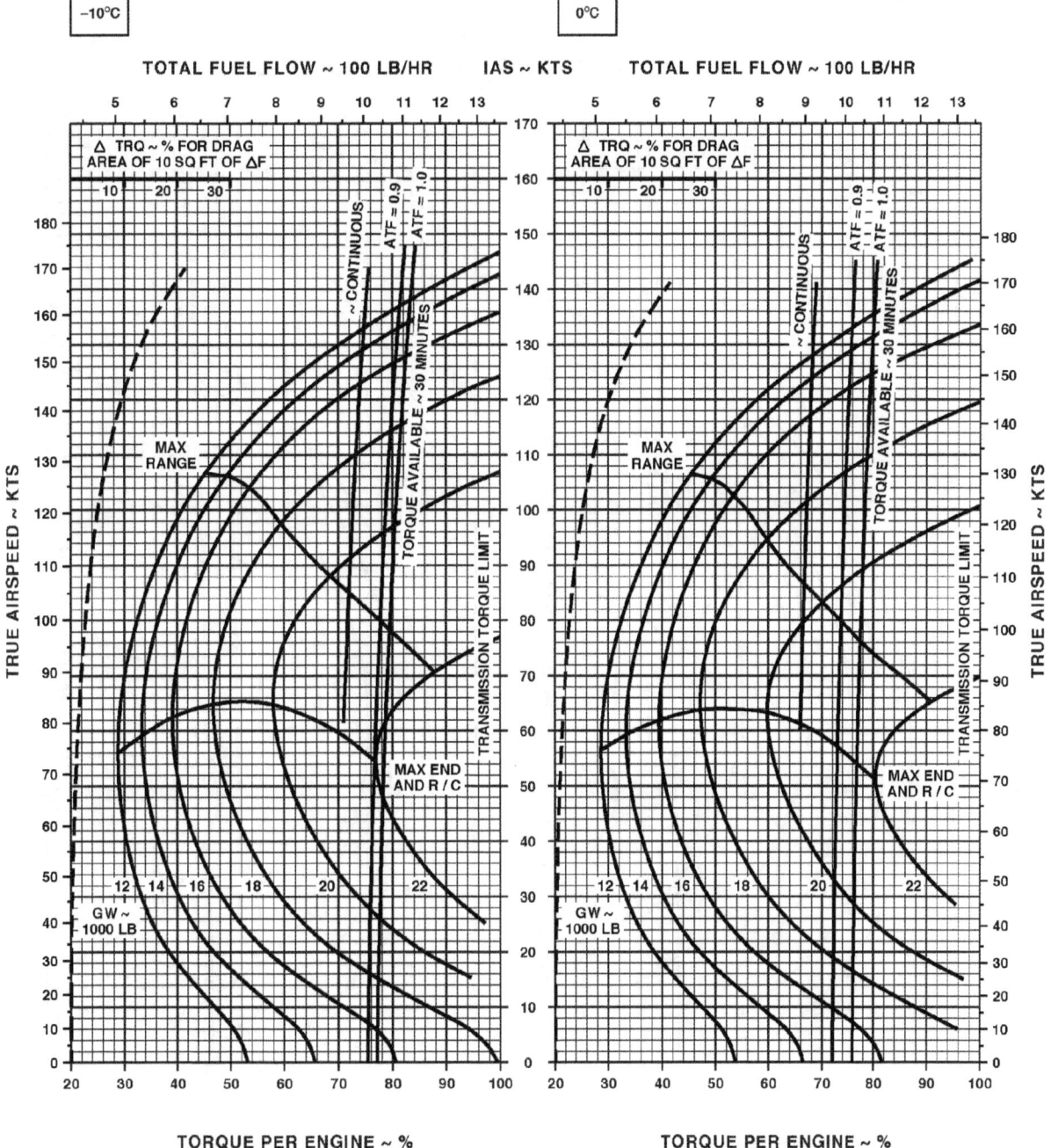

Figure 7-19. Cruise - Pressure Altitude 12,000 Feet (Sheet 3 of 5)

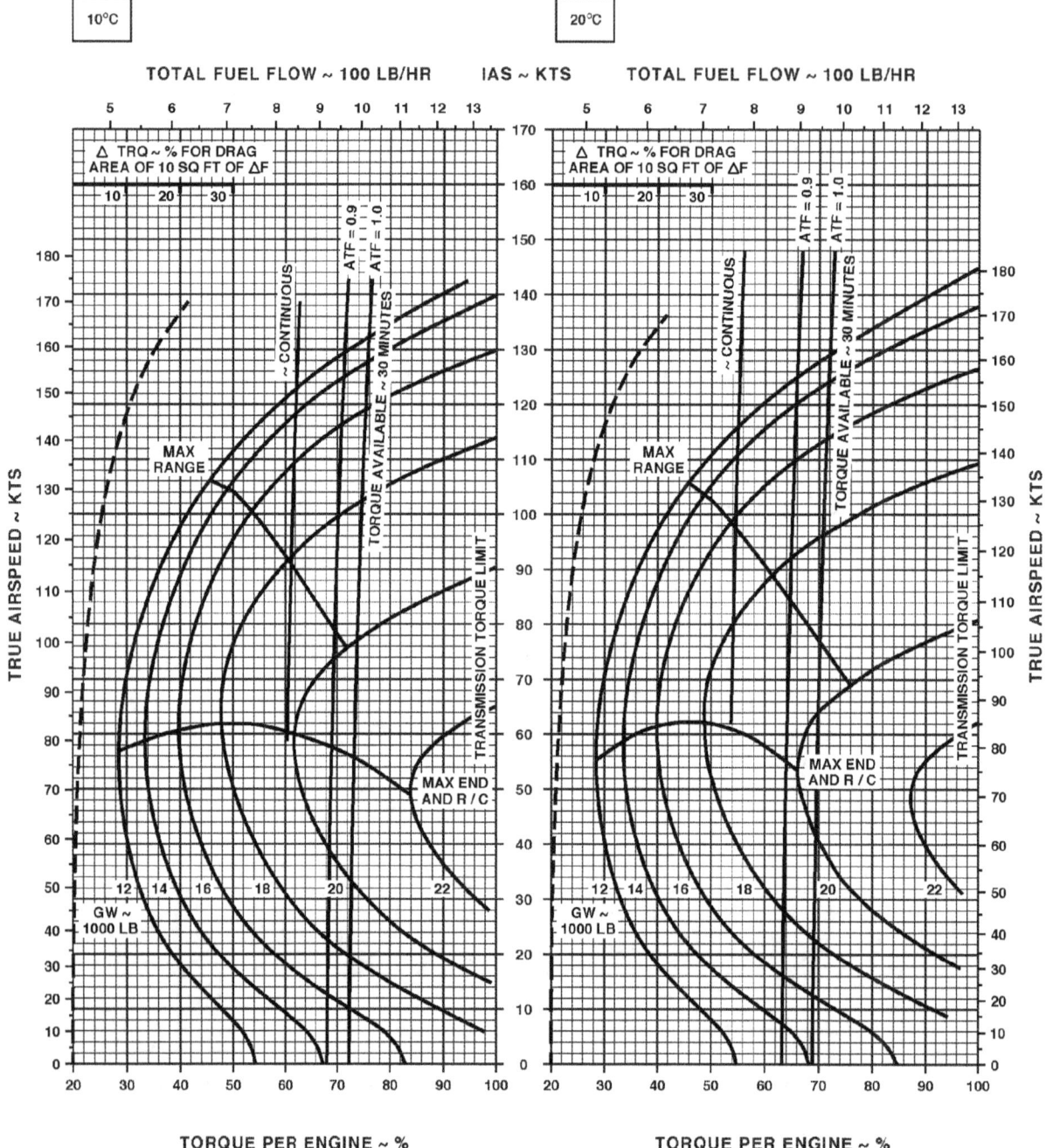

Figure 7-19. Cruise - Pressure Altitude 12,000 Feet (Sheet 4 of 5)

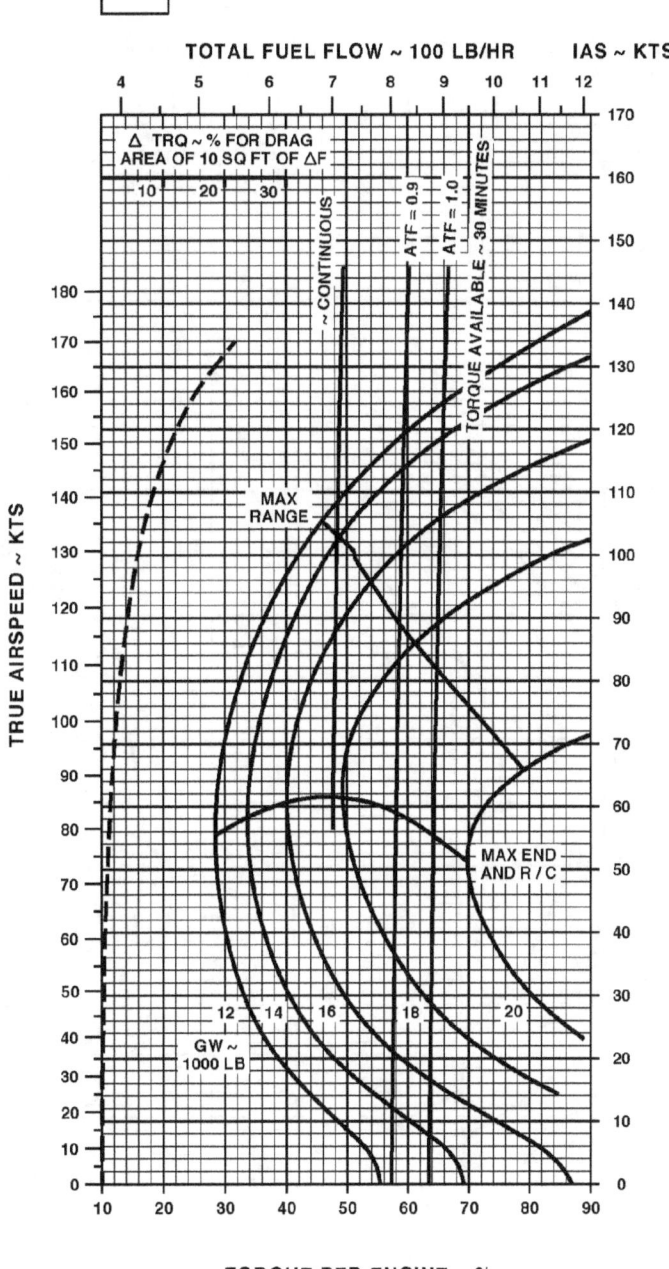

Figure 7-19. Cruise - Pressure Altitude 12,000 Feet (Sheet 5 of 5)

CRUISE

CRUISE
12000 FT
T700 (2)

PRESS ALT: 12000 FT

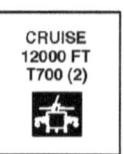

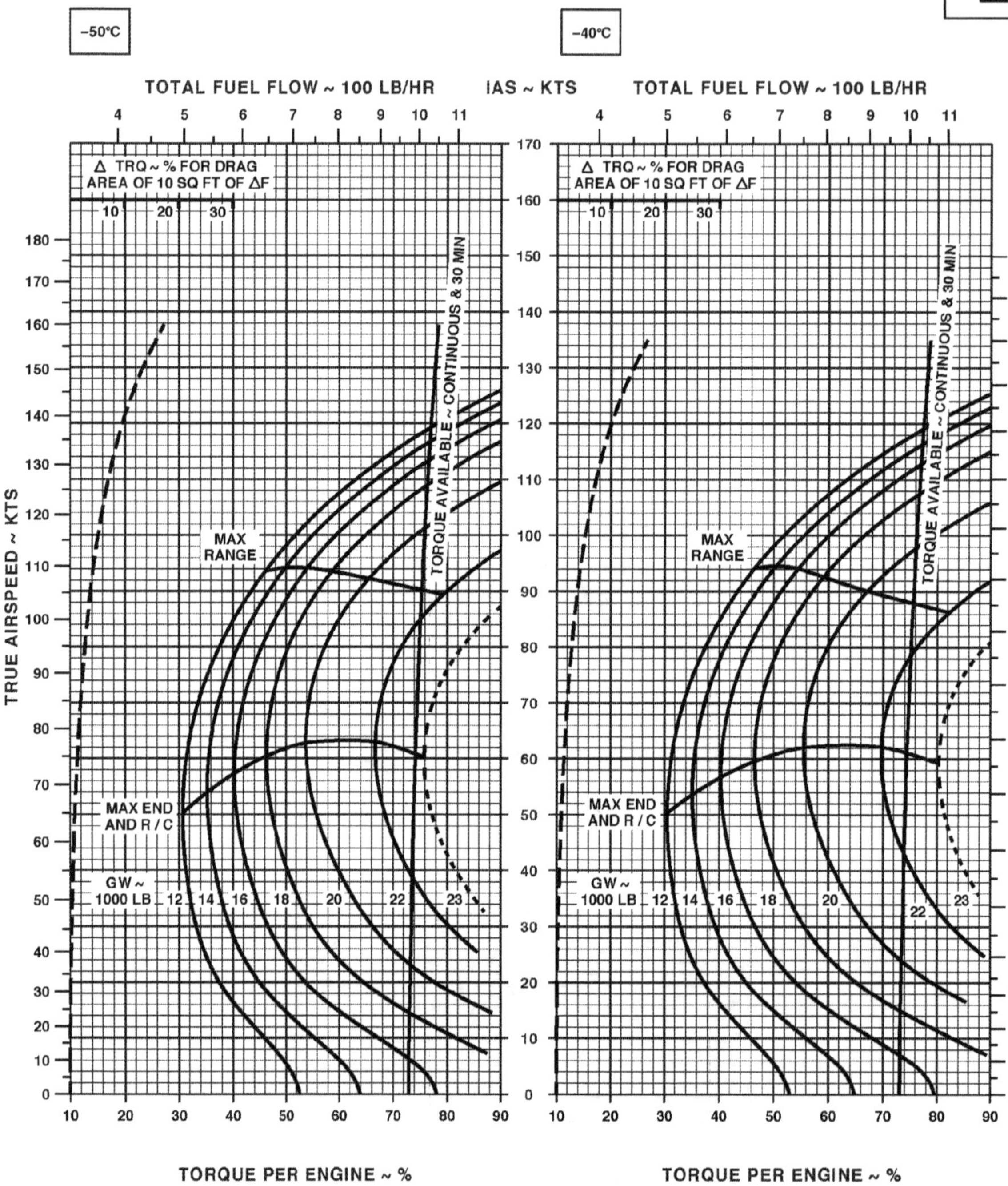

DATA BASE: FLIGHT TEST

AA0569
SA

Figure 7-20. Cruise High Drag - Pressure Altitude 12,000 Feet (Sheet 1 of 5)

CRUISE

PRESS ALT: 12000 FT

Figure 7-20. Cruise High Drag - Pressure Altitude 12,000 Feet (Sheet 2 of 5)

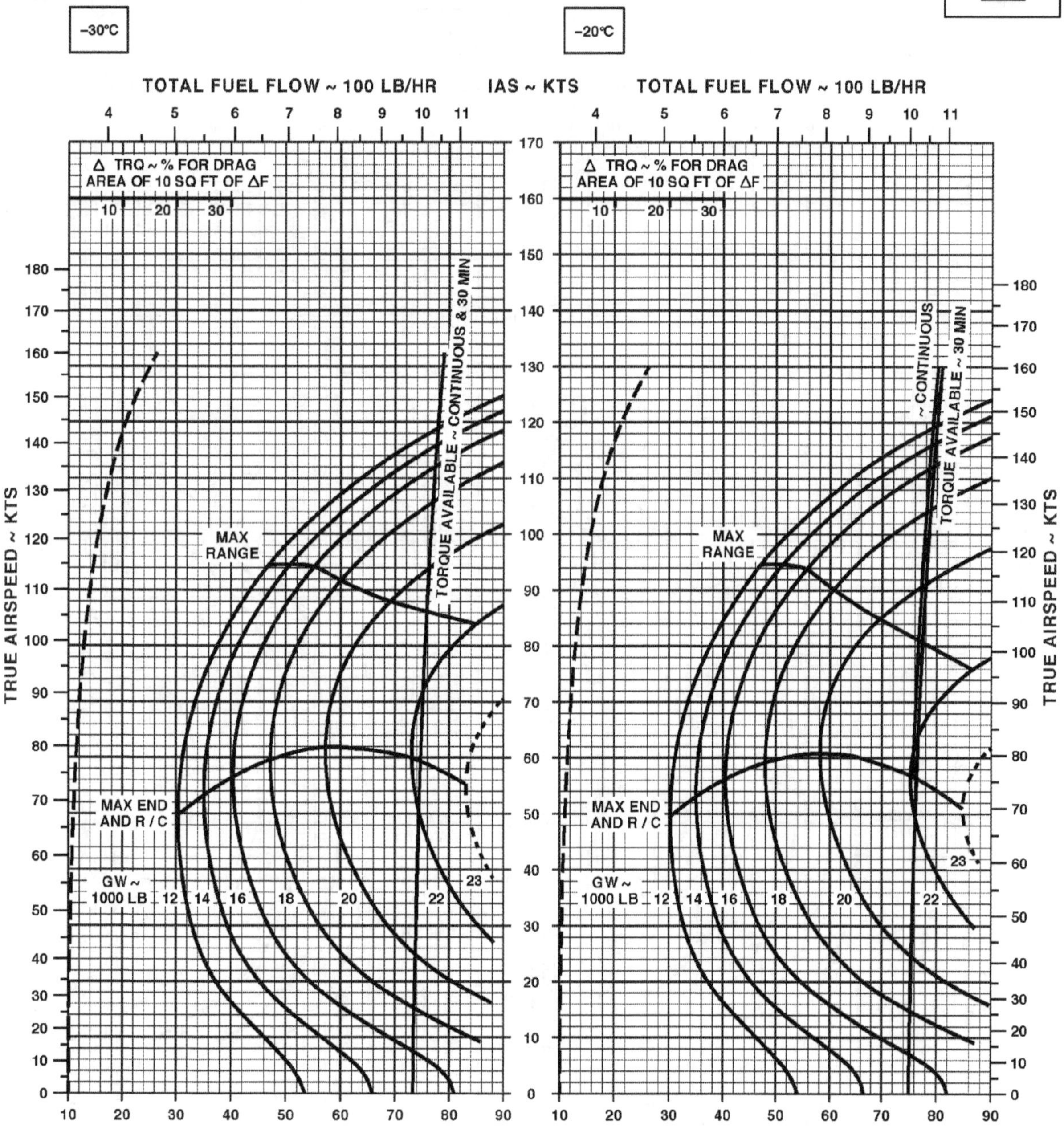

CRUISE

PRESS ALT: 12000 FT

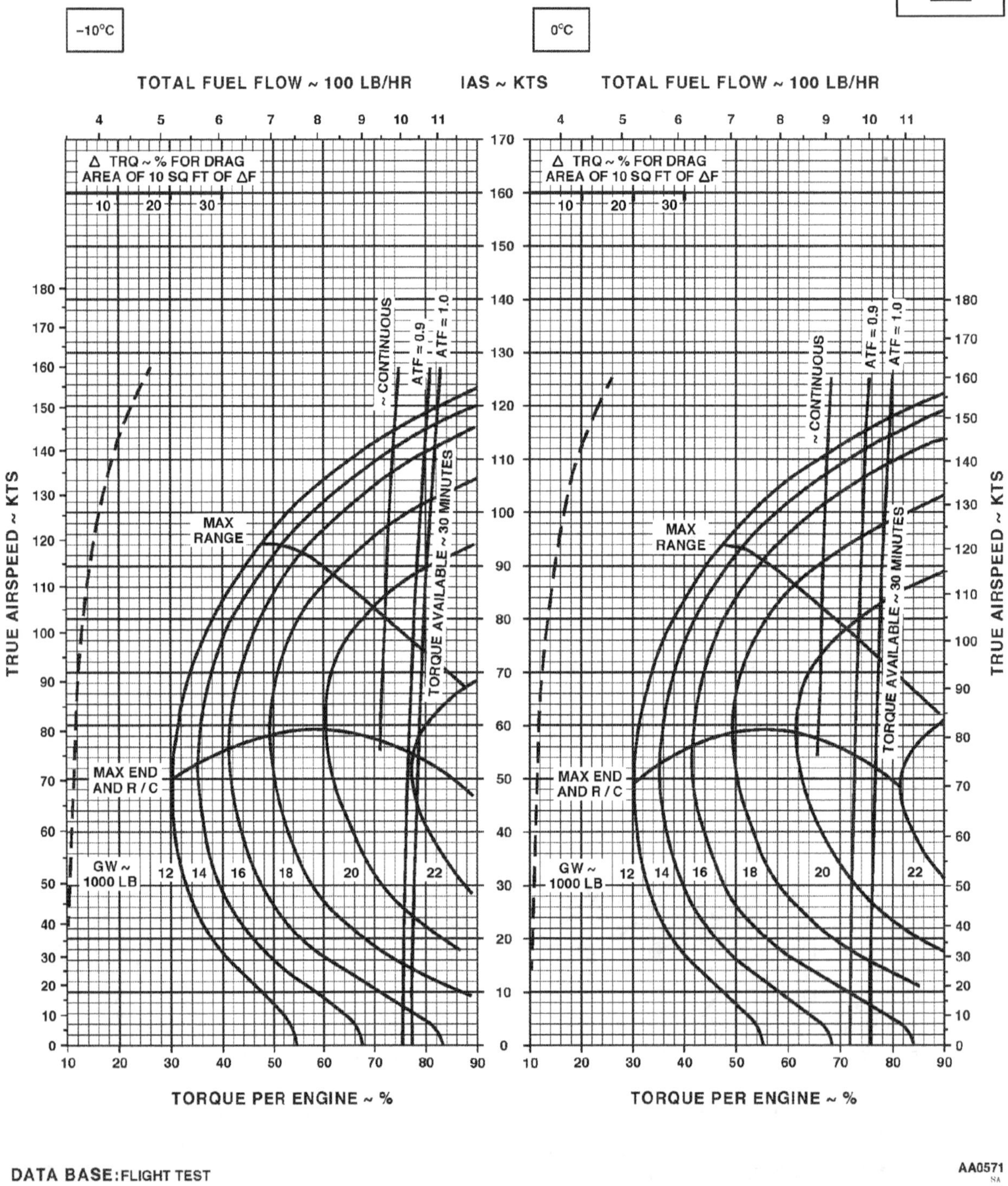

Figure 7-20. Cruise High Drag - Pressure Altitude 12,000 Feet (Sheet 3 of 5)

CRUISE

PRESS ALT: 12000 FT

CRUISE
12000 FT
T700 (2)

DATA BASE: FLIGHT TEST

AA0572

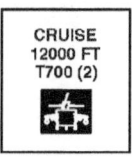

Figure 7-20. Cruise High Drag - Pressure Altitude 12,000 Feet (Sheet 4 of 5)

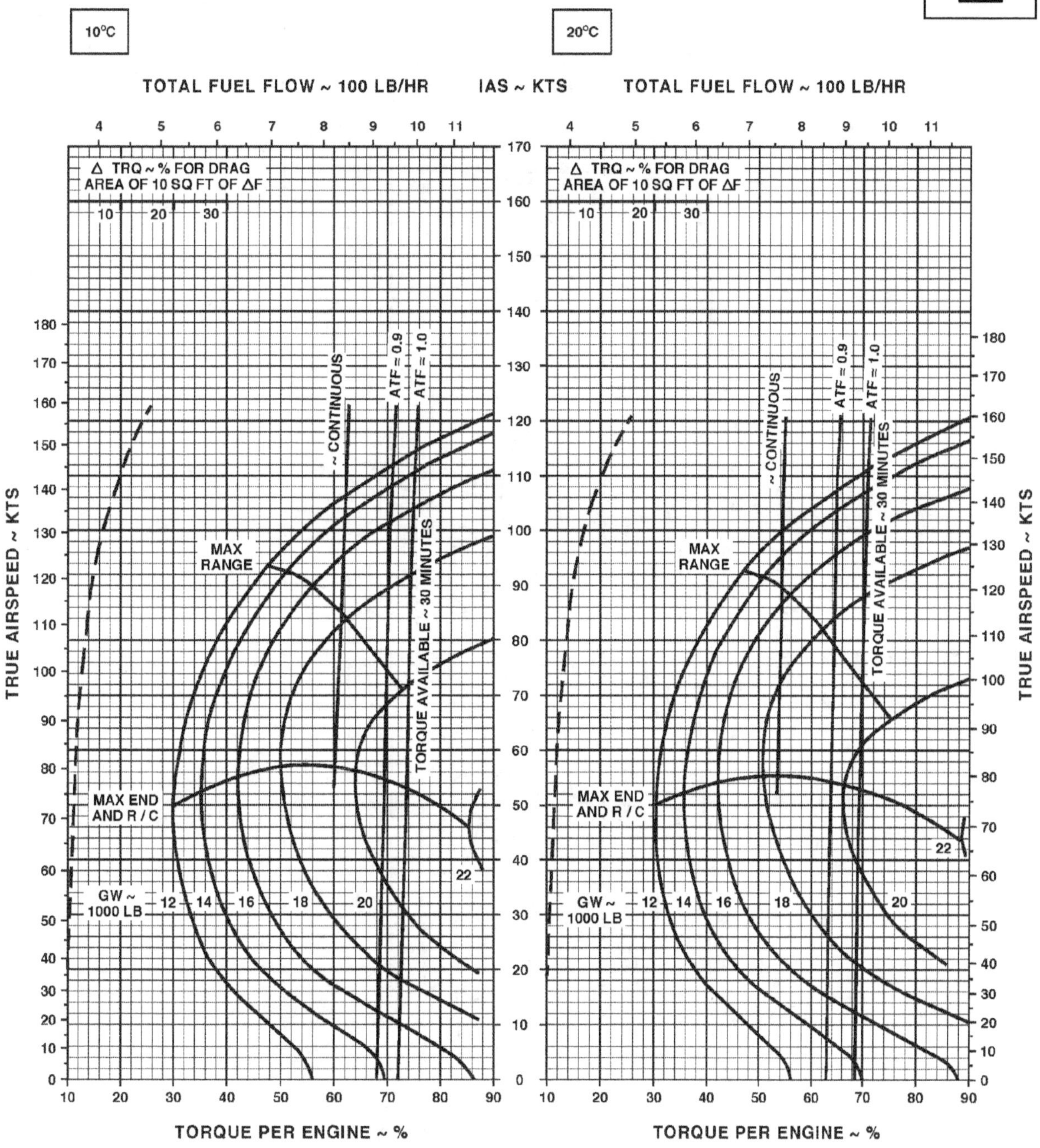

CRUISE

PRESS ALT: 12000 FT

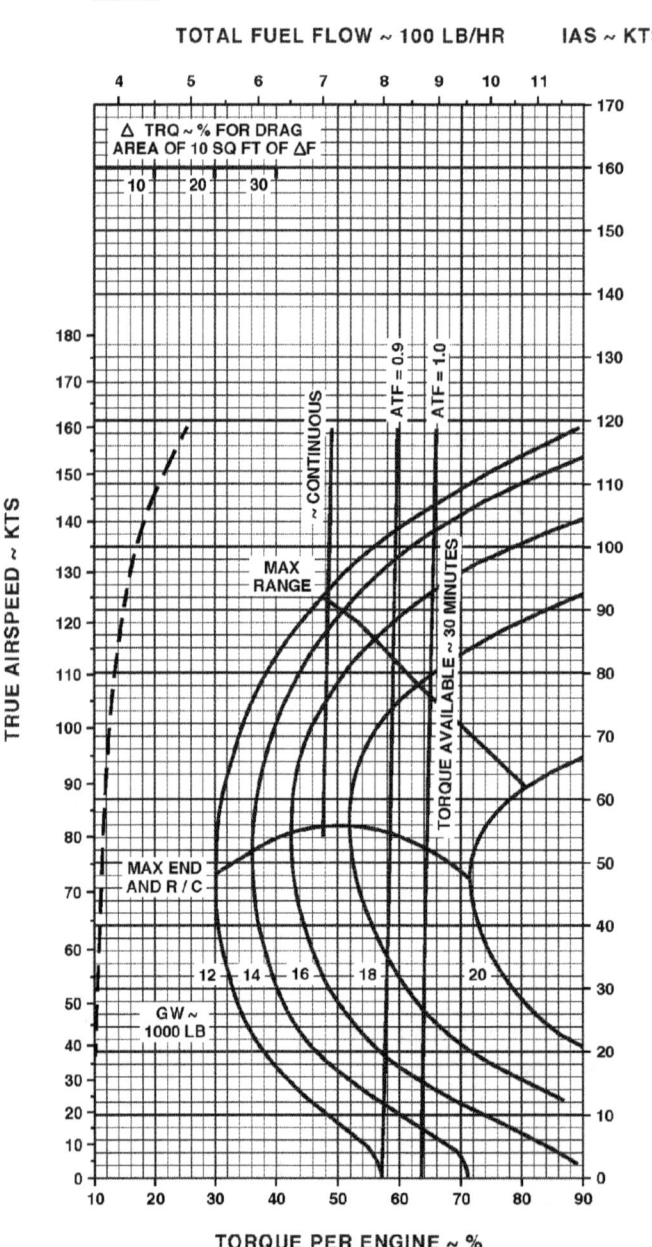

Figure 7-20. Cruise High Drag - Pressure Altitude 12,000 Feet (Sheet 5 of 5)

CRUISE
CLEAN CONFIGURATION
PRESS ALT: 14000 FT

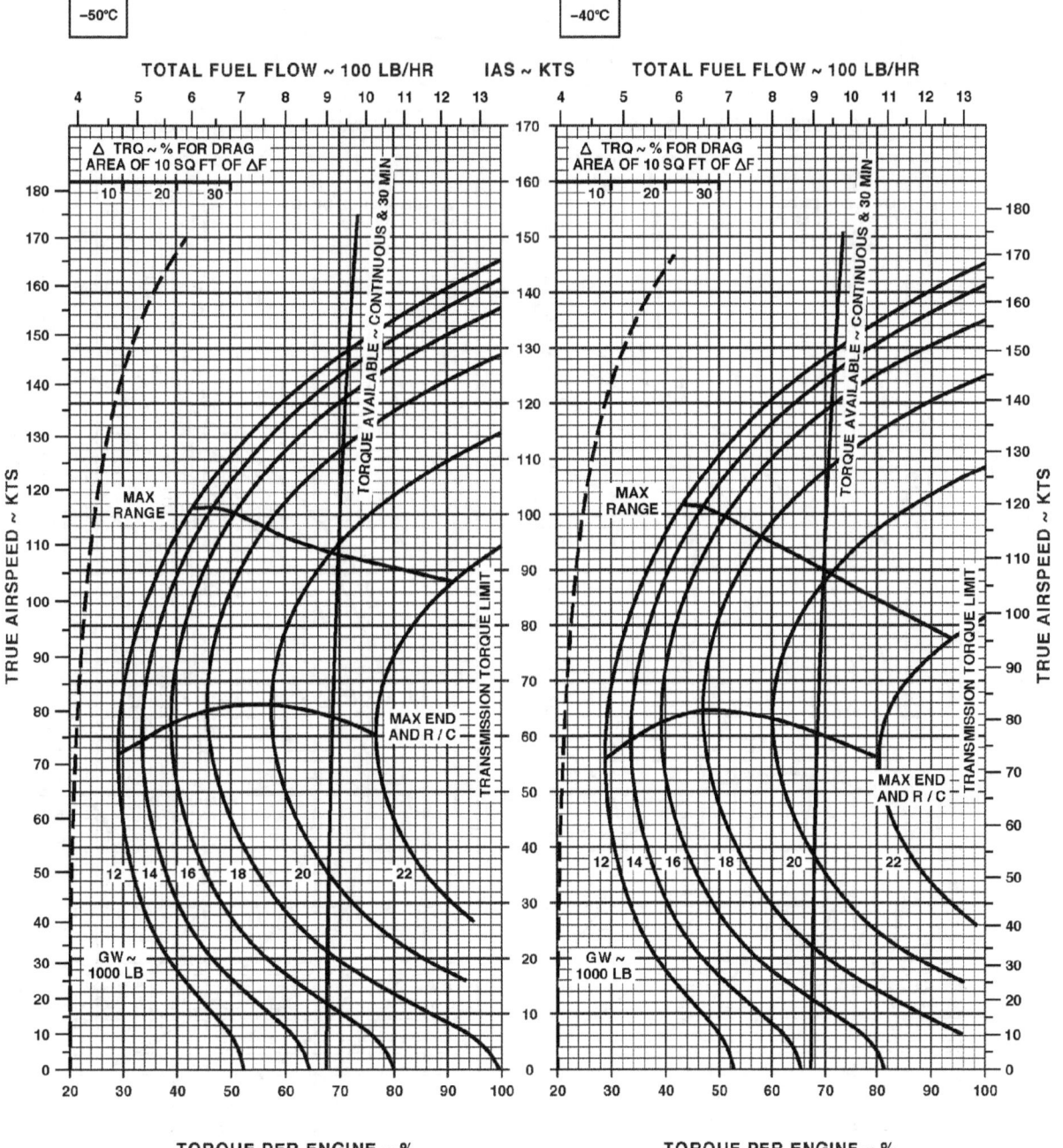

Figure 7-21. Cruise - Pressure Altitude 14,000 Feet (Sheet 1 of 5)

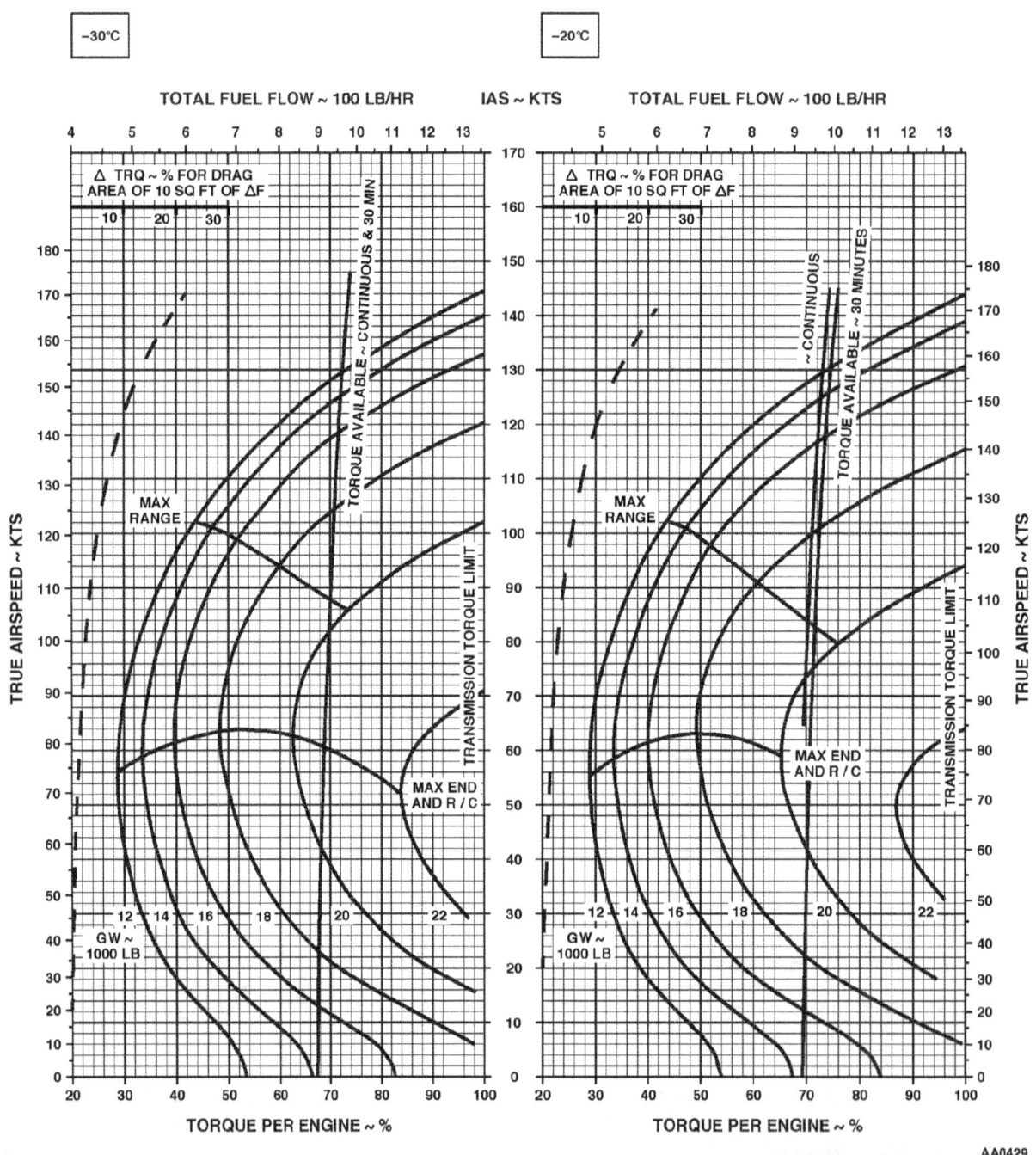

Figure 7-21. Cruise - Pressure Altitude 14,000 Feet (Sheet 2 of 5)

CRUISE
CLEAN CONFIGURATION
PRESS ALT: 14000 FT

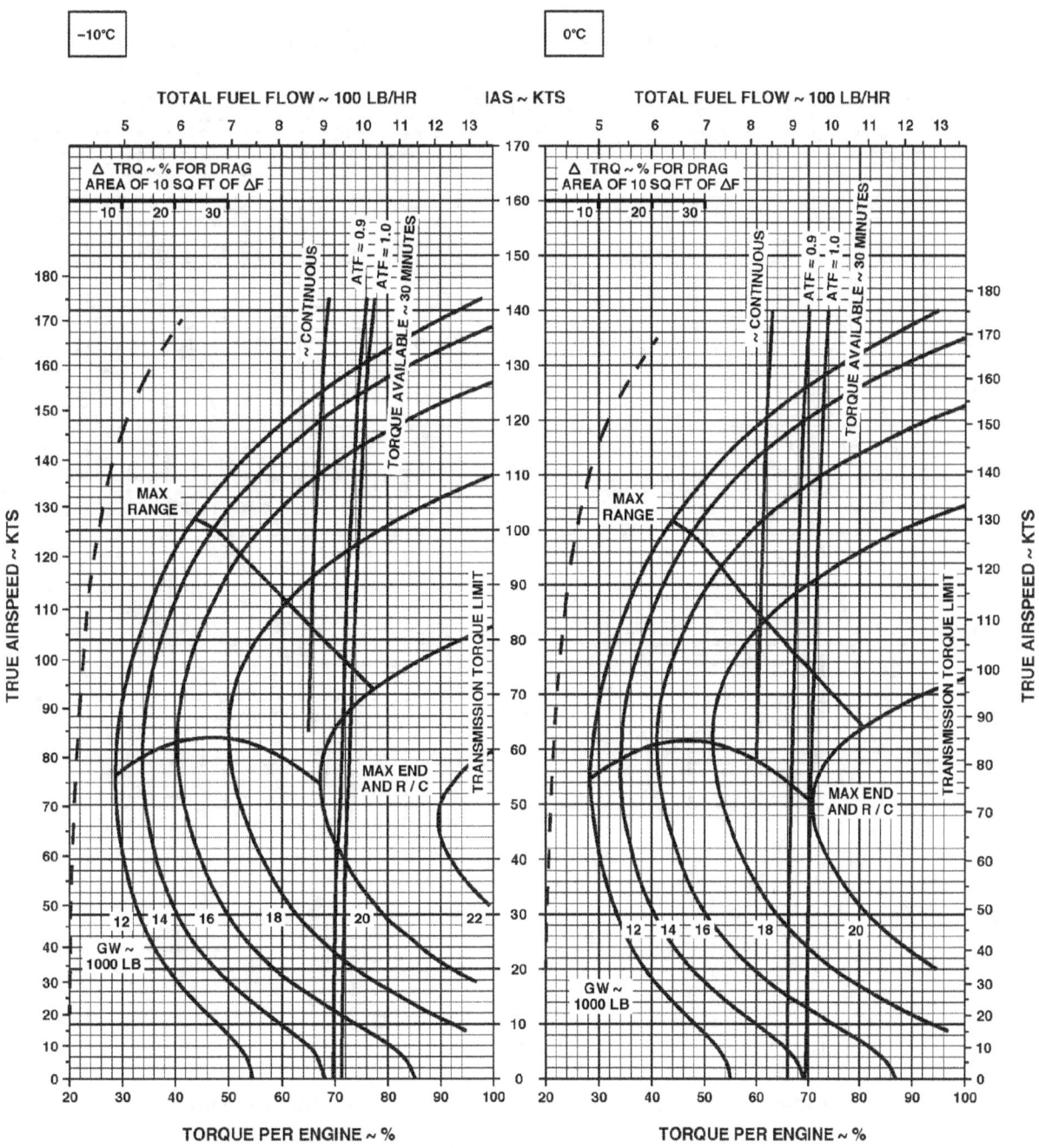

Figure 7-21. Cruise - Pressure Altitude 14,000 Feet (Sheet 3 of 5)

CRUISE
CLEAN CONFIGURATION
PRESS ALT: 14000 FT

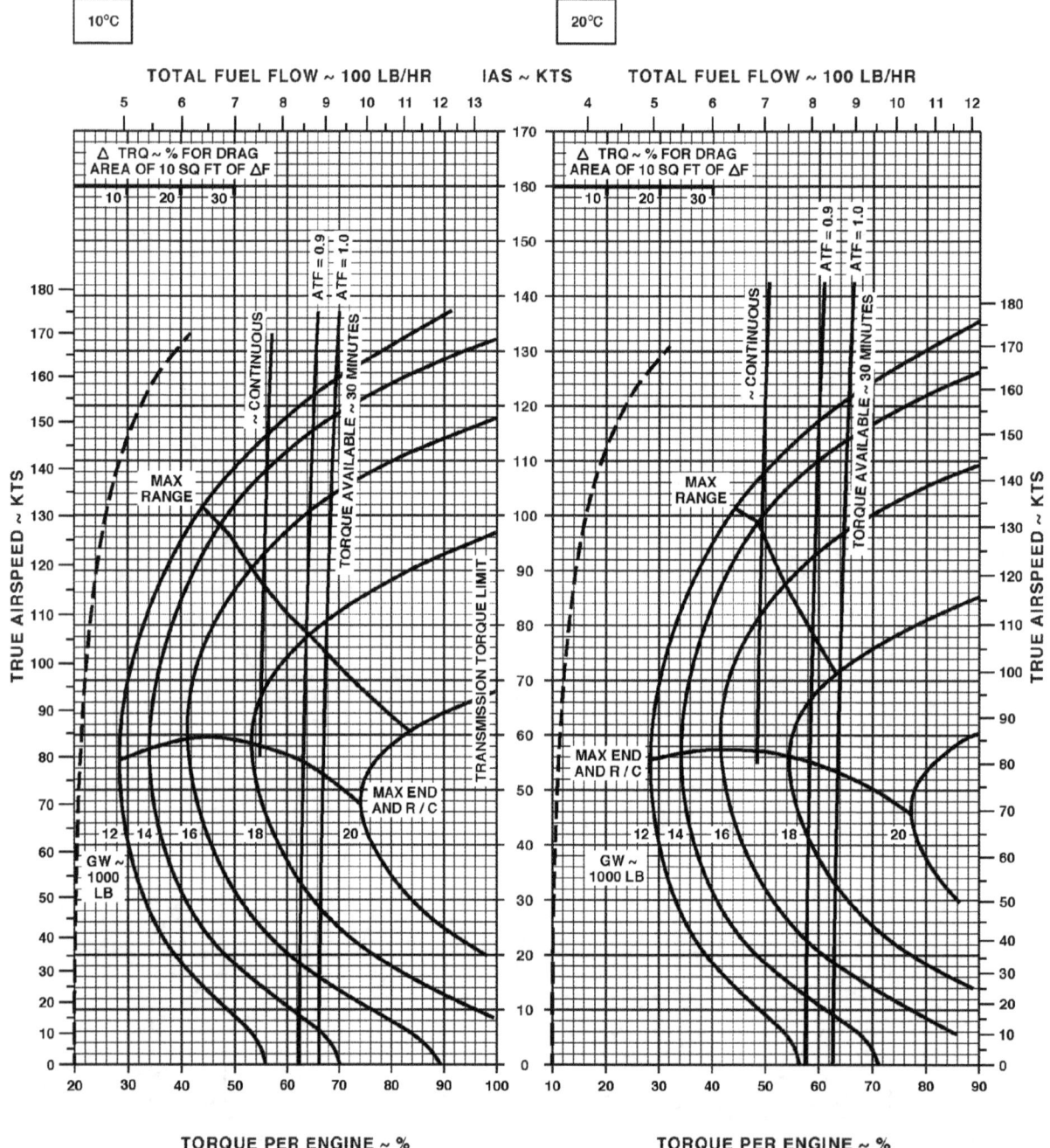

Figure 7-21. Cruise - Pressure Altitude 14,000 Feet (Sheet 4 of 5)

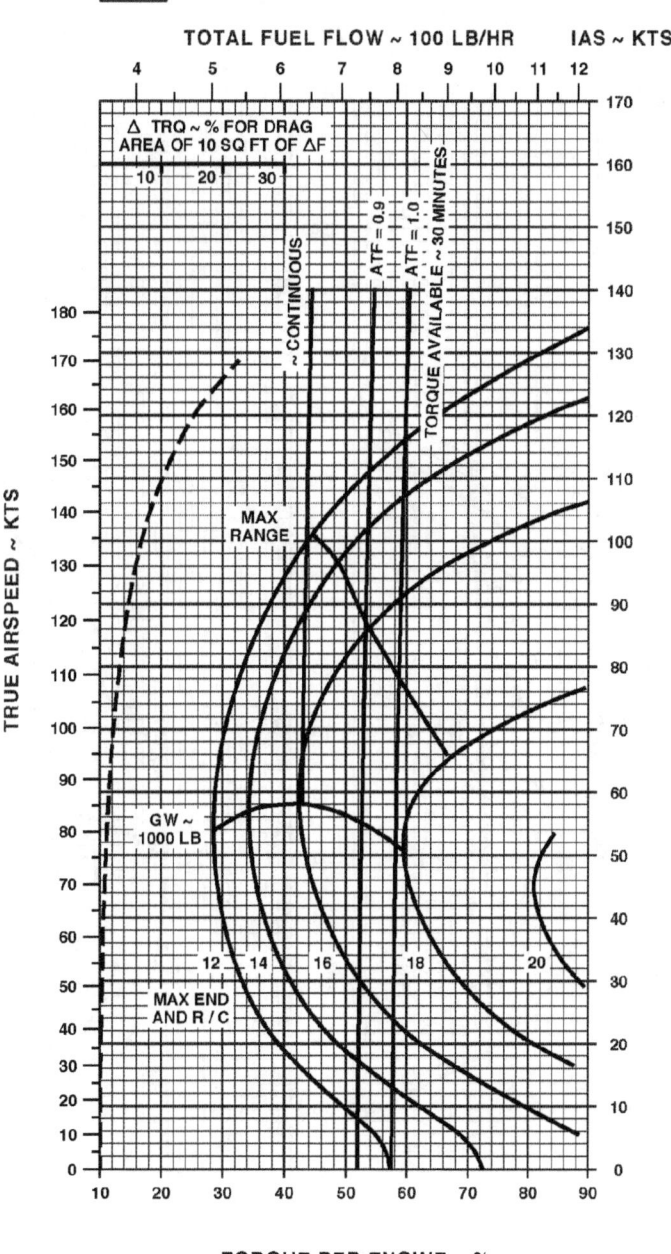

Figure 7-21. Cruise - Pressure Altitude 14,000 Feet (Sheet 5 of 5)

CRUISE

PRESS ALT: 14000 FT

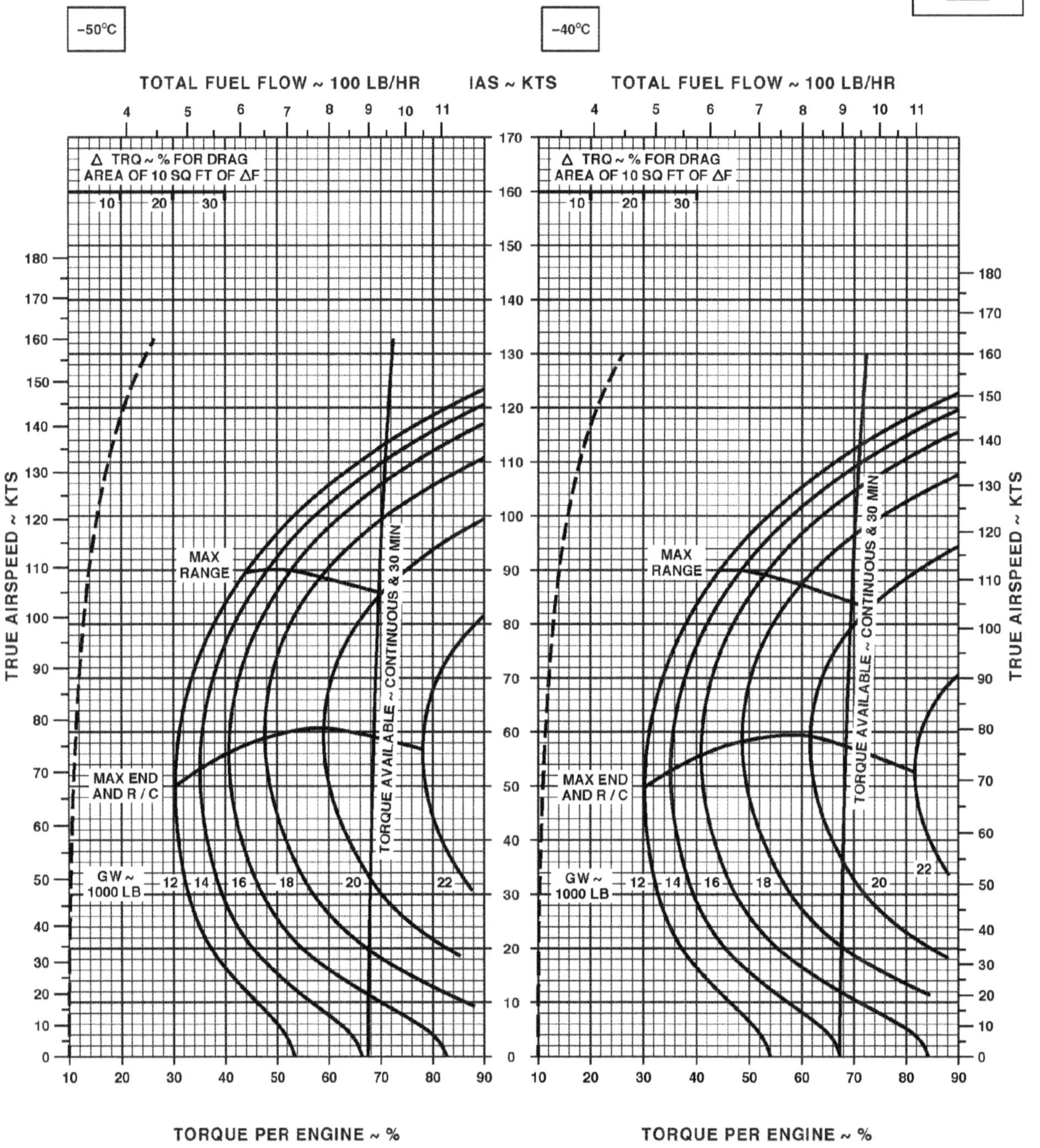

Figure 7-22. Cruise High Drag - Pressure Altitude 14,000 Feet (Sheet 1 of 5)

DATA BASE: FLIGHT TEST

CRUISE

PRESS ALT: 14000 FT

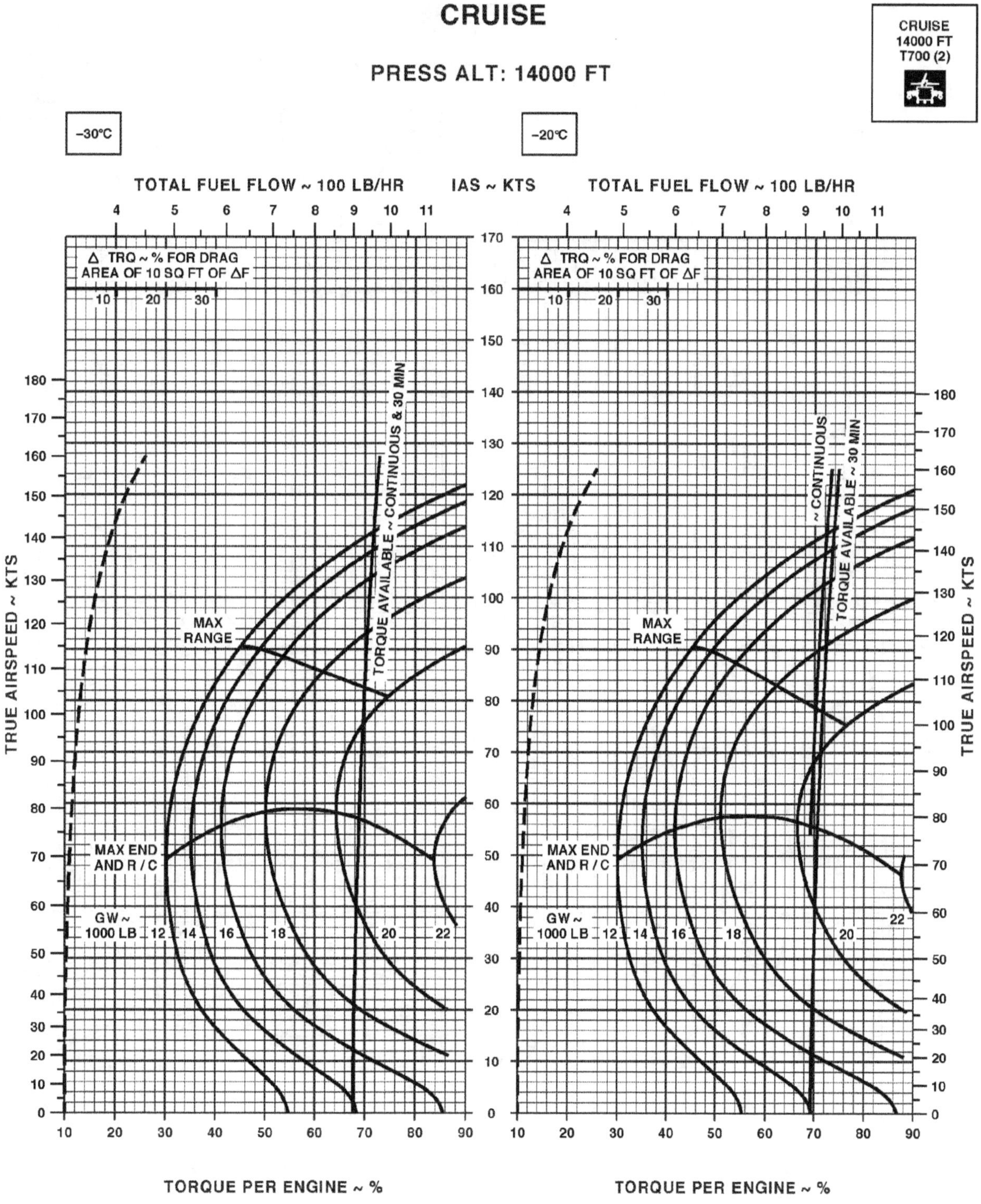

DATA BASE: FLIGHT TEST

AA0575

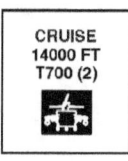

Figure 7-22. Cruise High Drag - Pressure Altitude 14,000 Feet (Sheet 2 of 5)

CRUISE

PRESS ALT: 14000 FT

CRUISE
14000 FT
T700 (2)

DATA BASE: FLIGHT TEST

AA0576

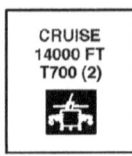

Figure 7-22. Cruise High Drag - Pressure Altitude 14,000 Feet (Sheet 3 of 5)

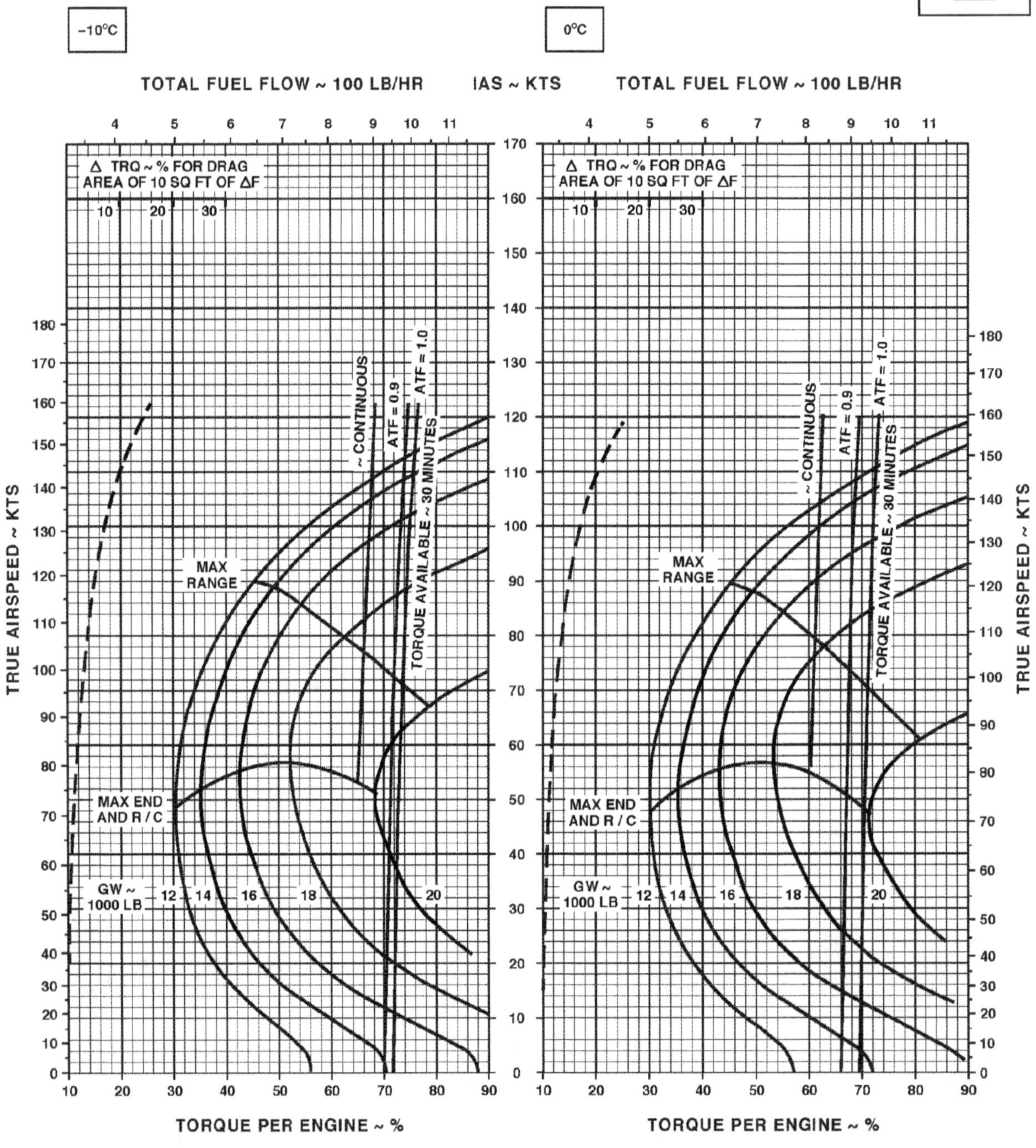

CRUISE

PRESS ALT: 14000 FT

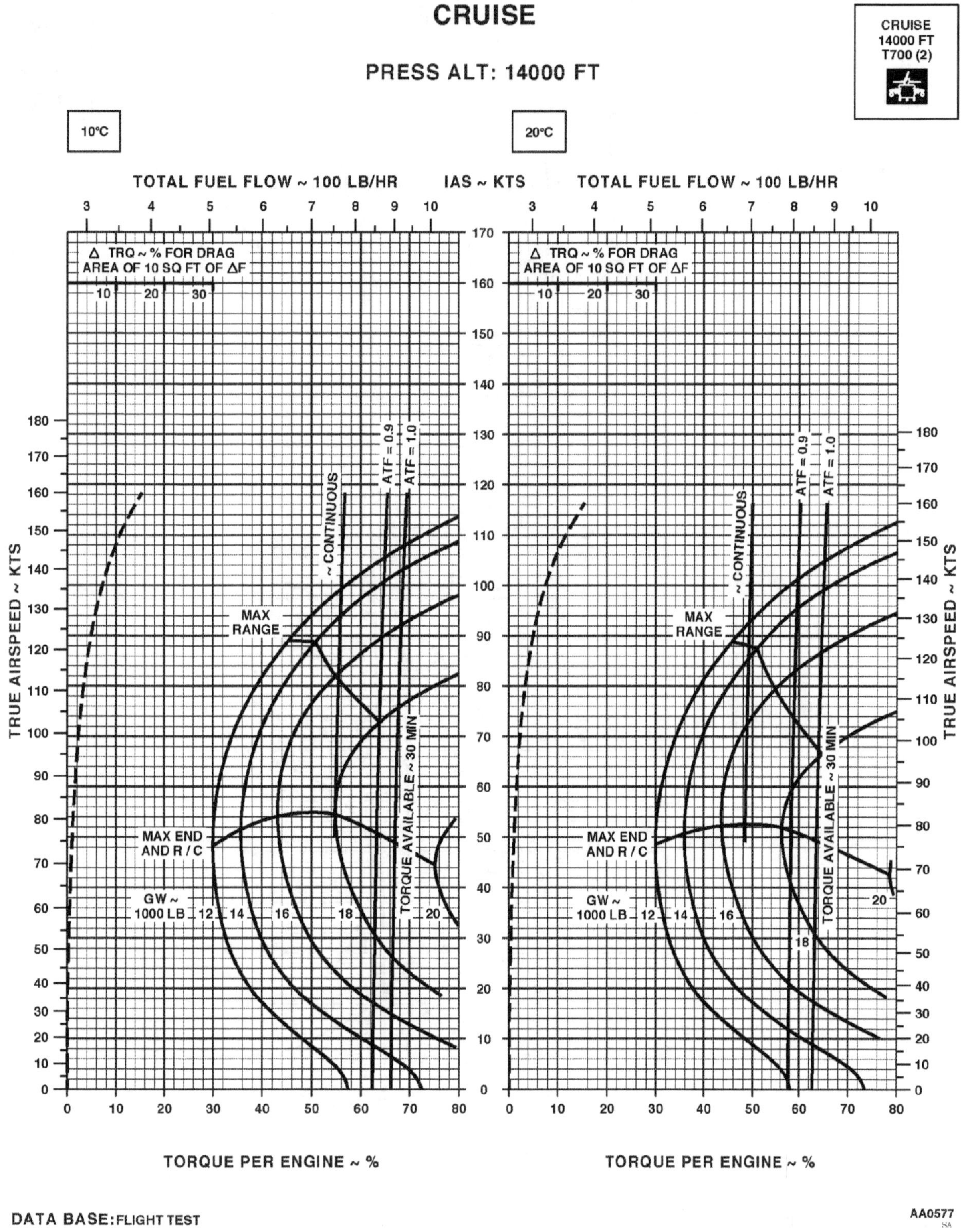

Figure 7-22. Cruise High Drag - Pressure Altitude 14,000 Feet (Sheet 4 of 5)

Figure 7-22. Cruise High Drag - Pressure Altitude 14,000 Feet (Sheet 5 of 5)

CRUISE
CLEAN CONFIGURATION
PRESS ALT: 16000 FT

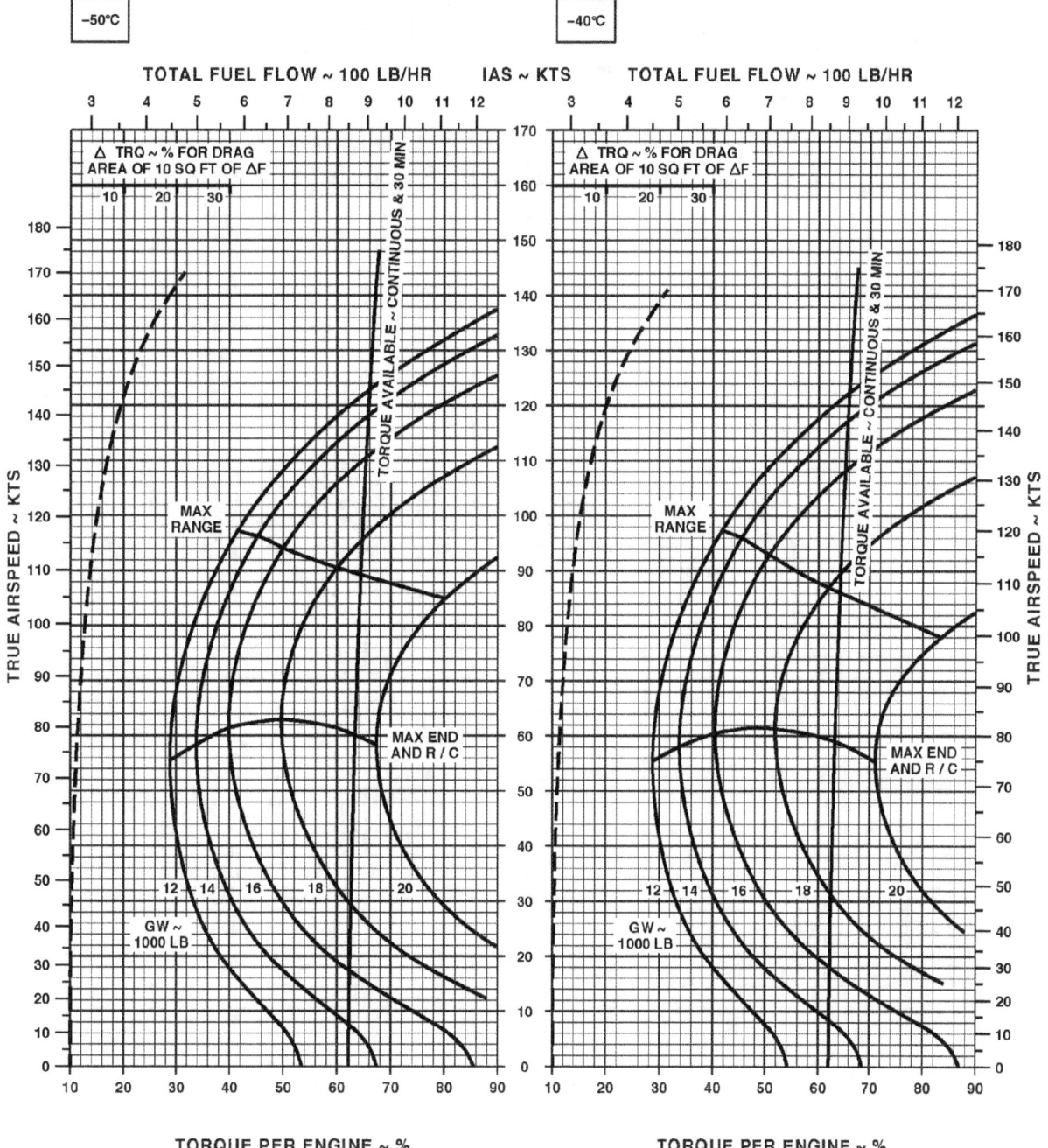

Figure 7-23. Cruise - Pressure Altitude 16,000 Feet (Sheet 1 of 5)

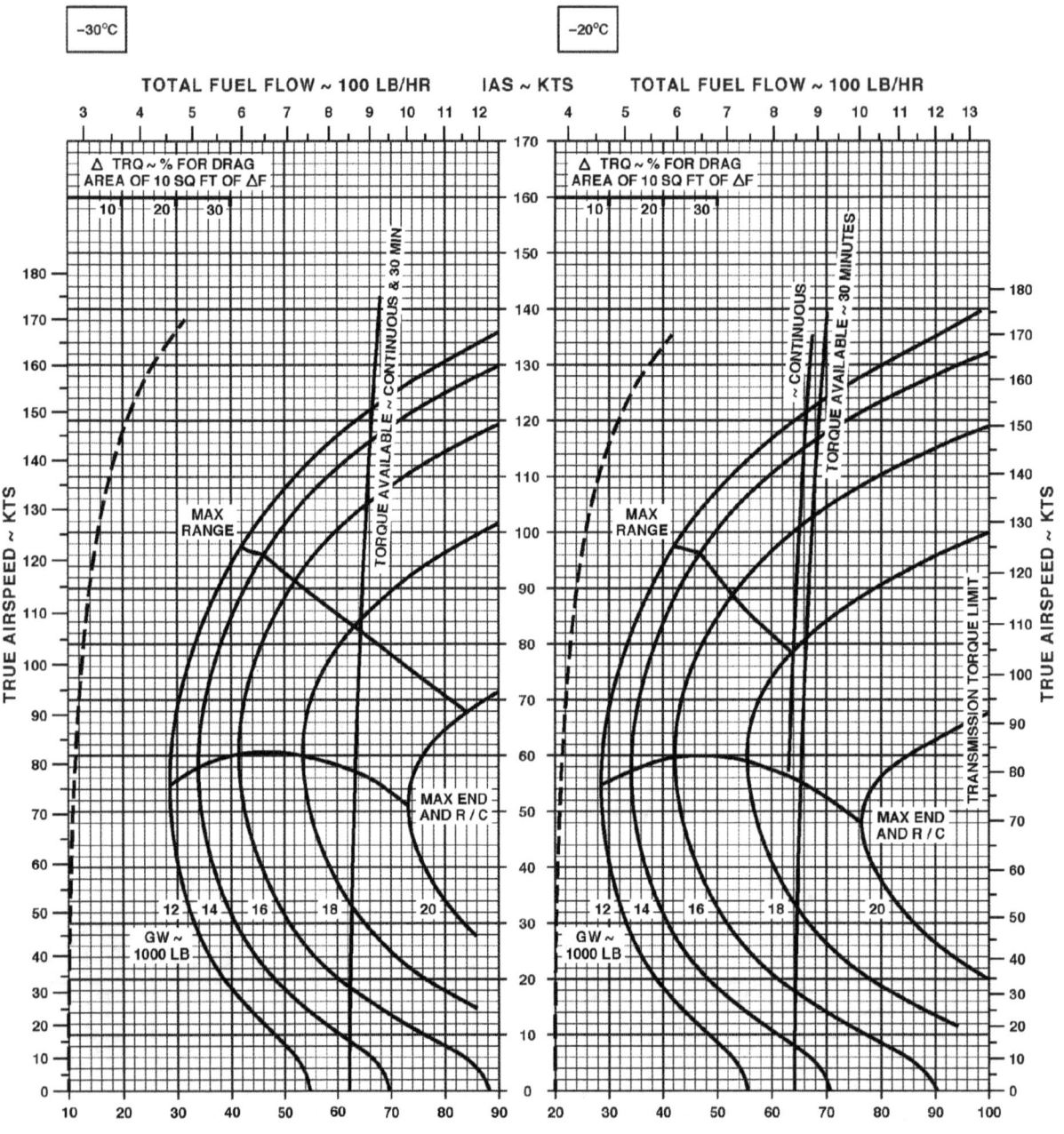

Figure 7-23. Cruise - Pressure Altitude 16,000 Feet (Sheet 2 of 5)

CRUISE
CLEAN CONFIGURATION
PRESS ALT: 16000 FT

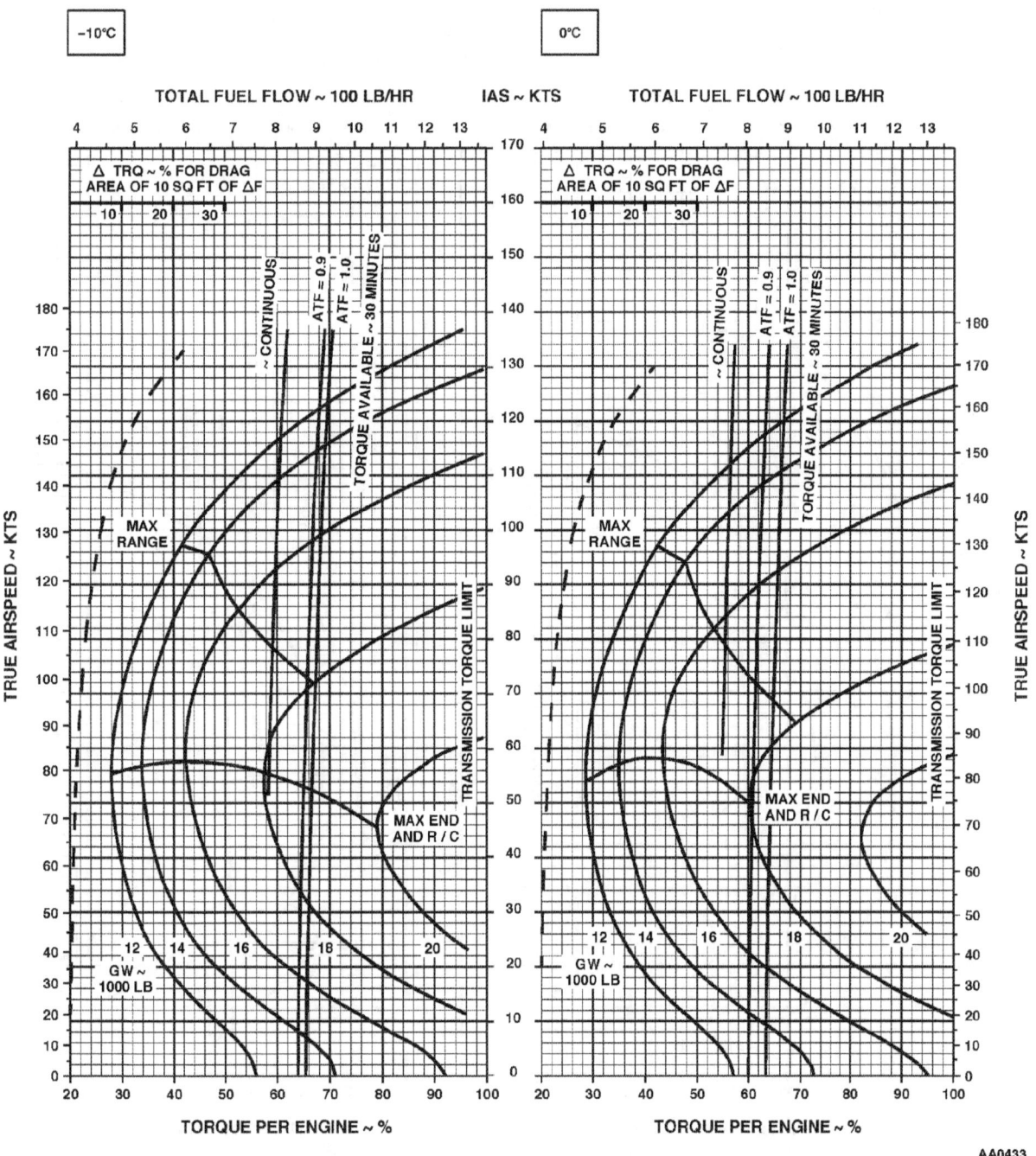

Figure 7-23. Cruise - Pressure Altitude 16,000 Feet (Sheet 3 of 5)

CRUISE
CLEAN CONFIGURATION
PRESS ALT: 16000 FT

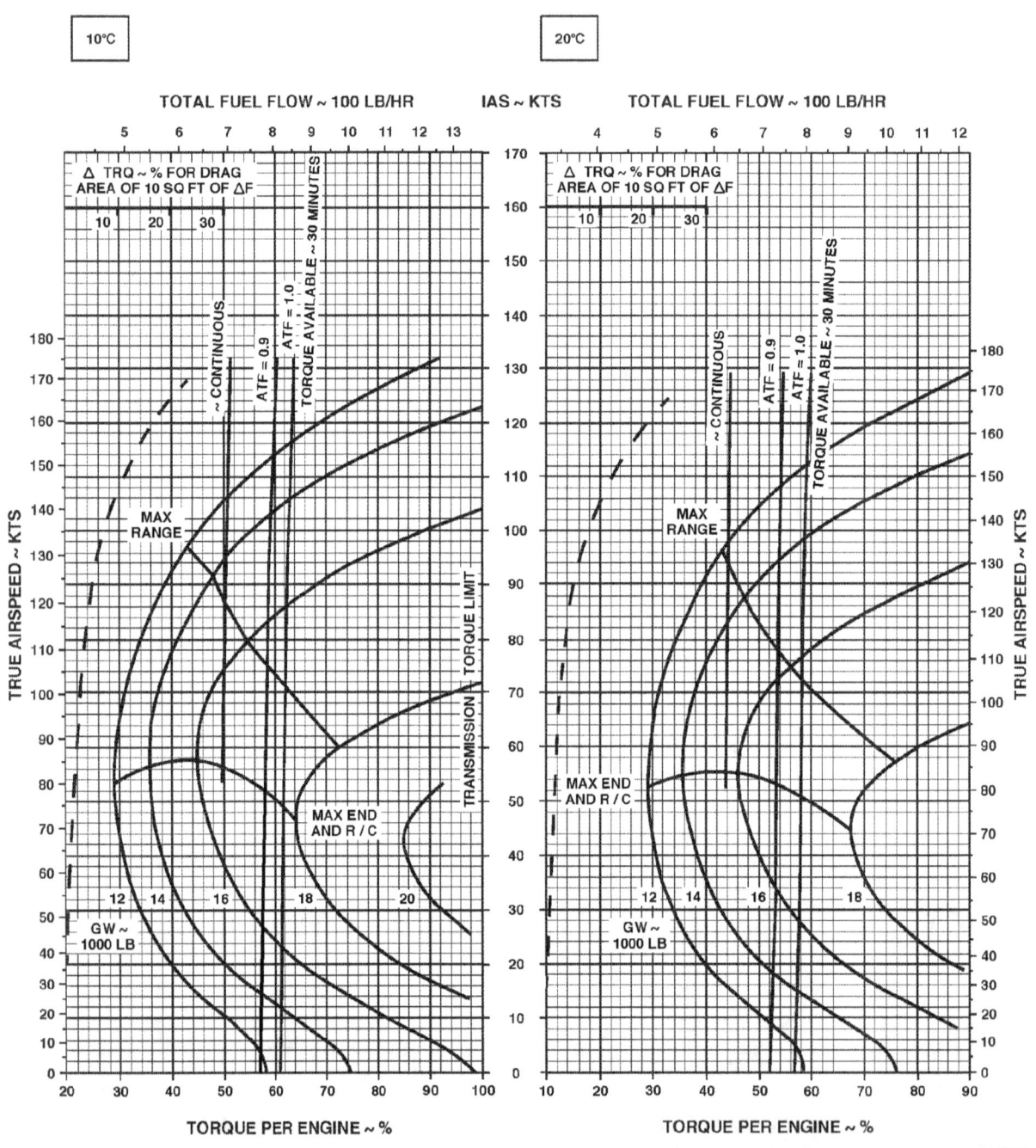

Figure 7-23. Cruise - Pressure Altitude 16,000 Feet (Sheet 4 of 5)

CRUISE
CLEAN CONFIGURATION
PRESS ALT: 16000 FT

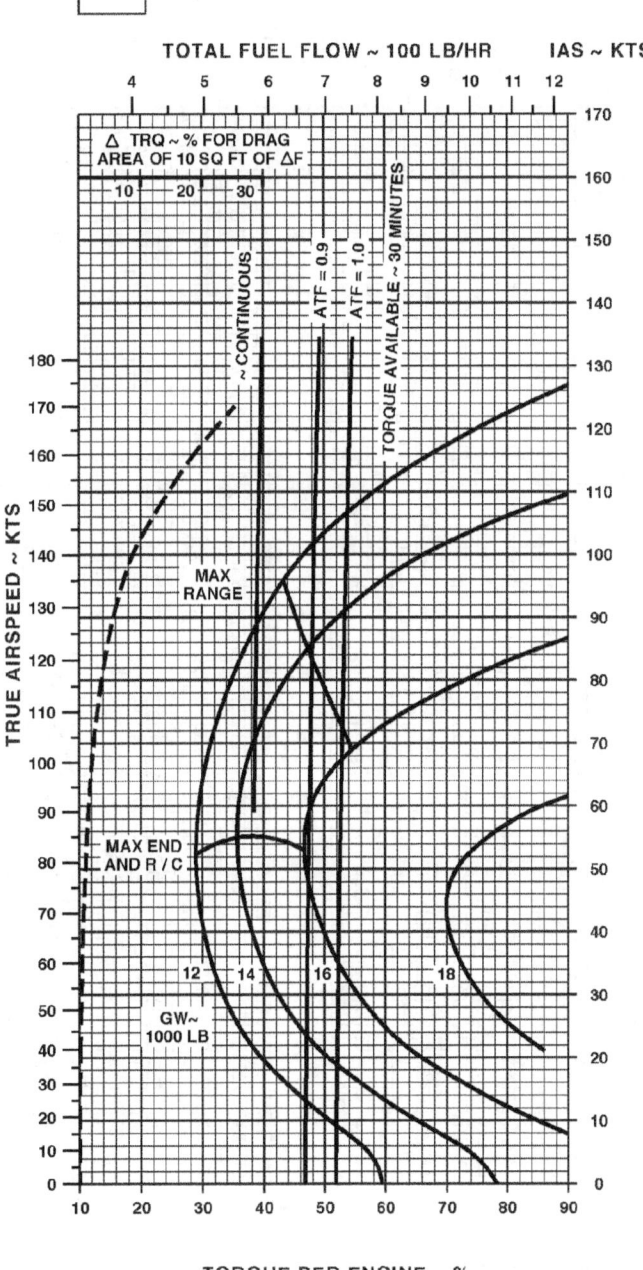

Figure 7-23. Cruise - Pressure Altitude 16,000 Feet (Sheet 5 of 5)

CRUISE

PRESS ALT: 16000 FT

CRUISE
16000 FT
T700 (2)

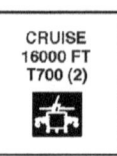

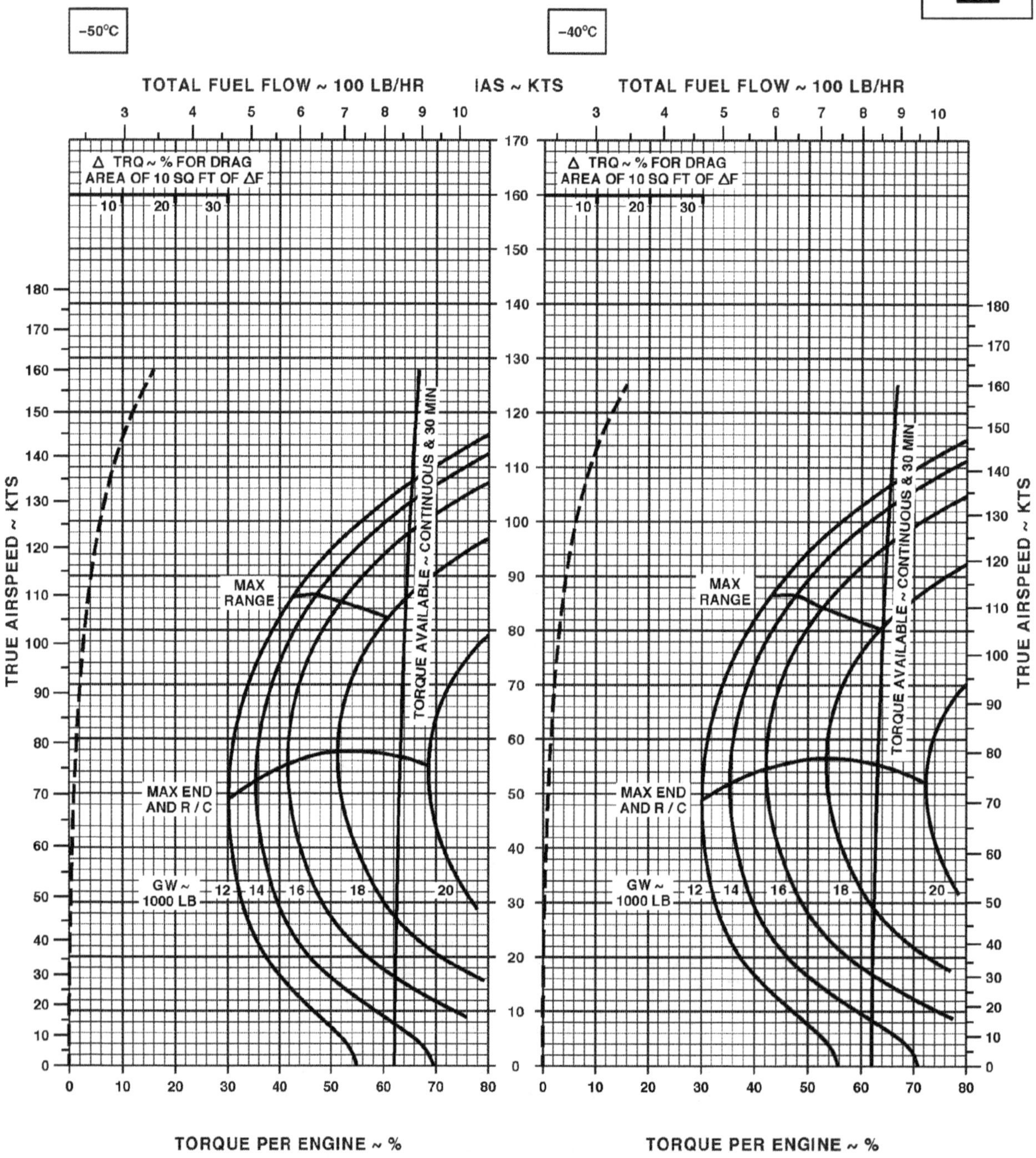

DATA BASE: FLIGHT TEST

AA0579
SA

Figure 7-24. Cruise High Drag - Pressure Altitude 16,000 Feet (Sheet 1 of 4)

CRUISE

PRESS ALT: 16000 FT

CRUISE
16000 FT
T700 (2)

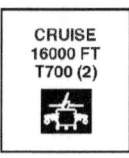

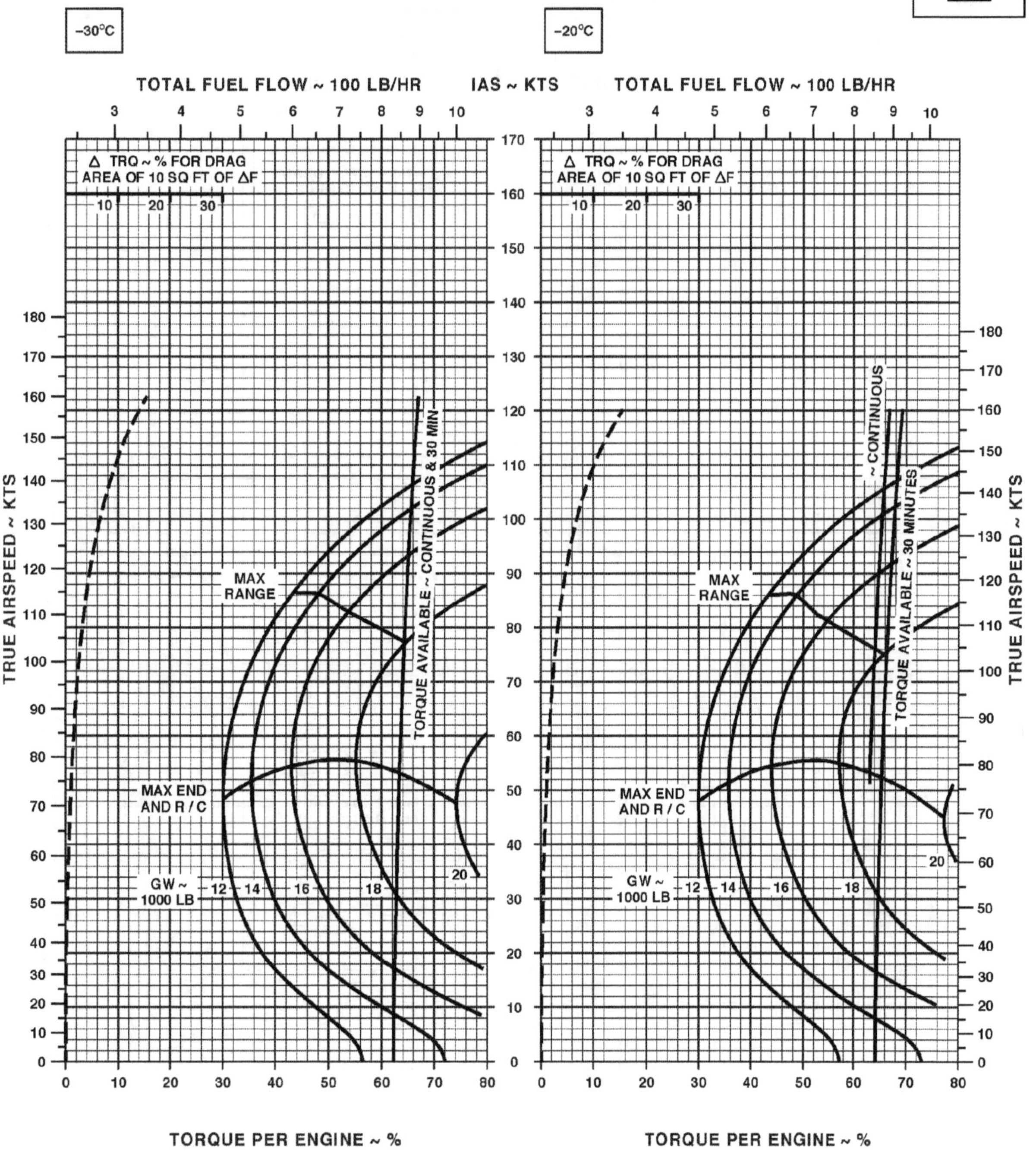

DATA BASE: FLIGHT TEST

AA0580
SA

Figure 7-24. Cruise High Drag - Pressure Altitude 16,000 Feet (Sheet 2 of 4)

CRUISE

PRESS ALT: 16000 FT

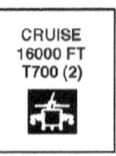

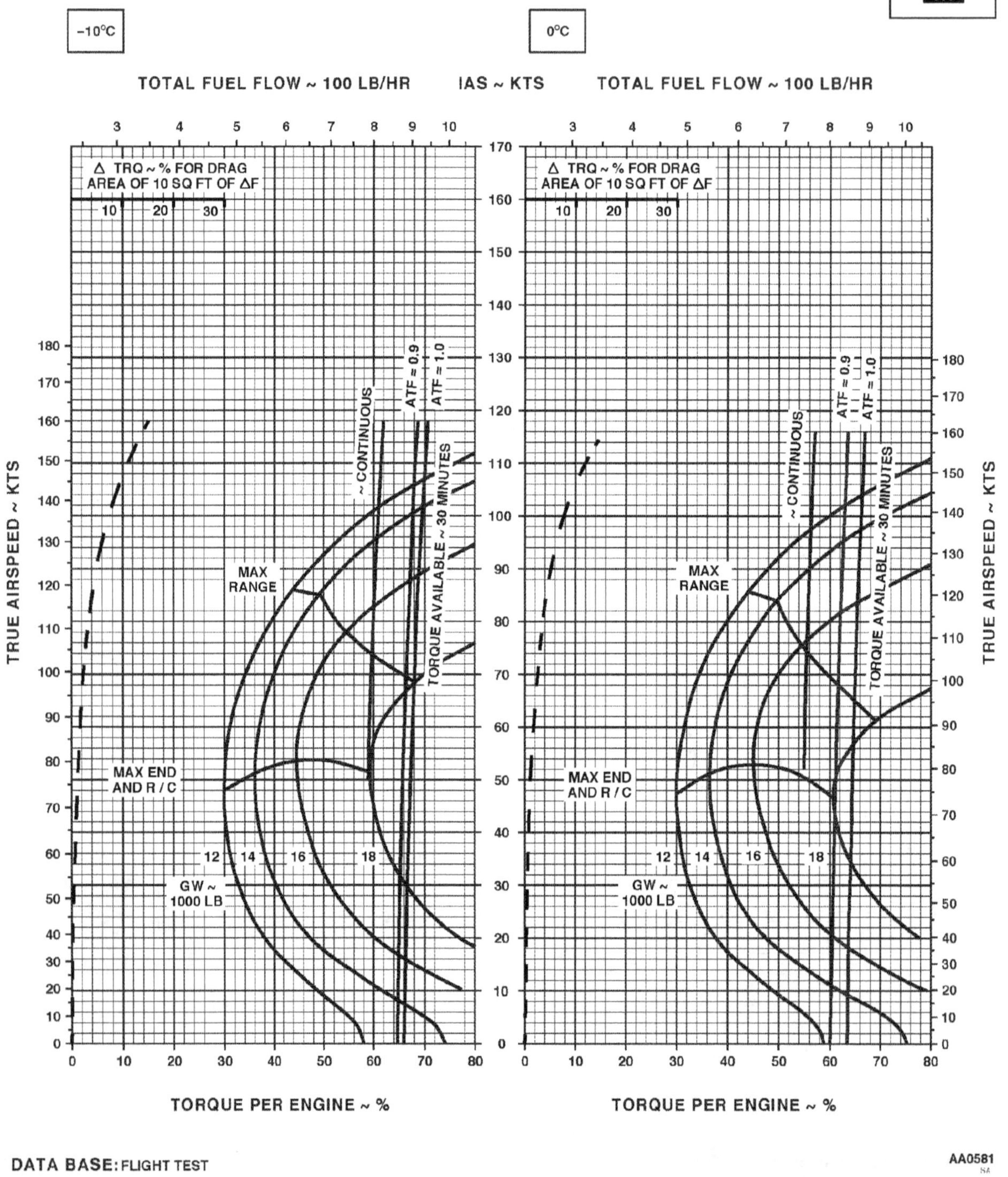

Figure 7-24. Cruise High Drag - Pressure Altitude 16,000 Feet (Sheet 3 of 4)

CRUISE

PRESS ALT: 16000 FT

Figure 7-24. Cruise High Drag - Pressure Altitude 16,000 Feet (Sheet 4 of 4)

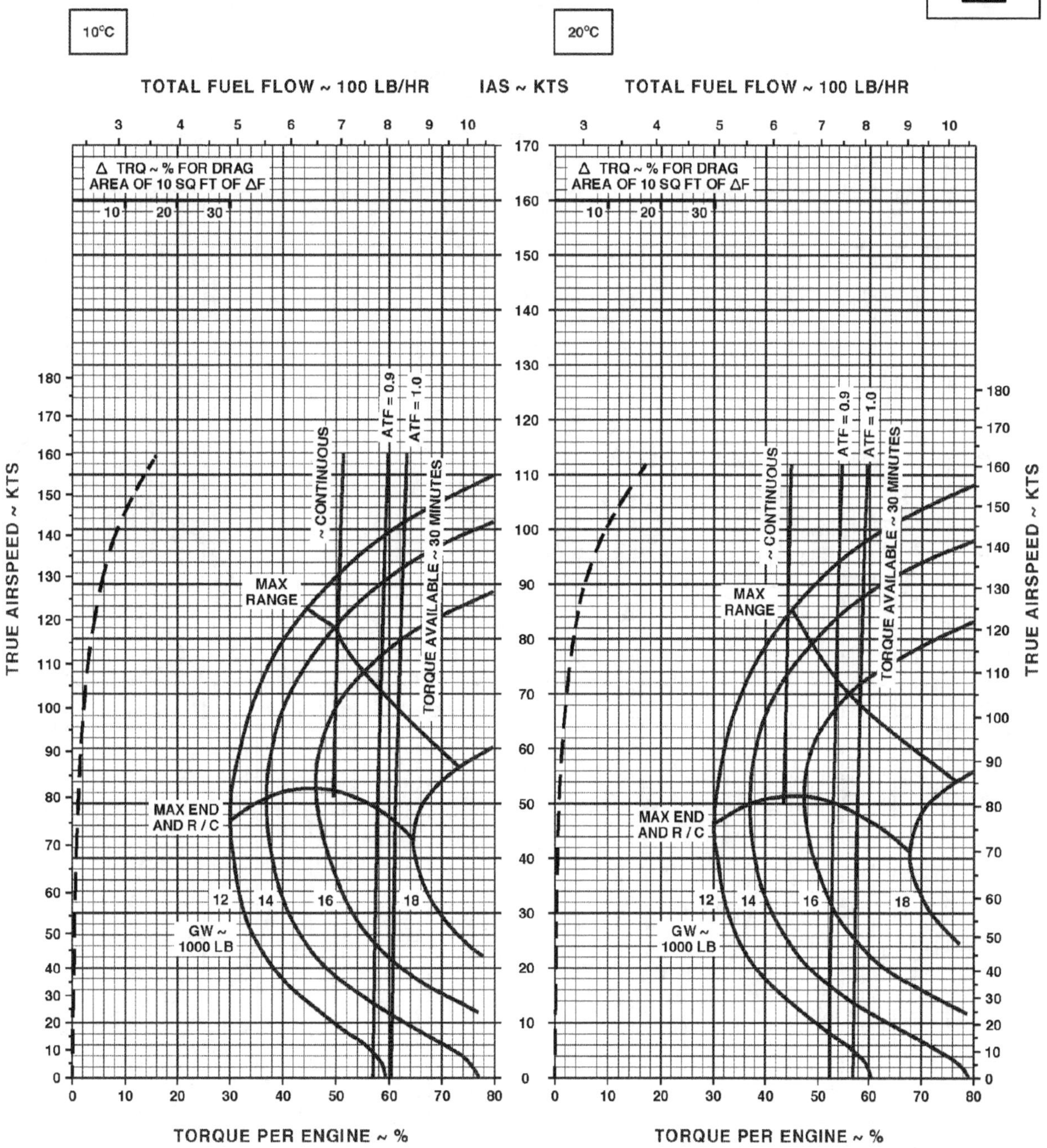

DATA BASE: FLIGHT TEST

CRUISE
CLEAN CONFIGURATION
PRESS ALT: 18000 FT

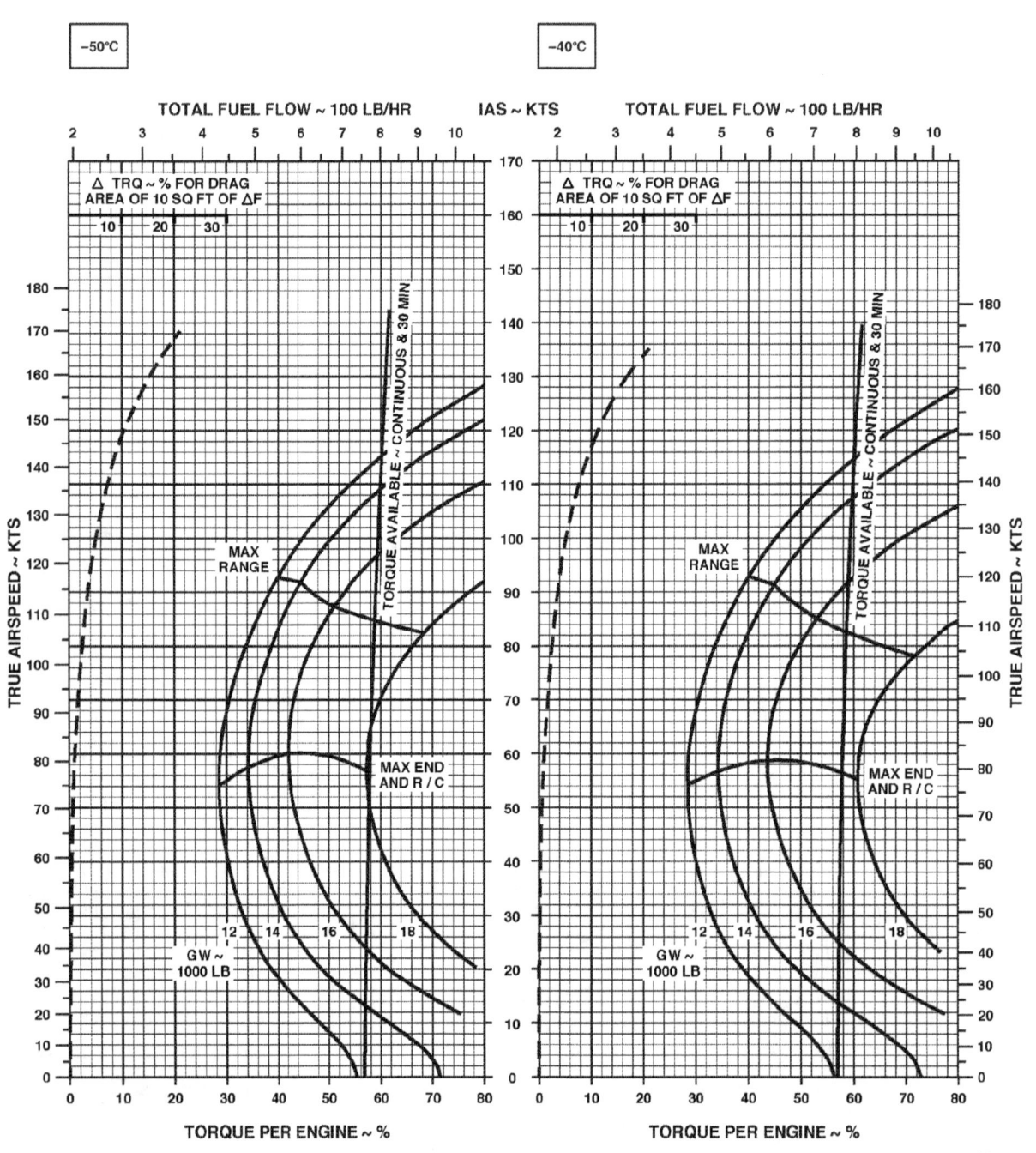

Figure 7-25. Cruise - Pressure Altitude 18,000 Feet (Sheet 1 of 5)

CRUISE
CLEAN CONFIGURATION
PRESS ALT: 18000 FT

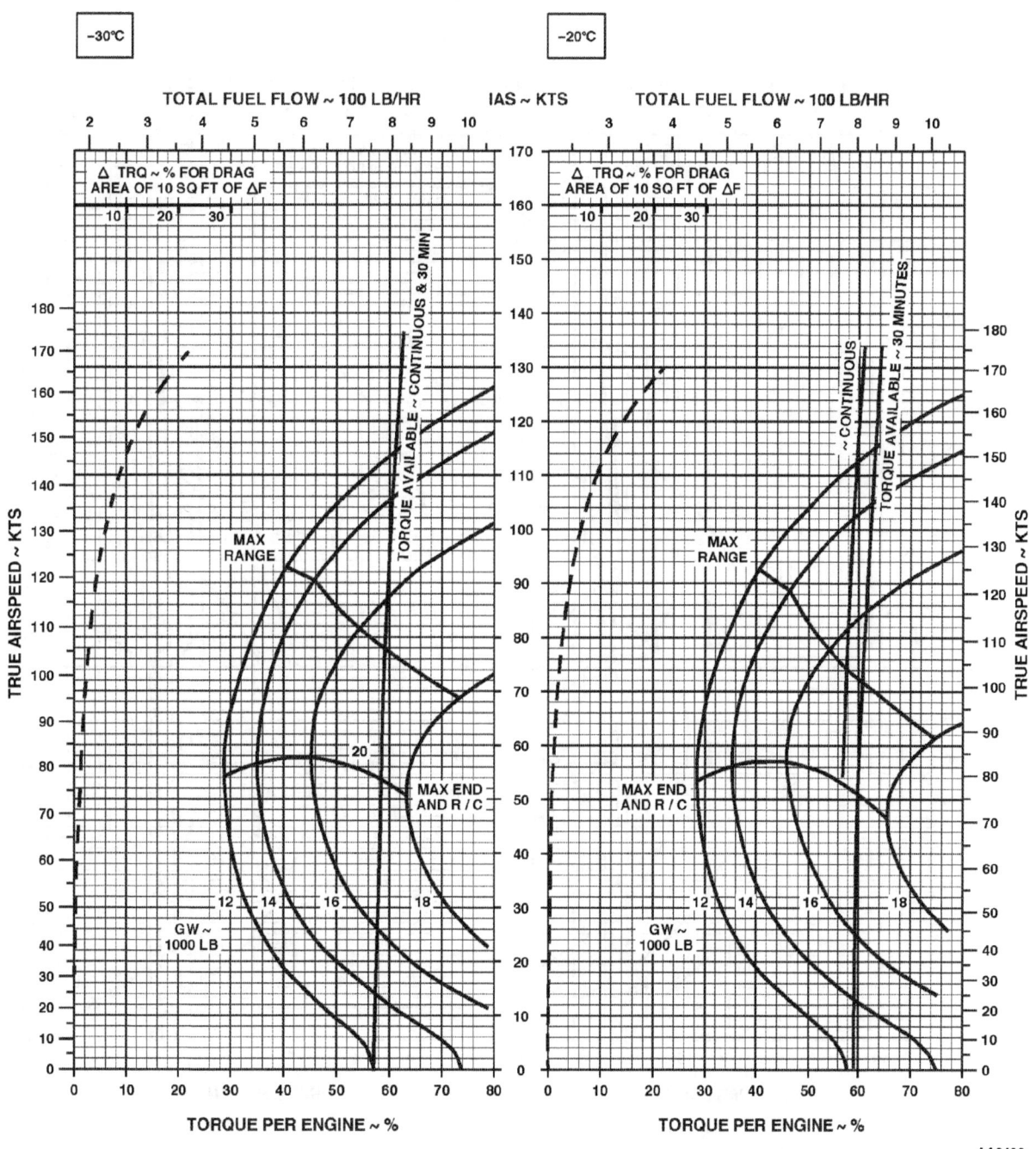

Figure 7-25. Cruise - Pressure Altitude 18,000 Feet (Sheet 2 of 5)

CRUISE
CLEAN CONFIGURATION
PRESS ALT: 18000 FT

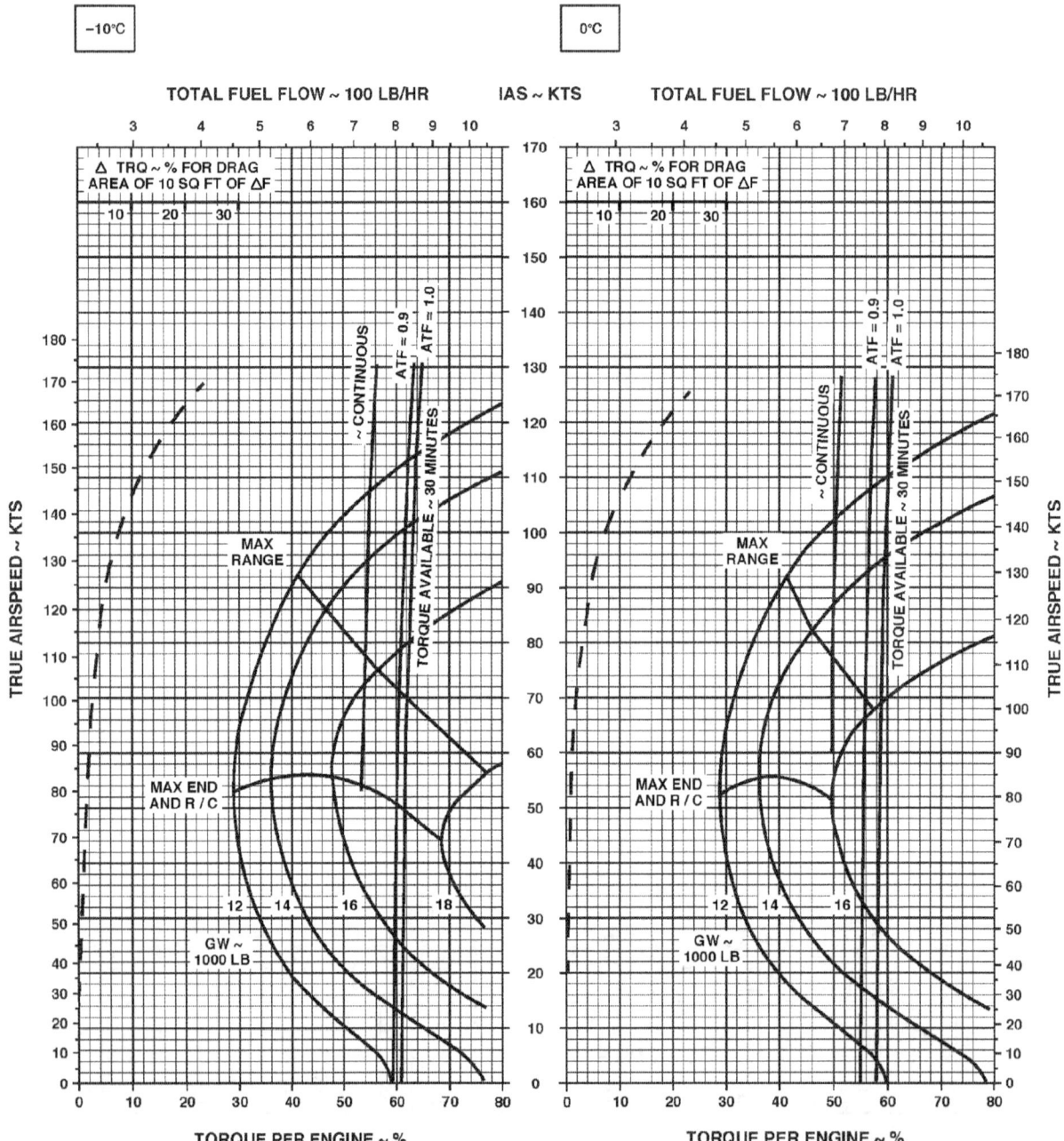

Figure 7-25. Cruise - Pressure Altitude 18,000 Feet (Sheet 3 of 5)

CRUISE
CLEAN CONFIGURATION
PRESS ALT: 18000 FT

CRUISE
18000 FT
T700 (2)

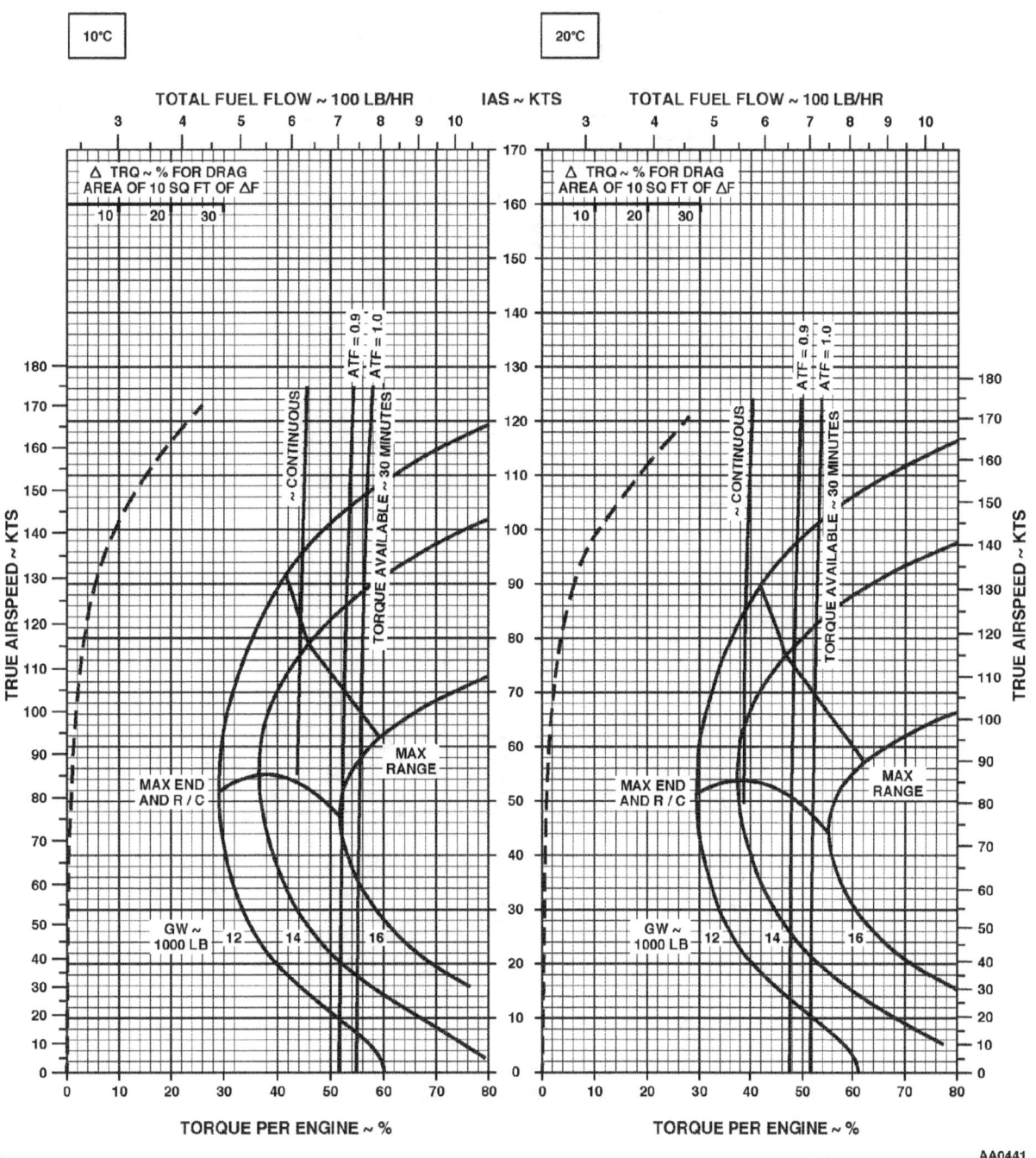

Figure 7-25. Cruise - Pressure Altitude 18,000 Feet (Sheet 4 of 5)

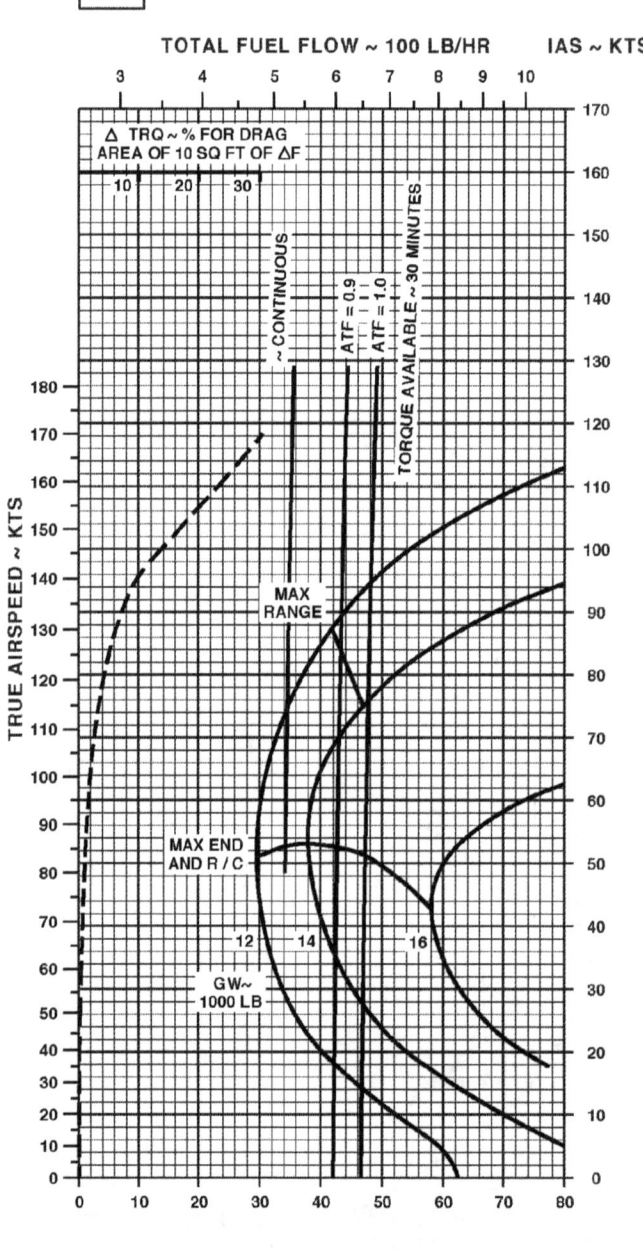

Figure 7-25. Cruise - Pressure Altitude 18,000 Feet (Sheet 5 of 5)

CRUISE

PRESS ALT: 18000 FT

CRUISE
18000 FT
T700 (2)

DATA BASE: FLIGHT TEST

AA0583
SA

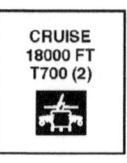

Figure 7-26. Cruise High Drag - Pressure Altitude 18,000 Feet (Sheet 1 of 4)

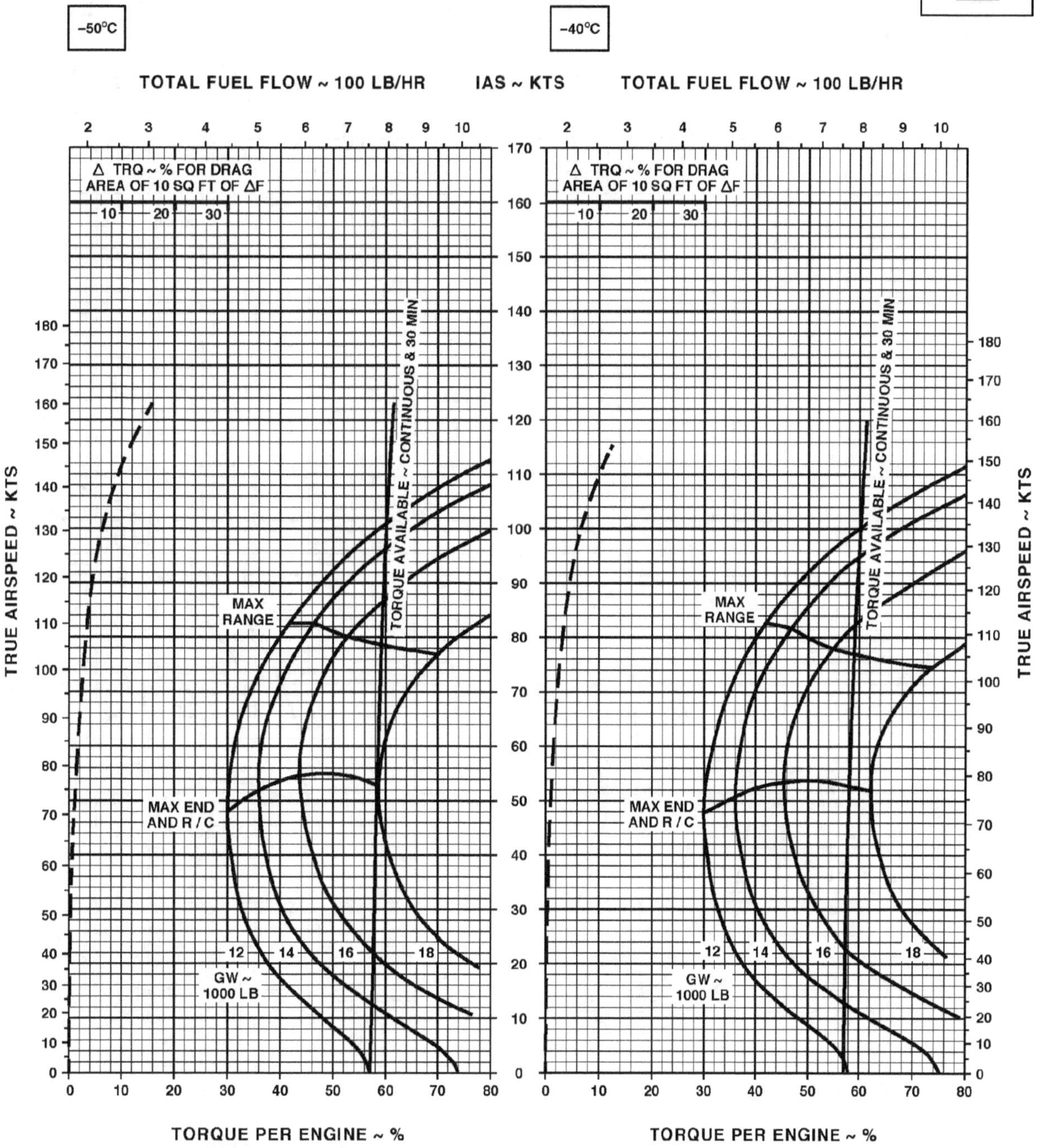

CRUISE

PRESS ALT: 18000 FT

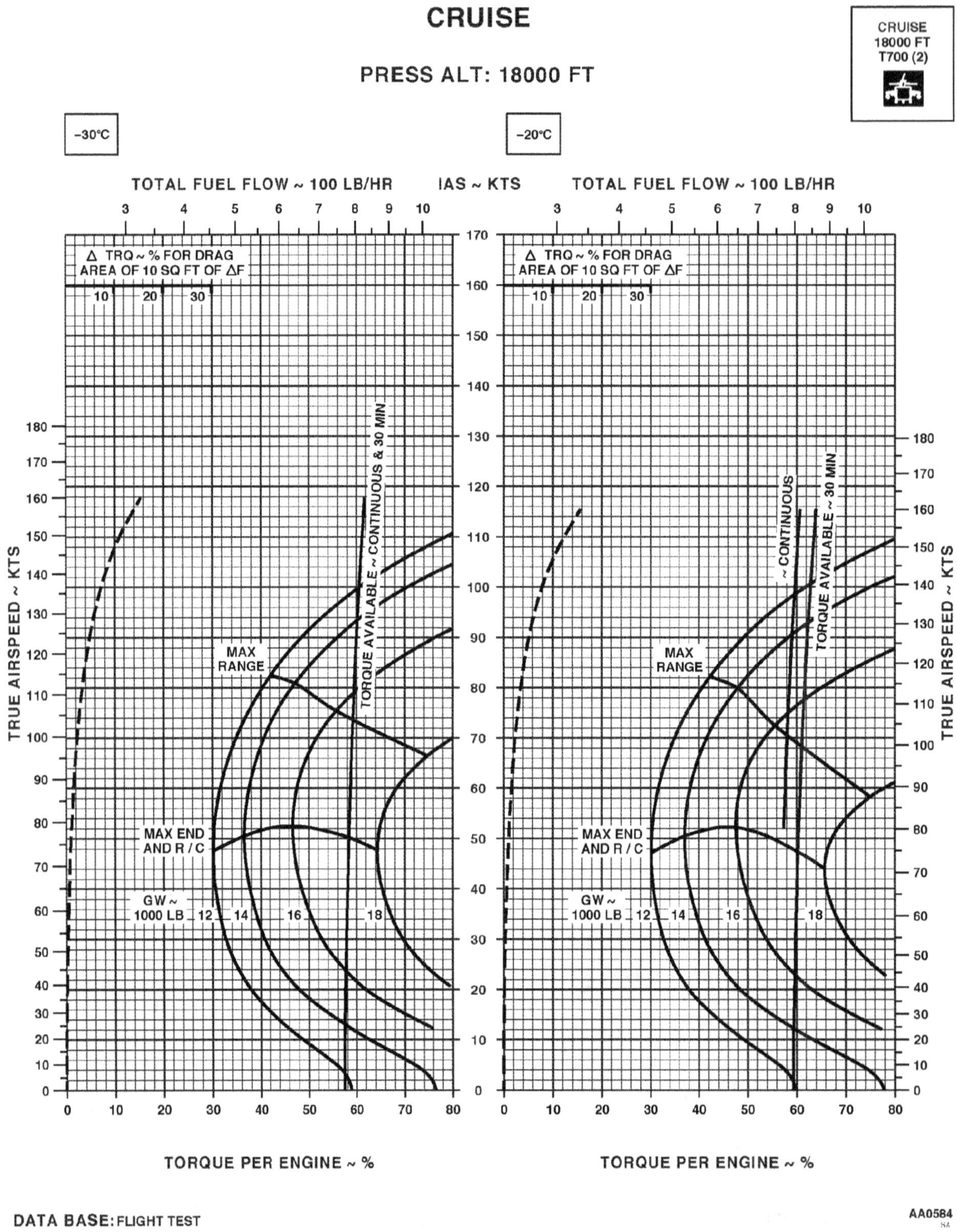

Figure 7-26. Cruise High Drag - Pressure Altitude 18,000 Feet (Sheet 2 of 4)

DATA BASE: FLIGHT TEST

CRUISE

PRESS ALT: 18000 FT

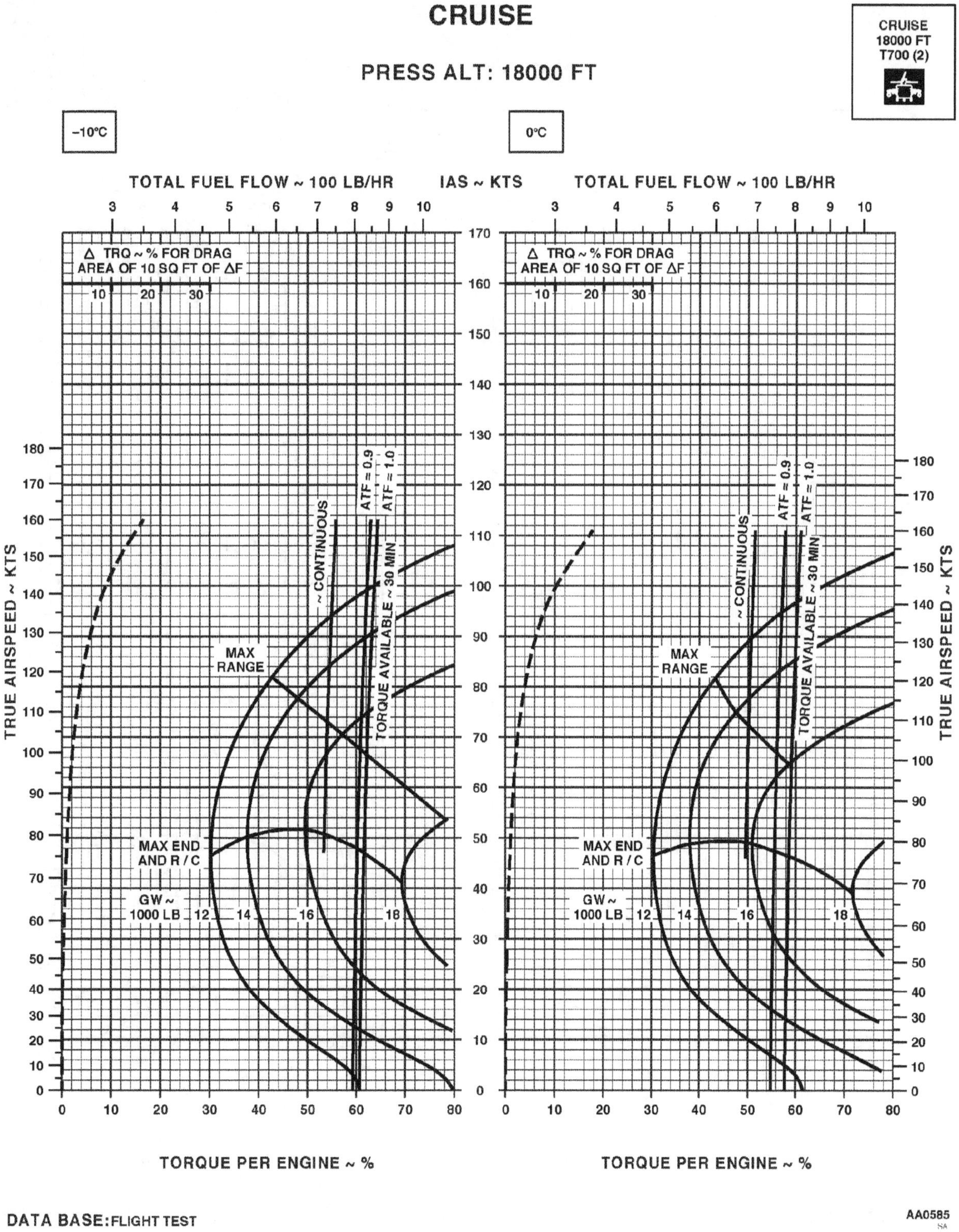

Figure 7-26. Cruise High Drag - Pressure Altitude 18,000 Feet (Sheet 3 of 4)

DATA BASE: FLIGHT TEST

CRUISE

PRESS ALT: 18000 FT

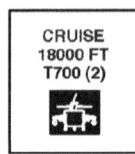

Figure 7-26. Cruise High Drag - Pressure Altitude 18,000 Feet (Sheet 4 of 4)

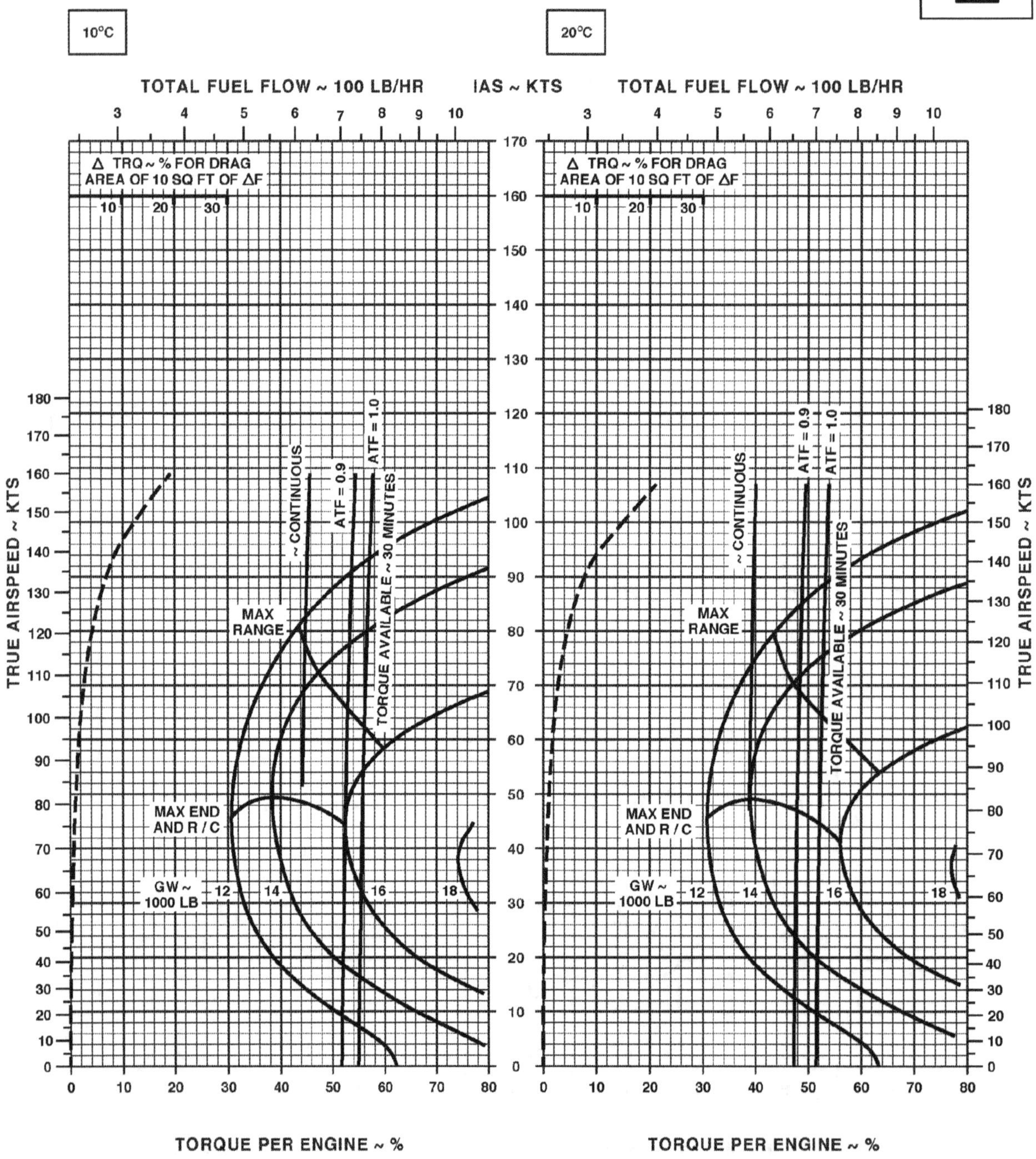

DATA BASE: FLIGHT TEST

CRUISE
CLEAN CONFIGURATION
PRESS ALT: 20000 FT

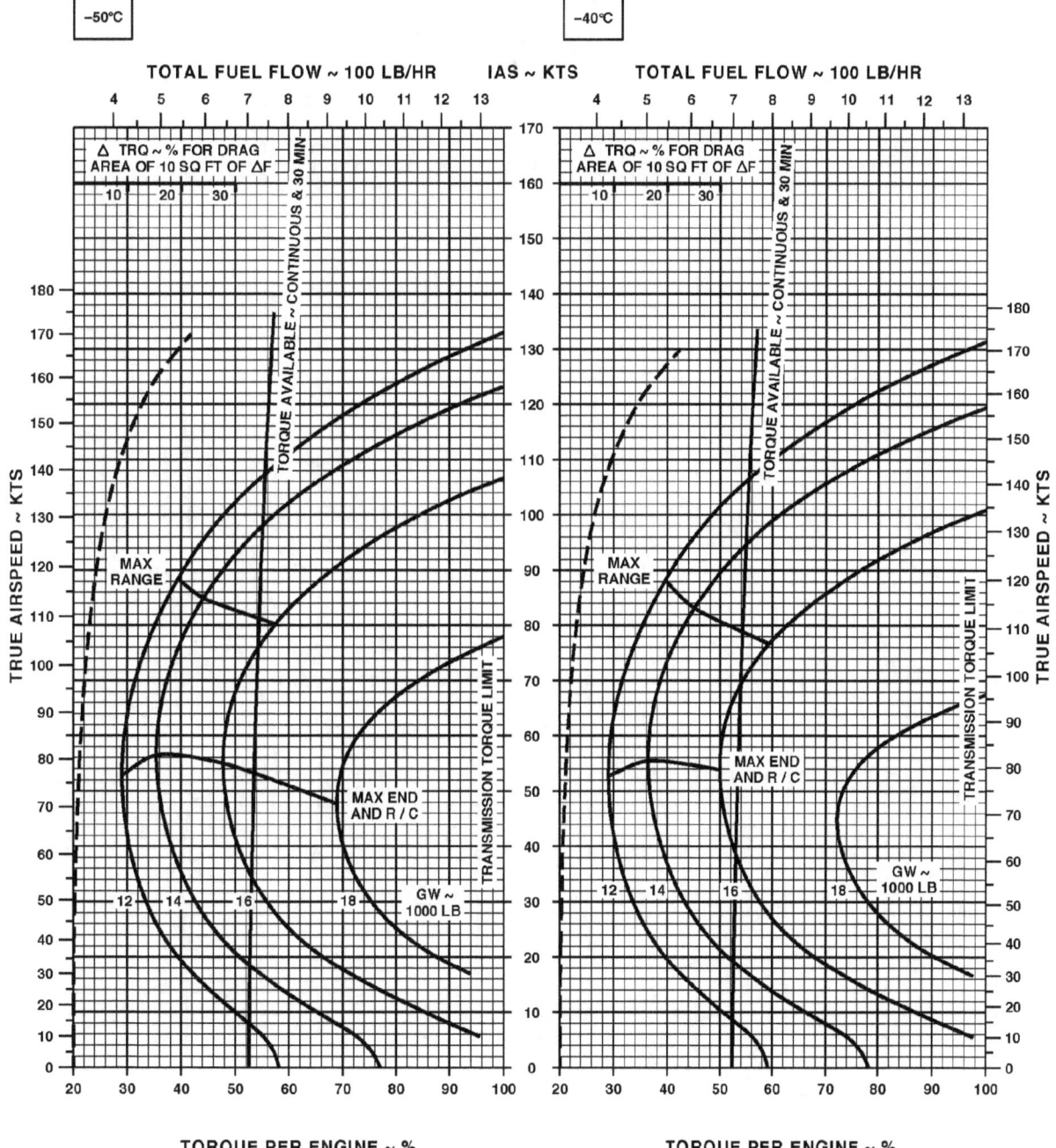

Figure 7-27. Cruise - Pressure Altitude 20,000 Feet (Sheet 1 of 4)

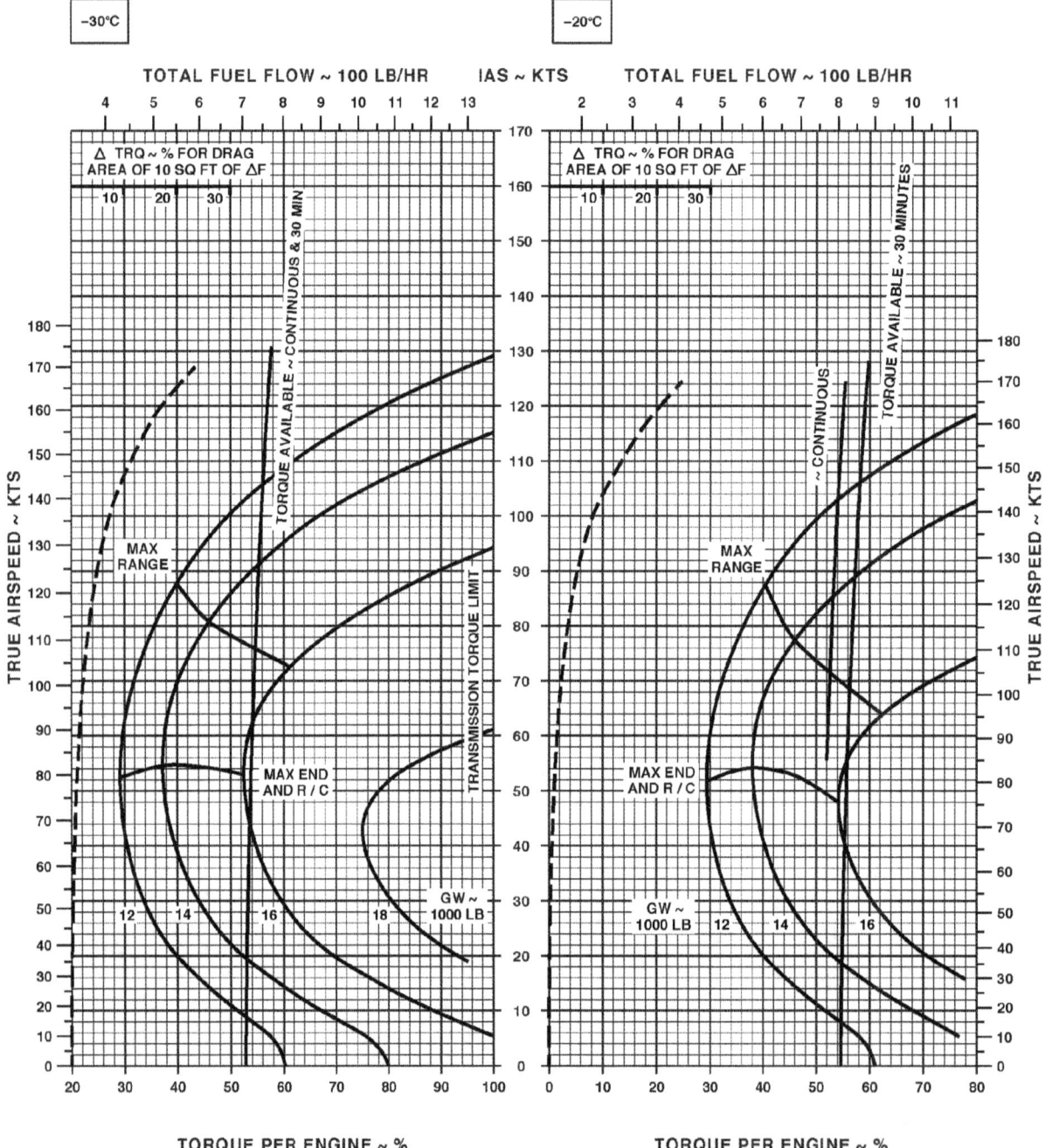

Figure 7-27. Cruise - Pressure Altitude 20,000 Feet (Sheet 2 of 4)

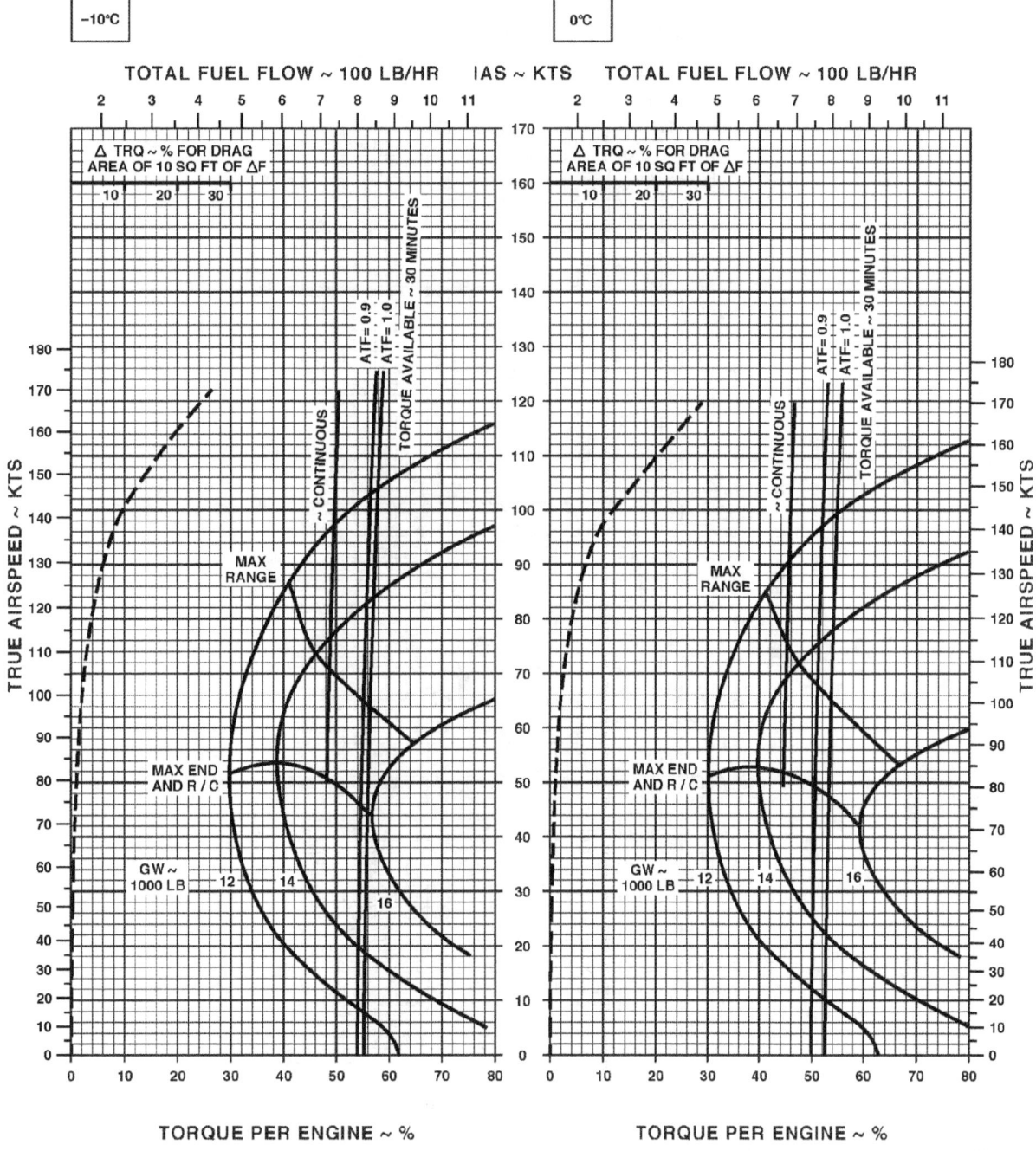

Figure 7-27. Cruise - Pressure Altitude 20,000 Feet (Sheet 3 of 4)

CRUISE
CLEAN CONFIGURATION
PRESS ALT: 20000 FT

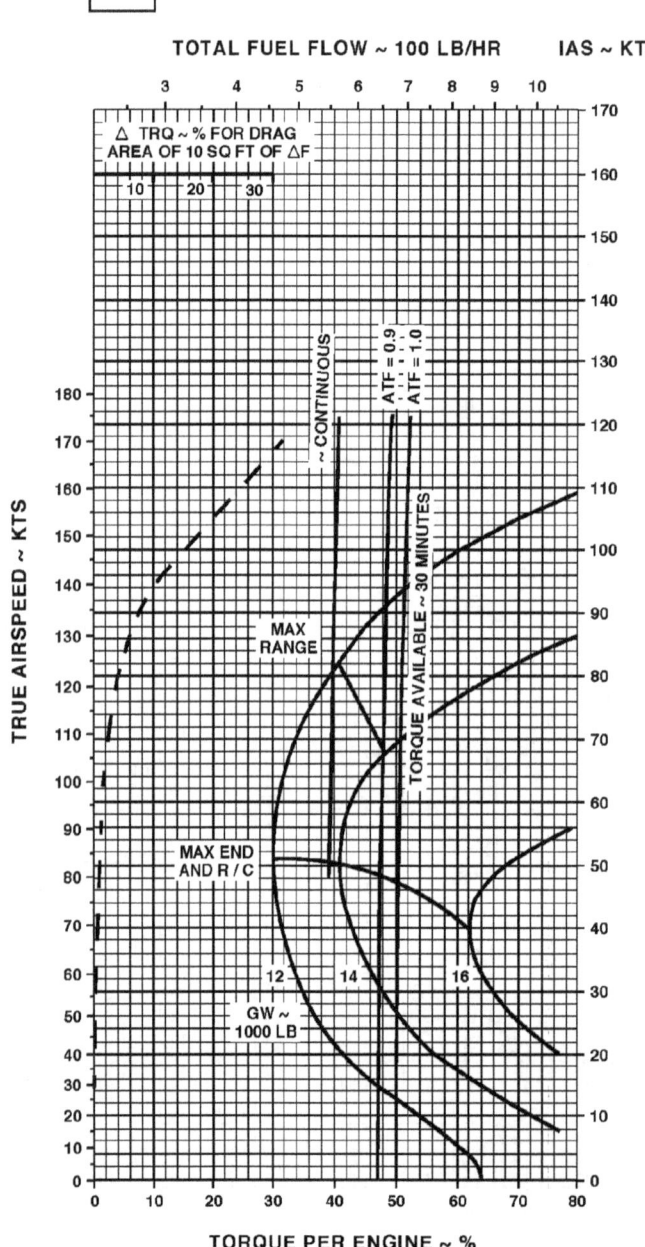

Figure 7-27. Cruise - Pressure Altitude 20,000 Feet (Sheet 4 of 4)

CRUISE

PRESS ALT: 20000 FT

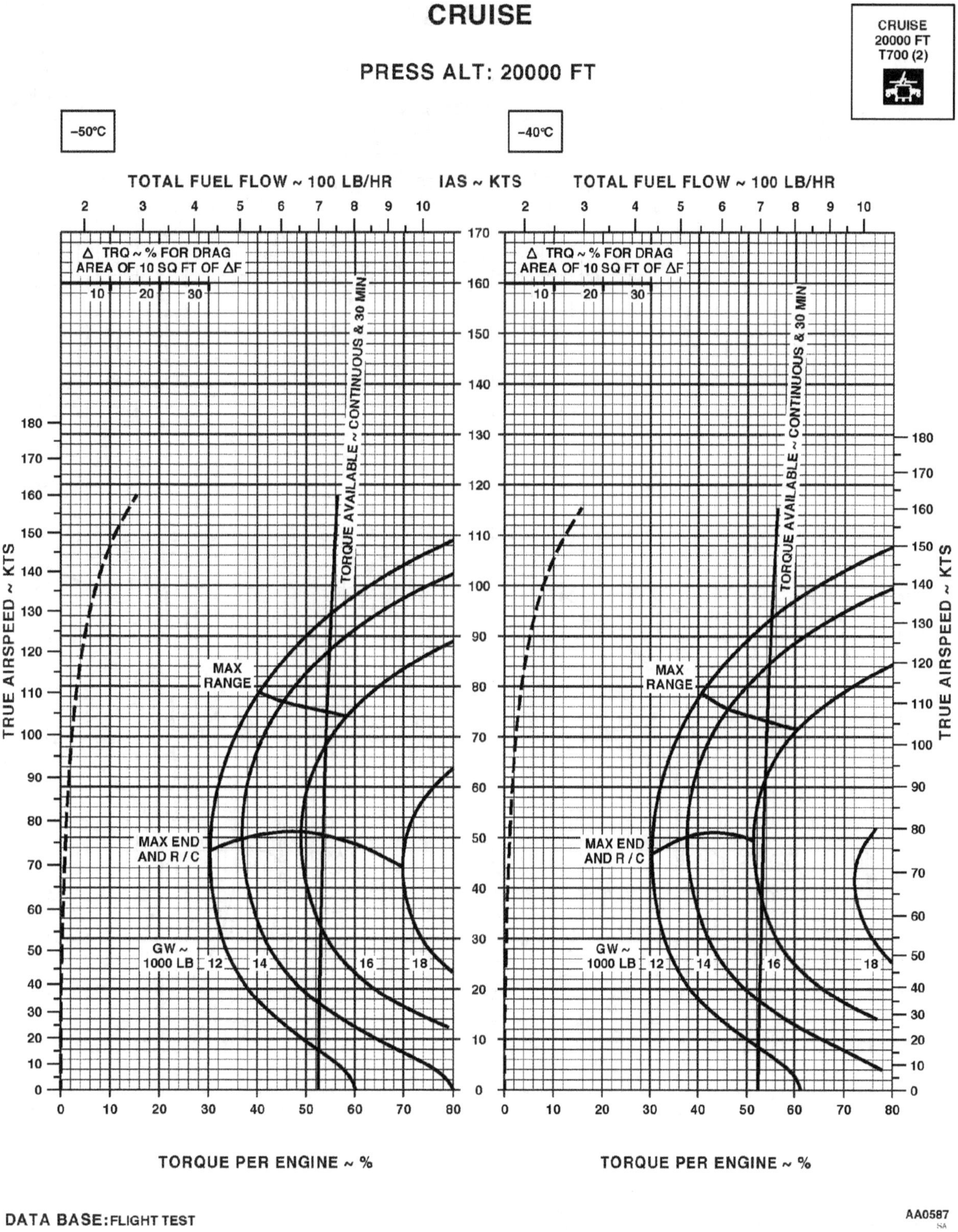

DATA BASE: FLIGHT TEST

Figure 7-28. Cruise High Drag - Pressure Altitude 20,000 Feet (Sheet 1 of 4)

CRUISE

PRESS ALT: 20000 FT

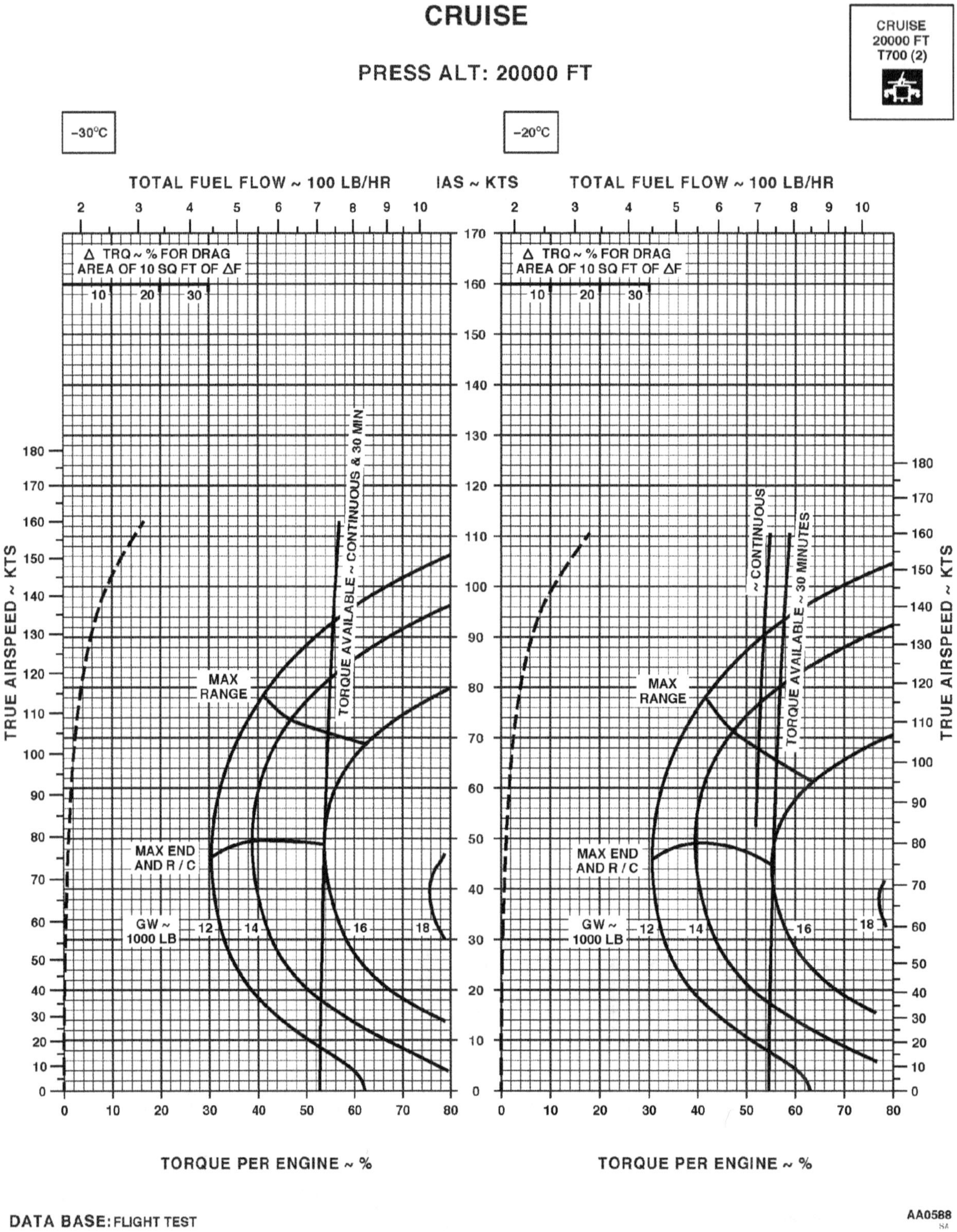

Figure 7-28. Cruise High Drag - Pressure Altitude 20,000 Feet (Sheet 2 of 4)

DATA BASE: FLIGHT TEST

CRUISE

PRESS ALT: 20000 FT

CRUISE
20000 FT
T700 (2)

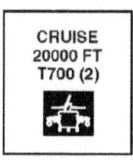

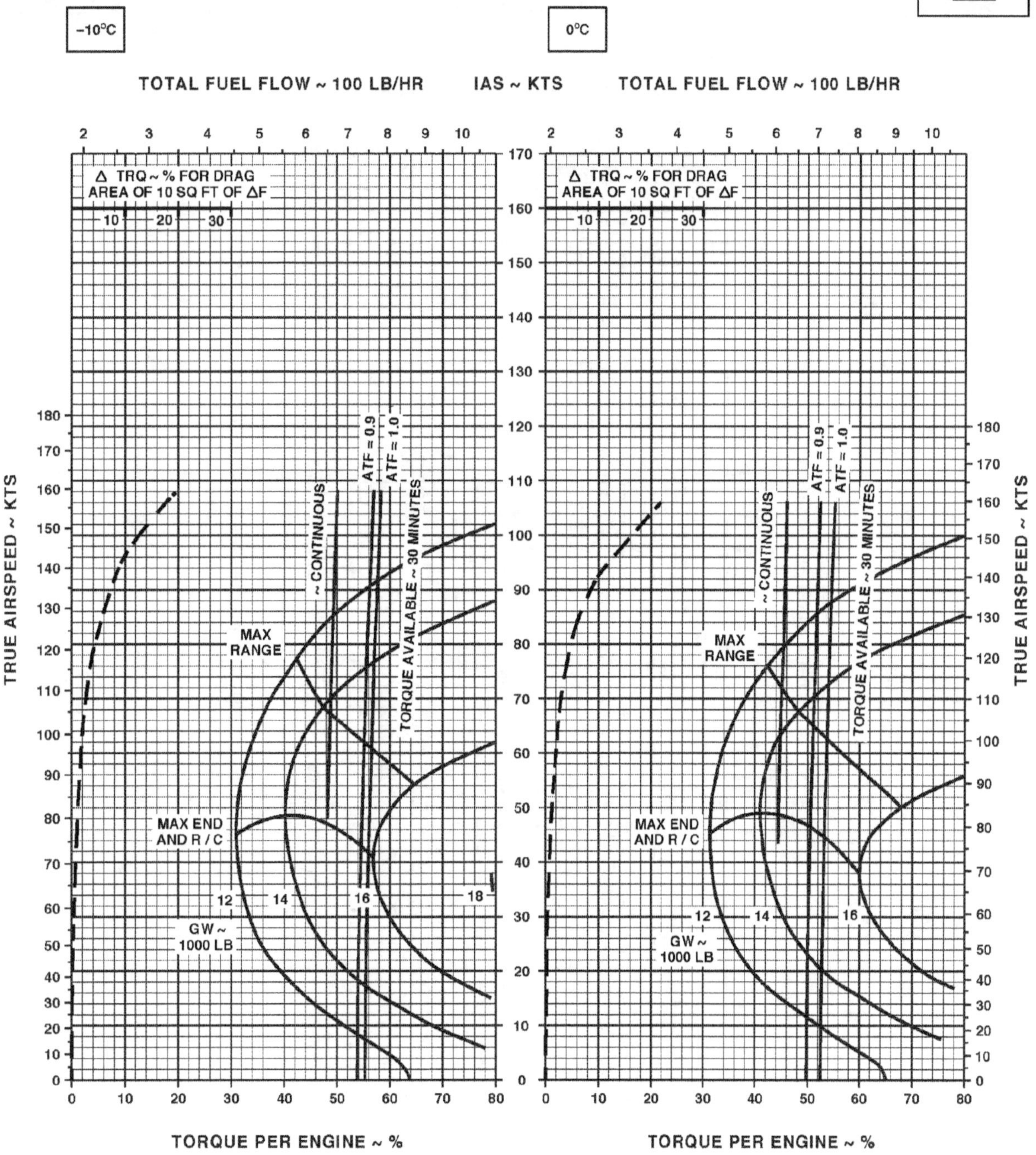

DATA BASE: FLIGHT TEST

AA0589

Figure 7-28. Cruise High Drag - Pressure Altitude 20,000 Feet (Sheet 3 of 4)

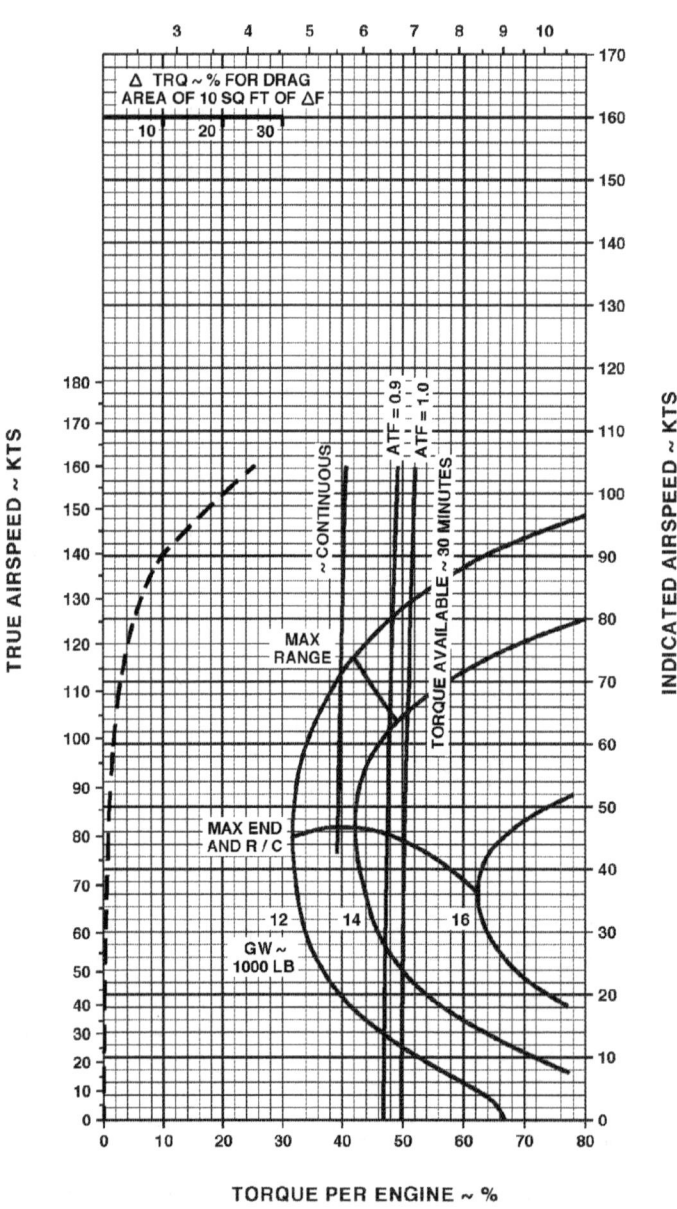

Figure 7-28. Cruise High Drag - Pressure Altitude 20,000 Feet (Sheet 4 of 4)

Section V OPTIMUM CRUISE

7.20 OPTIMUM RANGE CHARTS.

This section presents a method to optimize cruise performance for long range missions when the altitudes flown are not restricted by other requirements. The optimum altitude for maximum range chart (Figure 7-29) provides the pressure altitude at which to cruise to obtain the maximum possible range for any gross weight and FAT conditions. The altitude determined for optimum range may also be used for optimum endurance. Enter the chart at a current cruise or takeoff temperature condition and move along the temperature guide lines to the anticipated gross weight for cruise and obtain the optimum pressure altitude. Turn to the cruise chart closest to the altitude and temperature predicted by the optimum range chart for specific cruise information. The use of this chart is shown by the example.

OPTIMUM RANGE
CLEAN CONFIGURATION 100% RPM R
HIRSS (BAFFLES INSTALLED)

EXAMPLE

WANTED:

CRUISE ALTITUDE FOR OPTIMUM RANGE AND CORRESPONDING CRUISE CHART FOR FLIGHT CONDITIONS

KNOWN:

REFERENCE CONDITIONS OF:
PRESSURE ALTITUDE = 1,500 FT
FAT = 24 °C
GROSS WEIGHT = 16,500 LB

METHOD:

ENTER CHART AT FAT (24 °C), MOVE RIGHT TO REFERENCE / OPTIMUM PRESSURE ALTITUDE (1,500 FT). MOVE PARALLEL WITH THE TEMPERATURE TREND LINES TO AIRCRAFT GROSS WEIGHT (16,500 LB). MOVE LEFT OR RIGHT PARALLELING THE TEMPERATURE TREND LINE TO NEAREST EVEN THOUSAND REFERENCE / OPTIMUM PRESSURE ALTITUDE LINE (12,000). MOVE LEFT TO FREE AIR TEMPERATURE LINE (2.5 °C), MOVE UP OR DOWN TO NEAREST TEN VALUE ON THE FREE AIR TEMPERATURE SCALE (0 °C).

SELECT CRUISE CHART WITH ALTITUDE AND TEMPERATURE DATA AT THE NEAREST REFERENCE / OPTIMUM PRESSURE ALTITUDE (12,000 FT) AND THE NEAREST TEN DEGREE FREE AIR TEMPERATURE (0 °C).

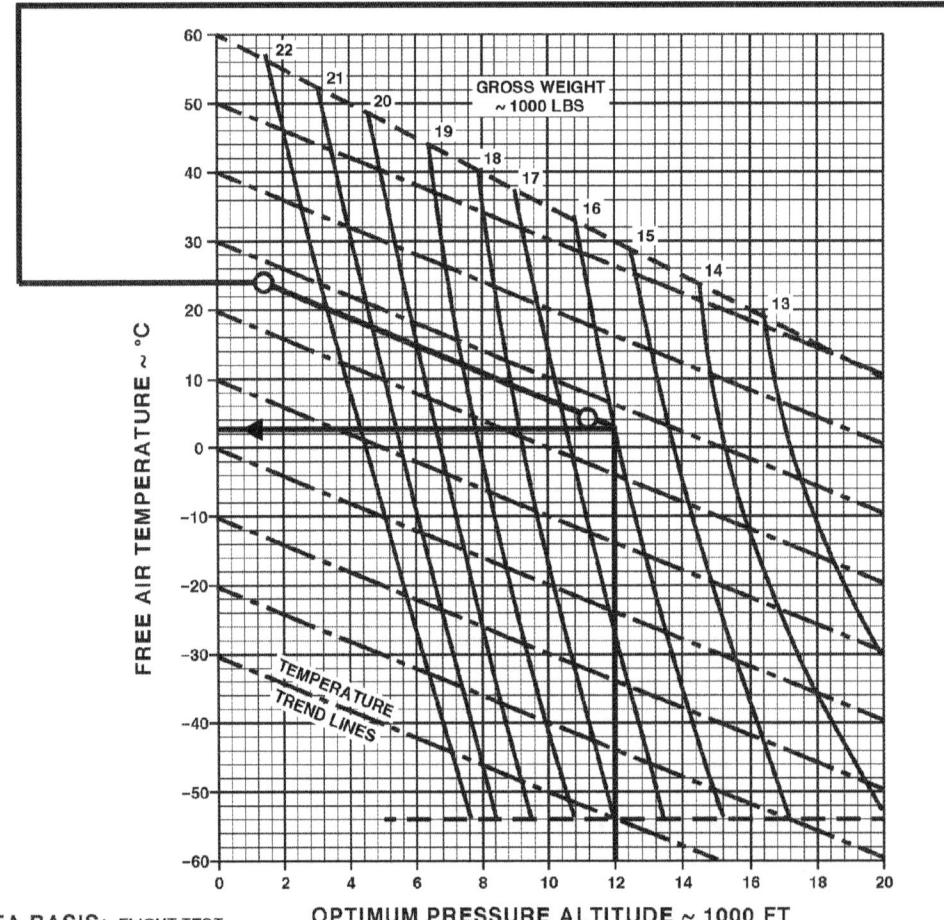

DATA BASIS: FLIGHT TEST

AA0683 1B
SA

Figure 7-29. Optimum Altitude For Maximum Range (Sheet 1 of 2)

OPTIMUM RANGE

HIGH DRAG CONFIGURATION 100% RPM R
HIRSS (BAFFLES INSTALLED)

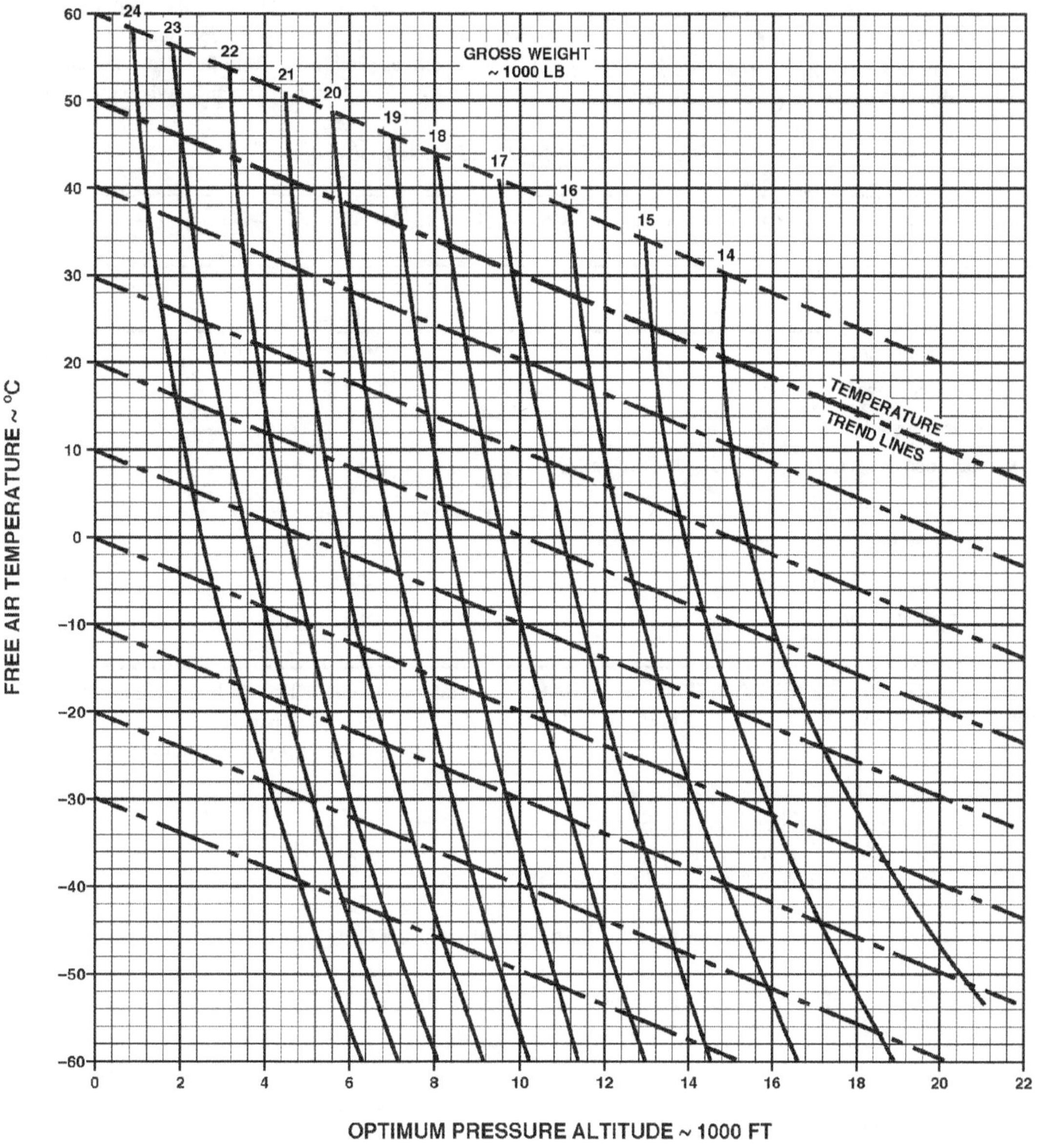

DATA BASIS: FLIGHT TEST

AA0683_2B
SA

Figure 7-29. Optimum Altitude For Maximum Range (Sheet 2 of 2)

Section VI DRAG

7.21 EXTERNAL LOAD DRAG CHART.

The general shapes of typical external loads are shown on Figure 7-30 as a function of the load frontal area. The frontal area is combined with the typical drag coefficient of the general shapes to obtain a drag multiplying factor for use with the 10 sq. ft. drag scale on each cruise chart. The ΔTRQ ~% value obtained from the cruise chart is multiplied by the drag multiplying factor and added to indicated torque to obtain total torque required at any airspeed.

7.22 AIRCRAFT CONFIGURATION DRAG CHANGES FOR USE WITH CLEAN CRUISE CHARTS.

When external equipment or configuration differs from the baseline clean configuration as defined in Section 1, a drag correction should be made similarly to the external drag load method. Typical configuration changes that have drag areas established from flight test or analysis along with their drag multiplying factor are shown on Table 7-1.

Table 7-1. Configuration Drag Change

DRAG CHANGES FOR USE WITH CLEAN CRUISE CHARTS

Item	Change in Flat Plate Drag Area- ΔF Sq. Ft.	Drag Multiplying Factor
a. Both cargo doors open	6.0	0.60
b. Cargo doors removed	4.0	0.40
c. Cargo mirror installed	0.3	0.03
d. IR Countermeasure Transmitter (ALQ-144) installed	0.8	0.08
e. Chaff Dispenser Installed	0.3	0.03
f. HIRSS not installed	-2.2	-0.22
g. Blade Erosion Kit	2.0	0.20
h. UH-60Q configuration	5.3	0.53

7.23 AIRCRAFT CONFIGURATION DRAG CHANGES FOR USE WITH HIGH DRAG CRUISE CHARTS.

When external equipment differs from the baseline high drag configuration as defined in this Section, a drag correction should be made using Table 7-2 similar to the external drag load method. Typical high drag configuration changes that have been established from flight test or analysis along with the drag multiplying factors are shown.

Table 7-2. Configuration Drag Change

DRAG CHANGES FOR USE WITH HIGH DRAG CRUISE CHARTS

Item	Change in Flat Plate Drag Area- ΔF Sq. Ft.	Drag Multiplying Factor
a. ESSS Clean, pylons removed	-4.0	-0.40
b. ESSS Four pylons - no stores	-1.7	-0.17
c. Skis installed	3.0	0.30
d. Both cargo doors open	6.0	0.60

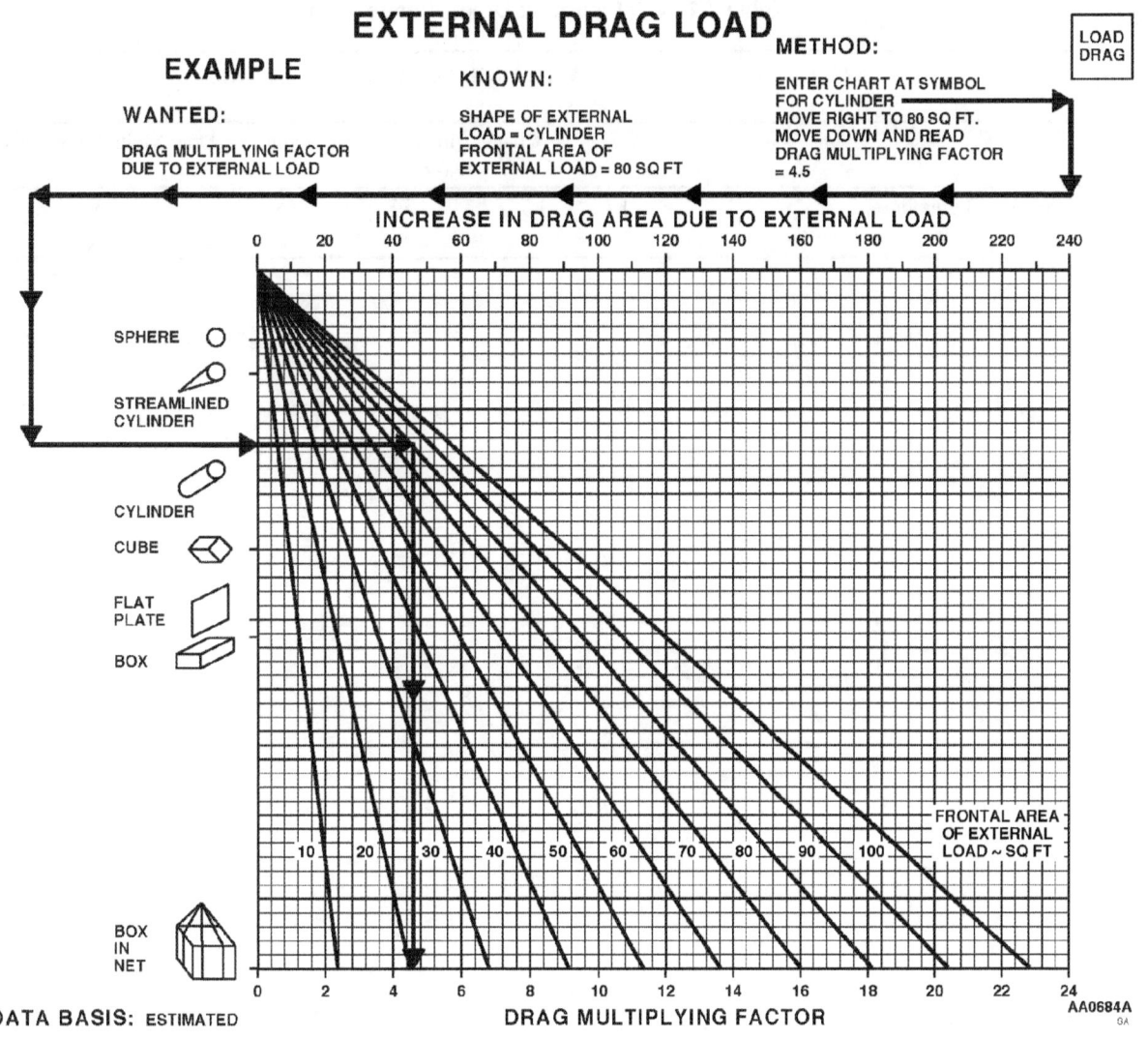

Figure 7-30. External Load Drag

Table 7-2. Configuration Drag Change (Cont)

DRAG CHANGES FOR USE WITH HIGH DRAG CRUISE CHARTS

Item	Change in Flat Plate Drag Area- Δ F Sq. Ft.	Drag Multiplying Factor
e. Both cargo doors removed	4.0	0.40
f. Cargo mirror installed	0.3	0.03
g. IR Countermeasure transmitter (AN/ALQ-144) removed	-0.8	-0.08
h. Chaff dispenser removed	-0.3	-0.03

Table 7-2. Configuration Drag Change (Cont)

DRAG CHANGES FOR USE WITH HIGH DRAG CRUISE CHARTS

Item	Change in Flat Plate Drag Area- Δ F Sq. Ft.	Drag Multiplying Factor
i. UH-60Q configuration	5.3	0.53

Section VII CLIMB - DESCENT

7.24 CLIMB/DESCENT CHART.

The CLIMB/DESCENT chart (Figures 7-31 and 7-32) presents the rate of climb or descent resulting from an increase or decrease of engine torque from the value required for level flight above 40 KIAS. The data are presented at 100% RPM R for various gross weights. The charts may also be used in reverse to obtain the torque increase or reduction required to achieve a desired steady rate of climb or descent. The maximum R/C may be determined by subtracting the cruise chart torque required from the maximum torque available at the desired flight conditions. Then enter the difference on the torque increase scale of the climb chart, move up to the gross weight, and read the resulting maximum R/C.

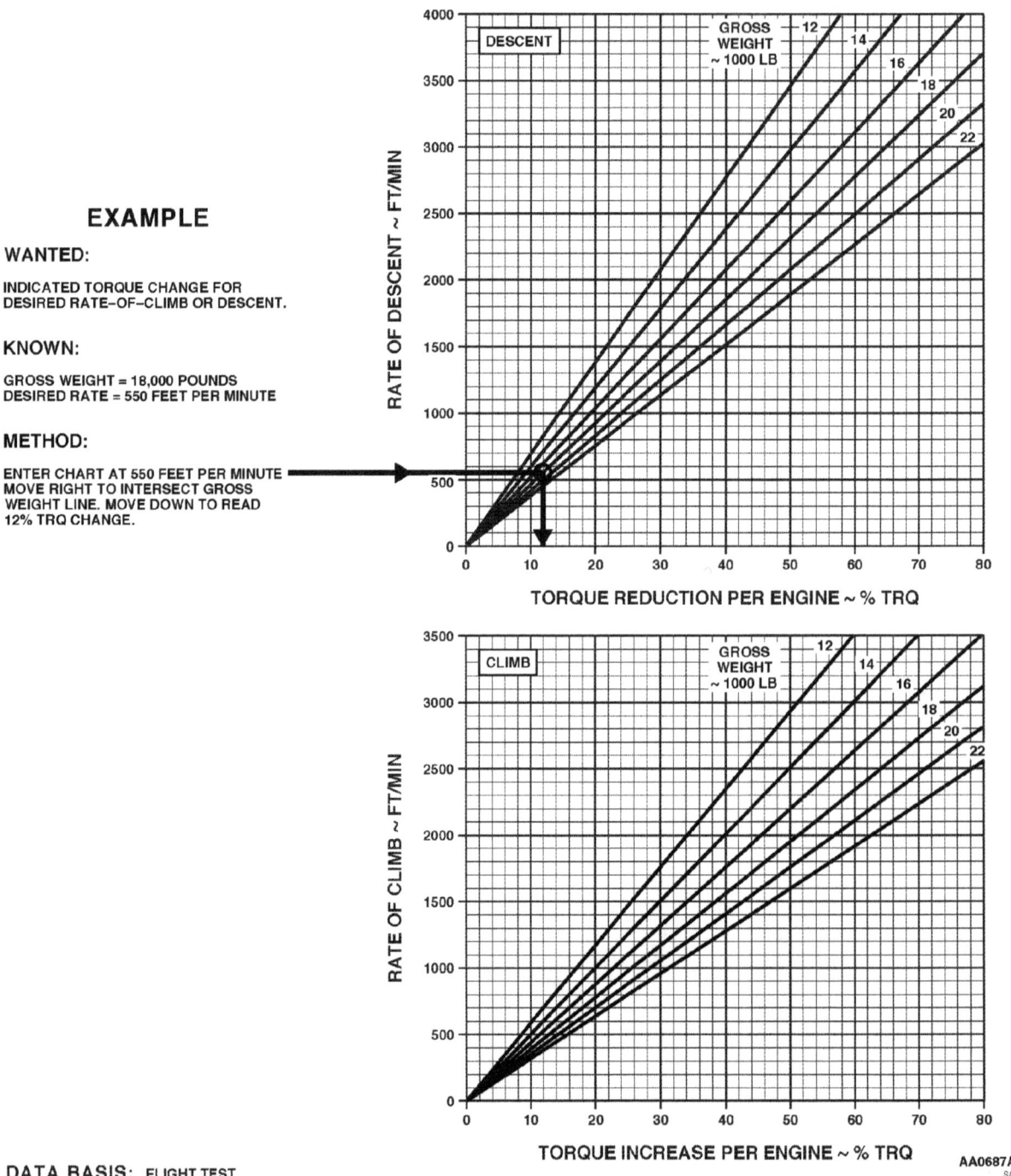

Figure 7-31. Climb/Descent

CLIMB/DESCENT

100% RPM R
AIRSPEEDS ABOVE 40 KIAS

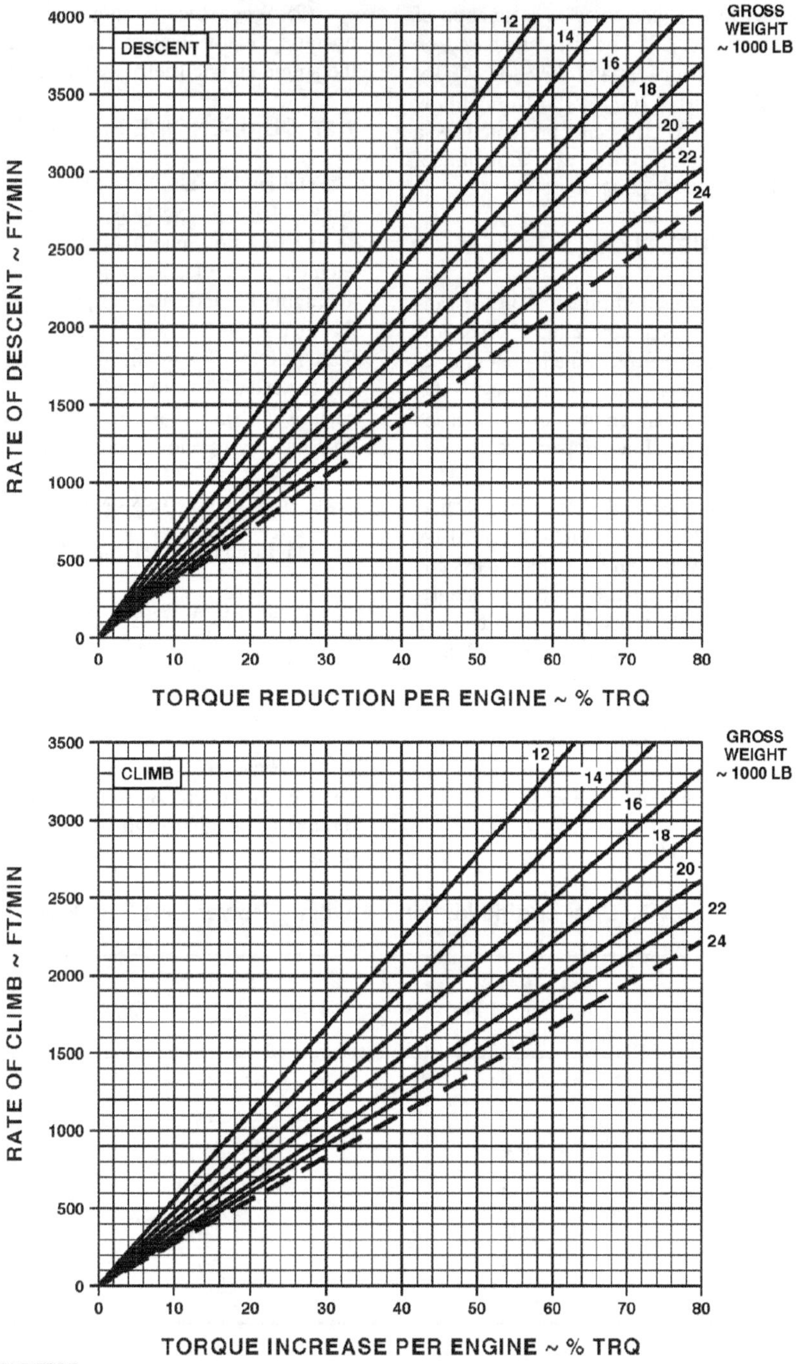

DATA BASIS: FLIGHT TEST

AA0688A
9A

Figure 7-32. Climb/Descent - High Drag

Section VIII FUEL FLOW

7.25 IDLE FUEL FLOW.

Dual-engine idle fuel flow is presented as a function of altitude at 0°C FAT in Table 7-3. The data are based on operation at 62% to 69% Ng for idle and 85% to 89% for flat pitch (collective full down) at 100% RPM R. Fuel flow for the auxiliary power unit (APU) is also presented for a nominal load of 80% maximum power as a function of altitude and 0°C FAT for general planning.

7.26 SINGLE-ENGINE FUEL FLOW.

a. Engine fuel flow is presented in Figure 7-33 for various torque and pressure altitudes at a baseline FAT of 0°C with engine bleed air extraction off. When operating at other than 0°C FAT, engine fuel flow is increased 1% for each 20°C above the baseline temperature and, decreased 1% for each 20°C below the baseline temperature.

b. To determine single-engine fuel flow during cruise, enter the fuel flow chart at double the torque required for dual-engine cruise as determined from the cruise charts and obtain fuel flow from the single-engine scale. The single-engine torque may not exceed the transmission limit shown on the chart. With bleed air on, single-engine fuel flow increases as follows:

(1) With bleed-air extracted, fuel flow increases:

(a) Engine anti-ice on - About 30 lbs/hr

(b) Heater on - About 10 lbs/hr

(c) Both on - About 40 lbs/hr

(2) When the IR suppressor system is installed and operating in the benign mode (exhaust baffles removed), the single-engine fuel flow will decrease about 8 lbs/hr.

7.27 DUAL-ENGINE FUEL FLOW.

Dual-engine fuel flow for level flight is presented on the cruise charts in Section IV. For other conditions dual-engine fuel flow may be obtained from Figure 7-33 when each engine is indicating approximately the same torque by averaging the indicated torques and reading fuel flow from the dual-engine fuel flow scale. When operating at other than the 0° FAT baseline, dual-engine fuel flow is increased 1% for each 20°C above baseline and is decreased 1% for each 20°C below baseline temperature. With bleed air on, dual-engine fuel flow increases as follows:

a. With bleed-air extracted, fuel flow increases:

(1) Engine anti-ice on - About 60 lbs/hr

Example: (760 lbs/hour = 820 lbs/hr).

(2) Heater on - About 20 lbs/hr

(3) Both on - About 80 lbs/hr

b. When the cruise or hover IR suppressor system is installed and operating in the benign mode (exhaust baffles removed), the dual-engine fuel flow will decrease about 16 lbs/hr.

Table 7-3. Dual Engine Idle and Auxiliary Power Unit Fuel Flow

Pressure Altitude Feet	Ng = 62-69% Ground Idle (No Load) Lb/Hr	Ng = 85-89% Flat Pitch (100% RPM R) Lb/Hr	APU (Nominal) Lb/Hr
0	350	580	120
4,000	326	500	105
8,000	268	440	90
12,000	234	380	75
16,000	206	320	65
20,000	182	270	55

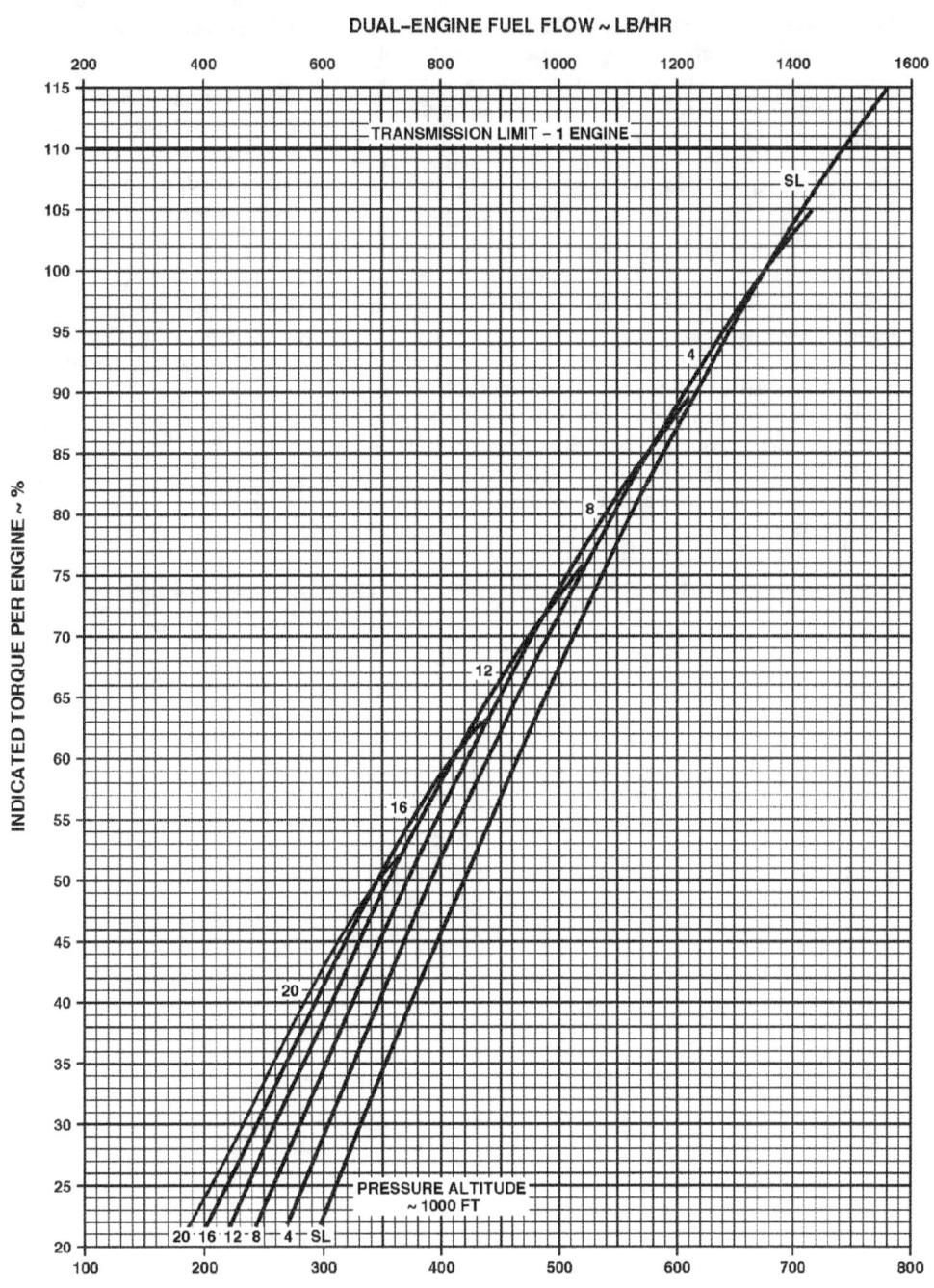

Figure 7-33. Single/Dual-Engine Fuel Flow

Section IX AIRSPEED SYSTEM CHARACTERISTICS

7.28 AIRSPEED CHARTS.

7.28.1 Airspeed Correction Charts. All indicated airspeeds shown on the cruise charts are based on level flight. Figures 7-34 and 7-35 provide the airspeed correction to be added to the cruise chart IAS values to determine the related airspeed indicator reading for other than level flight mode. There are relatively large variations in airspeed system error associated with climbs and descents. Figures 7-34 and 7-35 are provided primarily to show the general magnitude and direction of the errors associated with the various flight modes. If desired, these figures may be used in the manner shown by the examples to calculate specific airspeed corrections.

7.28.2 Airspeed System Dynamic Characteristics. The dynamic characteristics of the pilot and copilot airspeed indicating systems are normally satisfactory. However, the following anomalies in the airspeed and IVSI indicating system may be observed during the following maneuvers or conditions:

a. During takeoffs, in the speed range of 40 to 80 KIAS, 5 to 10 KIAS airspeed fluctuation may be observed on the pilot's and copilot's airspeed indicators.

b. Power changes in high power, low airspeed climbs may cause as much as 30 knot airspeed changes in indicated airspeed. Increase in power causes increase in indicated airspeed, and a decrease in power causes decrease in indicated airspeed.

c. The pilot and copilot airspeed indicators may be unreliable during high power climbs at low airspeeds (less than 50 KIAS) with the copilot system reading as much as 30 knots lower than the pilot system.

d. In-flight opening and closing of doors and windows may cause momentary fluctuations of approximately 300 feet per minute on the vertical speed indicators.

TM 1-1520-253-10

AIRSPEED SYSTEM CORRECTION
CLEAN

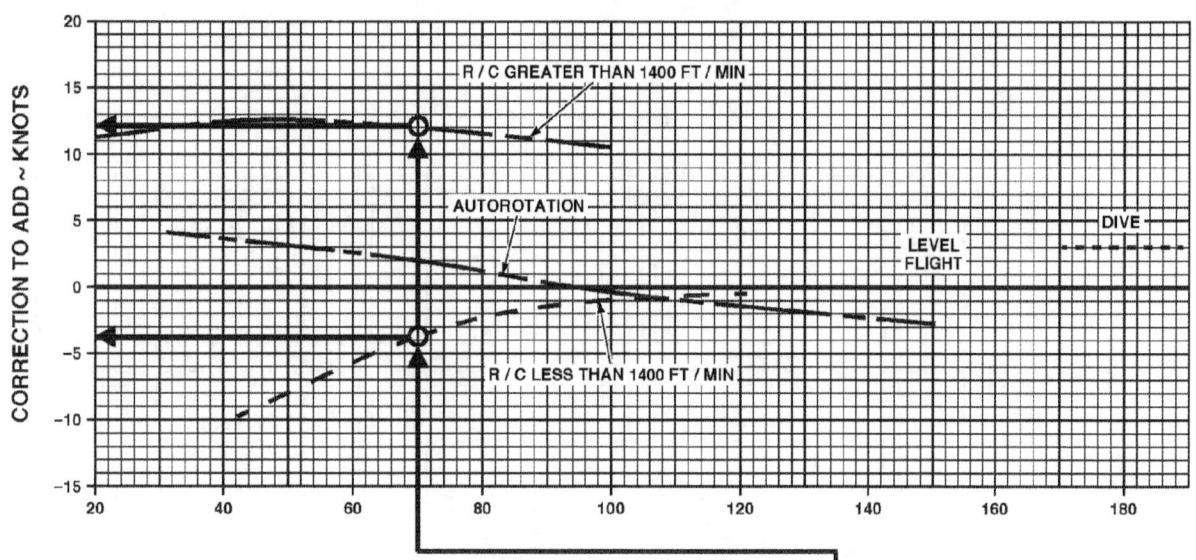

EXAMPLE

WANTED:

INDICATED AIRSPEED TO CLIMB AT MAXIMUM RATE OF CLIMB

KNOWN:

70 KIAS MAX END / AND R / C FROM APPROPRIATE CRUISE CHART FOR A GIVEN PRESSURE ALTITUDE, FAT, AND GROSS WEIGHT.

METHOD:

ENTER AT KNOWN IAS FROM CRUISE CHART, MOVE UP TO R / C GREATER THAN 1400 FPM, MOVE LEFT READ CORRECTION TO ADD TO IAS = + 12.5 KTS. RE-ENTER AT KNOWN IAS FROM CRUISE CHART, MOVE UP TO R / C LESS THAN 1400 FPM LINE, MOVE LEFT, READ CORRECTION TO ADD TO IAS = – 4 KTS CALCULATE IAS FOR MAX R / C WHEN:

FOR R / C GREATER THAN 1400 FPM, AIRSPEED = 70 KIAS + 12.5 KIAS = 82.5 KIAS

FOR R / C LESS THAN 1400 FPM, AIRSPEED = 70 KIAS – 4 KIAS = 66 KIAS

DATA BASIS: FLIGHT TEST

AB1089
SA

Figure 7-34. Airspeed Correction - Clean

AIRSPEED SYSTEM CORRECTION

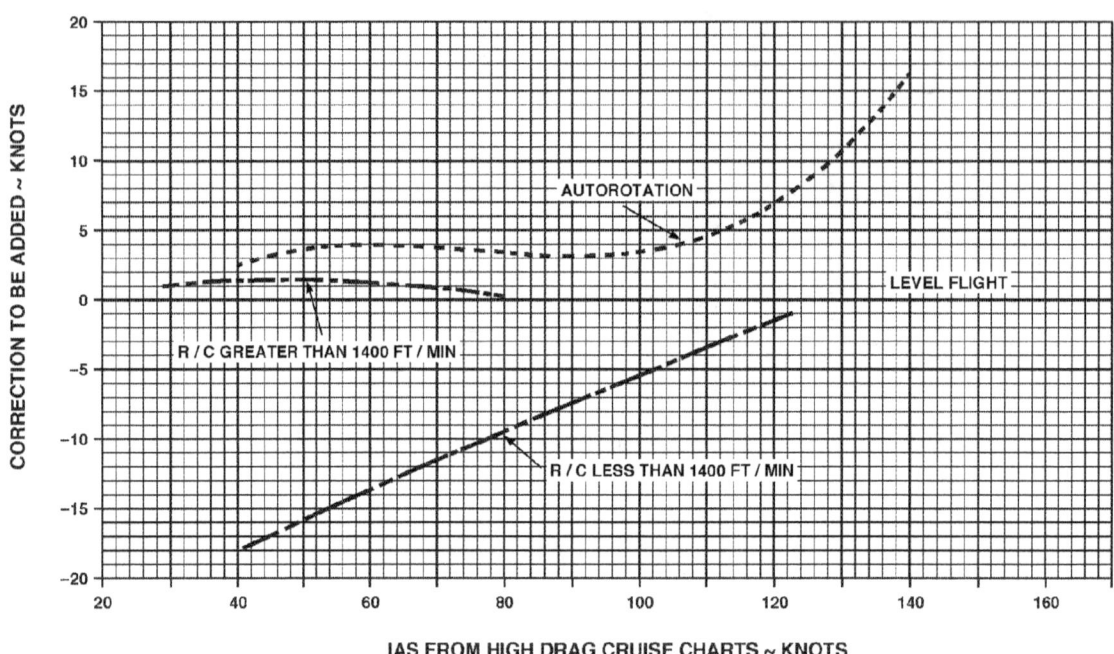

DATA BASIS: FLIGHT TEST

Figure 7-35. Airspeed Correction Chart - High Drag

Section X SPECIAL MISSION PERFORMANCE

7.29 SPECIAL MISSION FLIGHT PROFILES.

Figure 7-36 shows special mission flight profiles required to obtain near maximum range when equipped with ESSS and extended range fuel system. The upper segment of the chart provides the recommended altitude profile along with the IAS and average TRQ versus distance traveled. An average value of elapsed time is also presented on the lower axis of the altitude scale. The lower segment of the chart provides the relationship between fuel remaining and distance traveled resulting from the flight profile shown. This portion may be utilized to check actual inflight range data to provide assurance that adequate range is being achieved. The chart is divided into 3 regions of Adequate Range, Inadequate range-return to base, and Inadequate range-requiring emergency action. When an inflight range point is in the Adequate range region, the required mission range can be obtained by staying on the recommended flight profile. However, the range may not be achieved if stronger headwinds are encountered as the flight progresses, and normal pilot judgement must be used. These charts also assume that the flight track is within proper navigational limits. Standard temperature variation with PA is shown on the upper segment of the charts. A general correction for temperature variation is to decrease IAS by 2.5 KTS and total distance traveled by 0.5% for each 10°C above standard. Detailed flight planning must always be made for the actual aircraft configuration, fuel load, and flight conditions when maximum range is required. This data is based on JP-4 fuel. It can be used with JP-5 or JP-8, aviation gasoline, or any other approved fuels ONLY IF THE TAKE-OFF GROSS WEIGHT AND THE FUEL LOAD WEIGHT MATCH THE DATA AT THE TOP OF THE CHART. The Flight Time and the Distance Traveled data SHOULD NOT be used with any full tank configuration if the fuel density is not approximately 6.5 lb/gal (JP-4 fuel).

SPECIAL MISSION PROFILE - 2 tanks. The special mission profile is shown in Figure 7-36 with the ESSS configured with two 230-gallon tanks. In this configuration, the aircraft holds in excess of 5,300 pounds of JP4 fuel and assumes a take-off gross weight of 22,000 pounds which provides a maximum mission range of 630 Nm. with 400 lb reserve. This mission was calculated for a standard day with a zero headwind. Take-off must be made with a minimum of fuel used (80 lbs) for engine start and warm-up, and a Climb to 4,000 feet should be made with max power and airspeed between 80 and 108 KIAS. The first segment should be maintained at 4,000 feet and 108 KIAS for 1 hour. The average engine TRQ should be about 77% for this segment, but will initially be a little more and gradually decrease as shown on each segment. Altitude is increased in 2,000 feet increments to maintain the optimum altitude for maximum range to account for fuel burn. At this altitude, the airspeed for best range should also be reduced to 95 KIAS for the remainder of the flight.

EXAMPLE:

WANTED:

    Assurance of adequate aircraft range for mission defined.

KNOWN:

    Flight position: 150 nm from base
    Flight Track Within Limits
    Fuel Remaining = 3,900 pounds
    Elapsed flight time = 1 HRS, 20 MINS (1.33 HRS)
    Target: Normal Flight Conditions:

        Airspeed = 102 KIAS
        Press Alt = 6,000 feet
        Approx Torque = 70%

METHOD:

(1) Enter chart at total distance flown and at fuel remaining, move to intersection and plot point. If point falls on or above fuel remaining line (adequate range), remaining fuel is adequate to complete the mission. If point falls below the fuel remaining line in the inadequate range, abort mission region, immediately return to departure point while continuing to utilize altitide profile using total elapsed flight time (see item 2). If point falls below the fuel remaining line in the inadequate range, region, consult emergency procedures for corrective action.

(2) To determine target nominial flight conditions, enter upper chart at elapsed flight time and move up to determine target airspeed, approximate torque, and pressure altitude.

Figure 7-36. Special Mission Profile (Sheet 1 of 2)

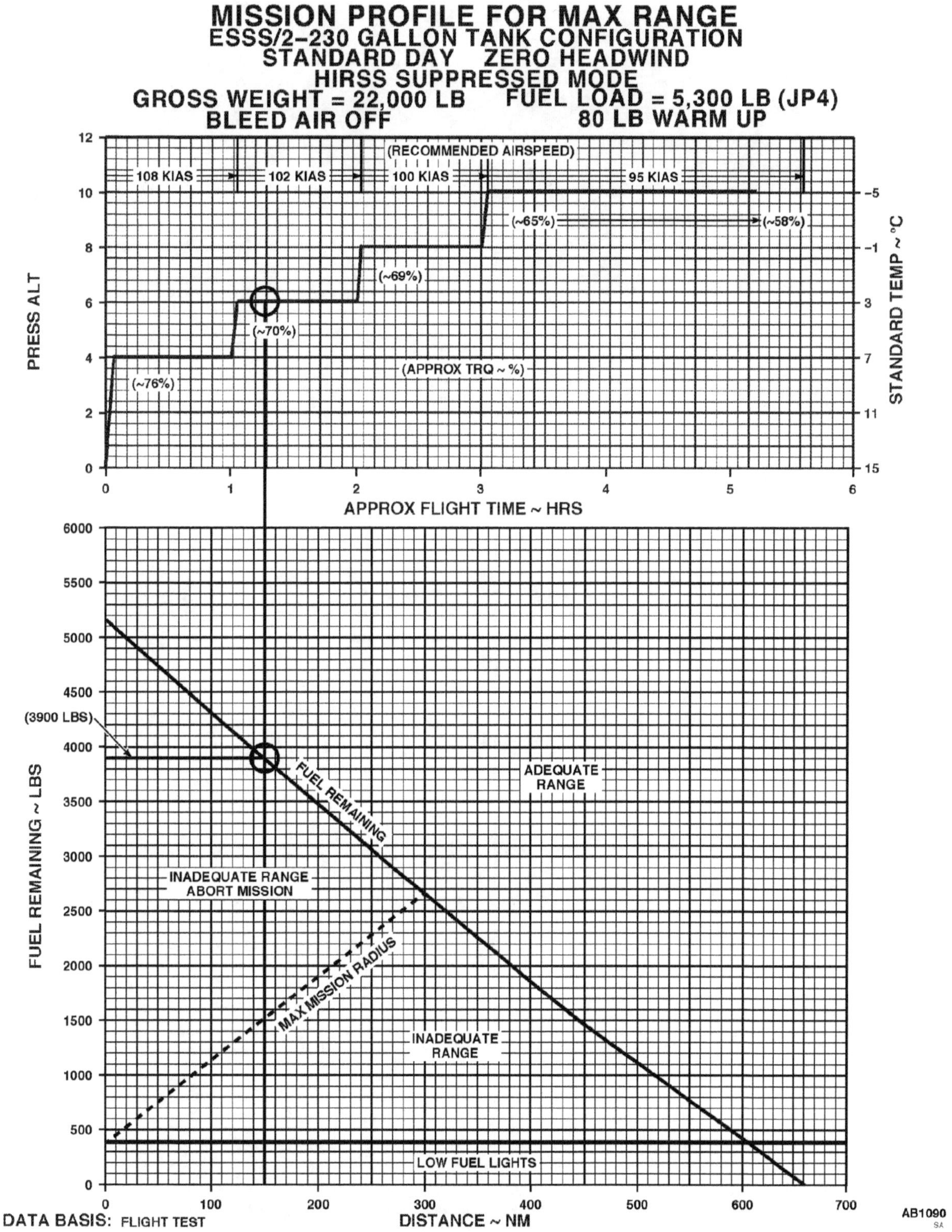

Figure 7-36. Special Mission Profile (Sheet 2 of 2)

CHAPTER 8
NORMAL PROCEDURES

Section I MISSION PLANNING

8.1 MISSION PLANNING.

Mission planning begins when the mission is assigned and extends to the preflight check of the helicopter. It includes, but is not limited to checks of operating limits and restrictions; weight, balance, and loading; performance; publications; flight plan; and crew and passenger briefings. The pilot in command shall ensure compliance with the contents of this manual that are applicable to the mission and all aviation support equipment required for the mission (e.g., helmets, gloves, survival vests, survival kits, etc).

8.2 AVIATION LIFE SUPPORT EQUIPMENT (ALSE).

All aviation life support equipment required for mission; e.g., helmets, gloves, survival vests, survival kits, etc., shall be checked.

8.3 CREW DUTIES/RESPONSIBILITIES.

The minimum crew required to fly the helicopter is two pilots. Additional crewmembers, as required, may be added at the discretion of the commander. The manner in which each crewmember performs his related duties is the responsibility of the pilot in command.

   a. The pilot in command is responsible for all aspects of mission planning, preflight, and operation of the helicopter. He will assign duties and functions to all other crewmembers as required. Prior to or during preflight, the pilot will brief the crew on items pertinent to the mission; e.g., performance data, monitoring of instruments, communications, emergency procedures, taxi, and load operations.

   b. The pilot in command must be familiar with pilot duties and the duties of the other crew positions.

   c. The crew chief will perform all duties as assigned by the pilot.

8.4 CREW BRIEFING.

A crew briefing shall be conducted to ensure a thorough understanding of individual and team responsibilities. The briefing should include, but not be limited to, pilots, crew chief, mission equipment operator, ground crew responsibilities, and the coordination necessary to complete the mission in the most efficient manner. A review of visual signals is desirable when ground guides do not have direct voice communications link with the crew.

8.5 PASSENGER BRIEFING.

The following guide may be used in accomplishing required passenger briefings. Items that do not pertain to a specific mission may be omitted.

   a. Crew introduction.

   b. Equipment.

     (1) Personal, to include ID tags.

     (2) Professional.

     (3) Survival.

   c. Flight data.

     (1) Route.

     (2) Altitude.

     (3) Time en route.

     (4) Weather.

   d. Normal procedures.

     (1) Entry and exit the helicopter.

(2) Seating.

(3) Seat belts.

(4) Movement in helicopter.

(5) Internal communications.

(6) Security of equipment.

(7) Smoking.

(8) Oxygen.

(9) Refueling.

(10) Weapons.

(11) Protective masks.

(12) Parachutes.

(13) Hearing protection.

(14) Aviation life support equipment (ALSE).

e. Emergency procedures.

(1) Emergency exits.

(2) Emergency equipment.

(3) Emergency landing/ditching procedures.

Section II OPERATING PROCEDURES AND MANEUVERS

8.6 OPERATING PROCEDURES AND MANEUVERS.

This section deals with normal procedures and includes all steps necessary to ensure safe and efficient operation of the helicopter from the time a preflight begins until the flight is completed and the helicopter is parked and secured. Unique feel, characteristics, and reaction of the helicopter during various phases of operation and the techniques and procedures used for taxiing, takeoff, climb, etc., are described, including precautions to be observed. Your flying experience is recognized; therefore, basic flight principles are avoided. Only the duties of the minimum crew necessary for the actual operation of the helicopter are included. Additional crew duties are covered as necessary in Section I Mission Planning. Mission equipment checks are contained in Chapter 4 Mission Equipment. Procedures specifically related to instrument flight that are different from normal procedures are covered in this section, following normal procedures. Descriptions of functions, operations, and effects of controls are covered in Section IV Flight Characteristics, and are repeated in this section only when required for emphasis. Checks that must be performed under adverse environmental conditions, such as desert and cold-weather operations, supplement normal procedures checks in this section and are covered in Section V Adverse Environmental Conditions.

8.7 SYMBOLS DEFINITION.

Items which apply only to night or only to instrument flying shall have an N or an I, respectively, immediately preceding the check to which it is pertinent. The symbol O shall be used to indicate "if installed". Those duties which are the responsibility of the pilot not on the controls, will be indicated by a circle around the step number; i.e., ④ . The symbol star ★ indicates an operational check is required. Operational checks are contained in the performance section of the condensed checklist. The asterisk symbol * indicates that performance of step is mandatory for all thru-flights. The asterisk applies only to checks performed prior to takeoff. Placarded items such as switch and control labels appear in boldface capital letters.

8.8 CHECKLIST.

Normal procedures are given primarily in checklist form, and amplified as necessary in accompanying paragraph form, when a detailed description of a procedure or maneuver is required. A condensed version of the amplified checklist, omitting all explanatory text, is contained in the operator's checklist. To provide for easier cross-referencing, the procedural steps in the checklist are numbered to coincide with the corresponding numbered steps in this manual.

8.9 PREFLIGHT CHECK.

The pilot's walkaround and interior checks are outlined in the following procedures. The preflight check is not intended to be a detailed mechanical inspection. The preflight order is a recommended sequence only. The expanded substeps do not need to be memorized or accomplished in order. The steps that are essential for safe helicopter operation are included. The preflight may be made as comprehensive as conditions warrant at the discretion of the pilot.

8.10 BEFORE EXTERIOR CHECK (FIGURE 8-1).

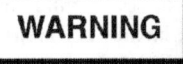

Do not preflight until systems are safe, switches off, safety pins installed and locking levers in locked position.

1. Publications - Check; required forms and publications, and availability of operator's manual(s) (-10) checklist (-CL).

*2. Helicopter covers, locking devices, tiedowns, and grounding cables - Removed and secured.

*3. Fuel - Check quantity as required.

4. Fuel sample - As required. Check for contamination before first flight of the day and after adequate settling time after cold refueling, or if fuel source is suspected contaminated.

8.11 EXTERIOR CHECK.

Exterior walkaround diagram is shown in Figure 8-1.

8.12 NOSE SECTION (AREA 1).

CAUTION

Do not deflect main rotor blade tips more than 6 inches below normal droop position when attaching tiedowns. Do not tie down below normal droop position.

*1. Main rotor blades - Check.

2. Fuselage - Nose area, check as follows:

   a. Windshield and wipers - Check.

   O b. Blade deice OAT sensor, FAT indicator probe(s) - Check.

CAUTION

Ensure avionics compartment door is closed and latches are secure prior to securing the FLIR door.

   c. Avionics compartment - Check equipment as required; secure door.

CAUTION

Optical lens of FLIR is easily scratched. To avoid damage, use cleaning procedures and supplies referenced in the maintenance manual.

   d. FLIR - Check condition (remove locking pin).

   . Landing and searchlights - Check.

8.13 COCKPIT - LEFT SIDE (AREA 2).

1. Cockpit area - Check as follows:

   a. Cockpit door - Check.

   b. Copilot seat, belts, and harness - Check.

   c. FM homing antenna - Check.

   d. Landing gear support fairing and step - Check.

   e. Position light - Check.

   f. Main landing gear - Check.

   *f.1 Drag beam - Check.

   O g. **ES** HSS, VSP, ejector rack locking levers locked, fairings, and external tanks - Check; refueling caps secure.

   h. Ambient sense port - Check.

*2. Left engine oil level - Check.

8.14 CABIN TOP (AREA 3).

1. Cabin top - Check as follows:

   a. Left engine - Check inlet.

   b. Left pitot tube - Check.

   c. Control access - Check flight controls, hydraulic reservoir, and filter indicators. Check tempilabels for safe indication and security. Check area.

   d. Control access cover - Close and check secured.

   e. Right pitot tube - Check.

   f. Right engine - Check inlet.

   g. Rescue hoist - Check.

   h. IRCM - Check.

   i. Antennas - Check.

2. APU - Check; oil level, use dipstick.

O 3. APU IPS - Check.

4. Gust lock - Check.

5. Main transmission - Check; oil level.

*6. Main rotor system - Check controls, dampers, head, and blades. BIM® indicators - Check for safe indication (yellow color).

8.15 INTERIOR CABIN (AREA 4).

1. Cabin - Check as follows:

    a. Fire extinguishers - Check.

    b. First aid kits - Check.

    c. Pilot's and copilot's tilt-back release levers - Lock position.

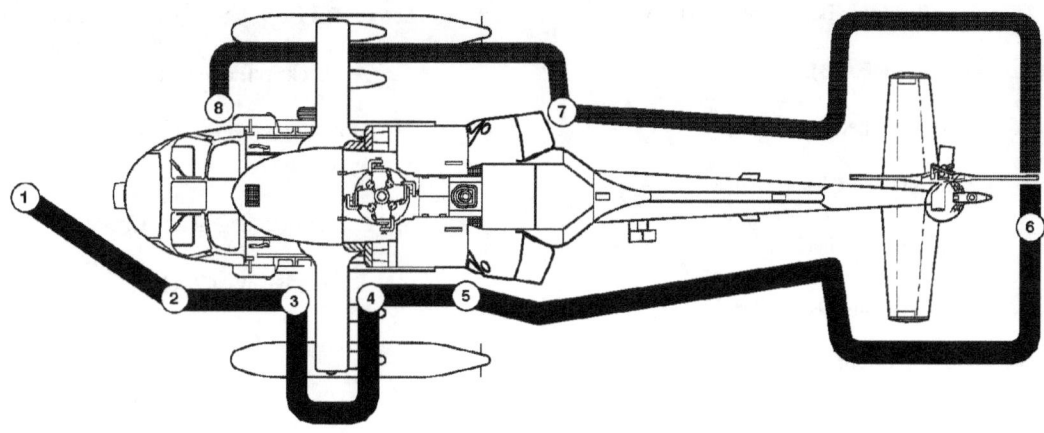

AREA 1 NOSE SECTION	AREA 5 FUSELAGE – LEFT SIDE
AREA 2 COCKPIT – LEFT SIDE	AREA 6 TAIL PYLON
AREA 3 CABIN TOP	AREA 7 FUSELAGE – RIGHT SIDE
AREA 4 INTERIOR CABIN	AREA 8 COCKPIT – RIGHT SIDE

Figure 8-1. Exterior Check Diagram

    d. Cabin interior - Check security of stowed equipment.

    e. Cabin seats and seat belts - Check.

    f. Litters - Check properly stowed and locked in position.

    g. Medical equipment cabinet - Check and secure equipment.

    h. Medical interior circuit breaker panels - Check.

    i. ECS control panel switch - **OFF**.

    j. Rescue hoist searchlight control panel switches - **OFF**.

    k. **ARM - TEST** switch - **TEST**.

    l. Cabin **CSC** panels - Set.

2. APU accumulator pressure gage - Check minimum 2,800 psi.

3. Transmission oil filter impending bypass indicator - Check.

4. Survival gear and mission equipment - Check as required.

8.16 FUSELAGE - LEFT SIDE (AREA 5).

1. Fuselage - Check as follows:

    a. Cabin door - Check.

    b. Fuel tank filler ports - Check; caps secure, doors secured.

    c. External pneumatic inlet port - Door secured.

    d. Engine exhaust - Check.

O   e. APU IPS exhaust - Check.

    f. APU exhaust - Check.

    g. OBOGS heat exchange vent - Check.

O   h. Chaff dispensers - Check; number and programmer settings.

    i. Lower anticollision light - Check.

j. Antennas - Check.

k. Tail landing gear - Check.

*2. Intermediate gear box - Check; oil level.

8.17 TAIL PYLON (AREA 6).

1. Tail pylon - Check as follows:

   a. Tail pylon - Check.

   b. Stabilator - Check.

   c. APR-39 antennas - Check.

   d. Position light - Check.

   e. Upper anticollision light - Check.

*2. Tail rotor - Check.

*3. Tail rotor gear box - Check; oil level.

8.18 FUSELAGE - RIGHT SIDE (AREA 7).

1. Fuselage - Check as follows:

   a. Antennas - Check.

   b. Aft avionics compartment circuit breakers, avionics, ECS screens and OBOGS - Check and secure door.

   c. Fire bottles thermal plug - Check.

   d. Engine exhaust - Check.

   e. Fuel tank gravity filler port - Check cap secure; door secured.

   f. Cabin door - Check.

O g. Rescue hoist - Check cable protection rail.

O h. Rescue hoist searchlight - Check.

   i. Antennas - Check.

8.19 COCKPIT - RIGHT SIDE (AREA 8).

*1. Right engine oil level - Check.

2. Cockpit area - Check as follows:

O a. Ice detector - Check.

   b. Ambient sense port - Check.

O c. ES HSS, VSP, ejector rack locking levers locked, fairings, and external tanks - Check; refueling caps secure.

   d. External electrical power receptacle - Door secured.

   e. Main landing gear - Check.

*e.1 Drag beam - Check.

   f. Position light - Check.

   g. Landing gear support fairing and step - Check.

   h. FM homing antenna - Check.

   i. Cockpit door - Check.

   j. Pilot seat, belt, and harness - Check.

★*3. Crew and passenger briefing - Complete as required.

8.20 BEFORE STARTING ENGINES.

NOTE

Before engine operation can be performed with the gust locks engaged, all main rotor tie downs shall be removed.

*1. Copilot's collective - Extended and locked.

2. Shoulder harness locks - Check.

3. **PARKING BRAKE** - Release, then set.

★4. Circuit breakers and switches - Set as follows:

   a. Circuit breakers - In.

   b. Data cartridge DC-902 - Insert in data loader DL-902 as required.

   c. **ENGINE IGNITION - ON**.

   d. AMS covers - Remove and stow.

e. Pilot **CSC** switches - Set.

f. PLS - Off.

g. **STORES JETTISON** panel switches - Set.

h. **BLADE DEICE POWER** switch - **OFF**.

i. **EMERGENCY CONTROL PANEL, CDU** control - **AUTO, EMERG COMM** and **EMERG IFF** to **NORM**.

j. FLIR and mode switches - **OFF**.

k. APX-100 - Set as desired.

l. Copilot **CSC** switches - Set.

m. **AUX SW** panel switches - **OFF**.

n. M-130 panel **ARM SAFE** switch - **SAFE**.

o. AN/APR-39 - **OFF**.

p. **IRCM** panel switch - **OFF**.

q. Rescue hoist panel **HOIST POWER** switch - **OFF**.

r. **AUXILIARY FUEL MANAGEMENT** panel switches - Set.

s. ANVIS HUD panel - Set.

t. Storm Scope - **OFF**.

*u. Radar altimeter - Set.

v. **BACKUP HYD PUMP - AUTO**.

*w. **ANTICOLLISION/POSITION LIGHTS** - As required.

x. **CARGO HOOK EMERG REL** switch - **OPEN, ARMING** switch - **SAFE**.

y. **APU CONTR** switch - **OFF**; **APU** T-handle - In.

z. **GENERATORS NO. 1** and **NO. 2** switches - Check **ON**.

aa. Ground power unit - Connected if required.

*ab. **AIR SOURCE HEAT/START** switch - **APU** (**OFF** for external air source).

ac. **EMER OFF** T-handles - Full forward.

*ad. **BATT** switch - **ON**.

NOTE

MASTER CAUTION light will not illuminate.

*ae. CDU - Check on.

af. CDU C/A softkey caution/advisory/warning - Check as required.

8.21 COCKPIT EQUIPMENT CHECKS.

*1. **FUEL PUMP** switch - **APU BOOST**.

*2. **APU CONTR** switch - **ON**.

NOTE

If the APU does not start and the **APU ACCUM LOW** advisory legend does not appear with the **APU CONTR** switch **ON**, the manual override lever on the accumulator manifold should be pulled to attempt another start, and held until the APU has reached self-sustaining speed.

If APU fails, note and analyze BITE indications before cycling **BATT** switch or before attempting another APU start.

WARNING

Stabilator will move to full trailing edge down position upon application of AC power. Assure stabilator area is clear prior to energizing stabilator system.

Potential radiation hazard exists at the TACAN antenna when the TACAN is turned on. Make sure that no person is within three feet of the antenna when power is applied to the helicopter. The HF radio transmits high power electromagnetic radiation. Serious injury or death can occur if you touch the HF antenna while it is transmitting. Do not grasp, or lean against the antenna when power is applied to the helicopter.

*3. **APU** generator switch - **ON**.

*4. **EXT PWR** switch - **OFF** and cable disconnected.

*5. APX-100 - **STBY**.

★*6. CDU AMS - Verify and setup:

NOTE

Initial battery power and/or initial APU generator on may cause COM 1, COM 2, and COM 4 to enter **CT** mode, COM 3 change to squelch off, and COM 5 to loose its band. Reset **PT** and band modes from individual **SETTINGS** pages. Squelch may be regained by cycling preset (use **PRV/NXT** key with edit box around preset number).

*a. CDU **COM** fixed function key - Press, set modes as required.

NOTE

M mode must be selected if no P codes are loaded. If no P codes are loaded and the Y mode is selected, the GPS will not update the navigation computer, which then will not send flight plan cues to the display systems.

b. Auto initialize GPS, press **INI** key. Enter **ENT** as required, initial position, system date (MMDDYY), system time (Zulu or local) and select M or Y mode (GPS could take up to 12 minutes to initialize) and press (GPS could take up to 12 minutes to initialize).

c. From the bus controller CDU press **DTS** key and then press **LOAD** key to down load DTS.

d. Press **NAV** soft key, press **DO-GPS** or the desired soft key to set the navigator mode.

e. CDU AMS **STS** soft key - Verify system status.

*7. MFDs - On. - Check as required. On MFD, press **ILLUM ALL**, check **NAV** mode, check **COM** mode.

8. Digital clocks - Check and set.

9. On CDU, **DAT** soft key - Press to verify the DTS information (COM/NAV/Waypoint presets) is loaded, or set manually as desired.

10. On CDU, **FPN** fixed function key - Press, and via **FPN1** or **FPN2** enter desired flight plan and **ENGAGE**.

11. **BRT/DIM-TEST** - Check as required.

NOTE

The switch legend on the VSI/HSI and **CIS** mode select panels may change when the panel **BRT/DIM-TEST** switch is set to **TEST**. (This can also occur in flight). The original indications may be restored by pressing the applicable switches.

a. Panel **BRT/DIM-TEST** switch - **TEST**. **CIS/MODE SEL**, and VSI advisory lights on. **AFCS FAILURE ADVISORY** lights will illuminate.

N b. **INSTR LT PILOT FLT** control - **ON**.

N c. Panel **BRT/DIM-TEST** switch - **BRT/DIM** momentarily and then to **TEST**.

N d. All **CIS/MODE SEL** and VSI advisory lights on at decreased intensity. **AFCS FAILURE ADVISORY** lights will not dim.

N 12. Interior/exterior lighting - Set.

O★13. Mission equipment - Check and set as required.

    a. Cargo hook.

    b. Rescue hoist.

    c. Auxiliary Fuel Management.

    d. **HUD**.

    e. **IRCM**.

    f. Chaff.

    g. Medical interior (OBOGS, suction, litter lift system).

★*14. Cold weather control exercise - Check if temperature is below -17°C (1°F).

*15. **AFCS FAILURE ADVISORY** lights - If on, **POWER ON RESET**.

*16. **SAS1** off, **SAS2**, **TRIM**, **FPS**, and **BOOST** switches - Push **ON**.

★17. Flight controls - Check first aircraft flight of day as follows:

    a. Collective - Midposition, pedals centered, friction off.

    b. **BOOST** switch - Press off. There will be a slight increase in collective and pedal forces. **BOOST SERVO OFF** caution legend and **MASTER CAUTION** light should be on.

    c. Right **SVO OFF** switch - **1ST STG**. No allowable cyclic stick jump. **#1 PRI SERVO PRESS** legend and **MASTER CAUTION** lights should be on.

    d. Move cyclic and pedals slowly through full range. There should be no binds or restrictions. Move collective full up to full down in about 1 to 2 seconds. Check **#2 PRI SERVO PRESS** caution legend does not illuminate during movement of collective.

    e. Right **SVO OFF** switch - **2ND STG**. No allowable cyclic stick jump. **#2 PRI SERVO PRESS** legend and **MASTER CAUTION** lights should be on.

    f. Repeat step d. above. Check **#1 PRI SERVO PRESS** caution legend does not illuminate during movement of collective.

WARNING

If **#1 PRI SERVO PRESS** or **#2 PRI SERVO PRESS** caution legend illuminates during collective movement, a servo bypass valve may be jammed. If this situation occurs, do not fly the helicopter.

    g. **SVO OFF** switch - Center.

NOTE

During steps h. and i., check for not more than 1.5 inches of freeplay in control.

    h. Collective - Move through full range in no less than 5 seconds. There should be no binding.

    i. Pedals - Move both pedals through the full range in no less than 5 seconds. There should be no binding.

    j. **TAIL SERVO** switch - **BACKUP**. **#1 TAIL RTR SERVO** caution legend and both **MASTER CAUTION** lights, and **#2 TAIL RTR SERVO ON** advisory legend illuminate. Move pedals through full range in no less than 5 seconds. There should be no binding.

    k. **TAIL SERVO** switch - **NORMAL**. Caution and advisory legends out.

    l. **BOOST** switch - **ON**. **BOOST SERVO OFF** caution legend should be off.

★18. Stabilator - Check.

WARNING

If any part of stabilator check fails, do not fly helicopter.

a. **STAB POS** indicator should be between 34° and 42° **DN**.

b. **TEST** button - Press and hold. Check **STAB POS** indicator moves up 5° to 12°. **MASTER CAUTION** light and **STABILATOR** caution legend on; stabilator audio heard.

c. **AUTO CONTROL RESET** switch - Press **ON**. Note that the **STABILATOR** caution legend and audio are off, and **STAB POS** indicator moves to 34° to 42° down. Press **MASTER CAUTION** to reset the light.

d. Either cyclic mounted stabilator slew-up switch - Press and hold until **STAB POS** indicator moves approximately 15° trailing edge up, release, stabilator should stop. **STABILATOR** legend and **MASTER CAUTION** lights on and beeping audible warning in pilot's and copilot's headsets. **MASTER CAUTION** - Press to reset audio tone.

e. Other cyclic mounted stabilator slew-up switch - Press and hold until **STAB POS** indicator moves approximately 15° trailing edge up, release, stabilator should stop.

f. **MAN SLEW** switch - **UP** and hold until stabilator stops. **STAB POS** indicator should be 6° to 10° up.

g. **MAN SLEW** switch - **DN** and hold until **STAB POS** indicator reads 0°.

h. **AUTO CONTROL RESET** switch - Press **ON**. **STAB POS** indicator should move 34° to 42° **DN**. **STABILATOR** caution legend off.

*19. Avionics - On, check as required.

a. PLS - **BIT**, modes as required.

b. AUX ARC-222 - Check on.

c. APX-100 - Check, then **STBY**.

*20. **COMPASS** switch - **SLAVED**. Set as required.

21. Barometric altimeters - Set.

*22. Cyclic and pedals centered. Collective raise no more than 1 inch (to prevent droop stop pounding).

23. **BACKUP HYD PUMP** switch - **OFF**.

O★24. Blade deice system - Test as required.

CAUTION

Do not perform blade deice test when blade erosion kit is installed.

To prevent overheating of droop stops, blade deice test shall not be done more than one time within a 30-minute period when rotor head is not turning.

a. Ice rate meter **PRESS TO TEST** button - Press and release.

b. Ice rate meter indicator - Moves to half scale (1.0) holds about 50 seconds; then falls to 0 or below. **ICE DETECTED** legend and **MASTER CAUTION** lights on after 15 to 20 seconds into the test, and FAIL flag should not be visible in flag window. Ice rate meter should move to zero within 75 seconds after pressing **PRESS TO TEST** button.

NOTE

PWR MAIN RTR, and **PWR TAIL RTR** fault monitor legends may flicker during tests in steps e. through q.

c. **BLADE DE-ICE TEST** panel select switch - **NORM**.

d. **BLADE DEICE POWER** switch - **TEST**.

e. **PWR MAIN RTR** and **TAIL RTR** monitor legends - Check. **MAIN RTR** monitor legend may go on for 2 to 4 seconds. If either legend remains on for 10 seconds or more:

(1) **BLADE DEICE POWER** switch - **OFF**. If either legend is still on:

(2) APU generator switch and/or **EXT PWR** switch - **OFF**.

8-10   Change 2

f. **TEST IN PROGRESS** light - Check. The light should be on for 105 to 135 seconds.

No other blade deice system lights should be on. **PWR MAIN RTR** and **TAIL RTR** monitor legends may go on momentarily near end of test. The **TEST IN PROGRESS** light should then go off.

WARNING

Droop stop hinge pins and cams may become very hot during test. Use care when touching those components.

    g. Crewman touch each droop stop cam - Cams should be warm to touch.

    h. **BLADE DEICE POWER** switch - **OFF**.

    i. **BLADE DE-ICE TEST** panel select switch - **SYNC 1**.

    j. **BLADE DEICE POWER** switch - **TEST**. **MR DE-ICE FAIL** legend and **MASTER CAUTION** lights on.

    k. **BLADE DEICE POWER** switch - **OFF**. **MR DE-ICE FAIL** legend and **MASTER CAUTION** lights off.

    l. **BLADE DE-ICE TEST** panel select switch - **SYNC 2**.

    m. **BLADE DEICE POWER** switch - **TEST**. **MR DE-ICE FAIL** legend and **MASTER CAUTION** lights on.

    n. **BLADE DEICE POWER** switch - **OFF**. **MR DE-ICE FAIL** legend and **MASTER CAUTION** lights off.

    o. **BLADE DE-ICE TEST** panel select switch - **OAT**.

    p. **BLADE DEICE POWER** switch - **TEST**. **MR DE-ICE FAIL, TR DE-ICE FAIL** legends, and **MASTER CAUTION** lights on.

    q. **BLADE DEICE POWER** switch - **OFF**. **MR DE-ICE FAIL, TR DE-ICE FAIL** legends, and **MASTER CAUTION** lights off.

8.22 STARTING ENGINES.

    *1. **ENG FUEL SYS** selector(s) - As required. **XFD** for first start of day.

    *2. Deleted.

    *3. **GUST LOCK** caution legend - Off.

    *4. MFDs - Set to C/A or as desired to utilize pop-up window.

    *5. Fire guard - Posted if available.

    *6. Rotor blades - Check clear.

★* 7. Engine(s) - Start as follows:

CAUTION

If start is attempted with **ENGINE IGNITION** switch **OFF**, do not place switch **ON**. Complete **EMER ENG SHUTDOWN** procedure.

    a. If any of these indications occur, perform EMER ENG SHUTDOWN as required.

        (1) No **TGT TEMP** increase (light off) within 45 seconds.

        (2) No **ENG OIL PRESS** within 45 seconds.

        (3) No % **RPM 1** or **2** within 45 seconds.

        (4) **ENGINE STARTER** caution legend goes off before reaching 52% **Ng SPEED**.

        (5) **TGT TEMP** reaches 850°C before idle is attained (Ng 63%).

CAUTION

To avoid damage to the engine start switch actuators, do not move the **ENG POWER CONT** lever from **IDLE** to **OFF** while pressing the starter button.

During engine start and runup ensure that cyclic is kept in neutral, collective no more than one inch above full down, and pedals centered until % **RPM R** reaches 50% minimum to prevent damage to anti-flap bracket bushings.

    b. Starter button(s) - Press until **Ng SPEED** increases; release.

NOTE

If an **ENGINE STARTER** caution legend goes off when the starter button is released, and the **ENG POWER CONT** lever is **OFF**, the start attempt may be continued by pressing and holding the starter button until 52% to 65% **Ng SPEED** is reached; then release button.

    c. **TGT TEMP** - Check below 150°C before advancing **ENG POWER CONT** levers.

    d. **ENG POWER CONT** lever(s) - **IDLE**. Start clock.

    e. System indications - Check.

    f. **ENGINE STARTER** caution legend(s). Check, off at 52% to 65% **Ng SPEED**. If **ENGINE STARTER** caution legend remains on after 65% Ng:

        (1) **ENG POWER CONT** lever - Pull out.

If caution legend remains on:

        (2) **APU** - **OFF** or engine air source remove as required.

* (8.) If single-engine start was made, repeat step 7 for other engine.

* (9.) Systems - Check.

    a. **Ng SPEED** - 63% or greater and within 3% of each other.

    b. **% RPM** - Check that **% RPM 1** or **2** is not in the range of 20% to 40% and 60% to 90%. Advance **ENG POWER CONT** lever(s) as required.

    c. **XMSN PRESS** - Check.

    d. **ENG OIL PRESS** - Check.

    e. **#1** and **#2 HYD PUMP** caution legends - Check off.

* (10.) **BACKUP HYD PUMP** switch - **AUTO**.

NOTE

Power interruptions between main and backup generators such as cycling backup pump from OFF to ON, or sudden high electrical demands may cause the MFD's to blank momentarily and the GPS to loose satellites.

★ (11.) Hydraulic leak test system - Check as follows:

NOTE

When performing the HYD LEAK TEST, all leak detection/isolation system components are checked electrically. Manually holding the **HYD LEAK TEST** switch in the test position does not allow the leak detection/isolation system to be checked automatically. It manually holds the circuits open. The switch must be placed in the **TEST** position and released.

    a. **HYD LEAK TEST** switch - **TEST**. **#1 TAIL RTR SERVO, BOOST SERVO OFF, SAS OFF, #1** and **#2 RSVR LOW, BACK-UP RSVR LOW**, and **MASTER CAUTION** lights and **#2 TAIL RTR SERVO ON** and **BACK-UP PUMP ON** advisory legends on. During this check, it is normal for the collective and pedals to move slightly.

    b. **HYD LEAK TEST** switch - **RESET**. The MFD legends in a. should go off. **MASTER CAUTION** light - Press to reset.

NOTE

If the backup pump is still running following the hydraulic leak test, cycle the **BACKUP HYD PUMP** switch to **OFF** then back to **AUTO**.

★ (12) Tail rotor servo transfer - Check.

    a. **BACKUP HYD PUMP** switch - **AUTO** with backup pump not running.

NOTE

Failure of the **BACK-UP PUMP ON** advisory legend or the **#2 TAIL RTR SERVO ON** advisory legend indicates a failure in the leak detection/isolation system.

    b. **TAIL SERVO** switch - **BACKUP**. **#1 TAIL RTR SERVO** caution legend on and **#2 TAIL RTR SERVO ON** and **BACK-UP PUMP ON** advisory legend on within 3 to 5 seconds.

    c. **TAIL SERVO** switch - **NORMAL**. **#1 TAIL RTR SERVO** caution legend and **#2 TAIL RTR SERVO ON** advisory legend off. **BACK-UP PUMP ON** advisory legend remains on for approximately 90 seconds.

*13. Engine warmup - Check if temperature is below -17°C (1°F).

    a. At temperatures between -17°C (1°F) and -43°C (-45°F), warm engines at **IDLE** for 3 minutes.

    b. At temperatures between -43°C (-45°F) and -54°C (-65°F), warm engines at **IDLE** for 5 minutes.

8.23 ENGINE RUNUP.

*1. Flight controls - Hold.

WARNING

Restrict the rate of **ENG POWER CONT** lever's movement, when the tailwheel lockpin is not engaged. Rapid application of **ENG POWER CONT** levers can result in turning the helicopter, causing personnel injury or loss of life.

* (2.) **ENG POWER CONT** lever(s) - **FLY**.

*3. Droop stops - Check out 70% to 75% **RPM R**.

* (4.) **#1** and **#2 GEN** caution legends - Off.

○★ (5.) **DEICE EOT** - Check as required.

CAUTION

In ambient temperatures above 21°C (70°F), operate rotor at 100% **RPM R** for 5 minutes before doing the deice EOT check, to prevent blade overheating. Do not do the deice EOT check if OAT is above 38°C (100°F).

    a. **BLADE DE-ICE TEST** select switch - **EOT**.

    b. **BLADE DEICE MODE** select switch - **MANUAL M**.

    c. **BLADE DEICE POWER** switch - **ON**.

    d. **TR DE-ICE FAIL** caution legend and **MASTER CAUTION** lights on after 15 to 30 seconds, and **MR DE-ICE FAIL** caution legend on after 50 to 70 seconds.

    e. **BLADE DEICE POWER** switch - **OFF**. **TR DE-ICE FAIL**, **MR DE-ICE FAIL** legends, and **MASTER CAUTION** lights off.

    f. **BLADE DE-ICE TEST** select switch - **NORM**.

NOTE

If helicopter engine was started using external air source and/or external ac power, the APU must be started to do APU generator backup check.

    g. **GENERATORS NO. 1** or **NO. 2** switch - **OFF**. Applicable **GEN** legend and **MASTER CAUTION** lights on.

Change 4   8-13

h. **BLADE DEICE POWER** switch - **ON**. Wait 30 seconds, no deice lights on.

i. **GENERATORS** switch(es) - **ON**. Applicable **GEN** caution legend(s) off.

j. **BLADE DEICE POWER** switch - **OFF**.

k. **BLADE DEICE MODE** select switch - **AUTO**.

*6. % **TRQ 1** and **2** - Matched within 5%.

* (7.) **FUEL PUMP** switch - **OFF**.

* (8.) **APU CONTR** switch - **OFF**.

* (9.) **AIR SOURCE HEAT/START** switch - As required.

* (10.) **ENG FUEL SYS** selectors - As required.

* (11.) **SAS 1** - **ON**.

*12. Collective friction - As required.

NOTE

A slight amount of collective friction (approximately 3 pounds) should be used to prevent pilot induced collective oscillations.

O *13. FLIR - **ON**, wait for self test complete, set as desired, focus 2X, and modes set.

*14. Storm scope - **ON**, set as desired.

N O *15. HUD - Adjust brightness, mode, barometric altitude, pitch, and roll as necessary.

CAUTION

During operation of the air conditioner system, the right cabin door should remain closed. If opening is required, the right cabin door should not remain open for more than 1 minute.

NOTE

Turning the ECS on may cause the AFCS computer **CPTR** capsule and the **TRIM** and **FPS** caution to illuminate. **PWR ON RESET** to clear failure.

ECS heater will operate with either backup pump or windshield anti-ice operating, but not with both at same time.

*16. **ECS** panel switches - As desired.

WARNING

Engine anti-ice bleed and start valve malfunction can cause engine flameout.

(17.) Engine Health Indicator Test (HIT)/Anti-Icing Check - Accomplish. Refer to ENGINE HEALTH INDICATOR TEST/ANTI-ICE CHECK IN HELICOPTER LOG BOOK. HIT/ANTI-ICE checks while operating in adverse conditions (e.g., dust, desert, coastal beach area, dry river beds) may be deferred (maximum of 5 flight hours) until a suitable location is reached.

*18. **FUEL BOOST PUMP CONTROL** switches - **ON** (for all fuel types). Indicator lights check - On.

O ★ (19.)  **AUXILIARY FUEL MANAGEMENT** panel - Test and fuel transfer check.

8.24 BEFORE TAXI.

WARNING

[ES] When on the ground, the ejector rack lock lever should be turned inward to allow the pilot visual confirmation from the cockpit. Prior to flight, the ejector rack lock lever must be in the unlock (vertical) position to allow emergency jettisoning of the tanks in flight.

O*1. [ES] Ejector rack lock levers unlocked.

O*2. Chaff electronic module safety pin(s) - Remove.

*3. Chocks - Removed.

*4. Doors - Secure.

*5. **PARKING BRAKE** - Release.

* ⑥ **TAIL WHEEL** switch - As required.

7. Wheel brakes - Check as required.

8.25 GROUND TAXI.

CAUTION

When performing these maneuvers, cyclic inputs should be minimized to prevent droop-stop pounding.

Landing and searchlight have less than one foot ground clearance when extended. Use caution when taxiing over rough terrain when landing light and/or searchlight are extended.

Increase collective and place cyclic forward of neutral to start forward movement. Minimize forward cyclic movement to prevent droop stop pounding. Reduce collective to minimum required to maintain forward movement. Soft or rough terrain may require additional collective pitch. The use of excessive collective pitch during taxi, especially at light gross weights, can cause the tailwheel to bounce. Regulate taxi speed with cyclic and collective and control heading with pedals. Use brakes as required.

8.26 HOVER CHECK.

1. Systems - Check for caution/advisory legends, CDU and PDU(s) for normal indication.

2. Flight instruments - Check as required.

3. Power - Check. The power check is done by comparing the indicated torque required to hover with the predicted values from performance charts.

8.27 BEFORE TAKEOFF.

WARNING

Pitot heat and anti-ice shall be on during operations in visible moisture with ambient temperature of 4°C (39°F) and below. Failure to turn on pitot heat on in icing conditions can cause the stabilator to program trailing edge down during flight. If this occurs, manually slew the stabilator to zero degrees.

* 1. ENG POWER CONT levers - FLY.
* 2. Systems - Check.
* 3. Avionics - As required.
* 4. Crew, passengers, and mission equipment - Check.

8.28 TAKEOFF.

WARNING

If the stabilator has not begun trailing edge up movement by 30 to 50 KIAS, abort the takeoff.

Refer to the height-velocity diagram, Figures 9-2 and 9-3, for avoid areas. Since suitable landing areas are often not available, operating outside avoid areas during takeoff and climb will provide the highest margin of safety.

8.29 AFTER TAKEOFF.

WARNING

ERFS Fuel transfer sequence must be carefully planned and executed in order to maintain CG within limits.

O★ 1. **ERFS** Extended range fuel system transfer - As required.

2. OBOGS - As required.

8.30 BEFORE LANDING.

1. **TAIL WHEEL** switch - As required.

2. **PARKING BRAKE** - As required.

3. Crew, passengers, and mission equipment - Check.

8.31 LANDING.

> **CAUTION**
>
> During roll-on landing aerodynamic braking with aft cyclic is permitted with the tail wheel contacting the ground. Once the main wheels touchdown, the cyclic must be centered prior to reducing collective. Excessive aft cyclic may cause droop stop pounding and contact between main rotor blades and other portions of the aircraft. Aerodynamic braking is prohibited once the main landing gear touches down. Use brakes to stop the aircraft.

NOTE

Because of the flat profile of the main transmission, pitching the helicopter nose up as in hover, may cause a transient drop in indicated main transmission oil pressure, depending on degree of nose-up attitude.

a. Roll-on landing. A roll-on landing may be used when the helicopter will not sustain a hover, to avoid hovering in snow or dust, if tail rotor control is lost, or when operating with one heavy external tank.

b. Slope landing. The tailwheel should be locked and the parking brake should be set. For slope landings and all ground operations, avoid using combinations of excessive cyclic and low collective settings. Where minimum collective is used, maintain cyclic near neutral position and avoid abrupt cyclic inputs. During nose-down slope landings, low-frequency oscillations may be eliminated by moving cyclic toward neutral and lowering collective.

8.32 AFTER LANDING CHECK.

1. **TAIL WHEEL** switch - As required.

2. Exterior lights - As required.

> **WARNING**
>
> Potential radiation hazard exists at the TACAN antenna when the TACAN is turned on. Make sure that no person is within three feet of the antenna when power is applied to the helicopter. The HF radio transmits high power electromagnetic radiation. Serious injury or death can occur if you touch the HF antenna while it is transmitting. Do not grasp, or lean against the antenna when power is applied to the helicopter.

3. Avionics/mission equipment - As required.

    a. TACAN - **REC**

    b. AN/ARC-220 - Not in ALE mode, and no transmit.

8.33 PARKING AND SHUTDOWN.

1. **TAIL WHEEL** switch - As required.

2. **PARKING BRAKE** - Set.

2.1. **FUEL BOOST PUMP CONTROL** switches - **OFF**.

3. Landing gear - Chocked.

O4. [ES] Ejector rack locking levers - Locked.

O5. Chaff/flare electronic module safety pin(s) - Install.

6. **ECS** panel switches - **OFF**.

7. **SAS 1** - Off.

8. **DEICE, PITOT, ANTI-ICE**, and **HEATER** switches - **OFF**.

9. **AIR SOURCE HEAT/START** switch - **APU**.

10. **FUEL PUMP** switch - **APU BOOST**.

11. **APU CONTR** switch - **ON**. The APU ON, BACK-UP PUMP ON, and **APU ACCUM LOW** advisory legends - On.

12. Mission equipment - Off, as required.

NOTE

If external electrical power is required for shutdown, it shall be connected and **EXT PWR** switch placed to **RESET**; then **ON**. If external ac power is not available, complete normal shutdown on right engine before continuing.

13. Collective raise no more than 1 inch.

14. Flight controls - Hold.

```
╔══════════════╗
║   CAUTION    ║
╚══════════════╝
```

During shutdown ensure that cyclic is kept in neutral or displaced slightly into prevailing wind, collective no more than one inch above full down and pedals centered.

Restrict the rate of ENG POWER CONT lever movement, when the tailwheel lockpin is not engaged. Abrupt application of ENG POWER CONT lever can result in turning the helicopter.

(15) **ENG POWER CONT** levers - **IDLE**.

(16) **ENGINE IGNITION** switch - **OFF**.

17. Cyclic - As required to prevent anti-flap pounding.

18. Droop stops - Verify in, about 50% **RPM R**. If one or more droop stops do not go in during rotor shutdown, shut down an engine to lower rotor idling RPM in an attempt to seat the droop stops. If droops still do not go in, accelerate rotor to above 75% **RPM R**. Repeat rotor shutdown procedures, slightly displacing cyclic in an attempt to dislodge jammed droop stop. If droop stops still do not go in, make certain that rotor disc area is clear of personnel and proceed with normal shutdown procedures while keeping cyclic in neutral position.

```
╔══════════════╗
║   CAUTION    ║
╚══════════════╝
```

To prevent damage to anti-flap stops, do not increase collective pitch at any time during rotor coast-down.

(19) **BACKUP HYD PUMP** switch - **OFF**.

20. Stabilator - Slew to 0° after last flight of the day.

(21) **BACK-UP PUMP ON** advisory legend - Check off.

```
╔══════════════╗
║   CAUTION    ║
╚══════════════╝
```

Before moving ENG POWER CONT lever OFF, engine must be cooled for 2 minutes at an Ng SPEED of 90% or less. If an engine is shut down from a high power setting (above 90%) without being cooled for 2 minutes, and it is necessary to restart the engine, the restart should be done within 5 minutes after shutdown. If the restart can not be done within 5 minutes, the engine should be allowed to cool for 4 hours before attempting an engine restart.

(22) **ENG POWER CONT** levers - **OFF** after 2 minutes at **Ng SPEED** of 90% or less.

(23) **ENG FUEL SYS** selectors - **OFF**.

(24) **TGT TEMP** - Monitor. If **TGT TEMP** rises above 538°C:

   a. Start button - Press.

   b. **ENG POWER CONT** lever(s) - Pull after **TGT TEMP** is below 538°C.

25. Avionics - Off.

26. Deleted.

Change 4   8-17

27. MFDs - Off.

28. Overhead switches - As required:

    a. **ANTICOLLISION/POSITION LIGHTS**.

    b. Left panel light controls.

    c. **WINDSHIELD WIPER**.

    d. **VENT BLOWER**.

    e. Right panel light controls.

29. **APU** generator switch - **OFF**.

30. **FUEL PUMP** switch - **OFF**.

31. **APU CONTR** switch - **OFF**.

32. **BATT** switch - **OFF**.

8.34 BEFORE LEAVING HELICOPTER.

1. Walkaround - Complete, checking for damage, fluid leaks and levels.

2. Mission equipment - Secure.

3. DC-902 data cartridge - Remove.

4. Complete log book forms.

5. Secure helicopter - As required.

Section III INSTRUMENT FLIGHT

8.35 INSTRUMENT FLIGHT.

Refer to FM 1-240 for instrument flying and navigation techniques.

Section IV FLIGHT CHARACTERISTICS

8.36 GENERAL.

a. Refer to FM 1-203 Fundamentals of Flight for explanation of aerodynamic flight characteristics.

b. The safe maximum operating airspeed range is described in Chapter 5. While hovering in high wind, sideward and rearward flight should be limited to low ground speeds. The helicopter is directionally stable in forward flight. In sideward and rearward flight, directional control is more difficult. During approach, or slow flight as the airspeed reaches about 17 to 20 KIAS, a mild vibration will be felt.

8.37 GROUND RESONANCE.

Ground resonance is a self-excited vibration created when a coupling interaction occurs between the movement of the main rotor blades and the helicopter. For this to happen, there must be some abnormal lead/lag blade condition which would dynamically unbalance the rotor and a reaction between the helicopter and ground, which could aggravate and further unbalance the rotor. Ground resonance can be caused by a blade being badly out of track, a malfunctioning damper, or a peculiar set of landing conditions. Ground resonance may occur when a wheel reaction aggravates an out-of-phase main rotor blade condition such as a hard one-wheel landing, resulting in maximum lead and lag blade displacement. This helicopter does not have a history of ground resonance. If it should occur, get the helicopter airborne. If this is not possible, immediately reduce collective pitch, place **ENG POWER CONT** levers **OFF**, and apply wheel brakes.

8.38 MANEUVERING FLIGHT.

8.38.1 Flight with External Loads. Refer to FM 55-450-1.

WARNING

Static electricity generated by the helicopter should be discharged before attempting a sling or rescue hoist pickup. Use a conductor between helicopter and the ground to discharge the static electricity.

Caution must be exercised when transporting external loads that exhibit unstable characteristics. These loads may amplify any oscillation and cause the load to contact the aircraft.

a. Load bobble. In forward flight at the higher external cargo hook load weights, a slight vertical bobble may occasionally be noticed. If experienced, this bobble will increase in amplitude with a corresponding increase in airspeed or aggressiveness of maneuver. This bobble is caused by an external disturbance (e.g. turbulence or a control input) that triggers the natural elastic response of the sling. To correct, airspeed shall be decreased or limit aggressiveness of maneuver until bobble is eliminated and pilot is comfortable with the aircraft's control.

b. Stabilator angle in level flight. Due to the increased drag of external loads, collective position for a given level flight speed will be higher. Correspondingly, the stabilator angle will be more trailing edge down than usual. Since the surface area and inherent drag of each external load varies, exact guidance relative to how much more trailing edge down angle that results is not possible.

c. Collective friction. With external cargo hook sling loads, it is especially important to have collective friction set at a minimum of three pounds.

8.38.2 Flying Qualities with External ERFS Installed. ERFS

a. Pitch Attitude vs. Airspeed. The ERFS installation naturally results in increased drag. Since this drag vector is below the center of gravity of the helicopter, the pitch attitude will be more nose-down for any speed beyond 60 to 70 KIAS. At mid to high gross weights (and most especially at a forward CG) there is a slight pitch down at 50 to 55 KIAS. The installation of the ERFS results in a small increase in this nose-down tendency.

b. Tank Vibration. It will be observed that the right hand tank(s) will vibrate more than the left tank(s). This is a normal occurrence.

c. Stabilator Angle vs. Airspeed. With the increased drag of the ERFS, a given airspeed will require more collective which, due to the collective to stabilator coupling, results in a more trailing edge down stabilator angle. This is normal as no stabilator program changes were made for the ERFS.

d. Roll Attitude Hold (FPS ON). With only the ERFS wings installed, the roll attitude hold feature of the FPS is not noticeably affected. With full 230-gallon tanks there is a very slight degradation of roll attitude stability, evidenced by a slower return to trim after an excitation (gust).

8.38.3 Collective Bounce/Pilot Induced Oscillation.

NOTE

The friction force refers to the breakaway force required to move the collective stick in an upward direction. The three pounds force is measured with the BOOST servo and SAS amplifiers operating and collective at mid-range.

To prevent vertical oscillation (collective bounce), the collective control system requires a minimum friction of three pounds measured at the collective head. Vertical oscillation can occur in any flight regime and may be caused by such events as SAS oscillation, turbulence, external load oscillation, and inadvertent pilot input into the collective. The oscillation causes the aircraft to vibrate. This vibration will be felt as a vertical bounce at approximately three cycles per second. If the severity of the oscillation is allowed to build, very high vibration levels will be experienced. During flight, if vertical oscillation is encountered, the pilot should remove the hand from the collective grip; this should eliminate the oscillation.

8.38A 700 TRANSIENT ROTOR DROOP CHARACTERISTICS

a. The T700 engine control system accurately maintains 100 % **RPM R** throughout the flight envelope for most maneuvers. However, pilots should be aware that certain maneuvers performed with minimum collective applied will result in significant transient rotor droop. High density altitudes, heavy gross weights and operation at less than 100% **RPM R** will aggrevate this condition.

b. During descent with little or no collective applied, **Ng SPEED** will be less than 80%. If % **RPM R** increases above 100%, the ECU torque motor input to the HMU is trimmed down in an attempt to restore 100% **RPM 1/2** and % **RPM R**. When collective is increased, the LDS input demands more power, but the ECU continues to trim down until % **RPM 1/2** returns to 100%. Since the **Ng SPEED** is at a slow speed, engine response time is greater. If rotor drag increases faster than the engine controller response, rotor droop occurs.

c. During aggressive level deceleration (quick stop) or right turn approach maneuvers as the collective is raised and the nose lowered, % **RPM R** may droop to 95% or lower for 1 - 2 seconds. % **RPM R** may then momentarily increase to 105-106% as the engine control system overcompensates for the reduced % **RPM 1/2**. Similar conditions of low collective, high % **RPM R**, and low **Ng SPEED** may be present during practice autorotations to a power recovery. After the flare as the nose is leveled and collective is increased, significant transient droop can occur. A rapid collective pull will aggravate the rotor droop.

d. Maneuvers that rapidly load the rotor system with no collective input can result in transient droops as low as 92%. Transient droop is more pronounced at higher altitudes since the HMU reduces **Ng SPEED** acceleration as barometric pressure decreases.

e. To minimize transient rotor droop, avoid situations which result in rapid rotor loading from low **Ng SPEED** and % **TRQ** conditions. Initiate maneuvers with collective inputs leading or simultaneous to cyclic inputs. During approach and landing, maintain at least 15% - 20% **TRQ** and transient droop will be minimal as hover power is applied.

Section V ADVERSE ENVIRONMENTAL CONDITIONS

8.39 GENERAL.

This section informs the crewmembers of the special precautions and procedures to be followed during the various weather and climatic conditions that may be encountered. This will be additional material to that already covered in other chapters regarding the operation of the various helicopter systems. Refer to FM 1-202 for cold weather operations.

8.40 COLD WEATHER OPERATION.

The basic helicopter with normal servicing can operate at temperatures down to −34°C (−29°F).

WARNING

Static electricity generated by the helicopter should be discharged before attempting a sling or rescue hoist pickup. In cold, dry climatic conditions static electricity buildups are large. Use a conductor between the helicopter and the ground to discharge the static charge. Delay lowering rescue hoist hook until helicopter is over the load, to lessen static charge buildup.

NOTE

During operation in cold weather, particularly when snow or moisture is present, the tail wheel locking indicating systems may give erroneous cockpit indications.

8.40.1 Cold Weather Preflight Check.

CAUTION

Ice removal shall never be done by scraping or chipping. Remove ice by applying heat or deicing fluid.

Blade deice operation with erosion strips installed may cause blade damage.

a. In addition to the checks in Section II check aircraft for ice or snow. If ice or snow is found, remove as much as possible by hand and thaw aircraft with heated air or deicing fluid before attempting start. Failure to remove ice and snow may cause damage.

b. Check main rotor head and blades, tail rotor, flight controls and engine inlets and hand holds for ice and snow. Failure to remove snow and ice accumulations can result in serious aerodynamic, structural effects in flight and serious foreign object damage if ice is ingested into the engine. Check **ENG POWER CONT** levers for freedom of movement.

c. On aircraft equipped with Extended Range Fuel System, check ESSS and 230-gallon fuel tank for ice or snow. Remove as much as possible by hand and then use heated air. Start APU and turn on pressure to OUTBD fuel tanks. Wing-mounted pressure regulator may require heated air applied directly onto the exhaust vent protruding from the ESSS wing. After regulator valve is operating and fuel tanks are pressurized, leave system on. DO NOT TURN OFF PRESSURE SWITCHES OR PRESSURE REGULATORS MAY FREEZE.

d. When parking the helicopter in temperatures below freezing, the gust lock may seize due to frozen moisture in rod assembly. Normal operations may be returned by warming the assembly. Main rotor tiedowns may be used in lieu of gust lock to meet parking requirements.

8.40.2 Cold Weather Control Exercise.
After starting the APU, the controls must be exercised when operating in a temperature range of -17°C (1°F) and below. The control exercise is required

  a. At temperatures between -17°C (1°F) and -31°C (-24°F), cycle collective control slowly for 1 minute.

   (1) Move collective stick grip up about 3 inches from lower stop, and down again 30 times during 1 minute of control cycling in step a.

   (2) Move each tail rotor pedal alternately through 3/4-inch of travel from neutral position 30 times during 1 minute of control cycling in step a.

  b. At temperatures between -31°C (-24°F) and -43°C (-45°F), cycle collective slowly for 2 minutes.

(1) Move collective stick grip up about 1-1/2 inches from lower stop and down again during first minute, and 3 inches of travel during second minute of control cycling in step b.

(2) Move each tail rotor pedal alternately through 3/8-inch of travel from neutral position during first minute and 3/4-inch of travel during second minute of control cycling in step b.

c. At temperatures between -43°C (-45°F) and -54°C (-65°F), cycle collective stick grip slowly for 5 minutes.

Move collective and pedals through travel for times shown below:

Collective Travel (Approximately)	Pedals Travel (Approximately)	Time Duration
3/4-inch	1/8-inch	First minute
1-1/2 inches	1/4-inch	Second minute
1-3/4 inches	1/2-inch	Third minute
2-1/2 inches	5/8-inch	Fourth minute
3 inches	3/4-inch	Fifth minute

8.40.3 Engine Operation.

a. Even though cold weather does not particularly affect the engine itself, it still causes the usual problems of ice in the fuel lines, control valves, and fuel sumps, which frequently prevent a successful cold weather start. It may be found that certain elements or accessories need preheating.

CAUTION

When starting an engine that has been exposed to low temperatures, watch for rise in TGT TEMP within 45 seconds. If no TGT TEMP rise is evident, manually prime the engine and attempt another engine start. If there is no overboard fuel flow during prime, inspect for ice in the sumps and filters. During cold weather operation, allow longer warm-up period

to bring transmission oil temperature up to desired operating range refer to Chapter 5. Monitor oil pressure and temperature closely. When advancing the power control levers, maintain transmission oil pressure in normal operating range.

b. When starting in cold weather below -40°C (-40°F), if light-off does not occur within 45 seconds after initial indication of **Ng SPEED** move **ENG POWER CONT** lever for the affected engine back to **OFF**, with the engine shutdown move the **ENG POWER CONT** lever from **OFF** to **FLY**, if the force required to move the **ENG POWER CONT** lever is higher than normal, suspect possible frozen PAS cable. This situation may require maintenance prior to attempting another start. If force is normal then attempt another start. If light-off still does not occur within 45 seconds, abort start and do the following:

(1) **ENG POWER CONT** lever(s) - Hold at **LOCKOUT**.

(2) **FUEL BOOST PUMP CONTROL** switch(es) - **ON** until crewmember reports fuel from the overflow drain.

(3) **FUEL BOOST PUMP CONTROL** switch(es) - **OFF**.

(4) **ENG POWER CONT** lever(s) - **OFF**.

(5) Attempt another start.

8.40.4 Engine Oil System Characteristics.

a. It is normal to observe high engine oil pressure during initial starts when the ambient temperature is 0°C (32°F) or below. Run engine at idle until oil pressure is within limits. Oil pressure should return to the normal range after operating 5 minutes. However, time required for warm-up will depend on temperature of the engine and lubrication system before start.

b. During starts in extreme cold weather (near -54°C (-65°F)), the following oil pressure characteristics are typical:

(1) Oil pressure may remain at zero for the first 20 to 30 seconds after initiating the start. Abort the start if oil pressure does not register within 1 minute after initiating a start.

(2) Once oil pressure begins to indicate on the gage, it will increase rapidly and it will exceed

the limit. This condition is normal. The time for oil pressure to decrease will depend on the ambient temperature, but should be normal within 5 minutes after starting the engine.

(3) Oil pressure may increase above the maximum pressure limit if the engine is accelerated above idle while oil temperature is within normal operating range. The pressure will decrease to within the normal operating range as the oil temperature increases.

c. It is normal for the **OIL FLTR BYPASS** caution legend to be on when starting an engine with oil temperatures below normal because of high oil viscosity and the accumulation of oil filter contaminants. When the engine oil temperature reaches about 38°C (100°F) during warm-up, the light should go off.

8.40.5 Taxiing. The helicopter should not be taxied until all engine temperatures and system pressures are within the normal range. All taxiing should be done at low speeds with wide-radius turns. If the tires are frozen to the surface, a slight yawing motion induced by light pedal application should break them free. Taxiing in soft snow requires higher than normal power.

DESERT AND HOT WEATHER OPERATION.

Prolonged hovering flight in hot weather 35°C (95°F) at higher gross weight may cause transmission oil temperature to rise into the yellow precautionary range. Hovering operations in the precautionary range under those conditions may be considered normal.

8.41.1 Taxiing and Ground Operation. Braking and ground operation should be minimized to prevent system overheating. During ground operations, if engine oil pressure falls into the red gage range when the power control lever is in the idle position and/or the engine oil pressure caution light comes on when the power control lever is in the idle position, slightly advance the power control lever. If the engine oil pressure returns to the yellow range and the engine oil pressure caution light extinguishes, engine oil pressure is acceptable.

8.42 IN-FLIGHT.

8.42.1 Thunderstorm Operation.

Avoid flight in or near thunderstorms, especially in areas of observed or anticipated lightning discharges.

a. Tests have shown that lightning strikes may result in loss of automatic flight controls (including stabilator), engine controls or electrical power. The high currents passing through the aircraft structure are expected to produce secondary effects whereby damaging voltage surges are coupled into aircraft wiring.

b. If a lightning strike occurs whereby all aircraft electrical power and electronics subsystems and controls are lost (including the engine ECU and the engine-driven alternator), both engines go immediately to maximum power with no temperature limiter or overspeed protection.

8.42.2 Turbulence.

a. Recommended maximum turbulence penetration airspeeds. For moderate turbulence, limit airspeed to the MAX RANGE (Chapter 7) or Vne minus 15 knots, whichever is less.

b. In turbulent air - Maintain constant collective and use the vertical situation indicator as the primary pitch instrument. The altimeter and vertical velocity indicator may vary excessively in turbulence and should not be relied upon. Airspeed indication may vary as much as 40 KIAS. By maintaining a constant power setting and a level-flight attitude on the vertical situation indicator, airspeed will remain relatively constant even when erroneous readings are presented by the airspeed indicator.

8.42.3 Ice and Rain Operation.

CAUTION

Operation in rain will result in significant damage to the blade erosion kit materials and should be avoided.

At airspeeds greater than 120 KIAS or during periods of reduced rain intensity the windshield wipers may slow noticeably. If this occurs, wipers must be parked immediately to avoid wiper motor failure.

8.42.4 In-Flight Icing.

CAUTION

Activation of anti-ice systems after entry into potential icing conditions creates the possibility of engine FOD caused by ice shedding. The ice detector has been designed primarily as a sensor to indicate the requirement for activation of the blade deice system.

a. All anti-ice systems must be turned on prior to entering visible moisture at ambient temperatures of 4°C (39°F) or less.

b. If icing conditions are encountered, turn on all anti-icing equipment immediately. If torque required increases 20% above that required for level flight at the airspeed being maintained before entering icing, exit the icing environment or land as soon as possible. A 20% torque increase indicates that normal autorotational rotor rpm may not be possible, should dual-engine failure occur.

c. When the helicopter is equipped with an operating blade deice, and icing conditions are encountered, a recurring torque increase up to 14% per engine may be experienced during normal operation of the blade deice system because of ice build-up. The crew should closely monitor engine instruments to prevent exceeding limits and/or rotor droop. Significant power losses and increased fuel consumption will occur with the activation of engine inlet anti-icing systems. Refer to Chapter 7 for torque available. The main rotor hub and the blades collect ice before initiation of a deice cycle. When enough ice has collected on the blades, moderate vibration levels of short duration can be expected in controls and airframe during normal deicing cycles. If the blade deice system is not operating, unbalanced loads of ice, resulting from asymmetric shedding, may cause severe vibrations. However, these vibrations normally subside after 30 to 60 seconds when ice from other blades is shed.

d. **ERFS** When helicopter is equipped with external extended range fuel system turn on pressure to OUTBD fuel tanks. This will prevent ice accumulation and assure pneumatic pressure for fuel transfer.

NOTE

After pressurizing the external extended range fuel tanks, DO NOT TURN OFF if ambient temperature is below 4°C.

8.42.5 Ground Operations.

a. Strong gusty winds may cause increased flapping of the main rotor blades during shutdown following an icing encounter, because the anti-flap restrainers may be frozen in the fly position.

b. During flight in icing conditions when droop stop heaters are not installed or fail to operate properly, the droop stop hinges may become iced, resulting in the droop stops not returning to the static position during rotor coast down. When the droop stops do not return to the static position, the main rotor blades may droop to within 4 feet of the ground during shutdown. Strong gusty winds may also cause excessive flapping of the main rotor blades, presenting the additional hazard of potential contact with the aft fuselage. If the droop stops are suspected to be stuck in the fly position, caution must be taken during shutdown to be sure personnel remain clear of the helicopter.

TM 1-1520-253-10

CHAPTER 9
EMERGENCY PROCEDURES

Section I AIRCRAFT SYSTEMS

9.1 HELICOPTER SYSTEMS.

This section describes the helicopter systems emergencies that may reasonably be expected to occur and presents the procedures to be followed. Emergency operation of mission equipment is contained in this chapter, insofar as its use affects safety of flight. Emergency procedures are given in checklist form when applicable. A condensed version of these procedures is contained in the condensed checklist TM 1-1520-253-CL.

9.2 IMMEDIATE ACTION EMERGENCY STEPS.

NOTE

The urgency of certain emergencies requires immediate and instinctive action by the pilot. The most important single consideration is helicopter control. All procedures are subordinate to this requirement. The **MASTER CAUTION** should be reset after each malfunction to allow systems to respond to subsequent malfunctions. If time permits during a critical emergency, transmit MAYDAY call, set transponder to emergency, jettison external stores if required, turn off boost pumps, and lock shoulder harnesses.

Those steps that shall be performed immediately in an emergency situation are underlined. These steps must be performed without reference to the checklist. Nonunderlined steps should be accomplished with use of the checklist.

9.3 DEFINITION OF EMERGENCY TERMS.

For the purpose of standardization, these definitions shall apply.

a. The term <u>LAND AS SOON AS POSSIBLE</u> is defined as landing at the nearest suitable landing area (e.g., open field) without delay. (The primary consideration is to ensure the survival of occupants.)

b. The term LAND AS SOON AS PRACTICABLE is defined as landing at a suitable landing area. (The primary consideration is the urgency of the emergency.)

c. The term <u>AUTOROTATE</u> is defined as adjusting the flight controls as necessary to establish an autorotational descent and landing.

d. The term <u>EMER ENG SHUTDOWN</u> is defined as engine shutdown without delay. Engine shutdown in flight is usually not an immediate-action item unless a fire exists. Before attempting an engine shutdown, identify the affected engine by checking **ENG OUT** warning lights, **% RPM**, **% TRQ**, **ENG OIL PRESS**, **TGT TEMP**, and **Ng SPEED**.

   1. <u>**ENG POWER CONT** lever(s) - **OFF**</u>.

   2. <u>**ENG FUEL SYS** selector(s) - **OFF**</u>.

   3. <u>**FUEL BOOST PUMP CONTROL** switch(es) - **OFF**</u>.

CAUTION

If TGT rises above 538°C after shutdown, place **AIR SOURCE HEAT/START** switch as required, turn **ENGINE IGNITION** switch **OFF**, and press starter to motor engine for 30 seconds or until **TGT TEMP** decreases below 538°C.

e. The term <u>LOCKOUT</u> is defined as manual control of engine RPM while bypassing ECU functions. Bypass of the engine control will be required when **% RPM 1** or **2** decreases below normal demand speed.

CAUTION

When engine is controlled with **ENG POWER CONT** lever in **LOCKOUT**, engine response is much faster and TGT limiting system is inoperative. Care must be taken not to exceed TGT limits and keeping **% RPM R** and **% RPM 1** and **2** in operating range.

Change 4   9-1

ENG POWER CONT lever - Pull down and advance full forward while maintaining downward pressure, then adjust to set % RPM R as required. Engine control malfunctions can result in % RPM R increasing or decreasing from normal demand speed. Under certain failure conditions, % TRQ, % RPM, and Ng SPEED may not be indicating and the possibility of the ENG OUT warning light and audio activating exists. The most reliable indication of engine power will be TGT TEMP.

f. The term EMER APU START is defined as APU start to accomplish an emergency procedure.

1. **FUEL PUMP** switch - **APU BOOST**.

2. **APU CONTR** switch - **ON**.

9.4 AFTER EMERGENCY ACTION.

After a malfunction of equipment has occurred, appropriate emergency actions have been taken and the helicopter is on the ground, an entry shall be made in the Remarks Section of DA Form 2408-13-1 describing the malfunction. Ground and flight operations shall be discontinued until corrective action has been taken.

9.5 EMERGENCY EXITS.

Emergency exits are shown in Figure 9-1. Emergency exit release handles are yellow and black striped.

WARNING

For helicopters without a roll-trim actuator, the cyclic shall be held at all times with the rotor turning. In cases where emergency exit is required prior to rotor coasting to a stop, make sure that the cyclic stick is centered until the last crewmember can depart the cockpit. Since the main rotor shaft has a 3° forward tilt, an exit to the right rear or left rear will provide the greatest rotor clearance safety.

a. Each cockpit door is equipped with a jettison system for emergency release of the door assembly. Jettison is done by pulling a handle marked **EMERGENCY EXIT PULL**, on the inside of the door (Figure 9-1). To release the door, the jettison handle is pulled to the rear; the door may then be jettisoned by kicking the lower forward corner of the door.

b. Cabin door window jettison. To provide emergency exit from the cabin, two jettisonable windows are installed in each cabin door. To release the windows, a handle (under a jettison lever guard) marked **EMERGENCY EXIT PULL AFT**, (left side; right side, **PULL FWD**) on the inside of the cabin door (Figure 9-1), is moved in the direction of the arrow, releasing the windows. The windows can then be pushed out.

9.6 EMERGENCY EQUIPMENT (PORTABLE).

Emergency equipment consists of two hand held fire extinguishers, one crash ax, and three first aid kits, as shown in Figure 9-1.

9.7 ENGINE MALFUNCTION - PARTIAL OR COMPLETE POWER LOSS.

WARNING

Prior to movement of either power-control lever, it is imperative that the malfunctioning engine and the corresponding power-control lever be identified. If the decision is made to shut down an engine, take at least five full seconds while retarding the ENG POWER CONT lever from FLY to IDLE, monitoring % TRQ, Ng SPEED, TGT TEMP, % RPM, and ENG OUT warning light on.

The various conditions under which engine failure may occur, prevent a standard procedure. A thorough knowledge of emergency procedures and flight characteristics will enable the pilot to respond correctly and automatically in an emergency. The engine instruments often provide ample warning of a malfunction before actual engine failure. The indications of engine malfunction, either partial or complete power loss, may be as follows: Changes in affected engine % **RPM**, **TGT TEMP**, **Ng SPEED**, % **TRQ**, **ENG OIL PRESS**, % **RPM R**, **LOW ROTOR RPM** and/or **ENG OUT** warning lights and audio, and change in engine noise. The amount of change in each depends upon the type of failure, e.g., compressor stall, as opposed to complete power loss on one or both engines.

9.8 FLIGHT CHARACTERISTICS.

DUAL-ENGINE FAILURE: The flight characteristics and the required crewmember control responses after a dual-engine failure are similar to those during a normal power-on descent. Full control of the helicopter can be maintained during autorotational descent. In autorotation, as airspeed increases above 70 - 80 KIAS, the rate of descent and glide distance increase significantly. As airspeed decreases below 64 KIAS, the rate of descent will increase and glide distance will decrease.

SINGLE-ENGINE FAILURE: When one engine has failed, the helicopter can often maintain altitude and airspeed until a suitable landing site can be selected. Whether or not this is possible becomes a function of such combined variables as aircraft weight, density altitude, height above ground, airspeed, phase of flight, single engine capability, and environmental response time and control technique may be additional factors. In addition, these factors should be taken into consideration should the functioning engine fail and a dual-engine failure results.

9.9 SINGLE-ENGINE FAILURE - GENERAL.

WARNING

When the power available during single engine operation is marginal or less, consideration should be given to jettisoning the external stores. The engine anti-ice and cabin heater switches should be turned off as necessary to ensure maximum power is available on the remaining engine.

Crewmember recognition of a single-engine failure and subsequent action are essential and should be based on the following general guidelines. At low altitude and low airspeed, it may be necessary to lower the collective only enough to maintain % **RPM R** (normal range). At higher altitude, however, the collective may be lowered significantly to increase % **RPM R** to 100 percent. When hovering in ground effect, the collective should be used only as required to cushion the landing, and the primary consideration is in maintaining a level attitude. In forward flight at low altitude (as in takeoff), when a single-engine capability to maintain altitude does not exist, a decelerating attitude will initially be required to prepare for landing. Conversely, if airspeed is low and altitude sufficient, the helicopter should be placed in an accelerating attitude to gain sufficient airspeed for single-engine fly away to a selected landing site. The light regions in the height velocity avoid region diagram (Figure 9-2) define the ground speed and wheel-height combinations that will permit a safe landing in the event of an engine failure for various gross weights at both sea level 15°C (59°F), and 4,000 feet/35°C (95°F), ambient condition.

9.10 SINGLE-ENGINE FAILURE.

WARNING

Do not respond to ENG OUT warning light and audio until checking TGT TEMP, Ng SPEED, and % RPM 1 and 2.

1. Collective - Adjust to maintain % **RPM R**.
2. External cargo/stores - Jettison (if required).

If continued flight is not possible:

3. LAND AS SOON AS POSSIBLE.

If continued flight is possible:

4. Establish single-engine airspeed.
5. LAND AS SOON AS PRACTICABLE.

9.11 ENGINE RESTART DURING FLIGHT.

After an engine failure in flight, an engine restart may be attempted. If it can be determined that it is reasonably safe to attempt a start, the APU should be used. Use of a cross-bleed start could result in a power loss of up to 18% on the operational engine.

9.12 DUAL-ENGINE FAILURE - GENERAL.

a. If both engines fail, immediate action is required to make a safe autorotative descent. The altitude and airspeed (Figure 9-3) at which a two-engine failure occurs will dictate the action to be taken. After the failure, main rotor rpm will decay rapidly and the aircraft will yaw to the left. Unless a two-engine failure occurs near the ground, it is mandatory that autorotation be established immediately. During cruise, reduce collective immediately to regain % **RPM R** and then adjust as required to maintain % **RPM** within power off rotor speed limits. The cyclic should be adjusted as necessary to attain and maintain the desired airspeed. The recommended airspeed for autorotation is 80 KIAS. Autorotation below 80 knots is not recommended because the deceleration does not effectively arrest the rate of descent. Adjusting the cyclic and collective control to maintain 100 % **RPM R** and 110 KIAS (100 KIAS high drag) will result in achieving the maximum glide distance. A landing area must be selected immediately after both engines fail. Throughout the descent, adjust collective as

TM 1-1520-253-10

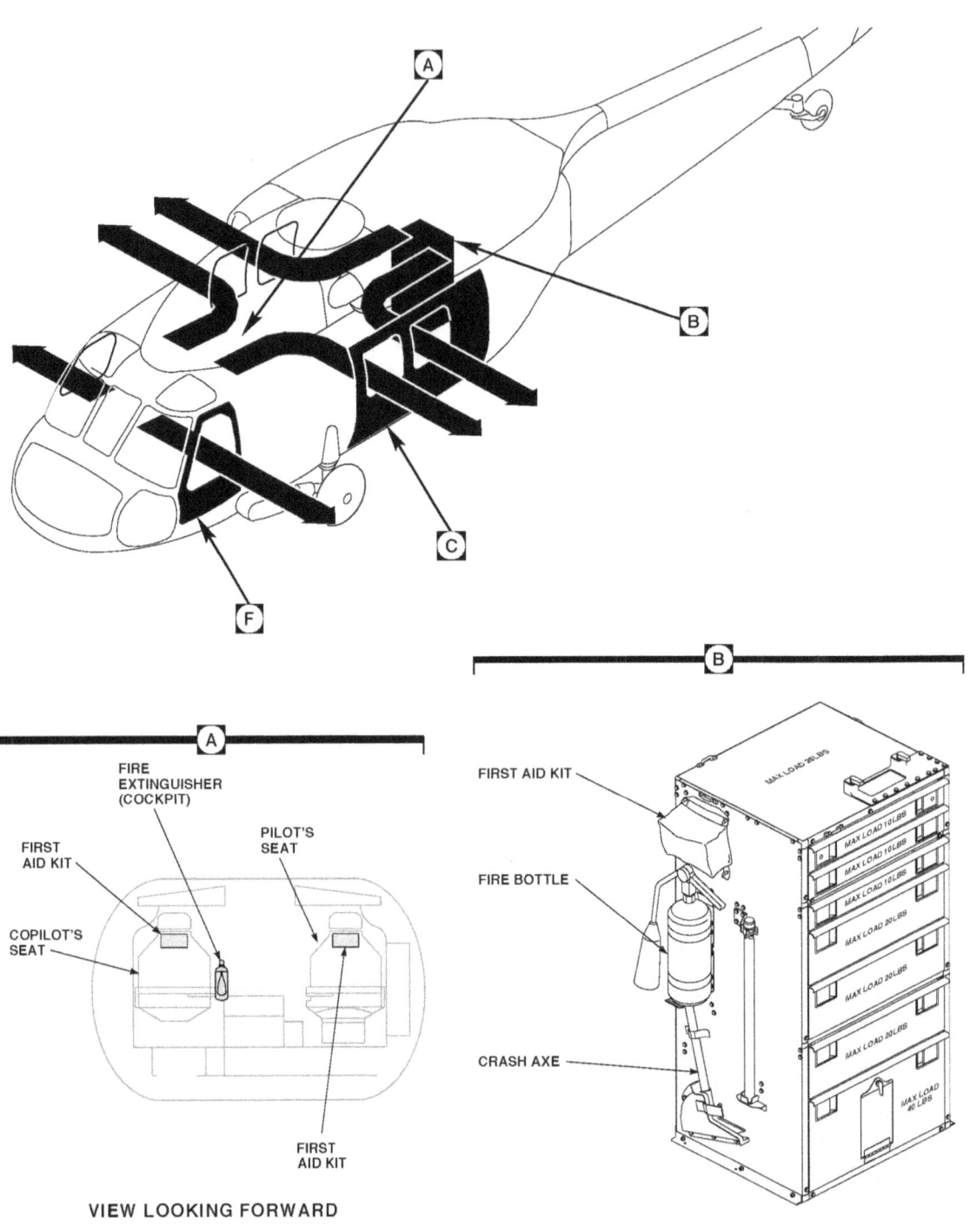

Figure 9-1. Emergency Exits and Emergency Equipment Diagram (Sheet 1 of 3)

9-4

TM 1-1520-253-10

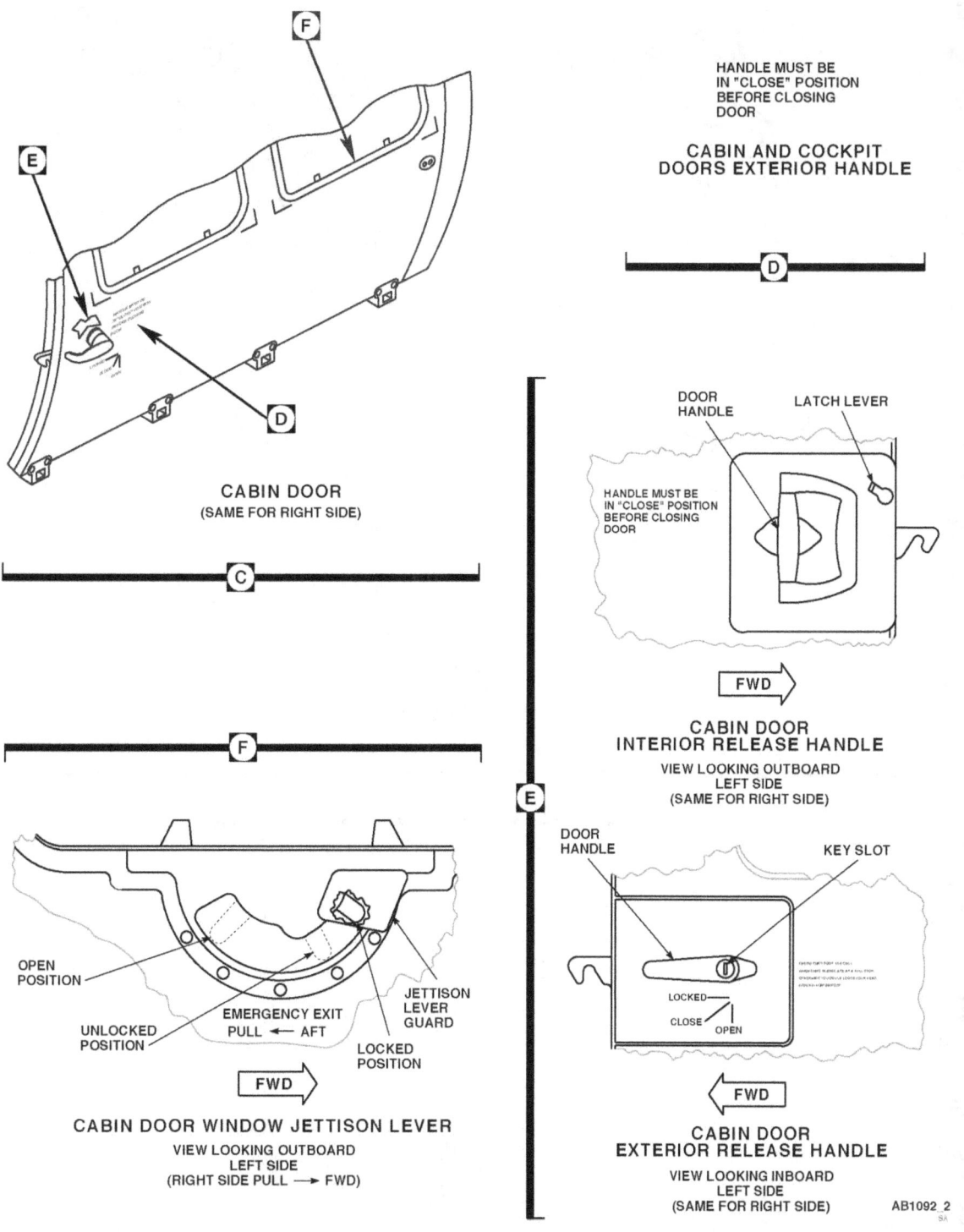

Figure 9-1. Emergency Exits and Emergency Equipment Diagram (Sheet 2 of 3)

9-5

TM 1-1520-253-10

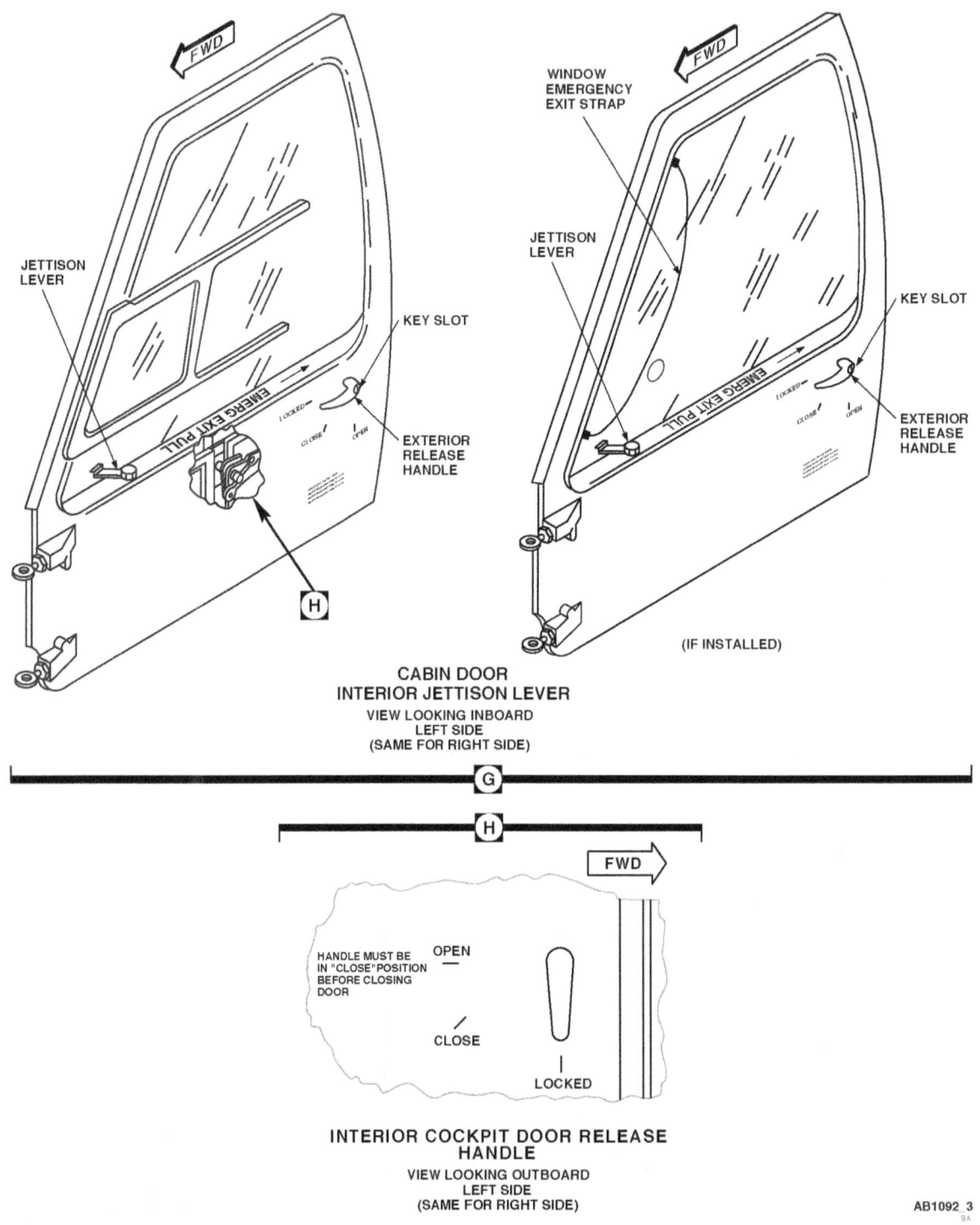

Figure 9-1. Emergency Exits and Emergency Equipment Diagram (Sheet 3 of 3)

necessary to maintain % **RPM R** within normal range. Figure 5-1 shows the rotor limitations. % **RPM R** should be maintained at or slightly above 100 percent to allow ample rpm before touchdown.

b. Main rotor rpm will increase momentarily when the cyclic is moved aft with no change in collective pitch setting. An autorotative rpm of approximately 100 percent provides for a good rate of descent. % **RPM R** above 100 percent will result in a higher rate of descent. At 50 to 75 feet AGL, use aft cyclic to decelerate. This reduces airspeed and rate of descent and causes an increase in % **RPM R**. The degree of increase depends upon the amount and rate of deceleration. An increase in % **RPM R** can be desirable in that more inertial energy in the rotor system will be available to cushion the landing. Ground contact should be made with some forward speed. Pitch attitudes up to 25° at the point of touchdown normally result in an adequate deceleration and safe landing. If a rough area is selected, a steeper deceleration and a touchdown speed as close to zero as possible should be used. With pitch attitude beyond 25° there is the possibility of ground contact with the stabilator trailing edge. It is possible that during the autorotative approach, the situation may require additional deceleration. In that case, it is necessary to assume a landing attitude at a higher altitude than normal. Should both engines fail at low airspeed, initial collective reduction may vary widely. The objective is to reduce collective as necessary to maintain % **RPM R** within normal range. In some instances at low altitude or low airspeed, settling may be so rapid that little can be done to avoid a hard-impact landing. In that case, it is critical to maintain a level landing attitude. Cushion the landing with remaining collective as helicopter settles to the ground. At slow airspeeds, where altitude permits, apply forward cyclic as necessary to increase airspeed to about 80 KIAS. Jettison external cargo and stores as soon as possible to reduce weight and drag, improve autorotational performance, and reduce the chance of damage to the helicopter on landing.

9.13 DUAL-ENGINE FAILURE.

WARNING

Do not respond to **ENG OUT** warning lights and audio until checking **TGT TEMP** and % **RPM R**.

AUTOROTATE.

9.14 DECREASING % RPM R.

If an engine control unit fails to the low side and the other engine is unable to provide sufficient torque, % **RPM R** will decrease.

CAUTION

When engine is controlled with engine power-control lever in lockout, engine response is much faster and the TGT limiting system is inoperative. Care must be taken not to exceed TGT limits and keeping % **RPM R** and % **RPM 1 and 2** in operating range.

NOTE

If % **RPM R** reduces from 100% to 95-96% during steady flight, check % **TRQ 1 and 2**. If % **TRQ 1 and 2** are equal, attempt to increase % **RPM R** with **RPM** trim switch.

1. Collective - Adjust to control % **RPM R**.

2. **ENG POWER CONT** lever - **LOCKOUT** low % **TRQ/TGT TEMP** engine. Maintain % **TRQ** approximately 10% below other engine.

3. LAND AS SOON AS PRACTICABLE.

9.15 INCREASING % RPM R.

% **RPM R** increasing will result from an engine control system failing to the high side. % **RPM 1 and 2** (Np) will increase with the rotor % **RPM R**. Increasing the collective will probably increase the malfunctioning engine's **TGT TEMP** above 900°C. If an engine control unit fails to the high side:

1. **ENG POWER CONT** lever - Retard high % **TRQ/TGT TEMP** engine, maintain % **TRQ** approximately 10% below other engine.

2. LAND AS SOON AS PRACTICABLE.

If the affected engine does not respond to **ENG POWER CONT** lever movement in the range between **FLY** and **IDLE**, the HMU may be malfunctioning internally.

UH-60Q
HEIGHT VELOCITY AVOID REGIONS
SINGLE-ENGINE FAILURE

EXAMPLE

WANTED:

A TAKEOFF PROFILE WHICH WILL PERMIT A SAFE LANDING AFTER AN ENGINE SUDDENLY BECOMES INOPERATIVE.

KNOWN:

AIRCRAFT GROSS WEIGHT = 22,000 LBS
AMBIENT CONDITIONS:
  TEMPERATURE = 15°C
  PRESSURE ALTITUDE = SEA LEVEL
  WIND = 0 KTS

METHOD:

TRACE ALONG GROSS WEIGHT LINE NOTING WHEEL HEIGHT / AIRSPEED COMBINATIONS WHICH WILL KEEP THE TAKEOFF PROFILE BELOW AND TO THE RIGHT OF THE AVOID REGION.

POINT	AIRSPEED	WHEEL HEIGHT
A	10	10
B	20	10
C	30	15
D	42	155

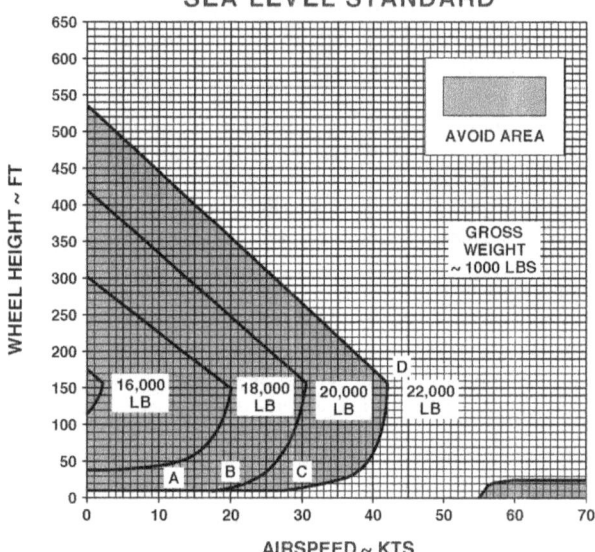

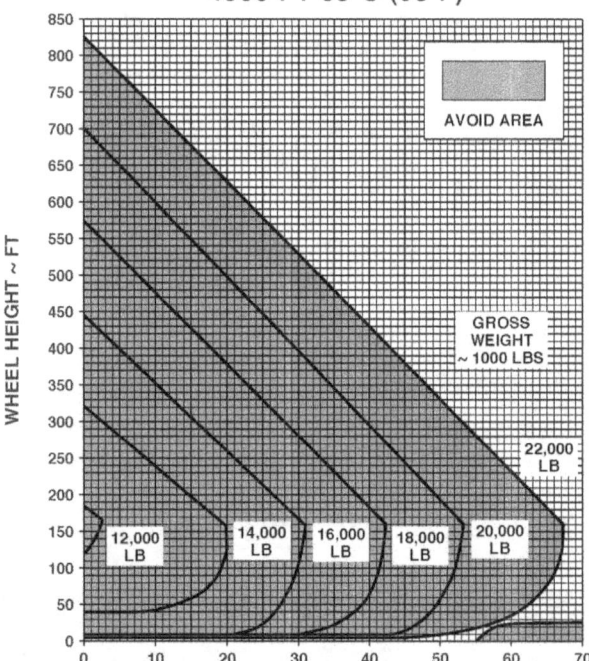

NOTE:
BASED ON AN ETF OF .85 OF MAXIMUM RATED POWER.

DATA BASIS: CALCULATED

Figure 9-2. Height Velocity Diagram

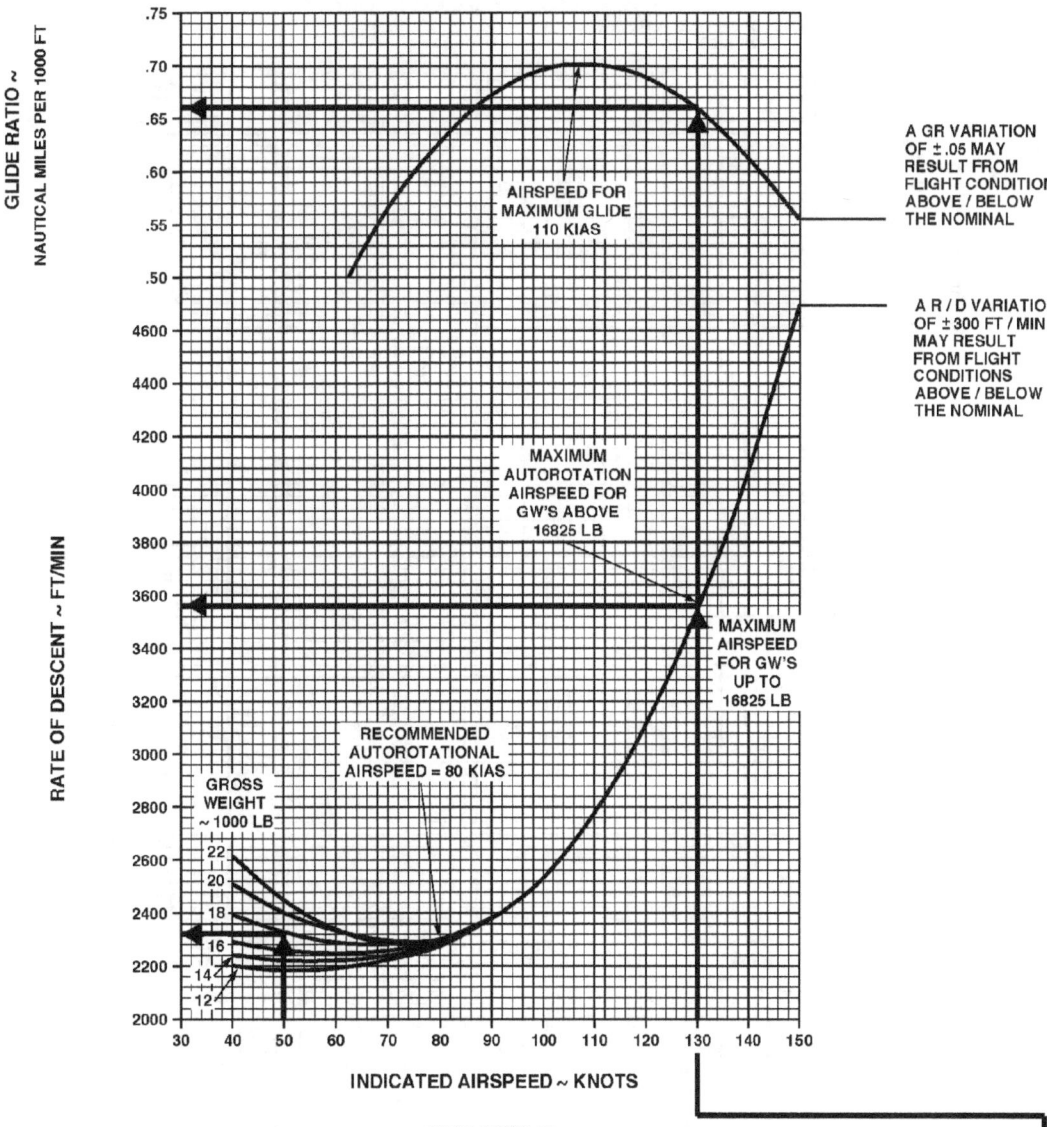

Figure 9-3. Autorotative Glide Distance Chart

AUTOROTATION

HIGH DRAG CONFIGURATION
100% RPM R ZERO WIND

DATA BASIS: FLIGHT TEST

AA1253A

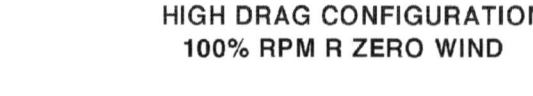

Figure 9-4. Autorotative Glide Distance Chart-High Drag

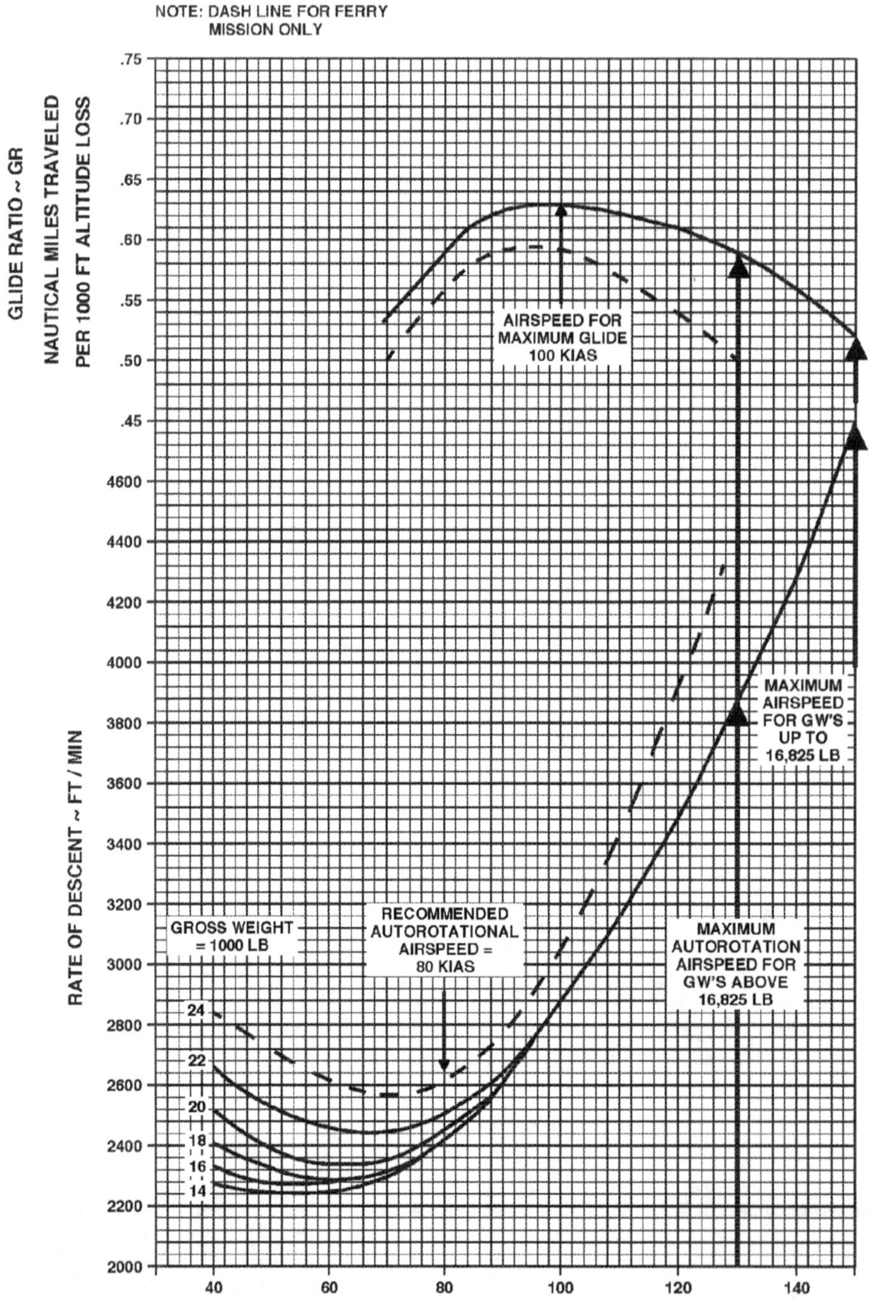

If this occurs:

    3. Establish single engine airspeed.

    4. Perform EMER ENG SHUTDOWN (affected engine).

    5. Refer to single engine failure emergency procedure.

9.16 % RPM INCREASING/DECREASING (OSCILLATION).

It is possible for a malfunction to occur that can cause the affected engine to oscillate. The other engine will respond to the change in power by also oscillating, usually with smaller amplitudes. The engine oscillations will cause torque oscillations. The suggested pilot corrective action is to pull back the **ENG POWER CONT** lever of the suspected engine until oscillation stops. If the oscillation continues, the **ENG POWER CONT** lever should be returned to **FLY** position and the other **ENG POWER CONT** lever pulled back until the oscillation ceases. Once the malfunctioning engine has been identified, it should be placed in **LOCKOUT** and controlled manually.

    1. Slowly retard the **ENG POWER CONT** lever on the suspected engine.

If the oscillation stops:

    2. Place that engine in **LOCKOUT** and manually control the power.

    3. LAND AS SOON AS PRACTICABLE.

If the oscillation continues:

    4. Place the **ENG POWER CONT** lever back to **FLY** and retard the **ENG POWER CONT** lever of the other engine.

When the oscillation stops:

    5. Place the engine in **LOCKOUT**, manually control the power.

    6. LAND AS SOON AS PRACTICABLE.

9.17 % TRQ SPLIT BETWEEN ENGINES 1 AND 2.

It is possible for a malfunction to occur that can cause a % TRQ split between engines without a significant change in % RPM R. The % TRQ split can be corrected by manual control of the **ENG POWER CONT** lever on the affected engine.

    1. If **TGT TEMP** of one engine exceeds the limiter 849°C, retard **ENG POWER CONT** lever on that engine to reduce **TGT TEMP**. Retard the **ENG POWER CONT** lever to maintain torque of the manually controlled engine at approximately 10% below the other engine.

    2. If **TGT TEMP** limit on either engine is not exceeded, slowly retard **ENG POWER CONT** lever on high % **TRQ** engine and observe % **TRQ** of low power engine.

    3. If % **TRQ** of low power engine increases, **ENG POWER CONT** lever on high power engine - Retard to maintain % **TRQ** approximately 10% below other engine (The high power engine has been identified as a high side failure).

    4. If % **TRQ** of low power engine does not increase, or % **RPM R** decreases, **ENG POWER CONT** lever - Return high power engine to **FLY** (The low power engine has been identified as a low side failure).

    5. If additional power is required, low power **ENG POWER CONT** lever, momentarily move to **LOCKOUT** and adjust to set % **TRQ** approximately 10% below the other engine.

    6. LAND AS SOON AS PRACTICABLE.

9.18 ENGINE COMPRESSOR STALL.

An engine compressor stall is normally recognized by a noticeable bang or popping noise and possible aircraft yaw. These responses are normally accompanied by the rapid increase in **TGT TEMP** and fluctuations in **Ng SPEED**, % **TRQ**, and % **RPM** reading for the affected engine. In the event of a compressor stall:

TM 1-1520-253-10

1. <u>Collective - Reduce</u>.

If condition persists:

2. <u>**ENG POWER CONT** lever (affected engine) - Retard</u> (**TGT TEMP** should decrease.)

3. <u>**ENG POWER CONT** lever (affected engine) - FLY</u>.

If stall condition recurs:

4. <u>EMER ENG SHUTDOWN</u> (affected engine).

5. <u>Refer to single-engine failure emergency procedure</u>.

9.19 ENGINE OIL FILTER BYPASS CAUTION LEGEND ON, ENGINE CHIP CAUTION LEGEND ON, ENG OIL PRESS HIGH/LOW, ENGINE OIL TEMP HIGH, ENGINE OIL TEMP CAUTION LEGEND ON, ENGINE OIL PRESS CAUTION LEGEND ON.

1. <u>**ENG POWER CONT** lever - Retard</u> to reduce torque on affected engine.

If oil pressure is below minimum limits or if oil temperature remains above maximum limits:

2. <u>EMER ENG SHUTDOWN</u> (affected engine).

3. <u>Refer to single-engine failure emergency procedure</u>.

9.20 ENGINE HIGH-SPEED SHAFT FAILURE.

Failure of the shaft may be complete or partial. A partial failure may be characterized at first by nothing more than a loud high-speed rattle and vibration coming from the engine area. A complete failure will be accompanied by a loud bang that will result in a sudden % **TRQ** decrease to zero on the affected engine. % **RPM** of affected engine will increase until overspeed system is activated.

1. <u>Collective - Adjust</u>.

2. <u>EMER ENG SHUTDOWN</u> (affected engine). Do not attempt to restart.

3. <u>Refer to single-engine failure emergency procedure</u>.

9.21 LIGHTNING STRIKE.

WARNING

Lightning strikes may result in loss of automatic flight control functions, engine controls, and/or electric power.

Lightning strike may cause one or both engines to immediately produce maximum power with no **TGT TEMP** limiting or overspeed protection. Systems instruments may also be inoperative. If this occurs, the flight crew would have to adjust to the malfunctioning engine(s) power-control lever(s) as required to control % **RPM** by sound and feel. If practical, the pilot should reduce speed to 80 KIAS. This will reduce the criticality of having exactly correct rotor speed 100%.

1. <u>**ENG POWER CONT** levers - Adjust</u> as required to control % **RPM**.

2. <u>LAND AS SOON AS POSSIBLE</u>.

9.22 ROTORS, TRANSMISSIONS AND DRIVE SYSTEMS.

9.22.1 Loss of Tail Rotor Thrust. Failure of the tail rotor gearbox, intermediate gearbox or tail rotor drive shaft will result in a loss of tail rotor thrust. The nose of the helicopter will yaw right regardless of the airspeed at which the failure occurs. Continued level flight may not be possible following this type failure. Loss of tail rotor thrust at low speed will result in rapid right yaw. At higher airspeed, right yaw may develop more slowly but will continue to increase. Autorotation should be entered promptly. **ENG POWER CONT** levers retard to **OFF** position during deceleration. Every effort should be made to establish and maintain an autorotative glide at or above 80 KIAS. This will maximize the effectiveness of the deceleration during the landing sequence. If autorotation entry is delayed, large sideslip angles can develop causing low indicated airspeed with the stabilator programming down. This can make it more difficult to establish or maintain adequate autorotative airspeed.

1. AUTOROTATE.

2. **ENG POWER CONT** levers - **OFF** (when intended point of landing is assured).

9.22.2 Loss of Tail Rotor Thrust at Low Airspeed/Hover.

Loss of tail rotor thrust at slow speed may result in extreme yaw angles and uncontrolled rotation to the right. Immediate collective pitch reduction should be initiated to reduce the yaw and begin a controlled rate of descent. If the helicopter is high enough above the ground, initiate a power-on descent. Collective should be adjusted so that an acceptable compromise between rate of turn and rate of descent is maintained. At approximately 5 to 10 feet above touchdown, initiate a hovering autorotation by moving the **ENG POWER CONT** levers - **OFF**.

1. Collective - Reduce.

2. **ENG POWER CONT** levers - **OFF** (5 to 10 feet above touchdown).

9.22.3 TAIL ROTOR QUADRANT Caution Legend On With No Loss of Tail Rotor Control.

WARNING

If the helicopter is shut down and/or hydraulic power is removed with one tail rotor cable failure, disconnection of the other tail rotor cable will occur when force from the boost servo cannot react against control cable quadrant spring tension. The quadrant spring will displace the cable and boost servo piston enough to unlatch the quadrant cable.

Loss of one tail rotor cable will be indicated by illumination of **TAIL ROTOR QUADRANT** caution legend. No change in handling characteristics should occur.

LAND AS SOON AS PRACTICABLE.

9.22.4 TAIL ROTOR QUADRANT Caution Legend On With Loss of Tail Rotor Control.

a. If both tail rotor control cables fail, a centering spring will position the tail rotor servo linkage to provide 10-1/2 degrees of pitch. This will allow trimmed flight at about 25 KIAS and 145 KIAS (these speeds will vary with gross weight). At airspeed below 25 and above 145 KIAS, right yaw can be controlled by reducing collective. Between 25 and 145 KIAS, left yaw can be controlled by increasing collective.

b. A shallow approach to a roll-on landing technique is recommended. During the approach, a yaw to the left will occur. As the touchdown point is approached, a mild deceleration should be executed to reduce airspeed. As collective is increased to cushion touchdown, the nose of the helicopter will yaw right. Careful adjustment of collective and deceleration should allow a tail-low touchdown with approximate runway alignment. Upon touchdown, lower collective carefully. Use brakes to control heading.

1. Collective - Adjust.

2. LAND AS SOON AS PRACTICABLE.

9.22.5 Pedal Bind/Restriction or Drive With No Accompanying Caution Legend.
If pedal binding, restriction, or driving occurs with no caution light the cause may not be apparent. A Stability Augmentation System/Flight Path Stabilization (SAS/FPS) computer induced yaw trim malfunction can produce about 30 pounds at the pedal. An internally jammed yaw trim actuator can produce up to 80 pounds until clutch slippage relieves this force. The pilot can override any yaw trim force by applying opposite pedal firmly and then turning off trim. A malfunction within the yaw boost servo or tail rotor servo can produce much higher force at the pedals and the affected servo must be turned off. Hardover failure of the yaw boost servo will increase control forces as much as 250 pounds on the pedals.

1. Apply pedal force to oppose the drive.

2. **TRIM** switch - Off.

If normal control forces are not restored:

3. **BOOST** switch - Off.

If control forces, normal for boost off flight are not restored:

4. **BOOST** switch - **ON**.

5. **TAIL SERVO** switch - **BACKUP**, if tail rotor is not restored.

a. If the tail rotor quadrant becomes jammed, collective control is available, except that

9-13

TM 1-1520-253-10

low collective with right pedal or high collective with a left pedal will be restricted. With a quadrant jam, complete collective travel is available for most control combinations, provided the pedals are allowed to move as the collective is displaced.

b. If tail rotor pitch becomes fixed during decreased power situations (right pedal applied), the nose of the helicopter will turn to the right when power is applied, possibly even greater than complete loss of tail rotor thrust. Some conditions may require entry into autorotation to control yaw rate. If continued flight is possible, a shallow approach at about 80 KIAS to a roll-on landing should be made. As the touchdown point is approached, a mild deceleration should be executed at about 15 to 25 feet to reduce airspeed to about 40 KIAS. As collective is increased to cushion touchdown, the nose of the helicopter will turn to the right. Careful adjustment of collective and deceleration should allow a tail-low touchdown with approximate runway alignment. Upon touchdown, lower collective carefully and use brakes to control heading.

c. If tail rotor pitch becomes fixed during increased power situations (left pedal applied), the nose of the helicopter will turn left when collective is decreased. Under these conditions, powered flight to a prepared landing site and a powered landing is possible since the sideslip angle will probably be corrected when power is applied for touchdown. Adjust approach speed and rate of descent to maintain a sideslip angle of less than 20°. Sideslip angle may be reduced by either increasing airspeed or collective. Execute a decelerated touchdown tailwheel first, and cushion landing with collective. Upon touchdown, lower collective carefully and use brakes to control heading.

6. LAND AS SOON AS PRACTICABLE.

9.22.6 #1 TAIL RTR SERVO Caution Legend On and BACK-UP PUMP ON Advisory Legend Off or #2 TAIL RTR SERVO ON Advisory Legend Off. Automatic switch-over did not take place.

1. **TAIL SERVO** switch - **BACKUP**.

2. **BACKUP HYD PUMP** switch - **ON**.

3. LAND AS SOON AS PRACTICABLE.

9.22.7 MAIN XMSN OIL PRESS Caution Legend On/XMSN OIL PRESS LOW/XMSN OIL TEMP HIGH or XMSN OIL TEMP Caution Legend On. Loss of cooling oil supply will lead to electrical and/or mechanical failure of main generators. If the malfunction is such that oil pressure decays slowly, the generators may fail before **MAIN XMSN OIL PRESS** caution legend goes on.

1. LAND AS SOON AS POSSIBLE.

If time permits:

2. Slow to 80 KIAS.

3. **EMER APU START**.

4. **GENERATORS NO. 1** and **NO. 2** switches - **OFF**.

9.22.8 CHIP INPUT MDL LH or RH Caution Legend On.

1. **ENG POWER CONT** lever on affected engine - **IDLE**.

2. LAND AS SOON AS POSSIBLE.

9.22.9 CHIP MAIN MDL SUMP, CHIP ACCESS MDL LH or RH, CHIP TAIL XMSN or CHIP INT XMSN/TAIL XMSN OIL TEMP or INT XMSN OIL TEMP Caution Legend On.

LAND AS SOON AS POSSIBLE.

9.23 FIRE.

WARNING

If AC electrical power is not available, only the reserve fire bottle can be discharged and fire extinguishing capability for the #2 engine will be lost.

The safety of helicopter occupants is the primary consideration when a fire occurs; therefore, it is imperative that every effort be made to extinguish the fire. On the ground, it is essential that the engine be shut down, crew and passengers evacuated, and fire fighting begun immediately. If

9-14   Change 4

time permits, a "May Day" radio call should be made before the electrical power is OFF to expedite assistance from fire-fighting equipment and personnel. If the helicopter is airborne when a fire occurs, the most important single action that can be taken by the pilot is to land. Consideration must be given to jettisoning external stores and turning FUEL BOOST PUMPS and XFER PUMPS off prior to landing.

9.23.1 Engine/Fuselage Fire On Ground.

1. **ENG POWER CONT** levers - **OFF**.

2. **ENG EMER OFF** handle - Pull if applicable.

3. **FIRE EXTGH** switch - **MAIN/RESERVE** as required.

9.23.2 APU Compartment Fire.

1. **APU** fire T-handle - Pull.

2. **FIRE EXTGH** switch - **MAIN/RESERVE** as required.

9.23.3 APU OIL TEMP HI Caution Legend On.

APU CONTR switch - **OFF**. Do not attempt restart until oil level has been checked.

9.23.4 Engine Fire In Flight.

> **WARNING**
>
> Attempt to visually confirm fire before engine shutdown or discharging extinguishing agent.

1. **ENG POWER CONT** lever (affected engine) - **OFF**.

2. **ENG EMER OFF** handle - Pull.

3. **FIRE EXTGH** switch - **MAIN/RESERVE** as required.

4. LAND AS SOON AS POSSIBLE.

9.23.5 Electrical Fire In Flight.
Prior to shutting off all electrical power, the pilot must consider the equipment that is essential to a particular flight environment which will be affected, e.g., flight instruments, flight controls, etc. If a landing cannot be made as soon as possible the affected circuit may be isolated by selectively turning off electrical equipment and/or pulling circuit breakers.

1. **BATT** and **GENERATORS** switches - **OFF**.

2. LAND AS SOON AS POSSIBLE.

9.24 SMOKE AND FUME ELIMINATION.

Smoke or fumes in the cockpit/cabin can be eliminated as follows:

1. Airspeed - 80 KIAS or less.

2. ECS panel switches - **OFF**.

3. Cabin doors - Open.

4. LAND AS SOON AS PRACTICABLE.

9.25 FUEL SYSTEM.

9.25.1 #1 or #2 FUEL FLTR BYPASS Caution Legend On.

1. **ENG FUEL SYS** selector on affected engine - **XFD**.

2. LAND AS SOON AS PRACTICABLE.

9.25.2 #1 and #2 FUEL FLTR BYPASS Caution Legends On.

LAND AS SOON AS POSSIBLE.

9.25.3 #1 FUEL LOW and #2 FUEL LOW Caution Legends On.

LAND AS SOON AS PRACTICABLE.

9.25.4 #1 or #2 FUEL PRESS Caution Legend On.

a. If the legend illuminates, flameout is possible. Do not make rapid collective movements. This emergency procedure has been written to include corrective action for critical situations. Critical situations are those where the loss of an engine represents a greater hazard than the possibility of pressurizing a fuel leak.

If the legend illuminates and the situation is critical:

1. **FUEL BOOST PUMP CONTROL** switches - **NO. 1 PUMP** and **NO. 2 PUMP** - **ON**.

2. LAND AS SOON AS PRACTICABLE.

b. This portion of the emergency procedure has been written to provide the best method of isolating the cause of the failure and prescribing the proper corrective action when the situation is not critical. This portion of the emergency procedure assumes the **FUEL BOOST PUMP CONTROL** switches are **OFF** when the malfunction occurs.

If the situation is not critical:

1. **ENG FUEL SYS** selector on affected engine - **XFD**.

If legend stays on:

2. **FUEL BOOST PUMP CONTROL** switches - **NO. 1 PUMP** and **NO. 2 PUMP** - **ON**.

If legend stays on:

3. **FUEL BOOST PUMP CONTROL** switches - **NO. 1 PUMP** and **NO. 2 PUMP** - **OFF**.

4. LAND AS SOON AS PRACTICABLE.

9.26 ELECTRICAL SYSTEM.

9.26.1 #1 and #2 Generator Failure (#1 and #2 CONV and AC ESS BUS OFF Caution Legends On).

1. **SAS 1** switch - Press off.

2. Airspeed - Adjust (80 KIAS or less).

3. **GENERATORS NO. 1** and **NO. 2** switches - **RESET**; then **ON**.

If caution legends remain on:

4. **GENERATORS NO. 1** and **NO. 2** switches - **OFF**.

5. EMER APU START.

6. **SAS 1** switch - **ON**.

7. LAND AS SOON AS PRACTICABLE.

9.26.2 #1 or #2 GEN Caution Legend On.

When the #1 ac generator is failed, and the backup pump circuit breaker is out, turn off ac electrical power before resetting the backup pump power circuit breaker, to avoid damaging the current limiters.

1. Affected **GENERATORS** switch **RESET**; then **ON**.

If caution legend remains on:

2. Affected **GENERATORS** switch - **OFF**.

9.26.3 #1 and #2 CONV Caution Legends On.

1. Unnecessary dc electrical equipment - OFF.

NOTE

When only battery power is available, battery life is about 38 minutes day and 24 minutes night for a battery 80% charged.

2. LAND AS SOON AS PRACTICABLE.

9.26.4 BATTERY FAULT Caution Legend On.

1. **BATT** switch - **OFF**; then **ON**. If **BATTERY FAULT** caution legend goes on, cycle **BATT** switch no more than two times.

If legend remains on:

2. **BATT** switch - **OFF**.

9.26.5 BATT LOW CHARGE Caution Legend On. **BATT LOW CHARGE** caution legend on indicates charge is at or below 40%.

If legend goes on after ground APU start:

1. **BATT** switch - **OFF**; then **ON** to reset charger analyzer logic. About 30 minutes may be required to recharge battery.

If legend goes on in flight:

2. **BATT** switch - **OFF**, to conserve remaining battery charge.

9.27 HYDRAULIC SYSTEM.

9.27.1 #1 HYD PUMP Caution Legend On.

1. **TAIL SERVO** switch - **BACKUP**; then **NORMAL**.

2. LAND AS SOON AS PRACTICABLE.

9.27.2 #2 HYD PUMP Caution Legend On.

1. **POWER ON RESET** switches - Simultaneously press, then release.

2. LAND AS SOON AS PRACTICABLE.

9.27.3 #1 and #2 HYD PUMP Caution Legends On.

LAND AS SOON AS POSSIBLE. Restrict control movement to moderate rates.

9.27.4 #1 or #2 HYD PUMP Caution Legend On and BACK-UP PUMP ON Advisory Legend Off.
Loss of both the No. 1 hydraulic pump and backup pump results in both stages of the tail-rotor servo being unpressurized. The yaw boost servo is still pressurized and the mechanical control system is still intact allowing limited tail-rotor control. Because of the limited yaw control range available, a roll-on landing 40 KIAS or above is required. Loss of both the No. 2 hydraulic pump and the backup pump results in the loss of pilot-assist servos.

1. Airspeed - Adjust to a comfortable airspeed.

2. **BACKUP HYD PUMP** switch - **ON**.

If **BACK-UP PUMP ON** advisory legend remains off:

3. **FPS** and **BOOST** switches - Off (for **#2 HYD PUMP** caution legend).

4. LAND AS SOON AS POSSIBLE.

9.27.5 #1 or #2 PRI SERVO PRESS Caution Legend On.
Illumination of #1 or #2 **PRI SERVO PRESS** caution legend can be caused by inadvertently placing the **SVO OFF** switch on either collective control head in **1ST STG** or **2ND STG** position. Before initiating emergency procedure action, the pilots should check that both **SVO OFF** switches are centered.

LAND AS SOON AS POSSIBLE.

9.27.6 #1 RSVR LOW and #1 HYD PUMP Caution Legends On With BACK-UP PUMP ON Advisory Legend On.

1. LAND AS SOON AS PRACTICABLE.

If the **BACK-UP RSVR LOW** caution legend also goes on:

2. **SVO OFF** switch - **1ST STG**.

WARNING

If **#2 PRI SERVO PRESS** caution legend goes on, establish landing attitude, minimize control inputs and begin a descent.

3. LAND AS SOON AS POSSIBLE.

9.27.7 #2 RSVR LOW and #2 HYD PUMP Caution Legends On With BACK-UP PUMP ON Advisory Legend On.

1. **POWER ON RESET** switches - Simultaneously press then release.

2. LAND AS SOON AS PRACTICABLE.

If **BACK-UP RSVR LOW** caution legend also goes on:

3. **SVO OFF** switch - **2ND STG**.

WARNING

If **#1 PRI SERVO PRESS** caution legend goes on, establish landing attitude, minimize control inputs, and begin a descent.

4. LAND AS SOON AS POSSIBLE.

9.27.8 #2 RSVR LOW Caution Legend On.

Pilot assist servos will be isolated; if they remain isolated, proceed as follows:

① BOOST and FPS switches - Off.

2. LAND AS SOON AS PRACTICABLE.

NOTE

Because the logic module will close valves supplying pressure to the pilot-assist servos, **BOOST SERVO OFF**, **SAS OFF**, and **TRIM FAIL** caution legends will be on.

9.27.9 Collective Boost Servo Hardover/Power Piston Failure. Hardover failure of the collective boost servo will increase control forces (as much as 150 pounds) in the collective. The increased control forces can be immediately eliminated by shutting off the boost servo. Resulting control loads will be the same as for in-flight boost servo off.

① BOOST switch - Off.

2. LAND AS SOON AS PRACTICABLE.

9.27.10 Pitch Boost Servo Hardover. Hardover failure of the pitch boost servo will increase the longitudinal cyclic control forces (approximately 20 pounds). The increased control forces can be immediately eliminated by shutting off SAS.

① SAS (1 and 2) and FPS switches - Off.

2. LAND AS SOON AS PRACTICABLE.

9.27.11 BOOST SERVO OFF Caution Legend On. Lighting of the **BOOST SERVO OFF** caution legend with no other caution legends on indicates a pilot valve jam in either the collective or yaw boost servo. Control forces in the affected axis will be similar to flight with boost off.

① BOOST switch - Off.

2. LAND AS SOON AS PRACTICABLE.

9.28 LANDING AND DITCHING.

9.28.1 Emergency Landing In Wooded Areas. Power Off.

1. AUTOROTATE. Decelerate helicopter to stop all forward speed at treetop level.

2. Collective adjust to maximum before main rotor contacts tree branches.

9.28.2 Ditching - Power On. The decision to ditch the helicopter shall be made by the pilot when an emergency makes further flight unsafe.

1. Approach to a hover.

2. Cockpit doors jettison and cabin doors open prior to entering water.

3. Pilot shoulder harness - Lock.

4. Survival gear - Deploy.

5. Personnel, except pilot, exit helicopter.

6. Fly helicopter downwind a safe distance and hover.

7. **ENG POWER CONT** levers - **OFF**.

8. Perform hovering autorotation, apply full collective to decay rotor RPM as helicopter settles.

9. Position cyclic in direction of roll.

10. Exit when main rotor has stopped.

9.28.3 Ditching - Power Off. If ditching is imminent, accomplish engine malfunction emergency procedures. During descent, open cockpit and cabin doors. Decelerate to zero forward speed as the helicopter nears the water. Apply full collective as the helicopter nears the water. Maintain a level attitude as the helicopter sinks and until it begins to roll; then apply cyclic in the direction of the roll. Exit when the main rotor is stopped.

1. AUTOROTATE.

2. Cockpit doors jettison and cabin doors open prior to entering water.

3. Cyclic - Position in direction of roll.

4. Exit when main rotor has stopped.

9.29 FLIGHT CONTROL/MAIN-ROTOR SYSTEM MALFUNCTIONS.

a. Failure of components within the flight control system may be indicated through varying degrees of feedback, binding, resistance, or sloppiness. These conditions should not be mistaken for malfunction of the AFCS.

b. Failure of a main rotor component may be indicated by the sudden onset or steady increase in main rotor vibration or unusual noise. Severe changes in lift characteristics and/or balance condition can occur due to blade strikes, skin separation, shift or loss of balance weights or other material. Malfunctions may result in severe main rotor flapping. The severity of vibrations may be minimized by reducing airspeed.

If the main rotor system malfunctions:

WARNING

Danger exists that the main rotor system could collapse or separate from the aircraft after landing. Exit when main rotor has stopped.

1. LAND AS SOON AS POSSIBLE.

2. EMER ENG(S) SHUTDOWN after landing.

9.29.1 SAS Failure With No Failure Advisory Indication. Erratic electrical input to a SAS actuator can result in moderate rotor tip path oscillations that are often accompanied with pounding sounds or "knocking" which may be felt in the cyclic or pedal controls. No SAS malfunction, however, can physically drive the pilots' flight controls. Failure of **SAS 2** is usually but not necessarily followed by a failure/advisory indication. Failure of a **SAS 1** component will not be accompanied by a failure/advisory indication as **SAS 1** does not contain diagnostic capabilities.

If the helicopter experiences erratic motion of the rotor tip path without failure/advisory indication:

1. **SAS 1** switch - Off.

If condition persists:

2. **SAS 1** switch - **ON**.

3. **SAS 2** switch - Off.

If malfunction still persists:

4. **SAS 1** and **FPS** switches - Off.

9.29.2 SAS 2 Failure Advisory Light On.

POWER ON RESET switches - Simultaneously press and then release.

9.29.3 SAS OFF Caution Legend On.

FPS switch - Off.

9.29.4 FLT PATH STAB Caution Legend On. An **FPS** malfunction will be detected by the SAS/FPS computer, which will disengage **FPS** function in the applicable axis and light the **FLT PATH STAB** caution legend and corresponding **FAILURE ADVISORY** light.

1. **POWER ON RESET** switches - Simultaneously press and then release.

If failure returns, control affected axis manually.

WARNING

If the airspeed fault advisory light is illuminated, continued flight above 70 KIAS with the stabilator in the AUTO MODE is unsafe since a loss of the airspeed signal from the remaining airspeed sensor would result in the stabilator slewing full-down.

If the airspeed fault light remains illuminated on the AFCS panel:

NOTE

Use of the cyclic mounted stabilator slew-up switch should be announced to the crew to minimize cockpit confusion.

2. Manually slew stabilator - Adjust to 0° if above 40 KIAS. The preferred method of manually slewing the stabilator up is to use the cyclic mounted stabilator slew-up switch.

3. LAND AS SOON AS PRACTICABLE.

9.29.5 Pitch, Roll or Yaw/Trim Hardover.

a. A pitch **FPS**/trim hardover will cause a change in pitch attitude and a corresponding longitudinal cyclic movement of about 1/2 inch. This condition will be detected by the SAS/FPS computer which will disengage **FPS** and trim functions in the pitch axis and light the **FLT PATH STAB** and **TRIM FAIL** caution legends.

Change 3   9-19

b. A roll **FPS**/trim hardover will be characterized by a 1/2 inch lateral stick displacement, resulting in a corresponding roll rate and a constant heading sideslip condition, caused by the yaw **FPS** attempting to maintain heading. The SAS/FPS computer will detect the hardover condition and disengage lateral trim and illuminate the **FLT PATH STAB** and **TRIM FAIL** caution legends.

c. A yaw **FPS**/trim hardover is characterized by an improper motion of the pedals, resulting in about 1/4 inch of pedal motion followed by a corresponding change in helicopter heading trim. This condition will be detected by the SAS/FPS computer, which will disengage trim and **FPS** functions in the yaw axis and light the **FLT PATH STAB** and **TRIM FAIL** caution legends.

If failure occurs:

> **POWER ON RESET** switches - Simultaneously press and then release.

If failure returns, control affected axis manually.

9.29.6 Trim Actuator Jammed. Both yaw and roll trim actuators incorporate slip clutches to allow pilot and copilot inputs if either actuator should jam. The forces required to override the clutches are 80 pounds maximum in yaw and 13 pounds maximum in roll.

LAND AS SOON AS PRACTICABLE.

9.30 STABILATOR MALFUNCTION - AUTO MODE FAILURE.

An Auto Mode Failure will normally result in the stabilator failing in place. The indications to the pilots of the failure are a beeping audio warning, and **MASTER CAUTION** and **STABILATOR** caution legends illuminating when the automatic mode fails. The position of failure may vary from the ideal programmed position by 10° at 30 KIAS to 4° at 150 KIAS. If an approach is made with the stabilator fixed 0°, the pitch attitude may be 4° to 5° higher than normal in the 20 to 40 KIAS range.

WARNING

If acceleration is continued or collective is decreased with the stabilator in a trailing edge down position, longitudinal control will be lost. The stabilator shall be slewed to 0° above 40 KIAS and full-down when airspeed is less than 40 KIAS.

Pressing the AUTO CONTROL RESET button after a failure occurs results in the automatic mode coming on for one second. If a hardover signal to one actuator is present, the stabilator could move approximately 4° to 5° in that one second before another auto mode failure occurs. Subsequent reset attempts could result in the stabilator moving to an unsafe position.

If the stabilator AUTO mode repeatedly disengages during a flight, flight above 70 KIAS is prohibited with the stabilator in AUTO mode.

If an **AUTO** Mode Failure Occurs:

NOTE

Use of cyclic mounted stabilator slew-up switch should be announced to the crew to minimize cockpit confusion.

1. <u>Cyclic mounted stabilator slew-up switch - Adjust if necessary</u> to arrest nose down pitch rate.

2. **AUTO CONTROL** switch - Press **ON** once.

If automatic control is not regained:

3. Manually slew stabilator - Adjust to 0° for flight above 40 KIAS or full down when airspeed is below 40 KIAS. The preferred method of manually slewing the stabilator up is to use the cyclic mounted stabilator slew-up switch.

4. LAND AS SOON AS PRACTICABLE.

If manual control is not possible:

5. **STAB POS** indicator - Check and fly at or below **KIAS LIMITS** shown on placard.

6. LAND AS SOON AS PRACTICABLE.

9.31 UNCOMMANDED NOSE DOWN/UP PITCH ATTITUDE CHANGE.

a. An uncommanded nose down/up pitch attitude change could be the result of a stabilator or other AFCS malfunction (SAS or FPS). There is a remote possibility that a stabilator malfunction could occur in the automatic or manual mode without audio warning or caution light illumination.

b. If an uncommanded nose down pitch attitude change is detected, the pilot should initially attempt to stop the rate

with aft cyclic. Maintaining or increasing collective position may assist in correcting for a nose down pitch attitude. If the nose down pitch rate continues, and/or inappropriate stabilator movement is observed, activate the cyclic mounted stabilator slew-up switch to adjust the stabilator to control pitch attitude. Continue to monitor the stabilator position when the cyclic mounted stabilator slew-up switch is released to ensure movement stops.

c. Uncommanded nose up pitch attitude changes at airspeeds of 140 KIAS and less should not become severe even if caused by full up slew of the stabilator and can be corrected with forward cyclic. If the nose up pitch attitude is caused by full up stabilator slew at airspeeds above 140 KIAS, full forward cyclic may not arrest the nose up pitch rate.

d. If an uncommanded nose up pitch attitude change is detected, the pilot should initially attempt to stop the rate with forward cyclic. At airspeeds above 140 KIAS, a collective reduction of approximately 3 inches, simultaneously with forward cyclic will arrest the nose up pitch rate. If these control corrections are delayed and/or a large nose up attitude results, a moderate roll to the nearest horizon will assist in returning the aircraft to level flight. After the nose returns to the horizon, roll to a level attitude. After coordination with the pilot, the copilot should adjust the stabilator to 0° at airspeeds above 40 KIAS and full down at airspeeds below 40 KIAS.

If an uncommanded nose down pitch attitude occurs:

1. Cyclic - Adjust as required.

2. Collective - Maintain or increase.

3. Cyclic mounted stabilator slew-up switch - Adjust as required to arrest nose down pitch rate.

4. **MAN SLEW** switch - Adjust to 0° at airspeeds above 40 KIAS and full down at airspeeds below 40 KIAS.

5. LAND AS SOON AS PRACTICABLE.

If an uncommanded nose up pitch attitude occurs:

1. Cyclic - Adjust as required.

2. Collective - Reduce as required.

3. **MAN SLEW** switch - Adjust to 0° at airspeeds above 40 KIAS and full down at airspeeds below 40 KIAS.

4. LAND AS SOON AS PRACTICABLE.

9.32 AVIONICS MANAGEMENT SYSTEM MALFUNCTIONS.

9.32.1 AMS DUAL CDU AND DUAL MFD FAILURE.

1. Place **EMERGENCY CONTROL PANEL**, **EMERG COMM** switch to **EMERG COMM** to activate the ARC-164 to 243.0 and to manually control the ARC-222.

2. LAND AS SOON AS POSSIBLE.

9.32.2 CDU SINGLE AMS FAILURE or BLANK CDU DISPLAY.

1. Verify operating CDU is bus controller (Boxed B on status line).

If operating CDU is not bus controller:

2. On the **EMERGENCY CONTROL PANEL** place **CDU 1-AUTO-CDU 2** switch to the good CDU.

3. Check status of good AMS.

If CDU bus controller assignment did not switch to the good CDU, go to **CDU DUAL AMS FAILURE**.

9.32.3 CDU DUAL AMS FAILURE or BLANK CDU DISPLAYS (NO CDU BUS FUNCTIONS CAN BE ACCOMPLISHED).

1. Wait 10 seconds for AMS CDUs to reinitialize self.

If AMS did not reinitialize self:

2. Place **EMERGENCY CONTROL PANEL**, **EMERG COMM** switch to **EMERG COMM** to activate the ARC-164 to 243.0 and to manually control the ARC-222.

3. LAND AS SOON AS PRACTICABLE.

9.32.4 MFD FAILURE.

1. CDU **STS** key - Press.

2. Verify and acknowledge system failures of MFD 1 or MFD 2 by indication of Fail (F).

If MFD went blank or locked up:

TM 1-1520-253-10

    3. Cycle MFD power switch to **OFF**, then back to **ON**.

    4. CDU **STS** key - Press.

    5. Verify and acknowledge MFD system status change of MFD **1** or MFD **2** by indication of Good (G).

If MFD cycling of power was unsuccessful:

    6. LAND AS SOON AS PRACTICABLE.

If both MFDs have failed:

    7. LAND AS SOON AS POSSIBLE.

9.32.5 DGNS FAILURE.

Failure of DGNS appears as status advisory Bad (B) or locked up MFD displays.

    1. CDU **STS** key - Press.

    2. Verify and acknowledge system failure of DGNS by indication of Fail (F).

If DGNS status is indicated Fail (F) on the CDU, or MFDs are locked up, or MFDs display "X":

    3. Press CDU (INI) function key - Verify GPS status (UTC) indicates the correct GPS time and date, and verify satellite vehicles used (SV-USED) is minimum of four.

    4. If four or less satellite vehicles are used verify the DGNS navigator mode has automatically changed from its present NAV mode in the header of **DG** or **GP** to **DOP**.

    5. If DGNS did not automatically change to a different mode, go to **NAV** page. Manually select **GPS** or **DOP** mode.

    6. Verify present position is updating.

    7. Monitor nav sensor alert in status line. If GPS reinitializes itself, change mode to **DO-GPS**, as desired.

Section II MISSION EQUIPMENT

9.33 EMERGENCY JETTISONING.

When conditions exist which require the jettisoning of external loads to ensure continued flight or execution of emergency procedures, the crew should jettison the load as follows:

CARGO REL or **HOOK EMER REL** button - Press.

9.34 EMERGENCY RELEASE OF RESCUE HOIST LOAD.

If the rescue hoist becomes jammed, inoperative, or the cable is entangled and emergency release is required:

9.34.1 HOIST CABLE CUT.

On either pilot's or crew panel:

NOTE

Crew's hoist control panel **ARM-TEST** switch must be in **ARM** to cut cable from either position.

CABLE CUT button - Press.

9.34.2 HOIST RUNAWAY.

1. Pilot's hoist control panel **PILOT OVERRIDE** switch **UP** or **DOWN** to control, as required.

If control is not possible:

2. Pilot's hoist panel **HOIST POWER** switch - **OFF**.

9.35 BLADE DEICE SYSTEM MALFUNCTIONS.

9.35.1 MR DE-ICE FAULT or MR DE-ICE FAIL, or TR DE-ICE FAIL Caution Legend On.

a. If the **MR DE-ICE FAULT** caution legend goes on, the system will continue to function in a degraded mode. The pilot must be aware of vibration levels and % TRQ requirements, which could be a result of ice buildup.

b. If the **MR DE-ICE FAIL** caution legend goes on, the main rotor deice will automatically turn off. Tail rotor deice will remain on.

c. If the **TR DE-ICE FAIL** caution legend goes on, tail rotor deice will automatically turn off. Main rotor deice will remain on.

1. Icing conditions - Exit.

2. **BLADE DEICE POWER** switch - **OFF**, when out of icing conditions.

If vibrations increase:

3. LAND AS SOON AS POSSIBLE.

9.35.2 PWR MAIN RTR and/or TAIL RTR MONITOR Light On.

If a **PWR** monitor light is on with **BLADE DEICE POWER** switch **ON** to stop power from being applied to blades:

1. Icing conditions - EXIT.

2. **BLADE DEICE POWER** switch - **OFF**.

If a **PWR** monitor light is still on with **BLADE DEICE POWER** switch **OFF**:

3. **GENERATORS NO. 1** or **NO. 2** switch - **OFF**.

4. **APU** generator switch - **OFF** (if in use).

5. LAND AS SOON AS PRACTICABLE.

9.35.3 Ice Rate Meter Fail or Inaccurate.
Failure of the ice rate meter should be indicated by appearance of the **FAIL** flag on the meter face. Inaccuracy of the meter will be indicated by increased torque required and/or increase of vibration levels due to ice buildup. If failure or inaccuracy is suspected, with no other indicated failures, the system can be manually controlled.

1. **BLADE DEICE MODE** switch - **MANUAL** as required.

If vibration levels increase or % TRQ required increases:

2. Higher icing **MODE** - Select as required.

If ice buildup continues:

3. LAND AS SOON AS PRACTICABLE.

9.35.4 Loss of NO. 1 or NO. 2 Generator During Blade Deice Operation.
Loss of one generator during blade deice operation will result in loss of power to the system. To restore system operation, the APU must be started and the **APU** generator switch ON. The **APU GEN ON** advisory legend will not go on because one main generator is still operating. The APU generator will supply power only for blade deice operation.

Pilot not on the controls:

<u>EMER APU START</u>.

9.36 EXTERNAL EXTENDED RANGE FUEL SYSTEM FAILURE TO TRANSFER SYMMETRICALLY IN MANUAL MODE. ERFS

a. Total failure of a single external extended range fuel system tank to transfer fuel could be the result of a loose filler cap, bleed-air regulator/shutoff valve, fuel shutoff valve, or line blockage failure.

b. Total failure of one tank to transfer fuel will turn on the associated tank's **NO FLOW** light. Reduced flow from one tank may not cause a **NO FLOW** light to go on, but will change the lateral CG of the helicopter. The pilot will notice a migration of the lateral cyclic stick position as the lateral CG offset from neutral increases. For example, a fully asymmetric outboard 230-gallon tank set (one tank full, one tank empty), on an otherwise neutrally balanced H-60, will result in a level flight lateral stick position offset of approximately two inches. If asymmetric transfer is suspected, stop transfer on the selected tank set and initiate transfer on the other tank set, if installed.

If asymmetric fuel transfer is suspected:

1. Stop transfer on tank set.
2. Select other tank set and initiate transfer.
3. LAND AS SOON AS PRACTICABLE.

WARNING

With asymmetric fuel loading, lateral control margin will be reduced in the direction opposite the heavy side. The aircraft has been flown from hover to 138 KIAS, with lateral CG's equivalent to a fully asymmetric outboard 230-gallon tank set, (full right tank, no stores on left side). The most critical maneuvers are turns toward the heavy side and approaches with a crosswind from the lighter side. These maneuvers are not recommended. The most adverse condition for lateral controllability is right side heavy, in the 20 to 50 KIAS range. Do not exceed 30 degree angle of bank. If controllability is in question, jettison the asymmetric tank set.

Should controlled flight with one heavy external tank become necessary, proceed as follows:

1. Make all turns shallow (up to standard rate), and in the direction away from heavy side (particularly when a right tank remains full).

2. Avoid abrupt control motions, especially lateral cyclic.

3. If possible, shift personnel to the light side of the helicopter.

4. Select a suitable roll-on landing area, and make a roll-on landing with touchdown speed in excess of 30 KIAS. To increase control margin, execute the approach into the wind or with a front quartering wind from the heavy side and align the longitudinal axis of the aircraft with the ground track upon commencing the approach. If a suitable roll-on landing area is not available, make an approach to a hover into the wind, or with a front quartering wind from the heavy side.

9.37 EXTERNAL STORES JETTISON. ES

At high gross weights and with one engine inoperative, or in an emergency or performance limited situation, it may be necessary to jettison a tank set. Circuitry prevents the release of any individual tank even if a single tank jettison has been selected at the **STORES JETTISON** control panel. The helicopter will remain controllable even if a single tank fails to release because of a malfunction in the jettison system.

If jettisoning of tanks is required:

1. **STORES JETTISON** switch - Select **OUTBD BOTH** or **ALL** as applicable.
2. <u>JETT</u> switch - Actuate.

If primary jettison system does not operate:

3. **EMER JETT ALL** switch - Actuate.

9.38 FUEL FUMES IN COCKPIT/CABIN WITH EXTERNAL EXTENDED RANGE FUEL SYSTEM PRESSURIZED. ERFS

If the bleed air check valve(s) is stuck in the open position when the heater is turned on, the resulting bleed air manifold pressure drops due to the heater bleed air demands. This allows fumes/mist above the tanks to backflow through the bleed air manifold, through the heater, and into the cabin. If fuel fumes or mist are noted during external extended range fuel system operation, perform the following:

If heater is on:

1. **HEATER** switch - **OFF**.

If heater is off or fumes persist:

2. **PRESS OUTBD** switch - **OFF**.

3. **MODE** switch - **OFF**.

4. **FUEL BOOST PUMP CONTROL** switches - As required.

9.39 LITTER SYSTEM MALFUNCTIONS.

9.39.1 LITTER LIFT RUNAWAY.

From any one of the four cabin medical control panels:

1. **EMERGENCY STOP** switch - **STOP**.

If litter continues to runaway:

2. Cockpit **AUX SW** panel **MED INT** switch - **OFF**.

After stopping the runaway:

3. Pull the appropriate bad litter lift system control **FWD** and **AFT LIFT MOT** circuit breaker on the medical interior circuit breaker panel.

4. Do not use bad litter lift system.

9.40 OBOGS SYSTEM MALFUNCTIONS.

9.40.1 OBOGS BIT/FAULT LIGHT ILLUMINATED.

If after initial start up of OBOGS the automatic BIT/FAULT cycle light on the monitor panel has not extinguished after five minutes:

1. Cockpit **AUX SW** panel **OBOGS** switch - **OFF**.

2. Utilize only the remaining O2 from the backup oxygen supply.

3. Do not use OBOGS system.

9.41 FLIR SYSTEM MALFUNCTIONS.

9.41.1 MODE PROBLEM, CAGE PROBLEM, GIMBAL RACHETING, IMAGE DISTORTION, MISC.

1. FLIR control panel **POWER** switch - OFF. Wait three minutes then, **ON**.

2. Perform BIT/FIT check. Allow 3 to 4 minutes for FLIR to complete BIT/FIT check.

If FLIR problem is not solved:

3. Press **STOW FLIR** control panel **POWER** button.

4. FLIR control panel **POWER** switch - OFF.

9.40.2 FAULT INDICATOR (BIT/FIT Error Reporting and Clear).

1. Enable the menus and hook on **FIT**.

2. Annotate the error code, hook on **CLEAR** label to clear the error report.

3. Hook on **FIT** to initiate FIT.

4. Hook on **EXIT** to end FIT.

If FLIR error code cleared and FLIR functions check out:

5. Continue mission and annotate FLIR error code at mission completion.

If FLIR error code did not clear or FLIR functions do not check out:

6. Press **STOW FLIR** control panel **POWER** button.

7. FLIR control panel **POWER** switch - **OFF**.

8. Do not use FLIR system.

9. Continue mission and annotate FLIR problem at mission completion.

APPENDIX A

REFERENCES

AR 70-50	Designating and Naming Military Aircraft, Rockets and Guided Missiles
AR 95-1	Army Aviation General Provisions and Flight Regulations
AR 95-3	General Provisioning, Training, Standardization, and Resource Management
AR 385-40	Accident Reporting and Records
DA PAM 40-501	Noise and Conservation of Hearing
DA PAM 738-751	Functional Users Manual for the Army Maintenance Management System Aviation (TAMMS-A)
DOD FLIP	Flight Information Publication
FAR Part 91	Federal Air Regulation, General Operating and Flight Rules
FM 1-202	Environmental Flight
FM 1-203	Fundamentals of Flight
FM 1-230	Meteorology for Army Aviators
FM 1-240	Instrument Flying and Navigation for Army Aviators
FM 10-68-1	Aircraft Refueling
FM 55-450-1	Army Helicopter External Load Operations
FM 55-450-2	Army Helicopter Internal Load Operations
TB 55-9150-200-24	Engine and Transmission Oils, Fuels, and Additives for Army Aircraft
TC 1-204	Night Flight Techniques and Procedures
TM 1-1520-253-CL	Operator's and Crewmember's Checklist, Army Model UH-60Q Helicopter
TM 1-1520-250-23	General Tie-down and Mooring Technical Manual Aviation Unit and Intermediate Maintenance. All Series Army Models AH-64, UH-60, CH-47, UH-1, AH-1, OH-58 Helicopters.
TM 11-5810-262-10	Operator's Manual for Communication Security Equipment TSEC/KY 58
TM 11-5841-283-12	Operator's Manual for AN/APR 39(V) Radar Signal Detecting Set
TM 11-5865-200-12	AN/ALQ 144 Countermeasure Set
TM 11-5895-1199-12	Operator's and Organization Maintenance for MARK-12 IFF System AN/APX-100, AN/APX-72
TM 11-5895-1037-12 & P	Transponder Set AN/APX-100(V)
TM 55-1500-342-23	Army Aviation Maintenance Engineering Manual: Weight and Balance
TM 750-244-1-5	Procedures for the Destruction of Aircraft and Associated Equipment to Prevent Enemy Use

APPENDIX B

ABBREVIATIONS AND TERMS

AJ	- anti-jam	ft	- feet
ALT	- altitude	GPS	- global positioning system
ANT	- antenna	GW	- gross weight
APU	- auxiliary power unit	HAT	- height above terrain
ATF	- aircraft torque factor	HMU	- hydromechanical unit (fuel control)
BL	- butt line		
°C	- degree Celsius	HQ	- have quick
CBIT	- continuous built in test	hr	- hour
CCU	- converter control unit	HSI	- horizontal situation indicator
CDU	- central display unit	HSP	- hot start preventor
CG	- center of gravity	HSS	- horizontal stores support
CL	- center line	HUD	- heads up display
DCU	- dispenser control unit	IAS	- indicated airspeed
DEG	- degree	IAW	- in accordance with
ECM	- electronic counter measure	IB	- inboard
ΔF	- change in flat plate drag area	IGE	- in ground effect
ΔTRQ	- change in torque	IN	- inch
ECU	- electrical control unit	IN HG	- inch of mercury
ENG	- engine	IPS	- inlet particle separator - inches per second
EOT	- element-on-time	IR	- infrared
ERFS	- extended range fuel system	IRCM	- infrared countermeasures
ESU	- electronic sequence unit	KCAS	- knots calibrated airspeed
ESSS	- external stores support system	KIAS	- knots indicated airspeed
ETF	- engine torque factor	KN	- knot
ETL	- effective translational lift	KTAS	- knots true airspeed
°F	- degree Fahrenheit	lb	- pound(s)
FAT	- free-air temperature		
FPM	- feet-per-minute		

APPENDIX B (Cont)

lb/gal	- pounds-per-gallon	PRESS	- pressure
lb/hr	- pounds-per-hour	PPM	- pounds-per-minute
LDI	- leak detection isolation	PSI	- pounds per square inch
LDS	- load-demand spindle	PSID	- pounds per square inch differential
LIM	- limit	PSIG	- pounds per square inch gauge
LLL	- low light level		
LRU	- line replaceable unit	R/C	- rate of climb
LWC	- liquid water content	R/D	- rate of descent
MAX	- maximum	RPM	- revolutions-per-minute
MGRS	- military grid reference system	SAR	- search and rescue
MIN	- minimum	SDC	- signal data converter
min	- minutes	SEL	- select
Ng SPEED 1 or 2	- No. 1 or No. 2 engine compressor speed % rpm	SL	- sea level
		SLAB	- sealed lead acid battery
NM	- nautical miles	SPEC	- specification
Np	- power turbine speed	STA	- station
NVG	- night vision goggles	STD TEMP	- 15°C at sea level
°	- degree	SQ FT	- square feet
% RPM R	- rotor rpm, percent	TAS	- true airspeed
% RPM 1 or 2	- No. 1 or No. 2 engine Np % rpm	TGT	- turbine gas temperature
		TOD	- time of day
OAT	- outside air temperature	% TRQ	- torque, percent
OB	- outboard	TRQ	- torque
ODV	- overspeed and drain valve	UTM	- universal transverse mercator
OEI	- one engine inoperative	VDC	- volts direct current
OGE	- out of ground effect	Vh	- maximum level flight speed using torque available - 30 minutes
PA	- pressure altitude		
PAS	- power available spindle		
PDU	- pilot display unit	VIDS	- vertical instrument display systems
POU	- pressurizing and overspeed unit		

APPENDIX B (Cont)

Vne	- velocity never exceed (airspeed limitation)	WOD	- word of day
VSI	- vertical situation indicator	WOW	- weight-on-wheels
VSP	- vertical support pylon	XMSN	- transmission
WL	- water line		

INDEX

Subject	Paragraph Figure, Table Number
% RPM INCREASING/DECREASING (OSCILLATION).	9.16
% TRQ SPLIT BETWEEN ENGINES 1 AND 2.	9.17

#1 and #2

Subject	Paragraph Figure, Table Number
#1 and #2 CONV Caution Legends On.	9.26.3
#1 and #2 FUEL FLTR BYPASS Caution Legends On.	9.25.2
#1 and #2 Generator Failure (#1 and #2 CONV and AC ESS BUS OFF Caution Legends On).	9.26.1
#1 and #2 HYD PUMP Caution Legends On.	9.27.3
#1 FUEL LOW and #2 FUEL LOW Caution Legends On.	9.25.3
#1 HYD PUMP Caution Legend On.	9.27.1
#1 or #2 FUEL FLTR BYPASS Caution Legend On.	9.25.1
#1 or #2 FUEL PRESS Caution Legend On.	9.25.4
#1 or #2 GEN Caution Legend On.	9.26.2
#1 or #2 HYD PUMP Caution Legend On and BACK-UP PUMP ON Advisory Legend Off.	9.27.4
#1 or #2 PRI SERVO PRESS Caution Legend On.	9.27.5
#1 RSVR LOW and #1 HYD PUMP Caution Legends On With BACK-UP PUMP ON Advisory Legend On.	9.27.6
#1 TAIL RTR SERVO Caution Legend On and BACK-UP PUMP ON Advisory Legend Off or #2 TAIL RTR SERVO ON Advisory Legend Off.	9.22.6
#2 HYD PUMP Caution Legend On.	9.27.2
#2 RSVR LOW and #2 HYD PUMP Caution Legends On With BACK-UP PUMP ON Advisory Legend On.	9.27.7

INDEX (Cont)

Subject		Paragraph Figure, Table Number
#2 RSVR LOW Caution Legend On.		9.27.8

A

AC Power Supply System.		2.59
Accessory Module.		2.41.2
Accessory Section Module.		2.14.4
Accumulator Recharge.		2.63
AFTER EMERGENCY ACTION.		9.4
AFTER LANDING CHECK.		8.32
After Takeoff.		8.29
Air Conditioner System.		2.56
Air Conditioning System Power Source Priority	T	2-2
Aircraft Configuration Drag Changes For Use With Clean Cruise Charts.		7.22
Aircraft Configuration Drag Changes For Use With High Drag Cruise Charts.		7.23
Aircraft Torque Factor (ATF)	F	7-2.
Airspeed Charts.		7.28
Airspeed Correction - Clean	F	7-34.
Airspeed Correction Chart - High Drag	F	7-35.
Airspeed Correction Charts.		7.28.1
Airspeed for Onset of Blade Stall.	F	5-5.

INDEX (Cont)

Subject		Paragraph Figure, Table Number
Airspeed Indicator.		2.69
Airspeed Limitations Following Failure of the Automatic Stabilator Control System.		5.20
Airspeed Operating Limits ES	F	5-4.
Airspeed Operating Limits.		5.18
Airspeed Operating Limits	F	5-3.
Airspeed System Dynamic Characteristics.		7.28.2
Altimeter Encoder AAU-32A	F	2-20.
Altimeter/Encoder AAU-32A		2.70
Ambulatory Patient Configuration.		4.12.3
Ambulatory Seat Arrangement	F	4-22.
Ambulatory (Seated) Patient Configuration.		4.12.18
AMS Control Display Unit	F	3-2.
AMS DUAL CDU AND DUAL MFD FAILURE.		9.32.1
AN/ARC-201D (COM 1 and 4) Communication Screen Flow	F	3-10.
AN/ARC-220 Messages	T	3-2.
AN/ARC-222 Control Panel	F	3-13.
AN/ARN-149 Control Screens	F	3-24.
AN/ARN-153 TACAN Control Screens.	F	3-25.
AN/ASN-128B DGNS Control Screens	F	3-22.

INDEX (Cont)

Subject		Paragraph Figure, Table Number
Antenna Arrangement.	F	3-1.
Antenna, AN/ASN-128B Doppler.		3.13.1
Antenna, Personnel Locator System.		3.17.1
Antenna, AN/APX-100 Transponder.		3.21.1
Antenna, AN/ARC-222 VHF Radio.		3.8.1
Antenna, AN/ARC-220 HF Radio.		3.9.1
Antennas, AN/ARN-147 VOR/ILS/MB.		3.14.1
Antennas, AN/ARN-149 ADF.		3.15.1
Antennas, AN/ASN-153 TACAN.		3.16.1
Antennas, Storm Scope.		3.20.1
Antennas, AN/APN-209 Radar Altimeter.		3.22.1
Antennas, AN/ARC-201D VHF/FM Radio.		3.6.1
Antennas, NA/ARC-164 UHF Radio.		3.7.1
Anticollision Lights.		2.65.3
Appendix A, References.		1.4
Appendix B, Abbreviations, and Terms.		1.5
Approved Fuels.	T	2-5.
APU Compartment Fire.		9.23.2
APU Controls.		2.62.1
APU Fuel Control System (Helicopters equipped with GTC-P36-150 APU).		2.62.3

INDEX (Cont)

Subject		Paragraph Figure, Table Number
APU Fuel Control System (Helicopters equipped with (T-62T-40-1 APU)).		2.62.2
APU Fuel Supply System.		2.62.4
APU Oil System Servicing.		2.81
APU OIL TEMP HI Caution Light On.		9.23.3
APU Operating Limitations.		5.30
APU Source Engine Start.		2.24.2
APU.		2.62
Area Navigation System.		3.12
Arm.		6.6.2
Army Aviation Safety Program.		1.7
Attitude Indicating System.		2.67
Automatic Flight Control System (AFCS) Switch Panel	F	2-12.
Automatic Flight Control System (AFCS).		2.33
Autorotative Glide Distance Chart-High Drag	F	9-4.
Autorotative Glide Distance Chart	F	9-3.
Autoscan Menu.	F	4-9.
Auxiliary AC Power System.		2.60
Auxiliary Fuel Management Control Panel Test.		4.10.5
Auxiliary Fuel Management Control Panel.		4.10.3

INDEX (Cont)

Subject	Paragraph Figure, Table Number	
Auxiliary Fuel Management Control Panel	F	4-18.
Auxiliary Power Unit (APU) System.		2.61
Auxiliary Power Unit (APU)	F	2-19.
Average Arm.		6.6.4
AVIATION LIFE SUPPORT EQUIPMENT (ALSE).		8.2
Avionics Equipment Configuration.		3.2
AVIONICS MANAGEMENT SYSTEM MALFUNCTIONS.		9.32
Avionics Management System.		3.4
Avionics Power Supply.		3.3

B

Subject	Paragraph Figure, Table Number
Back Up System Operation.	4.12.13.3
Backup Hydraulic Pump Hot Weather Limitations.	5.29
Backup Hydraulic System.	2.36.3
Balance Definitions.	6.6
Basic Moment.	6.6.5
Basic Principles of Operation.	4.4.1
BATT LOW CHARGE Caution Legend On.	9.26.5
BATTERY FAULT Caution Legend On.	9.26.4
Battery.	2.58.2
BEFORE EXTERIOR CHECK (Figure 8-1).	8.10

INDEX (Cont)

Subject	Paragraph Figure, Table Number
Before Landing.	4.7.9
BEFORE LANDING.	8.30
BEFORE LEAVING HELICOPTER.	8.34.
BEFORE STARTING ENGINES.	8.20
Before Takeoff.	4.7.6
BEFORE TAKEOFF.	8.27
BEFORE TAXI.	8.24
Blackout Curtains.	2.51
Blade Deice System Control Panel.	2.50.2
BLADE DEICE SYSTEM MALFUNCTIONS.	9.35
Blade Deice System Operation.	2.50.1
Blade Deice Test Panel.	2.50.4
Blade Deice Test.	2.50.3
BOOST SERVO OFF Caution Legend On.	9.27.11
Boost Servo.	2.32.4

C

Cabin Ceiling Tiedown Fittings.	5.15
Cabin Dimensions.	6.14
Cabin Dome Lights.	2.64.7

INDEX (Cont)

Subject		Paragraph Figure, Table Number
Cabin Doors.		6.15
Cabin Interior.	F	2-5.
CABIN TOP (AREA 3).		8.14
Cabin/Cargo Doors.		2.9.2
Cage Menu.	F	4-10.
Calibration Menu.	F	4-11
Cargo Center of Gravity Planning.		6.18.2
Cargo Configuration.		4.12.20
Cargo Hook and Rescue Hoist Moments.		6.13
Cargo Hook Control Panel.		4.7.2
Cargo Hook Moments.	F	6-5.
Cargo Hook Stowage.		4.7.1
Cargo Hook System.	F	4-15.
Cargo Hook System.		4.7
Cargo Hook System.	F	4-15.
Cargo Hook Weight Limitation.		5.16
Cargo Tiedown Arrangement.	F	6-7.
Carry On Medical Equipment Limitations.		5.37
Caution/Advisory and Warning Light Lighting Parameters	T	2-3.

INDEX (Cont)

Subject		Paragraph Figure, Table Number
Caution/Advisory BRT/DIM - TEST Switch.		2.75.3
Caution/Advisory Legend System.		2.75.1
CDU Caution/Advisory Grid.		2.75.2
CDU Caution/Advisory Grid	F	2-23.
CDU Controls and Functions.		3.4.1
CDU Display Screen Conventions.		3.4.2
CDU DUAL AMS FAILURE or BLANK CDU DISPLAYS (NO CDU BUS FUNCTIONS CAN BE ACCOMPLISHED).		9.32.3
CDU SINGLE AMS FAILURE or BLANK CDU DISPLAY.		9.32.2
Center of Gravity (CG).		6.6.6
Center of Gravity Limitations.		5.13
Center of Gravity Limits Chart	F	6-8.
Center of Gravity Limits Chart	F	6-9.
Center of Gravity Limits Chart.		6.20
Central Display Unit (CDU).		2.8.2
CG Limits.		6.6.7
Chaff and Flare Dispenser M130.		4.1
Chaff Dispenser M130.		4.1.1
Chapter 7 Index.		7.2
CHECKLIST.		8.8

INDEX (Cont)

Subject		Paragraph Figure, Table Number
CHIP INPUT MDL LH or RH Caution Legend On.		9.22.8
CHIP MAIN MDL SUMP, CHIP ACCESS MDL LH or RH, CHIP TAIL XMSN or CHIP INT XMSN/TAIL XMSN OIL TEMP or INT XMSN OIL TEMP Caution Legend On.		9.22.9
CIS Modes of Operation	F	3-31.
Class.		6.2
Climb/Descent - High Drag	F	7-32.
Climb/Descent Chart.		7.24
Climb/Descent.	F	7-31.
Clock.		2.74
COCKPIT - LEFT SIDE (AREA 2).		8.13
COCKPIT - RIGHT SIDE (AREA 8).		8.19
Cockpit Diagram	F	2-4.
Cockpit Doors.		2.9.1
COCKPIT EQUIPMENT CHECKS.		8.21
Cockpit Floodlights.		2.64.2
Cold Section Module.		2.14.1
Cold Weather Control Exercise.		8.40.2
COLD WEATHER OPERATION.		8.40
Cold Weather Preflight Check.		8.40.1
Collective and Cyclic Grips	F	2-11.

INDEX (Cont)

Subject		Paragraph Figure, Table Number
Collective Boost Servo Hardover/Power Piston Failure.		9.27.9
Collective Bounce/Pilot Induced Oscillation.		8.38.3
Collective Pitch Control Stick.		2.31.2
Collective/Airspeed to Yaw (Electronic Coupling).		2.31.4
COM Header.	F	3-3.
Communication/Navigation Equipment.	T	3-1.
Communications System Control (CSC) Panel.		3.5
Compartment Diagram.		2.5
Compass Control C-8021/ASN-75.		3.18.1
Compass Control Panel C-8021/ASN-75.	F	3-28.
Configuration Drag Change.	T	7-1.
Configuration Drag Change.	T	7-2.
Control Panel RT-1296/APX-100(V).	F	3-33.
Controls and Function, M130 Chaff Dispenser.		4.1.2
Controls and Function, AN/ALQ-144 IR Countermeasures Set.		4.3.2
Controls and Function, FLIR.		4.6.2
Controls and Function, Rescue Hoist Control Panels.		4.9.3
Controls and Functions, TSEC/KY-100 Secure Comm.		3.10.1
Controls and Functions, Emergency Control Panel.		3.11.1
Controls and Functions, AN/ARN-147 VOR/ILS/MB.		3.14.2

INDEX (Cont)

Subject	Paragraph Figure, Table Number
Controls and Functions, AN/ARN-149 ADF.	3.15.2
Controls and Functions, Personnel Locator System.	3.17.2
Controls and Functions, AN/ASN-43 Gyro Magnetic Compass.	3.18.2
Controls and Functions, AN/APX-100 Transponder.	3.21.2
Controls and Functions, AN/ARC-201D VHF/FM Radio.	3.6.2
Controls and Functions, AN/ARC-164 UHF Radio.	3.7.2
Controls and Functions, AN/ARC-222 VHF Radio.	3.8.2
Controls and Functions, AN/ARC-220 HF Radio.	3.9.2
Controls and Functions, Oxygen Generating System (OBOGS).	4.12.13.1
Controls and Functions, AN/APR-39 Radar Signal Detecting Set.	4.2.1
Controls and Functions, AN/AVS-7 Heads Up Display.	4.4.2
Controls and Functions, Multifunction Display.	4.5.1
Controls and Indicators, Horizontal Situation Indicator.	3.19.3
Controls, Displays, and Function, AN/ASN-128B Doppler.	3.13.2
Controls or Indicator Function, AN/APN-209 Radar Altimeter.	3.22.2
Converters.	2.58.1
Crash Axe.	2.12
Crash-Actuated System.	2.11.6
Create and Modify Waypoints, and Storepoints.	3.12.3.1

INDEX (Cont)

Subject	Paragraph Figure, Table Number
Create Storepoints	3.12.4
CREW BRIEFING	8.4
CREW DUTIES/RESPONSIBILITIES	8.3
Crew Seats	2.10
Crewmember's Cargo Hook Control Pendant	4.7.3
Crewmember's Cargo Hook Control Pendant	F 4-16
Crossbleed Engine Start System	2.24.3
Cruise - Pressure Altitude 10,000 Feet	F 7-17
Cruise - Pressure Altitude 12,000 Feet	F 7-19
Cruise - Pressure Altitude 14,000 Feet	F 7-21
Cruise - Pressure Altitude 16,000 Feet	F 7-23
Cruise - Pressure Altitude 18,000 Feet	F 7-25
Cruise - Pressure Altitude 2,000 Feet	F 7-9
Cruise - Pressure Altitude 20,000 Feet	F 7-27
Cruise - Pressure Altitude 4,000 Feet	F 7-11
Cruise - Pressure Altitude 6,000 Feet	F 7-13
Cruise - Pressure Altitude 8,000 Feet	F 7-15
Cruise - Pressure Altitude Sea Level	F 7-7
Cruise High Drag - Pressure Altitude 10,000 Feet	F 7-18
Cruise High Drag - Pressure Altitude 12,000 Feet	F 7-20

INDEX (Cont)

Subject	Paragraph Figure, Table Number
Cruise High Drag - Pressure Altitude 14,000 Feet	F 7-22.
Cruise High Drag - Pressure Altitude 16,000 Feet	F 7-24.
Cruise High Drag - Pressure Altitude 18,000 Feet	F 7-26.
Cruise High Drag - Pressure Altitude 2,000 Feet	F 7-10.
Cruise High Drag - Pressure Altitude 20,000 Feet	F 7-28.
Cruise High Drag - Pressure Altitude 4,000 Feet	F 7-12.
Cruise High Drag - Pressure Altitude 6,000 Feet	F 7-14.
Cruise High Drag - Pressure Altitude 8,000 Feet	F 7-16.
Cruise High Drag - Pressure Altitude Sea Level	F 7-8.
CSC Control Panel	F 3-9.
CSC Controls and Functions	3.5.1
Cyclic Stick	2.31.1
Cyclic-Mounted Stabilator Slew Up Switch	2.34.3

D

Dashed Line Data	7.5.1
Data Basis	7.5.2
Data Compartments	2.53
Data Prior to Loading	6.18.1
DC and AC Circuit Breaker Panels	F 2-18.

INDEX (Cont)

Subject	Paragraph Figure, Table Number
DC and AC Circuit Breaker Panels.	2.58.4
DC Power Supply System.	2.58
DD Form 365-3 (Chart C) Weight and Balance Records.	6.7
DD Form 365-4 (Form F).	6.9
DECREASING % RPM R.	9.14
DEFINITION OF EMERGENCY TERMS.	9.3
Description, Helicopter.	1.3
Description, Avionics Subsystem.	3.1
Description, Cruise Charts.	7.17
DESERT AND HOT WEATHER OPERATION.	8.41
Destruction of Army Materiel to Prevent Enemy Use.	1.8
DGNS FAILURE.	9.32.5
Dimensions.	2.3
Direction Finder Set AN/ARN -149 (LF/ADF).	3.15
Dispenser Assembly.	4.1.3
Display Modes.	4.4.4
Ditching - Power Off.	9.28.3
Ditching - Power On.	9.28.2
Door Locks.	2.9.3

INDEX (Cont)

Subject		Paragraph Figure, Table Number
Doors and Windows.		2.9
Doppler/GPS Navigation Set (DGNS)AN/ASN-128B.		3.13
Downwind Hovering.		5.22.2
Dual Engine Idle and Auxiliary Power Unit Fuel Flow	T	7-3.
DUAL-ENGINE FAILURE - GENERAL.		9.12
DUAL-ENGINE FAILURE.		9.13
Dual-Engine Fuel Flow.		7.27

E

Subject		Paragraph Figure, Table Number
ECS Control Panel	F	2-16.
Effects of Additional Installed Equipment.		7.16
Effects of Blade Erosion Kit.		7.15
Electrical Control Unit (ECU).		2.25.1
Electrical Fire In Flight.		9.23.5
Electrical Power Systems.		2.57
Electrical Power.		4.12.14
ELECTRICAL SYSTEM.		9.26
Electrical System	F	2-17.
Electronic Module Assembly (EM).		4.1.5
Electronic Navigation Instrument Display System.		3.19

INDEX (Cont)

Subject		Paragraph Figure, Table Number
Electronics Module Controls.		4.1.6
Emergency Control Panel (ECP).		3.11
Emergency Control Panel (ECP).	F	3-16.
Emergency Controls and Functions.		3.8.3
EMERGENCY EQUIPMENT (PORTABLE).		9.6
Emergency Exits and Emergency Equipment Diagram	F	9-1.
EMERGENCY EXITS.		9.5
EMERGENCY JETTISONING.		9.33
Emergency Landing In Wooded Areas. Power Off.		9.28.1
Emergency Operation.		3.7.6
Emergency Operation.		3.8.5
Emergency Release Circuit Tester.		4.7.4
EMERGENCY RELEASE OF RESCUE HOIST LOAD.		9.34
Emergency Release Procedure.		4.7.7
Engine % RPM Limitations.		5.8.2
Engine Alternator.		2.16
Engine Alternator.		2.16.1
Engine and Engine Inlet Anti-Ice Limitations.		5.28
Engine Anti-Icing Systems.		2.22
Engine Anti-Icing.		2.22.1

INDEX (Cont)

Subject		Paragraph Figure, Table Number
Engine Bleed Air.		7.12
Engine Bleed-Air System.		2.21
Engine Chip Detector.		2.23.4
ENGINE COMPRESSOR STALL.		9.18
Engine Control Quadrant.		2.25.2
Engine Control Quadrant	F	2-10.
Engine Control System.		2.25
Engine Driven Boost Pump.		2.15.1
Engine Emergency Oil System.		2.23.1
Engine Fire In Flight.		9.23.4
Engine Fuel Prime System.		2.29
Engine Fuel Supply System.		2.15
Engine Fuel System Components.		2.15.4
Engine Fuel System Selector Control.		2.28.2
ENGINE HIGH-SPEED SHAFT FAILURE.		9.20
Engine Ignition Keylock.		2.24.1
Engine Inlet Anti-Icing.		2.22.2
Engine Instruments.		2.27
Engine Limitations.		5.8

INDEX (Cont)

Subject		Paragraph Figure, Table Number
ENGINE MALFUNCTION - PARTIAL OR COMPLETE POWER LOSS.		9.7
ENGINE OIL FILTER BYPASS CAUTION LEGEND ON, ENGINE CHIP CAUTION LEGEND ON, ENG OIL PRESS HIGH/LOW, ENGINE OIL TEMP HIGH, ENGINE OIL TEMP CAUTION LEGEND ON, ENGINE OIL PRESS CAUTION LEGEND ON.		9.19
Engine Oil Pressure Indicator.		2.27.2
Engine Oil System Characteristics.		8.40.4
Engine Oil System Servicing.		2.80
Engine Oil System.		2.23
Engine Oil Temperature Indicator.		2.27.1
Engine Operation.		8.40.3
Engine Overspeed Check Limitations.		5.11
Engine Power Limitations.		5.8.1
Engine Power Turbine/Rotor Speed Indicator.		2.27.5
ENGINE RESTART DURING FLIGHT.		9.11
ENGINE RUNUP.		8.23
Engine Speed Control System.		2.25.4
Engine Start Envelope.	F	5-2.
Engine Start Limits.		5.10
Engine Start System.		2.24
Engine Starter Limits.		5.8.3
Engine T700	F	2-9.

INDEX (Cont)

Subject		Paragraph Figure, Table Number
Engine/Fuselage Fire On Ground.		9.23.1
Engine.		2.14
Equipment Loading and Unloading.		6.18
ESSS Fuel System Degraded Operation Chart ERFS	T	4-2
ESSS Side Position Lights.		4.11.3
Exceeding Operational Limits.		5.3
Explanation of Change Symbols.		1.10
Exterior Check Diagram.	F	8-1.
EXTERIOR CHECK.		8.11
Exterior Lights.		2.65
External AC Power System.		2.60.2
External Air Source/Electrical Requirements.		2.79
External Extended Range Fuel Quantity Indicating System.		4.10.4
EXTERNAL EXTENDED RANGE FUEL SYSTEM FAILURE TO TRANSFER SYMMETRICALLY IN MANUAL MODE. ERFS		9.36
External Extended Range Fuel System Kit Configurations.		5.33
External Extended Range Fuel System Kit. ERFS		4.10
External Extended Range Fuel System Tanks.		4.10.2
External Extended Range Fuel Transfer Check.		4.10.7
External Extended Range Fuel Transfer Modes.		4.10.1

INDEX (Cont)

Subject   **Paragraph Figure, Table Number**

Subject	Paragraph Figure, Table Number
External Load Drag Chart.	7.21
External Load Drag.	F 7-30.
External Source Engine Start.	2.24.4
External Stores Fixed Provisions.	4.11.1
External Stores Jettison Control Panel.	4.11.4
EXTERNAL STORES JETTISON. ES	9.37
External Stores Removable Provisions.	4.11.2
External Stores Support System (ESSS). ES	4.11

F

Subject	Paragraph Figure, Table Number
FAULT INDICATOR (BIT/FIT Error Reporting and Clear).	9.40.2
Fire Detection System.	2.11.1
Fire Detector Test Panel.	2.11.2
Fire Extinguisher Arming Levers (T-Handles).	2.11.4
Fire Extinguisher Control Panel.	2.11.5
Fire Extinguishing Systems.	2.11.3
Fire Protection Systems.	2.11
FIRE.	9.23
First Aid Kits.	2.13
FLIGHT CHARACTERISTICS.	9.8

INDEX (Cont)

Subject	Paragraph Figure, Table Number
Flight Control Servo Low-Pressure Caution Legends.	2.32.2
Flight Control Servo Switch.	2.32.1
Flight Control Servo Systems.	2.32
Flight Control Systems.	2.31
FLIGHT CONTROL/MAIN-ROTOR SYSTEM MALFUNCTIONS.	9.29
Flight in Icing Conditions.	5.27
Flight in Instrument Meteorological Conditions (IMC).	5.26
Flight Instrument Lights.	2.64.3
Flight Path Stabilization (FPS).	2.33.3
Flight Plan Control Screens	F 3-17.
Flight Plans.	3.12.1
Flight with Cabin Door(s)/Window(s) Open.	5.19
Flight with External Loads.	8.38.1
FLIR Menus (Basic)	F 4-8.
FLIR SYSTEM MALFUNCTIONS.	9.41
FLIR System Status Display	F 4-7
FLIR System Symbology Display	F 4-13
FLIR System.	F 4-6
FLT PATH STAB Caution Legend On.	9.29.4

INDEX (Cont)

Subject		Paragraph Figure, Table Number
Flying Qualities with External ERFS Installed. ERFS		8.38.2
Focus Menu	F	4-12.
Formation Lights.		2.65.5
Forms and Records.		1.9
Forward Looking InfraRed System AN/AAQ-22.		4.6
Free Air Temperatures.		7.9
Free-Air Temperature (FAT) Indicator.		2.73
Fuel and Lubricants, Specifications, and Capacities	T	2-4.
Fuel Boost Pump.		2.30.2
Fuel Filter.		2.15.2
Fuel Filter.		2.28.3
FUEL FUMES IN COCKPIT/CABIN WITH EXTERNAL EXTENDED RANGE FUEL SYSTEM PRESSURIZED. ERFS		9.38
FUEL LIMITATIONS.		5.12
Fuel Low Caution Legend.		2.30.1
Fuel Moments.		6.10
Fuel Moments	F	6-2.
Fuel Pressure Warning System.		2.15.3
Fuel Quantity Indicating System.		2.30
Fuel Sampling System.		2.78.5

INDEX (Cont)

Subject	Paragraph Figure, Table Number
Fuel Supply System.	2.28
Fuel System Servicing.	2.78
FUEL SYSTEM.	9.25
Fuel Tanks.	2.28.1
Fuel Transfer Sequence.	4.10.6
Fuel Types.	2.78.1
Function.	4.2.3
FUSELAGE - LEFT SIDE (AREA 5).	8.16
FUSELAGE - RIGHT SIDE (AREA 7).	8.18

G

Subject		Paragraph Figure, Table Number
Gas Generator Speed (Ng) Indicator.		2.27.4
General Arrangement	F	2-1.
Generator Control Switches.		2.60.1
Generator Control Units (GCU).		2.59.1
Gravity Refueling.		2.78.3
Ground Operations.		8.42.5
GROUND RESONANCE.		8.37
GROUND TAXI.		8.25
Gust Lock Limitations.		5.35

INDEX (Cont)

Subject		Paragraph Figure, Table Number
Gyro Magnetic Compass Set AN/ASN-43.		3.18

H

Hand-Operated Fire Extinguishers.		2.11.7
Handpump Reservoir Servicing.		2.82
HAVE QUICK (HQ) System.		3.7.3
Heads Up Display AN/AVS-7.		4.4
Heads Up Display AN/AVS-7.	F	4-2.
Heat and Ventilation Controls.		2.54.1
Heating System.		2.54
Height Velocity Diagram.	F	9-2.
Helicopter Compartment and Station Diagram.		6.3
Helicopter Compartment and Station Diagram.	F	6-1.
HELICOPTER SYSTEMS.		9.1
HF (COM 5) Communication Screen Flow.	F	3-14.
HF Radio Set AN/ARC-220 (COM 5).		3.9
High Drag Symbol.		1.12
History Recorder.		2.18
HOIST CABLE CUT.		9.34.1
Hoist Control Panel.		4.9.1

INDEX (Cont)

Subject		Paragraph Figure, Table Number
Hoist Operation.		4.9.4
HOIST RUNAWAY.		9.34.2
Horizontal Reference Datum.		6.6.1
Horizontal Situation Indicator.		3.19.2
Horizontal Situation Indicator.	F	3-30.
Hot Section Module.		2.14.2
Hover - Clean Configuration	F	7-4
Hover - High Drag	F	7-5.
HOVER CHART.		7.14
HOVER CHECK.		8.26
Hover Infrared Suppressor Subsystem (HIRSS).		2.26
Hydraulic Leak Detection/Isolation System.		2.37
Hydraulic Logic Module Operation Principle	F	2-13.
Hydraulic Pump Modules.		2.36
Hydraulic System.		2.35
HYDRAULIC SYSTEM.		9.27
Hydraulic Systems Servicing.		2.83

I

Ice and Rain Operation.		8.42.3

INDEX (Cont)

Subject		Paragraph Figure, Table Number
Ice Rate Meter Fail or Inaccurate.		9.35.3
Idle Fuel Flow.		7.25
Ignition System.		2.17
IMMEDIATE ACTION EMERGENCY STEPS.		9.2
INCREASING % RPM R.		9.15
Index.		1.6
In-Flight Icing.		8.42.4
In-flight Procedures.		4.7.8
IN-FLIGHT.		8.42
Infrared Countermeasure Set AN/ALQ-144(V).		4.3
Infrared Countermeasure System Control Panel.		4.3.1
Infrared Suppressor System.		7.13
INI Screen Flow	F	3-7.
Initialization Screen	F	3-6.
Input Module.		2.41.1
INSTRUMENT FLIGHT.		8.35
Instrument Marking Color Codes.		5.5
Instrument Markings	F	5-1.
Instrument Panel	F	2-8.
Instrument Panel.		2.8

INDEX (Cont)

Subject — Paragraph, Figure, Table Number

Subject	Paragraph Figure, Table Number
Intercommunication Keying System.	3.5.2
INTERIOR CABIN (AREA 4).	8.15
Interior Lighting System.	4.12.10
Interior Lighting.	2.64
Intermediate and Tail Gear Box Chip/Temperature Systems.	2.43.3
Intermediate Gear Box.	2.43.1
Introduction.	6.1

J

Subject	Paragraph Figure, Table Number
Jettison Limits.	5.34

K

Subject	Paragraph Figure, Table Number
KY-100 Secure Communication Control Screen	F 3-15.

L

Subject	Paragraph Figure, Table Number
LANDING AND DITCHING.	9.28
Landing Gear Limitations.	5.23
Landing Gear System.	2.7
Landing Light.	2.65.2
Landing Speed Limitations.	5.24
LANDING.	8.31

INDEX (Cont)

Subject		Paragraph Figure, Table Number
Lighted Switches Dimmer		2.64.4
LIGHTNING STRIKE		9.21
Limits		7.4
LITTER LIFT RUNAWAY		9.39.1
Litter Lift System Operation		4.12.15
Litter Lift System Patient Loading and Unloading		4.12.17
Litter Lift System		4.12.2
Litter Moments	F	6-4
Litter Platform	F	4-23
Litter Platforms		4.12.4
LITTER SYSTEM MALFUNCTIONS		9.39
Load Demand System		2.25.3
Loading Data		6.8
Logic Modules		2.38.4
Loss of NO. 1 or NO. 2 Generator During Blade Deice Operation		9.35.4
Loss of Tail Rotor Thrust at Low Airspeed/Hover		9.22.2
Loss of Tail Rotor Thrust		9.22.1
Lower Console	F	2-7

M

INDEX (Cont)

Subject		Paragraph Figure, Table Number
Main Landing Gear.		2.7.1
Main Module.		2.41.3
Main Rotor Blade and BIM® System.	F	2-14.
Main Rotor Blades.		2.45.1
Main Rotor Gust Lock.		2.45.2
Main Rotor System.		2.45
Main Rotor Tiedown.		2.88.2
Main Transmission Chip Detector/Fuzz Burn-Off System.		2.42.3
Main Transmission LubricationSystem.		2.42
Main Transmission Module Limitations.		5.7
Main Transmission Oil System Servicing.		2.84
MAIN XMSN OIL PRESS Caution Legend On/XMSN OIL PRESS LOW/XMSN OIL TEMP HIGH or XMSN OIL TEMP Caution Legend On.		9.22.7
Maintenance Light.		2.64.8
Maintenance Operational Checks (MOC).		5.38
MANEUVERING FLIGHT.		8.38
Maneuvering Limitations.		5.22.3
Manual Operation of the Stabilator.		5.22.1
Master Mode Display	F	4-3.
Master Mode Symbology Display (HUD)	T	4-1.

INDEX (Cont)

Subject		Paragraph Figure, Table Number
Master Warning Panel	F	2-21.
Master Warning System.		2.75
Maximum Cargo Size Diagram for Loading Through Cabin Doors.		6.16
Maximum Torque Available - 30-Minute Limit	F	7-3.
Maximum Torque Available Chart.		7.11
Medevac Equipment Moments.		6.12
MEDEVAC Seats Installation.		4.12.5
MEDEVAC System.	F	4-20.
Medical Attendant Seat Belt Operation.		2.10.4
Medical Attendant Seats.		2.10.3
Medical Cabinet.		4.12.8
Medical Cabinet.	F	4-25.
Medical Control Panels.		4.12.6
Medical Control Panels	F	4-24.
Medical Evacuation (MEDEVAC) System.		4.12
Medical IV Bags.		4.12.9
Medical Stations.		4.12.1
Medical Stations	F	4-21.
Medical Suction Controls	F	4-27.
Medical Suction System.		4.12.11

INDEX (Cont)

Subject		Paragraph Figure, Table Number
Messages		3.9.4
MFD Adjustments		4.6.5
MFD Caution/Advisory Grid	F	2-22.
MFD FAILURE		9.32.4
Minimum Crew Requirements		5.4
Mission Kits	F	4-1.
MISSION PLANNING		8.1
Mission Profile	F	Figure 7-36
Mission Readiness Circuit Breaker Panel		4.8
Mixing Unit		2.31.3
Mode of Operation		3.6.3
MODE PROBLEM, CAGE PROBLEM, GIMBAL RACHETING, IMAGE DISTORTION, MISC		9.41.1
Modes of Operation, Emergency Control Panel		3.11.2
Modes of Operation, Personnel Locator System		3.17.3
Modes of Operation, Storm Scope		3.20.3
Modes of Operation, Communications Systems Control		3.5.3
Modes of Operation, AN/ARC-164 UHF Radio		3.7.4
Modes of Operation, AN/APR-39 Radar Signal Detecting Set		4.2.2

INDEX (Cont)

Subject		Paragraph Figure, Table Number
Modes of Operation, AN/AVS-7 Heads Up Display.		4.4.3
Modes of Operation, FLIR.		4.6.4
Moment.		6.6.3
Mooring Instructions.		2.88.1
Mooring.		2.88
Mooring.	F	2-25.
MR DE-ICE FAULT or MR DE-ICE FAIL, or TR DE-ICE FAIL Caution Legend On.		9.35.1
Multi Function Display (MFD).		4.5
Multi Function Display (MFD).	F	4-5.

N

Subject		Paragraph Figure, Table Number
N AV Header.	F	3-4.
Navigation Calculator Control Screens.	F	3-21.
Navigation Calculator.		3.12.5
No. 1 Transfer Module.		2.38.1
No. 2 Transfer Module.		2.38.2
Normal Operation, Heating System.		2.54.2
Normal Operation, Ventilation System.		2.55.2
Normal Operation, TSEC/KY-100 Secure Comm.		3.10.3
Normal Operation, Personnel Locator System.		3.17.4

INDEX (Cont)

Subject	Paragraph Figure, Table Number
Normal Operation, AN/ARC-164 UHF Radio.	3.7.5
Normal Operation, AN/ARC-222 VHF Radio.	3.8.4
Normal Operation, Oxygen Generation System.	4.12.13.2
NOSE SECTION (AREA 1).	8.12
Number 1 Hydraulic System.	2.36.1
Number 2 Hydraulic System.	2.36.2
NVG Lighting System.	2.64.1

O

Subject	Paragraph Figure, Table Number
O BOGS BIT/FAULT LIGHT ILLUMINATED.	9.40.1
OBOGS Panel.	F 4-28.
OBOGS SYSTEM MALFUNCTIONS.	9.40
Oil Cooler and Filter.	2.23.3
Oil Tank.	2.23.2
OPERATING PROCEDURES AND MANEUVERS.	8.6
Operation, Area Navigation.	3.12.6
Operation, AN/ARN-147 VOR/ILS/MB.	3.14.3
Operation, AN/ARN-149 ADF.	3.15.3
Operation, TACAN.	3.16.3
Operation, AN/ASN-43 Gyro Magnetic Compass.	3.18.3

INDEX (Cont)

Subject		Paragraph Figure, Table Number
Operation, EFIS.		3.19.5
Operation, AN/APX-100 Transponder.		3.21.3
Operation, AN/APN-209 Radar Altimeter.		3.22.3
Operation, Avionics Management System.		3.4.3
Operation, AN/ARC-220 HF Radio.		3.9.3
Operation, M-130 Chaff Dispenser.		4.1.8
Operation, AN/ALQ-144 IR Countermeasures Set.		4.3.3
Operation, AN/AVS-7 Heads Up Display.		4.4.5
Operation, Multifunction Display.		4.5.4
Optimum Altitude For Maximum Range	F	7-29.
Optimum Range Charts.		7.20
Overhead Control Panel.		4.12.7
Overhead Lighting.	F	4-26.
Overlay Display Modes.		4.5.3
Oxygen Delivery System.		4.12.12
Oxygen Generating System.		4.12.13

P

PARKING AND SHUTDOWN.		8.33
Parking.		2.86

INDEX (Cont)

Subject	Paragraph Figure, Table Number
PASSENGER BRIEFING.	8.5
Payload Module Assembly.	4.1.4
Pedal Bind/Restriction or Drive With No Accompanying Caution Light.	9.22.5
Performance Data Basis - Clean.	7.7
Performance Data Basis - High Drag.	7.8
Performance Discrepancies.	7.6
Personnel Locator System (PLS).	3.17
Personnel Moments.	6.11
Personnel Stations.	F 6-3.
Pilot-Assist Controls.	2.32.5
Pilot-Assist Servos.	2.32.3
Pilot's Display Unit (PDU).	2.8.3
Pilot's Seats.	2.10.1
Pitch Boost Servo Hardover.	9.27.10
Pitch, Roll or Yaw/Trim Hardover.	9.29.5
Pitot Heater.	2.49
Pitot-Static System.	2.66
PLS Central Display Unit	F 3-26.
PLS Remote Display Unit	F 3-27.
Pneumatic Source Inlet Limits.	5.9

INDEX (Cont)

Subject		Paragraph Figure, Table Number
Pneumatic Subsystem.		2.40
Position Lights.		2.65.4
Power Turbine Section Module.		2.14.3
POWER UP AND MODE SET Operation.		4.6.7
Powertrain.		2.41
PREFLIGHT CHECK.		8.9
Preflight.		4.7.5
Preparation for Littered Patient Loading.		4.12.16
Pressure Refueling.		2.78.4
Pressurizing and Overspeed Unit.		2.15.4.1
Primary Controls and Functions.		3.16.2
Principal Dimensions.	F	2-2.
Prohibited Maneuvers.		5.21
Protective Armor.		2.10.2
Protective Covers and Plugs.		2.87
PWR MAIN RTR and/or TAIL RTR MONITOR Light On.		9.35.2
Radar Altimeter Set AN/APN-209(V).		3.22
Radar Altimeter Set AN/APN-209(V).	F	3-34.
Radar Signal Detecting Set AN/APR-39A(V)1.		4.2

INDEX (Cont)

Subject		Paragraph Figure, Table Number
Radio Receiving Set AN/ARN-147(V)(VOR/ILS/MB).		3.14
Radio Receiving Set AN/ASN-153 TACAN.		3.16
Radio Set AN/ARC-201D (VHF-FM) (COM 1 and 4).		3.6
Recommended Emergency External Fuel Tank Jettison Envelope	T	5-1.
Refueling/Defueling.		2.30.3
Rescue Hoist Limitations.		5.36
Rescue Hoist Moments.	F	6-6.
Rescue Hoist Pendant.		4.9.2
Rescue Hoist System	F	4-17.
Rescue Hoist Weight Limitations.		5.17
Rescue Hoist.		4.9
Reservoir Fill System.		2.39
Restraint Criteria.		6.18.3
Restricted Maneuvers.		5.22
Rotor Blade Deice Kit.		2.50
Rotor Blade Deice Kit.	F	2-15.
Rotor Limitations.		5.6
Rotor Speed Limitations.		5.6.2
Rotor Start and Stop Limits.		5.6.1
Rotor Systems.		2.44

INDEX (Cont)

Subject		Paragraph Figure, Table Number
ROTORS, TRANSMISSIONS AND DRIVE SYSTEMS.		9.22

S

Subject		Paragraph Figure, Table Number
Safety Procedures.		4.1.7
Sample Cruise Chart - Clean.	F	7-6.
SAS 2 Failure Advisory Light On.		9.29.2
SAS Failure With No Failure/Advisory Indication.		9.29.1
SAS OFF Caution Legend On.		9.29.3
Scope.		6.4
Search Pattern Control Screens.	F	3-18.
Searchlight.		2.65.1
Series and Effectivity Codes.		1.11
Service Platforms and Fairings.		2.77
Servicing Diagram.	F	2-24.
Servicing.		2.76
Shut Down.		4.12.11.2
Single/Dual-Engine Fuel Flow.	F	7-33.
SINGLE-ENGINE FAILURE - GENERAL.		9.9
SINGLE-ENGINE FAILURE.		9.10
Single-Engine Fuel Flow.		7.26

INDEX (Cont)

Subject		Paragraph Figure, Table Number
Single-Engine.		7.19
Sling/Hoist Load Maneuvering Limitations.	F	5-6.
Slope Landing Limitations.		5.25
SMOKE AND FUME ELIMINATION.		9.24
Special Mission Flight Profiles.		7.29
Special Mission Profile.	F	7-36.
Specific Conditions.		7.5.3
Stabilator Control Panel.		2.34.1
STABILATOR MALFUNCTION - AUTO MODE FAILURE.		9.30
Stabilator Position Indicator.		2.34.2
Stabilator System.		2.34
Stability Augmentation System (SAS).		2.33.1
Stand Alone Display Modes.		4.5.2
Standby Magnetic Compass.		2.72
STARTING ENGINES.		8.22
Starting Procedure, TSEC/KY-100 Secure Comm.		3.10.2
Starting Procedure, Storm Scope.		3.18.4
Starting Procedure, AN/ARC-201 VHF/FM Radio.		3.6.4
Starting Procedure, FLIR.		4.6.3

INDEX (Cont)

Subject		Paragraph Figure, Table Number
Status Line	F	3-5.
Status Screen Flow	F	3-8.
Stopping Procedure, AN/APX-100 Transponder		3.21.4
Stopping Procedure, AN/APN-209 Radar Altimeter		3.22.4
Stopping Procedure, M-130 Chaff Dispenser		4.1.9
Stopping Procedure, AN/ALQ-144 IR Countermeasure Set		4.3.4
Stopping Procedure, FLIR		4.6.8
Storepoint Control Screens	F	3-20.
Stores Jettison Control Operation		4.11.5
Stores Jettison Control Panel ES	F	4-19.
Storm scope Controls, Functions, and Displays		3.20.2
Storm scope Displays	F	3-32.
Storm Scope Error Messages	T	3-3
Storm Scope Normal Operation		3.20.4
Storm scope Weather Mapping System		3.20
Stow Ambulatory Patient Seats		4.12.19
Symbol Generator Test Mode	F	4-4.
Symbology/Status Menus	F	4-14
SYMBOLS DEFINITION		8.7
System Status / Symbology		4.6.6

INDEX (Cont)

Subject **Paragraph Figure, Table Number**

T

Subject	Number
Tail and Intermediate Gear Box Servicing.	2.85
Tail Drive System.	2.43
Tail Gear Box.	2.43.2
Tail Landing Gear.	2.7.3
TAIL PYLON (AREA 6).	8.17
Tail Rotor Control.	2.31.5
Tail Rotor Pedals.	2.31.6
TAIL ROTOR QUADRANT Caution Legend On With Loss of Tail Rotor Control.	9.22.4
TAIL ROTOR QUADRANT Caution Legend On With No Loss of Tail Rotor Control.	9.22.3
Tail Rotor Quadrant/Warning.	2.47
Tail Rotor System.	2.46
TAKEOFF.	8.28
Taxiing and Ground Operation.	8.41.1
Taxiing.	8.40.5
Temperature Conversion Chart.	F 7-1.
TGT Temperature Indicator.	2.27.3
Thermocouple Harness.	2.19
Thunderstorm Operation.	8.42.1

INDEX (Cont)

Subject	Paragraph Figure, Table Number
Tiedown Fittings and Restraint Rings.	6.17
Torque and Overspeed and % RPM Sensors.	2.20
Torque Factor Method.	7.10
Torque Factor Procedure.	7.10.2
Torque Factor Terms.	7.10.1
Torque Indicator.	2.27.6
Transfer Modules.	2.38
Transmission Chip Detector System.	2.42.4
Transmission Oil Pressure Indicator.	2.42.2
Transmission Oil Temperature Indicator.	2.42.1
Transponder AN/APX-100(V)1 (IFF).	3.21
Trim Actuator Jammed.	9.29.6
Trim System.	2.33.2
TSEC/KY-100 SECURE COMMUNICATION SYSTEM.	3.10
Turbulence and Thunderstorm Operation.	5.32
Turbulence.	8.42.2
Turn Rate Indicating System.	2.68
Turning Radius and Clearance.	F 2-3.
Turning Radius and Ground Clearance.	2.4

INDEX (Cont)

Subject		Paragraph Figure, Table Number
Turret		4.6.1

U

UH-60Q		2.2
UHF (COM 2) Communication Screen Flow	F	3-11.
UHF Radio, AN/ARC-164(V) (COM 2)		3.7
UNCOMMANDED NOSE DOWN/UP PITCH ATTITUDE CHANGE		9.31
Upper and Lower Console Lights		2.64.5
Upper and Lower Consoles		2.6
Upper Console	F	2-6.
Use of Charts		7.18
Use of Charts		7.5
Use of Fuels		2.78.2
Use of Words Shall, Should, and May		1.13
Utility Lights		2.64.6
Utility Module		2.38.3

V

Ventilation System	2.55
Ventilation System	2.55.1
Vertical Instrument Display System (VIDS)	2.8.1

INDEX (Cont)

Subject		Paragraph Figure, Table Number
Vertical Situation Indicator.		3.19.1
Vertical Situation Indicator	F	3-29.
Vertical Speed Indicator.		2.71
VHF (COM 3) Communication Screen Flow	F	3-12.
VHF Radio Set AN/ARC-222 (COM 3).		3.8
VOR/ILS/MB Control Screens AN/ARN-147(V)	F	3-23.
VSI/HSI and CIS Mode Selector Panels.		3.19.4

W

Warnings, Cautions, and Notes.		1.2
Waypoint Control Screens	F	3-19.
Waypoints.		3.12.3
Weight Definitions.		6.5
Weight Limitations.		5.14
Weight-On-Wheels Functions	T	2-1
Wheel Brake System.		2.7.2
Windshield Anti-ice Limitations.		5.31
Windshield Anti-Ice/Defogging System.		2.48.2
Windshield Wiper Control.		2.48.1
Windshield Wipers.		2.48

INDEX (Cont)

Subject   **Paragraph Figure, Table Number**

Wire Strike Protection System. 2.512.52

TM 1-1520-253-10

By Order of the Secretary of the Army:

DENNIS J. REIMER
General, United States Army
Chief of Staff

Official:

(signature)

JOEL B. HUDSON
Administrative Assistant to the
Secretary of the Army
05409

DISTRIBUTION:
To be distributed in accordance with Initial Distribution Number (IDN) 313811 requirements for TM 1-1520-237-10.

This manual is sold for historic research purposes only, as an entertainment. It is not intended to be used as part of an actual flight training program. No book can substitute for flight training by an authorized instructor. The licensing of pilots is overseen by organizations and authorities such as the FAA and CAA. Operating an aircraft without the proper license is a federal crime.

©2011 Periscope Film LLC
All Rights Reserved
ISBN #978-1-935700-61-6
www.PeriscopeFilm.com

www.ingramcontent.com/pod-product-compliance
Lightning Source LLC
Chambersburg PA
CBHW081753300426
44116CB00014B/2106